REAL LIFE DRAMA

REAL LIFE DRAMA

THE GROUP THEATRE AND AMERICA, 1931–1940

Wendy Smith

GROVE WEIDENFELD
New York

Published by Grove Weidenfeld
A Division of Grove Press, Inc.
841 Broadway
New York, NY 10003-4793

First published in the United States in 1990 by Alfred A. Knopf,
Inc., New York.

Owing to limitations of space, all acknowledgments of
permission to reprint previously published material will be
found following the index.

Published in Canada by General Publishing Company, Ltd.

Library of Congress Cataloging-in-Publication Data
Smith, Wendy, 1956–
    Real life drama : the Group Theatre and America,
  1931–1940 / Wendy Smith.—1st ed.
        p.   cm.
    "First published by Alfred A. Knopf, Inc."—T.p. verso.
    Includes bibliographical references and index.
    ISBN 0-8021-3300-2 (acid-free paper)
    1. Group Theatre (U.S.)   2. Theater—United States—
  History—20th century.   I. Title.
  [PN2297.G7S6   1990b]
  792'.0973'09043—dc20   91-44170
                                                             CIP

Manufactured in the United States of America
Printed on acid-free paper
First Evergreen Edition 1992
10 9 8 7 6 5 4 3 2 1

This book is for Joe,
who got me through it

and for Alberta Magzanian,
who taught me what history is

CONTENTS

Illustrations follow page 212.

PREFACE

I first encountered the Group Theatre when I was a teenager in the early 1970s. Roaming among my parents' bookshelves in my perpetual quest for something to read, I stumbled on an old hardcover copy of *The Fervent Years*, Harold Clurman's compelling memoir of the Group. I was already fascinated by American life in the 1930s, a period that seemed to me very like the turbulent decade recently ended that had indelibly marked the way my friends and I thought about our society. I liked the photographs I saw as I thumbed through the book: young people clustered together on the porch of a frame house, looking straight at the camera with a determination in their gaze to shape the world to their vision; an intense, angry man in a shabby suit standing on a dark stage, his fists clenched in the air—so that gesture hadn't been invented in the sixties! I took the book away to have a closer look.

I already knew in those days that my generation wasn't the first to see how grievously America had failed to live up to its promise of a good life for everyone, that we had a history and forebears slighted in the official texts. But I was troubled by a sense that I was not a political person as I understood the meaning of the word at the time, that literature meant more to me than manifestos, that I would rather go to the theatre than to a demonstration. I'd seen the way political activism consumed people—in the early seventies it seemed to be driving many of them insane—and I knew I didn't have that kind of stamina or determination. I felt I'd failed some sort of obscure but vital character test and condemned myself to a life of dilettantish irrelevancy, while better people went out and did the really important work.

The story of the Group Theatre told me something I should have known but didn't. Art is part of the real world, the Group said over and over again. It has content, meaning, and implications. There are all kinds of activism, and when art reveals to us our society and ourselves, it is a force for change at least as powerful as any political party. As I've grown older and studied the Group more closely, it has said many other things to me as well, important things about the conflict between individual and collective needs, the difficulties of a committed life, that in some ways have more deeply affected me. But the thrill of that initial revelation has never worn off, and I hope it never will.

I describe my embarrassingly ingenuous response to the Group to make a point: at a time when our day-to-day existence too often seems fragmented into a dozen different parts that have little connection with each other, when we feel isolated and powerless, we must insist—as the Group did—on wholeness. Culture doesn't exist apart from society; those who claim it does, that art should be "above" politics, are putting forward a social agenda all the more insidious for being dressed up in aesthetic clothing. The music we listen to, the movies we see, the books we read—even, for those of us crazy enough to believe that the theatre will someday escape the economic straitjacket that has made it an expensive and trivial entertainment, the plays we attend—these arts at their best express truths that can help us understand ourselves and our world and determine to improve them.

I read books and write about them and press them on my friends because I love them, but it would be an empty sort of love if I didn't believe—if I didn't know, from personal experience—that the right book at the right time can make a difference in someone's life. The members of the Group felt the same way about the theatre. Of course it's naïve to think that art can change the world, but it would be tragic to think that it can't. The fight to make a better life, as the Group called it, takes place on many fronts. The Group believed that the trade-union organizer, the mother struggling to feed her children, the civil-rights activist, the working-class kid trying to get a decent education, *and* the artist all wanted the same thing: a world in which everyone was free to pursue his or her dreams unhindered by prejudice, economic inequality, and the dead weight of tradition. If this belief is unfashionable today, that is our loss. When ordinary men and women are excluded from official culture—either because it's too expensive or its concerns are not theirs—and told that their own culture is junk, we are all poorer because of it.

I wanted to write about the Group Theatre because I sensed that the whole story about this seminal American theatre hadn't been told—and it's a wonderful story, filled with vivid personalities and dramatic events. But the history of the Group is more to me than a chronicle of a prestigious American acting company and a few famous plays. The Group grappled with issues of cultural, economic, and political empowerment that we have not yet resolved; people today still look longingly, as the Group did, for meaningful work that satisfies their financial needs and gives them personal dignity as well. Examining the Group's confusions, difficulties, and disagreements can help us to define the questions and take a step toward answering them.

It will hardly come as a surprise to anyone who's read this far to discover that this is an opinionated book. Any writing worth its salt has a definite point of view; authors (and critics) who pretend not to have one are kidding themselves and their audience. In addition to offering my own judgments, however, I have tried to let the members of the Group speak for themselves as much as possible. Their passionate declarations of faith, their confessions of doubt and despair, are as moving and thought-provoking now as they were in the 1930s. These voices of half a century ago have a great deal to tell us, if we would only listen.

REAL LIFE DRAMA

ONE

Genesis

In the beginning was the Word—a whole flood of words from a passionate idealist in search of a spiritual and artistic home.

One Friday night in November 1930 Harold Clurman, a twenty-nine-year-old playreader with the Theatre Guild in New York City, began a series of weekly talks for an audience of young actors he hoped to interest in the theatre he wanted to establish with his friends, an actor-director named Lee Strasberg and the Guild's casting director, Cheryl Crawford. When this quiet, stammering young man opened his mouth, out rushed an extraordinary monologue, the aggregate of everything he had ever thought, felt, hoped, and dreamed about American theatre and American life. When he paused for breath the following May, he had articulated a vision of a new kind of theatre: an ensemble of artists who would create, out of common beliefs and technique, dramatic productions that spoke to an equally committed audience about the essential social and moral issues of their times. By June, he and his two friends had set off for the country with twenty-seven actors who shared their determination to make that vision a reality.

The talks began in Clurman's room at the Hotel Meurice on West 58th Street. Soon word spread, the audience grew, and they moved to Cheryl Crawford's larger apartment on West 47th Street. When that filled to overflowing, they persuaded other friends to play host. The photographer Ralph Steiner had to rent chairs from a nearby undertaker to seat the crowd; his guests were so broke they couldn't reimburse him. Finally someone finagled a large room, rent-free, at Steinway Hall on West 57th Street, where as many as 200 people would come to listen to the weekly jeremiads.

Part of the attraction was the spectacle of Clurman in full cry. A shy man who sometimes spoke so softly he could hardly be heard, he was transformed by his intense need to communicate his ideas. Whatever names people called Harold Clurman after 1930, they would never call him shy. "I changed by the challenge of life," he later remembered. "I said, 'I've got to get over this shyness! I've got to get them to be interested in what I'm saying! I know I'm right, by God I know I'm right!' " He seemed almost possessed: his face turned red, veins stood out, his once hushed voice rose to a pitch clearly audible outside in the street. He would grab the nearest chair, pick it up and shake it at his audience before flinging it aside. One of his most potent weapons was a willingness to make himself ridiculous, to exaggerate wildly, scream and stamp his feet to get a point across—in a ringing Bronx accent somewhat at odds with his almost mystical message. The set designer Boris Aronson once compared him to Father Divine, and there was certainly something evangelical in the way he laid out for his listeners the sorry state of the American theatre and exhorted them to do something about it.

For if a few casual observers came once or twice to enjoy the show, those who returned week after week were drawn by Clurman's provocative analysis of the artistic and social difficulties they faced and his stirring portrait of the theatre they could build together to solve their dilemma. He defined their vague dissatisfaction with the theatre and their work in it; he offered hope for the future. The actress Stella Adler summed up the call to arms that engaged her and so many others: "He said, 'You are lost here. You won't be able to find your way alone. Please follow me.' "

Looking at the American theatre, Clurman saw an institution in such confusion that even its critics hadn't really grasped what was wrong with it. He scornfully dismissed as superficial the conventional list of problems: a shortage of good plays, the personal vanity of actors, the moneygrubbing of commercial producers. "If we were providentially blessed with a host of admirable plays and players, and an epidemic of virtue broke out over the entire theatre-world, we should still hardly have effected the establishment of any sort of Theatre. . . . Nothing can be wrong with the theatre when no Theatre exists. And America has as yet no Theatre."

This was a bold statement. The 1920s had been the American theatre's liveliest decade, crammed with glamorous stars, fired by the exciting emergence of native playwrights, vibrant with the rhythms of great popular music. On the surface, Broadway still boomed; despite the stock-market crash the previous October, there had been 249 productions during the 1929–1930 New York season. Even the majority of Clurman's listeners who considered such quantitative measures trivial could point to Eva Le Gallienne's success at the Civic Repertory Theatre, where she presented classical repertory at popular prices; to the Theatre Guild's tasteful productions of European and American drama; to the careers of respected actors like Katharine Cornell, Alfred Lunt and Lynn Fontanne, who consistently appeared in classics and important contemporary plays; to the ongoing contributions of such patently serious writers as Eugene O'Neill, Maxwell Anderson, Elmer Rice, Sidney Howard, Paul Green, and John Howard Lawson. Surely these were proof that worthwhile theatre existed.

Hardly, said Clurman. He was unimpressed by Broadway stars, unenthusiastic about their work in the classics, and doubtful that any existing organization could give adequate theatrical expression to the American dramatists he admired. His criticisms shocked many in his audience, yet in a fundamental way he was right, and they knew it. The American theatre was living off the dwindling artistic capital amassed in the heady years during and immediately after World War I, when an explosion of theatrical energy called the "little theatre" movement championed American playwrights, explored the possibilities of experimental theatre, and discovered an audience for serious drama. The little theatres had given a new vitality and credibility to American theatre, yet they had never comfortably made the transition from amateur to professional production; by 1930 such key organizations as the Provincetown Players and the Neighborhood Playhouse had folded and the movement itself seemed moribund. Its only lasting legacy in New York was the Theatre Guild, born from the ashes of the Washington Square Players in 1919 with a commitment to professionalism and, as its founding manifesto declared, to "the creation, as carefully and lovingly as lies within one's power, of the best drama of one's time, drama honestly reflecting the author's vision of life or sense of style and beauty."

To Clurman, that sincere and high-minded credo was fatally flawed and indicated a misunderstanding of the basic problem that had killed the little theatres and still stood in the way of real theatrical growth. "The only fundamental difference between the new theatre and the old is that the former sells better stuff," he declared rather cruelly. "These theatres always will begin with a play, and never with a group of actors that may be appropriately considered part of it. They will take a company of actors, usually trained in the petty realism of the average commercial play, and ask them to do French poetic-rhetorical drama, a modern German tragedy in the classic manner, or something equally foreign to them." For actors like Morris Carnovsky, Franchot Tone, Phoebe Brand, Ruth Nelson, and Sanford Meisner, who had all worked at the Guild, this was a liberating insight, helping them understand why they had been disappointed by such well-intentioned productions as Jacques Copeau's dramatization of *The Brothers Karamazov* and Franz Werfel's *Juarez and Maximilian*, which in the end seemed stagey and without coherent intent.

This lack of unity drove Clurman crazy. "We have, on the American stage, all the separate elements for a Theatre, but no Theatre. We have playwrights without their theatre-groups, directors without their actors, actors without plays or directors, scene-designers without anything. Our theatre is an anarchy of individual talents."

This was not the fault of the theatre so much as a reflection of a larger disorder in society. "Americans don't really talk to each other," Clurman told Cheryl Crawford around this time. "They make wisecracks to each other, they drink well together, but they don't really exchange with each other their hearts, their backgrounds, their souls. They don't really live together." She was moved by his comment, and many of the listeners at Steinway Hall shared their profound disquiet with the way things were. It was symptomatic of a sea-change in the national spirit.

To Clurman, the soulless materialism encapsulated in the word "Babbittry," the smart-alecky cynicism of intellectuals who despised it, and the vague idealism of bohemians who looked to "art" as an alternative were all part and parcel of the anarchic individualism of the 1920s, an era in which self-fulfillment was the ultimate goal and the only disagreement was over the best way to achieve it. He and his colleagues were looking for something very different:

> We feel the individualism of self-assertion which made the ego the sole and final reality of life is self-destructive and we believe that the individual can realize himself only by seeking his spiritual kindred and by making their common aspirations and problems the object of his active devotion. We believe that the individual can achieve his fullest stature only through the identification of his own good with the good of his group, a group which he himself must help to create. . . . We do not know—we believe. We have not found, we are seeking. But we are seeking not in the texts of ancient creeds or in those of the up-to-the-minute intellectual academies but in the maze of our own lives, in the lives of those closest to us, in the ordinary routine of our work and our pleasures. We know that the task we have appointed ourselves is not simple and we expect our period of discovery to take a long time, so that our efforts will be a record of continuous growth. What we find our work will show. We are sure at least that we are not alone in anxious waiting.

Words, words, and more words—every Friday night from the time the curtains went down on Broadway to the early hours of Saturday morning. Listeners who were too stirred up to sleep afterward repaired to Childs Restaurant on Columbus Circle to talk informally with Clurman. He held Sunday get-togethers, where an indignant young actress named Margaret Barker bombarded him with questions. "How dare you say these things about Lynn Fontanne?" she demanded, wondering plaintively why "all my gods had feet of clay for him." Many wondered where all this talk was leading. An actor named Clifford Odets used to walk home with Clurman after the Friday meetings. One night he confessed, "You know, you've been talking for ten weeks, and I'm just beginning to understand you." Clurman liked that; he didn't believe in quick (or short) answers.

Out of these rambling, impassioned lectures a picture slowly began to emerge of the kind of theatre the three aspiring directors wanted—for although Clurman was doing most of the talking, his ideas had been shaped over five years of discussion with Strasberg, and Crawford fully shared them:

A theatre is created when people with common interests and tastes *unite to devise ways and means whereby they may give their group feeling an adequate theatrical expression.* They seek out people who, for all the superficial differences of their temperament, fundamentally share the same feeling. They seek them amongst directors, actors, playwrights, scene-designers—confident all the time that the thing that binds them together must be a reflection of a sentiment that animates many people in the world about them. . . . If the theatre is an art, if it has any value beyond decorating the emptiness of our existence, it too, *collective art though it be,* must have an analogous *singleness of meaning and direction.* It too must say something, it too *must create* from the chaos which is the common experience of its members, *an expression that will have,* like that of the individual art- ist, *an identity and significance with which people, sharing the com- mon experience,* may *sense their kinship and to which they can attach themselves.*

This was the difference between Clurman's hoped-for theatre and exist- ing organizations like the Theatre Guild and the Civic Rep, which were places to work rather than communities. No unifying principle informed these older companies: they had no organic connection with the material they performed, no point of view they wished to express through their work, no sense of the theatre as an arena in which important ideas could be thrashed out. They thought of theatre as an outlet for "art"; Clurman knew that real theatre was an expression of life itself.

All very well, the more skeptical members of his audience said, but what *were* these important ideas—most crucial of all, what was this "Group Idea" to which Clurman kept referring? He hated to be pinned down: "Words are so inadequate for the definition of essences. You know Cheryl Crawford, Lee Strasberg and me. You have heard what we think about theatre; you have listened to our interpretation of plays, you know how we are attacking this project for a new theatre. In other words, you see us in action. If you are in sympathy with what we say and do, if your response is one of spon- taneous affirmation, then you probably share our Idea. You have the first qualification for work in our theatre."

Some people were so infuriated by this vagueness that they stormed out of the meetings, never to return. But for many, Clurman's fervent generali- ties struck a resonant chord. Though they might have little sense of what his broad pronouncements would mean in practice, they knew that the Group Idea in some way answered their individual hunger for a meaningful theatre and a committed life. Some knew more: they had attended the

American Laboratory Theatre, where Clurman and Strasberg had studied the acting and directing techniques employed at the Moscow Art Theatre, or worked on the two plays they rehearsed for seventeen weeks in 1928, or spent time hanging around with them in the corridors of the Guild and the smoky confines of the Double R Restaurant on West 44th Street. These initiates had a slightly clearer idea of the practical applications of all those abstract ideals.

From his statement of principles, Clurman drew two main conclusions. They had to do with the twin imperatives of art—form and content—and it was typical of the sharply contrasting personalities of the two men who pulled their group in often uneasy tandem for seven years that form was Strasberg's bailiwick and content was Clurman's.

Clurman wanted their new theatre to present contemporary plays by American writers that dealt in a vigorous, positive spirit with "the essential moral and social preoccupations of our time." At first glance, this might not have seemed far removed from the Theatre Guild's desire to do "the best drama of one's time," but the difference in emphasis was significant. The Guild defined "best" as "drama honestly reflecting the author's vision of life or sense of style and beauty"; for Clurman, however, "the criterion for excellence must be the degree to which [a] work responds to the profoundest spiritual needs of its audience." His frustration with the theatre of the twenties stemmed from his belief that it had nothing to say, no interest in the world beyond the stage door. *His* theatre would be vitally connected to real life, not alienated from it.

The Guild viewed the playwright in an abstract, rather romantic way, as an isolated genius who created art and need not necessarily have much to do with the actual production. Clurman believed that author and actor alike were "citizens of a community before they took on their dubious connection with 'art.'" In his theatre, playwrights would be treated not as "isolated purveyor[s] of literary goods" who visited dress rehearsals and made a few comments, but as full members of the group, which would grapple with them about the substance of their ideas, not just doctor lines for superficial effectiveness.

Strasberg, more knowledgeable about theatre than Clurman, with considerable experience as both an actor and a director, had convinced his friend that an idea could not be given satisfactory dramatic form, even by people who fully understood and shared it, unless they had developed a common technique to express it. The unity of a production stemmed not from the written word but from the way all its elements—acting, direction, scenic design—were fused to create a single vision. Most important of all was the actor, the basic unit of the theatre, who had been left in America to fumble around onstage, learning the craft through trial and error, with no coherent sense of how to relate a character to the themes of the play or any kind of deeper personal and emotional truth.

Ever since Strasberg had seen the Moscow Art Theatre, which electrified New York audiences with performances there in 1923 and 1924, he had known what he was after: "a superb ensemble able to fill each moment of a play with life, each actor concerned not with the importance of his part, but his relation to the scene, to the other characters, each moment played with full conviction and reality." The theatre he and Clurman dreamed of would commit itself to a permanent company of actors, then weld them together through a common technique that would enable them to bring the reality of life onto the stage. That technique, he believed, was the system developed by Constantin Stanislavsky at the Moscow Art Theatre and taught by Richard Boleslavsky and Maria Ouspenskaya at the American Laboratory Theatre in New York.

Some of the actors who flocked to Clurman's Friday-night talks already knew about the Stanislavsky system. Those who joined the new theatre learned much more over the next few years of rehearsal and production. What was important in the beginning was not just the content of the system, though its emphasis on the ability to produce truthful emotion revolutionized American acting, but the idea of systematic training for the actor, an alternative to the commercial theatre's hit-or-miss approach.

This, then, was what Clurman and his colleagues promised their audience. A permanent company that would present contemporary American plays reflecting on the life of their times. An organization that helped actors grow through intensive study of their craft and performance in a wide variety of parts. Unified productions, where script, acting, direction, sets, lights, and costumes would all be informed by a common set of values. A living theatre, expressing the spiritual and social concerns of Americans caught up in what by late 1930 was clearly a major crisis in their society. A chance to escape from the loneliness of American life into a group inspired by a shared ideal. A center. A refuge. A home.

It was a vision characteristic of the 1930s. It weighed the boisterous individualism of the twenties and found it lacking; it asserted that any art worthy of the name must have a living connection with the world around it. The actors who responded most intensely to Clurman's words were intrigued by the new techniques he spoke of, but what thrilled them was the idea that theatre could have something to say about the frightening state of American society. If few knew that one-fourth of all urban factory workers were out of work, they were all aware that their own industry was feeling the pinch, with almost 25 percent fewer productions on Broadway that fall than the preceding season. Only the most prescient sensed that an entire economic system lay in ruins about them, but no one could avoid seeing the pitiful apple sellers who shivered on every corner, trying to make a few cents from the willingness of the oversupplied Apple Shippers' Association to provide its product on credit to the unemployed for resale. Clurman's talks made explicit a growing feeling among American artists of all kinds that in the face of such suffering art for art's sake was empty; extreme individualism was self-destructive. Art and society *had* to change.

This feeling gained urgency from the devastation wrought by the Depression, but predated it by many years. Clurman's messianic lectures, which contained not a shred of specific social criticism, had an enthusiastic optimism about American culture that would have been inconceivable before the 1920s, when intellectuals discovered and nurtured an authentic native voice in literature, music, and photography. The committed theatre Clurman, Strasberg, Crawford, and their actors wanted would flower in the welcoming political climate of the 1930s, but its roots had been nourished in the fertile artistic soil of the twenties.

Clurman's ideas had been strongly influenced by his participation in that quintessential twenties experience, expatriate life in Paris. Though born on the Lower East Side, the son of Russian-Jewish immigrants, he was more privileged than most first-generation Americans. His father was a doctor, well enough off to send him to Columbia and, when he decided in 1921 to break off his studies there and go to Paris, indulgent enough to consent. With his friend Aaron Copland, Clurman plunged into the exuberant ambience of the City of Light during its most exciting era. He frequented the famous English-language bookstore Shakespeare and Company, where he saw James Joyce and Ernest Hemingway. He attended concerts of music by Schoenberg, Stravinsky, and the other radical innovators he and Copland admired. He viewed the paintings of Picasso, Matisse, and Duchamp. He heard Jean Cocteau lecture. He reveled in the spirit of experimentation and intellectual vigor that characterized all the arts in the 1920s.

All except the one he loved best. Clurman had been an avid playgoer since age six, when his parents took him to see Jacob Adler in *Uriel Acosta* at the Grand Street Theatre. The Yiddish theatre enthralled him with its productions of classic drama: Shakespeare, Tolstoy, Chekhov, and Gogol brought to life in performances of extraordinary realism by actors with an emotional fluency unknown to their English-language counterparts. Most of all, it was the intense relationship between and among actors and audience he adored, the sense of theatre as a gathering place for the community. When his family moved to the Bronx, he switched his attendance first to local stock companies there, then to Broadway during his high school years. As a teenager he wrote and directed plays in the neighborhood. (One was a melodrama about a small-town chemist he later realized he'd plagiarized from Ibsen's *An Enemy of the People*.) While at Columbia, he found the early work of the Theatre Guild and the daring dramas presented by producer Arthur Hopkins far more absorbing than his studies.

In Paris his feelings about theatre slowly changed. He admired the productions of the Théâtre du Vieux-Colombier and attended lectures by its director, Jacques Copeau, who espoused a unified theatre with organized training for actors similar to what Clurman would later call for in his own talks. He wrote a thesis for the Sorbonne on French drama; he was dazzled by the Moscow Art Theatre when it stopped in Paris in 1922 en route to New York. But theatre began to seem somehow . . . trivial. The excitement he heard in the voices of his friend Copland and fellow musicians when they talked of creating music that captured the rhythms of modern life, the adventurous spirit expressed in books like Waldo Frank's *Our America* as they attempted to define the national essence—theatre had no such electric connection with the real world. Its most lavish productions paled in comparison to the lively pageant Clurman could see on any contemporary street.

Yet when he returned to New York in June 1924, he quickly decided, after a desultory attempt to get a job in book publishing, that the theatre was where he belonged. For four months he read every book on modern theatre he could get his hands on, though when he got to Gordon Craig he had the uneasy feeling that his lack of experience prevented him from really grasping what Craig was driving at. He knew theatre as it was didn't satisfy him; he hadn't yet figured out how he wanted it to be different.

In October he landed work as an extra in Stark Young's *The Saint* with the Provincetown Players. Recently reorganized under the leadership of Kenneth Macgowan, Eugene O'Neill, and Robert Edmond Jones, the organization had expanded into a second theatre, the Greenwich Village in Sheridan Square, where *The Saint* was rehearsed. Clurman learned little from the production, but a good deal from a vague and embarrassingly artsy speech made by Jones, who informed the baffled cast that "To me, theatre is like a light that blind people are made to see for the first time," then exited without further explanation. Jones's inability to communicate his ideas to the actors, Clurman later concluded, was symptomatic of the lack of a common artistic language that prevented even the best-intentioned people in American theatre from doing good work together. He also noted that the idealistic Jones was an amateurish director; when Richard Boleslavsky was brought in to shape up the production, Clurman had his first direct contact with the techniques developed at the Moscow Art Theatre, though as yet they made little impression on him.

Aaron Copland met an aspiring young actor with a musical background and, recognizing someone as passionate about theatre as his friend Clurman, introduced the two. Sanford Meisner had graduated from Erasmus Hall in 1923 and studied piano for a year at the Damrosch Institute of Music before talking his way into a job as an extra in a Theatre Guild production. He'd always wanted to act, and watching the intense, naturalistic performance of Pauline Lord in Sidney Howard's *They Knew What They Wanted* he began to realize that "acting which really dug at me was what I was looking for." His parents, Hungarian-born Jews who hoped he would make a career in the clothing industry, were horrified, but Meisner persisted.

Soon he and Clurman were spending a lot of time talking together at the

Double R, a dingy place opposite the Belasco Theatre that served terrible coffee but was tolerant of ardent young people swapping grandiose ideas about theatre. When Meisner got his first decent part in a special Guild production of Pirandello's *Right You Are If You Think You Are*, he invited his friend to come see it. Clurman thought he was "picturesque," but was more struck by the "disagreeable though effective" performance of the man playing the lead. With his harsh voice, faint foreign accent, and receding hairline, Lee Strasberg hardly seemed like an actor at all.

In fact, his choice of acting as a profession came relatively late. Books were the consuming passion of young Israel Strassberg. Born in Poland in 1901, he arrived at age seven on the Lower East Side, where he found himself isolated in a country whose language he didn't speak, and emotionally distant from overworked parents with neither time nor inclination for intimacy. He took refuge in voracious reading and the companionship of his older brother, Zalmon. As a boy he was lured by a brother-in-law into playing a few small parts in Yiddish-language productions, but an unpleasant incident when he was still quite young—a lamp blew up onstage and scorched his hands—soured him on theatre.

Zalmon's death in the influenza epidemic of 1918 was so traumatic for the young Strassberg that the straight-A student dropped out of high school. Not until the early 1920s, did Strassberg—desperate for human contact, and profoundly bored with his work as a partner in a company that manufactured women's hairpieces—join the Students of Arts and Drama Club at the Chrystie Street Settlement House.

SAD, as its members called it, was part of the lively network of settlement-house drama groups that had recently sprung up, inspired by the Neighborhood Playhouse and its insistence that theatre had a vital role to play in the community. Through these groups, young immigrants who previously thought they had no connection with American culture became part of the excitement of the little theatre movement. Though SAD's main purpose—and Strassberg's reason for joining it—was social, the new member soon began to feed his insatiable reading habit with books on his new hobby. Gordon Craig's *On the Art of the Theatre* excited him as it did Clurman, but other books were also influential, especially those that dealt with the art of acting: Ludovico Riccoboni's *Pensées sur la déclamation* (Strassberg read French and German as well as English and Yiddish), *The Illusion of the First Time in Acting* by William Gillette, the English tragedian William Macready's memoirs and diaries, and many, many more. From the beginning, he was fascinated by the question of how an actor could summon up real emotion during a performance rather than simply relying on external skills to imitate feeling.

Strassberg learned enough from books to win a prize as outstanding settlement-house actor during his first year there. (On one of the Chrystie Street playbills he dropped the extra "s" and altered his first name to become Lee Strasberg.) He knew so much more than the ostensible head of the drama club that his fellow students insisted he be named director; they were the audience for the first of what would be a lifetime of lectures based on his voluminous reading. Yet despite his newfound eminence, Strasberg thought of theatre as a sideline, something to fill the hours after the wig business shut down at six o'clock. After all, he was hardly the physical type to be a leading man. The stars of the time were glamorous, romantic figures; their personalities as much as their acting sold tickets. Strasberg knew he lacked that appeal. When the Theatre Guild's casting director, Philip Loeb, impressed by one of his performances, asked if he wanted to act professionally, he replied in typically brief fashion, "No."

The Moscow Art Theatre changed his mind. On January 8, 1923, Stanislavsky's company burst like a thunderclap on the New York theatrical world, which had never seen anything like its productions of *The Cherry Orchard, The Three Sisters, The Lower Depths,* and *The Brothers Karamazov.* The intense psychological realism of the acting, the sense of the characters' inner life resonating in every line and movement, thrilled New York audiences. Used to watching one or two stars surrounded by supporting players, they marveled at the Russians' devotion to an ensemble in which all the actors subordinated their personalities to the demands of the characters and the play.

Strasberg was overwhelmed. He had seen great acting before—Pauline Lord in *Anna Christie,* Jeanne Eagels in *Rain,* Jacob Ben-Ami in *Samson and Delilah,* Fyodor Chaliapin at the Metropolitan Opera. For him, what made a great performance were those moments when the actor and the character seemed one, when the audience felt "that it was a person living, breathing on stage, not acting." But such performances were rare. Too often, he witnessed affectation of the worst sort, down to phony British accents and trite gestures. Even the artists he admired seemed to achieve brilliance only in flashes; the emotional reality that excited him was seldom sustained over the course of an evening, let alone the long run. Yet here was a company performing plays that had been in its repertory for years, and the acting was as spontaneous and emotionally charged as if the lines were being spoken for the first time.

Two things about the Moscow Art Theatre particularly impressed him, and both had a personal significance. The first was that every actor on the stage was giving a performance of equal caliber: Maria Ouspenskaya in the minor role of the governess in *The Cherry Orchard* had the same conviction and inner truthfulness as Stanislavsky, who portrayed Gayev; Leo Bulgakov playing a small part in *The Sea Gull* was in no way inferior to Vassily Katchalov as the Baron in *The Three Sisters.* For a good actor who didn't have star quality, a company in which every actor was great, no matter what the size of the part, was a revelation and an inspiration.

The second revelation grew out of the first. Stanislavsky's *My Life in Art,* which discussed the evolution of his system, wasn't published until 1924, but Strasberg understood immediately that the consistently fine acting of the Moscow Art Theatre hadn't happened by accident: "Obviously, this truth and reality was achieved by some singular process or procedure of which we in the American theatre had little knowledge." The idea that someone had discovered a solution to the essential actor's problem was intoxicating. The promise of a methodical approach to acting was especially appealing to a voracious reader and largely self-taught intellectual like Strasberg, studious by nature and inclined to look for answers in books. Like Clurman, he loved the theatre but was dissatisfied with what he saw. Now that he had glimpsed what theatre could be, he was ready to take the plunge: quit the wig business, commit himself to a career as a professional actor, and get some training.

With the money he received from his erstwhile partner, Strasberg enrolled in the Clare Tree Major School of the Theatre, where he studied speech, voice, and ballet; declaimed Shakespeare, and acted in a few plays. It was the standard training of the time, all surface and imitation, not at all what he had in mind. A younger classmate, Phoebe Brand, who seven years later would worship Strasberg as a teacher and director, in 1924 found him strange and unapproachable; she couldn't imagine why such an untheatrical man wanted to be an actor. Strasberg certainly didn't want to be the kind of actor the Clare Tree Major School turned out. When a fellow student told him that two former members of the Moscow Art Theatre were teaching acting at a place called the American Laboratory Theatre, he rushed to audition.

The Lab had been founded in June 1923 by four well-to-do Americans and Richard Boleslavsky, a Polish-born actor who had worked with Stanislavsky at the Moscow Art Theatre from 1906 to 1919, when he fled the Russian Revolution. He reached America in late 1922 and was on hand to greet his old MAT comrades when they docked there the following January. Just ten days after their triumphant New York premiere, he began a series of lectures at the Princess Theatre that laid out for his American audience the philosophy of actor training behind the MAT's extraordinary performances. He bemoaned the fact that the American theatre existed simply to sell a product, no matter how shoddy, and that "there are no laboratories of the theatre . . . to contemplate, to search, to create." It was only natural that Miriam and Herbert Stockton, patrons of the arts who dreamed of establishing an American art theatre similar to the MAT, should ask Boleslavsky to direct it. He in turn enlisted Maria Ouspenskaya, who decided to stay behind when the MAT went back home in 1924.

At the Lab's new quarters at 139 MacDougal Street, Strasberg first encountered Stanislavsky's system, the effort to prepare an actor consciously for the unconscious flights of inspiration embodied in a great performance. "This is it. This is what it really means. This is what it is all about," he exulted as he scribbled furiously in his notebook during Boleslavsky's lectures and Ouspenskaya's classes. Just as an actor's voice and body could be trained, so too it was possible to discipline and hone the intangibles: emotion and imagination. Inspiration couldn't be taught, but the groundwork for inspiration could be laid. Ouspenskaya drilled her students in concentration, showing them how much more relaxed and natural they appeared when they were actually thinking about something onstage rather than trying to show the audience what they were thinking. Exercises with nonexistent objects sharpened the actor's powers of observation and trained the senses to respond to imaginary stimuli, giving the actor the tools to create a specific, genuinely felt physical and emotional reality in the dream world of a theatrical performance.

The Lab was the first school in America to offer comprehensive actor training. The Stanislavsky-based classes were its most famous element, but external means of expression were not neglected: students took courses in speech, voice, and movement. Boleslavsky also emphasized the actor's need to develop intellectually and culturally, to study history, read literature, look at paintings, listen to music—an approach that meshed comfortably with Strasberg's own scholarly instincts. It was all a revelation to Strasberg; the exercises and general attitude he learned at the Lab formed the basis of his work for the rest of his life. But he didn't stay long. Once he'd absorbed the basics, the youthful autodidact preferred to study on his own and explore the ramifications of the system through his work as an actor and director. Ironically, Boleslavsky himself sowed the seeds for Strasberg's departure. In his prospectus for the Lab, he said that an art theatre based on Stanislavsky's acting principles needed to be grounded in American reality, to become "a living social force, recreating itself each generation from the thoughts and material of its own times." Strasberg didn't think this goal could be achieved in a theatre run by Russian expatriates; he set out to see if it were attainable anywhere else.

Philip Loeb remembered the strange young actor who had said he didn't want to be a professional; he didn't hold Strasberg's change of heart against him and gave him a batch of small parts in *Processional*, John Howard Lawson's "jazz symphony of American life." Also in the cast was Sandy Meisner; the two were among the young actors given the chance to appear in a trial production of a play the Guild wasn't sure would work as a regular subscription offering: *Right You Are If You Think You Are.*

Just a few months later, at a casting call for the Guild's *Garrick Gaieties* in the spring of 1925, Harold Clurman met the man whose performance in the Pirandello play had so intrigued him. Strasberg got parts in a few of the revue's sketches, Meisner landed a job in the chorus, and Clurman (who demonstrated in his audition with the Flower Song from *Carmen* that singing was not his forte) was hired as stage manager. They discovered and defined their shared dream of a serious American theatre while working on a musical revue that epitomized the insouciant wit of the 1920s. For six months, they listened to the strains of Rodgers and Hart's delightful songs and enjoyed the script's satiric thrusts at the Theatre Guild's penchant for "important drama." Backstage and after hours, Clurman and Strasberg talked about a completely different kind of theatre, quickly realizing that their individual ideals were compatible and in many ways complementary. Their discussions over the next five years would be summarized and polished into a call for action in Clurman's talks during the winter of 1930–1931.

Only the most compelling vision could have drawn two such different men together. Clurman was still timid with strangers in those days, but among friends he was flamboyant, almost overpowering. He loved to talk and had a spellbinding way with words, an ability to inflame listeners with the fire of his ideas. Profoundly intellectual—widely read in several languages, numbering critics, photographers, and musicians as well as theatre folk among his friends—he was also earthy (with a penchant for profanity unusual in those days), warm, and gregarious. His belief that all meaningful activity took place in groups sprang as much from his need to surround himself with companions as it did from intellectual conviction. He loved to make his friends laugh, as often as not by making fun of himself: this man of ideas was so physically inept that he found peeling an orange a difficult task and had been known to stand by a ringing phone saying, "Hello? Hello?"—unaware that he had neglected to pick up the receiver. But he wasn't entirely oblivious to the real world; his fanaticism was tempered by an irony that added tang to his enormous zest for life.

If Clurman embraced life, Strasberg appeared to have been wounded by it in some indefinable way. He was serious, aloof, and so rigidly self-possessed as to be intimidating. Intense feelings seethed under his icy exterior, but the only one that ever broke through was rage, when he felt an actor wasn't trying hard enough for the true emotion that was his passion and obsession. It was difficult to feel close to this frightening young man, who went stiff with embarrassment and incomprehension when effusive people made the mistake of touching him. The give-and-take of friendship with peers was hard for him; he preferred to lecture or hide from direct contact altogether behind the sports section of a newspaper, rustling its pages when whatever was going on displeased him. "In those days I wasn't too easy to have a dialogue with," he admitted.

Clurman managed. "We were drawn together by our common dissatisfactions, our still unshaped ideals," he wrote. With their diverse temperaments and interests, they challenged each other's ideas; out of their sometimes heated debates, a fuller, more well-rounded program for a new theatre emerged.

Neither had much professional experience, though Strasberg had done a lot of acting and recently begun to direct down at Chrystie Street. Like most young intellectuals, they formed their ideas out of books. Clurman had read widely in classic and contemporary drama, was familiar with most important works of literary and cultural criticism, had dipped into the philosophy of Spinoza and Kant, and avidly read novels and poetry. He was fascinated by works of the imagination and how they related to the world around him; his friendship with Aaron Copland introduced him to many creative artists, and he understood his desire to create meaningful theatre as part of a larger effort in all the arts to capture and comment on the teeming reality of American life.

Strasberg's knowledge was deeper and narrower. He'd read virtually every handbook on acting and design and was well versed in theatre history. Since childhood he'd also immersed himself in Egyptology and archeology; in his lonely post-high-school forays to the New York Public Library, he'd discovered Oriental and Biblical history; he'd read Freud and studied the origins of Zoroastrianism and Buddhism. He liked dense factual books that told him how things worked; his careful attention to detail stood him in good stead as a director and acting teacher. Clurman was the theorist, Strasberg the one who anchored those theories in theatre practice.

Throughout 1925 and into 1926, as they played small parts at the Guild, they talked and talked. Clurman learned that a play was more than words spoken on a stage, that a great production embodied its ideas in living experience: a fusion of acting, direction, and stage design whose significance lay deeper than the surface text. Strasberg learned that good acting and an interesting concept were not enough to redeem a trivial play, that the talents of the theatre's interpretative artists were most deeply realized when put in service of ideas important to them and the audience. They were young, their jobs were nowhere near commensurate with their aspirations, they had plenty of free time; they talked some more. In the summer of 1926, Clurman went to Europe with Copland while Strasberg stage-managed the second *Garrick Gaieties* and continued his work at Chrystie Street.

In the fall the Guild cast Clurman in a few minor roles in *Juarez and Maximilian.* He had studied the play over the summer—his article about it was published in *Theatre Guild Magazine*—and knew a good deal more about its historical background than the director, a fact he wasn't shy about imparting to select backstage companions. One of them was the assistant stage manager, Cheryl Crawford, who was amused by his arrogance and taken with his ideas about theatre. But she didn't have much time to spend listening to Clurman: she played two bit parts, fired a pistol offstage, conducted a small backstage orchestra, called the actors for entrances, and shot off a cannon in the basement. Still, they continued their meetings—he talking, she listening—during the infrequent moments she could snatch from her daytime duties as the Guild's casting director.

At first glance, the calm, sensible, and reserved Cheryl Crawford seemed very different from her volatile colleagues-to-be. She hated arguments and

would respond to people yelling around her by talking so softly that eventually they would quiet down just to find out what she was saying. Her
origins were a long way from the Lower East Side. Born in Akron, Ohio,
the daughter of a well-off real-estate entrepreneur, she had a quiet, unevent-
ful childhood and dreamed of becoming a missionary. She attended Smith
College, where she was head of the Dramatic Association, built sets and
props for the Provincetown Players during the summer before her senior
year, and after graduating in 1925 landed a berth in the Theatre Guild's
new acting school despite her admitted desire to be a director, not an actress. A year later when Theresa Helburn, executive director of the Guild,
offered her the thankless job of replacing Philip Loeb as casting director,
she bargained her way into the assistant stage manager slot on *Juarez*. She
was practical, efficient, and clearly destined for a long and rewarding career
at the Guild.

But Crawford wasn't nearly so conventional as she appeared. At Smith,
her Sunday school precepts were largely abandoned in favor of the intoxicating bohemianism of the twenties. She read Nietzsche and passed on his
ideas to impressionable younger students. She smoked and drank; rumors
about her sex life were of a nature that a women's school found particularly
unnerving. She lost the Phi Beta Kappa membership her grades had earned
and was nearly expelled when a professor spotted her at an off-campus inn
smoking after lunch with a group of fellow students. Her theatrical efforts
were no less avant-garde. As leader of the drama club, she eschewed conventional plays in favor of an outdoor production of an Oriental drama,
complete with a water curtain that ruined the president's back garden. She
hadn't shed her idealism along with her desire to become a missionary,
merely refocused it on the theatre.

To her mind, the Guild was a commendable organization that did important plays with fine actors. She was intrigued by Clurman's ideas, but
wrapped up in her demanding duties. For the moment, she was a sympa-
thizer rather than a convert.

Clurman and Strasberg were exploring alternatives to the Guild. Working with his devoted amateurs at Chrystie Street, Strasberg experimented
with many theatrical styles: psychological realism in the Moscow Art mode,
the flamboyant expressionism of the German director Max Reinhardt, con-
structivism, poetic lyricism. When Clurman came to visit while Strasberg
was directing Racine's *Esther*, he marveled at the originality of his friend's
work with the actors. It was based on the Stanislavsky system as taught by
Boleslavsky, but Strasberg had made some changes inspired by his own
reading. He found that nonprofessionals were too inexperienced to make
creative use of Stanislavsky's "magic if" ("What would I do if I were the
character?") and turned to the approach favored by Stanislavsky's disciple
Eugene Vakhtangov, in which the director suggests an "adjustment," a substitute reality not necessarily related to the text that helps make the quality

the director seeks personally meaningful to the actor. In *Esther,* Strasberg told his actors to think of themselves not as Biblical kings and queens, which might seem impossibly remote to them, but as priests and nuns, who were more familiar but whose behavior would give them the appropriate dignity. Professional actors later complained that this method could be manipulative and disorienting, but it was highly effective. Clurman was so impressed that he urged Sandy Meisner, unhappy with the superficial acting classes at the Guild school, to come down and see what he could learn from Strasberg.

In November, Strasberg and Clurman enrolled in Boleslavsky's course for directors at the Lab. It was somewhat disorganized, with Boleslavsky absent from February through April staging a play in London, but it was the backdrop for a momentous event in Clurman's life: he met Stella Adler.

She was the youngest daughter of Jacob Adler, the "great eagle" of the Yiddish theatre, whose bravura performance in *Uriel Acosta* had been the six-year-old Clurman's first theatregoing experience. Jacob's wife, Sarah, was a prominent actress herself, and all their children shared their life in the theatre. Stella made her debut at age five, when her father held her out to the audience at the curtain call, crying, "She's yours too!" As a child and teenager she acted in the wide range of repertory characteristic of the Yiddish theatre: contemporary folk drama, Shakespeare, European classics. She made her English-speaking stage debut in 1922, when she was twenty, in Karel Čapek's peculiar insect comedy *The World We Live In.* Shortly thereafter she contracted tuberculosis and spent three years away from the theatre. When she came back and decided to enroll at the Lab, "she was roundly laughed at by her brothers and sisters for her 'seriousness.' " The gay, laughter-loving Adlers saw no need to study acting: you simply went out there and did it; it was your life.

Stella Adler was in a vulnerable state at the time she met Clurman. Her beloved father had recently died. (Half a million people turned out to pay their respects at the Hebrew Actors Club where he lay in state.) A youthful marriage to an Englishman was strained by her need to travel and act. The Yiddish theatre was home: its intimate, quarrelsome atmosphere was familiar, its actors the best she had ever seen, there was always work. But she was an American and sensed she wanted something more. Her cousin Francine Larrimore was a Broadway star, and that possibility tempted her glamour- and luxury-loving side even as its commercialism and coldness repelled her. Her studious, intellectual instincts were nourished by the Lab course of study, which she found "thorough and complete, well-rounded and systematic." The question was: where could she put these exciting new ideas into practice as a working actor?

Clurman as yet had no definite answer for her. She continued her work at the Lab, toured Europe and South America, and acted with the Yiddish Art Theatre, whose founder, Maurice Schwartz, envisioned it as a fusion of the ideals of the little theatre movement and the older traditions of the Jewish stage. When she was in town, she and Clurman drew closer together through their talks; he did not realize he was in love with her for another year.

In the spring of 1927 Jacques Copeau came to New York to direct his dramatization of *The Brothers Karamazov* for the Guild, and Clurman joined the production as unofficial translator. To honor this visionary theatre artist, whom they both admired, Strasberg staged Copeau's autobiographical drama *The House into Which We Are Born* at Chrystie Street. Neither event was an entire success. Watching Copeau struggle to impart his ideas to American actors, Clurman was once again struck by the fact that, without a common artistic language, even the most talented people couldn't work together to create effective theatre. He took Copeau downtown to see Strasberg's production, but was appalled by his friend's utter silence when Copeau murmured a few words of praise; it was almost as though Strasberg had to prove to the actors that this was *his* production and he didn't care what the author thought. Strasberg, never one to waste words, had simply felt he had nothing to say.

Nonetheless, Copeau's presence and his lectures at the Lab inspired the friends to speak more definitely of founding a theatre of their own. As they scoured New York in search of new theatrical experiences—Max Reinhardt's imported productions on Broadway, the Chinese theatre in the Bowery, the powerful emotional acting of the Sicilian artist Giovanni Grasso—they talked about how their own theatre would draw on all these traditions yet create a uniquely American institution. They believed in American culture with an assurance made possible by the spirit of the 1920s and with a special passion common to the children of immigrants.

Clurman's life outside the theatre was giving him ideas as well. Underneath the Jazz Age frenzy of the smart parties he attended, he sensed a new current of doubt and loneliness. In the frustrated, despondent tone of books by Joseph Wood Krutch, Lewis Mumford, and Waldo Frank, he saw a hunger for something their art wasn't giving them. At Alfred Stieglitz's gallery, he felt a spirit that moved him profoundly: "[Stieglitz] was committed to the artists, not simply as individual talents, but as representatives of something astir in the country, something bigger than the art world— life in America itself." Could he and Strasberg create a theatre with that commitment?

In early 1928 they got a chance to try. A real-estate entrepreneur named Sidney Ross, who planned to put some of his money into theatrical production, hired Clurman as an assistant. It quickly became apparent that Ross had no exact idea of what he wanted to do; finally he asked his new aide for suggestions. At a hasty council of war in Childs Restaurant on Fifth Avenue and 49th Street, equidistant between the apartment Strasberg shared with his new wife in Astoria and Clurman's residence with his parents in the Bronx, the pair drew up a proposal. Ross would let them use the roof garden of a building he owned, they would select a company of actors to rehearse a play using their new methods, and if he liked the results he could finance them. The idea was not to get backing for a single production, but to convince Ross and perhaps others to fund a new theatre group.

Ross agreed to the plan, and they set to work. Clurman introduced himself to Waldo Frank, who'd just finished revising a play called *New Year's Eve* that he'd been mulling over for nearly a decade. Clurman had adopted Frank as one of his literary heroes the moment he read *Our America*, a book that discussed critically but hopefully the nation's raw energy and the vital culture that might arise from it. As an editor at the short-lived but influential *Seven Arts* magazine, which had expired in 1917 because of its opposition to America's entrance into the World War, Frank had championed American writers and urged intellectuals to come out of their ivory towers and grapple with the pressing social and political issues of the day. He was flattered to hear how greatly his outlook on culture had influenced Clurman's ideas and intrigued by the request to let a new, untried company give his script the kind of in-depth, philosophical approach Clurman assured him it needed.

Frank agreed to let them rehearse *New Year's Eve*, and they invited a group of young actors to join the project. What Clurman and Strasberg offered was the first practical formulation of the ideas they'd been shaping over the past three years. Rehearsals would be a training ground; they would use the Stanislavsky system to help actors explore their craft more fully than was possible in the commercial theatre, paying attention to the artistic growth of each actor as well as the shaping of the production. They would draw the actors closer to the ideas in the script, trying to make the playwright's vision personally meaningful to them. Form and content would be intertwined to create a whole that expressed the vision of actors and director as well as playwright.

Sandy Meisner signed up as a matter of course; by virtue of his participation in many an all-night talk and his work with Strasberg on *Esther*, he could be counted on as their first disciple. Stella Adler preferred to observe; she was intrigued, but wary of what to her professional eye seemed amateur. Others responded favorably to Clurman's enthusiastic proselytizing, including two who became close associates.

Clurman had spotted Franchot Tone in a New Playwrights production of John Howard Lawson's *The International* in January 1928. Tall, handsome, always well dressed, this affluent young Cornell graduate seemed out of place in a company founded the previous year to present radical plays—which may have accounted for the stiffness Clurman observed in his performance. But Tone had a serious side not evident to those who saw him squiring beautiful women around New York nightclubs; his lively interest in social and economic issues had steered him toward New Playwrights and made him receptive to Clurman's ardent formulations.

Morris Carnovsky shared Tone's intellectual nature, though his background was more akin to Clurman's and Strasberg's. The child of immigrant Jews in St. Louis, as a boy he had "made a damn nuisance of myself through an inordinate demand for sincerity." After graduating Phi Beta Kappa from Washington University in 1920, he studied with the German actor Emmanuel Reicher, then acted with two Boston stock companies and at the Provincetown Players and the Theatre Guild, always in search of a more definite technique and a permanent company to call home. The Guild seemed the perfect place for him, and he was delighted to be added to its small band of regular actors after the 1926–1927 season. By 1928 he was a respected character actor, but despite the praise he won in *Juarez and Maximilian*, *The Brothers Karamazov*, and *The Doctor's Dilemma*, he was dissatisfied. "I had good instincts, I think; I got along in the theatre, even without training. . . . I was capable of acting truthfully up to a certain point." Yet he felt he couldn't get beyond that point; the sincerity he had demanded since childhood eluded him onstage, and he was frustrated. Perhaps this promised new method of rehearsal would help.

The group rehearsed for seventeen weeks—at a time when the average commercial production took only four—in a rooftop hall at 128 Riverside Drive, near 85th Street. *New Year's Eve* was not a great script; the dialogue was stilted, and it had the lugubrious tone common to seriously inclined playwrights working under the not-always-beneficial influence of Eugene O'Neill. But the theme as defined by Clurman appealed to idealistic young people: "man had to face living realities rather than be guided by the nomenclature of institutions and dogmas." The twists and turns of the plot, which involved infidelity and disillusionment among a group of upper-middle-class intellectuals, offered a good opportunity for the kind of in-depth work on the actors' emotional equipment that was Strasberg's specialty.

In fact, Clurman began as the director but decided he was "insufficiently secure, technically speaking, to convince the actors of the validity of our methods." ("What is this hocus pocus?" snapped the normally polite Carnovsky when Clurman tried to give him an emotional exercise of the sort taught at the Lab.) He asked Strasberg to take over, and a division of labor began that endured for seven years: Strasberg exploring and expanding the horizons of the actor's art in daily rehearsals, Clurman speaking outside the hall on the historical and theoretical issues underpinning the script.

Waldo Frank was impressed by the result of their work, and the company planned to go away for the summer to rehearse another play with money provided by Ross. At the last minute, Ross changed his mind; he was unready to finance a group of virtually unknown actors using what must have seemed to him an incomprehensible and suspiciously arty new technique. He was willing to let them continue using the roof, however, and for an additional six weeks in July and August they worked on *Balloon*, an expressionistic comedy by the Irish poet Padraic Colum. Much better written than *New Year's Eve*, it seemed to the actors rather slight, though its fantastical mood and good-natured insistence on the hollowness of success were very much in the spirit of the times. A performance for an invited audience including the author's wife was enthusiastically received, but the hoped-for financing wasn't forthcoming.

"The work of my group will have to be discontinued for a month or so," Clurman wrote to his friend Paul Strand, adding optimistically, "After that there will be a regathering of forces and a renewal of the effort." For the moment, they scattered: Carnovsky and Meisner to the Guild's touring production of O'Neill's *Marco Millions*, Tone to *The Age of Innocence* with Katharine Cornell, Strasberg back to Chrystie Street, and Clurman to deal with his personal life.

Somewhat to his dismay, he'd fallen in love with Stella Adler. The romance waxed and waned. Despite the fact that she was still married to someone else, he was sure: "Here was the personification of something I wanted to integrate with my whole sense of life, someone who indeed was a living symbol of so much I treasured in life." She was not so sure. She wondered if he loved her or some idea he had of her, mixed up with his love for the Yiddish theatre and yearning for a theatrical tradition that didn't exist in America. His symbol was a flesh-and-blood woman who doubted that he measured up to the larger-than-life standard set by her father ("I can't compete with a dead man," he told her) and found him lacking in the sophistication she expected in the men in her life. Yet she was impressed by his intellect and loved to talk with him about the theatre. When he spoke of the new theatre he and Strasberg would found, she glimpsed the possibility of an organization with all the values that sustained her on the Yiddish stage—ensemble acting, good plays, steady work—in an American incarnation. She was excited, she was interested, she was unsure. They began a relationship of flight and pursuit, deep affection and terrible cruelty, that would amaze and appall their friends for decades. Cheryl Crawford sardonically suggested that a book about their "hazardous interdependence" might be entitled *Wolf on the Carcass*.

The graduates of *New Year's Eve* and *Balloon* continued to meet whenever they could. They attended productions and analyzed the acting. They gathered in one another's apartments and talked about "our group" and "our theatre." They had no money and no standing: "Strasberg and I, as far as the theatre world was concerned," wrote Clurman, "were minor actors who talked a lot to whoever would lend an ear." There seemed nothing to be done about it at the moment. Clurman was so depressed and at loose ends that one night he turned up in Astoria to ask Strasberg if he should go to Russia to pursue advanced studies in theatre. His friend sensibly pointed out that when he returned their own theatre would be just as far from reality, and Clurman calmed down. When Theresa Helburn offered him a job as playreader at the Guild, he took it.

He admitted later that he was much too difficult about the scripts he

read in those days. Despite years of talks with Strasberg, he was still inclined to judge a play on the basis of its ideas, with little attention to
whether they had been given a workable dramatic form. His contempt for
craftsmanship devoid of thought was in many ways commendable; his inability to see merit in work whose conclusions he disagreed with and his
belief that incoherent plays whose values he shared could somehow be
shaped up in production would be drawbacks for years to come.

During his stint in the Guild play department, his severity stemmed in
part from his frustration with his job and his life. Here was the Guild,
rolling in money, with a guaranteed subscriber list of 30,000 in New York
and 30,000 more on the road, able to produce any play they wanted with
comparatively little risk. And what did they do? They took good actors,
plunked them down in worthwhile plays for which the Guild board had no
real feeling, and left them to flounder, without any sense of what the author
was trying to say or how it might relate to their own lives. He contemp-
tuously dismissed the board members as "Ethical Culture people"—cosmopolitan German Jews (though of course they weren't all Jewish) with
intelligence and taste but none of the moral passion he demanded.

He also despised their faith in an unhappy ending as a guarantee of a
play's seriousness. "They had a fixation on pessimism. If you felt BADLY and
said life stinks! it STINKS! you were really an advanced person. There's something about pessimism that gives people an aura of grandeur. If you think
everything is hopeless and down and wretched and dirty, then you really
are an exalted person. I've never understood why." Clurman and his friends
believed that out of the struggle and confusion of American life, something
true and worthwhile could be born. They took their credo from Walt Whitman's *Democratic Vistas*, a book Clurman was always pressing on people:
"America demands a poetry that is bold, modern, and all-surrounding and
kosmical, as she is herself. . . . It must bend its vision toward the future,
more than the past." While their theatre, which would express this optimism, hung in limbo for want of financing, the Guild wallowed in cash and
facile nihilism.

It was maddening. He grew a beard to make visible his discontent. He
ranted to Cheryl Crawford and Herbert Biberman, a Guild stage manager
who had some of the same complaints. The Guild board, sensing unrest in
the ranks, decided to give the lunatics charge of a small asylum; it created
a subsidiary to present the kinds of experimental productions that had
marked the Guild's early days and made Clurman, Crawford, and Biberman
heads of the project. The plan was to present three productions a year in
special Sunday performances for subscribers who might care to sample
something beyond the Guild's usual diet of sophisticated Middle European
comedy, emasculated Shaw, and ponderous American tragedies. The implicit promise was that, just as the Moscow Art Theatre's First Studio had
grown into the Second Moscow Art Theatre, so this new group might some-

day become a full-fledged independent organization. In tribute to that dream, the triumvirate called its venture the Theatre Guild Studio.

For their initial production, Clurman chose a Soviet play, first presented in Moscow in 1927, that had caused quite a stir in Paris and London as well. *Red Rust* was a swaggering melodrama whose overwrought plot was less interesting than the extensive and frank discussions among the characters about various political and moral problems that faced the young nation. Biberman directed and played the villain, an opportunist who uses the slogans of the Revolution to mask his nefarious personal misdeeds. Clurman recruited Franchot Tone to play Fedor, a young Communist under suspicion because of his bourgeois background, and Strasberg for a small part as Pimples, a student. He also brought into the fold a few other actors who had been giving his ideas a sympathetic hearing.

Luther Adler, Stella's younger brother, had a "slightly depressed air" at the time that Clurman felt suited him for the part of Piotr, the disenchanted idealist who gives the play's title speech about the "red rust" of apathy and laziness discoloring the bright metal of Soviet society. Luther was a charismatic and ambitious young actor struggling to carve out a career in the shadow of his father's mighty reputation. He loved the serious attitude of the actors and the intense involvement of the audience in the tradition he was born to, but by 1920 he had concluded that the Yiddish theatre's great days were over and joined the Provincetown Players to see if he could find its equal elsewhere. His father lured him back into Yiddish repertory in 1922, and for seven years he swung uneasily between Broadway and Second Avenue, finding neither wholly satisfying.

Two actresses who had studied and acted at the American Laboratory Theatre took roles as students. Ruth Nelson, who as the daughter of a vaudeville performer was part of a more instinctual theatrical tradition, had been terrified and bewildered by Maria Ouspenskaya's classes at the Lab. Only when she worked with Boleslavsky on *Martine*, a French drama in which the main action was the emotional progress of the title character, did she begin to see how the Stanislavsky system could help her as an actress. Critics lavishly praised her performance when *Martine* bowed in April 1928, and she hoped to continue acting at the Lab. But it was in the throes of the organizational and financial chaos that led to its dissolution in 1930, and she began the disheartening seesaw between engagements and layoffs that was—and is—the usual lot of young actors in the commercial theatre. She was as disappointed by Broadway as it was unwelcoming to her and eagerly snapped up the chance to try something different in *Red Rust*.

Eunice Stoddard's parents were among the affluent, cultivated New Yorkers who had been excited by the Moscow Art Theatre and subsequently took interest in the Lab; her father was a partner in the same law firm as Herbert Stockton, one of the organization's founders. Stoddard studied singing, dancing, and music for three years in Europe, where she met Stanislavsky, before returning to America to enroll in the Lab. Her classic ingénue good looks—pale blond hair, peaches-and-cream complexion—won her parts on Broadway even while she was appearing in the Lab's experimental productions. But her parents had raised her to aspire to more than stardom; she found the work at the Lab fascinating and shared their hope that an American company to equal the MAT might grow out of it.

William Challee, who played a male student in *Red Rust*, had met Nelson earlier that year in a production called *Judas*, in which they discovered their mutual dislike of the commercial theatre. They continued their friendship while playing small parts in Leo Bulgakov's famous 1929 revival of *The Sea Gull*. Since running away from home at age eighteen, Challee had acted in stock and then for three years at Provincetown, where the dedication to serious native drama was more to his taste. He was a fiery man with strong convictions, looking for a theatre that could contain them.

Red Rust was not rehearsed in the careful manner Strasberg had employed in 1928. Herbert Biberman was a conventional director who, to Eunice Stoddard's knowledgeable eye, "just blustered through" the highly colored melodrama. The critics were very taken with the enthusiasm and vigor of the young cast, however; they especially liked the crowd scenes and were surprised by the candor with which the characters discussed the Soviet Union's faults. Joseph Wood Krutch of *The Nation* put his finger on what had attracted Clurman to the play and excited the actors: *Red Rust*, he wrote, was typical of the Soviet theatre, which was "a theatre closer and more literally faithful to the contemporary life of its age than any other theatre in the world." The anonymous critic in *Vogue*, sounding a good deal like Clurman, noted the contrast between this vibrant play of ideas and "the American drama of to-day [which] lacks genuine vitality; rarely, if ever, does it give the impression of having been written because it had to be written. For the most part, it says what it says carefully; it is arranged; it employs tricks generously and seems satisfied. That kind of play may interest, amuse, thrill, but it can not make a really lasting dent in the spectator's consciousness. *Red Rust* does."

Originally planned for three special matinees, the play was successful enough to be given a regular production, opening at the Martin Beck on December 17, 1929, and running through mid-February. Given the favorable reception, the triumvirate assumed the Studio would continue. Clurman wanted to try a new production of *Balloon*, but the Guild board saw nothing in the script. Cheryl Crawford began directing *Dead or Alive*, a folk play by Philip Barber, but after the board attended a run-through that too was shut down. (These command performances, an ordeal undergone by every Guild production, were referred to in the ranks as "the death watch.") With those two decisions, the Theatre Guild Studio came to an end.

In part, it was a matter of finances. *Red Rust* lost about $13,000 despite the good reviews, and the Guild was very nervous about money in the uneasy months immediately following the stock-market crash. Other factors came into play as well. The board generally considered politics outside the province of art—its productions of Shaw had achieved the remarkable feat of removing his plays from the political context in which they were written—and could only have been dismayed by people in the audience at *Red Rust* cheering as "The Internationale" was played before the curtain. The Guild's rather abstract concern for the "integrity" of the author's words also conflicted with the Studio's more hands-on approach; shortly after *Red Rust* opened word began to circulate among the board that the triumvirate was taking too many liberties with scripts. Reluctant to assert their authority openly over the endeavor they had funded, yet unwilling to let the Studio go its own way, the Guild simply shut the project down.

Once again, Clurman and Strasberg saw a road leading toward their own theatre turn into a dead end. But they were at least partly consoled by their acquisition of a fellow trailblazer: Cheryl Crawford was disillusioned by the Guild's autocratic termination of the Studio, and months of close contact with Clurman and Strasberg had convinced her that the theatre they dreamed of was her dream too. They in turn realized how much they needed her executive experience and practical abilities. (The Guild recognized Crawford's gifts too, making her assistant to the board after the Studio folded.) In April 1930, picking up the pieces of the shattered Studio, they began to hold informal get-togethers for small groups of friends.

It was a difficult time for all of them. Strasberg's young wife had died of cancer just before *Red Rust* opened. Clurman was tormented by his stormy affair with Stella Adler and infuriated by the closing of the Studio. Personal unhappiness giving an edge to his words, he argued that their individual problems in the theatre were symptomatic of society's sickness. America was boiling with energy, yet it all seemed to evaporate without issue. People were swamped in a sea of furious activity, unable to set a steady course, lacking a vehicle to transform their ideals into action, blaming themselves for their failures. We have to reach out to each other, he said. We can overcome the isolation and desperation we feel by working together. He quoted Waldo Frank's new book, *The Re-discovery of America:* "With tragic intensity, America needs groups." He spoke of theatre as a healing force, theatre as redemption, theatre as salvation. He yoked private and public life together, implicitly promising that their theatre would mend the breach between the two. He was stirring and inspiring as always, but offered no concrete plan, no way to move forward.

Nineteen-thirty was a restless, nervous year for everyone in America. The economy didn't instantly grind to a halt after the crash of '29; it underwent a series of slow, agonizing contractions while President Hoover insistently declared that conditions were fundamentally sound and business would be picking up any day now. Everyone wanted to believe it, especially the three million people thrown out of work in the immediate aftermath of Black Tuesday. Wall Street desperately tried to make it true: in the first three months of 1930 the stock market surged briefly as investors rushed to buy at bargain prices, and it rallied slightly again over the summer. Business itself was not so easily fooled. Production levels and commodity prices sank steadily throughout the year. Farmers faced ruin. The incredible figure of three million unemployed had doubled by winter. The majority who still had jobs anxiously wondered how long the decline could last and whether they would be next on the bread line. If many agreed with Hoover that federal aid was not the answer, that private charity would relieve the hungry without damaging the American tradition of independence and self-reliance, those hit hardest by the economic crisis found these words increasingly hollow. Clurman and his friends were not the only ones feeling isolated and powerless that year.

They were lucky; they could act. Cheryl Crawford, ever the pragmatic one, suggested a more structured series of meetings for a larger group of actors who might be interested in a new theatre. She would discuss its organizational basis, and Strasberg would explain the acting technique they planned to employ, but the main burden of delineating the philosophy behind their endeavor, which everyone had begun to call "the Group," would fall on Clurman. In November he faced his first audience not composed exclusively of intimate acquaintances, took a deep breath, and began to speak.

He struck a vein of longing and idealism no one had entirely anticipated. To those most moved by his talks, he seemed to be articulating ideas they'd held for a long time without knowing it. They took them as their own. "The conclusions we drew seemed to me, personally, to ideally solve most of my own disillusionment about the Broadway theatre," said Dorothy Patten. She was a Tennessee-born actress who had decided after three reasonably successful years in New York, capped by a featured part in the 1930 Guild production of Maxwell Anderson's *Elizabeth the Queen*, that the commercial theatre gave actors little opportunity to demonstrate their abilities and none to develop them. Others shared her feelings: "inspiring," "thrilling," "overwhelming" were the words young actors all over town used as they told their friends about the meetings. Soon Ruth Nelson, always eager to be helpful, was rattling around in her old Ford roadster, cramming people into the rumble seat and carrying them off to the meetings.

The ideas Clurman propounded were intoxicating, but not everyone was convinced. An oft-told story concerns a pretty young understudy who attended a few meetings with her friend Eunice Stoddard. Asked what she thought of the Group Idea, she replied, "This may be all right for you people, if you want it, but you see, I'm going to be a star." Then, as always, Katharine Hepburn knew what she wanted.

Her fellow Bryn Mawr graduate Margaret Barker was torn. She was playing "clearly about the best part that any young ingénue could have" in

The Barretts of Wimpole Street. She admired its star, Katharine Cornell, enormously, and part of her wanted to be that kind of glamorous, successful actress. Yet Clurman's vision of meaningful theatre sparked her idealism. She might be a Baltimore debutante (with the decidedly upper-crust nickname of "Beany"), but she was also the daughter of a doctor, dean of The Johns Hopkins Medical School, and had been raised with the idea that service to others was important. She had worked with Franchot Tone in *The Age of Innocence* and respected him; she asked what he thought. "If you want to be a star, don't come to the Group," he replied. "If you want to be a good actress, do."

By March Clurman, Strasberg, and Crawford, now calling themselves the Group's directors, had decided on a course of action. They would select their actors, go away for the summer (as both Stanislavsky and Copeau had done before them), and rehearse two plays for fall production in New York. They would pay no salaries during rehearsals—managers were not required to in those days—but they would cover room and board. More important, they would offer the actors a chance to forge their common technique and get to know each other by living as well as working together.

Strasberg, on tour as the comic peddler in Lynn Riggs's folk play *Green Grow the Lilacs*, sent back suggestions. Crawford and Clurman interviewed the actors they didn't know, examining their character, temperament, education, background, feelings, and opinions as well as professional credentials. A certain amount of technical proficiency was a prerequisite; they prided themselves on being professionals, with no taint of little-theatre amateurism. But in the end personal qualities were more important; they were seeking comrades, not hiring employees. "We needed thinking actors, people who cared," said Crawford, who felt that the actors chose the Group as much as the directors chose them. "The real basis of choice," Clurman later admitted, "was the degree of the actor's desire to be part of such a theatre."

Robert Lewis was one who literally refused to be left out. Short, plump, and round-faced, he knew he was fated to be a character actor and would work best in a permanent company. His parents had been beside themselves when he gave up the cello, which at least offered the opportunity to make a living as a music teacher, to devote himself full-time to acting. It was a relief to all concerned when he left home in 1928 (for good, as it turned out) to tour with a marionette company where his appearance was no hindrance. He was barely twenty when he sneaked into the balcony at the Civic Rep and landed a spot as an apprentice during the 1929–1930 season. His parts were tiny, but he began directing and was delighted to have a theatrical home. Eva Le Gallienne let him go after one season, declaring, "I feel you definitely have a place in the theatre; but it is not as an actor." He was determined not to be rejected again; he convinced Clurman to give him a chance.

Clifford Odets too was chosen for reasons other than his acting ability.

An intense, unhappy twenty-four-year-old with deep psychic wounds in-flicted by his parents' miserable marriage, he'd begun to write short stories and a novel while playing small parts in the Guild's 1929–1930 tour. Clur-man saw him in S. M. Tretyakov's *Roar China* at the Guild that fall and thought he was terrible, but at Cheryl Crawford's urging went backstage at another short-lived production to invite him to attend their meetings. Eager to impress his visitor, Odets began a high-flown monologue linking acting with the polyphonic music of Beethoven (whom he worshipped), rattling on and on in an incoherent yet oddly moving fashion. Clurman remained silent, until finally Odets burst into laughter and explained, "I'm laughing because I don't know what the hell I'm talking about." His humor and candor appealed to Clurman, who nonetheless continued to find him strange as he hung around Steinway Hall, sat silent at postmeeting gather-ings in Childs, and followed Clurman home, virtually inarticulate yet ob-viously seething with thoughts and emotions. When the time came to decide, Clurman said, "Let's take Odets. That fellow has something—not as an actor: humanly."

In May, after Strasberg's return, they finally settled on twenty-seven ac-tors, including Stella Adler, Margaret Barker, Phoebe Brand, Morris Car-novsky, Bill Challee, Bobby Lewis, Sandy Meisner, Ruth Nelson, Clifford Odets, Dorothy Patten, Eunice Stoddard, and Franchot Tone. The fifteen others had diverse backgrounds and experience. J. Edward Bromberg, com-monly called Joe, was a young character actor who had studied with Leo Bulgakov and acted with the Civic Rep; he'd been drawn in by his friend Carnovsky. Walter Coy, a bit player from the Guild, was a big, handsome, athletic man, a type the Group was notably short on. Virginia Farmer was a seasoned Broadway and radio actress who also wrote plays. Her husband, Lewis Leverett, had acted with Jasper Deeter's influential Hedgerow com-pany in Pennsylvania, at the Civic Rep, and with Ruth Nelson and Bill Challee in Bulgakov's *The Sea Gull*. Sylvia Feningston had worked on *New Year's Eve* with Clurman and Strasberg; she was one of the few actors in those early days with a definite, and very left-wing, political point of view. Friendly Ford, a graduate of George Pierce Baker's famous playwriting course at Yale, had worked at Chicago's Goodman Theatre before coming to New York. Gerrit Kraber (known everywhere except in theatre playbills as Tony) had acted at Jacques Copeau's Vieux-Colombier in Paris; after finishing his degree at Carnegie Tech he landed a small part in *Elizabeth the Queen*. Gertrude Maynard, usually called Mab, played a lady-in-waiting in the same production; she was the girlfriend, later the wife, of Maxwell Anderson, who was friendly with both Carnovsky and Clurman and drawn to the Group's ideals. Paula Miller was another Civic Rep graduate. Mary Morris was a veteran of the Washington Square Players and Provincetown, where she had created the role of Abbie in *Desire Under the Elms*. Herbert Ratner, another Guild bit player, was tagged as the youngest group member; Bobby Lewis hid the fact that he was a few months younger, feeling this romantic, naïve boy was more suited for the role. Philip Robinson played clarinet and saxophone in jazz bands as a teenager, then studied and acted at the Goodman. He was brought to the meetings by Art Smith, who had grown up touring the country with a stock company run by his father; after the elder Smith died, his fourteen-year-old son held a variety of tough jobs—mess boy, shipyard laborer, longshoreman—before landing at the Goodman. Alixe Walker shared an affluent background with her friends Eunice Stoddard and Margaret Barker; they had worked together on *The Age of Innocence*. Clement Wilenchick, primarily a painter, had acquired an enthusiasm for the Stanislavsky system while designing sets and costumes at the American Laboratory Theatre.

No Group member was chosen lightly, or as a supporting player. The directors were looking for "a unity of background, of feeling, of thought, of need." But at first glance, this unity was hardly evident. Many were Jews, the children of immigrants, or foreign-born themselves; many were not. Some came from the heartland of the Midwest and the middle class; some were from affluent East Coast families, members of the American aristocracy. Many were beginning actors with few credits but a fervent willingness to learn. Others were seasoned professionals with years of experience and well-developed artistic credos. In short, they were an oddly assorted bunch, wildly different in background, temperament, and habits, and the directors must have wondered how on earth they would all get along.

Yet there were similarities. None of them was a conventional Broadway actor. They had worked in organizations with ideals beyond commercial success: the Guild, Civic Rep, Provincetown, the Yiddish theatre, New Playwrights, Hedgerow. They were studious. They had sought out places like the American Laboratory Theatre, Baker's courses at Harvard and Yale, the Goodman's well-known training program, and Bulgakov's classes in order to develop their craft. They cared deeply about theatre, and they cared about more than their personal success. They were willing, even eager, to subordinate their egos and their desire for stardom to a group that aimed at a higher goal. They had responded to Clurman's talks with the "spontaneous affirmation" that marked them as Group material. They were optimists rather than pessimists, believers rather than cynics. They were idealists, of course. If Broadway sneered at their ideals, well, they would soon show Broadway what real theatre was.

The Guild heard about the meetings and asked its employees what they were up to. Crawford submitted a report listing the actors and playwrights who had expressed interest in the Group and outlining a plan for the Guild to finance them in a modest way and attach the Group to it as a Studio. Neither she nor Clurman seems to have considered that this name, with its memories of the *Red Rust* days, was perhaps not the best choice. Clurman wrote a decidedly tactless paper discussing the Group's artistic and spiritual goals, filled with alarming comments about "collaborating" with play-wrights and urging the Guild to prove by funding the Group that "the theatre has a future, that something permanently valuable may still be accomplished"—a comment that might well have offended the board, with its implication that the Guild was *not* the theatre's future.

Instead, the board was supportive. It did attempt to lure Crawford back into the fold by offering her a raise and full membership on the board, but she refused: "It had taken four years, but Harold and Lee had seduced my mind." Resignedly, the board acceded to her request that it release a play it had under option, Paul Green's *The House of Connelly,* and permit Tone and Carnovsky, who were contract players, to go away for the summer. It also allowed Crawford and Clurman to retain their status as Guild employ-ees while organizing the new group. It threw in $1,000 toward the Group's summer expenses and promised to consider financing and sponsoring the production of *Connelly* in the fall.

At last the Group was under way. Clurman solicited money from friends and sympathizers: Maxwell Anderson contributed $1,500; Dorothy Nor-man, whom Clurman knew through Alfred Stieglitz, added another $500; so did Mary Senior, an acquaintance via Aaron Copland. Crawford got $500 from the writer Edna Ferber and organized a symposium on "What Chance Has the Theatre?" that netted another $800. She located a "vacation resort" in Brookfield Center, Connecticut, five miles from Danbury, with a barn which the owner was willing to refurbish for rehearsals, enough small buildings to house their flock, and a main dining hall where the clan could gather after working hours. In 1931, $4,800 was almost enough to rent the complex and provide summer-long room and board for three directors, twenty-seven actors, assorted spouses, and children. They would scrape up the rest of the money when and where they could.

In mid-May the directors sent telegrams to the chosen twenty-seven. The large contingent on the road in *Elizabeth the Queen* erupted in jubilation, hugging each other and declaring it the happiest day of their lives. Margaret Barker, still undecided, went to her mentor, Katharine Cornell, and sat up all night talking in the star's Beekman Place home; as dawn was breaking, Cornell said, "Beany, if I were twenty years younger it's what I would want to do." Barker sent her note of acceptance that morning. Bobby Lewis, who'd been asked to provide ninety dollars to cover his expenses, spent days hunting among his impoverished acquaintances for someone with that kind of money. He finally located a stock-market investor he knew slightly and offered him "a chance to invest in someone's life." The man took it, and Lewis was in.

On the morning of June 8, 1931, the Group assembled in the pouring rain in front of the Guild Theatre on West 52nd Street to pack themselves and their few belongings into the motley fleet of cars collected for the ride to Connecticut. The mood was gay, excited, nervous, expectant. They stood on the verge of a great unknown. They were about to embark on a voyage of self-discovery and artistic exploration that would change the American theatre.

Clifford Odets had been up for two days reading *Our America*. Waldo Frank's passionate essay was one of Clurman's favorite books, and he quoted it frequently as an example of the ideals American artists should hold themselves to in their work. Looking south to the clustered Broadway theatres—bereft of their electric glitter in the gray light of a rainy day, a symbol of everything the Group wanted to change—Odets may very well have recalled one of Frank's most beautiful passages:

> Let us step out from the American theatres into the streets of American life. These clamorous buildings drip with energy. This iron world is a tissue of complex human wills. Underneath, walks the multitude: colorless, cowed, the abject creature of its own creation. But this delirium of stone, for all its seeming mastery, is but a scum on the energies of men. The multitude has better powers. Can it not build higher than these buildings?

The Group intended to try.

TWO

First Love

Now closes another beautiful day in the happiest summer of my life.
. . . In this almost paradisical interlude life is straightforward, sound
and healthy. . . . I wish I could put all the wonder and beauty of the
Group in these pages. . . . The feeling that's most completely satisfying
is the fact that I don't know where the work finishes, and life begins.
. . . Our life is part of the group, or rather the group is our life. . . .
Someday the words individual and group should be almost synonymous. . . . My individuality grows as it contributes to the whole. . . . I
believe—as I have wanted to believe for almost ten years—in some
person, idea, thing outside myself. . . . Here's to you, comrades—God
speed us all!

In the collective diary the Group kept at Brookfield Center, the actors
wrote with joy, love, and an almost preternatural serenity of their first
summer together, an idyll never to be repeated or forgotten. The directors,
with heavier responsibilities, wrote more candidly of their doubts and worries. There were crises inside and outside the rehearsal hall as people struggled to tame their egos and dedicate themselves to the service of the play
and the Group. None of it mattered. For ten enchanted weeks time seemed
to stand still, the outside world vanished, nothing mattered but their work
and each other. The barn they rehearsed in was sacred; one overexcited
member compared it hyperbolically to the stable where Christ was born.
The hills of Connecticut were the backdrop for an exhilarating drama of
collective self-discovery, the forging of a bond that was to hold the Group
together for a decade. Forever after, they looked back on Brookfield as a
kind of Paradise Lost, the place where theatre and life became one. There
would be other summers, but this one had the magic of first love.

It began stormily. In the caravan leaving New York in the driving rain, Dorothy Patten rode with Clurman and Stella Adler. He had been up all night; his face was unshaven, his eyes hollow with excitement and fear. Adler, just back from a three-month tour of one-night stands, was as edgy as he. In a move calculated to arouse her lover's personal as well as professional jealousy, she flourished a telegram from a theatrical manager, her former leading man, asking her to tour with him that summer. Clurman snatched it from her hand and ripped it up. Patten, from a genteel Southern family that didn't go in for this sort of display, wondered, *"What* kind of people I was having to spend the summer with!"

Lunch could not have reassured her. The food was awful; clearly the expatriate Russian who ran Brookfield and had rented it to the Group at a relatively low rate intended to widen his profit margin with the meals. In the afternoon, after rooms had been assigned, everyone wandered about at loose ends: some explored the surrounding countryside, a few tried out the swimming pool, others took naps. Franchot Tone decided to break the ice with an impromptu baseball game for the men on a netless tennis court. It seemed to help, though Clurman spotted Stella Adler gazing at these shenanigans with bewilderment, an adult adrift in a gang of overgrown kids.

The rambunctiousness was merely an expression of nerves. By eight-thirty, when the Group gathered in the barn for their first meeting as a working company, the mood was hushed, expectant, emotional. Strasberg began, faltered twice, overcome by his feelings, and admitted he was nervous. Crawford spoke briefly, then turned away, tears spotting her glasses. Clurman was uncharacteristically laconic, awed by the charged atmosphere.

Helen Deutsch, a young writer and press agent who'd attended some of their winter meetings, had given the Group an imitation black-leather notebook and urged them to make a daily record of their work, which she guessed would be of historic importance. Her typed instructions assigned two days to each individual, and she suggested, "Be as personal as you like, within the limits of conscience." Lewis Leverett, charged with the first entry, summarized the directors' speeches: "They spoke of the meaning of a true theatre and of this one in particular. They impressed upon us again, not merely the uniqueness of the Group but its great importance to us, to the theatre and to our civilization." This burning sense of mission, of the Group as something far more significant than just a new theatrical organization, set the tone for the whole summer.

The next morning they assembled in the main parlor to hear Crawford read *The House of Connelly,* Paul Green's somber drama about the decline of the Old South and the emergence of the New. (As was customary Group practice throughout their years together, the play was read before parts were assigned so that actors would pay attention to the whole script, not just their own lines.) The protagonist is Will Connelly, scion of an aristocratic family fallen on hard times, living on memories of a more gracious past. The love of a young woman from the rising tenant-farmer class offers him a chance at redemption. Only by rejecting the corruption and falsehood of his family's lives and dedicating himself to hard work, with the capable and determined Patsy as his wife, can Will halt the decay of the Connelly estate and face the future. The play was an apt metaphor for the fledgling Group, turning away from the empty brilliance of Broadway in favor of a sterner, more fulfilling goal.

Their choice of playwright also fit neatly with the Group's aspirations. Paul Green, an associate professor of philosophy at the University of North Carolina, had been content to see his work produced by the university's Carolina Playmakers; only two of his plays had been presented in New York. The second, a tragedy of black American life entitled *In Abraham's Bosom*, had won the Pulitzer Prize in 1927. It wasn't a popular choice, as the play hadn't made money, but Green couldn't have cared less. Financial success wasn't his aim; he was an outsider who forced the commercial theatre to take him on his own terms. He cared about "plays representing the traditions and various phases of present-day life of the people," and he wanted "to extend influence in the establishment of a native theatre." If this ideal wasn't precisely the same as the Group's, the two were certainly compatible.

The Theatre Guild hadn't known quite what to make of either Green or *The House of Connelly*, which had been languishing under option for several years (a common fate for Guild-owned scripts). The only suggestion the board could come up with was "Cut it. It's too long," so by the time Crawford came across it *Connelly* existed in two versions, one more than 200 pages, the other a scant 96. She pieced together a working script that she hoped combined the strengths of both, though she was concerned about its pessimistic ending. When Clurman decided that Strasberg should direct it, she was hurt: after all, she had found the play, her background was much closer to the characters', and one of the reasons she had joined the Group was because her partners seemed receptive to the idea of a woman director. But she swallowed her pride—her first lesson in Group spirit—and agreed to participate as codirector, working with Rose McClendon and Fannie Belle De Knight, the black actresses playing the Connellys' servants.

Clurman, still uncertain of his own directorial skills, insisted on Strasberg as the person best equipped to train the actors in the technique that would unify Group productions. Stanislavsky called his approach to acting a "system"; Strasberg preferred the more modest name "method" (as in "method of work") for the version he had devised from his studies at the Lab, his reading, and his experiences as a director and actor. The discovery and exploration of the method galvanized the Group that summer, giving them a chance to put into action the ideals that had inspired them in Clurman's talks. Even actors who had encountered it before were excited by the way Strasberg employed this technique in rehearsals for *The House of Connelly*.

They were more than rehearsals, really; Strasberg was shaping a company as much as he was rehearsing a particular play. "Lee took it upon himself to give us a complete technique, from A to Z, and we worked our heads off," Phoebe Brand remembered. Some of the work involved basic training in observation and recall, as Strasberg had learned it at the American Laboratory Theatre. They had three minutes to examine an object— for example, a matchbox; when it was removed, they had to describe it as completely as possible. Initially, they were shocked by how little they remembered; it brought home the need to observe carefully in order to avoid generalized, fake behavior while acting. They also worked with nonexistent objects: enacting the slicing and eating of an apple, the drinking of a glass of tea, picking up pearls or nuts from the floor and showing by the movement of their fingers which was which. By learning to respond concretely to imaginary stimuli, they tried to create reality out of unreal circumstances, just as they would have to do onstage.

Improvisational work was more directly related to the play. The actors playing small parts as tenant farmers in *Connelly* had few individual lines, yet the Group's ideas about production demanded that they too have strong identities, as real to the audience as those of the principals. Strasberg devised improvisations that stimulated them to create characters and relationships without the help of written dialogue. In one, they were trapped in a burning mine shaft and crawled down imaginary corridors in search of an escape route. In another, townspeople attending a wedding began to gossip among themselves about the bride: one said she was already married, another that she had an illegitimate child; others denounced them as slanderers. The actors had to create individual characterizations and interact with those around them while also following the general movement of the improvisations. It taught them to pay attention to what was actually happening in a scene rather than relying solely on lines and business worked out in advance.

At the same time, the actors were reading *Connelly* and discussing its meaning. They did improvisations based on scenes in the play. Confronting Paul Green's situations without the support of his text, Strasberg and Clurman believed, helped them to respond honestly and spontaneously to his ideas instead of simply mouthing dialogue with what they thought were the appropriate emotions. Slowly the improvisations grew closer to the actual scenes. "First thing you know, we'd be doing the play with our own words," Ruth Nelson recalled. "If we remembered words from Green we'd use them —but the main thing was that the moment was clear. We would re-read the play. We would never memorize . . . never did any work on the book."

All this was exciting and stimulating, but what really electrified them that first summer was an exercise that would soon make the Group notorious in the New York theatre world. Stanislavsky called it "emotional memory"; at the Lab, Boleslavsky had dubbed it "memory of emotion." Strasberg, borrowing a phrase coined by the nineteenth-century French psychologist Théodule Armand Ribot, termed it "an affective memory exercise." This central tenet of Stanislavsky's system was a process by which an actor used a personal experience from his or her past to summon up an emotion—the real feeling, not a surface imitation of it—required of their character in a scene. The actual exercise involved sitting comfortably (complete muscular relaxation was a prerequisite for all work with the method) and concentrating on an incident from the actor's own life that had produced the desired emotion. The actor didn't try to recall the feeling directly, but rather to reexperience the sensory impressions surrounding it: the size of the room it happened in, the color of the walls, the fabric on the furniture, the time of day, how the people there were dressed, what they looked like, and so on. Then the actor went over the exact sequence of events, concentrating on re-creating as precisely as possible the physical reality of the moment. When done properly with a strong situation, the exercise almost invariably brought the emotion flooding back in the present. The actor could then play the scene with the appropriate feeling.

Neither Stanislavsky nor Strasberg invented the idea of true emotion on stage. Since at least the eighteenth century, debate had raged among theatre people as to whether actors should actually experience the feelings of their characters or rely on external technique to put across the characters' development in a more disciplined fashion. Stanislavsky's contribution was to see that the inspirational and craft approaches were not mutually exclusive. His system gave the actor a coherent way of preparing for the moment when inspiration struck, of training the physical, intellectual, and emotional instrument so that real feelings could be sought out and, when they arrived, flow naturally into a characterization already carefully conceived and analyzed in terms of its relationship to the play. Emotional memory was crucial to achieving this result. It was the obvious tool of choice for Strasberg, whose idea of great theatre had always been those thrilling moments when the actor and character merged, when emotion filled the stage and spilled out into the audience.

Working on *The House of Connelly*, Strasberg directed the actors to "take an exercise" for virtually every moment in the script. It was an intensely psychological production, "the play in which I think we followed most purely the inner, emotional line of the work," he said later. "I was not afraid to take time which as a director I would ordinarily not take in some of the scenes to permit them to develop their own kind of mood and aroma." This deliberate approach, coupled with the use of affective memory exercises, gave the characters a compelling inner life that resonated under and around the text, enriching the play with a sense of truth and reality seldom seen in the American theatre.

For the Group actors, the new level of truth and real feeling they were able to reach through affective memory was a revelation. "One quavers before the 'method' as if one were facing for the first time some grand, majestic idol," wrote Friendly Ford, in dead earnest. "It is as clear and as sound as a theorem of Euclid." Strasberg, the man who gave them the method, gained new eminence. He was "General Lee," leading his troops into battle. He was "Dr. Strasberg," patiently probing his actors' psyches "to penetrate and to make apparent simple truths obscured by evasion, habit, and the ego that clings to old and comfortable masks." The ugly, ill-fitting yellow slicker he wore—it rained almost all summer—gave him "a curious priest-like quality" appropriate to the prophet of a new religion. Many of the actors rated him even higher: "He was God that summer," said Bobby Lewis.

A decidedly Old Testament God, given to terrifying rages, upholding what sometimes seemed an impossibly high standard of dedication. You did not smoke during rehearsals, you did not eat, drink, or read magazines in between your cues. All your attention was focused on the work at hand. Those who failed to maintain Group discipline felt his wrath. During a scene in the first act, the farmers enter the Connelly home on Christmas Eve dressed as mummers, singing and dancing and toasting the family. At one point, Morris Carnovsky, playing Uncle Bob Connelly, had to climb up on a table and raise his glass, giving a long speech while his sister-in-law entered, the revelers backed up as a group, then exited slowly one by one. It would have been a tricky moment to stage even for a conventional director satisfied with merely getting everyone on and off in good order. Strasberg, intent that each movement be properly motivated for the individual, took a long time with it, requiring Carnovsky to climb up on the table and raise his glass over and over again. Already a prominent actor with the Guild, considerably less awed by the method than some of the younger Group members, Carnovsky seethed. After a number of repetitions he took the slightly childish revenge of dropping his glass on the table.

Everyone stopped dead. It was an unthinkable gesture of revolt. "Try it again," Strasberg said, and there was an ominous silence while they ran the blocking one more time. Then the director hit the roof. White with fury, trembling all over, he informed Carnovsky, at the top of his lungs, that this sort of irresponsible behavior would not be tolerated. The Group was engaged in an unprecedented endeavor, the creation of a wholly new kind of theatre; there was no room for petty egoism and actors unwilling to work. On and on he raved, raking Carnovsky over the coals in front of the entire company. He was so out of control that the object of his anger found himself murmuring soothingly, "Lee, don't. You'll hurt yourself, Lee."

Strasberg lived for his work—"he hardly seems a person outside the theatre," Clurman noted—and he expected the actors to do the same. One Sunday afternoon the Group went to visit Eunice Stoddard's parents, who had a summer home nearby. The good food, handsome house, and well-kept grounds made a pleasant contrast with the awful meals and ramshackle buildings of Brookfield; the atmosphere was festive, and a lot of people consumed too much applejack, the only strong drink available in Prohibition-era Connecticut. Strasberg, naturally, had not attended; he had no interest in parties given by well-to-do WASPs. When the company returned for the evening rehearsal, he angrily informed them that they were in no shape to work. Abashed, resentful, and a little drunk, the actors straggled off to swim in the lake; later the men had a pillow fight and spread feathers all over the sleeping quarters. Everyone was upset, Strasberg most of all, but he had made his point.

For in spite of his fits of anger and aloof manner, perhaps because of them, Strasberg won the actors' respect and devotion that summer. They might not always live up to his lofty ideals, but they took them to heart. His teaching and direction gave them an entirely new sense of the possibilities of theatre and their own work in it. "All my acting training, everything I had done up till then, was copying: copying other actors, copying my teachers," said Phoebe Brand. "I had completely phony ideas about acting; I never had any sense of using myself, of having it come from me. I didn't resist Lee, I opened myself completely because I wanted to learn." For Beany Barker, "It was that sense that the barn itself was sacrosanct; it was the place where you came to do creative work. It was the first time I'd ever thought of myself as an artist."

Being an artist as Strasberg defined it sometimes hurt. The affective memory exercises, which probed the actor's most intimate and disturbing emotions, could be agonizing. On occasion people were so shattered by the feelings the exercises aroused that they couldn't speak for hours afterward. Many in the Group eventually came to reject Strasberg's emphasis on true emotion, arguing that it damaged actors psychologically and inhibited them as performers. But in the early days they found affective memory liberating and accepted the suffering it sometimes caused as the necessary consequence of shedding comfortable old habits and seeking something deeper. "Now we throw out the well-oiled but useless machinery and start painfully with building blocks," wrote Art Smith. "Simplicity is elusive and the truth hard to tell." The Brookfield Diary entries are filled with images of birth; the labor might be long and hard, but the actors trusted Dr. Strasberg to deliver their new American theatre "rich with all the possibilities in Heaven and Earth and born out of great need and great love."

Strasberg's rising star partially eclipsed those of his fellow directors, who were grappling with problems of their own. Crawford, by nature private and reserved, found communal life with a volatile bunch of actors "battering . . . like living in a goldfish bowl." She was worried about the Group's finances, which had been blithely declared her responsibility by her impractical partners. What would they do, she asked herself, if the Guild refused to put up the money for *Connelly*? Where on earth were they going to find backing for the play in the middle of an economic crisis?

More fundamentally, she was anxious about her role in the Group. Her status as codirector of *Connelly* was hardly justified in her eyes by her work with Rose McClendon and Fannie Belle De Knight. The Group, not as immune from the prejudices of the time as they should have been, didn't make these distinguished black actresses members of the company, nor were their scenes rehearsed according to Strasberg's method. They were treated with personal friendliness—Bobby Lewis could often be seen strolling arm in arm with McClendon—and they slept and ate with everyone else; but the line was drawn, all the same. Lewis, who had reasons of his own for feeling like an outsider (the directors had chosen him hesitantly and even asked him to pay for his room and board), was outraged one day to find McClendon listening intently from her bedroom window while Clurman talked to the company on the lawn below. She hadn't been invited to attend the afternoon lectures.

Crawford, though fond of McClendon and De Knight, accepted their subordinate position unquestioningly. She was less sanguine about her own. She didn't feel like an equal member of the triumvirate. Strasberg was the director, imparting a revolutionary new technique to the actors. Clurman was the inspirer, keeping their goals before them in private and public talks. She seemed to be relegated to the thankless tasks no one else wanted, in particular finance and administration, for which she felt ill equipped. A scant two weeks after they arrived at Brookfield, she went to Clurman and told him she wanted to resign as codirector of *Connelly*.

Clurman was brutally frank. It was her ego that was suffering, he told her; she didn't feel her job was big enough. Her main adjustment within the Group, he suggested, would be "making her contribution on the basis of her real competence without regard to a preference that might stem from the aura of importance a particular task might have in her or other people's eyes."

For Crawford, who'd turned her back on a well-paying job and an assured future with the Guild to join this visionary new theatre, it was galling to be told her real usefulness lay in such mundane areas as raising money and drilling actors in minor roles. Too upset to attend rehearsal, she drove out into the hills and stopped by a quiet riverbank to sit and think. What was she doing with the Group? she wondered. If she was going to be stuck with the thankless task of taking care of practical matters for a gang of hotheaded visionaries, why not go back to the Guild and do it with far greater ease for a fat salary?

The answer was that the Guild wasn't the Group, and she believed in the Group. Observing Strasberg, she saw him training and stretching the actor's abilities in an exciting new technique she knew would transform American acting. With *Connelly*, which she'd helped shape for production, they were using the theatre to say something truthful and vital about American life. Paul Green was to arrive that evening, and the directors were going to try to convince him to change the play's pessimistic ending to reflect the

Group's deep optimism about America, their sense that with struggle the future could be better than the past. This was essential work, grappling with real issues, and she could be part of it if she put aside her pride. She got in her car and drove back to Brookfield Center. In the collective diary that night, she wrote of her decision, "It wasn't easy. It was damned hard."

Crawford's lonely battle with herself was reenacted time and again throughout the 1930s, a decade that drew much of its energy from the drama of the individual within the group. In many ways the thirties went against the grain of traditional American ideology, rejecting the oft-cited pioneer spirit of rugged individualism and reclaiming a communal ideal that was more nurturing and embedded just as deeply in the national psyche. (The pioneers, in fact, had not crossed the plains one by one, but in family groups and wagon trains.) The problems of the times were too overwhelming to be faced alone; they demanded collective action. It gave all kinds of different people—artists, workers, even a few politicians—enormous satisfaction to join hands and struggle together. It also caused pain and confusion, as they tried to balance the need for personal fulfillment against the demands of the collective.

Some found group life more natural, if no less difficult. Clurman was in his element at Brookfield. "Human relationships are the most important thing in the world to me," he wrote to Paul Strand, "and if they are not right, if 'art' doesn't affect them, if I do not feel that everything is sound and clear in that respect then everything becomes unimportant or even futile to me. So the summer was spent in fighting within myself (or puzzling!) the endless, confused, tragic enigmas of the personal, human relationships of people in the group."

For Clurman, the moral problems posed by group living were exemplified in the struggle of Stella Adler, whose ambivalent bond with the Group had a direct impact on her feelings for him. She'd been uncertain about coming; she was uncertain about staying. Her entry in the communal diary reflected her divided emotions. She wrote with passion and excitement about the rehearsals. "For the first time I don't close my 'part,' and with a tired spirit say 'this is "theatre"—now get yourself a little of "life." ' I'm straightening out." She wondered, "Is it possible that I'm a perfect specimen for the group?" Then she backed off: "Lee said 'no' a few years ago." She didn't much like Strasberg, and no matter how enthusiastic she was for the time being about the method, playing a faded Southern belle (she was cast as Franchot Tone's elder sister) was hard for a beautiful 29-year-old woman.

The Group spoke to her idealistic side, the part of her that had been nourished by acting in European classics on the Jewish stage and influenced by her father's belief that the theatre must impart moral lessons to its audience. It appealed far less to the young woman who was fond of expensive clothes and jewelry, who had been raised in luxury on the Upper

East Side, miles north of the teeming ghettos where her parents had made their fortune. Jacob and Sarah Adler had been reserved, almost cold, with their children and hadn't taught them how to mingle. Communal life was difficult for Stella; she was by nature a queen who liked to be surrounded by acolytes, not a pal who enjoyed hanging around with the gang.

Because Clurman loved her and wanted her with him, her problem was his problem. He grappled with it all summer, to no definite end, as he also sought to define his own position in the Group. He wasn't consciously jealous of Strasberg's new prominence; he knew how frustrated his friend had been by the slights and dead ends they'd encountered before the Group began. He was concerned by Strasberg's increasing self-satisfaction and blithe acceptance of the actors' worship, but told himself that the brilliant work done in rehearsals justified a certain amount of arrogance, which would soon pass. He contented himself with giving private instruction on the method to those with small parts in *Connelly* who had less chance to practice it during rehearsals. He also worked with the playwright Gerald Sykes on an adaptation of a Soviet play, *The Man with the Portfolio*, which they hoped to put into rehearsal as the Group's second production.

On June 23, two weeks after their arrival at Brookfield, Clurman began a series of afternoon lectures in which he laid out the general principles of the Stanislavsky system and continued his winter discussion of the values on which the Group was founded. Whether he realized it or not, the talks were intended to restore his status as the Group's spiritual leader, keeper of the flame if not director of the day-to-day work.

He began by defining the terms they used. Tellingly, the first one he discussed was action, summarized by Sandy Meisner in the diary as "the thing to do irrespective of emotion or characterization, the actor's basic function, the foundation of a part through which the fundamental idea of the play is revealed." Only by concentrating on the character's basic action, said Clurman, could the actor achieve the relaxation necessary for the free flow of emotion that gave life to the play's ideas. He then spoke about adjustment, the process by which the characters' individual lines of behavior were shaped to suit the direction of a scene, always in relationship to the play's larger meaning and overall action.

In his most electrifying talk, Clurman moved away from Stanislavsky to discuss Gordon Craig's famous dictum, "After we've reformed the art of the Theatre, we must remake the life of the Theatre." His subject was the kind of person a true theatre artist must be. The average actor, obsessed with status and the size of a part, was no artist at all, he declared. This kind of actor saw the theatre as an escape from the real world, whereas a true theatre embraced life and made itself part of the society around it. He urged the actors to think less about what the theatre could do for them and more about what they could contribute to the theatre. In the theatre they were trying to create, their individual talents would find fullest expression by serving the play and its message. A good actor, in short, was also a good person.

Clurman directed the actors' attention outward to the theatre's basic intent, its significance for their lives and American society. Strasberg, who gave a few talks on the rehearsal process and emotion, turned them inward to their own feelings and how they could use them within the play. It was a fruitful partnership of opposites—tense, as such relationships always are—in which each man's temperament led him to emphasize a particular element of theatre, even though both recognized that the other's contribution was also crucial.

Their respective entries in the Brookfield Diary pointed up sharply the different roles they played within the Group. Strasberg, of course, wrote about their work. In a warm, moving passage praising improvisations by Beany Barker and Art Smith (referred to by their characters' names), he displayed the intense satisfaction over creative work well done that was the goal and the reward he held out to Group actors. "To watch life being born in any object is always a fascinating thing—but to watch it transform one person into another under your very eyes—to know that you have helped to do it—that the thing is so near to yours and yet so far—I wish the actor would sometimes realize how much the director's joy and happiness depends on him." Then came the kicker: "Maybe sometimes he might work even when he doesn't feel like it."

Characteristically, Strasberg drew on his formidable fund of learning to give the point he wished to make the imprimatur of a learned authority. Paraphrasing the philosopher John Dewey, he criticized Americans' (i.e., the actors') "magical attitude" toward achievement:

> We [but he clearly didn't include himself] have a feeling that somehow things will happen—we gamble—we hope—we dream—but we don't *Work!* We have lost our self-respect, our faith in our own activity—we use work only as a means—as a necessity—namely as a *means to an End.* Work is not the time spent on any object—it is not the desire, the wish—it is the energy—the determination—the will power—it is inherent in all creation. It is contained in the struggle—not in the achievement—the achievement is the enjoyment of *work done . . .* I wish I could drive this into our actors in some way. But I guess the only way is just to work.

"I am pleased with our group," he added coolly. "The one great thing that pleased me in today's rehearsal—and at notes—is that our people are beginning to learn to *work.*"

The tone was that of a schoolmaster exhorting lazy students, and it was a measure of the actors' dedication and devotion that they hardly ever balked at it. Any resentment they might have felt was tempered by their realization that Strasberg drove himself harder than anyone else and that the work was good enough to be worth a lecture. That halcyon summer their attitude toward all three directors, but especially Strasberg, was that of trusting children. Clurman found it both appealing and unnerving.

His diary entry, as intimate and personal as Strasberg's was lofty and abstract, showed how deeply immersed he was in the life of the Group, how closely he shared their feelings:

> Never have I so desired to cut myself off from time—past and future —and from the rest of the world. Never have I had so little desire to receive mail, to write letters or to acknowledge in any way the existence of a world outside the group! When I hear that one of our people has gone to N.Y. or requests permission to go I feel almost pained that they can remember other obligations and harbor desires unrelated to our immediate life here; and contact with other people in the hell of N.Y. inspires in me the dread of contamination. It is as if everything outside the group were somehow impure.

Having established his kinship with the actors and their happiness, Clurman subtly shifted his ground:

> The actors seem to have lost sight of the future more completely than I have. . . . They act as if this were an eternal summer, as if they were going to be able to discuss their parts, do affective memory exercises, run the victrola, swim, play tennis and dress in pyjamas for ever and ever. There is not enough—*pathos!*—in their enjoyment of their new life! I would have them realize for all their carefree pleasure how difficult the achievement of this summer's "paradise" has been, how terribly hard it is going to be to perpetuate it amidst the sterner realities of the winter and its N.Y. season.

He contrasted this carefree attitude with the worries of their leaders, who

> question the future, ask themselves whether they will be permitted to go on as they dreamed—ask themselves these questions with tremendous fervent hope and passionate fear, for the group has come to mean the *only* life for them and for their actors. . . . These are the things I secretly wish the actors would feel more often, so that this confidence would become something more than the childlike passivity it generally is, and their contentment have in it that strength that comes from the oppression of realizing its possible destruction. Paradise is real only when one knows the imminence of hell!

Clurman too was urging the Group to change, though he did so with considerably more finesse than Strasberg. In a lengthy paragraph praising his partner's work as a director, he inserted just enough irony to goad the actors into reexamining their unquestioning belief that "There is one God, and Lee is his prophet." Strasberg was content to have the Group blindly follow the directors; Clurman's leadership style was very different. He wanted less faith and more active participation: "A little more pathos, my brothers, a little more of the suffering and the struggle of a healthy and legitimate doubt!"

In years to come he would get what he wanted with a vengeance. For the present, he couldn't shake the actors' trust. "No, you can't expect pathos from us—or doubt," wrote Eunice Stoddard. "The setting is too perfect for pathos—and doubt in our leaders is impossible, since we wish to believe and follow the ideal, their ideal, which we have consciously or subconsciously cherished for years."

The directors might worry about the future and each other; for the actors, everything was well-nigh perfect. Inside the barn, they worked almost as hard as Strasberg wanted. Outside, their excitement over the artistic discoveries they were making spilled over into the exuberant play of a group of young people away for a summer in the country. When the sun shone, they swam, fished, played tennis, sunbathed—two actresses perfecting all-over tans on a remote hill discovered to their dismay that they were clearly visible to motorists from the road. Herbie Ratner packed his Victrola into a rowboat and floated for hours, playing music and reading Shakespeare. Those who knew how went horseback-riding; the horses grew so fond of Tony Kraber, who volunteered to take care of them, that they would whinny from their stables below the rehearsal space whenever they heard his voice. In their spare time, the more restless souls cruised into nearby Danbury, where the men's beards attracted a good deal of unfavorable comment. (Shaving had been forsworn by many, owing to a perpetual lack of hot water.) They would return with huge bottles of applejack, which serious drinkers like Franchot Tone, Art Smith, and Beany Barker kept underneath their beds, out of sight of the teetotaling General Lee.

The more sober refreshment of milk and crackers was served in the main living room, where they gathered in bad weather and at night after rehearsal. Clem Wilenchick drew caricatures. At the piano, Sandy Meisner created musical portraits of his comrades. Clifford Odets, less accomplished on the keyboard, drove everyone to distraction by playing endless, rolling chords. Bobby Lewis brought his cello but never played it. Odets and Morris Carnovsky played classical music on the Victrola. Kraber and Carnovsky played chess with Joe Bromberg, defeating him so soundly that he vowed to "pay more attention to this game of gods." Phoebe Brand and Meisner played backgammon. Tone, Wilenchick, and a few of the other men played poker with the innocent Ratner, cheating him so outrageously that Clurman finally turned to Strasberg one night and asked, "Shall we interfere in this?" His partner thundered, "We should interfere in everything!"

There were intellectual activities as well. At Clurman's suggestion, the entire company read D. H. Lawrence's *Studies in Classic American Literature,* to get a better sense of recurring native themes their own work would also explore. Odets and Bromberg argued about Whistler's merits as a painter. Strasberg, Odets, and Bill Challee had a lengthy discussion over breakfast about whether Michelangelo or Beethoven would have been great even if born in different eras, concluding that artists could flourish only in an atmosphere conducive to creation. "We have not yet established such an atmosphere in America," Strasberg noted. Odets, who was working on an autobiographical play, was particularly interested in the problems of the artist in relation to society, but the entire Group was caught up in an exhilarating sense of themselves as peers of other creative people, past and present, struggling to make a meaningful contribution to the world. As Clurman had declared in his talk on the life of the theatre, "Art is not a plaything."

Love affairs flourished in this feverish environment. Clurman and Adler were the stormiest couple, Carnovsky and Brand the steadiest, though unable to marry as he was not yet divorced from his first wife. Ruth Nelson and Bill Challee, who were to marry in the fall, were so rapturously in love that they were often absent from communal activities, including the first Group photograph, even though it was taken in front of their house. Spouses were equally ardent. Fannie De Knight, observing one woman kissing her husband at length in the dining room, suggested posting a sign: "Osculation Prohibited For Fear Of Contagious Feelings Permeating The Group." But permeate they did. Even Strasberg succumbed, responding to the forthright blandishments of Paula Miller, an earthy, aggressive blonde unintimidated by his forbidding demeanor. The gay men discreetly found partners; Dorothy Patten had a fling with another actress before settling down in a long-term liaison with Crawford. Clifford Odets was not so preoccupied by art that he neglected more fleshly pursuits: he chased anything in skirts and was especially taken with Eunice Stoddard, who was engaged to an architect and unimpressed by Odets' daily love letters. He had no better luck with Beany Barker, who had a serious beau at Yale.

Though the more staid denizens of Broadway sometimes viewed the Group as a hotbed of free love, they were no more bohemian than any other gathering of artists working and living in close quarters. Their pleasure in the rehearsals was matched by their joy in getting to know one another. Romantic relationships were part of a larger sense of comradeship that knit them closer together as the summer progressed.

Becoming a collective unit took time. Group members came from virtually every segment of American society, and these diverse elements didn't always mix well or comfortably. In the beginning, people from similar backgrounds tended to split off into smaller groups. Beany Barker, Dorothy Patten, Eunice Stoddard, and the stage manager, Alixe Walker, all from relatively wealthy families, went off for picnics in the woods and spent time together reading books Strasberg had recommended. They gave each other nicknames: Barker was called "Huzzybitch," which was how the servants in *Connelly* referred to the ambitious young tenant farmer she played; Patten's role was a Southern belle who would "sashay her tail off" to attract Will Connelly—"Sashytail," her friends dubbed her. Just as idealistic as the other Group members, they had a streak of high-spirited silliness that they were naïvely surprised to find their comrades didn't share.

The less affluent members of the Group—"slops together," Clifford Odets dubbed them—found the foursome's girlish ways irritating, and resented their calm assumption that outdoor activities were their birthright. "You don't know how to live in the country," one of the women tactlessly told Morris Carnovsky. She wasn't entirely wrong—there were a few especially citified actors who hardly ever stirred from the front porch—but the comment added nothing to her popularity.

Gerald Sykes struck a nerve late in the summer when he suggested that the Group could "gain valuable clarity by considering the racial problem that it presents . . . your amalgamation of native and foreign elements— roughly, of Anglo-Saxons and Jews." The actors protested vehemently: they were all Americans, striving to create an American theatre; categorizing people by background led to the kind of typecasting and isolation they had joined the Group to fight. Yet Sykes' comment had a certain validity. He'd sensed a division within the company that wasn't entirely ethnic—convent-educated Ruth Nelson fit fairly comfortably into the Group, Jewish Stella Adler didn't—but nonetheless fell roughly along ethnic lines. Some Group members, most of them affluent Protestants, were taken aback by the extent to which the company's serious approach to work spread beyond the re-hearsal hall. "I think I expected people to perhaps take life a little more lightly than they did," Eunice Stoddard confessed. For many in the Group, life wasn't something to be taken lightly. Some were Jews who bore the scars of poverty and prejudice. Some had experienced hard times at the bottom of American society as manual laborers. Some were tempera-mentally disposed to seize upon an ideal and make it their whole reason for being. They may have viewed their more easygoing comrades with suspi-cion, feeling that commitment to the Group couldn't be as strong when it arose from a less consuming need.

Franchot Tone, who had a noticeable fondness for life's more frivolous pleasures, often felt his peers judged him as somehow morally inferior. He and Stella Adler were the actors most openly and agonizingly conflicted about their relationship with the Group. Like her, Tone was not a mixer. The convivial discussions that kept Morris Carnovsky, Joe Bromberg, and Lewis Leverett up late at night in the living room were not for him. In the years since he'd first worked with Strasberg and Clurman on *New Year's Eve,* he'd become a sought-after leading man; conventional Broadway stardom still tempted him. He found fault with Strasberg and the rehearsals, as if looking for flaws in the Group ideal that might justify his abandoning it. He staged minor rebellions against Group discipline. He seldom showed up for the afternoon talks. During rehearsals he was constantly ducking outside for a forbidden cigarette; indoors he scored the barn wall with his hunting knife, obviously giving the work less than his full attention. He went out of his way to provoke people, infuriating Carnovsky on the Fourth of July by setting off batches of firecrackers outside the main building and drowning out the tranquil strains of Mozart within. When Carnovsky protested the noise, Tone shouted, "I can't stand *your* noise!" and slammed into his car for a visit to New York and less elevated entertainments.

Observing the strains of individual adjustment to Group life, the directors conducted personal interviews with each member of the company to help them better understand their problems. They analyzed character defects and pointed out how they contributed to difficulties in the work. Phoebe Brand, who was shy and introspective, was urged to become more outgoing and bolder in her acting. Bill Challee, who didn't like feeling that he was *"required* to be personal," was criticized for holding back in his relationship to the Group. He replied that he had to make himself whole before he could be of full value to the company.

Unsurprisingly, it was Clurman who did most of this analysis. "He was very good to us, very warm," said Brand. "We all felt if we had any personal problems it was Harold you went to." Unlike the remote Strasberg, he was happy to listen to people's worries and doubts, to struggle with them toward an "objective" (a favorite thirties word) understanding of the factors influencing their feelings. He felt strongly that artistic problems often remained unsolved because directors were reluctant to deal with the human issues that lay underneath. Just as Strasberg taught actors to use their personal emotions to create a part, Clurman encouraged Group members to consider their own and others' private difficulties as appropriate subjects for communal discussion insofar as they affected the Group's work. "The individual actor's total personality was supposed to be dealt with," Stella Adler explained later. "His economic, personal and artistic problems were of direct concern to the theatre. The actor's growth depended to some degree on his being understood and helped."

This stance would have explosive consequences. Although Clurman frequently warned the actors against the dangers of destructive criticism of their comrades, his own stress on the interconnection of personal and professional problems made a zealous involvement in one another's lives virtually inevitable. It could give Group existence an almost unbearable intensity, yet it also contributed strongly to the company's cohesiveness. The members broke down inner resistances in order to become more truthful artists, and they broke down the barriers between them to become a true ensemble. They were making a commitment to one another as human beings, and that included an obligation to acknowledge and overcome the conflicts that arose from differences of class, ethnicity, and temperament. Personal criticism could be painful, but it was comforting to know that their directors and fellow actors cared about more than their ability to produce the right cue during performance. Like a family, the Group provided an intimacy and warmth none of the members had known in the commercial theatre. "There were no failures, there were no people that didn't count," said Stella Adler. "Everybody counted." Brookfield Center was alive with the excitement of discovering new brothers and sisters. "We loved each other that summer," said Phoebe Brand. "Everyone did, even the group that went off on picnics."

The Group's passionate and rapidly evolving bond made them wary of outsiders who couldn't share it. "The visitors who are group friends are part of us," wrote Virginia Farmer. "All others look funny to us—they hang around the edges at meeting and rehearsal and peer, and cup their ears—maybe we look funny to them." When Theresa Helburn came up to see how the Guild's rebellious offspring were making out, she got a chilly reception. Her presence at rehearsals made the actors self-conscious, and Franchot Tone cheered her decision not to return. "The kindest thing she could do would be to stay home," he wrote in the diary. "Let all the old women in the theatre stay home, I say, and give the youngsters a chance for a while."

Helen Deutsch, who had given the Group their diary, discovered that even sympathetic visitors were denied entrance to the charmed circle of collective life. When she visited in late July, she stayed up half the night reading the entries, enthralled by their fervor. "This book fairly sings," she wrote. "You've got something, you people, that most of us gave up looking for when we turned twenty-or-so and settled down to a life of quiet desperation." She urged them, however, to be more specific, noting that the diary "sounds like a chapter of testimonials: 'I could hardly sleep and had no appetite. I tried the Group and also the Method, also dear Cheryl-Lee-Harold, now I am healthy, cheerful, and have much less trouble with gas.'"

The Group might joke among themselves about their fervor; they didn't appreciate levity from others. Art Smith slapped Deutsch down in the next day's entry, responding to her plea for more detailed information by writing a two-page description of the notebook's physical appearance similar to the daily observation exercises they performed for Strasberg. He lectured her on the importance of the Group's work, adding, "Naturally we feel more impelled to shout and sing when first we are inspired, than to narrate how Whoositz and Beulah Zilch came to see us and looked with great interest at the swimming pool." Deutsch, who had previously praised the Group's "good humbleness," now discerned "more than a touch of smugness" in their attitude. She was one of the first to encounter the Group's clannishness, a source of strength that prompted both amusement and hostility from the outside world.

Those the Group considered kindred spirits got a warmer welcome. The photographers Paul Strand and Ralph Steiner, who aspired to capture and comment on American life in their work, were greeted as artistic brothers-in-arms. Aaron Copland, by virtue of his friendship with Clurman and his own compositions, gained a receptive audience for his talks on modern music. The set designer Mordecai Gorelik, whose sharply analytical approach to scenery was ideally suited to the Group's method of work, was an obvious future collaborator; tough and critical by nature, even he responded enthusiastically to the ecstatic mood of that summer. Luther Adler came to see his sister and bed down with the available women; Clurman had been urging him to join since their work together on *Red Rust*, but he wasn't yet convinced he belonged in the Group.

Maxwell Anderson was closely linked to the Group by his romance with Mab Maynard and his friendships with Clurman, Morris Carnovsky, and Phoebe Brand. He was intrigued by, though not entirely in agreement with, the Group's ideas about drama; he shared their belief in theatre with a serious moral purpose, but differed as to the form in which it should be conveyed. (Anderson could never understand why Clurman preferred his racy prose in *What Price Glory?* to the lofty blank verse he'd fashioned for *Elizabeth the Queen.*) He rented a house just off the Brookfield Center grounds, attended a few rehearsals, continued his cordial arguments with Clurman, and came up with more money when the Group ran out during the summer. To please Maynard, he gave parties for the company—one so riotous that state troopers descended to find out where all the noise was coming from.

When Waldo Frank came to give two talks on the Group's place in American life, speaking of the sickness of false individualism in capitalist societies and the need to discover the collective values inherent in Spanish and Native American cultures, he voiced virtually the only political note of the summer, aside from joking references to communism in the diary. They had not joined the Group just to become better actors, he told the company; they had embraced an entire attitude toward life. He urged the Group to see their brave new theatre as part of a larger effort to reshape and revitalize America.

With Clurman's talk on remaking the life of the theatre, Frank's was the most inspiring speech of the summer. They would make a difference, wrote Beany Barker. "We will act in the theatre. He, Waldo, will write. The agitator will address the mob." Nearly sixty years later, she could still see the strange, blue-green tinge of the light in the barn and the excited, emotional faces of the actors: "We were all sort of teary-eyed that anything so wonderful might come into being."

The visit that had the most immediate impact on the Group's work was from Paul Green, who had been summoned by the directors to discuss *Connelly's* ending. In the script they were rehearsing, the young woman who offers the weak Will Connelly a chance to save himself and the family estate is smothered by the two black servants. This gloomy conclusion was completely contrary to the Group's desire to deal affirmatively with the problems of American life, violating their optimism about the future, their conviction that a vigorous, positive person like Patsy could change her world. Clurman felt the ending was phony, based on Green's vision of the servants as Fates in the manner of classical drama rather than on the play's basic intent. Crawford, who knew Green, assured her colleagues that the tragic finale contradicted the playwright's own beliefs.

The directors approached Green cautiously, beginning by asking him whether he saw hope for the South. Certainly, he replied. But then by killing Patsy, who personifies hope, they argued, he was saying the South had no future, which surely wasn't what he had intended. Perhaps a more appropriate ending would at least allow for the possibility that she could liberate Will from his bondage to the past. Green was startled; it was highly unusual for a producing organization to ask a playwright to make such a fundamental change in a script. In the end, he rewrote the last few lines to show the newly determined hero overcoming the servants' resistance, offering hope that Will might triumph over the obstacles that faced him with the help of Patsy's courage and strength. Green wasn't entirely convinced—he restored the original ending in later productions—but he was moved by the actors' devotion to the play and willing to be swayed. He allowed the directors to sweep him up with their faith in human perfectibility.

The actors were delighted. Now the play made a statement they could wholeheartedly agree with. As rehearsals progressed, their excitement and pleasure in the work deepened. Bill Challee voiced their communal sense of the possibilities opening up for them as artists and human beings: "In the 'method' of the group I have found a means which will eventually enable me to express most deeply and rightly what I want to express in the theatre."

The continuity and coherence Clurman had promised them were becoming a reality. They were simultaneously creating a great production and laying the foundations for a permanent institution. At last, they had found a home. "I came in this group like one leaping almost hopelessly for a raft in the open sea," wrote Walter Coy. "I found it solid and to be believed in." They took as their byword a phrase uttered by Beany Barker during an encounter that quickly became Group legend. Shortly before she left New York for Brookfield, a commercial manager had offered her a part, which she refused. "How long do you think you'll be busy with your present engagement?" he asked. She answered, "If our play is a success—twenty years. If not—twenty years." Soon the response to any difficulty was, "Ah, well— we have twenty years." In his talks, Clurman spoke of "twenty years from now," and Herbie Ratner happily commented, "It's nice to think of the Group in terms of 'twenty years.' "

That faith survived Clurman's abortive efforts to put *The Man with the*

Portfolio on its feet. He was eager to have a second production in the works, to demonstrate that the Group was a permanent theatre rather than the producer of an individual play. Unfortunately, *Portfolio* wasn't the right project, and Clurman wasn't ready to direct. He read it to the actors on June 15, and the lengthy discussion that followed revealed a distinct lack of enthusiasm for the existing script. Like *Red Rust*, it was of interest more for its depiction of the intriguing new Soviet society than for its intrinsic artistic merits. Clurman worked with Gerald Sykes on revisions throughout the summer, but the adaptation never jelled. Rehearsals began on July 25, a scant three weeks before their scheduled return to New York, and were terminated four days later. "I was not in a working mood," Clurman confessed in a letter to Paul Strand. "That is, I wanted to work but for various reasons I was unable to. Being so close to everybody at all times made it difficult to get the necessary perspective for work."

By midsummer, Clurman was feeling overwhelmed by the Group:

> You are all my constant concern. I worry about you, make conjectures and respond to you all in pleasure and pain like a great father! . . . It is as if I am not permitted here to have a personal life outside the life of the group—which is the life of our actors. If I were in New York I should be able to retire at moments into the dark of my apartment, go to a movie, commune with a non-theatrical friend, possibly read a book that might take me away from the pressure of the group's demands. But here I have to draw strength constantly from within—and the supply doesn't always seem inexhaustible.

Strasberg, less wrapped up in collective life, kept the Group active and alert with the rehearsals of *Connelly*. Under his assured, effective direction, the actors grew daily more confident and enthusiastic about the production. Certain scenes and performances had special meaning for the company. Stella Adler and Eunice Stoddard, playing Will Connelly's older sisters, touched everyone with an improvisation based on their last scene, in which they left the beloved ancestral home knowing that life had passed them by and the future belonged to the energetic Patsy. Adler and Stoddard were confident, assertive actresses, familiar with the Stanislavsky system from the Lab and not inclined toward the hero worship many others lavished on Strasberg. The depth and power of their work affirmed his ability to collaborate with more fully developed artists as well as to shape unformed ones.

The growth of Beany Barker's performance as Patsy in many ways encapsulated the artistic journey they had all taken that summer. From the first reading, when Strasberg had stood behind her rubbing her shoulders and murmuring "Relax" while she spoke her lines, she had struggled with the method. She was confused when Strasberg told her to use affective

memory exercises to summon up anger for her love scenes with Franchot
Tone; it seemed to contradict the meaning of the speeches. She listened
carefully as he explained that she was searching too consciously for mood,
that it was the effort to overcome a mood that created drama. She tried to
understand: "My small pride wanted to say, 'Lay off, and let me do it!' But
you submitted, because this was the way." By the end of July, Clurman was
praising the "purity and sweetness" of her work. She came to love Patsy,
whose fight to win Will and the Connelly estate symbolized for Barker the
Group's effort to bring new life and energy to the moribund Broadway
theatre. She even learned to love Strasberg, who demanded more from her
as an actress than she had ever demanded of herself.

Emotions mounted as the play fell into final form. The diary entries
began to contain notes of doubt and worry, not so much about the work
but about the members' individual difficulties in relating to the Group;
Clurman was not the only one who felt swamped after more than six weeks
of collective life. The mood was pitched so high by late July that one night
during rehearsal Joe Bromberg, whose comic demeanor masked deep feelings, retreated behind the piano to weep after an especially powerful scene.
He spoke for them all when he said, "None of us will ever be really satisfied
anywhere else in the theatre again."

Everything the actors had felt during their "hard, exciting, bewildering,
profound, inscrutable, *fast* summer" was poured into the last run-through
of *Connelly* in Brookfield on August 15. It had the passion, unity, and spiritual exaltation Strasberg had spoken of in his lectures on primitive theatre.
It was the vehicle for all their hopes, the weapon they would brandish in
the face of a complacent Broadway. Patsy's final speech was their battle
cry: "To grow and live and be something in this world you've got to be cruel
—you've got to push other things aside. The dead and the proud have to
give way to us—to us the living. We have our life to live and we'll fight for
it to the end. Nothing shall take that away from us." It was an intoxicating
moment, the summation of all their work thus far—a religious rite as much
as a rehearsal.

They were quickly yanked back into the secular world. Winifred Lenihan,
director of the Guild school, who had been invited to attend the run-
through, gave them a disquieting preview of the kind of obtuse reaction
they could expect in New York. She praised individual scenes, but declared
the production overall "too slow." Never, as far as the Group was concerned, had a critique been so completely beside the point. With all the
arrogance of youth, and more than a little justice, they believed they were
doing work of a depth no one had ever attempted before in the American
theatre. Lenihan's criticism of their pacing was like the Guild's earlier inability to suggest any improvements in Green's script other than making
cuts. It indicated an appalling lack of interest in the play's ideas, a superficial view of drama as purely a matter of style.

After ten weeks in paradise, this jolting contact with a hostile reality was disheartening. A large group of the actors responded by getting drunk and noisy, keeping Strasberg up most of the night. Incapable of finding consolation in alcohol, he was hurt by what he viewed as a profanation of the high seriousness they'd displayed in the run-through. The next morning he appeared, pale and drawn, bitter emotions simmering within. An innocuous comment by one of the actors pushed him over the edge; he rushed from the room, barely repressing a sob. The burden of their forthcoming encounter with New York weighed most heavily on him as director of *Connelly*, and Lenihan's criticism of the production struck directly at his prestige with the company. He was exhausted and he felt alone; the previous night's ruckus had underscored his alienation from the light-hearted side of Group life.

Everyone's nerves were wearing thin. It was time to leave the womb. On the Group's last night at Brookfield, Clurman spoke alone. He praised the originality and daring of Strasberg's work, reiterating his belief that "no director—not even Stanislavsky—directs just this way." He warmly assessed the actors' progress, reminding them that whatever faults might remain in individual performances, the Group's approach to acting and the script was "a new thing and an exciting and creative thing in the American theatre." Heaping scorn on the kind of limited theatrical mind that responded to this creativity with the words "too slow," he warned them that they would encounter such stubborn incomprehension again. "Your life is going to be *hard!* You won't succeed easily!" he shouted, inviting their complicity through laughter as he'd done so often in his winter talks.

As he intended, the promise of opposition drew them together. Strasberg's temper, difficulties with the method, clashes of temperament, struggles with the imperatives of collective life were all forgotten. What they remembered was the vision of a true American theatre that had brought them to Brookfield, the enormous strides they had taken toward their goal, the love they felt for their comrades who shared the work and the dream. They would face New York in the spirit Clurman suggested: not with bitterness, but with an energy and warmth that would melt the city's cold heart.

They would face it with a name as well. They had debated all summer about what the Group should be called. The Brookfield Players? The New Theatre Commune? The Atlantic Theatre? None of these seemed right. Shortly before their departure, Gerald Sykes grasped the obvious. The title they chose for their theatre should be as naturally appropriate as the one they had spontaneously given themselves. "There is no need to look about for a name," he wrote in the diary's last entry. "You have as it is the best kind of name, one that means something to all of you: Group Theatre. . . . You are new. There has never been anything like you before. You can't go to the past for a name. Let them turn up their noses at the bareness of Group Theatre. Five years from now others will be imitating it." The directors agreed, and the Group Theatre it was.

THREE

The Real World

Back in New York, nervously awaiting the all-important visit of the Guild board to their rehearsals, the Group received tribute to the intensity and realism of their work from an unexpected source: the doorman at the Guild Theatre.

They were rehearsing the climactic second-act scene in which Uncle Bob Connelly commits suicide. Strasberg had carefully directed Franchot Tone, who was left alone onstage after a gunshot was fired in the wings, to allow the actor maximum spontaneity in his emotional reaction while still fulfill-ing the scene's technical requirements. Tone was to wait until the fact of his uncle's death hit him, then run toward the door through which the body would be carried. He was not to time his run or worry about getting to the door too soon and leaving the stage empty; these considerations would interfere with the truthfulness of the moment. Once he made his move, he had two options: if he got to the door before the farmers entered, he would see them carrying the body and recoil back into the room; if the realization took longer to strike and he ran later, he would be pushed back into the room by the people bearing Uncle Bob's corpse. It made absolutely no difference when he began to run, said Strasberg. What was important was that his movement should be impelled by the proper belief and logic.

The actors accompanying the body started preparing for their entrance in the wings, each one taking an exercise to elicit his character's response to the death, forming and re-forming in small knots of keening mourners as Art Smith and Joe Bromberg picked up the prostrate Morris Carnovsky and the entire group entered to confront Tone. Strasberg loathed crowd scenes where a mass of undifferentiated characters made meaningless sounds, and he had worked patiently to help each individual create a con-crete, personal reaction.

The doorman knew none of this. He heard a lot of noise from inside the theatre and stuck his head in to investigate. Instead of one of the Guild's artfully arranged, pictorially pleasing crowd scenes, he saw a group of hysterical people clustered around an actor who was clearly in serious trouble. He dashed up onstage and was restrained only with difficulty from tossing a bucket of water over Carnovsky. He was the first spectator to encounter the Group's ability to vividly capture life's tumult and clamor. A Guild board member, Helen Westley, later remarked that seeing a Group Theatre production was like witnessing a real accident.

Better-prepared viewers were also impressed. When Waldo Frank, Robert Edmond Jones, Ralph Steiner, Theresa Helburn, and the set designer Lee Simonson attended a rehearsal, they all seemed enthusiastic. Jones said it was one of the most creative productions he had ever seen in New York. The Group had reason to hope for the best when Helburn and Simonson returned with the rest of the Guild board on August 25 to decide whether the Guild would finance *The House of Connelly*.

They were in for a shock. The board members were polite but hardly effusive about the overall production. They praised the mood Strasberg had created without seeming very interested in how it had been accomplished. They proceeded to pick at particular performances: Morris Carnovsky was unconvincing as a Southern aristocrat; Mary Morris was weak as the mother. They hardly listened as Strasberg explained, with icy self-control, that the play had been rehearsed for nearly three months and was an ensemble effort that would be badly damaged by replacing individual actors. These were minor skirmishes. It quickly became clear that what really upset the board members was the new ending; they were horrified that the Group had presumed to alter Green's tragic finale, even with his consent. "Some of them spoke as if we had violated an aesthetic law," Clurman noted. In Crawford's recollection, the reaction was blunter: "You have murdered the play," the board told her.

There it was again: the Guild's infuriating belief that tragedy was the only true art. Clurman, Strasberg, and Crawford defended the Group's very different view as best they could, but there was little point in arguing across a philosophical divide. The next day the directors received the board's decision. If they replaced Carnovsky and Morris and restored the original ending, the Guild would put up the full $10,000 required to produce *Connelly* and offer it as a regular subscription production. If not, the Guild would contribute only $5,000 and, provided the directors could raise the other half, would allow them to present the play under Guild auspices, though not as part of the subscription season.

As far as the directors were concerned, there was no choice. It would have violated every pledge they had made to their actors about permanency and commitment to replace any of them on the say-so of outsiders for mere financial considerations. They didn't even tell Carnovsky and Morris about the Guild's suggestion. As for the ending, they had been through all that with Paul Green. The play as it stood beautifully expressed their hopes for

America, and they weren't about to change it because of the board's abstract and wrong-headed notions. They stuck to their guns and agreed to raise the additional $5,000 themselves.

It was a brave stance, especially since Clurman and Crawford were still under contract to the Guild and had no means of support aside from their salaries as playreader and assistant to the board. Crawford immediately began looking for backers, and the company spent a discouraging few weeks giving performances for commercial managers to no avail. They had a stroke of luck when Eugene O'Neill, in town to prepare for the opening of *Mourning Becomes Electra*, saw Crawford fretting in her Guild office and asked what the problem was. She told him of the Group's dilemma.

By 1931 O'Neill was America's preeminent playwright, wealthy and se-cure. His increasing fatalism about human nature was more in tune with the Guild's ideas than with the Group's optimism. Yet he hadn't forgotten that his first steps in the theatre were taken with the support of an idealistic company, the Provincetown Players, and in an interview given that fall he bemoaned "the passing of the experimental group theatre." His additional comments could have been made by Clurman: "I believe that we have the best directors, the best writers, the best actors and the best scenic artists in the world right in this country, but all of them are going each his own way. If all this talent could be made to work together, I am certain that produc-tions could be given here that would be unequalled." He hadn't read *Con-nelly* or seen the Group's work on it, but he was sympathetic to what Crawford told him of the company's goals. He wrote out a check for $1,000 and handed it to her on the spot.

She managed to raise another $2,000 from an executive at the Samuel French Company, which had published *Connelly*. Franchot Tone provided the final $2,000, the first of a decade's worth of contributions he would make to the Group. With the money finally in hand, the directors scrambled to ready the scenic elements. Time constraints prevented them from work-ing with the artists and having the design grow organically out of the pro-duction concept, as they hoped to do in the future. Cleon Throckmorton was hired to produce three sets in eight days; they arrived a scant forty-eight hours before the opening. The costume designer Fania Mindell bought or rented most of the clothes ready-made, and Group actresses helped her alter them to fit the performers. Capable Ruth Nelson made her own.

The directors met to discuss the company's salaries. The guiding princi-ple was that actors would be paid on the basis of their general usefulness to the Group, with some account taken—insofar as the organization's straitened circumstances permitted—of such personal financial obligations as spouses and children to support. Salaries were set for the entire season, without regard to the size of the role an actor played in a particular produc-tion. Initially the directors hoped to insure the Group's permanence by paying the actors, and themselves, throughout the year. In practice, this proved impossible and was later revised to commit the organization to giving everyone a weekly salary whenever any Group production was playing, whether or not an individual actor had a part in it.

For the first season, Franchot Tone and Morris Carnovsky, still under contract to the Guild, received their regular salary of $300 a week. The top fee below that was $140, accorded to husband and father Joe Bromberg even though he had only a small role in *Connelly*. Beany Barker, the female lead, was offered the same salary and refused, saying she didn't need that much. She remained at the higher end of the Group's wage scale along with Stella Adler and Mary Morris, who both had young children. In the middle range were Dorothy Patten, Eunice Stoddard, Art Smith, Ruth Nelson, Walter Coy, and Phoebe Brand. Salaries went down as low as $30, which was still nearly double the standard Broadway extra's fee. The ratio of top to bottom salaries was 10 to 1; as Strasberg later pointed out, that was much lower than the average of 23 to 1 in the commercial theatre, where, even during the Depression, stars' salaries might top $1,000 a week. Clurman, Strasberg, and Crawford paid themselves each $50 a week and split the $1,500 they had budgeted as the director's fee for *Connelly;* they agreed that they would continue to share it in the future, regardless of who actually directed the individual productions.

It was an unconventional arrangement, with the leaders receiving less than some of the followers and those at the bottom making less of a sacrifice vis-à-vis the commercial theatre than their better-paid comrades. (A solid character actor like Bromberg could have made double his Group wages working for a Broadway producer.) But it reflected the directors' vision of the Group as a community, where members contributed to the best of their artistic abilities and were rewarded with at least some consideration for their economic needs. Breaking the link between a big role and high salary confirmed the importance of every actor to the Group, and the promise to pay the actors for the season, not show by show, affirmed the Group's long-term commitment to them. Idealism was demanded, particularly from the more successful Group actors, who were asked to take lower salaries than they would have received elsewhere so that others could get living wages. This policy also, perhaps unwittingly, made salaries an emotional issue because it acknowledged that they were based on the directors' evaluation of each actor's status within the organization.

In any case, no one would receive the projected new salaries until *Connelly* opened. Everyone in the Group was broke and nervous in the uneasy interim between their return from Brookfield and the premiere on which all their hopes rested. They had six weeks—more than the entire rehearsal period for most commercial productions—with little to do besides tinker with their performances, hear progress reports on Crawford's fund-raising efforts, and try as best they could to settle themselves back into the rigors of New York life after their summer romance. Clurman, himself feeling strained and worried about money, tried to keep the Group spirit alive by holding more meetings. A talk he gave on Alfred Stieglitz, however, failed to ignite the actors, who regarded Clurman's friend as a bit passé and were at the moment concerned more with the Group's future than with their cultural antecedents. They also felt, for the first time, slightly impatient with Clurman's endless capacity for talk, especially at a time when they were all desperate for action.

In this tense atmosphere, minor difficulties provoked full-scale battles. The worst was set off by the Guild's publicity department, which prepared the press releases, advertising, and billboards for *Connelly*. The Group had decided that members of the company would be listed alphabetically in all material relating to the production and that no individual actors would be featured in the ads. The directors instructed the publicity department accordingly, but the company arrived at the theatre for rehearsal one day to discover that the house boards billed Tone, Carnovsky, and other better-known Group members above the rest of the actors. They were outraged, none more so than Stella Adler, who despite her difficulties within the Group was rapidly assuming the position of spokeswoman for the actors' discontents.

Strasberg, who ought to have been sympathetic, wasn't. Though the actors had no way of knowing it, he had his own quarrel with the billing. He resented sharing the director's credit with Crawford but had suppressed his feelings, not even telling Clurman about them, for the sake of Group morale. Under the circumstances, he found the actors' complaints trivial and irritating. Adler's leadership of the protest annoyed him further; despite his respect for her acting ability, he considered her a temperamental trouble-maker. "If you're not satisfied, you know what you can do—leave!" he shouted. Clurman, stunned by everyone's vehemence over an inconsequential mistake, smoothed matters over, and the boards were restored to alphabetical order. It was the directors' first inkling that the actors had their own conception of the Group Idea and were prepared to defend it when their leaders wouldn't.

The House of Connelly opened at the Martin Beck Theatre on September 29, 1931. Though there had been little advance publicity, critics and other veteran theatregoers were extremely curious about this new company; rumors about the Group and their strange rehearsal methods had been floating around New York all summer. The directors and actors were terrified. Whatever they thought of the shabby standards of Broadway, their ability to raise money and continue on their chosen course was dependent on how their work was received that night. Clurman and Strasberg stood tensely at the back of the orchestra; Crawford and Paul Green sat worrying upstairs in the mezzanine. The actors, their nerves stretched to the limit, performed with less energy than usual; several of them were almost inaudible. The audience was also quiet; the directors couldn't tell what the response was.

When the final curtain fell, tears came to Clurman's eyes. He was fiercely proud of his young company, stirred to his depths by thoughts of all they had been through together. "Bravo!" he cried—and discovered to his delighted surprise that a large portion of the audience was cheering with him. Up in the mezzanine, Crawford began counting curtain calls. When she got to sixteen and heard the shouts of "Author!" she seized Green and hustled him down to the stage. The rafter-rocking reception continued for a total of twenty-two curtain calls.

The elated company assembled in Walter Coy's walk-up flat on West 47th Street to celebrate. In her apartment down the block, Crawford could hear their revels as she anxiously waited for the Guild press agent to phone with the reviews. She knew the audience response didn't guarantee that the critics would also be pleased. At 2:00 a.m. she got the word: the reviews were great, everything they could have hoped for. She reported the good news by phone, dressed, and ran to join the party. Clurman and Odets had gone to Times Square to get the papers, and Strasberg read them aloud.

The acting was lauded beyond their wildest imaginings. Brooks Atkinson in the *New York Times* wrote, "What beauties Mr. Green has imparted to his play these young actors have discovered. They play it with delicacy and tenderness, with imagination, with a remarkably affecting sincerity. . . . They play like a band of musicians." Arthur Ruhl of the *Herald Tribune* grasped the quality of "emotional inwardness" that made the Group's performance so different from anything else to be seen on Broadway. In the New York *American* Gilbert W. Gabriel made a comparison that gave particular pleasure to Strasberg: "They gave it so smooth, so finely dovetailed and error-proof and enamelled a performance . . . they may have convinced the fascinated audience that their way is the only way to prepare a play for all the play is worth. I cannot remember a more completely consecrated piece of work since the Moscow Art masters went home."

True, there was criticism as well as praise; most reviewers found the Group's attempts at Southern accents unconvincing and complained that some of the actors spoke too softly. But what was most important and exciting about the press reaction was not the discussion of the performances but the critics' warm acceptance of the Group as a company and an ideal. John Mason Brown in the New York *Evening Post* cheered the organization for offering "the young blood and new ideas for which most of us have been praying. . . . Their first production is one that deserves the attention—and support—of playgoers who ask more of the theatre than that it should be a mere passage of time." He continued in a second column a week later, "It has a group feeling about it that is as rare as it is welcome on Broadway. It is unselfish and co-operative . . . the healthiest thing that has happened to our theatre in the past five years." All summer the Group had wondered whether it would be possible to work as they hoped in the hostile environment of Broadway; now they found that even in New York others shared their hunger for a new kind of theatre. Atkinson voiced all their aspirations when he wrote, "Between Mr. Green's prose poem and the Group Theatre's performance, it is not too much to hope that something fine and true has been started in the American theatre."

The actors cheered and applauded each critical bouquet. When Strasberg finished, the room quieted and a mood of hushed exaltation settled over the company. Paul Green, "happy as a lark on bourbon and the notices," stood up to read from the Bible. "In the beginning was the Word, and the Word was with God, and the Word was God. . . . In him was life; and the life was the light of men. And the light shineth in the darkness; and the darkness comprehended it not." As he read on about the law handed down by Moses, the truth and grace incarnated in the life of Christ, tears poured down everyone's cheeks. He seemed to be talking about their own dedication, the quest for unity of form, content, and spirit that was the Group's reason for being. They had worked so hard, they had come so far. At that radiant moment, anything seemed possible.

The directors were brought down to earth almost as quickly as Beany Barker, who woke up the next morning under a bush in Central Park without the slightest idea how she'd got there. Clurman assumed that after the excellent reviews for *Connelly* the Group wouldn't have too much trouble getting the backing they needed. He and his partners wanted more than a few dollars for their next production; they were hoping for a long-term financial commitment that would allow them to operate as a permanent institution, developing scripts and actors without having to scramble for money on a show-to-show basis. Since the press often referred to the Group as a Guild offshoot, and since the older organization had given them a good deal of money and sympathy, the Guild seemed the natural place to turn.

The directors' meeting with the Guild board was a textbook example of how not to win friends and influence people. Flushed with the success of *Connelly*, Clurman was at his most arrogant and abrasive, all the while convinced that he was speaking in the accents of sweetest reason. He began by stating "the incontrovertible fact" that the Guild's least satisfactory productions in recent years had been contemporary plays such as *Juarez and Maximilian*, which the admirable Guild actors were not trained to perform properly. Such new plays—and there would be many more of them in these unsettling times—demanded a new company: the Group Theatre. The Group would be more than a producing organization, it would be a Theatre, "a homogeneous body of craftsmen to give voice to a point of view which they shared with the dramatist, whose work might be described as the most clearly articulated and eloquent expression of the Theatre's conscience." This idea wasn't new, he said, but there was no such Theatre as yet in America. By funding the Group, the Guild could help start one.

If Clurman had come right out and said that the Group despised the Guild's achievements and wanted nothing from the board but money and the right to go their own way, he couldn't have been more tactless. The Guild board was understandably offended; the fact that he happened to be right hardly made his comments less infuriating. As Crawford watched in horror, Clurman and Strasberg got into a shouting match with two board members, Philip Moeller and Lawrence Langner. The latter, appalled by Clurman's confident statement that the Group would work with playwrights and help shape their ideas, asked, "Do you think you would have anything to tell Eugene O'Neill?" "Certainly," Clurman shot back. End of conversation—and of any hope for sustained Guild support.

Several currents were running underneath the surface of this absurd encounter. The Guild had just emerged from a period of acrimonious internecine warfare; while the Group directors had been happily choosing their actors in the spring, Guild board members had been firing off angry memos and ultimatums that evenutally led to a restructuring of the organization. The conflict had been resolved at the cost of a good deal of bitterness, and no one on the board was now eager to take under their wing a bunch of difficult personalities likely to cause still more friction within the battered Guild. In addition, the board was annoyed by reports that Clurman and Crawford were using their positions at the Guild to make artistic contacts for the Group. Maxwell Anderson, John Howard Lawson, Lynn Riggs, and Sidney Howard, playwrights whose work had been produced at the Guild, were all talking with the Group, and Clurman had gone so far as to request that the board release another play it had under option, *Son of God*, by Paul and Claire Sifton.

The Guild agreed to let the Group have the play, and threw in $5,000 toward its production, though it would not be accorded even the marginal benefit *Connelly* had of being presented "under the auspices of the Theatre Guild." For the moment, Clurman and Crawford retained their jobs, although it was clear that there was no future for the Group as an adjunct to the Guild. The philosophical differences were simply too great: as the Guild took refuge in nostalgic comedies like O'Neill's *Ah, Wilderness!* and historical dramas such as Anderson's *Mary of Scotland*, the Group were propelled forward by their ideals into plays reflecting the contemporary turmoil in American society.

Son of God, which the Group retitled *1931—* to stress its topicality, was a case in point. It was a swift, savage piece that set the story of Adam, a warehouse worker who loses his job, against the larger drama of mass unemployment. Interspersed with Adam's rapid descent to the bottom are scenes at the warehouse; in each one, signs announce a decreasing number of men being hired, while the crowd of people looking for work grows larger and more desperate, until a placard proclaiming "No Men Wanted" is posted and the mob rebels. In the last scene Adam joins the rioters, and the curtain falls to the sounds of gunfire and screams. The authors' preface to the published edition made clear the lesson they wished to be drawn: "The contrapuntal design . . . suggests a ground swell that is bearing Adam, his group, and the audience itself, on to revolution of one sort or another."

The Siftons belonged to a radical political and theatrical world which viewed the Group with great interest as potential allies, though the company had as yet expressed only a generalized and fairly romantic social consciousness. Paul Sifton was a journalist who had turned to theatre to expose the horrors of the assembly line in *The Belt*. Produced by New Playwrights in 1927, the play became a favorite of the small workers' theatre groups just beginning to spring up around the country. His wife, Claire, joined him to write *Midnight*, an attack on capital punishment that the normally cautious Guild had presented in the fall of 1930. (It was after seeing Clifford Odets in *Midnight* that Clurman invited him to attend the Group's Friday night meetings.) *1931—* was painfully relevant that fall, when there were ten million unemployed and the closing of 827 banks in September/October promised that their ranks would soon swell. Much more than *The House of Connelly*, it promised the Group an opportunity to achieve their publicly stated desire "to give the most expert and complete dramatic expression . . . to the living forces of our day."

Yet Clurman had hesitated. His early encounters with New York's radical intellectuals had not disposed him to be sympathetic to their aims. He and Strasberg had been invited to speak shortly after *Connelly* opened at the John Reed Club, a group founded by the Communist party's cultural organ, the *New Masses* magazine, to encourage proletarian artists. When Clurman argued mildly that even plays without an obvious social message might be understood as commentaries on their times, he was astonished to hear himself denounced as a "liberal" and a "social fascist." The radicals' slogan, "Theatre is a weapon," seemed to him "a caricature of all I had said in my Group talks."

1931— had all the flaws inherent in this rather crude conception of theatre. The dialogue was bad: an intellectual's idea of how workers talked. The characterizations were weak as well; it was difficult to care much what happened to the swaggering Adam and his tearful girlfriend—referred to, Expressionist-style, merely as The Girl. Clurman may very well have feared that association with this kind of left-wing amateurishness would jeopardize the Group's status as a serious, professional theatre. He was inclined to think *1931—* was not for them.

Cheryl Crawford changed his mind. Less given to picking apart scripts than he was, she looked beyond the play's problems to its important message. She was always quick to feel others' misfortunes, a quality that had made her unhappy as Guild casting director, and during her walks around New York she winced at the bread lines in Times Square, the makeshift huts crowded with destitute people underneath the 59th Street bridge. "It is our theatre's duty to produce such a play," she told Clurman, and he deferred to her judgment.

Strasberg, always quicker than Clurman to spot a script's theatrical (as opposed to literary) values, quickly realized that *1931—* would play like a house afire. As director, he was attracted by the opportunity it offered to display the Group's versatility. Where *Connelly* was private, probing individual psychology as much as class relations, *1931—* was public, outlining in broad strokes wrenching social change. The intimate tone of *Connelly* would not do for *1931—*, which required vivid, physical acting. The numerous crowd scenes would give Strasberg a chance to further explore the method's possibilities as a tool in creating visually exciting mass groupings that were also fully realized emotionally for each individual actor.

1931— went into rehearsal during the run of *Connelly*. The directors optimistically planned to present the two plays in repertory, then add a third later in the season. They cast Franchot Tone as Adam, Phoebe Brand as The Girl, and Joe Bromberg as a villainous foreman. True to the Group's philosophy, Stella Adler, Beany Barker, and others who had leading roles in *Connelly* were assigned small parts in the new project. Because of the large cast, a number of additional actors were hired. One was made a Group member at the end of the season: Grover Burgess had worked extensively at Provincetown and in 1928 played the lead in a New Playwrights production, Upton Sinclair's *Singing Jailbirds*, a play about a California longshoremen's strike led by the radical Industrial Workers of the World.

October and November were busy, fruitful, and generally happy months for the Group. As they rehearsed *1931—* they continued to refine their performances in *Connelly*, based on a long paper written by Strasberg analyzing the production's strengths and weaknesses. Since the Group expected to work and grow together for many years, it was natural that they should look for areas that needed improvement, even when they were pleased with their overall achievement. The director's post-mortem became a tradition, rendered for each play during Strasberg's years with the Group. Later on, as the actors became more actively involved in the organization's direction, they would deliver their own comments as well. The habit of self-criticism, although healthy in the abstract, would sometimes have disastrous consequences. Nonetheless, it was one of the foundations of Group life.

Not long after *Connelly* opened, the actors were invited to decide Group policy for the first time when Bill Challee was offered a major role in *Wonder Boy*, a Broadway production being prepared by the noted producer-director Jed Harris. Challee had only a bit part in *Connelly*, Harris would pay him four times as much money, and he confessed when he went to the directors that he would like to take the job. In principle, no Group actor was supposed to accept outside work. To have people coming and going from other engagements would make the unity they sought in their productions impossible. Since the Group couldn't afford to pay salaries comparable to those of a commercial manager, it would also open up a dangerous avenue of financial temptation. The directors had made a year-round commitment to the actors; they expected the same commitment in return. Lee Strasberg felt especially strongly about this.

Nonetheless, there was a pragmatic reason to grant Challee's request. Before the Group began, Joe Bromberg had signed a contract with Harris that was still legally in effect. If the directors let Challee appear in *Wonder Boy* the producer might not complain about the Group's holding on to Bromberg. It was too important an issue to be dealt with by the directors alone; they asked the actors for their opinion. There was a long discussion, and several actors were hurt that Challee would even consider acting outside the Group, but in the end they voted to let him go. The show flopped, and Challee was back in time to join rehearsals of *1931—*.

The larger question of when it was all right for Group actors to work elsewhere and when it wasn't would continue to plague the company. By giving the actors a voice in the policy-making process, the directors were acknowledging that the nature of the Group demanded that crucial decisions be reached by consensus, not handed down from the top.

In November, the directors announced the formation of an advisory committee, the Group Associates. Most of its members were long-time Group friends: Maxwell Anderson, Aaron Copland, Waldo Frank, Mordecai Gorelik, Theresa Helburn, Robert Edmond Jones, Ralph Steiner, Alfred Stieglitz, Paul Strand, Gerald Sykes. Newcomers included Philip Barber, a playwright and assistant professor at Yale, and a critic, Barrett H. Clark. The committee's precise function was unclear, but its existence affirmed Clurman's vision of the Group not just as a theatrical organization but as an integral part of American cultural and intellectual life. His talks to the Group that fall made the same point.

The excitement engendered by the Group's activities stimulated some of its members to creativity outside the rehearsal hall as well. During the run of *Connelly*, Clifford Odets asked Clurman to read *910 Eden Street*, the autobiographical play he had been working on at Brookfield. Dissatisfied with his tiny roles in the first two productions, concerned that the directors apparently didn't think much of his abilities as an actor, Odets was desperately looking for another outlet for his explosive feelings and confused thoughts. Clurman's response to his new effort wasn't encouraging. Rather than focusing on its artistic shortcomings, he used it as an opportunity to analyze Odets' personal problems. "It gave evidence of an internal injury in the writer," he told Odets. "Something in his past life had hurt him. He was doubled up in pain now, and in his pain he appeared to be shutting out the world." Characteristically, Clurman urged him "to stand up straight and see the world more objectively."

Odets wasn't the only actor to undergo Clurman's psychological scrutiny that fall. In conjunction with Strasberg's paper on *Connelly*, Clurman took it upon himself to discuss in private interviews the individual problems of each member of the company with the Group. He was particularly concerned by the method's troubling effect on some of the more inexperienced actors. They seemed to be obsessed with affective memory, pursuing true emotion to the point where it paralyzed their ability to play an actual part. It was supposed to be a tool, and the wiser Group actors used it as such: to make contact with their feelings and to create a truthful performance. But it tied some people up in knots, and the blame had to be laid largely on Strasberg. If a few of the Group members were overly concerned with affective memory, they were only reflecting their director's preoccupation with it. As for the tenseness it induced, that was also a product of Strasberg's general demeanor. Even though the Stanislavsky system required muscular relaxation as an absolute prerequisite of all work, the atmosphere at a Group rehearsal was by no means easygoing. The quintessential Strasberg command was "Relax!"—uttered with suppressed anger through clenched teeth. Clurman had observed the bad results of his partner's imperious attitude, but for the moment he tended to see individual actors' difficulties with the method as personal maladjustments that could be cleared up by a friendly chat.

Phoebe Brand got a taste of Strasberg's ability to send conflicting signals during the rehearsals of *1931—*. She was having trouble working with Franchot Tone, who in the middle of their scenes would suddenly shut her out and dive deep inside himself, taking an exercise to find the emotion to fuel his performance. Brand was left with the feeling of being alone onstage with no one for her character to respond to. When Tone was with her, she loved the power of his acting, but his tendency to go in and out of the scene confused and disoriented her. Observing their difficulties, Strasberg came over and asked Brand, "Why can't you work the way Franchot does? Don't you see how marvelously he's working?"

"Marvelous?" she retorted. "He's not giving me a thing! He's going away all the time!" No, Strasberg told her, she was the one who wasn't working properly. He was clearly annoyed at her resistance, yet at the same time he was stroking her arm—petting her, she felt, as if to say he wasn't really angry. The baffled actress wondered, "Which message shall I take?"

Though the characters' emotions and motivations were always Strasberg's principal concern, in *1931—* he took great care with the physical elements of the production as well. He had a strong visual sense: his reading of Gordon Craig had drawn his attention to the necessity for a director to study great paintings, and he was particularly influenced by the work of Giotto, Goya, and Carpaccio, strongly narrative artists whose vivid groupings of figures taught him a great deal about arranging human beings within a picture frame. The scenic tableaux he created for *1931—* were strikingly dramatic, aided by Mordecai Gorelik's remarkable set. The huge corrugated iron walls of the warehouse dominated the stage. Sliding doors within them were raised and lowered to reveal the play's numerous other settings—a park, a Bowery street, a shabby rooming-house interior—but the warehouse itself was always present, an ominous reminder of the merciless economic forces bearing down on the characters.

The set helped Strasberg create an atmosphere of menace and despair that made the play's apocalyptic finale credible. It also made the last weeks of rehearsal slow and difficult, as the company worked to adjust their blocking to the demands of a large, complex, and multileveled playing area. Yet Strasberg insisted that the actors never lose sight of their characters' inner life or the play's message, and he was always willing to stop a rehearsal to answer questions or work out a bit of staging so that it was psychologically as well as physically appropriate. The playwrights, who had never seen anyone work like this before, grew understandably nervous as opening night approached and the production seemed a long way from finished. One encounter between Strasberg and Paul Sifton quickly became a favorite Group story, repeated with a greater or lesser degree of malice according to the narrator's feelings about the method in general and Strasberg in particular.

Depending on who was telling the story, Strasberg was either expounding on some philosophical point, trying to justify a move for an actor who felt it didn't make emotional sense for his character, or explaining how to find an individual reality to play in the middle of a chaotic crowd scene. In all versions, the actor in question was Friendly Ford, a sincere and not especially gifted fellow who didn't fit into the Group very well, and Strasberg spent a half-hour or more talking the problem over with him while the company watched—with keen interest, said Strasberg's supporters; with boredom and exhaustion, averred the nay-sayers. There was no question about the Siftons' reaction; they were stunned that the director could waste so much time with a minor actor over a small point when their play was due to open in a very few days. Paul Sifton finally interrupted, suggesting acidly that Strasberg could give acting lessons some other time, meanwhile they had a show to put on. "Please don't interfere with what you don't understand," the director replied angrily. According to some of the more imaginative accounts, he went so far as to declare, "Mr. Sifton, we are not here to rehearse your play!"

It's highly unlikely that Strasberg would have said that outright. Reverence for the play was one of the Group's central tenets; it was the company's belief that a playwright had something to say and their job was to make sure it was said as lucidly and powerfully as possible. But he might have thought it. The technique he was developing was, for him, the most important thing the Group had to offer, and he was well aware that Broadway was not yet convinced; he'd heard the mocking tales making the rounds about Group actors praying before they went onstage. If the playwright didn't understand that the quest for inner truth outweighed trivial concerns about time and money, that was too bad.

In fact, *1931—* opened on time (December 10 at the Mansfield Theatre) and in a polished form praised even by critics who detested the play. And detest it they did: the gentlemen of the press, who admired *Connelly* as an example of American art theatre, were appalled by the brutal realism and left-wing sentiments of *1931—*. "If propaganda drama is your dish, here you will find it served piping hot," sneered the *Daily News* critic, Burns Mantle, who went on to suggest lamely that if the Siftons' story was true, there ought to be an investigation of charitable relief organizations. In *The New Republic* Stark Young fastidiously complained, "When you present the raw spectacle of these hungry, exhausted, caustic or ironic or brutalized men, to be perceived no doubt as the result of economic conditions, you have only begun." In order to have "import," he explained, the play needed "the comment of something larger"—unemployment apparently being too small a subject for the sensitive Mr. Young. The Group's favorite hostile comment came from Percy Hammond in the staunchly Republican *Herald Tribune*. Depressed by the long lines of hungry workers filling the stage, he asserted that when he went outside onto Broadway, the only lines he saw were of moviegoers at the Paramount, Rialto, and Loews theatres. "None of them was cold or hungry. They were warmly clothed and they had the price of admission. No symptoms of destitution were present." Apparently the huge crowd of shabbily dressed people who queued up in Times Square every night for hot soup had escaped his notice.

Repelled as they were by *1931—*'s crudeness, the critics couldn't deny its power. "Seldom has a bad play stunned an audience quite so completely," wrote Brooks Atkinson in the *Times*. *Commonweal*'s Richard Dana Skinner, who found the play shrill and occasionally dishonest, admitted that "it moves forward with an emotional intensity and a fire of impassioned protest all too rare in the theatre." The Group's work garnered nothing but praise. Everyone liked Gorelik's stark set and Strasberg's masterful handling of crowds. Franchot Tone was hailed as the finest young actor in New York, and critics also admired Joe Bromberg in his varied roles as a cruel foreman, meek snow shoveler, and callous restaurant owner. Many commented on the dedication of well-known actors playing small parts and declared the ensemble work even better than in *Connelly*. A number of critics noted the Group's versatility in performing two such different plays; they didn't grasp that a single vision—the belief that meaningful theatre reflected the life of its times—informed the Group's decision to do both plays. The despised *1931—* was as integral to that vision as the admired *Connelly*.

The Group pointed this out in a letter reprinted by John Mason Brown in the *Post* (it was signed by Crawford, but the phrasing sounded more like Clurman):

The Group, though fully aware of [its] faults, was glad to produce this play because it was a simple presentation of material that was perhaps

more immediate socially than any other in America today, and because it could be made moving, exciting and expressive on the stage.
. . . If our critics insist on pointing out the play's literary shortcomings, we can only reply that to us such a play for all its defects is better
theatre than, let us say, some slick piece of craftsmanship innocuously
reflecting the sickened spirit of Middle Europe. Moreover, the production of such a play as *1931—* opens up a new vein in the American
theatre and encourages the writing and further production of more
and, let us hope, solider plays of the same type.

This salvo inaugurated a Group tradition of openly debating the critics'
response to their plays, not a policy calculated to endear them to the press.

The critics had the last word on *1931—;* it lasted a scant twelve performances. *Connelly* had played ninety-one times—not a hit, but not a flop—
and made back its costs, though nothing more. The Guild, Franchot Tone,
and the other backers of *1931—* lost every nickel. Yet the play marked a
crucial stage in the Group's development: they made their first contact with
their audience.

Connelly had been warmly received, but the spectators were fairly typical
Broadway theatregoers of the more serious sort, attracted by the good reviews and the promise of a worthy cultural experience. The audience that
found its way to *1931—* despite the critics was very different. To begin with,
its members had less money; the balcony was packed every night, while the
orchestra remained empty. These viewers were noisier than the average
theatre crowd, but that was because the play stirred more than theatrical
passions. They followed the action with an intensity and "smoldering conviction" Clurman had never seen. They came backstage to ask what they
could do: for the Group? for the unemployed? It wasn't clear, but the play
made them want to help. Several newspapers noted with amusement that
the Christmas Seals fund-raiser outside the Mansfield was getting more
donations from the modest patrons of *1931—* than her co-workers solicit-
ing money from better-heeled audiences elsewhere on Broadway. When the
Group announced the play was closing, they received letters begging them
to keep it running. On the last night, the auditorium fairly seethed with
emotion, creating an electric current between actors and audience. During
the curtain call someone in the balcony called out, "Long live the Soviet
Union!" Franchot Tone, startled and a bit taken aback, responded, "Hurrah
for America!" The theatre had entered the ferment of contemporary life.

The Group had aspired from the very beginning to create a new audience
for their new kind of theatre. The unity of which Clurman spoke in his early
talks was not just of the various artists who created a production; it included the people who watched it. In the *1931—* program, freed from the
constraints of Guild sponsorship, he wrote that the Group's fundamental
goal was to create a constituency. "When an audience feels that it is really
at one with a theatre; when audience and theatre-people can feel that they

are both the answer to one another, and that both may act as leaders to one another, there we have Theatre in its truest form."

Clurman's vision of a vital theatre intimately linked to the world around it demanded that the Group look beyond the traditional circle of affluent culture lovers for their support. They had an inkling that their intended audience was not a Broadway crowd. Ticket prices for both *Connelly* and *1931—* had been set below the norm: the balcony had been slashed from $1.00 to 50 cents, and orchestra seats cost $2.50 rather than the standard $3.00. Even at those reduced rates, they couldn't fill the orchestra. In the wake of *1931—*'s closing, Mordecai Gorelik urged the Group to move outside the commercial theatre, to relocate to a less expensive milieu, as Eva Le Gallienne had done with the Civic Rep down on 14th Street, so that they could offer theatre at prices their natural constituency could afford.

Gorelik, called Max by his friends, was a set designer whose commitment to his craft matched the Group members' devotion to theirs. He had studied with Robert Edmond Jones and Norman Bel Geddes. He carried a sketch pad everywhere, believing that "in order to put dramatic scenes on the stage one must have a richly stored imagination and a background of a million pictures." It was the visual equivalent of Strasberg's emphasis on the actor's duty to observe keenly different kinds of people and build up a fund of knowledge about a wide variety of physical and emotional behavior. Though not yet thirty, Gorelik had years of eclectic experience: he had painted backdrops for vaudeville and burlesque shows and created scenery for the Yiddish theatre, the Provincetown Players, and New Playwrights. He began a long, fruitful relationship with the playwright John Howard Lawson in 1925 with the controversial burlesque-style design of *Processional* and went on to do the sets for *Nirvana* and *Loud Speaker*. His ideas about scenery made him perfect for the Group. A set was not simply an atmospheric background but "a machine for the purpose of projecting a play visually to its audience." Like the Group, he rejected the idea that an artist created in an unconscious frenzy of inspiration; he believed in analyzing a script carefully and totally in order to create scenery that conveyed its essential message.

His nine-year relationship with the Group would produce some of their most imaginative, resonant sets. But it was stormy from the very beginning. Gorelik was a forceful man—"all iron and spit," Beany Barker thought— who had his own ideas about what the Group Theatre should be. It was just the kind of company he'd been looking for, but he wanted it to move in certain directions, and wasn't shy about sharing his ideas with the directors. He would fix them with an angry stare, piercing even through his wire-rimmed glasses and a perpetual haze of cigarette smoke, and tell them just what they were doing wrong. He infuriated them, but his talent was so great, and so compatible with the Group's way of working, that they always came back for more.

In late 1931, Gorelik pointed out the obvious contradiction inherent in the Group's effort to work in the commercial theatre with a noncommercial philosophy. His experience at the Neighborhood Playhouse on the Lower East Side had given him a deep respect for the downtown audiences shut out of Broadway, and his understanding of theatre as part of a community was in many ways better defined than the directors'. Gorelik was also a convinced radical, excited by the early stirrings of a whole new labor audience that was just beginning to be stimulated by the burgeoning workers theatre movement. The Group's future, he argued, lay among these kinds of theatres, not on Broadway.

Everything in the Group's philosophy supported Gorelik's view. Their ideals, particularly their desire to run plays in repertory, were simply not compatible with the financial imperatives of the commercial theatre. Yet the directors resisted Gorelik's suggestion of setting themselves up on a more modest basis elsewhere. For all its faults, Broadway was the heart of the American theatre, and they wanted to be part of it. Working downtown to them meant the artiness and amateurism of the little theatre movement, which they judged a dead end. They wanted to change the mainstream, not abandon it. The Group didn't intend to be a fringe theatre or an experimental avant-garde outfit appealing only to a small elite. They didn't yet realize that the new alternative theatre Gorelik had in mind could be populist and vibrant as the little theatres no longer were. When they did, by the end of 1932, the workers' theatre movement drew many Group members into its orbit. Yet they always chose to present their own productions on Broadway.

It was the only world they knew, really. For all their high ideals, they'd grown up as theatre people in an environment where the ultimate standard of professional achievement was success on the Broadway stage. Some of them had joined the Group only after a struggle with their desire for the glamour and fame the commercial theatre offered. They wanted to show Broadway what real theatre was, and they wanted its respect at the same time—and they never resolved the fundamental contradiction in these goals. Still, it may have been a necessary contradiction: certainly they would never have received the press attention they did if they had moved off-Broadway. And how could they reach their audience or their backers without the press?

They knew little about financing a theatre outside the commercial system. The only Group director with any fund-raising experience was Crawford. What she knew how to do was approach managers like the Shuberts with a script and get backing and the lease of a theatre on the standard Broadway terms. She was conscientious and devoted: she studied the subscription plans and financial organization of various European theatres in an attempt to devise a method whereby the Group could be permanently funded. None of her efforts—and she made many—enabled the Group to escape the necessity of raising money show by show, just like any commercial producer.

So the Group continued their tricky course, on Broadway but not of it. Until December they had kept a low profile, preferring to let *Connelly* speak for itself about their methods and beliefs. A single interview in October found Clurman, "the self-appointed spokesman of the group," eager to stress the company's professionalism and its independence from the Guild, although he also talked briefly about the Stanislavsky system and the Group's desire to present contemporary plays. As relations with the Guild became strained during the preparation of *1931—*, the directors made stronger efforts to foster public awareness of the Group as a separate entity. A number of newspaper stories based on Group press releases appeared in early December. Capping this small flurry of publicity was an article by Clurman which appeared in the *Times* on December 13, the first major published statement of the Group's goals and aspirations.

"The Group Theatre Speaks for Itself" contained little that Clurman hadn't already said in his talks to the Group about the organization's central aims, but its shape, and the subjects Clurman chose to discuss at length, were revealing. He made almost no mention of the method, which, he already feared, had assumed disproportionate importance for the press. He wanted the public to think more about the kind of plays the Group did, less about how they were done. So he wrote a great deal about the role of the playwright within the Group, brandishing the names of prominent writers who were "preparing plays for the Group Theatre" (a slight overstatement of fact) and asserting the uniqueness of the Group's attitude: "The playwright is approached not merely with the thought of the immediate practical availability of each of his separate scripts but with the idea of helping him to the most mature theatric incarnation of his particular nature and artistic direction." In fact, the Group hadn't exactly been deluged with scripts since they set up shop, and Clurman was distressed by the quality of the few scripts they had received. The cultivation of playwrights was as important now as the recruiting of actors had been the previous winter. Without plays that expressed their ideas, the Group would be mute.

Clurman concluded with a lengthy discussion of finances, a completely new concern for him. The traditional show-by-show backing of the commercial theatre, he declared, was unsuited to the Group's larger aims. "It would not be impossible—though difficult and wearing—to go on . . . in this way. But, whatever the nature of our productions or the success they might win, this would not be establishing the Group Theatre so that it could carry out the real objective it has set itself. To do that it needs an endowment of $100,000." That figure, which Clurman had more or less pulled out of the air, would allow the Group to function as an institution: to work year-round, paying the directors and actors low salaries in return for a cooperative share in the (presumed) profits, and presenting as many as ten plays, possibly in repertory, while continuously developing new scripts and honing technique.

A few short months in New York had reminded Clurman of something he'd forgotten during the idyllic months at Brookfield: no artistic goal in the theatre could be reached without money, and lots of it. A radically new idea like the Group's required a new kind of financing as well. Unfortunately, Clurman had no idea how to go about getting it save by asking plaintively in his article, "Are we wrong then to ask whether in our extravagant city there is some person or group of persons willing to help realize an entirely feasible, desirable, necessary project?" He *was* wrong; the extravagant city he addressed had vanished with the bull market, and patrons were not to be found. He and Crawford spoke with several potential backers and listened to these wealthy New Yorkers in their lavish apartments tell them that they had been devastated by the crash. Even Otto Kahn, the shrewd investment banker receptive enough to experimental theatrical ventures to pour money into New Playwrights for two years, said he couldn't help the Group.

Eager to keep the company active as a unit after the failure of *1931—*, the directors decided to revive *Connelly* for a week at Christmas, then take it to Philadelphia, Baltimore, Washington, and Boston while they looked for a third play to present in New York. The tour was hard on everyone. Reviews were good, but business wasn't. By the time they got to Boston, the actors were receiving only half their normal salaries. There, Clurman had to tell them that they would get only one-third the following week.

Everyone was becoming irritable. Clurman, immersed as usual in the Group's complex personal interactions, worried that they were "contracting minor diseases—spiritual measles or something." The spirit of dedication and devotion that had flourished at Brookfield had been somewhat frayed by the actors' contact with the rigors of New York and the cynicism of their non-Group friends: the more established actors, especially, found themselves under virtual attack from well-meaning acquaintances who told them they were crazy to give up their hard-won status and salaries for a nebulous ideal. It was hard not to think of these comments while sitting in a bleak hotel room looking at a laughably small paycheck.

Franchot Tone had been a disciplinary problem throughout the fall, when the pleasures of Manhattan night life often kept him from wholehearted involvement in Group life and work. Crawford and Strasberg had resisted Clurman's desire to reprove him because they feared it might prompt him to quit. Volatile and difficult Tone might be; he was also one of the Group's best actors and the only one with the looks and appeal of a conventional leading man, which they could hardly do without. The fact that he had money of his own and was willing to invest it in the Group made him even more important to the organization. By the time they reached Boston, however, his behavior had become so disruptive of Group discipline that Clurman finally went ahead and sat him down for a three-hour talk, urging him to be true to his idealistic instincts and not fall prey to the temptations proffered by his worldlier companions. "I succeeded, I feel, in cheering him up and strengthening his belief in the Group and in 'reforming' his action," Clurman wrote to Paul Strand. "I believe I managed to draw him more wholeheartedly into the Group." Tone was so moved by Clurman's concern that he wept, though he later confessed sardonically, "The feeling didn't last."

Clurman had even less success with Stella Adler, who was tearing herself apart—and Clurman as well—over her conflicts with the Group. She was dissatisfied with her parts, she mistrusted Strasberg as a director, she felt ill at ease and out of place in the Group. She wanted to leave, but then again she didn't; she felt the same ambivalence toward the company as she did toward Clurman himself. They seemed to demand something from her she didn't necessarily want to give, a commitment she wasn't ready to make to a group she wasn't sure was worth it. Clurman "struggled with her doubts, bore her personal blame" because "it was a personal drama in which was mirrored my whole attitude toward the Group. Stella's love and hatred of it, her self-torment over it, her objective battle against it, symbolized for me all that the Group had to overcome within itself, within the world, and each member within his own nature."

To the rest of the Group, the private nature of the drama was more obvious. Clurman might emphasize the artistic differences that troubled his relationship with Adler; his friends also observed the personal anguish she inflicted on him by flirting with every attractive man she met. At least once, just after they returned from Brookfield, she made him so jealous that he'd been driven to the point of violence. Over the years, the actors would come to think that Clurman's battles with Adler sapped his energies for the important work he ought to be doing within the Group. They didn't necessarily agree with his contention that her problem with the Group was typical; even if it was, it certainly received a lot more attention than most. Though Clurman was a warm father figure to everyone in the company, always willing to console and advise, the suspicion arose that he favored some people. Adler, because of her relationship with Clurman, and Tone, because of his financial contributions and important position in the acting hierarchy, seemed to be privileged, partially exempt from the discipline expected of everyone else. Thrown together in uncomfortable circumstances by the tour, wondering what their future held, the Group found these differences looming large.

Rehearsals of their third play, which began in Washington, D.C., didn't improve the mood. *Night over Taos*, which Maxwell Anderson had written specifically for the Group, should have been an exciting opportunity: a romantic costume drama that presented completely different technical problems from *Connelly* and *1931—*, with a leading role for the well-liked Joe Bromberg. Inspired by a series of articles in *The American Mercury* about the semifeudal society of the Rio Grande valley in the mid-nineteenth century, Anderson fashioned a tale about the violent overthrow of an ancient way of life. A proud Spanish grandee, Pablo Montoya, fights to maintain absolute sovereignty over his family, the local aristocrats, and the town's peasants while holding off an invading Yankee army, which threatens to bring with it the democracy Montoya dreads. After melodramatic maneuverings involving discarded wives and a treacherous son, the forces of change win out and Montoya commits suicide, declaring as he does, "This is what Death is for: to end old fashions."

The play didn't suit the Group in terms of either philosophy or style. Like *Connelly*, it was a play about the death of an old order, but it had little of the hope for the future the Group had invested in the earlier production. Much more than Paul Green, Anderson was drawn to the glamour of the past; he might acknowledge the necessity of change, but the play suggested he rather regretted it—an attitude the Group emphatically didn't share. To make matters worse, he insisted on writing *Taos* in the blank-verse style he had developed for *Elizabeth the Queen;* the Group was neither sympathetic nor particularly well equipped to deal with the special problems of verse drama. Clurman, who didn't much care for the play, nonetheless pushed hard for it. It had heroic, larger-than-life aspirations, he argued, that would be good for the company after the Chekhovian intimacy of *Connelly* and the gritty realism of *1931—*. It wasn't as though they had stacks of scripts to choose from: it was *Taos* or nothing, and the Group's principal imperative was to keep working. His arguments were given additional force by the fact that Anderson, who had already been a generous supporter of the Group, promised to put up $2,500 toward the production.

The Group's decision to produce *Night over Taos* prompted their official break with the Guild, which declined to back it. Clurman submitted his resignation, and Crawford, though asked to stay, did the same after brief reflection. "I think it is a shame that the organization which brought me up should not have the benefit of what I might do," she wrote the Guild board, "but I have puzzled and found no solution within the Guild. I feel there is more creative work for me to project and accomplish within the Group." On February 19, newspapers announced, "Group Theatre Now Independent" and quoted the Guild business manager as saying that the connection between the two had always been a working arrangement, not a permanent plan. Crawford's resignation was mentioned; Clurman's was not. Though Broadway at large was surprised, the directors of both organizations had known for months that the split was inevitable.

Rehearsals for *Taos* continued in New York, with Franchot Tone and Dorothy Patten's father putting up the additional money required. Strasberg worked conscientiously with the actors to give shape and depth to the many long speeches, while Clurman pleaded with Anderson to make major cuts in the verbose script. When Anderson unwillingly complied, the revisions only made the play seem sketchy, and it remained static. Strasberg's deliberate and carefully thought out direction was true to the cold, academic tone of Anderson's drama; perhaps a more active and romantic production would have enlivened *Taos* and given spirit to the author's heroic intentions.

Two things brightened the subdued rehearsals. Luther Adler had at long last decided to throw his lot in with the Group; he gave up a good role on Broadway to take a small part in *Taos.* The addition of an actor they all admired, and a good companion to boot, boosted morale. They also loved working with the gentle, charming designer Robert Edmond Jones, who spent hours with them choosing fabrics and colors for even the most insignificant characters' clothing. The gorgeous costumes were universally popular. Strasberg and Clurman were less enthusiastic about Jones's scenery, which they thought too spare for an already austere production. Strasberg, though ferociously outspoken within the Group, felt less confident when dealing with outsiders; unwilling to argue with America's most prominent designer, he held his tongue. Clurman, always ready to put in his two cents, suggested that the set needed a few touches of color. Jones was startled by this remark coming from someone who wasn't the director, but he agreed, and added a large crucifix to the back wall.

Night over Taos opened March 9, 1932, at the 48th Street Theatre. The critics were unimpressed, though more welcoming than they had been to *1931—.* Several praised the Group for their courage in producing such an obviously uncommercial play. Most had kind words for Joe Bromberg as Montoya, Franchot Tone as the treacherous son, and Morris Carnovsky as the idealistic priest who warns Montoya that his privileged way of life is doomed. But Strasberg's low-keyed direction was deemed insufficient and the Group's diction inadequate to the demands of a verse drama; Walter Coy as the good son received some especially hard knocks for mumbling from Stark Young in *The New Republic.* The general reaction was profound indifference, and most reviewers devoted a large portion of their space to admiring descriptions of the set. The Group would have preferred hostility. Although the actors attempted to keep the show on the boards by voting to take whatever salary the management could afford, *Taos* closed ten days later.

So ended the first Group Theatre season, after one artistic success and two outright flops. Still, they had brought a sense of idealism and commitment to the theatre that had been absent from Broadway for years. If their belief that theatre must be intimately related to the world around it wasn't yet well understood by outsiders, the passion and truthfulness this belief brought to their performances couldn't be ignored. The quality of Group acting was so strikingly different from the norm that professional theatre-goers—other actors and the journalists who covered their doings—spent a lot of time trying to figure out just what it was they did.

A fairly sympathetic article that appeared shortly before *Taos* opened gave a good sense of the intense curiosity the Group aroused and the wild rumors their method bred:

> Stories about the Group began to drift around town. One heard that they kept a ton of dirt in the cellar of the theatre and puttered around in it before every performance to get into trim for the earth impulses in the Paul Green play; it was rumored that an actor had to pass an arduous written exam "not unlike a College Entrance Board, only much harder," before he became eligible to act in the Group; and that every evening before the performance all the company arrived an hour earlier than is customary, hurried into their costumes and then stood about on the stage "thinking beautiful thoughts." It was said that they rehearsed each play for eleven weeks with the scenery and costumes; it was whispered that they rehearsed without costumes or scenery or even a script of the play for just three weeks and they learned their lines on the evening before the performance; and it was also said that they insisted on having two months in the country to prepare a play, with the author, the scenic designer, the stage carpenter and the property man all on the spot to get into the spirit of the thing.

All these stories, the article noted, were based in a farfetched way on fact. The ton-of-dirt tale stemmed from an offstage improvisation by the farmers in *Connelly* that in fact began in the Martin Beck's cellar. (The actors mimed the motions of hoeing, though they didn't use real dirt.) The Group's unusual process of selecting actors through personal interviews gave rise to the rumors of a written exam. "Beautiful thoughts" was a garbled version of the affective memory exercises. The wildly varying stories about the Group's rehearsal methods made it clear just how unorthodox their preparations for a play were in an era when memorizing the script and setting the blocking as quickly as possible were the foundation of most productions.

Clurman was frustrated that the press devoted most of its attention to the Group's technique rather than to what it had to say. Since Strasberg had directed all the productions to date, while Clurman had been largely responsible for the play selection, the widespread comments that the company's acting was superior to the scripts struck at him personally. In an article defending *Taos* he wrote, "The Group Theatre insists that its plays should not be judged on their separate merits alone, but should be seen in relation to the plays that preceded them; should be regarded, in other words, as parts of the message which the Group Theatre as a whole hopes to communicate through its work with ever increasing scope and clarity." All three plays dealt with the death throes of an old order and the painful, chaotic struggle for birth of something new. In their very different ways, all "affirm[ed] the dignity, breadth and power toward which human activity must aspire. . . . To survive and develop, men will either have to develop a muscular, dynamic attitude toward life or perish. Such an attitude . . . in relation to the contemporary scene will inform many of the future Group Theatre plays."

The Group worked hard that spring to prepare for the future. Crawford organized a campaign to create a Group Theatre audience. To assist her in this massive task she hired a number of people, including the redoubtable M. Eleanor Fitzgerald. Fitzgerald had been the administrative mainstay of the Provincetown Players and also had close ties to the radical community, thanks to her work in California on the defense of the labor leader Tom Mooney, sentenced to death for his alleged participation in the bombing of the 1916 San Francisco Preparedness Day parade. For the Group, Fitzgerald wrote letters and held teas for wealthy theatre lovers, progressive political people, and various community organizations, trying to convince them all to invest in the new theatre.

Crawford also had the Group incorporated and issued a stock offering at $100 a share. "At the end of the fiscal year," a pamphlet optimistically forecast, "all monies over the original investment will be declared as dividends and will be divided, half to the investors and half to the Group Theatre, Inc., until each investor has received 100% profit for each share issued." Would-be shareholders didn't exactly come charging up the one hundred steps that led to the Group's offices at the top of the 48th Street Theatre. The spring of 1932, some two and a half years after the Crash, was not a good time to be floating stocks.

The subscription drive Crawford launched in mid-March was only slightly more successful. What the Group offered subscribers, in return for $2.00, was a 20 percent reduction in box-office prices and one free seat per season. She had chosen this unusual approach because the directors didn't want to commit the Group to producing a specific number of plays. Given their past experience with scripts, they feared they might end up obligated to their subscribers with no viable play at hand. Since the company's goal was to present "new plays rather than old," filling in with a classic was not considered an option.

The most interesting aspect of the subscription plan was its goal of drawing the audience into the life of the Group. In addition to their box-office reduction and free seat, subscribers were told, they would be asked to submit their criticisms and comments on each play; the directors would respond to them in open meetings of the entire Group, including the audience, during the runs of the plays. Crawford in particular felt strongly that "the audience is just as much a part of the theatre as the actor or playwright. In order to create the sort of theatre we want, we have to have the right audience, just as we have to have the right actors and the right plays." The subscription campaign was her project, though Clurman and Strasberg gave their share of talks as well and the actors valiantly plugged the Group to drama clubs, women's organizations, Jewish groups, political associations, trade unions, and anyone else who would have them to lunch, tea, or dinner.

"It is our intention to be self-supporting," stated the subscription brochure. "We do not believe that any theatre which aims to be the best representation of its time and place has any significance except through the recognition of its importance by an audience. . . . The Group Theatre hopes to create an audience that will identify itself with and can become constructively active in the Group's work. Since we are a theatre with a particular direction, we desire an audience that shares that direction." As always, the Group declined to define the direction precisely. This wasn't due to coyness; it reflected Clurman's belief that the Group Theatre must embrace the chaos and contradictions of America, not tie itself down to a specific ideology. Part of his unease with the left-wing theatre stemmed from his belief that its scope was too narrow, its beliefs too constricting; it shut itself off from too much of American life. The most he would do this first season was to indicate what kind of plays were most in line with the Group Idea: "We prefer the robust tragedy of a Gorky in 'The Lower Depths' to the slightly ornamental (romantic) ache of an Andreyev; we prefer the frank Rabelaisianism of such people as P. Conkle to the mincing cosmopolitan naughtiness of Noel Coward; we prefer the O'Neill of the last act of 'The Straw' to the O'Neill of 'Diff'rent.' . . . plays that have a life-affirming rather than a life-negating, a yea-saying rather than a nay-saying spirit."

Finding suitable plays was the Group's other main concern that spring. The subscription brochure's list of possible productions for the following season indicated how little success they were having. The list included *Balloon* and *New Year's Eve*, which no one really wanted to tackle again; *Donogoo*, by the French author Jules Romains, which went against the company's stated policy of presenting "American plays rather than foreign"; and only the promise of new scripts from Sidney Howard, Waldo Frank, and Paul Green, none of which materialized. Planning ahead, the brochure stated, "Through a form of subsidy, the Group Theatre proposes to incorporate playwrights as an integral part of its organization." To that end, Crawford announced in late March that the Group would take six playwrights away with them for the summer, in hopes of giving the writers a sense of the requirements of a working theatre and stimulating new plays more closely linked to the Group's philosophy. The chosen six were named in June: Paul Green; Lynn Riggs, author of *Green Grow the Lilacs;* Albert Bein, an unproduced playwright and protégé of Maxwell Anderson; the poet George O'Neil, who was preparing his first script; Albert Maltz and George Sklar, students at the Yale Drama School whose scathing drama of municipal corruption, *Merry-Go-Round,* caused an enormous stir at the old Provincetown Playhouse in April.

These steps laid the groundwork for future plays, but they didn't answer the Group's immediate need for a script. Clurman had planned to do the first play by the novelist and labor writer Charles R. Walker, *Crazy American*, which he felt was an interesting parable of American life in their unsettled times. When Walker returned from a cross-country trip, however, he announced that he had given the play to another manager. The Group had none of the advantages of a commercial theatre, he told Clurman, and because it wasn't a real revolutionary theatre either he wasn't willing to make a financial sacrifice for it. Walker was already thinking about setting up a radical theatre himself, although the Theatre Union wouldn't present its first play for another eighteen months.

Desperate for scripts, Clurman turned to one he had read at the Guild. *The Party*, by the novelist Dawn Powell, was a tough, bitingly funny drama about an advertising man who almost pushes his wife into bed with an out-of-town buyer. It was bitter, more nay-saying than yea-saying, and the characters were unsympathetic, but Clurman admired the dialogue and decided it was worth doing. As luck would have it, around the same time in mid-May John Howard Lawson submitted *Success Story*, a ferocious drama of an ambitious young Jew, deeply at odds with society, clawing his way to the top of an advertising agency. Clurman, who had read it at the Guild when it was titled *Death in an Office*, found the revised version vastly improved and immediately accepted it. The Group finally had two viable scripts for the fall season.

Now all they had to do was survive until June, when they would assemble for their summer work period at Sterling Farms, an old summer camp in Dover Furnace, New York, a tiny town just across the state line from their former digs at Brookfield Center. Survival wasn't easy, with no production on the boards and no money in the till. Crawford had regretfully terminated the audience campaign, which wasn't bringing in sufficient funds to justify its expenses. The Group's financial situation was so bad that they lost their office at the 48th Street Theatre and were forced to relocate to Clurman's apartment at 52 West 58th Street. It was a stark setting, with only a bed, a few chairs, and a table left over from the *Taos* set as furnishings. The landlady, unhappy about groups of noisy actors trooping in and out at all hours, complained that Clurman was using the apartment as an office (which he was) and exhausting the building's electricity supply—as well as being behind on his rent.

Despite their poverty, the Group had plenty of work to do. Everyone pitched in to raise money for the summer. Crawford added up the $2.00 checks and solicited additional donations from her list of wealthy sympathizers. Capitalizing on people's curiosity about the company's method, Franchot Tone, Eunice Stoddard, Ruth Nelson, Morris Carnovsky, Stella Adler, and Beany Barker gave the first public display of Group improvisations at the MacDowell Club on East 73rd Street; Strasberg came along to explain what they were doing and drum up contributions.

There was organizational work to be taken care of as well. The directors held long interviews with each of the actors, discussing their achievements in the past season and what the future held for them in the Group. Two were dropped: Friendly Ford, who simply didn't fit in, and Clem Wilenchick, whose gifts were more as a painter than as an actor. Mary Morris resigned; older than the rest of the Group, she had been troubled all along by what she felt was Strasberg's and Clurman's arrogance and their tendency to treat the actors like wayward children. She cared enough for the Group Idea to stick it out for one season, but found life among the fanatics too wearing.

A number of actors were warned that the directors saw no great potential in their work to date, though they could stay if they wished and continue in small parts. Clifford Odets was one of these, and a memorandum he wrote gives a good sense of what a Group interview was like in those days:

> Lee sat there wordlessly, seemingly uninterested, almost, I thought, a little annoyed. Harold said . . . he didn't think I was yet ready for big parts because I held to my original emotion, the one with which I'd start a scene . . . It seems I'm not slated for large parts this coming season. All right, I must work on what I get and work. The truest thing to be said is what the directors have said of some people: "He or she is busy trying to be a great actor. No, be busy doing your work and what you have will come out, greatness or otherwise."

This kind of criticism was hard to take, and Odets was hurt and disappointed. Yet he exhorted himself, as most Group actors did, to quell his ego and trust the directors: "Let them say what you have, Lee and Harold, let them help you by being relaxed and open to them all the time. This is really belief."

Two new members were added: Russell Collins from the Cleveland Playhouse and Roman Bohnen, a friend of Art Smith's from the Goodman Theatre. Philip Barber was elevated from Group Associate to technical director; since he was also a playwright, the Group hoped he would perform double duty. Barber recommended two enterprising young students from Yale Drama, Alan Baxter and Elia Kazan. They weren't experienced enough to be made members of the Group, but their energy and enthusiasm so impressed Crawford that she convinced her partners to take them along for the summer as apprentices. The Group would get to know all these newcomers when they joined forces at Dover Furnace.

In the meanwhile, they waited, hoped, and planned. Those with a little money, like Beany Barker and Dorothy Patten, helped out their comrades who were broke. Crawford bustled around taking care of practical details for the summer. Strasberg, exhausted after directing three productions, made one of his periodic withdrawals into himself, retreating to his beloved books to restore his energies. As so often happened in moments of inactivity and uncertainty, Clurman became the Group's emotional and intellectural cheerleader. They might grow impatient with all his talking when deeds were required, but when there was nothing to do but sit and worry, his fervent belief in the Group always restored their faith in themselves.

He was obsessed with America that spring. "The word 'America,' and talk of American character, American society, were always on my lips," he wrote later. He urged Group members to look around them at the clamorous streets of New York—vibrant with conflicting currents of hope and fear as the economic crisis gripped the city ever more fiercely—and see their natural subject matter. These times of dislocation and liberation offered overwhelming opportunities for personal and artistic growth. He called a lecture he gave to the Group in late April "The Awakening of America" because "today we are privileged to watch this very thing happening; to see for the first time a national drama actually being born in our own days and before our own eyes in our own country." In that talk, he ranged over the recent history of American theatre, picking out the plays he felt had helped to define this new national drama: Anderson's *What Price Glory?* and *Gods of the Lightning*, Lawson's *Processional, The Adding Machine* by Elmer Rice, Sidney Howard's *The Silver Cord, Hotel Universe* by Philip Barry, *In Abraham's Bosom* and *The House of Connelly* by Paul Green, and virtually everything written by Eugene O'Neill, who "embodied in his very breath the spirit of his times, the struggle and groping of his own day."

As Clurman went through his long list, explaining the importance of these plays to the development of native theatre, his excitement grew. What a wonderful time to be an American theatre artist! How much had been accomplished, how much remained to be done! The Group would help playwrights become articulate and self-conscious about the vast changes that were occurring in American society just as they had helped Paul Green with *Connelly*. They had shown Green that the central conflict of *Connelly* was the characters' struggle to realize one of the great new truths of American life: "that social distinctions are past; that it doesn't matter that once you were a great slave owner. What matters is to buckle down to your farm and live in the tempo of your age."

On June 19, 1932, the Group set off for their summer farm to nurture two plays that were very much in the tempo of the age.

FOUR

New Horizons

The Group's sojourn at Dover Furnace was a period of intensive experiment and rapid growth. At Brookfield their goals had been few and fundamental: the development of a unified technique, the preparation of a single play, the creation of a Group spirit. They had been self-absorbed, all their energies focused on learning to live and work together. At Dover Furnace they turned their attention outward, and a whole world of new ideas and possibilities rushed in. The result was an explosion of creativity that was a catalyst for the entire exciting, unsettling summer.

The season in New York had tested their commitment. *Connelly's* success showed them how much they could hope for; the failures of *1931—* and *Taos* reminded them how long and hard their road would be. They came to Dover Furnace with renewed resolve and deeper confidence in their aspirations and abilities. They knew each other better now, they were ready to work together more boldly, to explore new aspects of their craft. Many visitors that summer remarked on the relaxed, serious atmosphere, fostered by a sensible routine of classes and rehearsals.

The layout of the old summer camp they'd rented proved ideal for their diverse activities. Both a main building and a barn contained rehearsal space, so different kinds of work could be carried on simultaneously. Clustered around were cottages; one standing slightly apart was reserved for the playwrights, who needed a little distance from the hurly-burly of Group life. There was a main dining room where the company could gather in their spare time and a billiard table for indoor recreation; open-air facilities included a tennis court, a croquet lawn, and a swimming pool. The accommodations weren't fancy and the surrounding undergrowth harbored mice and rattlesnakes, but the scenery was beautiful—wooded hills dotted with lush orchards—and the food considerably better than the year before. The improved practical arrangements were largely due to Strasberg's friend Ben Slutzky, whose family was in the hotel business and who cheerfully agreed to manage the camp for the Group.

Nearly fifty people spent the summer at Dover Furnace; in addition to the usual complement of spouses and well-wishers, a small band of apprentices paid twenty dollars a week to study with the Group. (The difference between that and the twelve dollars per person the camp's owner charged the Group went to Ben Slutzky for his work.) There were a lot of new faces, and those viewed with the most interest were the two new Group members.

Born in New Orleans, Russell Collins spent his childhood moving around the Midwest with his restless father, who went from city to city and job to job alternating between linotype operation and rewrite work for various newspapers. In his first year at Indiana State University, Collins discovered a love for drama and transferred to Carnegie Tech in Pittsburgh, where he acted in many plays and made money on the side teaching diction to the blind. In 1922 he joined the Cleveland Playhouse and played in some ninety productions during ten years there. While on tour with *Elizabeth the Queen*, Morris Carnovsky had seen Collins at the Playhouse and admired the emotional intensity of his acting; he seemed like good Group material. Collins, a tall, gaunt, and often unhappy man who lived for his work, was attracted by the Group's dedication and agreed to join for the 1932–1933 season. Talkative and basically sweet despite a fiery temper, he made a lively addition to the collective life.

Roman Bohnen came to the Group after five years with the Goodman Theatre in Chicago and eighteen months in New York, where he struck a blow against the typecasting system he detested when he won a part by turning up for the audition in full make-up and character. The unsuspecting producers, thinking him a natural for the role, hired him before they realized he was giving a performance. Bud, as his friends called him, fit easily and naturally into the Group. He shared their idealism about the theatre and already possessed the social conscience many of them were just developing. (He'd written a play, *Incubator*, about young men turned into hardened criminals by the reform-school system.) Scrambling for money was nothing new to him: he was the son of a well-known but perennially impoverished portrait painter and had spent his youth thinking up ways to keep the family solvent. Everyone in the Group liked him. He was warmhearted, funny, sensitive, and brimming over with enthusiasm. He'd been a cheerleader at the University of Minnesota, and was still a cheerleader for any cause that attracted him. When he joined the Group, he turned some of the unselfish generosity he had always lavished on his friends to the service of the company, working tirelessly in the office as well as onstage to help keep the Group thriving.

Among the band of apprentices were two who became full members the following year. Alan Baxter and Elia Kazan had become friends at Williams College and decided to room together when they got to the Yale Drama School in the fall of 1930. The friendship endured even after Baxter's girlfriend, an aspiring playwright named Molly Day Thacher, left him for Kazan. Baxter was a good-looking, good-natured young man who didn't

take life too seriously; he later supplemented his meager Group earnings by
writing humorous sketches for Broadway shows. But he was deeply devoted
to the theatre, much to the disappointment of his father, a vice president at
the Cleveland Trust Company who wanted his son to follow him into banking. Baxter was determined to make his name as an actor, though as yet his
work gave no indication that he had the passion and power the Group
looked for in performance.

His pal Kazan was another story altogether. Even during his first summer with the Group, when few knew him well, the more perceptive members sensed there was a lot going on underneath his ever-agreeable exterior.
They were right. Born in Constantinople in 1908, Kazan had come to America at the age of five and never lost his feeling of being an outsider in his
new country. He was desperate to fit in, and with the help of his devoted
mother he plotted to escape his father's plans to apprentice him to the
family rug trade. He concluded early "that the most precious things in life
were forbidden by authority (my father)." Therefore, he would have to fulfill
his desires secretively, and if he had to fulfill them at the expense of other
people . . . well, life was like that. Kazan smiled a lot, but he was angry: at
his father, at the upper-crust classmates who had patronized him at Williams, at the world that seemed determined to keep him down. He was
equally determined to rise.

At Dover Furnace with the Group, for the first time, he felt he belonged.
This odd, ardent bunch of dreamers, mocked by Broadway for their idealism, were outsiders too. They were his natural kin, even though they hadn't
accepted him as an equal. He would have to make them see that he was one
of them. He set out to make himself indispensable; his eagerness to help
out in any capacity earned him the nickname "Gadget," which he detested.
He concealed his anger behind an amiable mask. He made friends with
fellow Group malcontent Clifford Odets and settled down to observe the
interpersonal dynamics and power structure of his adopted family.

The sharp-eyed Kazan soon realized that the company was united by
their work and ideals, yet subdivided day-to-day into smaller groups based
on friendship and compatible temperaments. Gathered around Clurman
were those who shared his fondness and admiration for Stella Adler. This
gay, fun-loving bunch included Bobby Lewis, who could always make Clurman laugh with his slightly malicious jokes, and sardonic Sandy Meisner,
whose musical caricatures sometimes made people squirm. (Beany Barker,
though very fond of Meisner, wasn't entirely flattered to be told that she
was Schubert's Unfinished Symphony but would rather have been a piece
by Mozart.) Just as dedicated to the Group's quest for a new kind of acting,
the Clurman-Adler crowd was perhaps more attached to traditional theatre
than some members. Bobby Lewis was a rabid opera lover and worshipped
the glamorous, flamboyant style of the great Yiddish stars. He and Meisner
listened avidly to Stella's and her brother Luther's stories about the golden

days of the Yiddish theatre, roaring with laughter over the gaffes of a hapless actor named Honigman, who once drove an entire company to distraction by delivering a tear-jerking first-act curtain line, "Why? Because he's a Jew!" as "Why? Because he's a goy!"—necessitating a hasty revision of the plot during intermission.

More serious in demeanor were the actors close to Morris Carnovsky, dubbed "the Dean" by Sandy Meisner because at the advanced age of thirty-four he was among the oldest Group members, fond of taking younger actors under his wing. (The sobriquet may also have been a sly poke at Carnovsky's naturally dignified manner, given added authority by a beautiful baritone voice in which he took justifiable pride.) Phoebe Brand, whose mother was a suffragette and a liberal, had a strong interest in social issues that Carnovsky came to share. Lewis Leverett, Virginia Farmer, Joe Bromberg, and several others had a similar inquisitiveness about the state of the world; virtually the whole Group would be swept up into his spirit over the course of the summer.

The women who had picnicked together at Brookfield remained good friends, though Eunice Stoddard was also building a life outside the Group with her new husband. Strasberg was aloof to all except Paula Miller, content to make his connection with Group life solely as director and prophet of the method. Franchot Tone, also essentially a loner, gathered around him a group of hard drinkers, including the new member Collins and the apprentice Baxter, who joined him almost nightly to down a few bottles after rehearsals. None of these small clusters was hostile to the others; boundaries between them were fluid and friendships across boundaries were numerous. Their existence, however, testified to the fact that not even the Group Idea could erase every barrier between individuals.

That was why the work was so important: in that they were truly one. Yet debates over how to organize the summer were fraying the directors' nerves, even as they presented a united front to the actors. Strasberg flatly refused to direct *The Party*, and both he and Crawford felt Clurman was temperamentally best suited to *Success Story*. Clurman, on the contrary, argued that Strasberg should continue the Group's training, and his partners suspected this stance was largely a rationalization of his continuing reluctance to direct. It wasn't clear whether Clurman felt intimidated by the actors' worship of Strasberg, unsure of his own abilities, or just plain incapable of action (which he sometimes was), but weeks of argument failed to budge him. Strasberg finally agreed to undertake *Success Story*, but remained steadfast about *The Party;* it fell to Crawford by default.

On their first night at Dover Furance, Clurman spoke passionately to the assembled company, "roaring defiance at the rest of the theatre world, relighting the fire for the members," as Kazan remembered it. The actors were moved, but they were also beginning to be a little skeptical of their beloved Harold. Was talk all he was good for? Was he ever going to direct a play, or was he going to spend his time on grandiose schemes? His current obsession was a Group restaurant, which he saw not just as a place for the members to gather with their friends but as a center for the many different kinds of creative people interested in their ideas. And that was only the beginning: he dreamed of the Group inspiring a magazine, a school, a film, an art gallery, a lecture program, a publishing house. He held on to that dream for years, asserting, "It is an intrinsic part of the Group idea to make the Theatre not merely a show-shop but a cultural center."

In fact, the Group eventually did have a magazine and a school, both run by members other than Clurman and both short-lived, but important manifestations of the Group spirit. The power of Clurman's dreams was considerable. It was easy to laugh at his inchoate notions—the restaurant in particular became a standing Group joke—but they all affirmed his vision of the Group as more than a theatre. He wanted to share a way of life with as many people as possible, to respond creatively to compelling spiritual questions faced by every American.

He made this point in talks he gave about the plays the Group was preparing, both of which examined in scathing terms the American drive for money and power. Oddly enough, considering the company's desire to present drama of their times, both had been written in the late 1920s; they reflected their authors' response to the cynicism and corruption of the boom years, epitomized by the advertising world in which both were set, and had little to say about the desperate new social situation the Group had addressed in *1931*—. Yet the *The Party* and *Success Story* were not untypical of the early thirties, when Americans were looking back at the recent past to see where they had gone so terribly astray, to find out what insufficiency in their values had provoked the financial recklessness that led to the Crash.

Success Story, the more provocative and compelling of the two plays, needed extensive revisions before it went into rehearsal. The Group began with *The Party*, which Dawn Powell read to the company on June 20. Its story concerns Ed Bonney, a salesman for an advertising agency desperate to land the account of Bert Jones, an important buyer in town for a spree. Ed's wife, Myra, is a former dress model who married in the belief that Ed would take her away from a life where she was expected to flirt with the customers to get their business. Jones had been attracted to Myra before her marriage, and in the first act, as they prepare for a party in his honor, Bonney urges his wife to be nice to their guest in terms that suggest he wouldn't necessarily mind if she had to seduce the buyer. The second act is the drunken party, observed in grisly detail. In the third act, Myra, fed up with her husband, goes off with Jones, but the closing lines make it clear that he wants to use her sex appeal to get ahead, just as Ed did.

This savagely witty play was the work of a writer who surgically dissected human weakness but felt no obligation to stitch up the wounds her literary scalpel inflicted. Compassion was foreign to Powell, at least as an author;

even in the cynical twenties her four published novels were notable for their matter-of-fact acceptance of life's cruelty. She viewed the dreadful behavior of her characters with a detached amusement quite foreign to the Group, which was more comfortable with the righteous indignation of *1931—*. Many of the actors found the play brutal, though undeniably funny. Bud Bohnen took comfort in his belief that it was "really a terribly ghastly exposé of American Life, and for that reason . . . significant social drama." That may have been Clurman's rationale as well; his talks about *The Party* elucidated layers of social and psychological meaning in this bitter farce that Powell may or may not have intended, though Clifford Odets for one found the lectures brilliant.

Rehearsals began with Franchot Tone as Bonney, Stella Adler as his wife, and Joe Bromberg as Jones. Crawford, a neophyte director, was nervous and fully aware of Clurman's doubts about her readiness for the assignment. She worked conscientiously with the actors along the lines laid out by Strasberg the summer before: they discussed the characters' backgrounds, then the actors explored through improvisation the relationships they had discovered. At one session, they improvised the entire second-act party, based on the motives and adjustments she suggested to them. "In this way we become acquainted with the characteristics of the roles, away from the set lines in the play," Bohnen explained to his father, adding that an audience of Group actors and friends had found it hilarious. On the whole, however, the rehearsals were tense and unproductive. Crawford was unhappy with her work; she felt she wasn't getting her vision of the play across to the actors. Tone, who hated his part, was openly hostile, reading murder mysteries during rehearsals. Unable to discipline him, Crawford felt her authority being undermined.

The Group's real creative energies were focused elsewhere. Less than half the company was cast in *The Party,* and until rehearsals of *Success Story* began in July everyone devoted most of their time to experimental work designed to broaden their stylistic horizons. At Brookfield the discovery of affective memory had been so overwhelming that every other aspect of technique had been subordinate to it. This summer they were eager to stretch, to stimulate their imaginations with new technical challenges designed to make them more flexible and versatile actors. They embarked on a series of classes and exercises so radically unconventional that they would not become commonplace in the American theatre for another twenty years.

To develop their physical instrument, they took lessons in body movement from Helen Tamiris. Born Helen Becker on the Lower East Side, Tamiris was a fiery, earthy dancer deeply interested in the relationship between dance and drama. She'd studied at the Henry Street Settlement with Irene Lewisohn, codirector of the Neighborhood Playhouse, and created dances for a New Playwrights production. Her varied career included stints in the Metropolitan Opera ballet corps and a specialty act in night-clubs before she made her concert debut in 1927. Beautiful and glamorous, she was considered by some dance colleagues too theatrical, maybe even a little vulgar. Her choreography tended to be narrative and socially conscious, including works like "Revolutionary Machine" and "Dance of the City," whose musical accompaniment consisted of a siren. Like the Group, she believed in artists working together; she organized the Dance Repertory Theatre in 1930, but by 1932 it had failed, partly because other members feared losing their individuality within a collective. Tamiris never worried about this: no group could dim her luster.

A strong believer in using American music and rhythms in her own work, Tamiris was naturally sympathetic to the Group's ideals. Her classes aimed to help the actors delineate character and illuminate dramatic situations through movement. "It is not my object," she explained, "to turn [actors] into finished dancers. I strive, instead, to teach them three things—a sense of rhythm or time, a sense of the body moving in space in relation to other objects within that space, and a knowledge of the wonderful adaptability of their bodies." Like Stanislavsky, she stressed physical relaxation and concentration. She began with basic exercises that taught the actors to isolate various portions of their bodies and control them so that each movement they made onstage could be completely realized and physically accurate. She disliked physical "indicating," the external reproduction of a clichéd gesture, as much as Strasberg hated emotional superficiality.

Tamiris believed that the rhythm of a movement had to grow naturally out of the requirements of the play rather than be imposed from the outside. To that end, she devised exercises involving physical action with a definite goal. In one, an actor was given the simple task of going from one chair to another, with the understanding that the second chair represented freedom from pursuit. Between the two chairs, the actor had to leap over a bench, crawl under a table, squeeze between two stands, pick up a flag, adjust to a loud noise, and turn a somersault, making each movement with a tempo appropriate both to it and to the ultimate aim of reaching the second chair. Learning how to interact with objects was particularly important, she felt, because actors needed to be able to move freely in onstage space broken up by scenery and props.

The body training was grueling, and the Group humorously complained of their bruises and sore muscles, but most of them rather enjoyed it. Gadget Kazan, eager to be part of all Group activities even if it meant being addressed by his hated nickname, never missed a class. Years later he could still remember Tamiris standing over him with her foot on his back, proclaiming "The floor is your friend" as she pushed his recalcitrant spine toward the ground. Bobby Lewis was an especially ardent student; he strove always in his work for a stylized, heightened theatricality in which movement played an important part, along with music and visual effects.

Lewis was something of a renegade in the Group, whose belief in emotional truthfulness and relevant contemporary drama meant that most of their productions were in the realistic tradition of nineteenth- and twentieth-century European and American theatre. Yet the actors were well aware of other traditions; Strasberg had lectured at Brookfield on primitive, Greek, and Indian theatre, and he addressed these subjects again at Dover Furnace. That summer they were eager to expand their technique beyond the intense naturalism that had been the hallmark of their first season. They took keen interest in the innovations of Stanislavsky's protégés Vsevolod Meyerhold and Eugene Vakhtangov, who had shifted from the psychological focus of the Moscow Art Theatre to stress greater theatricality and visual and spatial creativity. Mark Schmidt, a Russian-born acquaintance of Strasberg's who worked at Dover Furnace as a dishwasher, also served as translator of current Soviet books. Before dinner, the Group would gather in the dining room and listen to him read aloud: from Pavel Markov's history of the First Studio, an offshoot of the MAT where Vakhtangov developed many of his ideas; B. Alpers' study of Meyerhold; and a profile of Vakhtangov, who died in 1922, by his disciple B. E. Zakhava.

Strasberg had long admired Vakhtangov, who united the true emotion of Stanislavsky's actors with the stylistic daring of Meyerhold's company, adding his own distinctive emphasis on the socioeconomic context in which the characters acted. Before rehearsals of *Success Story* began, Strasberg taught a series of classes (later continued by Clurman) consisting largely of exercises designed to stimulate the Group's imagination and encourage the actors to experiment with interpretation and characterization along the lines suggested by the Soviets' work.

The simplest exercises were based on a single word. Clifford Odets took "America" and created a whole scenario of a businessman rushing to work: he pantomimed waking with a start to the sound of an alarm clock, dressing hastily, hurrying out of an apartment and down to the subway station, pushing onto a train, dashing into a elevator, racing into an office, whisking off his jacket and arranging everything on a desk, then settling back in his chair, putting his feet up and lighting a cigar—with nothing else to do. One actress interpreted "liberty" as the Statue of Liberty, whose arm began to waver as her torch turned into a cocktail glass and she lowered it to her lips; the exercise ended with Miss Liberty getting drunk. In more complicated improvisations, two actors were given three unrelated words— "moon," "skeleton," and "baloney" or "iron," "fish," and "jitterbug," for example—and had one minute to come up with a skit making these words the springboard for an action. One pair took "explosive," "poison," and "M.O." and created a melodrama of FBI agents using them as code words.

Strasberg wanted to emphasize the fact that words didn't have a fixed meaning. He had actors say "I must see you" in half a dozen different ways, creating different dramatic situations with intonation alone. A play could be enriched by actions and motivations that might even contradict the sense of the text, he told them. He instructed Ruth Nelson in one class to carry on a conversation with another actor about anything at all except what they were really thinking about, a terrible deed by her partner's brother. He added a technical complication by directing Nelson to have at least one part of her body in motion throughout the scene. She found that the search for motivation to move her hand, leg, or head enriched the characterization.

Clurman gave the actors poems to recite and instructed them to create physical actions unrelated to the words' literal meaning. An actress might recite a poem by E. E. Cummings as if she were a prostitute entering a bar; someone else would deliver Keats's "Ode to a Nightingale" in the character of Shakespeare's drunken Sir Toby Belch. Bobby Lewis was particularly good at this; two of his classroom exercises would be a staple of Group benefits for years to come. In "Red Hamlet" he performed the "to be or not to be" soliloquy as a radical agitator enacting the class struggle for a crowd. On "to be" he was a victorious worker breaking his chains; "not to be" was a bloated capitalist reclining at his ease, and so on until the last phrase, "and lose the name of action," which became a rabble-rousing call to revolution complete with clenched-fist salute on the word "action." His version of a famous Walt Whitman poem was equally popular: a meek little man taking his morning shower discovered there was no hot water and, as the cold spray hit him, shrieked, "I sing the body electric," then proceeded to soap each organ praised in the poem before drying himself off and leaping back into bed.

Gibberish improvisation trained the actors to express vocal emotion independent of articulate speech. A large group improvisation about a factory strike required the actors to interact and move the action forward without the aid of words. Morris Carnovsky and Joe Bromberg invented several hilarious gibberish set pieces, usually involving an optimistic Carnovsky trying to cheer up a depressed and angry Bromberg. In one, Bromberg was a painter disgusted with his work and ready to give it up. As a fellow artist, Carnovsky tried to convince him (in gibberish) to persevere, but to no avail. The scene ended with Bromberg hurling a sponge at his canvas; then, as they both looked at the spatter of paint it made, enthusiastic gibberish poured from their lips and they began to paint again. Their most popular sketch portrayed two bums on a park bench: one (Bromberg) in a fit of profound depression over the state of the world, the other trying to cheer him up by reminding him of life's pleasures. Carnovsky's bum set an imaginary table full of good food and "champagnsky" to drink. When Bromberg downed the "boobly" he developed a severe case of hiccups, which subsided only after Carnovsky shook him and reminded him it was all unreal. Silence descended on the park bench, broken by a final single hiccup from Carnovsky's character.

Animal improvisations also encouraged the actors to look beyond words, to make their characterizations physically expressive as well. The movements of a particular beast, Strasberg explained, might translate into human motions that illuminated the psychology of a character. The deeper purpose, Phoebe Brand thought, "was not to copy the animal exactly but to try and place yourself into the life of the animal and his point of view. For that we'd really have to study the animal and see how he'd behave in certain circumstances."

The actors' visual sense was stimulated by a form of charades in which they were given a half-hour to create costumes from whatever scraps of material they could find around the cottages, then return to the rehearsal room dressed as literary or historical figures. Alixe Walker was a blowsy Toulouse-Lautrec washerwoman with a messy topknot and disheveled white blouse. Bobby Lewis parted his hair in the middle, stuffed his cheeks with cotton, and fashioned a cardboard collar to portray Herbert Hoover. Apprentice Wilhelmina Barton (soon to marry Tony Kraber) transformed herself into Ariel by stripping down to her bra and underpants and festooning herself with toilet paper—"very daring for the modest and shy, naïve young girl that I was!"

Drawing on his reading of Gordon Craig, Strasberg had the actors study dramatic poses in classical and modern art. They would duplicate the expressions and gestures in a specific painting by Rembrandt or El Greco, try to feel the mood it suggested, then step out of the picture frame and improvise dialogue in character. They also worked with music: Tony Kraber sang the Toreador Song from *Carmen* as a depressed bullfighter; a group of actors improvised the death of a child during an operation to the music of a Brahms quintet; Virginia Farmer played a world-weary woman swaying to the strains of Ravel.

In more ambitious projects, the actors combined elements explored separately in individual exercises to create longer experiments that were prepared and rehearsed over a period of weeks. Beany Barker and Sandy Meisner did a scene from *Twelfth Night;* she used a series of statuesque figures in Giotto's paintings as an inspiration for her stylized movements as Olivia, while Meisner played the Clown as a commedia dell'arte figure. The rhythms and tempos of the two characters were completely different, expressing the gulf between their perceptions. Barker also worked with Ruth Nelson to develop an improvisation based on German artist Käthe Kollwitz's lithographs of working-class women and their starving children, set to Mahler's "Songs on the Death of Children." Art Smith devised and directed an elaborate piece based on George Grosz's satirical sketches of the fat, complacent German bourgeoisie: a large number of Group actors reproduced poses from Grosz's drawings and recited portions of the Book of Psalms, while a recording featuring a tinny piano and the sultry singing of Marlene Dietrich played in the background.

This remarkable work was quite unlike anything they had done before and tremendously exciting. It allowed them to experiment, to try out new approaches, even make fools of themselves in a way that was impossible in the commercial theatre, where actors had to quickly impress results-oriented directors, whose main rehearsal concern was getting a presentable performance in four weeks. It gave the actors a new sense of their own creativity—shaped by Strasberg's guidance, to be sure, but independent of the detailed, step-by-step direction he gave during rehearsals. For the first time they were doing large portions of their work among themselves: many of them took their first steps as directors, and entire scenes were conceived and rehearsed without Strasberg or Clurman. They grew closer to those whose ideas and acting styles they found most compatible; they began to feel a unity that in some ways excluded the directors. Their devotion to their leaders remained firm, but it was no longer the childlike, unquestioning worship Clurman had found so disturbing at Brookfield. They read books the directors recommended, but they read other books as well. They got new ideas from Strasberg's lectures and Clurman's impassioned speeches, but they had ideas of their own too. They were growing up.

And they were branching out. The spirit of experiment and inquiry that characterized the Group's theatrical work led them to take a closer look at the world around them. It was impossible to be indifferent to political and economic questions in America during the desperate year of 1932. The fabric of society seemed irreparably torn. Some fifteen million people were unemployed. For those who were working, the average weekly wage had dropped 60 percent since 1929, to a mere seventeen dollars a week. A million people roamed across the country, without homes or jobs; 200,000 of these drifters were children. More than 1,500 banks failed in 1932; 20,000 businesses went bankrupt. The gross national product was half its 1929 level, industrial production one-third what it had been before the crash.

Former Secretary of the Treasury, Andrew Mellon might assert that spring that there was nothing fundamentally wrong with "the social system under which we have achieved, in this and other industrialized countries, a degree of economic well-being unprecedented in the history of the world"; people who saw men fighting for scraps of food out of restaurant garbage pails no longer believed him. Ugly scandals like the spectacular collapse of Chicago magnate Samuel Insull's public utilities empire shook Americans' faith in the financial leaders who were supposed to be doing something about the Depression. Word began to circulate about a Senate investigation of the stock market that showed it was manipulated for personal gain by corporate executives with inside information at a time when they were touting Wall Street's solidity and fiscal responsibility to the rest of the world.

Events that summer suggested the nation's powerful had no intention of alleviating the suffering of the unemployed and dispossessed. The most shameful moment came on July 28, the day the Dow Jones average hit an all-time low (41.22, as opposed to 381.17 on September 3, 1929). Since May, impoverished World War veterans had been assembling in Washington, holding demonstrations to demand the bonuses that had been voted for them by Congress in 1924. The monies weren't slated to be delivered until 1945, but the veterans needed them now, and by the end of July 25,000 of them were camped out with their wives and children in parks, dumps, and empty lots all over the city. On July 28, the U.S. Army rolled out tanks, infantry, and cavalry on the veterans' main camp at Anacostia Flats, using grenades and bayonets to disperse the unarmed crowd and setting fire to their pitiful homemade shacks. More than a hundred people were injured, and the Group shared the nation's shock at the use of violence against a peaceful demonstration. Odets hoped in his diary that this display would "hasten the day when the people will make a just government." John Howard Lawson, back home in Long Island working on revisions of *Success Story,* agreed with his friend John Dos Passos that "the class nature of our society was more clearly exposed than it had ever been." The entire system seemed morally as well as economically bankrupt.

In this atmosphere the Soviet Union was more than a theatrical mecca for the Group; it was also the home of a brave new experiment that seemed to offer a better way of life than the discredited capitalist order. American intellectuals had been intrigued by the Russian Revolution long before the Crash; so had the Group's founders, as witness the Guild Studio production of *Red Rust.* By 1932 this rather abstract interest in a foreign society had been made concrete by the crisis at home. Drastic times called for drastic solutions. Radicalism seemed to be entering the mainstream of American thought. In the summer of 1932, V. F. Calverton's *Modern Quarterly* asked seventeen writers, including a number of conservatives, if capitalism was "doomed to inevitable failure and collapse," and only two answered no. The spirit of revolt gathering force among intellectuals would culminate in the September publication of an open letter signed by fifty-three writers, including Clurman's friend Waldo Frank, declaring the Republican and Democratic parties hopelessly corrupt and urging Americans to vote Communist in the forthcoming election. (Socialism, once such an important force on the American left, now seemed irrelevant; John Dos Passos quipped in *Modern Quarterly* that joining the Socialist party "would have just about the same effect on anybody as drinking a bottle of near-beer.") Frank was also among those who responded that same month to a request from the *New Masses* for comments on "the marked movement among the intellectuals toward the left."

The Group was ripe for a similar movement. Some members, like Sylvia Feningston, were already politically committed. Morris Carnovsky, Phoebe Brand, Lewis Leverett, Art Smith, Virginia Farmer, Joe Bromberg, and Bud Bohnen were strongly inclined to the left. Everyone was interested, including the directors. Strasberg's brother, Arthur, read aloud from *Das Kapital* and lectured on Marxism. (He was a dentist by trade but reasonably well versed in left-wing theory—the Group were short on experts.) Strasberg, like his brother, had grown up immersed in the Jewish socialist tradition of the Lower East Side, reading Lenin and Marx as a teenager. He loaned his copy of Trotsky's *History of the Russian Revolution* to Tony Kraber, both of them too naïve in those days to realize that Trotsky was a nonperson as far as orthodox communists were concerned.

Clurman, always more inclined to examine ideas in terms of their impact on American life, urged everyone to read Vernon Parrington's *Main Currents in American Thought*. Though the third volume was only half finished at the time of the author's sudden death in 1929, this massive text had great influence in the 1930s, partly because of its emphasis on literature's integral connection to social and economic developments but primarily owing to its staunch affirmation of liberalism as the deepest and truest expression of the American spirit. To an idealistic young actor reading Parrington's ardent and well-argued book in the summer of 1932, it seemed obvious that radical ideas like communism were simply the natural extension of an American tradition of collectivism, compassion, and liberal social change.

Given the Group's belief that art must be vitally concerned with contemporary life and ideas, it wasn't surprising that this new interest in politics was, as Clurman described it, "like a fever running through our camp." Mealtimes were clamorous with argument, each table the center of a separate discussion. The actors' new social consciousness spilled over into their work, informing the content of many improvisations. Strasberg, more influenced by Vakhtangov than ever, emulated the Soviet director's political emphasis in his lectures on acting. "Every action must be a definite comment on the character," he told the actors. "The tie this man wears will show just what class he belongs to and the sort of person he is." Clurman himself, though he later liked to believe he had been more skeptical of big words and foreign ideas than the unsophisticated actors, was very much swept up in the militant mood. Everyone was. Stella Adler, whose family were socialists by tradition (though aristocrats by temperament), declared her sympathy with Marxist ideology. She later joked that she could live in any communist country provided she could be queen.

The Group's increasing radicalism had a profound impact on their interpretation of *Success Story*, which Strasberg put into rehearsal in July while Clurman worked with John Howard Lawson on the final revisions. Lawson was in many ways the most sympathetic and compatible playwright they had yet discovered; Clurman considered him "the hope of our theatre." From *Roger Bloomer* in 1923 through *Processional* (1925), *Nirvana* (1926), *Loud Speaker* (1927), and *The International* (1928), his challenging and stylistically innovative plays had criticized the brutality of American life even as they reveled in its vitality: "The grotesque of the American environment, the colorful exaggeration of the American language . . . these are Rabelaisian in their intensity," he wrote in the introduction to *Processional*. His belief that "the blood and bones of a living stage must be the blood and bones of the actuality around us" was in essence a summary of the Group Idea. He shared with his friend Max Gorelik, who designed the sets for *Success Story*, a hope that the Group would be their theatrical home.

Lawson's political commitment long antedated the Group's. He had been considered something of a radical as an undergraduate at Williams and disapproved of America's involvement in the World War. His experiences as an ambulance driver for the Red Cross during the war reinforced his conviction that the old order was dying; he became a pacifist and a socialist. He had gone against the apolitical temper of the times when he founded New Playwrights in 1927 with Dos Passos and their fellow leftists Michael Gold, Em Jo Basshe, and Francis Farragoh. He seemed a natural Group ally, and as he and Clurman talked of the work that needed to be done on *Success Story* and the play he planned to write about the international revolutionary movement *(Red Square)*, they both anticipated a long and fruitful association.

Yet there were philosophical and emotional disparities between Lawson and his new partners that flamed into a furious debate over the last act of *Success Story*. The play chronicles the rise of Sol Ginsberg, an angry and ambitious young Jew working in an advertising agency where his childhood friend Sarah Glassman is also employed. Sol has discarded the youthful radicalism Sarah retains and has focused his energy on rising to the top and displacing the agency's owner, Raymond Merritt. In the second act he forces Merritt to make him a partner and marries his rival's mistress, shocking Sarah with his greed and duplicity. By the third act Sol is rich, yet still unhappy and unfulfilled. When he tries to reclaim Sarah, who has always loved him, she violently rejects him and in a final struggle—whether accidentally or deliberately is left vague—shoots him. The dying Sol takes the gun in his hand so the death will look like a suicide.

The Group directors were enthusiastic about the play and cast some of the company's best actors in it: Luther Adler as Sol, his sister as Sarah, and Franchot Tone as Merritt. Everyone agreed with Lawson that *Success Story* was "an indictment of the whole system of values which capitalism imposed upon us" and that Sol had betrayed everything that was best in himself during his brutal climb to the top. But the utter pessimism of the last scene troubled the Group; they wanted to find some redeeming note of hope in Sol's debacle. In a series of letters sent to Lawson on August 6, 7, and 8, Clurman argued that, while Sol has lost his integrity, Sarah has been true to her moral obligations and that the difference between them must be made explicit in the scene preceding the shooting. "Sarah must *tell* Sol very clearly and passionately what is really the matter with him and what is really the tragedy and significance of his story . . . Sarah in this way will acquire a more positive, exultant quality which is good for the finale."

Lawson was appalled. He didn't want the finale to be exultant; he considered Sarah as confused and neurotic as Sol. He felt the Group was searching for "heart's ease and moral certitude" in a play that had neither. "When Clurman wrote me that Sarah was 'a person with a definite point of view,'" he remembered later, "I did not need three guesses to identify her belief." He knew how strong an impact communist philosophy had made on the Group that summer, though he doubted any of them had actually joined the party. He responded to Clurman's letters with an impassioned memo addressed to the entire Group, entitled "Communism in Relation to *Success Story.*" He flatly stated that Sarah was by no means a serious communist, that her radicalism was just as much an escape as Sol's pursuit of money. The essential key to her feelings in the last act, he wrote, was a line Clurman wanted to cut, which read, "I'm so high-strung that it crosses the borderline of common sense." The half-accidental killing wasn't the purposeful act of a determined revolutionary, but an emotional, unpremeditated response to an unbearable situation. Sarah would live with the guilt of having killed the man she loved for the rest of her life.

Lawson wasn't Paul Green; he knew what he wanted to say and resisted the Group's attempt to inform the ending with their own optimism. Faced with such a determined and articulate response, the directors backed down. When Lawson arrived at Dover Furnace just a few days after his memo, Clurman and Strasberg emphasized that their primary concern was getting the script into workable shape, as the play was scheduled to open on Broadway in just over a month. They asked Lawson to consider their objections, but acknowledged he must write the final revision as he saw fit. Mollified, Lawson promised to address structural weaknesses they discerned in the second act in return for their promise that his conception of the play's climax would be respected. The disagreement hadn't been resolved, merely smoothed over; Lawson admired the passion of Stella Adler's performance as Sarah but felt that it was still "guided by the idea of moral integrity . . . designed to win sympathy and not to expose 'estrangement' and sterile idealism."

It was a fascinating debate, utterly typical of the 1930s. It revealed how much the temper of the times had changed in a few short years and how wide a gulf could exist between people separated in age by less than a decade. Lawson, born in 1895, was just enough older than most Group members to have been shaped by a very different set of experiences: the tragic futility of the World War, the alienation and reckless gaiety of the Jazz Age. The Depression, which added economic chaos to the moral chaos he had already condemned in American society, frightened him in ways that the Group, filled with ardent faith in their new theatre and the exciting social ideas they were discovering, could barely comprehend. His involvement in the freewheeling political debates of the 1920s made him far more conscious of the flaws in the Soviet system than younger people caught up in the first flush of a romance with radicalism. Yet he shared the Group's militant contempt for the corrupt capitalist system and felt obliged to bolster his stance on *Success Story* with a lengthy discussion of his attitude toward communism, asserting that he had read widely in Marxist literature and was moving in the direction of "a more revolutionary point of view," though he continued to reject communism as a solution. (He finally concluded years of struggle and doubt by joining the Communist party in 1934.) He was uneasily aware that, although the Group's answer to the ethical dilemma posed by *Success Story* was too simple, "I had no answer at all."

Lawson felt the Group viewed him as a Greenwich Village bohemian, well intentioned but lacking in the firm resolve the times demanded. He found the Group politically naïve and theatrically conventional. The Stanislavsky system—still the core of the rehearsal process despite all their experimenting—seemed old-fashioned to a man deeply influenced by the European avant-garde. He took sardonic amusement in the fact that outside of their disciplined work regimen, the actors could be as eccentric and neurotic as the flightiest Village nonconformist.

Indeed, many Group members were acting—and looking—pretty peculiar that summer. Franchot Tone and Joe Bromberg maintained the Brookfield tradition and grew beards; Clifford Odets and Bud Bohnen startled the locals even more by shaving their heads. Everywhere you went, at all hours of the day or night, it seemed, you could hear Tony Kraber wailing mournful cowboy songs, accompanying himself (not very skillfully) on the guitar. Love affairs abounded, as did thwarted passions. "The camp had become a veritable cauldron of rapturous discontent," Clurman recalled; from friends in New York he heard that word on Broadway was "the Group was a free-love farm and we had all been converted to Communism." The Group did nothing to discourage those rumors. They were distant with outsiders— even those who had written plays for them, as Lawson discovered from a disastrous attempt to get closer to the actors by taking them out to a speakeasy. Only visitors from the magical "real" world beyond the arts—the radical activist Mother Bloor or a wild Irish rebel named Ernest O'Malley, who had served in the IRA—were greeted with interest and enthusiasm.

Perhaps their rapid artistic growth had Group members so keyed up that they needed to challenge one another outside the rehearsal hall as well. Possibly their new social consciousness encouraged a confrontational manner toward the bourgeois world. Whatever the reasons, everyone seemed a little cranky, and none more so than Franchot Tone. He certainly looked odd, as he wandered around the camp clad only in a jockstrap. His manner was aloof and his behavior disruptive. He was giving a wonderful performance in *Success Story* but put hardly any effort into *The Party*. After a few sessions he refused to attend Tamiris' classes, and he took no part in the experimental work. He drove onto the lawn after late-night drinking sessions and destroyed the garden furniture; he went hunting and shot off guns dangerously close to the rehearsal rooms. He left camp for days on end to see his current flame, the film actress Lilyan Tashman, who had not been made welcome by the Group. Halfway through the summer he disappeared altogether, and rumors swept the camp that he was in New York talking to movie studios. Strasberg gave an angry speech saying that Tone might be one of the finest actors in America, but he lacked the dedication the Group demanded; several actresses wept as the director said he no longer wanted Tone in the company. Bud Bohnen read his part in *Success Story*, and it seemed Tone's association with the Group was over.

Five days later, gunshots announced that he was back, and it appeared that he had patched matters up with the directors. It was a temporary truce, however, and by August Clurman and Strasberg confronted him again. He freely admitted that he had already decided to leave the Group and go into the movies. He would stay to play Merritt in *Success Story* until November, when his film contract began, but he wanted nothing more to do with *The Party*.

It was a painful moment for the Group. Only one other member had ever resigned, and Mary Morris hadn't been as integral a part of the collective. Tone was one of the earliest Group believers, a participant in the 1928 sessions on Riverside Drive, and their principal leading man. If his difficult temperament made him less than the most popular member of the company, everyone respected his acting ability and was shocked that he'd decided to squander his talents in the movies. Strasberg spoke to the actors, declaring that the Group remained strong and healthy; in fact, they would be better off without someone whose heart was no longer with them. They knew he was right, but Tone's departure wounded the Group's confidence. It would heal, but the scar remained. In Group mythology Tone's defection became the original sin, the shocking deed that forced them to face the fact that idealism could fade and worldly success mean more than artistic integrity. The six-foot rattlesnake spotted by Bud Bohnen on an adjacent farm wasn't the only serpent that had entered their Garden of Eden.

There were other unhappy people at Dover Furnace besides Tone. The plan to incorporate playwrights as part of the company wasn't working out as well as Crawford and Clurman had hoped. Of the six originally selected, only Albert Bein and George O'Neil turned up, although several others dropped in. Philip Barber wrote when his technical services weren't required, and Clurman's friend Gerald Sykes was there most of the time. Powell and Lawson appeared at scattered intervals to work on rewrites; Maxwell Anderson was a frequent visitor to see Mab Maynard. But the two authors who had been brought along specifically to produce Group drama had a rough summer. About the only aspect of it they found useful was the rehearsal of scenes from uncompleted plays with the actors, which gave them the opportunity to revise their work based on seeing it in performance.

The problem was getting that work written. The playwrights' cottage wasn't isolated enough from the others; aspiring authors like Clifford Odets came by to borrow typewriters and work space, bringing the tumult of Group life with them. O'Neil in particular found the noisy, intense atmosphere at Dover Furnace not at all conducive to creation. Despite this he managed to finish a trilogy called *American Dream*, but apparently preferred to give it to the Theatre Guild, which presented it the following season. Albert Bein would have liked the Group to produce the play he wrote that summer and was disappointed when Clurman told him *Heavenly Express* needed more work.

The apprentices were restless and at loose ends, largely because the Group hadn't planned their program very carefully. Theoretically, Clurman was holding classes for them, but his relationship with Stella Adler was in one of its periodic states of turmoil and about half the time he simply didn't show up. Most of them had made real financial sacrifices to be there—both Gadget Kazan and Willy Barton ran out of money halfway through the summer—so they were eager to get as much training as they could. They weren't usually allowed to attend rehearsals, but they subjected themselves to Tamiris' bone-cracking sessions and sat in on Strasberg's classes. Along with the new members who hadn't used it before, they practiced affective memory. Kazan kept a notebook listing the separate emotions he might need in a scene and the exercises that would awaken them; this was the "golden box" each Group actor created in his individual work on the method.

While most apprentices were discontented, Kazan was actively miserable. He was determined to make the grade as a full Group member, and depressed when word got back to him of the directors' judgment that he had "no actor's emotion." He would prove them wrong. He got a job as a waiter in the dining room to pay for his keep. He made extra money by typing *Heavenly Express* for Bein. He attended every class, every lecture; he took notes on everything. He resented it when Clurman, seeing him in a white jacket serving dinner, made no comment about his obvious dedication to the Group.

Clurman had more important things on his mind. As the summer drew to a close, the Group's theatrical hopes were centered on *Success Story*, which the directors decided would precede *The Party* as their first fall production. Despite their debate with Lawson over the ending, the Group loved the play and felt it made an important statement about American life. Rehearsals were going well. Luther Adler was superb as Sol, delineating his evolution from an angry, ambitious boy to a jittery, disoriented man astonished to find success so empty, with a wealth of precisely observed detail that gave shape and meaning to the character's ferocious appetites. As Sarah, Stella Adler was profoundly moving. Strasberg had fought to rein in her open emotionalism behind the modest façade appropriate to Sarah's repressed nature; the result was a performance of purity and restraint glowing with internal fire, all the more powerful because it burst forth only in the final scene. Franchot Tone invested the dignified, defeated Merritt with an air of bewildered resignation that reflected many of his own feelings and was perfect for the character. Playing a banker whose loyalties were determined solely by his financial interests, Morris Carnovsky gave a wonderfully subtle performance of cool menace. The minor parts were interesting as well, given bite and color by Strasberg's new emphasis on the socioeconomic forces that determined character. It was shaping up to be their best production to date.

When Crawford went to New York to find a backer, she decided the most likely candidate was Lee Shubert, owner with his brother, Jacob, of a vast and powerful empire of theatres. (It was an irony not lost on Lawson that the Group was seeking support for his stinging play, which spat in the face of capitalism, from "the most commercial figure in the commercial theatre.") She persuaded Shubert to come up to Dover Furnace and installed him in a red velvet chair in one of the rehearsal rooms, where the actors gave a run-through of the play with an intensity made even more compelling by the fact that they were playing almost in his lap. He was impressed; he agreed to finance the production and put it in his Maxine Elliott Theatre.

Shubert also pointed out *Success Story*'s one glaring weakness: Dorothy Patten's performance as Agnes, the seductive blonde Sol steals from Merritt and later makes his wife. It was a crucial role: Agnes incarnates in the flesh all the enticements that lure Sol from his better nature, and her suspected infidelity prompts his final breakdown. Patten was a hardworking actress, devoted to the Group Idea, but in addition to the minor drawback of not being blond she was by no stretch of the imagination the sexy plaything the script called for. Any number of Group actresses would have been more suitable. Phoebe Brand wasn't blond either, but she had Agnes' sizzle; half the men in the Group had tried to pry her loose from Carnovsky, at least for a night. Eunice Stoddard had the right looks for the part, but she thought Strasberg didn't like her, and Clurman viewed her as a character actress.

The directors passed over several more obvious choices to cast Patten as Agnes. They were committed to challenging their actors. One of Clurman's principal claims back in the winter of 1930–1931 was that the Group would allow actors to grow by giving them roles far beyond the range they were confined to by the stereotyping of the commercial theatre. He and Strasberg had rejected Lawson's initial suggestion that Stella Adler play Agnes because they felt she would bring interesting qualities to bear on Sarah, even if their personalities weren't superficially similar. In Adler's case they were right. With Patten, however, the directors' commendable distaste for typecasting led them to violate the iron law of plausibility.

"We believed in those days that proper direction could make any com-

petent actor give a satisfactory interpretation of a role," Clurman acknowledged later. Rather than replace Patten, they worked harder with her. She
had individual rehearsals with Strasberg; he attempted to instill in a woman
who loved dogs, outdoor activities, and casual clothes the sensuous narcis-
sism of a character described by Sol as "blood sister to a streetwalker." She
tried hard, but she didn't get much better. Nonetheless, she remained in the
play. The directors stuck by their choice.

Lee Shubert prompted another crisis within the Group's leadership when
they sat down to discuss the production budget. The amount he was willing
to provide for salaries was more than they needed to pay the small cast of
Success Story, but not enough for the entire company, even though the
directors waived their weekly $50 and Tone and Carnovsky both agreed to
have their wages reduced from $300 to $200. As Crawford saw it, the directors had no choice; they would simply have to restrict their payroll to the
Group actors working on *Success Story* and *The Party*. They would free the
rest of the company to look for work elsewhere but still consider them
Group members.

Strasberg strongly opposed this stratagem. The actors were in a sense
his particular responsibility, and he felt it was a betrayal of their trust to
toss them out into the cold the first time the directors felt a financial pinch.
He argued that it made the Group no different from any other commercial
theatre, which hired actors from play to play and didn't bind them together
in a real ensemble. Clurman agreed, but thought Crawford's course was the
only practical one. Outvoted, Strasberg put his doubts behind him and
presented a united front with Clurman and Crawford when they announced
to the actors that only the eighteen members with parts in the two fall
productions would be paid.

It wasn't a happy way to end the summer. It hurt those who weren't in
the productions; they suspected (with some justification, at least in regard
to Clurman) that their omission reflected the directors' opinion of their
lesser value to the Group. Even those who were on the payroll thought the
directors were setting a dangerous precedent by violating a basic Group
tenet. The new arrangement might be the only sensible solution to their
financial difficulties, but when had the Group ever been sensible?

The actors' nascent sense of themselves as an entity separate from the
directors gained definition from this disturbing announcement. It certainly
gave additional sharpness to the caricatures of the triumvirate they presented in a sketch they put on late in the summer. Beany Barker played
Crawford as a laconic cowgirl, trying to rope her starry-eyed partners into
rational behavior. Strasberg as portrayed by Art Smith was a scholar literally weighted down with learning—books protruded from his pockets, trou-
ser waistband, and anyplace else they could be stuffed. Morris Carnovsky
turned Clurman into a heavyset, bearded angel with an electric light on his
forehead and a shapely female leg (a stuffed silk stocking) under his arm;

he introduced every high-flown and incomprehensible remark with a sputtered "Goddammit!" These were basically affectionate portraits; later spoofs would be less gentle.

Personal problems loomed large in the tense atmosphere. Strasberg was shocked when Paula Miller's estranged husband turned up at Dover Furnace; he'd had no idea she was married. Clurman and Stella Adler quarreled so violently that Bobby Lewis, whose attic bedroom was directly over their quarters, could hear them shouting at each other night after night. Gadget Kazan wrestled with mingled feelings of guilt and anger toward Molly Thacher, who had undergone an abortion earlier in the summer and was now talking about coming to some kind of understanding about where their relationship was headed. He and Alan Baxter were both bitterly disappointed when Clurman told them they wouldn't be made full Group members this season. They were slightly mollified when Clurman said they could attend Group classes in New York, and Crawford helped Kazan out by getting him a job as assistant stage manager of *The Pure in Heart*, another new play by Lawson that the Theatre Guild was presenting.

Kazan's friend Clifford Odets was possibly the unhappiest and most frustrated Group member, even though he was one of the lucky ones with a part and the promise of a paycheck. His writing seemed to be going nowhere. Clurman had read his new play based on the life of Beethoven, *Victory*, and told him unequivocally it was terrible; the director suggested he'd be better off working along the lines of his earlier drama, *910 Eden Street*, whose more personal material better suited his gift for observation and characterization. Odets still thought of himself primarily as an actor, but his small role in *The Party* and thankless job as Luther Adler's understudy simply exacerbated his irritation over the chasm between the opportunities he was given and those offered to others. He consoled himself by deciding that Luther, admittedly an excellent actor, was softening his tough portrait of Sol, possibly because the Jewish Lee Shubert had been put off by the character's arrogance. Odets studied the part and the play intently, inspired by Clurman's incisive analysis of its significance for American life. He may also have heard in the unabashedly urban rhythms of Lawson's earthy dialogue an authentic American sound that he too might try to capture in his writing.

None of this was enough for Odets, desperate to win the Group's respect with significant creative work. He'd just turned twenty-six, and a sense of all the things he hadn't accomplished was driving him crazy. He was touchy, quick to take offense when he thought Group members like Sandy Meisner were sneering at him. He was argumentative, debating with more prominent actors over the interpretation of *Success Story* and delighted when Clurman agreed with a point he made. He was combative, yearning to slap the sulky Franchot Tone in the mouth. Most of all, he was angry: at Clurman, who hadn't liked his play; at the Group women, who failed to respond to his pleas for sexual solace; above all, at himself.

Odets' simmering emotions finally boiled over one crazy, drunken night at the end of August. His wild rampage through the camp, as funny as it was frightening, gave vivid physical expression to the Group's nervous mood as their stimulating, demanding, and exhausting summer drew to a close.

Virginia Farmer, one of those without a part for the coming season, had rustled up a job in a radio show and was scheduled to leave September 1. She invited some of the company up to her room after the evening class to have a drink. "She was serious, that girl," Odets remembered, "for there was a gallon of applejack and gingerale and rye." He polished off a good portion of it, and "began a drunk such as I've never had before." He started by running from room to room, kissing everyone and laughing hysterically. He tore off his sweater and, bare-chested, dragged Franchot Tone's bicycle upstairs. Then his mood darkened: he threw a sugar bowl at Farmer, collected a batch of glasses and cups, and tossed them out the window. He went out to the barn's rehearsal hall and overturned all the tables. At 2:00 a.m. he decided to go back to the main house and play the piano. His musical hunger sated, his thoughts turned to other appetites. Beany Barker, one of the objects of Odets' wide-ranging affections ever since Brookfield, had the misfortune to sleep in a bedroom not far away. When she heartlessly refused to let him in, he threw billiard balls at the door, leaving deep dents in the wood and rousing any Group members who'd managed to sleep through his crashing piano recital. Paula Miller and Phil Barber lured him away to his room, where they had to listen to a lengthy diatribe about Beethoven before he finally passed out. He woke the next day to find an orange squashed in his back pocket and his underwear ripped in half.

Though badly hung over, Odets was oddly pleased with himself. "It's the first time in my life I had an extroverted drunk," he wrote in his diary. "It is symptomatic of a new inner man, of a new line of life and conduct." The Group enjoyed it too. As they clustered around their battered comrade, filling in the gaps in his fuzzy memory with every gory detail of his riotous behavior, they could laugh with an ease and affection that had often been absent in recent weeks. Stella Adler's wisecrack was quickly enshrined in Group folklore. "Clifford," she warned, "if you don't turn out to be a genius, no one will ever forgive you."

Everyone howled. Odets had cleared the air. Whatever their individual difficulties and disappointments that summer, they had made important discoveries and grown beyond all measure. They were returning to New York with two new productions that expressed provocative ideas about contemporary America. Their acting in these plays was deeper and bolder because of their adventurous experimental work. The Group's stylistic range had broadened enormously; their increasing command over form enabled them to serve the play's content with greater power.

They were beginning to realize how precious these summers together were. It wasn't just that three months of uninterrupted work allowed them to develop their productions with a care and a level of detail impossible in the conventional four-week rehearsal period. Nor was it solely the chance to experiment that made the Group summers such a crucial element of the collective life. They were spiritually necessary as well. Away from the cynicism and backbiting of Broadway, whose self-serving wisdom was that everyone in the theatre looked out for themselves first and only fools passed up opportunities for the sake of an ideal, they could replenish their faith.

One playwright wrote to the company after he had left Dover Furnace, "It wasn't until I was away that I realized how sappy and idealistic I must have sounded. The place does that to me. I blush now to think of some of the things I said . . . I couldn't possibly have said them anywhere else, yet I know that I meant them, that they are true, that you accepted them and that someday it may be possible to say them anywhere without apology." Clurman, Strasberg, Crawford, and the actors had created the Group because they needed a home, a place where they could share their most cherished aspirations—artistic, political, personal—with kindred spirits. In their summer retreats, isolated from the world and liberated (at least temporarily) from financial worries, they found spiritual shelter. The rafters would inevitably be rocked by quarrels—an intense bond like theirs was bound to be stormy—but the foundations were firm. They returned to Broadway in early September, determined to make New York sit up and listen to the things they had to say.

FIVE

Hard Times

Early fall was always the most difficult time of year for the Group. They were usually penniless, the money amassed for the summer gone and salaries in abeyance until their first production opened. September 1932 was particularly tough, with one-third of the company off the payroll altogether and looking for work outside, the others finding their ability to scrape by on loans and odd jobs drastically hampered by the worsening economic situation.

The most impoverished Group members banded together and moved into a bleak top-floor apartment at 440 West 57th Street, near Tenth Avenue. It was damp and virtually unheated, but there were ten rooms and the rent was only fifty dollars a month. Art Smith talked the gas company into waiving the required deposit so they could cook on the dilapidated stove. They pooled what little money they had, Paula Miller and Willy Barton (now engaged to Tony Kraber) did the grocery shopping, and some of the men prepared the communal meals. Clifford Odets fried up potato pancakes, Grover Burgess stretched a little bit of food a long way in his soups, Gadget Kazan (when he returned from the Guild's unsuccessful out-of-town tryout of *The Pure in Heart*) introduced the Group to bulgur: cracked wheat boiled in a pot with tomatoes, onions, and kidney. Alan Baxter amused and irritated his hungry cohabitants by always managing to squeeze out a few cents to buy himself an individual dessert, which he ate surreptitiously and never offered to share.

They called their down-at-the-heels collective Groupstroy, paying sardonic tribute to the recently completed Dnieperstroy Dam in the Ukraine. This giant hydroelectric plant on the Dnieper River was always turning up in newsreels as a symbol of heroic Soviet achievement; for the Group in 1932 it was a heroic achievement just to make the rent. Articles written in later years would claim that the suffix "stroy" meant "collective" in Russian; in fact, it signified a construction (like the dam) or—taken very loosely—a settlement, but the widely reported version suited journalists' notions of Groupstroy as some sort of Soviet-inspired commune.

Strasberg lived there, burying himself in books behind the closed door of the room he shared with Miller. Kraber and Philip Robinson bunked down with Baxter; Morris Carnovsky and Philip Barber were roommates. A few weeks after Groupstroy began, Clurman joined the community; Stella Adler had asked him to move out of her comfortable apartment at 52 East 58th Street. Her mother and daughter were staying with her, which made Clurman's presence awkward, but the real reason was she was furious with him. She felt he'd let her down by not supporting her in disagreements with Strasberg over her interpretation of Sarah and, more fundamentally, by failing to become the strong leader the Group—and Adler—needed.

Even those not forced into "the Group's poorhouse," as Clurman called it, were living hand to mouth. Phoebe Brand and Herbie Ratner economized by moving back in with their parents. Bud and Hildur Bohnen found a cheap apartment in the wilds of Brooklyn Heights; Joe and Goldie Bromberg took their children to Sunnyside, Queens, in search of lower rent. Cheryl Crawford hung on to her apartment on West 55th Street but spent most of her time in the Group's makeshift office, a dressing room at the Maxine Elliott, where she and the new subscription secretary, Claire Leonard, devised strategies to woo their audience and get publicity for the struggling Group. Everyone hoped that *Success Story* would put them on a firmer financial footing.

It didn't. When *Success Story* opened on September 26, it was greeted with mixed notices that, while mostly praising the Group's production, discussed the play itself in terms calculated to make average theatregoers stay away in droves. "Shrill" was the word almost universally employed by critics to describe Lawson's impassioned indictment of American society's sick values. Even sympathetic reviewers like *The Nation's* Joseph Wood Krutch, who wrote that "for the first time this season Broadway has seen a play about which audiences may disagree with some point and passion," found *Success Story* graceless, murky, and lacking in variety—technical points which begged the question of whether or not Lawson and the Group had something worthwhile to say. The critics couldn't help noticing Lawson's "moral fervor," as Brooks Atkinson put it, but they chose to concentrate on his sins as a craftsman.

Clurman was infuriated by the reviews, not because they were bad, he wrote to Paul Strand, "but because they were confused, lukewarm, grudging. Above all they were *stupid*—even the better ones didn't really *see* the play." Looking back on the reception more than a decade later, he concluded that the essential problem with New York theatre critics was that they "represent[ed] nothing definite, [had] no intellectual identity." He contrasted them with someone like George Bernard Shaw, whose reviews might have been arbitrary and unfair, but always expressed a coherent and easily discernible point of view the reader could then agree with or not. It was impossible to defend a production against the kind of opinions that presented themselves as abstract esthetic judgments based on a play's "artistic" merits and wholly unrelated to its message. "Unlike other people," Clurman wrote, "our reviewers are powerful because they believe in nothing."

This analysis of *Success Story*'s reception gave the critics both too much and too little credit. Clurman assumed that they refused to discuss the play's theme because they didn't understand it. On the contrary, their affectation of impartiality masked a profound hostility toward Lawson's ideas about American society and the sort of people he chose to write about. When Richard Dana Skinner commented that in portraying an ambitious Jew as a tragic hero, "Mr. Lawson has chosen too cramped a frame for his picture," when Robert Garland described the protagonist as "a sad, sick genius adrift in the morass of his own mentality," they were reducing Sol's story to the level of an individual neurosis with no connection to larger questions about the validity of a society that rewarded his rapaciousness with money and power. (The anti-Semitism lurking just below the surface of some reviews also suggested their authors didn't feel Jewish problems were American problems.) When John Mason Brown regretted that Lawson had not yet recovered from a tendency to write "murky manifestoes," he expressed the conventional wisdom of critics who for ten years had described Lawson as a promising playwright whose unfortunate radicalism prevented him from writing "good theatre."

Disparaging comments about the audience response to *Success Story* further revealed the reviewers' underlying assumptions about what theatre was and whom it was for. "A large part of the audience evidently came from the East Side," noted the New York *Sun*, which clearly felt that the "many strange types [including] earnest bespectacled 'intellectuals' who are interested in plays of protest" were not appropriate attendees at a Broadway premiere. John Mason Brown mentioned disapprovingly that the opening-night crowd applauded the entrance of every actor, no matter how small the part. (Apparently it was all right to clap for the stars, but not for the theatrical proletariat.) When he wrote, "It was hard to tell where the group left off and the theatre began," he wasn't paying the Group a compliment. He couldn't conceive of any bond between actors and audience other than that of civilized intercourse between the ladies and gentlemen on the stage and those in the orchestra.

The idea of theatre as a public arena for social commentary and intellectual debate wasn't just foreign to Broadway reviewers; it was anathema. Theatre was entertainment, and they judged a play's value in terms of its ability to entertain. They might be won over occasionally by the emotional thrill of a passionate production infected with the disease of ideology, but their basic conception of culture was essentially hostile to the Group's.

When Clurman had written the preceding spring of "the message which the Group Theatre as a whole hopes to communicate through its work with ever increasing scope and clarity," he hadn't anticipated that this increasing clarity might change the initially friendly response to the Group into a skepticism eager to prove their ideals foolish and empty. By the time their second production opened in January, the *Herald Tribune*'s Percy Hammond thought he knew enough about the Group to write, "They regard current civilization as a flop, and they believe that by writing plays and acting in them they can change the sorry scheme and remold it nearer to their heart's desire." As far as he was concerned, this was an absurd enterprise. The critics' defense of the status quo was no less powerful for being largely implicit. Indeed, as Clurman grasped, it was much harder to argue with someone who pretended not to have a point of view.

The Group took little comfort from reviewers' lavish praise of "a smooth and effective performance which shows the best results of the Group Theatre's method of long summer rehearsals." Whatever their feelings about Sol Ginsberg as a character, most critics were enthralled by Luthur Adler's "precision, definition and rich fury," as Robert Benchley described it in his paean to "a distinguished performance that frequently made me tremble." His sister, said John Mason Brown, was "even better . . . warm, simple and vibrant," although, like most of his colleagues, he found her last scene too overwrought. Audiences didn't agree: Sarah's wrenching monologue as she held the dying Sol in her arms was delivered by Stella Adler with such overpowering emotion and technical brilliance that stars like Noel Coward frequently slipped in for the final few minutes just to marvel at her virtuosity.

Everyone liked Max Gorelik's sleek, modernistic set, though few realized the innovative designer had been inspired by a cubist painting by Braque. The miscast Dorothy Patten was the only actor generally panned; Franchot Tone and Morris Carnovsky received excellent notices for the depth and detail of their work. Once again, the critics made no connection between the superb performances and the actors' commitment to the play's message, concluding with a superficiality that annoyed the entire company, "[the Group Theatre] has done better by 'Success Story' than 'Success Story' has done by it."

The enthusiastic opening-night response had led the Group to expect better from the critics; they were stunned by the reviews. They wondered if Broadway was simply too hostile an environment for the Group; "Everyone seems to be trying to keep people out of our theatre," one actor disconsolately told a friend at the New York *Telegraph*. For about ten days it seemed certain the play would close. Rehearsals began anew on *The Party*, now retitled *Big Night*, with Lewis Leverett taking Franchot Tone's part.

At the same time, spurred by their faith in *Success Story* and belief that there was an audience for it, the Group fought to keep the play on the boards. Using money they didn't have, the directors took out ads stressing the Adlers' highly praised performances, a departure from the Group's no-star policy that caused some resentment but seemed necessary under the circumstances. The Group distributed free tickets to fill the house and build word of mouth; they sold blocks at cut rates to theatre parties, even though seats were already priced below the Broadway average, at $2.50. They landed a weekly radio spot, beginning October 16 with a fifteen-minute segment from *Success Story*.

They talked about the Group and the play anywhere and everywhere. Crawford turned up at a meeting of speech teachers in New York City high schools, Clurman spoke to the Doctors Club of Brooklyn, Philip Barber gave an informal talk to the Friends of Workers' Theatre, Lawson appeared at a Women's City Club dinner. They tried especially hard to reach Jewish groups: although Clurman and Lawson had never even mentioned the subject during their discussions about the play, it was deeply imbued with a Jewish tradition of social and moral responsibility of which the Adlers, at least, were certainly aware—Luther was one of the first to urge the Group to go out and hunt for *Success Story*'s audience. They worked around the clock; in a letter to his brother, Bud Bohnen referred to "the 24 hour a day system that seems to prevail," quite different from his experiences at the Goodman and in the commercial theatre, where actors didn't make it their personal mission to drum up business.

Their most interesting effort to reach their audience was a symposium for subscribers held October 16 at the Maxine Elliott. It was the first of the series of meetings with actors and directors they had promised back in the spring to people who paid two dollars to support the Group. The entire company turned out and brought along not only Gorelik and Lawson but also the head of the stage crew. (Newspaper reporters were stunned that an electrician would come down to the theatre on a Sunday night.) The idea was that the Group would answer questions from the audience, which de-served to be more than a silent partner in their theatrical endeavor. The subscribers turned out to be as passionate about *Success Story* as the Group, peppering Lawson in particular with sharp queries about the advis-ability of making Sol so unlikable. "There was little hint of Sabbath calm in the proceedings," noted the *New York Times*, which also reported that on occasion individual audience members were so stirred up by the debate that they took it upon themselves to answer questions addressed to the stage. The fervor of the spectators moved the Group; it made them realize, as *1931—* had, that their productions meant something to people, had an immediate and personal impact much stronger than that made by the av-erage evening at the theatre.

All these efforts paid off. By mid-October *Variety* reported "some im-provement" in attendance at *Success Story* and estimated its gross at $4,000, just about the break-even point. In November business had risen to roughly $5,000 a week, not enough to put the play in the smash-hit category but a comfortable income. The Group actors, however, didn't benefit from the result of their labors. After the third week, when *Success Story*'s prospects were still uncertain, Lee Shubert announced that he would withdraw his support, and the use of his theatre, unless the Group allowed him to take his money up front at the box office. Even though this meant they might not receive their full salaries, the actors agreed; keeping the play alive was more important. Their paychecks slipped lower and lower. Luther Adler joked, "I'm the only actor who ever starred on Broadway and got seven dollars a week." Though *Success Story* ran for 121 performances and made the *Daily News* "Golden Dozen" list of box-office hits, the Group didn't make a penny from it.

They kept going nonetheless. They resumed body movement classes with Tamiris, studied voice, continued the experimental work they'd begun at Dover Furnace. They took classes in special acting problems, taught by Clurman because Strasberg was in his usual postopening state of exhaustion. Since *Success Story* and the newly rechristened *Big Night* had small casts, many actors didn't have enough to do, so they shared parts: Bill Challee and Walter Coy alternated in a supporting role as a copywriter in *Success Story;* Russell Collins and Grover Burgess did the same in a small comic turn as a statistician. Bud Bohnen was busier than most with rehearsals for *Big Night* and for his own play, *Incubator,* slated to open in early January. Bohnen also had to be ready to go on for Franchot Tone, whose recurrent bronchitis kept threatening to make him miss performances. Tone's chronic illness may have reflected his divided state of mind; after making the break and signing a contract with MGM, he was having second thoughts and trying to put off going to the West Coast.

The directors appeared to be having second thoughts about their entire lives. Strasberg simply retreated to his room and slept. Crawford tried to put a good face on things: she gave optimistic interviews about the Group's future plans; she spoke of their desire to create a studio where they could train actors and directors for the company, try out new plays, and offer small-scale productions of their experimental work. She was basically whistling in the dark while she waited for her partners to recover from their separate traumas. Clurman, who by November had moved out of Group-stroy and into the Montclair Hotel, was bitterly unhappy over his separation from Stella Adler and discouraged by the relative failure of *Success Story,* which he considered the only worthwhile production on Broadway. "The Group has been tense and tired with me," he wrote to Paul Strand. "Cheryl claims this is no accident. That the Group has suffered from my suffering."

Crawford was right. With their leaders so downcast, it was hardly surprising that the troops were disheartened as well. Luther Adler let the general mood of weariness affect his acting, sometimes barely going through the motions of his part. He had been on the stage almost since birth, and every now and then he seemed simply to be tired of the whole preposterous business. His sister, who impressed even Strasberg with her ability to keep a performance at the same high-energy level night after night, was irked by his laziness. She would do almost anything to shock him back into the play, and as a result they fought constantly—not just backstage but during the curtain calls as well. Gentlemanly, punctilious Morris Carnovsky found their behavior unprofessional and complained about it to sympathetic residents of Groupstroy. He got his revenge (albeit unintentionally) one night when he missed his cue and the Adlers had to ad-lib for minutes before he finally made his entrance. When Clurman asked what had happened to the normally reliable Carnovsky, a mischievous fellow actor informed the director that he had been reading *The Communist Manifesto* in his dressing room and forgot about the time. True or not, it was typical of the sharp humor Group members aimed at each other that difficult winter.

Clifford Odets proved himself once again a sensitive barometer of the Group's mood. At Groupstroy he began writing his third play, a biting comic drama that vividly captured the edgy, expectant atmosphere of the early Depression years. He called it *I Got the Blues*, and it concerned a Jewish family in the Bronx struggling for economic security and emotional fulfillment in a hostile, chaotic world. Odets had taken Clurman's advice that he write about people and places he knew, drawing on observations of his own family, Group members, and the people he met wandering aimlessly through the shabby streets of New York to create a gallery of strongly imagined, furiously alive characters. They expressed the confused brew of feelings Odets sensed percolating within the Group and himself: fear inspired by the inability to make a living in a collapsing economic system, anger at their individual and collective failure to create a viable life despite the circumstances, and, paradoxically, hope—a powerful though still largely incoherent notion that things *had* to get better, that, however empty and desperate the present, the future was rich in possibility.

"I was sore; that's why I wrote that play," Odets said two years later when it was finally produced under the title *Awake and Sing!* "I was sore at my whole life. Getting nothing done. Stuffed in a room waiting for Luther Adler to perish so I might get a chance to play in *Success Story.*" Passing the too abundant spare hours by reading Emerson, listening to Beethoven, and looking at El Greco,

> I got to have a pretty fine idea of what a man could be if he had the chance. But I saw [that] girls and boys were not getting a chance. I saw . . . much terror in life. I went over my boyhood and tabulated people's lives which had touched mine. I wrote small sketches on yellow paper, and when I read back I saw a strange and wonderful sort of "Spoon River Anthology," but deeper and more hurting to me because the memories were self-experienced.

His typewriter perched on his lap in his tiny room at Groupstroy or, when the cold drove him into the kitchen, balanced atop the breadbox, Odets turned his scribbled memories into dialogue richly seasoned with the salty cadences of Jewish lower-middle-class speech. He had been inspired in part by *Success Story*'s tart language, but Odets' style, vibrant with the explosive rhythms and homely metaphors of ordinary speech, was dramatically different from the polished prose of the better-educated, more affluent Lawson. As he finished sections of the play he would read them aloud to the Group, assuring the actors that there would be good parts for everybody. Odets the playwright remembered the frustration of Odets the actor.

His friends at Groupstroy were struck by his pungent dialogue; some recognized phrases from real-life conversations that Odets had jotted down in the notebook he carried everywhere. Through his deeply authentic characters he was exploring an area of national life, the urban immigrant experience, seldom touched in the theatre. If he could write a third act with the vigor and originality of the two he was reading to them, this might be the play that most truly fulfilled the Group's ambition to bring real life into the theatre. They were moved by the transformation of this strange, unhappy boy from a mediocre actor into a promising playwright. Out of the turmoil and anxiety of these trying months, something new and exciting was being born.

Meanwhile, they struggled to keep the Group intact despite their straitened circumstances and the demoralizing departure of Franchot Tone. He stayed with *Success Story* two months longer than initially planned, raising the hope that he might have a change of heart and rededicate himself to the Group. Finally, in early January, able to avoid a decision no longer, he left for the West Coast to fulfill his MGM contract. It was a painful moment for everyone, especially Tone. He wept over his farewell drink with Clurman in a 52nd Street speakeasy. When Bobby Lewis and Sandy Meisner took him down to Grand Central Station and put him aboard the Twentieth Century, he stood on the steps of the club car and called to them, "Keep your line"— hoping that others would be more faithful to the Group Idea than he had been.

Beany Barker, who'd been close to Tone and was saddened by his departure, had temptations of her own to deal with. She was offered a good part in a Broadway play that she wanted very much to take. Her role in *Success Story* was small, she had no part at all in *Big Night*, and though she needed money less than other Group members (her parents supported her in lean times), the prospect of a regular paycheck was also appealing. She went to Clurman and asked for his permission to accept the role. He refused. What would happen to the Group, he asked, if every actor not cast in a leading part simply went elsewhere? Barker wept; it seemed unfair that Bill Challee had been allowed to do *Wonder Boy*, but she was being denied a similar opportunity, especially since several other Group actresses were unemployed and could easily take her place. Clurman, who had a knack for forgetting inconvenient facts or brushing them aside as irrelevant, was adamant. In the end, she submitted. The Group's policy on actors working outside the organization remained arbitrary and often unfair.

Bud Bohnen felt the tug of conflicting loyalties as well. His first effort as a playwright was being presented on Broadway, but he'd been unable to devote much time to *Incubator* because of *Big Night* rehearsals and his preparation to replace Tone in *Success Story*. He stepped into the role of Merritt on January 2; his own play opened one day later. Both experiences were difficult. *Incubator* received decent reviews but minimal attendance and closed quickly. Hard though he tried in *Success Story*, Bohnen soon realized that Tone was sorely missed. Stella Adler in particular found that Sarah's flirtatious relationship with her boss didn't work with this new actor; she dropped it, leaving an awkward hole in the play's fabric. Because of the Group's insistence that every performance express the emotional truth felt by the actors, a change in the cast also meant alterations in the nature of the characters' interactions. Bohnen had to accept the fact that he'd been judged insufficiently sexy by the demanding Adler.

The actors' salaries in *Success Story* had gone from inadequate to impossible—on New Year's Eve there was no pay at all—and the play closed hardly more than a week after Bohnen's substitution. *Big Night* opened January 17. The production had been troubled from the start, marked by Franchot Tone's distaste for it and Crawford's uncertainty as a first-time director. Rehearsals had been limping along, off and on, for six months. The performances had been embroidered with the thoughtful, character-revealing detail that was a trademark of the method, but it wasn't really appropriate for a comedy whose principal virtue was its snappy dialogue and whose characters didn't need the depth the Group was giving them.

Typical of the company's conscientious but misguided approach was a speech by Stella Adler, who asks her husband in the first scene, "Ed, did you ever feel as if there was something you was missing? . . . A feeling that there's something you want more than anything—something like the Atlantic Ocean or the sky—something you never could have only it's swell just to be wanting it. It's a feeling that just lasts a minute and then you see a fur coat in Jaeckel's window and you think, I guess that's what I meant." Adler delivered the lines with real emotion, investing them with her personal ambivalence between the desire to be a serious actress with the Group and the equally strong longing to be a glamorous star and wear mink. It was a touching, bittersweet moment, but it made Myra Bonney too smart and self-aware, killing the point of the joke. Dawn Powell, watching a rehearsal, said, "Isn't that remarkable? I thought that was a funny line when I wrote it."

The actors knew something was wrong with *Big Night*. They expressed their unease by finding fault with Crawford and requesting odd alterations in the script. Joe Bromberg persuaded Powell to change his character's name from Jones to Schwartz because it "felt better" to him; she complied reluctantly, fearing she would be accused of anti-Semitism for making the lecherous buyer a Jew. (As it turned out, Bromberg's exuberant comic portrait was about the only thing in the production the critics liked.) Relations between the actors and Crawford became so strained that Clurman ended up directing for the last few weeks. He later concluded that their essential mistake with *Big Night* had been the attempt to humanize the characters and make their repellent behavior more understandable, but also less funny.

The Group didn't soften the play enough to placate reviewers, who loathed it almost to a man precisely because it was so unpleasant. "Miss Powell is simply too savage an artist to be allowed loose with a box of greasepaint," wrote the *American*'s Gilbert W. Gabriel, who urged his readers to try her novels instead: "She knows the human race too well, too hatefully, to be able to treat it to the courtesies of a palatable play." Critical of their work though they were in this instance, the Group vehemently rejected Gabriel's implication that certain gritty subjects were suitable only for the more serious art of the novel while the theatre did best to confine itself to "palatable plays." They found the critics' response to *Big Night* prissy: "They ran from it," Clurman noted caustically, "screaming like so many maiden aunts."

What particularly offended the press was the drab lower-middle-class milieu. Percy Hammond called it "as sordid a play as I've seen since the Muscovites were here," and John Anderson found it "realistically tiresome" to watch "a stage-ful of dull and quarrelsome drunks." Spoofing his colleagues' squeamish reaction, Robert Benchley, who had rather enjoyed the play, asked, "Are we only to have high-class cads on our stage?"

Audiences shared the critics' distaste, and *Big Night* closed a scant four days after its premiere. The actors didn't even get the two weeks' salary guaranteed by the Equity bond all Broadway productions were required to post. Arch Selwyn, a commercial producer who had enjoyed rehearsals, promised to put up the money, but Claire Leonard forgot to mail him the necessary papers promptly. By the time he received them, he'd read the reviews and refused to honor his commitment, which wasn't legally binding without his signature. The directors went without pay for *Big Night;* Clurman had even gone into debt, borrowing $500 from his brother to raise the curtain opening night. The Group's financial situation was now desperate.

Their script prospects were no better. They hoped to present *Yellow Jack*, a new play by Sidney Howard about the conquest of yellow fever in Cuba. This examination of modern heroism was well suited to the Group's interests and abilities, and Clurman, who planned to make his official directorial debut with the script, had a strong emotional investment in it. Howard had promised them *Yellow Jack* the preceding spring, but after the chilly reception given both *Success Story* and *Big Night* he began to have his doubts. A year earlier he'd told reporters that only an ensemble like the Group could properly present his play; now he worried that the actors were too young to portray the older characters of central importance to the story. He "hemmed and hawed, vacillated, prevaricated, lied," Clurman wrote bitterly to Paul Strand, before finally telling the Group he didn't want them to produce it.

With no money and no play, the directors decided they must bow to the inevitable. After the closing performance of *Big Night*, they announced to the actors that the second Group season was over and the company was free to seek other engagements.

It was a terrible blow to the Group, which had been founded on the idea of continuous work. Stella Adler laid her personal blame on Clurman for failing to provide her with an atmosphere in which she could feel professionally secure, as she had in the Yiddish theatre. The rest of the actors weren't so openly hostile, but they too were disappointed in the directors. If Harold, Lee, and Cheryl couldn't come up with scripts or backing, they asked one another, what was the point in letting them make all the decisions? The closing-night meeting was grim and indecisive; many members left the theatre wondering if this was the end of the Group.

The press suggested the same thing in its coverage of the Group's announcement. Asserting that the Group would go on in a letter printed in the *New York Times* on January 29, Clurman revealed his own apprehensions about the almost impossible task the company had set itself. "The establishment of any permanent theatrical organization with a coherent policy is rendered particularly difficult in our New York theatre," he wrote. "What the Group Theatre aimed to do was something fundamentally different from Broadway, and its position as a competing producing organization was entirely irrelevant and was even injurious to its aims." As he had in the fall of 1931, he deplored the fact that the Group was forced to raise money show by show and depend on reviews to attract an audience. Given the Group's commitment to presenting provocative scripts and sustaining a permanent company, he acknowledged, "persistence in pursuing the ordinary course of theatrical production becomes folly."

"The Group Theatre might continue this season as it has for the past two years," he claimed (though this was hardly true at the moment).

But it refuses to strain itself along lines that do not advance or clarify its aims but that, on the contrary, impede and falsify them. [It] has decided not to resume production unless it can create conditions for itself that will permit it to carry on freely to do what it really wants to do, of which its first two years of activity give only the first bare indication. The Group Theatre continues the training of its actors, its quest of suitable plays, and is even now considering plans for a method of organization which will afford the most adequate conditions for the fulfillment of its purpose.

Though most of his letter essentially made a virtue of necessity, in this last phrase Clurman spoke the exact truth. Their bumpy season had shocked the Group into reconsidering the feasibility of trying to survive in the New York theatre; the directors may very well have recalled Max Gorelik's warning that their ideals were simply incompatible with the exigencies of commercial production. In a meeting held January 27 at Crawford's apartment, the company explored the possibility of making their headquarters in Boston, where subsidy for the Group as an institution rather than a producer of individual plays might be easier to find. Members had been asked to bring lists of people they knew who might be helpful; most of the actors had one or two names, but the better-connected—Eunice Stoddard, Beany Barker, Alixe Walker—knew dozens of affluent culture lovers. They were asked to write instantly, "as going up there is contingent on response we get from these people." In addition, Crawford obtained an introduction from the Guild's Theresa Helburn to Marguerite Hopkins, a wealthy society matron, and went up to present the Group's Boston plan to her in person, hoping that she would organize support for the idea.

What the Group suggested initially was a subscription series of five plays, some new and some classics, to be presented in Boston over the first two-thirds of the theatrical season, after which the company would come to New York for a limited engagement. Their long-range plan called for the establishment in Boston of a permanent theatre and affiliated school, where all the theatre arts would be taught. The Group would develop playwrights, present a season of plays followed by a tour each year, and build a repertory of lasting theatrical productions. To give prospective sponsors an idea of what they planned, they had prepared a list of eighty-six plays they might do in repertory; one advantage of their present inactivity was that they were free to dream of a more ambitious program combining new plays with the best of the past.

A week later Bud Bohnen wrote to his brother Arthur, who lived and worked in Chicago, suggesting that city as a good home for the Group. The letter was a hilarious and charming mixture of blatantly self-serving PR for the Group and astute analysis of the American cultural scene. "Never before has a theatre . . . left New York at the very moment when it was most wanted and needed," he wrote, at a time when three of the last four Group productions had been outright flops and the actors were scrambling for jobs. Bohnen presented a list of the shows Group members had reluctantly joined when *Big Night* closed as proof of "how quickly commercial Broadway gobbled up the services of our actors" and the immense prestige they would confer on Chicago if they came there.

His selling job concluded, Bohnen moved on to the question of why the Group would want to leave New York. His comments, made nearly half a century before regional theatres gained equal status with Broadway in the eyes of the press, were remarkably prescient.

[The projected move] has vast cultural implications—the beginning
of a de-centralization of New York's stranglehold on American art-life.
The Group has the clairvoyance to see through the futility of the New
York MYTH and the courage to fly in the face of it. It CAN continue in
New York and be America's finest theatrical institution, BUT that isn't
enough. . . . To do its *best* work, the Group must operate in a place
where it has a maximum control over the factors that influence its
work. From a sheer TECHNOCRATIC point of view, it is smarter to operate in Chicago (or Boston) . . . to go where people are hungry for
theatre, where the conditions are more favorable,—and merely de-
scend on New York to collect your annual LAURELS for your cultural
importance, without having to compete in a thieves' game for your
economic independence.

Crawford favored relocation to a saner environment; Strasberg opposed
it. Clurman wasn't sure. "All of [these schemes] must be tried," he wrote to
Paul Strand. "But damn it all, if we had $60,000 (which managers often
drop on one show) we could start a fine repertory season in New York, *order*
plays we want, revive plays like *Processional* and *Hairy Ape*, carry out the
real program of the Group Theatre." He still wanted the Group Theatre to
make its mark on Broadway, not out in the sticks, and he vowed to try once
more to raise the longed-for subsidy in New York.
    The Group would pursue both Boston and Chicago as potential homes
for several years; they finally presented a three-play season in Boston in the
fall of 1934. But they were never really committed to the idea of leaving
New York, nor, for all their talk about it, did they ever make a serious effort
to present plays in repertory. This failure was partly a matter of economics:
the Group never had enough of a financial guarantee to make moving
worthwhile, and repertory was too expensive for a Depression-era theatre
to consider. The deeper cause was the Group's urgent desire to present
contemporary American plays on Broadway *right now*. Despite Clurman's
high-principled talk of not resuming production until they had created
more favorable conditions, whenever a promising script came their way
they dropped everything and committed themselves to it then and there.
Establishing the Group in a new city, or as a repertory company in New
York, required long-term planning, the hiring of a full-time fund-raiser, and
a radical rethinking of the organization's financial structure. None of the
directors cared enough about business matters to bother. In fairness, it
should be noted that they were almost always too hard-pressed to look that
far ahead.
    At the January 27 meeting, the Group looked far enough ahead to assert
that they *would* have a summer session, no matter what. To obtain funds
for it, Beany Barker suggested presenting a program of improvisations at
social and professional clubs for a small admission fee; Sylvia Feningston,

Clifford Odets, and Paula Miller agreed to help her investigate the idea. Bobby Lewis proposed a benefit production, with short skits or songs performed by as many distinguished theatrical friends as the Group could muster. Dorothy Patten, Art Smith, Luther Adler, Joe Bromberg, Bud Bohnen, and Clurman formed a committee with Lewis to plan it. Since they had no professional business staff, they would have to handle these matters themselves.

In the meantime, they also had to make a living. Luther Adler landed a job costarring with Katharine Cornell in *Alien Corn* and told its author, Sidney Howard, how badly his refusal of *Yellow Jack* had hurt the Group. Several actors went back to the Guild: Morris Carnovsky, Joe Bromberg, and Russell Collins in Maxwell Anderson's *Both Your Houses;* Dorothy Patten in *The Mask and the Face;* Sandy Meisner in *American Dream,* the play George O'Neill had written at Dover Furnace. Beany Barker and Lewis Leverett appeared in *Black Diamond* at the Provincetown Theatre. Clifford Odets had a small part in a comedy called *They All Come to Moscow.* Eunice Stoddard acted in a screwball farce, *Three-Cornered Moon.* Stella Adler went home to the Yiddish theatre, touring with Jacob Ben-Ami; when she returned in May, she appeared in an undistinguished and short-lived Broadway production, *Hilda Cassidy.* Bohnen was up for a couple of roles, but confessed to his brother, "I'm not certain of either one, and am I sweating!" Virginia Farmer and Art Smith directed the Sunday-night radio broadcasts, which put a few dollars in the actors' pockets. Clurman taught a course, "The World of Theatre," at the New School for Social Research; he cleared about twenty-five dollars a week from the poorly attended lectures.

They were all scrambling to make ends meet, like so many other Americans. "We were very poor," said Phoebe Brand. "I remember searching an old purse to find a nickel to get downtown; if I couldn't find it, I walked." On her chilly treks from 71st Street, she saw people going through garbage cans, lying on the sidewalk with the inert helplessness of those who have no further to fall, walking coatless in the middle of January: "You wanted to take your coat off and give it to them, it was really so painful." Brand hardly had a coat to give; her father, who had managed a Remington typewriter plant in upstate New York, was out of work and the family in desperate financial straits. Alixe Walker and Mab Maynard gave her presents of clothing and small amounts of cash to tide her over.

That was the Group spirit. Beany Barker and Dorothy Patten made donations to help out fellow actors who were destitute. Patten shared her East Side town house with Crawford, who could no longer afford the apartment on 55th Street and rented it to Aaron Copland; he in turn made room there for Clurman, unable to pay his rent at the Montclair. Groupstroy ran chiefly on handouts: Theresa Helburn brought bundles of food; so did Strasberg's brother Arthur, who was always good for some spare change if anyone was desperate. The collective mood alternated between depression—there were days at Groupstroy when every door was shut, each member locked away with private fears—and a kind of grim gaiety. Clifford Odets would get Alan Baxter drunk and incite him to phone up Guild director Philip Moeller in the middle of the night; Baxter would pretend it was an emergency, then (coached by Odets in the background) mercilessly criticize Moeller's work on such O'Neill plays as *Mourning Becomes Electra*. The actors would try to cheer themselves and their visitors with improvised entertainments—one so bawdy that the dismayed Helburn said to her friend Crawford, "If that's the kind of theatre these youngsters are indulging in, Cheryl, then I just don't know . . ."

Into this peculiar setting one day that winter came a young theatre lover just married to Motty Eitington, a wealthy Russian-born furrier. Bess Eitingon had been trying for weeks through her acquaintance Sandy Meisner to get in touch with Strasberg. Her new husband had given her $50,000 as a wedding present, and she wanted to invest it in the Group, which impressed her as an important American theatre. Strasberg, in a state of deep depression over the Group's and his own future, refused to believe that anyone would give them money; he didn't bother to call her. Finally, Eitington came across town to West 57th Street and clambered the three flights of stairs that led to Groupstroy.

Paula Miller, who opened the door, was flustered to see a well-dressed, obviously affluent woman asking to come into their dismal abode (reeking that particular afternoon of the cabbage Miller was cooking) and speak with Mr. Strasberg. She ushered Eitington in and disappeared down the hall to get him. Strasberg walked into the room and waited to hear what his visitor had to say. Group members had long since grown accustomed to Strasberg's habit of never saying either hello or good-bye, but Eitington was startled by his silence. She hesitantly explained, disconcerted by the fact that this odd man appeared to be looking off in the distance and hardly listening to her, that she had with her a check for $50,000, that she wanted him to take it for the Group. Strasberg made no response; he seemed completely uninterested. Eitington tried several more times to give him the money, telling him how much the Group meant to her and how pleased she was to be able to help them, but she was met with the same blank wall of indifference. She finally ran out of the apartment and down the stairs to the street, weeping with humiliation and bewilderment. She couldn't understand what she had done wrong. Shortly thereafter she took her money and set up a partnership with two men who lost virtually all of it on their first production.

It was an incredible thing for Strasberg to have done. At a time when Clurman was writing disconsolately to Paul Strand of all the Group could accomplish if they only had $60,000, his partner was offered nearly the entire amount and turned it down, in deed if not word. "I honestly couldn't think at the moment what we could use the $50,000 for," Strasberg would say in later years, when he took perverse pleasure in telling this story on himself. That was obviously nonsense. The Group actors were doing improvisations in social clubs and working on radio to make food money, the organization was considering moving out of town in order to raise the funds needed for a coherent program of activity—even Strasberg, who preferred to have nothing to do with the company's practical affairs, could hardly have thought they had no use for $50,000.

Why, then, did he let it slip through his hands? There are a number of possible reasons, all linked to the complex personality of the man whose ferocious dedication had helped forge the Group's unity. Strasberg liked to be in control. He enjoyed the blind trust the actors placed in him at Brookfield and resented the growing independence evidenced by their suggestions about how to raise money and the involvement of several members with the new workers theatres. The production of *Success Story*, good though it was, had consumed and exhausted him: directing the experienced, argumentative Adlers and the fractious Franchot Tone had been difficult; the only leading actor who put herself totally in his hands, Dorothy Patten, had given a performance he knew was inadequate. His relationship with Clurman was always tense, given their disparate temperaments, and his normally steadfast ally Crawford had recently differed with him on several policy issues.

Was he angry enough at his Group comrades to punish them by throwing away an unprecedented opportunity? Not consciously—he loved the Group, which was, after all, in large part his creation. That may have been the point: it was *his* company, and perhaps the woman who wanted to give them all this money would expect some authority over them in return. In artistic matters he was still preeminent, but financial security might loosen his grip. Any of these thoughts may have floated through Strasberg's subconscious as he stood listening impassively to Bess Eitington, or he may have been so severely depressed that her offer simply seemed unreal. So much of Group life seemed unreal in these hungry, hallucinatory months as they drifted anxiously, waiting for a script, a job, the summer, new faith that their creative life together would continue.

At Groupstroy they clung to each other, getting what comfort they could from their mutual plight. They lost even that fragile refuge in February, when they were evicted for failure to pay the rent. The Group was now fragmented, with no real center to hold on to. Strasberg and Miller moved to an apartment on West 11th Street above a bakery; Odets came with them and wrote the last act of *I Got the Blues* on a wooden table in the kitchen. He worked there to avoid waking Strasberg, who spent a frightening amount of time hiding from his life and thoughts in the trancelike sleep of the deeply depressed. Philip Robinson resigned; he had no parts that season, had been unhappy in the Group for some time, and once his cheap room at Groupstroy was gone there seemed no reason to stay. Bud Bohnen also thought in passing about leaving to found his own company in Chicago with his brother's help. Hard times were forcing all members to assess their commitment to the Group.

The only cheerful notes were struck by two Group weddings, which provided the company with a certain ironic amusement because both their impoverished associates were marrying women listed in the Social Register. Gadget Kazan had married Molly Thacher in December, but he didn't tell anyone at the time. The news gradually seeped out over the winter, and Kazan responded to all congratulations with an embarrassed grin. The Group actors were happy for him. None of them yet knew Thacher well, but her passionate interest in political theatre—as a student, she'd written an antiwar play that caused a huge stir at Vassar—was in line with the Group's developing tendencies. Though Kazan was still technically an apprentice, his friendships with Clurman and Odets and his constant presence at Group activities made membership seem inevitable.

In late February the newspaper society pages were filled with the impending marriage of Art Smith and Betty Upjohn, an art student whose wealthy family planned a huge wedding in Scarsdale. "Poor little Arthur Gordon Smith [isn't] even accredited with having any parents or anything," Bud Bohnen wrote to his brother. "It's all too mad for words, as he truly hasn't got carfare to get to Scarsdale for the Marriage!" The Group found the disparity between the Smith and Upjohn estates particularly hilarious because Art was one of the most ardently left-wing members of the company. By the following year his bride was sporting proletarian-style clothes and trying to organize the kitchen help at the Group's summer camp.

That kind of thing happened in the thirties. "The world around you just wouldn't leave you alone," said Morris Carnovsky. "You could see desperation in front of your eyes." The Depression was becoming personally real to the Group that winter. Those who had been affected initially by the crash were the most vulnerable members of American society: blacks, unskilled laborers, factory workers. A grocer in St. Louis or a printer in Philadelphia, the kind of modest, middle-class Americans who were the parents of many Group members, made economies, dipped into their savings, and felt sorry for people selling apples and standing in bread lines. They were worried, but not terrified. Not until early 1933 did real fear creep into their homes, as large numbers of them began to wonder if they too would be thrown into the streets.

The Group's hard times in the wake of *Big Night*'s closing coincided with the worst crisis to date in the national economy. In February, as Americans waited to see what President-elect Franklin Roosevelt would do when he assumed office, the banking system went under. Thousands of banks across the country had failed since 1929, but the Federal Reserve and the Reconstruction Finance Corporation had poured in enough money to avoid an institutional collapse. By February, the strain caused by the questionable investments, mismanagement, and corruption of the boom years had become intolerable. On the 14th, the governor of Michigan closed every bank in the state, forcing the city of Detroit to default on its $400 million debt. All over the country, people panicked at the prospect of their life's savings disappearing. On the 24th, runs on Baltimore banks forced the governor of Maryland to declare a bank holiday there. The panic spread through Ohio, Indiana, Kentucky, and Pennsylvania, as account holders rushed to withdraw their money before the banks shut down. By March 2, twelve more states had closed their banks and New York and Chicago, the financial centers of the country, were badly battered. On the morning of Roosevelt's inauguration, March 4, the governors of New York and Illinois simultaneously declared statewide bank holidays. America's financial system had simply ceased to function. Never before had Marxism's apocalyptic predictions about the impending doom of capitalism so closely approximated reality.

It was around this time that several Group members joined the Communist party, the completion of a stage in their political evolution inaugurated with the feverish readings and discussions of the previous summer. The Group, founded on the principle that theatre must be vitally connected to real life, tended to attract people who believed in art's responsibility to engage itself with the issues of the day. To some, that responsibility implied an obligation on the part of artists to get out there and act, not just sit on the sidelines. With people starving in the streets and unemployed workers being brutalized by police, Phoebe Brand remarked, "You couldn't help but say, 'Gee, that's terrible. Gotta do something!' " For a good many idealists in 1933, doing something meant becoming a communist.

Communism dominated intellectual life on the left to an unprecedented extent in the 1930s. In a time of frightening chaos, it offered a coherent analysis of what had gone wrong and a straightforward program for putting it right. To those outraged by the human suffering they saw around them, the Communist party said it was the inevitable result of fundamental inequities in the capitalist system and would never be alleviated by conventional political parties. The callousness of the Republicans and the vacillations of the Democrats were the natural response of organizations owned by the propertied class, which had destroyed the nation's economy with its greed and stupidity; the massive restructuring of the economy necessary to ensure jobs and a decent life for everyone would happen only after the revolution, when power passed into the hands of the working people whose labor had created America's wealth but who had been robbed of their share in it. This made a lot of sense, particularly before Roosevelt inaugurated the sweeping social and economic reforms of the New Deal. Even then, the fierce resistance of Wall Street convinced many radicals the party was right: the nation's rulers would never give up their privileges willingly.

The calm middle ground happily occupied in more prosperous times by the American middle class from which most intellectuals and artists came was disintegrating under their feet. The triumphant rise of fascism in Germany, where Hitler's National Socialist party had just swept into power, seemed to bear out the communist assertion that bourgeois democracy was doomed and the middle must inevitably go right or left. Given the generally liberal backgrounds of most Group members, their direction was obvious and, for the more politically active, communism the logical destination. The socialists had been around too long and accomplished too little. Communists had made a revolution in Russia, and in America they stood at the forefront of the struggle for unemployment relief, trade-union recognition, justice for black Americans, and food for the hungry—or, at least, so their well-organized publicity claimed and those not seasoned in earlier ideological wars believed.

For performing artists like the Group actors, the allure of communism was enhanced by the glamour of Soviet culture in its heyday. The dramatic power and sheer visual excitement of films like *Potemkin, Mother,* and *Ten Days That Shook the World* were far beyond anything accomplished in the West. As for Russian theatre, it was the most exciting in the world. Stanislavsky's pre-Revolutionary discoveries, the basis of the Group's work, had been enhanced by Meyerhold's and Vakhtangov's thrilling innovations, which they'd studied at Dover Furnace. They learned from their reading that the Soviet Union boasted an incredible diversity of theatre: more than nine hundred companies, everything from a State Jewish Theatre to a Theatre of the Revolution, each with its own stylistic trademark and outlook on life. And these weren't theatres for a sleepy elite passing the time between a big dinner and bed; audiences were large, noisy, and involved with the subject matter of the plays. Contrasting this vigor with the deadly atmosphere on Broadway, it was easy to idealize Soviet theatre as the natural product of a country where both society and culture were being radically revamped to better serve the common man and woman.

Yet, as the Group was slowly learning, Broadway was not all there was to the American theatre. They'd thought they might have to move to Boston or Chicago in order to escape from the commercial theatre, but under their very noses in New York a completely different kind of theatre was developing. It had the same belief in drama as a living expression of contemporary experience that animated the Group, but its point of view was more frankly radical and it looked for new audiences in a far more concerted way than the Group had ever done. That fall and winter, with so little of their own work to do, several Group members had their first contact with this alternative theatre when friends like Max Gorelik and Charles Walker invited them to organizational meetings for two new outfits: the Theatre Collective and the Theatre Union.

The Theatre Collective's roots lay in the workers theatre movement that had sprung up across the country since 1929—amateur companies, staffed by unpaid young radicals (many of them communists, virtually all Marxists), that specialized in short skits outlining the class struggle in broad strokes and calling on their working-class audiences to organize and fight for better treatment. Agitprop (short for "agitation and propaganda"), it was called, and European radicals had been doing it for years before the German-language Prolet-Bühne (Proletarian Stage) introduced it to German-American workers in 1930. Crude and simplistic agitprop certainly was; it was also vividly theatrical and experimental, using rhythmic chanting, expressionistic staging, and a bare minimum of scenery and props to make its revolutionary points. Most exciting of all was the way agitprop troupes broke out of traditional theatrical venues to go directly to their audience: they acted in union halls, on picket lines, at May Day parades— on University Place in New York, one company, with props tied up in bundles, was hoisted through a window to give a performance for workers engaged in one of the earliest sit-down strikes.

By April 1931 there were enough groups nationwide to support a mimeographed magazine, *Workers Theatre* (in its early days a militantly and openly communist publication); a year later the League of Workers Theatres held its first annual conference in New York. Preeminent among these pioneering troupes was the Workers Laboratory Theatre, the company which had gone through the windows on University Place. Initially sponsored by the Workers International Relief organization, which was run by the Communist party, the WLT went independent in early 1933 so it could have greater freedom in choosing material. This signaled the beginning of a trend among the left-wing theatres away from the kind of strict party-line propaganda summarized by Marxist wits as "in the first act we suffer, in the second we pass out leaflets, and in the third we go on strike." Perceptive theatrical leftists realized this rigid format was effective only for the already converted and began to shape their productions to express a more general radicalism that reached out to all those disillusioned and frightened by the collapse of the American economic system. The party lagged behind its theatrical allies by more than two years; by the time the Seventh Comintern Congress declared a United Front policy in August 1935, American workers theatres had long since dropped the schematic preachifying of traditional agitprop in favor of a style more closely linked to American vaudeville than European drama, containing more human characters and leavened with some much-needed humor.

Among the leaders of the WLT were Jack and Hyam Shapiro, brothers who ran a metal shop on Second Avenue and had worked with Strasberg at the Chrystie Street Settlement House. In late 1932 the Shapiros began talking to interested friends about the possibility of moving beyond workers theatre to present full-length Marxist plays on a more professional basis. By early 1933 they had a name, the Theatre Collective, an abandoned loft to use as an office, and the support of Max Gorelik and Philip Barber, who

joined them in running the new organization. (The first production was a
revival of *1931—*, rewritten to have a more openly revolutionary ending.)
Virginia Farmer was also closely involved; she would eventually leave the
Group to direct the Collective's actor-training program.

Just as militant as the Collective but even more eager to avoid sectarianism, the Theatre Union was the brainchild of Charles Walker, the playwright who had taken *Crazy American* away from the Group because their
outlook was insufficiently revolutionary. (That was before their radicalizing
summer at Dover Furnace.) Like the Shapiros, he wanted to present full-
length plays with a Marxist slant on contemporary issues, but he was far
more concerned than the Collective with attracting the attention of the
mainstream press and with building a large, stable audience composed not
just of labor groups (though the Union worked hard to develop them)
but also middle-class sympathizers. He and his wife, Adelaide, gathered together an ideologically diverse executive board, running the gamut from
committed communists through members of the Socialist party (which CP
stalwarts hated more than they did fascists in those pre–United Front days)
to traditional liberals. One of the board members was Sylvia Feningston,
who decided that the Union's more openly political theatre was more to her
taste and resigned from the Group. Gadget Kazan's new wife, Molly
Thacher, also took a job at the Union, which she considered the kind of
brave new theatre she had worked toward at Vassar.

It was only natural that many Group members should be interested in
these new organizations, which espoused similar ideals and seemed to have
a firmer sense of direction than their own floundering company. The commercial theatre had proved hostile to the Group; the workers theatres promised contact with a new audience that would be more receptive to the kind
of plays the Group wanted to present. The move of formerly amateur companies toward professionalism coincided with the Group's tentative steps
away from Broadway; they met at a point on the theatrical spectrum where
skilled acting and good production values were considered essential but the
empty slickness of the commercial theatre was disdained. In their effort to
give agitprop a human content, the workers theatres looked to the Stanislavsky system to help their actors find personal truth in their dramatizations of the class struggle. Group members like Joe Bromberg and Clifford
Odets were flattered to be asked to give talks on the Group's acting technique, and the directors were also sympathetic; both Strasberg and Crawford would later teach at the Collective. During the depressing winter of
1933, with their own theatre closed, working with the Collective and Union
gave Group members a sense of meaningful activity they desperately
craved.

Clurman attended a few early meetings for the new companies, but he
was too wrapped up in the Group to have much energy for other theatres.
He got together frequently with Strasberg and Crawford to plan the Group's

future, but their discussions went nowhere; they had no money, no scripts, no prospects. Crawford devoted herself to searching for plays, plowing through piles of unsolicited manuscripts moldering in the offices of Lee Shubert, with whom she'd pragmatically maintained a cordial relationship despite his shabby treatment of the Group over *Success Story*. Her partners marked time in their individual ways: Strasberg withdrew even more deeply within himself, while Clurman turned his attention outward, wandering the streets of New York and reflecting on the transformation of the once glamorous cityscape into a gray, gloomy wasteland where, as he remembered later, "my own bleak state seemed to be reflected in thousands of faces, signs, and portents."

Joining him in his desolate peregrinations was Clifford Odets, who hadn't previously been close to Clurman but now stepped in to fill the emotional void created by the temporary collapse of his affair with Stella Adler. In his memoir about the Group, Clurman wrote evocatively of their growing friendship:

> We began to see each other nightly, and with hungry hearts wandered aimlessly through sad centers of impoverished night life. We would drop in at some cheap restaurant and over a meager meal make dreams of both our past and future. . . . We listened to queer conversations on street corners, visited byways we had never suspected before. There grew between us a feeling akin to that which is supposed to exist between hoboes in their jungles, and we were strangely attracted to people and places that might be described as hangdog, ratty, and low.

The intense relationship they were forming would have an enormous impact on Group life, uniting as it did two powerful personalities whose collaboration as writer and director would eventually supplant Strasberg as the company's dominant artistic leadership. It was surprising that it had taken the two so long to find each other, for only Odets looked to the Group for his artistic, spiritual, emotional, and intellectual salvation with a single-minded devotion as fierce as Clurman's. (Strasberg's dedication equaled theirs, but his ingrained aloofness made it seem more narrowly artistic, less personal.) They were drawn together by many things: their mutual love for music and literature, their fondness for cheap cigars, their enthusiasm for the opposite sex—though Odets, who had many lovers, was far more experienced than his rather strait-laced friend. Above all, they shared a burning curiosity about the strange world they saw taking shape around them, as the Depression destroyed old ways of living and thinking, leaving in their place nothing much beyond a sense of limitless possibility.

They explored the city's grimier quarters, visiting burlesque houses and cheap movies, usually winding up their evenings in Sheridan Square at

Stewart's Cafeteria, a favorite hangout for impoverished artists because the food was good as well as cheap. Here a large group of desperate young people were marking time, often in dangerously self-destructive ways, while they waited for an inkling that there might be something for them to do with their lives in a society that offered them no jobs and no future. Odets knew many of them from his dismal pre-Group days, when he lived in the grungy, bedbug-ridden Circle Hotel on West 60th Street. He introduced them to Clurman, who later admitted that his initial reaction was "a middle-class shrinking" from these spooky kids and their loose ways, so unlike his own proper bourgeois upbringing. He was moved by Odets' obvious love for these lost souls; he came to share his friend's belief that their confusion and dissipation were in fact the seedbed for something fresh and important in American life—though neither of them had any idea what it might be.

They got to know each other during these late-night expeditions. Odets, who'd never finished high school, had always been in awe of Clurman's intellect, and he continued to bombard him with questions about the state of the theatre, what he should read, where the Group was headed, what the director thought of his new play. He also developed a more intimate affection for the man behind the brain; he was amused by Clurman's clumsiness, charmed by his helplessness in the practical world, and sympathetic about his tormented love affair. "No Adler could ever be made a Group person," he warned Clurman, a remark that reflected his rivalry with Luther as well as his dislike of Stella.

Clurman appreciated Odets' warm interest in his problems and was fascinated by a personality completely different from Waldo Frank, Alfred Stieglitz, and his other intellectual companions. Group members constantly kidded Clurman about his tendency to divide the world into people who were "sensitive" and those who weren't; the Group's new Marxists in particular found this a sentimental and suspiciously elitist distinction. For Clurman, who was in his most militantly left-wing phase from 1932 through 1935, part of Odets' attraction was his ease in the seamy underside of American life, the "real" world artists found so compelling in the 1930s. Part of it was his acute physical awareness—a revelation to Clurman, who was capable of traveling through Europe's most exotic landscapes, talking nonstop, without taking even a glance at his surroundings. Odets "reacted to everything, not with words or articulate knowledge, but with his body," Clurman wrote later. "His senses were extraordinarily alive, though he was not professionally 'sensitive.' To be near him was like being near a stove on which a whole range of savory foods was standing ready to be served." Spiritually and emotionally hungry, Clurman drew nourishment from his new friend, while Odets found direction for his ardent but chaotic thoughts under the director's guidance.

The Group struggled on into the spring. They got a temporary financial boost in late March, when they began a brief East Coast tour of *Success*

Story. Luther Adler and Morris Carnovsky were still engaged in other productions, but Stella Adler and the rest of the cast were relieved to get advances on their salaries from the Union Theatre League (which handled the tour) and to have assured paychecks for a few weeks. The directors had initially hoped to take a small percentage of the sum due the Group and put it in the general treasury, but the actors were in such dire straits that the Group as a body decided that all money from the tour should go directly to the cast members.

In fact, the directors discovered this spring that the actors were no longer content to leave all decisions concerning the Group to the triumvirate; they felt they should have a voice in the organization's policy-making as well. A number of outside factors may have influenced their desire to participate in the Group's management. Many of them were impressed by the organization of the Theatre Union and Theatre Collective, which were both committed to democratic, collective leadership vested in an executive committee. The experience of some members in the Communist party probably played a part; although the party hierarchy was rigid, a good deal of the work and discussion went on in small groups. The actors were also reflecting in their own sphere the general sense fostered by Roosevelt that America could rise out of the Depression only if every citizen had the opportunity—and the responsibility—to take part in the struggle. The first National Recovery Administration signs, emblazoned with a blue eagle and the motto "We Do Our Part," didn't go up in store and factory windows until August, but Roosevelt had stressed that spirit of cooperation and collective effort in every speech since his inauguration. It seemed to many the first sensible thing that had been said by a public official since the Crash.

The primary reasons for the actors' new assertiveness, however, had to do with the internal evolution of the Group. The directors had acknowledged the actors' right to shape policy at the beginning of the first season, when they asked the company to vote on whether or not Bill Challee could accept a role in an outside production. Since then, the actors had from time to time sent delegations to Clurman, who was closest and most receptive to them, to express their worries about individual members: Alixe Walker, who as stage manager was bossy and difficult to get along with; Phil Robinson, who voiced open skepticism about the method; and Crawford, whose standing had been severely weakened by the debacle of *Big Night*. Clurman seldom did anything about these complaints, but he listened, and an implicit understanding was established, whether he intended it or not, that Group life was the concern of everyone and that, if final authority rested with the directors, the actors' opinions would nonetheless be taken into account.

By the spring of 1933, this wasn't enough. The actors were disillusioned by the directors' failure to protect them from Lee Shubert's predatory manipulation of the *Success Story* box office, the rapid closing of *Big Night* before it had a chance to find an audience, and their inability to acquire another script for the season. Clurman's initial talks about the Group had promised a new dignity for actors: as thinking people capable of understanding a script's ideas, which they would be encouraged to discuss and then bring to life in performance; as artists, rather than commodities, who would be given the chance to grow through rigorous training in a unified technique and by playing a variety of roles not limited by physical typecasting; and as human beings with financial needs, who would be given economic security by membership in a permanent company with year-round salaries and a program of continuous production. The actors' devotion to the Group and (more or less) to the directors was based on the artistic satisfaction they had found in their first five productions, especially *Connelly, 1931—*, and *Success Story*. As far as the practical matters of salary and production went, however, they felt the directors hadn't lived up to their commitments. How could they continue to grow as artists when they had no play to rehearse and even their classes were intermittent owing to the inertia of one director and the problematic personal life of another?

The actors made a number of concrete suggestions for the better management of the Group. First and foremost, they wanted to establish an Actors Committee, elected by the members, that would represent their views to the directors and have a recognized institutional role in making Group policy. Arguing that the directors had proven themselves bad business people, they urged that the company hire a business manager to get the best possible deals for them with commercial producers and to develop a Group audience so that they would be less at the mercy of reviews. They expressed dissatisfaction over the directors' violation during the 1932–1933 season of the Group principle that every member of the company should be paid when any production was running; they suggested that greater parity between the highest and lowest salaries would make that possible and also be more in keeping with the Group Idea. Finally, they reiterated their desire to make the Group a repertory theatre, which they argued would help keep the company active when there were no satisfactory new plays available.

The directors were offended by these proposals, especially since simmering under their surface were specific criticisms of the direction of *Taos* and *Big Night*, the leadership's inability to develop and acquire scripts, and the bad judgment, or possibly favoritism, displayed in casting and apportioning salaries. They felt they were being unjustly blamed for problems that were largely the result of conditions in the commercial theatre they had no control over; they viewed the actors' suggestions as unrealistic. At the same time, they felt guilty about their failure to provide the security that had, at least by implication, been promised the actors when the Group was founded. Under the circumstances, they were at first inclined to agree to share responsibility with an Actors Committee—partly on the grounds that the actors couldn't criticize decisions quite so easily if they had taken part in them.

No sooner had they expressed their willingness, however, than they began to have doubts. Clurman argued that the solution to the Group's troubles was to vest final authority in a single director, with the other two acting as advisers and the actors remaining in their current, subordinate position. He nominated himself for the job, accurately perceiving that he was psychologically better equipped to deal with the actors' discontents. Crawford responded to criticism with an air of injury, reminding people of all the dirty jobs the Group had dumped on her and asserting that no one appreciated her. Strasberg simply blew up, and while he might silence the actors temporarily with his terrifying rages, their underlying dissatisfaction remained. Clurman had an ego strong enough to listen quietly to even the most irrational complaints, and he had a clever trick of responding with lengthy discourses that took off from whatever the initial subject was and roamed amidst the fields of history, philosophy, and contemporary politics to explain why what his petitioners wanted was unreasonable or impossible or both. By the time he finished, the confused supplicants had often forgotten what it was they'd been angry about in the first place; at the very least, they went away feeling Harold had given serious thought to their suggestions.

Strasberg and Crawford rejected Clurman's proposal. They saw no signs that their impractical colleague had the organizational or artistic skills to head the Group. They'd wounded him at an earlier planning session when he expressed his desire to direct a new production of Lawson's *The Pure in Heart*, which the Guild had botched the past fall. Strasberg bluntly declared that Clurman had given no evidence of being ready to direct, and Crawford agreed. Unwilling to trust him with a single play, they were even less receptive to the idea of his having ultimate authority over the entire organization. Clurman acquiesced, and his idea went no further than the ears of his two partners.

The directors responded to the actors with a lengthy paper analyzing the Group's reason for being, the difficulties that had arisen as it was translated from idea into reality, and the actors' discontent. Although Clurman and Odets later identified the paper as being written by Strasberg, his widow feels strongly that it could not have been his work, as he always wrote out important memos by hand and this document is typed. The question of authorship isn't crucial here; the fact that the directors called a meeting to read the paper to the actors indicates that it expressed the opinions of all three. The way they laid out the issues facing the Group also revealed a great deal about the social and political assumptions shared by the entire membership.

On the sticky question of salaries, the paper began by situating the Group in society in a manner utterly typical of the 1930s:

Complete freedom from the domination of economic and practical considerations can never fully occur under the present capitalist system of society. It is unfortunate that this last consideration has neither been sufficiently stressed nor sufficiently recognized and has led therefore to a wrong, Utopian and somewhat naive belief that the Group Theatre can solve its economic problems all by itself on the basis of some ideal equality—has divorced the actor from the scene where his protest against the economic and political system *should* arise as part of the entire working class—and has created dissatisfaction with the Group Theatre economic organization without recognizing the benefits derived therefrom.

The actors' call for equality in salaries, the paper argued,

represents simply a personal desire as against the needs of the Group as a whole. True equality does not mean everyone share alike—that is silly, childish and impossible: true equality means ideally "From each according to his ability—to each according to his needs," and at the present stage of society that each one be judged by the same standard —group activity and *group* importance—instead of part of his labor going to someone who does not work. No one in the Group is paid except in relation to their importance to the Group . . . I cannot here go further into the theoretic problem except to ask those who are interested to look up this problem as elucidated by the two leading exponents of Karl Marx and Lenin.

It noted that in the beginning the ratio of highest to lowest Group salaries was 10 to 1, as opposed to 23 to 1 in the commercial theatre, that the second year it was voluntarily reduced to 6⅔ to 1, and that the directors intended to reduce it still further, to 4 to 1.

Having disposed of the salary question with the help of Marx and Lenin, the directors vigorously defended their management of the Group's business affairs, which "in all its looseness and irregularity has functioned miraculously well. We do not need a business manager," they stated flatly. "The Group . . . needs a staff of some kind to organize unions, clubs, etc. . . . who have an interest in plays of [our] sort. This cannot be done on a business basis."

Addressing the actors' desire for repertory, the directors admitted that "the great mistake of this period was the play problem": the Group's undue optimism about the right scripts simply coming their way and their inability to make playwrights feel an integral part of the company. The directors argued that they had already moved to solve these problems by suggesting themes and plots to playwrights, giving them books that might be adapted for the stage and paying out advances to commission new plays. Repertory wasn't the answer, as witness Eva Le Gallienne's difficulties in maintaining the Civic Rep and Lawrence Langner's abortive attempt to run a similar company in Connecticut. It should be an ultimate goal, not an immediate task.

Whether Strasberg wrote it alone or in collaboration with his fellow directors, the paper certainly displayed his tendency to treat the actors as recalcitrant children who had to be instructed in the realities of life. Both Strasberg and Clurman often turned questions of Group organization into lofty discourses on the nature of capitalism and the theatre.

Concerning the question of the Actors Committee, the directors asserted that the very nature of the actors' involvement in Group life made them unfit to run the organization:

> Each person in the Group has individual interests of his own, but while the actor's interest is not entirely satisfied even if the Group is successful if his own growth has not been fostered, the director's success comes only through the success of the entire group and cannot be separated from it. . . . There might be three other directors, but the form of organization should remain the same. . . . In the theatre a director with complete authority is an absolute necessity. You cannot decide things by majority vote.

The paper urged the actors to spend less of their time second-guessing the directors and more on much-needed self-criticism, on consideration of ways in which they could improve individually as artists within the Group.

The "growing division between the members of the Group and the three directors" was not healed by these comments. The directors were right, of course, about the practical difficulties they faced, and the actors knew it. But they hadn't joined the Group because they believed in submitting to unfavorable circumstances; they'd been drawn by the directors' promise that the Group would overcome these problems and create a better artistic environment *despite* commercial imperatives. The actors expected a lot from their leaders—they'd been encouraged to—and they weren't satisfied by a lecture on the state of the world and the nature of different people's functions within the Group. Many of them felt that the paper's generalizations simply evaded discussion of their specific complaints; Odets, his self-confidence bolstered by his new intimacy with Clurman, was especially vociferous in his disagreement.

The general feeling of the actors was that, while repertory and equal salaries might indeed be impractical at the moment, there was no reason other than the directors' reluctance why the Group shouldn't hire a business manager. As for the establishment of an Actors Committee, they insisted on it. Strasberg finally lost his temper with his once docile followers and yelled, "I don't care what you say!" To which Odets rejoined, "I don't care what *you* say!" Shocked and disheartened by this new boldness, Strasberg responded quietly, "I know." It was a sad moment for the man who had once reigned supreme as General Lee.

The meeting ended with a chastened Group searching for a means of compromise. It may have been in response to this dialogue that Helen Thompson, like Molly Thacher a graduate of Vassar's famed Experimental Theatre program, was hired to help plan the Group's audience strategy. The directors also promised to consider hiring a business manager; an aspiring young manager, Phil Adler (no relation to the actors), joined them in the fall. Salaries were not made equal, though this issue was largely academic at the moment, since no one was drawing a salary at all. The directors remained in charge, but an Actors Committee was formed. Quiescent in the beginning, it was to have a decisive impact on the Group's history in years to come.

As the paper noted, the directors had been taking steps to remedy the Group's lack of scripts. Most of the work had been done by Crawford while her partners were sunk in their personal problems. She met a young writer named Melvin Levy at a cocktail party and recalled that someone in the Group had thought Levy's novel *The Last Pioneers* might make a good play. When she asked him about it, he suggested instead an original script about a grasping shipping magnate in nineteenth-century San Francisco. Crawford, who had a strong personal interest in American history, was enthusiastic and, after consultation with Strasberg, gave Levy an advance. (Clurman, who didn't find out about it until later, was hurt by this new example of his partners' low estimation of his current value to the Group.) Levy seemed like just the kind of playwright the Group was looking for: young, politically involved—he had taken part in a 1931 investigation led by Theodore Dreiser of conditions in the Harlan County coal fields—and eager to portray American life. She was hopeful he would write something worthwhile for a future Group season.

More important for the present, Crawford had found an immediately viable script among the stacks in Lee Shubert's office. *Crisis,* by Sidney Kingsley, had been making the rounds for several years. It had been optioned by three different managements, but none of them could raise the money for a hospital drama which required a huge cast and a complicated set. Sidney Harmon and James Ullman, a pair of young producers in their twenties who had recently formed a partnership, still held an option when Kingsley was advised by a friend to send it to Shubert. Crawford saw the script there and brought it to her partners, who weren't initially enthusiastic. She took it to her old friend Theresa Helburn, who suggested that they might produce it together independently, but Strasberg and Clurman refused Crawford's request to work outside the Group. By May, with no other play in the offing, her partners looked on *Crisis* with a more favorable eye. They made a deal with Harmon and Ullman to coproduce it, with expenses and profits to be shared equally. Lee Shubert, who brought them together and agreed to provide a theatre for the production, also received a small share of the profits.

The directors committed the Group to *Crisis* over the objections of the actors, who found the play a conventional piece of playmaking without strong social commentary. Indeed, on the page *Crisis* seemed pretty tame. The story of a young doctor torn between a commitment to his profession and the love of his spoiled fiancée, who feels his work takes him away from her too much, was the stuff of a hundred earlier melodramas. The more radical members argued that Kingsley said nothing about the appalling fact that medicine was run for profit in the United Unites; others felt the interesting hospital backdrop hardly redeemed the trite love story. Clurman, who didn't much like the play himself, was uncharacteristically silent during the debate; it was Strasberg, who had come around to Crawford's belief that the script would play wonderfully and might very well be a hit, who defended it most strongly. *Crisis* might lack specific social criticism, he admitted, but it was a play about idealism; surely the Group could sympathize with that. It presented great opportunities for creative staging and in-depth characterization; after two plays with small casts, it would provide everyone in the Group with parts. He was tired of the Group's (what he really meant was, Clurman's) tendency to be hypercritical of scripts. They needed a play, and this was what was available.

That was the bottom line: they didn't have anything else. Having flexed their muscles and obtained an Actors Committee, the members were willing to back off and let the directors have their way. They reserved the right to complain and criticize—although no one was likely to have much leisure for even such agreeable pursuits during their summer retreat. Crawford had negotiated an agreement with the owners of an adult camp named Green Mansions, located near Lake George in Warrensburg, New York. Since they couldn't afford to pay rent, the company would provide entertainment four nights a week for the camp's guests; in exchange, thirty-five Group members received free room and board. Preparing *Crisis* for fall production, devising revues and one-acts for the nightly program, plus continuing their traditional schedule of classes would keep everyone very busy. The directors asked hardworking Gadget Kazan to come along as stage manager and jack-of-all-trades; his friend Alan Baxter was also invited to join the Group.

With Franchot Tone gone, they needed a leading man for the role of the idealistic young doctor in *Crisis*. They chose Alexander Kirkland, who had made a splash at the Guild in *Wings over Europe* in 1928, then gone to Hollywood, where he was disenchanted by a series of mediocre parts and the studios' authoritarian attitude toward actors. Kirkland's clean-cut good looks belied his broad interests—he'd managed the Berkshire Playhouse in Stockbridge, Massachusetts, and written several plays—and he disliked being a flunky. He was delighted to join the Group and quickly became one of the method's most dedicated practitioners, an ardent admirer of Strasberg. He was also a tireless worker and excellent public speaker; the Group benefited greatly over the years from his heroic efforts on the social club/trade union/drama society lecture circuit. The company's low morale received a salutary boost from their new member's high-spirited enthusiasm, and they welcomed Billy (his real first name) into the fold.

The benefit performance Bobby Lewis had proposed back in January took place May 21 at the Majestic Theatre; the well-known journalist Heywood Broun was master of ceremonies, and an array of prominent artists, including Martha Graham, donated their services. The evening netted $2,000, which meant that the Group's most impoverished members would be able to survive until they left for Green Mansions, but they were still in dire need of funds to pick up their share of Kingsley's option, commission more plays, and cover office expenses. Clurman appealed to Franchot Tone, who had written that he missed the Group but intended to stay in Hollywood because he'd fallen in love with Joan Crawford. Tone promptly sent a check to tide them over.

On Memorial Day Clurman went up to Green Mansions with a contingent of ten actors to give a holiday performance of a one-act play by John Galsworthy and a hastily improvised musical revue. The camp's weekend guests loved it, and it appeared that the Group's unconventional arrangement was going to work out nicely. Clurman settled in to await the entire company's arrival on June 19, when rehearsals for *Crisis* and the regular summer entertainment program would begin. He had no desire to return to New York City, the site of so many shattered hopes and painful experiences during the past year.

The Group had been severely tested during their second season, and it wasn't yet clear whether the collective spirit had survived intact. They'd given an important contemporary play their finest production to date, and it had been trounced by a hostile press. True, they'd managed to find their audience and keep *Success Story* afloat for sixteen weeks, but only at the cost of enormous personal sacrifices by every member of the company. *Big Night* had been an artistic disappointment and financial disaster. The strain of confronting a hostile theatrical establishment had badly damaged the Group's internal relationships; at a few distressing winter and spring meetings, it seemed as though the once-devoted creative family was splintering into acrimonious factions. The actors' faith in their leaders had been shaken; the directors' bond of mutual respect was battered. The Group had been born out of the members' love for the work and the people they shared it with—now they weren't even sure they liked each other very much. They faced the future with a play many of them disdained.

More than anyone else, Clurman was personally demoralized by the Group's trying year. His friendship with Odets was almost the only accomplishment he could point to. He'd directed no plays, found no scripts, raised no money. His fellow directors had made it clear how low they rated his energy and abilities. His rocky relationship with Stella Adler, who decided to join the Group summer only after an agonized debate that made them both miserable, kept him in a state of perpetual emotional turmoil. The past six months had nearly killed him; he looked forward to the next six with apprehension, feeling that for better or worse they would decide the course of his life. "The Group's life too—bound up more intimately than *it* realizes with mine—will blossom this year or die its first death," he wrote to Paul Strand.

Well, no one had ever told them it would be easy. Despite everything, Clurman had no desire to give up the impossible task he'd set himself and his comrades. He had an astounding resilience, an ability to roll with the punches life and the Group threw him, that came from a rich inner life nourished by his extensive reading and deep immersion in American culture. The same man who was so traumatized by the Group's difficulties and his own personal problems that his partners regarded him as virtually nonfunctional could spend hours with his friend Aaron Copland discussing the history of American ideology, from Emerson through Theodore Dreiser to the Group. (Somehow, all his conversations eventually came back to the Group.) He could stand back and view the things that mattered most deeply to him—the Group, Stella Adler—with a detachment that allowed him to surmount crises without succumbing to rages (like Strasberg) or hurt feelings (like Crawford). His letter to Strand on the eve of the Group's third summer reflected tangled feelings of exhaustion, fear, and dogged determination, but it closed on a characteristic note of hope. "The Group is still together," he wrote proudly. "Still a center, still a life, still struggling."

SIX

Broadway Success

When the majority of the Group arrived at Green Mansions on June 19, 1933, the signs were bad. Clurman was surprised to discover Stella Adler wasn't among them and embarrassed that Clifford Odets had to tell him she wouldn't be joining the company for a few more days. Their estrangement made him unhappy all summer; he was dejected and took little interest in *Crisis*. Crawford was worried about raising the Group's share of the production costs and harassed by the complicated logistics of assigning rooms and responsibilities for the largest gathering yet assembled for a Group retreat. Grover Burgess decided to come away for the summer only at the last minute, and Bud Bohnen didn't turn up at all. Strasberg was angry with the actors because they had voted to give Bohnen a leave of absence so he could take a better-paying role in a play being tried out by the Broadway producer John Golden. Granted, Bohnen was badly in debt and had pressing family responsibilities, but many Group members were in the same spot. Besides, Strasberg resented any infringement on the directors' authority.

In this troubled atmosphere, the Group had to rehearse *Crisis* and come up each week with four evening programs, a task many of them regarded as demeaning and damaging to their prestige, especially since the Broadway columnists had already evinced much amusement at the notion of the oh-so-serious Group serving up entertainment to a bunch of summer campers.

In fact, almost everyone had fun; Morris Carnovsky and Phoebe Brand later remembered it as the Group's most enjoyable summer. Green Mansions itself, with its well-maintained facilities and excellent food, made a welcome change from their rundown quarters at Brookfield Center and Dover Furnace. After the intense debates of the spring, it was something of a relief to mingle with outsiders and listen to their lavish praise of the nightly programs. Clifford Odets struck up a flirtatious friendship with the younger sister of the camp's owner; Carnovsky, Brand, and Joe Bromberg sat up late at night in the canteen chatting with sympathetic guests; Luther Adler made passes at the women who struck his fancy.

It wasn't all sweetness and light. There were stormy meetings about Group policy: two five-hour marathons hashing and rehashing the bad precedent set by Bohnen's leave and ongoing debates sparked by Max Gorelik, who was designing his fourth play for the Group and felt he deserved to be recognized as a full member of the organization. Everyone avoided the speech teacher who was charged with improving the actors' diction, and the new dance instructor didn't work out either. Nonetheless, there was a general atmosphere of good cheer, and enough work to keep people from dwelling unduly on personal difficulties.

Rehearsals for *Crisis* began immediately. Whatever the actors' feelings about the play, they quickly realized that Strasberg was directing it with an authority and imaginative freedom surpassing even his previous distinguished work. He was always at his best when engaged in an actual production, and with Clurman and Crawford both at a low ebb, his artistic leadership was crucial to Group morale. He more than rose to the occasion. As far as he was concerned, there was nothing exceptional about holding the Group together while his partners recuperated; they did the same for him when he was exhausted after a play opened. That was how the directorate worked. "While each of [us] in a way found [our] own niche," he told an interviewer years later, "it didn't mean you were set there, and you didn't attend to anything else. What happened was, when anybody got tired, somebody just took up. Nobody ever said, 'Gee I don't feel—' They said, 'Okay, I'll do it.' "

Strasberg saw that the principal strength of Kingsley's script lay in its detailed portrait of hospital life. While writing the play, the young Cornell graduate convinced college friends who had gone into medicine to introduce him in their hospitals as a visiting medical student so he could observe the daily routine. He hung out with the staff, noting the joking camaraderie with which the overworked doctors and nurses blunted the ever-present knowledge that their jobs involved matters of life and death. He tried the interns' favorite drink: ginger ale, soda, and lemon spiked with alcohol from the pathology lab. He observed half a dozen operations and was struck by the almost balletic physical poetry of the rigidly prescribed scrub-up ritual that preceded surgery. He captured all this in *Crisis*, which teemed with sharply drawn minor characters and vignettes. The vividly textured rendering of the medical environment gave weight to the hero's dedication to his profession and a realistic underpinning to the melodramatic plot involving an illicit affair and a young nurse's death after an abortion. It was custommade for the Group's ability to invest even the smallest roles with a fully imagined inner life, to discover a whole world of experience underneath the surface of the text.

Strasberg began by exposing the actors to that world. They visited hospitals near Green Mansions and talked to doctors and nurses, several of whom advised on the proper handling of instruments and the correct scrubbing procedure. Beany Barker, whose brother was one of the experts consulted, was amused when every time a new adviser appeared they had an entirely new routine to learn. (Strasberg eventually selected the movements that worked best onstage.) The actors worked meticulously to get every gesture just right; those playing doctors took to carrying stethoscopes around in their pockets to produce the appropriate medical gait.

For the first five weeks they did nothing but improvise. Strasberg devised situations that would give them a sense of what it meant to be a doctor, possessed of an almost godlike power over a patient, or a nurse charged with the daily burden of caring for dozens of sick people. They used the observations made on their hospital visits to capture the external reality of medical life; they used their personal emotions to explore how such grave responsibilities shaped their characters. Kingsley, whose work as an actor at Cornell and in a Westchester stock company had been along more conventional lines, was at first taken aback by the actors' use of their own words in scenes based only loosely on his plot—"Five weeks, and I haven't heard more than four or five of my lines," he remarked to Clurman, who assured him he would hear them in due time—but came to value this preliminary exploration of the reality behind the text.

Much of the improvisational work was devoted to the climactic operating-room scene at the end of the second act. Billy Kirkland's character has a brief affair with a young nurse, played by Phoebe Brand, who becomes pregnant and is brought to the hospital on the verge of death after an illegal abortion. While his unwitting fiancée (Beany Barker) watches from the sidelines, the young doctor and a team of hospital staff scrub up and perform an operation in a desperate attempt to save the woman's life. Strasberg envisioned the scene as a stylized ballet, expressing the essence of the surgeon's work as a somber ritual invoking the forces of life and death. To give the actors the weight of familiarity with surgery that real doctors and nurses had, he had them improvise it over and over. To sharpen their tempo, he did the scene twice in succession: the first time in solemn slow motion to the strains of Beethoven's Seventh Symphony, the second time as a double-quick farce, with doctors accidentally sewing instruments up in the patients to the rollicking rhythm of Offenbach's "Gaîté Parisienne."

Once the operating-room choreography was set, they practiced it religiously: it was rehearsed more than one hundred times over three months. It had to be, because the first five minutes of the scene were completely silent; nurses with sterilized gloves and doctors with freshly washed hands had to meet at the same spot onstage at the same moment without any dialogue to cue them. Individual actors worked on their moves outside the rehearsal hall as well. "For six weeks, all of us who played a doctor or nurse went through this process in pantomime every morning when we got up, before we could have breakfast," recalled Dorothy Patten, who played the head nurse. "By the end of that time we could do the routine backwards and forwards, eyes closed, and sound asleep, almost." Joe Bromberg, cast as the chief surgeon, startled the locals by doing his preparation al fresco: "You couldn't blame the poor folk, could you, if the story circulated that I was off my rocker after a farmer had discovered me in an open field going through the operating room motions."

Kingsley and the director soon formed a close relationship. The playwright had been apprehensive about working with Strasberg; their only previous encounter hadn't been promising. In 1928, when Franchot Tone was working on *New Year's Eve* at 128 Riverside Drive, he'd invited his college friend Kingsley over to visit a rehearsal. "A very studious young man came over to me and asked me a few questions and said, 'No, I'm sorry, you won't do.' And that was my first meeting with Lee Strasberg."

Working on *Crisis,* Kingsley found his new colleague much more receptive. Early in rehearsals, the author was troubled by Bromberg's performance. The character was based on an actual doctor Kingsley had met, a kindly man with a wonderful smile that instantly put people at ease in even the most trying situations. Kingsley felt Bromberg was giving the part a sinister quality that was all wrong. He wouldn't let a surgeon like that operate on his little toe, he told Strasberg. Couldn't the director get him to smile every now and then?

Strasberg nodded noncommittally, saying neither yes nor no. What Kingsley didn't know was that the quality he disliked was largely the director's doing. Strasberg thought Bromberg, who'd acted primarily in comic parts, lacked the authority necessary to portray the chief of surgery. He suggested a substitute reality he called "the FBI adjustment." He told the actor to pretend to himself he was an FBI agent sent to investigate the Group Theatre. "He could not give away the fact that he was an FBI agent, nor could he tell any of the actors . . . this created a strange, new quality appropriate to the character." Strasberg had used a similar tactic with Stella Adler in *Success Story,* giving her a private adjustment that he felt would help her project the emotions required by the play.

This was a central departure from the basic Stanislavsky technique. With his "magic if," Stanislavsky asked actors to imagine what they would do and how they would feel *if* they were the characters in the given circumstances of the play. Strasberg worked from Vakhtangov's revision of this premise, which he defined as: "The circumstances of the scene indicate that the character must behave in a particular way; what would motivate you, the actor, to behave in that particular way?" This shifted the emphasis from the character's emotions within the play to an actor's internal work on a part, encouraging an introspection that often shut out the other people in a scene. Taken to an extreme, it could result in a stageful of actors each playing an individual adjustment that had nothing to do with the text. That wasn't Strasberg's intention—he believed that his adjustments helped the actor better serve the play—but the potential for distorting the script was there.

In Bromberg's case, the actor solved the problem himself. The same day Kingsley had spoken to Strasberg about his worries, writer and director were eating lunch in the Green Mansions dining room when Bromberg came over and sat down with them. "You know," he said, "the most wonderful thing happened to me today—I don't know how it happened—but suddenly I found myself smiling sweetly and it worked; and if you don't mind, Lee, I'm going to work on it." The director indicated that would be fine; Kingsley nearly fell out of his chair. Then the sober, serious Strasberg turned to the playwright and did something entirely unprecedented: he winked. Bromberg's performance ultimately displayed both the authority Strasberg wanted and the kindliness Kingsley considered essential.

Despite his insistence that a performance be motivated by the actor's inner feelings, Strasberg was a pragmatic director who knew that a character's behavior couldn't contradict the meaning of the lines unless the script called for it. In an emotional scene between the young doctor and nurse before they begin their affair, both characters are exhausted and tense. The nurse, recognizing that the doctor is as fed up as she, says, "You too?" and he replies, "Up to here," holding his hand to his neck to indicate he's had about as much as he can stand. During rehearsals Kirkland, a slightly overzealous new disciple of the method, would deliver the line with his hand at his stomach, or his chest, or wherever it "felt right" to him at that particular moment. Kingsley, who didn't much like his leading man in any case, was infuriated. It made nonsense of the line, he complained to Strasberg, who agreed and directed Kirkland to hold his hand at his neck. "But I don't always feel it up to there," the actor protested. Strasberg lost his temper. He didn't care if the actor felt it up to *there*, he shouted, holding his hand at the level of his genitals. If Kirkland played it the right way, he'd feel it the right way.

Prodded by a playwright he liked, Strasberg was willing to redirect the actors toward external reality, but left to his own devices he was still primarily concerned with their internal emotions. By the summer of 1933, not all Group actors were as devoted to this approach as new converts like Kirkland. Both Beany Barker and Phoebe Brand had doubts about the way Strasberg wanted them to use affective memory in their portrayals. "I'd be sitting in Billy Kirkland's lap in the love scene, supposedly doing a sense memory of some great evening I'd had in Sorrento, Italy," Barker remembered. "Well, that was mad! It took me out of the reality of the play. Strasberg saw me the way Duse played *The Lady from the Sea*, like a lovely object that this intense young intern would have fallen in love with. I thought she was a straightforward, spoiled American girl with very little awareness of anything except herself, and I played it that way." She reflected the growing self-assurance of many Group actors, devoted to Strasberg and the method but ready to make their own choices.

Brand was still trying to do it Strasberg's way. "Those damned exercises!" she said, years later. "They helped in a way, to let us know that you had to put your whole self into something and use all your emotional equipment. It revealed to you that you couldn't just act the lines; they weren't enough. You had to *be* in that situation." But she found affective memory made it harder, not easier. "In that little, simple part I played, I started way offstage: I went this far and took an exercise; I went this far and changed my action —I wasn't onstage yet. Then I went this far and thought of something else, got to the door and opened it, took a new adjustment and a new action, went in. By the time I got to the table and was talking to [Kirkland], I was so full of I don't know how many different conflicting emotions! Maybe I was good, but I couldn't play the scene. People got tied up."

The confusion Brand felt may have been the quality Strasberg was look-ing for in her character, an ardent young woman attracted to a handsome doctor engaged to someone else. Certainly his painstaking direction nicely complemented Kingsley's technique as a playwright, which was to create a carefully detailed environment and show how strongly it affected the people working within it. The highly stylized operating-room scene (which had nothing to do with affective memory) infused the doctors and nurses with a dignity and moral stature that underscored the play's positive view of the medical profession and its espousal of the ideal of service to society. In that, at least, it expressed a point of view the Group could share. Though many members continued to dislike the play, which they considered conventional and superficial, they knew they were giving it a fine production highlighting every theatrical and social value it possessed.

Meanwhile, singing for their supper turned out to be more enjoyable than they'd expected. They treated their audience to everything from a nine-teenth-century temperance melodrama (*Ten Nights in a Barroom*, directed by Clifford Odets) to the experimental work from Dover Furnace. The Bromberg-Carnovsky gibberish sketches were especially popular with the Green Mansion guests, who roared with laughter at the Yiddish-Russian nonsense words and the absurd situations the duo created. The Group also presented their corrosive improvisation based on George Grosz's drawings, and Ralph Steiner made a film of it; still photos of the bare-chested Brom-berg, Art Smith, Gadget Kazan, and Russell Collins, clad in trousers, hel-mets, and boots, striking poses on a desolate plain strewn with tree trunks, turned up that fall in *Theatre Arts* magazine. They threw together a couple of musical revues: Tony Kraber sang his cowboy songs, and for the Fourth of July Barker, Patten, Stella Adler, and three other Group actresses donned skimpy costumes patterned like American flags and danced in a chorus line.

The more conventional entertainments included performances of the second act of *Big Night*, two acts of *Success Story*, and a revival of *Gods of the Lightning,* Maxwell Anderson's 1928 drama about Sacco and Vanzetti. Clurman directed an outdoor production of O'Neill's *The Emperor Jones* with Collins, Odets, and Bobby Lewis, and they also did one of O'Neill's short sea plays. They presented one act of *Marco Millions,* another O'Neill play, in which Carnovsky had made a personal hit as Kublai Kaan in the Theatre Guild tour. Carnovsky directed *The Bear,* their first encounter as a company with Chekhov, whose full-length plays had been the proving ground for the Stanislavsky technique and continued to be the showpieces of the Moscow Art Theatre.

The evening programs stretched the actors, much as the experimental work had at Dover Furnace. They had a chance to direct, and got a glimpse of what it would be like to do repertory. But the most significant production was a new work. Odets had been urging Clurman to give his play a chance, and the director decided to try out Act Two of *I Got the Blues* in this informal setting. The four-day rehearsal period was strained: Luther Adler never bothered to learn his lines properly; his sister considered both the play and her part vulgar and possibly anti-Semitic. Nonetheless, the show went over with a bang, as Odets had assured Clurman it would. The audience, mostly city dwellers themselves, loved the urban snap of Odets' dialogue and his characters' tough humor in the face of life's woes, and responded heartily.

Odets laughed too, with the sheer joy of hearing his words spoken by Group actors. Given the audience's enthusiasm, he was hurt and disappointed when it became clear the directors had no plans to give *I Got the Blues* a full-scale production. Clurman thought the first act cluttered and the conclusion too pessimistic; he told Odets the script needed more work. Strasberg actively disliked the play; he shared Stella Adler's distaste for its realistic portrayal of lower-middle-class Jewish life, believing it would offend Jewish audiences and alienate everyone else. Their reaction was especially galling to Odets in light of the script they *had* chosen; he was among the Group members who considered *Crisis* unworthy of their efforts.

Ironically, Odets, who had joined the Group partly in search of the warmth lacking in his own family, was being rejected by his theatrical parents at a moment when his real father had decided he showed some promise after all. Lou Odets, detested by most of the Group as a vulgar, materialistic salesman type, had a shrewd eye for the main chance, and the audience response told him that his son's play might be worth something. He advised Clifford to forget the directors, who were jealous of his success, and try to sell *I Got the Blues* elsewhere. The budding playwright was angry enough briefly to consider leaving the Group; instead, he began making notes for a new play he hoped would be more acceptable to Strasberg.

The Group was also rehearsing, rather desultorily, one additional play for fall production. Clurman had acquired *Gallery Gods,* a German piece about a theatre troupe, because he thought it would show off the company's ensemble work and make a nice contrast with *Crisis*. He directed a cast that included both Adlers, Joe Bromberg, and Bobby Lewis, but they had little time to devote to it since rehearsals of Kingsley's play had first call on the services of everyone except Stella Adler. It wasn't an auspicious project for Clurman's directorial debut, and his depressed state of mind didn't help matters. His status within the Group was low that summer; he heard Billy Kirkland and others saying, "The Group has only one director," and knew they weren't referring to him. His customary role as script adviser had been preempted by Kingsley's close working partnership with Strasberg. He felt frustrated, deprived of the chance to devote his best efforts to the Group. Sometimes he wondered if directing was what he really wanted to do after all. The Group's not-so-gentle ribbing about his gift of gab reminded him that thus far his most striking talent was his way with words. He began to think about writing professionally, but realized it would do nothing to improve his troubled relationship with the Group.

One of the translators of *Gallery Gods* was Clurman's friend John Houseman, who would soon make his own mark as an adventurous director and the producer of a series of brilliant classical revivals directed by his volatile young partner, Orson Welles. Houseman spent two weeks at Green Mansions making minor adjustments in the play's text and observing with fascination the Group's intense collective life. He attended their meetings, "which all were highly emotional and conducted with a curious combination of communal spirit and arbitrary authority." He heard Max Gorelik rail against the directors and listened to Strasberg reply at the top of his lungs for nearly three hours. He noted Stella Adler's unease within the Group and the hard time she was giving his friend Harold. He was impressed by the Group's dedication but taken aback, as many outsiders were, by the high-strung way they carried on together. Group life was not for everyone.

It wasn't always comfortable for Group members either. Gadget Kazan isolated himself from the collective by sleeping in the wings of the Green Mansion theatre and taking his meals in the kitchen, where he could read Lenin and not feel left out of conversations about rehearsals he wasn't invited to attend. He felt lonely—his wife had elected to spend the summer in Mexico writing a play—and excluded from full participation in the Group. Even camp guests noticed that the directors didn't take Kazan very seriously, though they relied on his boundless energy to cope with the huge number of backstage chores their ambitious entertainment program entailed. He built, painted, and lit all the sets; he fixed broken props; he took thankless small parts in various productions. "My goal that summer was simple: to make the Group feel they couldn't get along without me . . . I was simply there, on the spot, behind every production, somewhere or other in every play, eager, energetic, ready for anything, slam-bang, jaunty, never down." He was rewarded in August with a job as assistant stage manager of

Crisis, and Clurman and Crawford officially made him a permanent member just before the Group's return to New York. Strasberg was annoyed by their decision, which had been taken without consulting him; if Kazan learned of this, it would only have reinforced his belief that he was in the Group on sufferance, by virtue of his hard work rather than any real appreciation of his artistic abilities.

Crawford had persuaded Doris Warner, daughter of the film mogul Harry Warner, to put up the Group's $6,000 portion of the production costs in exchange for half their share of the profits. She came up just before Labor Day to see a run-through of *Crisis,* which had been renamed *Men in White.* The directors had never liked the original title, and Kingsley finally came up with a new one that shifted the emphasis from the plot to the people and their profession. The run-through was a disaster. The actors still didn't really know their lines, although that hardly mattered, since the rain pounding down on the theatre's roof was so loud they could barely be heard. The play seemed slow, too heavy, and it didn't engage the audience's emotions. Warner made it clear she was very disappointed, but didn't threaten to withdraw her backing—yet. On this ominous note, the Group returned to New York to put the play on its feet with Gorelik's complex set.

Strasberg, Crawford, and Clurman conferred anxiously about the production, trying to figure out where it had gone wrong. They knew every technical detail was correct; they'd researched it all. They saw how deeply the actors had immersed themselves in hospital routines and lore to gain an understanding of medical life. The script had the same strengths and weaknesses it had always possessed; there didn't seem to be any tinkering they could do on that. As for the lines, well, the actors would learn them. But something more fundamental was awry: the atmosphere they'd worked so hard to create wasn't coming across. Finally, they realized that all of them had become so caught up in the high drama of life and death a hospital presented that the actors were performing the medical scenes with the emotional sensitivity of artists instead of the impersonal objectivity of trained professionals. "The actors are all suffering so much the patients don't have to," Crawford told Strasberg. "The doctors' and nurses' job is to get on with it; they should be firm, cool and in control." The three directors had come to this understanding together, but it made sense that Crawford should be the one who best defined the proper medical attitude. It was the role she played within the Group: the calm, collected professional taking care of business.

As *Men in White* entered its final rehearsals at the Broadhurst Theatre, Strasberg instructed the actors to make what he called "the professional adjustment." It made all the difference: where scenes had dragged, they moved briskly with a sense of purpose; the personal struggles of the doctors and nurses were much more moving when contrasted with their ability to be objective and authoritative in their dealings with patients. Now that the

Group had left improvisations behind and begun rehearsing the play as
written, Kingsley could see the flaws in his script and make adjustments.
He realized the third act didn't quite work and added a scene in which
Beany Barker's character and the head surgeon discussed her fiancé's responsibilities as a doctor; it brought into sharper focus the play's central
theme of the overriding commitment demanded of men and women in the
medical professions.

To aid the Group in bringing to life the hospital environment, Max Gorelik contributed once again a brilliant set that physically illuminated the
script's basic motifs. The vista of an endless hospital corridor gave each
scene a sense of being played out against the vast backdrop of an institution
that contained many other scenes, many other stories. The permanent set
had a varnished blue rear wall with three sliding panels; the openings in the
side walls, also deep blue, were covered by white draw-curtains; the floor
was polished black. Three platforms parallel to the proscenium opening
reinforced the sense of horizontal movement; one was mobile and could be
dressed with props and small flats offstage for the play's many quick scene
changes. Nothing about the set was realistic; Gorelik believed that "the
mere reproduction of familiar scenes on a stage is as unnecessary as it is
essentially untheatrical." The wall color, for example, was chosen because
white would have been glaring, whereas blue was soothing and quiet. The
realism came from the props, especially the surgical instruments, purchased from a medical-supply company with a doctor's assistance. The
interplay between abstraction and realism gave a mythic quality to the
setting, visually underscoring the drama and nobility of the surgeon's
calling.

For the climactic operating-room scene, Strasberg wanted bright white
light focused on the table where the dying nurse lay. Ed Kook, whose Century Lighting Company was providing the electrical equipment, flooded the
area with four huge spots that made the doctors' gowns and the sheet
covering the patient stand out sharply against the blue walls, increasing the
scene's tension. At the curtain line—Joe Bromberg lifting his hand and
saying, "scalpel"—the director called for even more light as the instrument
was passed to him. But nothing Kook added created the effect Strasberg
wanted. Finally, Crawford ran down the street to a nearby drugstore and
bought a tall gooseneck lamp, which they placed next to the actor playing
the surgeon's assistant. When he handed Bromberg the scalpel, he switched
on the lamp; as the instrument was lowered toward the body it glittered in
the extra light. The effect, Crawford recalled, was breathtaking, "as painful
as the scalpel making the incision."

The Group was uncertain enough about *Men in White*'s reception to
announce, just before the opening, plans to present five other plays that
season, including *Gallery Gods* and a revival of *The Weavers* by Gerhart
Hauptmann. (They were still dreaming of a repertory company, though

they'd taken no concrete steps to make it happen.) As Crawford remembered it, the first preview justified their fears; the ending still wasn't quite right. In her recollection, the preview performance closed with the protagonist alone, guilt-stricken over the nurse's death and rejected by his fiancée. The directors thought this was too depressing, and, after discussion with Kingsley, a few brief lines were added. The doctor remains alone onstage for a few seconds, then the phone rings: an Italian woman whose son was brought to the hospital in an earlier scene is anxiously inquiring about him; as the doctor reassures her that her son will live, the curtain falls, leaving the audience with the understanding that despite his unhappiness the young doctor will continue his work and dedicate his life to healing.

Kingsley later vehemently disputed Crawford's account, claiming that he had made all changes in the play after final rehearsals revealed the script's weaknesses, not because of anything the directors said to him. The larger point he wanted to make was that the Group hadn't been exclusively responsible for the success of the play, which was performed to great acclaim by many other companies all over the world after the New York premiere. There was some bitterness between the author and the organization during the run of *Men in White* when word got back to Kingsley that Group actors were telling friends their production had given distinction to a mediocre play. However the revisions were made, the version of *Men in White* that premiered on September 26 ended on a note of hard-won optimism that expressed both the mood of the 1930s and the Group's own philosophy. It was the same spirit the directors had persuaded Paul Green to instill in *The House of Connelly* and failed to convince John Howard Lawson to provide in *Success Story*.

Unlike those two productions, *Men in White* was a hit from the moment it opened. The play's belief in the spiritual necessity of devotion to the greater good of humanity was very much in tune with the mood of New Deal America, and it struck a responsive chord in audiences and critics alike. The reviews were the best the Group had received since *Connelly*, and they lacked the daunting references to "art" that had made the earlier play a critical success rather than a box-office smash. Joseph Wood Krutch's lengthy analysis in *The Nation* was among the most enthusiastic, but by no means untypical:

To say that [*Men in White*] is by far the best thing which has appeared this season would be praise too faint; even to say that it may very probably remain the year's most satisfying demonstration of what the theatre can do would still not be enough. The thing must, on the contrary, be praised in terms absolute rather than relative. . . . The effectiveness of the production can be credited less to any one element in it than to its remarkable wholeness, to the way in which everything in the acting and direction, as well as in the script itself, works with everything else to produce an unbroken continuity of interest and to leave behind a complete, unified impression. . . . Not since the Theatre Guild *grew* up and the Neighborhood Playhouse *gave* up, has any noncommercial organization so triumphantly justified its existence as the Group Theatre here does.

Krutch touched on two elements that made the Group's production appealing: its brilliant theatricality and the artistic unity of the direction, acting, and scenic design. His fellow reviewers agreed; they were especially taken with the operating-room scene, which *Theatre Arts* called "a joint effect of sight and sound that has seldom been equalled in American group playing." The Group's ensemble performance was lauded to the skies: Joe Bromberg, said several critics, was the finest character actor on the American stage; they judged Billy Kirkland a worthy successor to Franchot Tone; and they respected such established performers as Morris Carnovsky and Luther Adler for their willingness to take small roles. The only sour note (sounded in more than one review) was about the script; hospital drama was almost a cliché in the movies, after all, and Kirkland himself had played a doctor in the recently released film *Humanity*. John Mason Brown spoke for many when he concluded that *Men in White* was "not much of a play . . . fake[d] into life by means of an excellent production." The actors weren't entirely displeased by such comments.

It was frustrating, however, to realize that the critics preferred to see the Group at work in a play they could condescend to rather than one that challenged them, as *Success Story* had. The patronizing tone toward the text of *Men in White* was coupled with an air of distinct satisfaction that the Group had at last given New York a production that was "professional in every meaning of the word," without distressing scenes of mass unemployment or tiresome speeches about the American lust for success. Despite a few provocative lines—a reference to the barbarity of the abortion laws, the suggestion that medicine should be state-controlled—*Men in White* threatened no one very profoundly. It was an excellent piece of traditional playmaking, far more polished than many of the Group's previous efforts but also more conventional.

Few in the Group appreciated the irony of the fact that this relative conventionality contributed to making *Men in White* the organization's first real hit. It began selling out almost immediately. In its first two weeks it broke the Broadhurst's three-year record for box-office receipts. *Variety* noted in early October that the show's weekly gross was $14,500, more than double that of *Success Story* in its best days. Bud Bohnen, who remained a member in good standing even though he was appearing in a commercial production, wrote to his brother in mid-October that the Group's portion of the profits came to about $5,000 a week. (An aside in the letter indicated the kind of comments many members' families must have made in the past:

"Dad was very superior about the Group last winter. He might be interested in the above figures.") Film rights were snapped up by MGM in November for $36,500; the Group's share added another $8,000 to their coffers. For the first time in their history, they were financially secure.

They were also receiving more, and more favorable, press coverage than they had since their first winter. The intense realism of the hospital scenes aroused renewed interest in the Group's technique; a flood of stories breathlessly reported on the actors' visits to hospitals, the three-month preparation of the operating-room scene, the consultations with doctors about accurate medical procedures and equipment. Theatrical journalists found these more superficial aspects of the method easier to grasp than confusing talk about affective memory, and they were better equipped to describe the company's expert ensemble playing in *Men in White* than the intense psychological work in *Connelly*, let alone the complex emotional and intellectual currents underlying *Success Story*.

Strasberg now gained his first real prominence outside the Group. "All the methods and theories of acting technic as practiced by this company have their roots in Strasberg's own philosophy and dramatic convictions," declared the New York *Sun*, revealing to the general public what Group members had known for years. Profiles in several other papers also credited Strasberg as creator of the company's unified technique and respectfully reported his reasons for the lengthy rehearsal period, formerly the subject of amusement among theatre folk.

The Group's way of life attracted at least as much attention as their method. Reporters assigned to interview the stars of *Men in White* quickly discovered that there was no way to get an actor alone backstage at the Broadhurst. A *Herald Tribune* writer looking for Beany Barker had trouble picking her out in the crowd of Group members making themselves comfortable in her dressing room. "I have never been in an atmosphere quite like that of the . . . Group Theatre players," wrote Dorothy Goulet in the *Telegraph*. "It's much more a family affair than anything else." Phoebe Brand, the proposed subject of her story, explained to her that this was indeed the spirit of the Group. The very idea of a star was negated by the organization's policy of listing all members alphabetically on the house boards and taking curtain calls as a company, with no separate bows for the principals. Group programs didn't even include biographies of the actors; it was the play and the ensemble that were important, not individual careers.

When actors could be pried loose from their comrades, the press found them more eager to talk about the Group than their personal history. A Queens reporter who knew Joe Bromberg as a pillar of the Sunnyside community and ardent participant in a local Sunday-night chess game (he'd improved since the days when Tony Kraber and Morris Carnovsky beat him soundly at Brookfield) discovered that beneath the jovial exterior of a well-liked family man beat the heart of a rabid Group enthusiast. It was "a new direction for the theatre and an ideal of co-operation, of collective effort among individuals for the sake of the theatre," Bromberg told the journalist.

The actors now expected the company to be shaped by their opinions as well as the directors'. "It's a swell organization," Billy Kirkland happily commented to a magazine called *Gotham Life.* "We vote on the plays, we actually have something to say." This hadn't been the case to date—the actors certainly hadn't voted on *Men in White*—but it reflected the members' ideals. Even General Lee understood that the evolution of the Group demanded that the directors lead by consensus. "When planning productions and in rehearsal," he remarked to the *Herald Tribune,* "the actors themselves, whether they have leading parts or minor ones, have been consulted as to their views and have been free at any time to offer criticism or suggestions, yet there has been absolutely no lack of harmony, discipline or co-ordination. We think we have discovered a real working basis for play production."

As *Men in White* settled in for a long run, the Group planned for the future. Crawford and Helen Thompson, at least, weren't fooled by their new prosperity into thinking New York had become an easier place to work. They continued with plans to finance a Group season, and possibly a permanent home, in Boston. Thompson set up an office in the Park Square Building and renewed contact with Marguerite Hopkins, the Boston matron Crawford had first approached the previous winter; Hopkins committed herself to the project and set about drumming up wealthy subscribers. Crawford set a minimum goal of 1,000 guarantors to ensure that the Group didn't lose money on the trip, and went several times to Boston to speak with potential supporters; she invoked her Revolutionary War ancestors, buried on Bunker Hill, and spoke passionately of the theatre's responsibility to deal with important social issues. She bought herself some chic new clothes with her *Men in White* salary and brought handsome Billy Kirkland along on one trip to impress the society ladies. The campaign progressed well, and in December the Boston newspapers reported that the Group would bring its current hit to town in the spring and present an entire season in the fall of 1934.

Crawford was very good at this kind of work, which assuaged her feelings of standing somewhat outside the Group's emotional and intellectual center. She disliked the noisy, argumentative meetings at the core of Group life, and indeed they were hard to take for anyone without iron nerves. (Clurman once compared their volatile mix of high-minded idealism and intimate personal complaints to the demented gatherings of the Stavrogin circle in Dostoevsky's novel *The Possessed.*) Crawford found most of the actors' criticisms of the directors unfair, not to mention unproductive and destructive. She had other complaints as well: still frustrated by her partners' willingness to leave in her hands the myriad thankless practical tasks that kept the company running, she worried that this was all they thought she was good for. What she really wanted to do was direct, and she continued her voracious script-reading in hopes of finding a suitable project. If the thought crossed her mind that Strasberg and Clurman felt free to dump the Group's dirty jobs in her lap because she was a woman, she kept it to herself.

Meanwhile, she and Thompson worked to solidify the Group's audience base in New York. Crawford sent the actors out on the usual round of luncheons, drama-club dinners, impromptu lectures, and radio spots. Thompson, taking a lesson from the Yiddish theatre, began to organize benefits, evenings when a social or professional club bought a block of tickets at a discount and sold them to its members at a profit. The theatre traded a small amount of profit for greater security: large batches of a play's tickets were presold, guaranteeing a certain amount of income and a minimum run. *Men in White* didn't need this kind of help, but over the years benefits would keep many floundering Group shows on the boards despite bad reviews. Benefits also built up a sense of attachment to the Group among the diverse organizations which sponsored them, everything from the Socialist party of New York to the New York Ladies' Auxiliary Jewish Consumptive Relief Society.

Group members were thinking once again about their audience that fall. The *Men in White* program included a short article which endeavored to squelch the idea that the company "wished to avoid presenting plays the public wanted." On the contrary, asserted the anonymous author, "this organization was very definitely interested in an audience,—not, however, in a casual here-today-gone-tomorrow audience that visits the theatre when there is nothing better to do; but in an audience sincerely interested in plays that reflect the contemporary human comedy, the passions and problems of our world today." The Group's aim was "to create an audience which will consciously follow its efforts, observe its development, encourage it, enjoy it, and, if need be, criticize it. If the Group Theatre can succeed in creating such an audience it will be doing in the best sense exactly 'what the public wants.' "

The Group held their spectators to as high a standard as they held themselves; they expected passion, commitment, and engagement in the issues their plays raised. It was a noble, slightly crazy ideal; a lot of theatregoers simply wanted, in Clurman's scornful words, "a pastime between supper and bed." But over the years the Group discovered—in fact, helped to create —a new audience whose enthusiasm and dedication matched their own, people previously shut out of the theatre by high ticket prices and subject matter that meant nothing to them. Even the audience for *Men in White*, a solid hit that attracted the conventional, well-heeled Broadway crowd in search of an evening's entertainment, displayed the usual Group demographics: attendance in the orchestra was variable, while the balcony sold out every night. These were the people who stopped the show with their applause for an inflammatory interchange between Kirkland's character and a doctor played by Morris Carnovsky: "Maybe someday the State will take over medicine," Carnovsky suggested, to which Kirkland replied, "Before we let the State take over medicine we'd have to put every politician on the operating table and cut out his acquisitive instincts." It was hardly a revolutionary sentiment, but it wasn't standard Broadway fare either.

Clurman continued to rehearse *Gallery Gods*, but John Houseman was convinced the Group would never produce it. Although the directors periodically announced that the play would be presented on alternating nights with *Men in White* or at a series of special matinees, their partnership with the commercial management of Harmon and Ullman meant they could neither close their hit show nor reduce the number of performances per week to make room for a new production.

Still, it was odd that the Group didn't present *Gallery Gods* at a matinee, especially since they hoped to create an entire program of special performances that season. Even before *Men in White* opened, Crawford told the *Herald Tribune* the Group planned to present the improvisations created at Dover Furnace and refined at Green Mansions in a series of Sunday-evening shows or additional matinees. *Men in White*'s success, and the unprecedented flow of cash it generated, made such a project seem eminently feasible. In December the *Herald Tribune* reported that the Group would inaugurate these experimental matinees, featuring "plays which could never be self-supporting or profitable if presented as commercial ventures," in early 1934. "We feel that such a program is part of the justification of our existence as a dramatic organization," Strasberg commented. Nonetheless, it never happened. Possibly the Group didn't want to do *Gallery Gods* at all (some members had doubts about its effectiveness) and feared they would hurt Clurman by presenting something else instead. Or they may simply have been preoccupied with other projects.

No one in the Group just sat back and enjoyed the financial security provided by *Men in White;* they hurled themselves into a wide variety of activities. Clifford Odets reworked *I Got the Blues*, still hoping to persuade the directors to buy it for the Group. The company had other aspiring writers: Virginia Farmer sold options on two of her plays to outside managements; Grover Burgess wrote short stories in his spare time; Alan Baxter specialized in humorous sketches, one of which turned up the following summer in the popular Broadway revue *Life Begins at 8:40;* and Billy Kirkland continued to work on plays.

Stella Adler looked for intellectual stimulation beyond the theatre and enrolled in courses at the New School. Her friend Bobby Lewis revived his puppeteering skills and put on a marionette show at a Brooklyn department store. Sandy Meisner and Beany Barker, who shared Lewis' interest in heightened theatricality, began an experimental project with several other Group actors to explore the possibilities of stylized production along the lines of the *Twelfth Night* scene they had performed at Dover Furnace. The directors read scripts, searching for a play that wouldn't require too many members of the *Men in White* cast; they still wanted to present a second Group production that season. They also discussed adding new actors to the company, and Strasberg began preparing a class to be given for prospective Group members. Strasberg also spoke with Ralph Steiner, whose film of the Grosz improvisations was shown in December and judged a failure, about doing some experimental film work for their mutual instruction.

They were a disciplined and hardworking band, dedicated to constantly improving their art and themselves through classes, lectures, and experiment. Unfortunately, not every member always lived up to the Group's high ideals. A painful meeting during the run of *Men in White* concerned the ongoing problem of Russell Collins. He had done excellent work for the Group in supporting parts in *Success Story* and *Big Night;* his performance as an incompetent doctor in Kingsley's play won him special notice from Stark Young, who praised him in *The New Republic* as one of the company's most natural, subtle actors. Collins had one big problem: he drank. Not the way their old comrade Franchot Tone had—enthusiastically, but with a sense of restraint when there was work to be done; Collins was an alcoholic, and he later estimated that he was a drunken liability to the Group about 75 percent of the time. The directors had been warned when they hired him, but decided to take a chance on his talent. Much of the time he justified their faith, but one night at the Broadhurst he was so drunk he was unable to go on. The company reluctantly decided to dock his pay, and they worried about what they would do if he didn't shape up, but there was no question of simply dropping him from the organization. When the Group made a commitment to an actor, they stuck by it.

Many Group members were finding revolution, both theatrical and social, far more intoxicating than liquor. They were swept up in the excitement of the radical theatre movement, which was making its first real impact on the mainstream that season. The Theatre Union's triumphant debut seemed to justify Charles Walker's belief that a large American audience was ready and waiting for militant theatre. *Peace on Earth*, the Union's inaugural production, was received coolly by Broadway critics when it opened on November 29 at the old Civic Rep, but the scathing antiwar drama by Albert Maltz and George Sklar (the team the Group had tried unsuccessfully to lure to Dover Furnace) attracted enthusiastic crowds nonetheless. The Union's executive board spearheaded a determined audience campaign, selling blocks of tickets to radical political organizations, trade unions, and social clubs at prices far lower than Helen Thompson could offer Group supporters uptown. (Top price at the Rep before any discount was $1.50, as opposed to $3.00 for *Men in White* on Broadway, and half the seats in the house sold for less than a dollar.)

The Union's second production, *Stevedore*, was virtually review-proof thanks to advance sales guaranteeing six weeks of performances. Even the critics were impressed by the vitality of Paul Peters' and George Sklar's sympathetic portrait of black Americans' struggle for justice. Left-wing activists were even more impressed by the Union's resolute stand against Broadway's de facto segregation. Although New York had no law requiring Negroes to sit in the balcony, at every commercial theatre a black person attempting to buy an orchestra ticket would be told that none was available. The Union seated blacks in the orchestra and refused to sell tickets to white theatregoers who objected. The integrated audiences loved *Stevedore* and its message of interracial working-class solidarity. They responded with a fervor that reminded Group members of the heady days of *1931—*. Pretty soon taxicabs were pulling up in front of the Rep, as bourgeois theatregoers came downtown to see what all the fuss was about.

Politically uncommitted audiences were becoming more receptive to left-wing theatre just as the movement decided to reach out to them. In October *Workers Theatre* changed its name to *New Theatre,* following a summer-long editorial overhaul to make the publication more accessible to noncommunist readers. In January the mimeographed sheet became a printed magazine which covered art theatre, film, dance, even the despised Broadway, from a radical though nonsectarian perspective. The arrival in May 1934 of Herbert Kline, an energetic twenty-five-year-old from Davenport, Iowa, completed the transformation; under his editorship, *New Theatre* urged revolutionary drama groups to pay more attention to human issues and less to dogma. The Workers Laboratory Theatre stood at the forefront of these changes; in November it premiered an innovative new agitprop piece, *Newsboy,* which showed off the company's increasing theatrical and ideological sophistication while making an uncompromising and trenchant criticism of the corrupt triviality of the commercial press.

To the Group's activist members all this seemed much more relevant than *Men in White,* dismissed by the radical press as "expert trivia" and, worse, "merely good Broadway theatre." The fact that the show and Joe Bromberg's performance made almost every critic's Ten Best list at the end of the year merely reinforced their fears that the Group had become too conventional, too much a part of the commercial theatre, while groundbreaking work was being done elsewhere. It was fun to perform the improvisations, many of which made strong social statements, at various outside events; as early as October 1933, the Group participated with the Theatre Collective and the WLT in a Workers Theatre Night, at which Bobby Lewis amused a highly receptive audience with "Red Hamlet." But many of them, particularly those with small parts in *Men in White* and a lot of energy to spare, yearned for more sustained activity.

They got their chance when Sylvia Feningston recruited several Group friends to teach the Stanislavsky system to inexperienced actors enrolled in the Theatre Union's free workshop. Clifford Odets, still smarting over the

Group directors' refusal to produce *I Got the Blues*, threw himself ardently into this work. He was basically instructing the young actors in the affective memory exercises and improvisations that were the foundations of the Group's technique, but he did it with a warmth entirely different from Strasberg's authoritarian attitude. Though no one (except Odets himself) thought he was much of an actor, he proved to be an excellent teacher. Even actors who considered the Group's psychological approach all wrong for a revolutionary theatre like the Union were impressed by his sensitivity, his attention to detail, and his strong emotional commitment to both the Group's method and the Union's radical politics.

In a talk he gave that fall to his students entitled "Toward a New Theatre," Odets emulated Clurman by discussing drama's historical and spiritual origins, arguing that the contemporary theatre's sorry state arose from its lack of "a central and common purpose, a purpose deeply understood and realized by all present." On occasion, he lifted whole phrases and ideas from his friend's speeches and essays. But in the three years since Clurman's first talks, subtle but substantive changes in rhetoric had occurred. Clurman had argued in the intellectual mode of the 1920s, even as he decried the decade's "smartness, cynicism, negativism." Odets expressed the tougher sentiments of artists who had lived through three years of economic depression. "Our theatre's work is undoubtedly the communication of a materialistic sense of life," he said, a remark that would have horrified Clurman in 1930. He discerned "class distinction" among actors, he quoted Vakhtangov's famous assertion that "a theatre is an ideologically cemented collective," he referred to "capitalist theatre" where Clurman had talked of the Broadway show-shop. He spoke, in short, like someone who had recently discovered Marxism and the Communist party.

According to his congressional testimony nearly twenty years later, Odets didn't actually join the party until the fall of 1934. His friend Kazan was recruited by a fellow Group member shortly after *Men in White* opened, and discovered that several other actors already belonged. Because of the ugly situation created by the House Committee on Un-American Activities in the 1950s, when people who refused to answer questions when subpoenaed by the Committee lost their jobs and saw their careers irreparably damaged, many former party members remain reluctant to discuss their involvement in detail. The simple act of naming people who exercised their constitutional right to join an unpopular political party has become fraught with controversy. It's a matter of public record, however, that in his HUAC testimony Kazan identified eight Group actors as members of his Communist party unit: Lewis Leverett and Joe Bromberg, who were co-leaders; Phoebe Brand ("I was instrumental in bringing her into the party," Kazan said); Morris Carnovsky; Tony Kraber, who'd recruited Kazan; Paula Miller;

Odets; and Art Smith. Several other Group members joined after Kazan left the party in 1936.

Long after the Group's demise and the HUAC hearings, two conflicting opinions about the Communist party's influence on the Group arose. Some of the less political Group members—Beany Barker, Cheryl Crawford, Lee Strasberg, Stella Adler—considered the party responsible for creating factions within the Group and undermining the directors' authority, possibly contributing to the company's eventual dissolution. Others, particularly Harold Clurman, argued that the communists in the Group were romantic idealists with only the most rudimentary understanding of politics and that therefore, whatever they may have thought or done at the time, the party's impact on the Group was negligible.

Both views oversimplify a complex issue. Certainly Americans entered— and left—the Communist party far more casually in the 1930s than they had in earlier decades or ever would again. Artists especially, because the party was eager to recruit them in order to reach a larger portion of the American public, were encouraged to believe that becoming a communist wasn't too different from joining any other political party, except that it was more useful and effective. Party discipline was waived to an extent that would have astonished working-class members out on the front lines of the class struggle. Accounts by former communists often include hilarious tales of young writers being assured that they wouldn't have to attend too many boring meetings, of earnest groups getting together once a week to read Marxist pamphlets and discuss such burning issues as why they didn't have clean drinking glasses in their dressing rooms, of an entire cast trooping down to see V. J. Jerome (who supervised the party's cultural activities) to hash out the problem of an actor "reacting all over the place" in a workers theatre production.

It was symptomatic of the relaxed standards of discipline among the party's artistic adherents that the co-leader of the Group's unit—in the 1930s they were called units, not cells—was Lewis Leverett, whose habit of simply disappearing for weeks on end, then turning up without any explanation of where he'd been, was a running gag among his fellow actors. Joining the Communist party as a member of the Group Theatre entailed a dramatically different level of commitment than volunteering to get your head cracked open as a union organizer in Tennessee.

Yet it was a commitment nonetheless. Communists within the Group weren't naïve about how the government, at least, viewed their activities. "In all the meetings that were going on, you knew that there would be an FBI agent or a provocateur," said Phoebe Brand. They also knew and accepted the fact that the party had a vested interest in shaping the message that sympathetic cultural organizations sent to the general public. Debates within the Group on the content of their plays and the structure of the organization were unquestionably influenced by discussions held within the

CP unit. It wasn't only communists who felt that *Men in White* was sorely lacking in social commentary and that actors deserved to have a greater voice in Group policy, but they were among the most vocal in expressing those opinions and they may very well have swayed less committed friends in their direction. Noncommunists who performed at radical benefits, marched in May Day Parades, taught at the Union and the Theatre Collective were impressed by the certainty and resolve of people with a well-defined political credo. "There was a certain kind of professionalism," remarked Odets, explaining why he assumed that a "quick, smart girl" he met must havë been a communist.

The discipline and solid organizing capabilities of party members won them a respected place at the left end of a broad consensus of progressive opinion that encompassed everyone who believed fascism overseas must be fought, hungry people in America must be fed, workers had a right to trade-union representation, and black people deserved equal treatment. Few people were utterly apolitical in the 1930s, certainly not in the Group: Strasberg considered himself a socialist, he and Crawford were both on the advisory board of the Theatre Collective, Stella Adler took courses on Marxism at the CP-run Worker's School, her brother, Luther, devoted considerable time and ingenuity to saving *New Theatre* from its periodic financial crises. The Popular Front as a real expression of shared basic values existed years before it was adopted by the Communist International as a tactical move. No one in the Group's unit believed that his or her membership in the party was contrary to the Group's best interests—when Kazan decided it was, he quit—and whatever other Group actors concluded in hindsight, at the time they saw no conflict either. The discipline the Communist party imposed was not so different from the commitment the Group demanded: subjugation of the ego to the collective will, hard work and financial sacrifice in service of a greater goal, whether it was a classless society or a serious American theatre. To want both at once didn't seem contradictory at the time.

No one expressed the Group's twin desires for mainstream success and radical credibility more clearly than Harold Clurman. Though never a communist, Clurman would have made a good party official; he combined a genuine intellectual enthusiasm for Marxist ideas with a streak of cynicism that enabled him to maneuver without undue regard for consistency. He thought nothing of criticizing *Men in White* publicly as "not distinguished by any particular social comment or definite intellectual value" and then, a scant three weeks later, writing privately to Paul Strand that the production was a necessary compromise with the uncultured Broadway environment because "only by such compromise can we attain the ends we have set ourselves." The importance of *Men in White*, he wrote in the *Daily Worker*, was that it showcased the Group's technique in a popular play. "We hope that the Group Theatre, having found a modicùm of recognition for its methods, advances toward an increasingly important employment of them."

Clurman's remarks were published under a pseudonym, which was probably why he felt so free to criticize a production by his own company. During the 1933–1934 season he wrote a regular drama column in the *Daily Worker*, using his middle name to form the by-line Harold Edgar. It was part of his effort to find an artistic outlet outside the Group; neither the rehearsals of *Gallery Gods* nor the perpetual playreading chores he shared with Crawford fully satisfied him. "All I fret about is that I have so much more to give than I seem to get the opportunity to give," he wrote to Strand. He thought about going to Moscow "to freshen my eyes and heart." He looked ahead two years, when he expected the Group to be firmly established, and planned to found a cultural magazine "written from a Group standpoint—which is a really creative, critical, seeking, profoundly and solidly communist and revolutionary point of view (without narrow communist sectarianism and dogmatism and without liberal vagueness or meaningless tolerance)." This casual aside, assuming the Marxist sympathies of any thoughtful person, said much about the contemporary intellectual climate.

"I know I could run such a magazine," he told Strand. "I feel in me creative talents of a type peculiar in that they are not of the routine critic who wants to be only a critic, or the theatre director who wants only to be that . . . but rather the leader who gets things started and set and *working* —and sees that they continue along certain lines without deviation and without false 'idealism.' " For the moment, Clurman seemed to have accepted the view generally held within the Group that he was an inspirer rather than a hands-on director like Strasberg. He tried to convince himself that this was what he wanted, but the depressed tone of his letter indicated he hadn't been entirely successful. Other than his reconciliation with Stella Adler, he found little to be cheerful about in his life and work.

He was sustained in this difficult period by his active theatregoing and his reports on it in the *Daily Worker*, which reveal a great deal about the complex relationship between Clurman's theatrical and political views. Immediately obvious was his detestation of Broadway. "What indifference of feeling, what emptiness of ideas, what lack of true personality are betrayed here," he wrote. "The whole set-up of the Broadway theatre leads inevitably to artistic sterility and death."

Clurman believed, as he always had, that "there is no creative way in the theatre except the collective way." Only a year earlier he had seen the Group as a lonely island of collectivity in a sea of hostile commercialism; now he saw workers theatres as welcome new exponents of the communal ideal. They brought a desperately needed "sense of joy, of youthful vigor, of fresh enthusiasm, of confidence" to the theatre, and Clurman reviewed productions by Artef, the Workers Laboratory Theatre, and other radical groups with sympathy and enthusiasm. He was not uncritical, however: he deplored their tendency to rely on slogans and noted the technical incompetence of many productions. He urged these young companies to develop better technique, which would make their plays' crude caricatures more human, and more polished presentations, not an imitation of the bourgeois theatre's empty slickness but an organic style growing naturally out of their structure and goals.

There was no question that Clurman shared the workers theatres' political sentiments. His columns were filled with matter-of-fact references to "Marxist objectivity," "our cause," and "workers' splendor," and on occasion he expressed his opinions at greater length. "Today the choice is clear," he wrote in an unfavorable review of *Ah, Wilderness!* which made slighting reference to O'Neill's residences in a French chateau and a Georgia mansion. "Either one sinks into a suicidal despair or one goes forward toward the revolution as envisaged by Marx and Lenin." Such a comment would have been inconceivable to Clurman as recently as 1930; in 1933 he didn't bat an eyelash over it. Looking around at the suffering caused by the Depression, many people found it easy to believe not only that capitalism was doomed, but that it deserved to die, that something much better would replace it. They were wrong—capitalism proved hardier than anyone imagined—but American culture in the thirties gained much of its fire and passion from their belief.

In the end, it was that passion that was really important to Clurman. Deeply concerned with the human response that theatre generated, he contrasted the passivity of Broadway spectators with the enthusiasm of radical audiences to underscore the difference between a moribund theatre and one that offered hope for the future. "Their whole idea of art is something that 'moves' you without disturbing you," he wrote of the Theatre Guild's subscribers. "They do not want to be involved: they prefer to sit contemplatively in their seats and regard the spectacle solely as a 'show.' Such an attitude, of course, has practically nothing to do with art." Downtown, at the League of Workers Theatres' annual competition, he heard "applause and cheers of . . . the abandoned kind one never hears on Broadway and which make the workers theatre when its efforts 'click' a truly complete theatre." The Group had sparked that kind of exciting communion before; he knew they would do it again.

Yet Clurman remained cool to a play that within a year brought Group actors and their audience together with a thrill of recognition that would enduringly shape the company's destiny. Clifford Odets had been rewriting *I Got the Blues* all fall, and in December he brought the new draft to the directors once again, begging them to show their faith in him by promising to give it a Group production. He had been offered an option by another management—ironically, it was the partnership set up by Bess Eitingon after Strasberg rejected her $50,000—and he threatened to take it there if the directors turned him down. After an angry scene in which they did just that, he stormed out and sold it to the firm of Merlin, Eitingon and Simon for $500.

It was more money than Odets had ever seen at one time, and if it couldn't quite soothe his injured feelings it gave him the chance to go on an eccentric shopping spree. He bought one bottle each of every kind of booze in a local liquor store. He purchased a Victrola so he could listen to his beloved Beethoven at home. He moved his new belongings into a tiny apartment on Horatio Street, giving Strasberg and Paula Miller some time alone after his ten-month stay with them. He began serious work on the new "de-Jewished" family play he called *Paradise Lost*. Even though he was furious with the directors, in his working notebook he listed Group actors next to each name in the list of characters. He created his plays with their performances in mind, and the brief "spine" he wrote outlining each character's basic motivation showed how strongly his ideas about drama had been shaped by the Group's interpretation of the Stanislavsky system. The other major influence on his thinking at the time could be seen in the clippings from the *Daily Worker* and quotations from Lenin he pasted into the notebook.

Recovering from several painful love affairs the previous year, Odets acquired a young girlfriend, a seventeen-year-old he met at a National Student League party where Bobby Lewis was performing his popular "Red Hamlet" and "I Sing the Body Electric" pieces. They had a tempestuous relationship, but there were happy evenings when they listened to records and had dinner together, often inviting Joe and Goldie Bromberg, or Odets' new friend Jules Garfield, to join them.

Julie, as everyone called him, had taken Odets' class at the Theatre Union while he was appearing in *Peace on Earth*. Born Julius Garfinkle in 1913, raised on one of the Lower East Side's tougher blocks, the boy began to get into trouble after his mother died when he was seven. His father, a presser in a factory, was eager to get him out of an environment in which playing hooky, stealing, and running away from home were the accepted pastimes. He sent Julie to P.S. 45 in the Bronx; the school's principal, Angelo Patri, had a reputation for dealing compassionately and creatively with troubled kids. Sensitive and affectionate under his street-smart swagger, the boy blossomed in this sympathetic environment. He excelled in the school drama program and at the age of fourteen won a prize for oratory. In 1930 he dropped out of high school, with Patri's blessing and a thirty-dollar loan, to study acting. The following season he was an apprentice at the Civic Rep, but after a year there he felt the spirit of the times urging him to learn more about real life. He hitchhiked through the United States and Mexico, working as a wheatfield harvester, a fruit picker, a waiter, and a firefighter before coming back East to land a small part in the Chicago company of Elmer Rice's *Counsellor-at-Law*. His work impressed the producers enough to get him transferred to the New York company, and he played the same role in a lengthy tour with the original star, Paul Muni.

Odets was drawn to Garfield by his candor, his zest for work, and an ardor for learning and personal growth the two young men shared. His acting also excited the playwright, who found himself thinking of the youthful intensity Garfield could bring to the part of Ralph in *I Got the Blues*. He seemed like natural Group material, and Odets sent him up to meet the directors. They were struck by his charm and his smoldering good looks, but they weren't ready to accept new members just then. They told Garfield to keep in touch.

By January, *Men in White* looked as though it would run forever—sometimes the actors felt it already had. Their first long run challenged them to keep their performances fresh, to avoid mechanically repeating themselves night after night until they ended up giving imitations of their original interpretations. Theoretically, doing an affective memory exercise would summon up the true emotion that made each performance real, but the effect of the exercises tended to lessen over time. "[It] gets worn out," Morris Carnovsky found. "It's almost as if you tread the same road again and again until the net result is zero." They tried to keep themselves alert and creative by using improvisation: sometimes people slightly revised their lines so the actors playing with them had to respond naturally instead of waiting for the usual cue. Bobby Lewis, whose comic character burst into song in one scene, tried out different ditties. Joe Bromberg and Billy Kirkland, with the biggest roles, had as many as a dozen variations to play in their scenes: changes in blocking, or the pitch of their voices, or slightly different attitudes.

It didn't help enough. Several actors, frustrated and bored by the long run, held secret meetings to discuss the possibility of breaking away to form "a more vital theatre." Nothing came of these meetings, but they were a sign that the actors expected more from the Group than a steady paycheck. They wanted continuous stimulation and activity, and if the directors didn't provide it, they would go looking for it themselves.

Men in White got an additional shot of new life when the smaller parts were shuffled to allow Carnovsky, Lewis Leverett, and Russell Collins to join the cast of *Gentlewoman*, the new play by John Howard Lawson the Group had decided on as their second production. It had been optioned by the Guild, but the proposed star wanted Lawson to revise the last scene and make it less pessimistic, which he was unwilling to do. When the Group came up with full financing, courtesy of a Hollywood producer named D. A. Doran who wanted to break into the theatre, Lawson agreed to let them do it.

Gentlewoman is a confused play that says a great deal about its author's troubled state of mind at the time it was written. Ostensibly it tells the story of a love affair between a wealthy woman and a bohemian writer with radical tendencies, but it is really an examination of the nature of personal and political commitment. Gwyn Ballantine finds her sheltered, aristocratic world empty, its bankruptcy shockingly demonstrated by the news of her husband's suicide in the first act. Rudy Flannigan attracts her as a representative of a bolder, freer life outside her drawing room; he is drawn to her sensitivity and cultivation, qualities created by the social privileges he despises. As Lawson saw it, their affair is doomed because it is false: "their dependence on each other prevented them from being truly themselves." The downbeat ending, in which the lovers separate—he to ally himself with "people who work and fight hunger and death," she to bear his child and hope for a better world to come—was essential to Lawson, because "it was the end of my life as a frustrated middle class rebel seeking romantic solutions." Unfortunately, in the context of the play their parting seems more the result of Rudy's philandering than of any spiritual imperative, and Gwyn's apocalyptic final speech, in which she sees "cities burning and marching armies . . . blood in the sky," comes out of nowhere.

Muddled though it was, *Gentlewoman* drew considerable emotional power from Lawson's anguished personal search for a meaningful form of action. It expressed the painful confusion of middle-class leftists, dissatisfied with the comfortable, cultivated environment they had grown up in, yet frightened and uncertain of their place in a harsh new world that seemed to be divided between workers and capitalists—neither of which they were, though many Marxist intellectuals made valiant attempts to define themselves as "brain workers," the natural allies of the "muscle workers." (*New Theatre*, when writing of actors, directors, or designers, rejected the term "artist" in favor of the more class-conscious "theatre worker.") Rudy was in part a Lawson self-portrait, especially when he voiced sentiments like those of the last act: "Books are all right if you can make 'em spit fire and lead . . . I don't want to sail over the battle on a pink cloud pounding a typewriter." These were also the sentiments of many Group members, fearful lest the revolution happen somewhere else while they were marking time in a Broadway hit.

The production prompted bad feelings within the Group from the moment it was announced in late January. Eunice Stoddard, already disappointed over losing the female lead in *Men in White* to her friend Beany, was very upset when the directors cast Stella Adler as Gwyn. Stoddard thought, rightly, that she was far more suited to the role of a quiet, reticent gentlewoman, but Stella was (in the parlance of the time) Harold's girl, Stella had no part in *Men in White*, Stella was unhappy and uncertain of her faith in the Group, Harold wanted Stella to be happy and remain with the Group; therefore, she would play Gwyn. Stoddard, an up-and-coming ingénue when she joined the Group, was one of the actors who suffered the most from being relegated to small parts. "You went in there for the purpose of acting, and unless you were given opportunities to really act something, it tore people apart." She wasn't the only one to feel that certain favored members of the company got an unfair number of the best roles.

A less personal, more general question of principle was raised by the casting of Rudy. Billy Kirkland was originally slated for the part, but a brief newspaper announcement resulted in the Broadhurst box office being swamped with protesting phone calls; the directors decided to leave him where he was. Then they looked outside the Group for a replacement. One actor under contract to a movie studio was ordered back to Hollywood on the threat of a lawsuit if he didn't comply. Another was a bit shorter than the statuesque Stella Adler; the disparity in height emphasized her commanding stage presence, which wasn't appropriate for Gwyn. They reluctantly settled on Walter Coy, a Group stalwart who'd had no parts at all the previous season and whose only featured role had been the good son in the short-lived *Night over Taos*. When non-Group actor Lloyd Nolan became available, however, the directors cast him and assigned Coy to serve as his understudy.

The directors chose Nolan in part because they were considering him for Group membership. In fact, they'd asked him to join the company as the lead in *Men in White* the previous spring, but he'd just made a hit in a play called *One Sunday Afternoon*, was weighing movie offers, and decided against it. Clurman considered Nolan "of great potential value" to the Group and hoped that through *Gentlewoman* they could attach him to the company permanently.

All fall the directors had been talking of adding new actors. The success of *Men in White* had hampered their efforts to do a second production and encouraged them to believe they could afford to support more people. Clurman in particular thought it would be good for the Group; they were, he feared, growing too clannish. The actors didn't see it quite that way. "The whole idea of the Group was to use your own people," said Stoddard. It was one thing to cast nonmembers in small parts because they needed a few extra actors, quite another to give outsiders like Nolan, Claudia Morgan, and Zamah Cunningham substantive roles in *Gentlewoman* that could perfectly well have been played by people who had struggled and starved with the Group for three years. (When the program for the show included biographies of the performers, which the Group had always disdained, it struck the membership as an additional betrayal of principle.) Perhaps they should have been more receptive to the idea of bringing new acolytes into the Group fold, but the fact that so many members felt underutilized made it understandable that they didn't.

Rehearsals of *Gentlewoman* thus began under a cloud, although Bud Bohnen was happy to be back with the Group after a lean season in the commercial theatre. The cast had difficulty understanding the script, and Lawson was only intermittently available to answer their questions, as he was also in rehearsal at the Guild, which had decided to give *The Pure in*

Heart another try. Though Clurman was close to Lawson, indeed had "practically collaborated" on *The Pure in Heart*, Strasberg again directed the Group production. *Gentlewoman* posed real problems of form for him, as Lawson had deliberately written what appeared on the surface to be a conventional drawing-room drama, examining the characters within that context and showing their development "to a point where they [could] no longer live within this shell of sentiment and sex." Strasberg agreed with Clurman and Crawford that the play required a more sophisticated style than some of the Group's previous work, but a light touch wasn't his leading quality as a director.

He had a hard time with the non-Group actors, who weren't used to the extensive improvisations and affective memory exercises that were the cornerstones of Strasberg's method. Lloyd Nolan was willing to learn, and he gave a good-natured interview to the *Brooklyn Eagle* discounting Broadway's jeering stories about Group actors wrestling with "beautiful thoughts" during rehearsals. "It seems to me that the interval [Nolan's term for taking an exercise] is a very common sense thing," he remarked, adding that improvisation "gives the actor the opportunity to develop the part in all its aspects." But Clurman felt, observing rehearsals, that Nolan was confused by the play and in consequence tended to emphasize Rudy's drunken, boorish side, which made the love affair unappealing to audiences and the underlying social themes even more unclear.

Strasberg's major problem, however, was with Stella Adler. As he had during rehearsals of *Success Story*, he battled to subdue what he caustically described as her "Jewish emotionalism" to the demands of the part. In a particularly tense moment, he threatened to kill her if she let herself cry. Strasberg was correct in his analysis that Gwyn wasn't the sort of woman who wept or displayed her feelings openly, but he didn't succeed in giving Adler a coherent attitude to play instead. She was miserable. She worked hard and invested her performance with carefully worked out gestures and speech rhythms designed to illuminate Gwyn's personality, but she remained unable to feel any real connection with the character. Her bitter dissatisfaction with her work and Strasberg's direction brought to a crisis Adler's long-standing doubts about the method; when she met Stanislavsky in Paris the following summer, she told him his system had made her hate acting. Lawson, who admired Adler as an actress, felt that not only was she all wrong for Gwyn, but the method made her worse: "In trying to immerse herself in the part through such devices as affective memory, she gave Gwyn a 'soul' and made her love for Rudy pitiably sincere, and thus eliminated the basic reason for their separation, their inability to love."

In fairness to Adler and Strasberg, it should be noted that this conclusion was hardly obvious from the script. If the director and cast were puzzled by but sympathetic to Lawson's rather incoherent drama, the critics were irritated by it. Their annoyance may have been compounded by the fact that they had to review two plays by Lawson in one week: *The Pure in Heart* opened March 20, *Gentlewoman* followed on March 22, and the press liked neither. Some of them ignored Lawson's social concerns in *Gentlewoman* altogether; Joseph Wood Krutch sneered that Adler's character "comes straight out of one of those novels which teach nursemaids to pity the broken-hearted aristocracy." Others found the relationship between the love affair and what they regarded as Lawson's "Red" concluding speeches unclear and unconvincing. The critics divided about fifty-fifty on whether Stella Adler was miscast or not: quite a few praised her intelligence and attention to detail in the role, and even those who found her mannered and ill at ease went out of their way to mention how good her work had been in the past. The rest of the actors received similarly mixed notices, though several critics agreed with Clurman that Nolan was unnecessarily brutish as Rudy. Strasberg's direction was mildly commended. It was the play and Lawson himself that drew the reviewers' fire: they found *Gentlewoman* talky, muddled, and dull; they disliked Lawson's politics almost as much as they deplored his contempt for the rules of good stagecraft.

Lawson wrote to several critics protesting that their reviews misrepresented the play and expressed a personal dislike of him more than an objective criticism of the script's faults. He was particularly angry about their comments on the ending. "You may disagree with the thesis of the final act of *Gentlewoman*," he wrote, "the thesis that these people find a new balance and reason for their lives in Communism. You may not like this conclusion; you may regard it as absurd, subversive, or ridiculous. But I don't see how you can call it indefinite."

Unfortunately for Lawson, his political allies on the left considered the play even more indefinite than did the Broadway reviewers, and criticized it much more harshly. The most sustained assault came in the *New Masses*, which wasn't deterred by the fact that Lawson was on the magazine's editorial board. Under the headline "A Bourgeois Hamlet of Our Times," Michael Gold wrote, "Lawson has once again taken what might have been a revolutionary theme and botched it dreadfully. He has again projected his own confused mind on the screen of history, and tried to convince an audience that it was the face of 'Revolution.'" He found Lawson a "bewildered wanderer" filled with the "adolescent self-pity" typical of the fellow traveler who hadn't made a firm commitment to communism. Lawson would never be a great writer, Gold argued, until he "found out what he actually believes. Yes, to be a great artist one must greatly believe in something." He also took a moment to slap down the Group for their bourgeois tendencies. "This is its second play of the season with as 'boxoffice' an intent as anything ever thrown together by Al Woods. What has become of all those tremendous manifestos with which it promised us to change the American theatre?"

Clurman, who'd already had a few run-ins with the *Daily Worker* over the question of revolutionary discipline, was appalled at the meekness of his friend's response to left-wing criticism. Not only did Lawson write a reply in which he "unhesitatingly admit[ted] the truth of 70% of Mike's attack" and said that he was a fellow traveler because "I have not demonstrated my ability to serve the revolutionary working class either in my writing or in practical activity," he was just as apologetic in person. At a meeting of the John Reed Club where Lawson spoke on "Fellow Travelers and Marxian Criticism," Clurman watched with shock and anger as speaker after speaker from the floor assailed the playwright for his lack of ideological clarity while Lawson listened politely, hoping for guidance as to how he could become a better artist and human being. Such criticism sessions were among the less attractive aspects of left-wing cultural life in the thirties, but what really upset Clurman was Lawson's failure to stand up for himself: "I could not bear to see him refuse to defend the qualities [his plays] had, rare and valuable qualities which his critics spoke of patronizingly as if they were common and easily come by."

Clurman's first commitment was always to art, and he was disenchanted by this glimpse of political criticism. He wrote only two more columns for the *Daily Worker* after *Gentlewoman* opened, and although he continued to express strongly radical opinions in private for a few more years he slowly returned to his habitual stance as a keenly interested observer of society with no specific political allegiance. He asserted his faith in Lawson by advancing the playwright $1,000 as an option on his next two scripts; on April 7 the Group announced that the first of these, *Marching Song*, would be their initial fall production.

Gentlewoman closed March 31, a week after *The Pure in Heart;* more than thirty years later, Lawson still found the memory of this double debacle so painful he could hardly bring himself to write about it. He fled to Alabama to cover a bitter local strike and the repercussions of the controversial Scottsboro rape trial of nine young black men; he discovered an atmosphere of terror and intimidation so total he feared America might be going the way of Germany under Hitler. In the face of these real-life struggles, his personal doubts seemed less important. He finally joined the Communist party in the latter half of 1934. The Group would wait two more years for him to deliver *Marching Song*.

The directors had made a half-hearted attempt to keep *Gentlewoman* running by asking the cast to take salary cuts. For the first time in the Group's history, they balked: one actor explained he was dissatisfied with Strasberg's direction, several criticized the play's confusion, others complained about the hiring of non-Group actors. They may have wondered why the production couldn't be subsidized with some of the *Men in White* profits rather than out of their pockets. "Every year around this time the Group gets troubled in spirit," Clurman wrote to Paul Strand. "The actors grow restive. . . . The Group doesn't please them anymore. 'Rebellion' is in the air."

Clurman was wrong to believe the actors were simply having an attack of ideological spring fever; they were acting on their new sense that they too should help shape Group policy. Actors outside the Group were also asserting themselves that spring, and several Group members were closely involved in the effort to make their union, Actors Equity, more responsive to the grass roots. Equity had alienated many of its members in early March, when it declined to take part in the controversy over a comedy called *Sailor, Beware!* Although the show was a hit, the producer asked the cast to take a 30 percent salary cut; convinced the production was making money, they refused. He then fired the three actors who had spearheaded the protest, and the entire company resigned on March 5. When they took their case to Equity, the union told them a manager could fire anyone he liked so long as he gave them two weeks' notice. This wasn't good enough for the aroused actors, who used the support of other Broadway companies, including the cast of *Men in White,* to force the producer to rehire them and promise to ask for salary cuts only when the show's gross dropped below $8,000 a week.

Their victory only made them angrier at Equity, and an open meeting was held March 19 to consider how to get better representation on the Equity Council, which ran the union. Bobby Lewis, Virginia Farmer, and Bud Bohnen were the most outspoken Group members to attend; they and several others argued that the union's rules should be revised to require more general membership meetings, a more democratic nominating procedure for the Council, and greater membership input into Equity bylaws. The rebels came up with an independent slate for the forthcoming Council elections, and at the annual Equity meeting on March 23 they shouted down a representative of the union leadership who tried to dismiss them as troublemaking Reds. Equity president Frank Gilmore was furious, but he couldn't prevent the nominating committee from including four of the dissidents on its slate. (Three were ultimately elected.) The Council grudgingly agreed to three additional meetings per year and made it slightly easier for the membership to amend the bylaws, but that was as far as they would go to conciliate "the so-called 'young group.' " Equity's intransigence would provoke renewed revolt the following year, but for now the actors were satisfied to have saved the *Sailor, Beware!* company's jobs and gained the council's approval for some of their demands.

Group actors had been asked to confer on the structure of their own organization earlier that spring, when they gathered on the Broadhurst stage after a performance of *Men in White* to discuss Max Gorelik's position in the company and his complaints about the way it was run. Gorelik began by arguing that because of his long association *(Gentlewoman* was his fifth set for them) and general sympathy with the Group he deserved to be made a full member. The actors had no problem with that, and though the directors didn't much care for the idea—Gorelik might be their favorite designer, but his perennial griping made him less than their favorite human being—

they raised no specific objections. The actors promptly voted to upgrade him from associate to member.

But Gorelik had other things on his mind as well. He voiced a number of complaints the actors had been making privately: that salaries were decided arbitrarily, that some favored actors got better parts, that the actors as a body were shut out of the Group decision-making process. He went considerably further than any of them had by demanding to see the organization's account books, a request Clurman angrily rejected. The meeting was loud and acrimonious, with the actors caught in the middle between the insurgent designer and the outraged directors. They affirmed their faith in their leaders, but justified it by stating that the Group was essentially democratic. Art Smith offered a rather threatening example when he pointed out that he could "go over and punch Harold in the nose, and not be fired for it." It was clear, under their protestations of support for the directors, that many of the actors agreed at least in part with Gorelik's criticisms.

Many of these points were raised again in early April when the Group met to read *Gold Eagle Guy*, the play Crawford and Strasberg had commissioned from Melvin Levy the previous spring. Levy's drama chronicles the rise of Guy Button, a ruthless shipping magnate in booming nineteenth-century San Francisco. The script he handed in to the Group was highly episodic, with the story taking place over a period of more than forty years, and, despite a huge cast, the only fully developed character was the title role. Some actors were troubled by what they thought was Levy's romantic attitude toward his protagonist—a capitalist exploiter, after all—and his insufficient criticism of the society that permitted such a person to thrive. More fundamentally, they viewed the directors' choice of a historical drama as a regrettable lapse from the Group's stated goal of examining in the theatre the vital issues of their day.

The directors were distressed by the actors' comments. Crawford had spent a lot of time working with Levy on the script, and she was hurt that the company didn't like it better. Strasberg, who thought Clurman was often overly critical of scripts, worried that the actors had picked up his nit-picking tendencies. Clurman worried about the Group's state of mind in general and wanted to discuss the matter with the entire company before individual vacations took people out of town. Strasberg and Paula Miller had casually legalized their union in mid-March; as a combined wedding present and thanks for his work on *Men in White*, Sidney Kingsley was taking the director to Moscow, and they were scheduled to depart April 11. Stella Adler was also going abroad; she planned to join Strasberg in Russia after visiting London, Paris, Vienna, and Warsaw. Before they left, Clurman presented a forty-two-page paper analyzing the Group's problems that took him over an hour to read.

The actual text of the paper has apparently been lost, and Clurman's highly selective account of its contents, written ten years later, made no mention of how he addressed such touchy subjects as salaries and casting. Nor did he say what he thought about the idea that the actors should have a voice in running the Group, although the directors' attitude could be discerned in a letter they sent Max Gorelik in late July revoking the membership the actors had bestowed on the grounds that only people who had faith in the authority of the directors could be part of the Group. Gorelik was furious; he didn't design for them again for three years.

Clurman did recap at some length his response to actors who argued that the Group's play selections were too conservative: "I pointed out that our aim was not and never had been to become a political theatre, but to be a creative and truly representative American theatre. . . . just as we had done the first depression play in *1931*—not from any political bias but from a sense of what was going on in our day, so in the future we would do more socially conscious plays than any other theatre then functioning." He pleaded for time, reminding the Group of Gordon Craig's assertion that "it takes ten years to build a real theatre." A letter to Paul Strand broadly outlined his talk: he had summarized the Group's achievements to date, he wrote, affirmed his belief in their work, and called for "strict discipline in the ranks" to ensure their future. "The paper did its work," he added optimistically. "All is quiet again!"

If so, it wasn't quiet for long. Clurman hadn't initially intended to go to Moscow—Crawford thought the Group needed him in New York—but he changed his mind in May. The strain of the previous year had taken its toll on his health; he was in such a nervous state that his father finally insisted on examining him and discovered that he had an occasional extra heartbeat. Dr. Clurman urged his son to take a vacation and get some rest; though not every Group member would have considered a visit with Stella Adler restful, Clurman decided to meet her in Moscow and see the Soviet theatre for himself.

Before he left on May 19, however, he had to endure one more stormy Group meeting. *Men in White* had been running since September, and many of the cast members felt tired and stale. It was clear by early May, when the play surprised everyone by winning the Pulitzer Prize (the Pulitzer committee overrode the drama judges, who had selected Anderson's *Mary of Scotland*), that it would run for another few months. The actors proposed that each member of the company get two weeks' paid vacation, giving them a much-needed respite and showing off the versatility of the Group's actors by putting people with small parts in the leads and adding unemployed members and friends like Bud and Hildur Bohnen to fill out the cast. Clurman objected that the Group treasury couldn't afford such generosity. The actors replied that it could be done by suspending Stella Adler's $200 weekly salary while she was abroad.

Clurman was incensed. Group policy was to pay every actor while any Group production was on the boards, he said, conveniently forgetting that the directors themselves had abrogated this policy the previous season. The actors argued that this was intended to apply to Group members who were in New York and could understudy, work in the office, or otherwise help out if not actually in a cast. Some bitter remarks were passed about Adler's privileged position in the Group, and her brother came under fire as well for general laziness and lack of responsibility. Clurman stood firm; as far as he was concerned, the debate was closed and Adler would continue to receive her salary. But in fact, no sooner had he sailed than the actors persuaded Crawford to stop the Group's payments to her.

Clurman didn't learn this until he arrived in Moscow, but the whole episode left a bad taste in his mouth. "There was a good deal about [that last meeting] that wearied and worried me," he wrote to Crawford. "Not any of the things said or decided so much but evidence of pettiness and 'pride' and small frustration (I mean a kind of combativeness without a point or object: which shows people are wasting a lot of themselves and are capable of hurting others without aim)." He acknowledged that Adler's relationship with the Group was difficult, "but certainly surrounding people with venom or allowing them to give vent to it at will—and finding good reasons for such expression—will not help build the Group—but will end by poisoning all of us."

It had been a long season; everyone was on edge. Clurman's letter indicated that even the normally tight-lipped Crawford had been talking to him about her frustrations. He promised "to see if I can communicate with Lee and make him realize your need" and urged her to take a vacation herself. He sent regards to Dorothy Patten, whose liaison with Crawford was now an established and accepted relationship. "You have been very fine this winter," Clurman told Crawford, "very helpful and sane in all ways and I want you to know that you have my respect and love as ever."

The love he spoke of bound the Group together even in their worst moments. Their troubles and quarrels arose out of their fierce devotion to the company, their desire to do what was best for the Group and the theatre. Under those circumstances, arguments became rude, passionate, and personal; disagreements couldn't be masked by a polite veneer of indifference, for no one was indifferent. Clurman looked forward with relief to a break from collective life, even in the company of Strasberg and Adler.

The rest of the Group relaxed somewhat in the absence of their most problematic member and the leaders whose authority they weren't always inclined to accept. (Crawford remained in New York, but she never asserted herself as strongly as her partners.) Everyone was glad to take a vacation: their trips ran the gamut from Patten's visit to Bermuda to "smell the lilies" to Gadget Kazan's journey through the South to educate himself in the realities of the class struggle. Crawford spent her time reading scripts and trying to find a suitable summer residence where they could prepare *Gold Eagle Guy*. In the days before air conditioning, even the biggest Broadway hits usually succumbed to the New York heat by July or early August, so the Group planned to delay rather than cancel their customary country sojourn.

In the meantime, they weren't idle. The radical theatre continued to benefit from their energies. The first "New Theatre Night," a benefit performance to raise funds for the perennially broke *New Theatre* magazine, took place on May 20; 1,400 left-minded theatregoers packed the Civic Rep, while 500 more were turned away. Bobby Lewis and Tony Kraber joined a bill that included the Theatre Collective doing a scene from *Marion Models*, the WLT Shock Troupe performing *Newsboy*, and a group of black singers from *Stevedore*. Lewis and Kraber, who were billed as offering satirical sketches and songs, probably dusted off their Dover Furnace work: Lewis as "Red Hamlet" or Herbert Hoover, Kraber doing his cowboy songs. Or they may have debuted a piece that would become a Group benefit staple, a farcical operation in which a pair of doctors operated on a mysterious patient, extracting all kinds of odd items from the body before discovering that it had no heart. The patient turned out to be Hitler.

A second New Theatre Night in June featured the premiere of a one-act drama written by Kazan and Art Smith, performed by Group actors. *Dmitroff: A Play of Mass Pressure* dealt with the trial of communists accused of setting the Reichstag fire that swept the Nazis into power in 1933. Joe Bromberg played Dmitroff, the Bulgarian communist who was the first to accuse Hitler's followers of setting the fire themselves. The sympathetic *New Theatre* reviewer acknowledged that the play was woefully underrehearsed, but praised it as the Group's "first concerted and sustained effort at revolutionary production." In fact, it marked another step in the evolution of American agitprop, going even further than *Newsboy* in telling a human story with individual, though hardly subtle characters while retaining the pointed political commentary and dramatic structure (a succession of short, swift scenes) that gave the form its power. Nothing could have been more different from the deliberate, meticulous pace of a Strasberg production, where every pause was impregnated with meaning: it was the difference between political and psychological intensity. Group actors learned from the contrast, as the company's later productions showed.

They were exploring other questions of style independent of the directors. Since the Group couldn't go away to the country until August, they decided to begin the traditional summer program of intensive training and experiment in the basement of the Broadhurst Theatre. The First Studio, as it was unofficially dubbed, opened its doors in late May; the company accepted twelve apprentices, including Odets' friend Julie Garfield, to work with the regular members in four separate workshops directed by Group actors. Each workshop, explained an article on the Studio in the *New York Times*, "represent[s] a different phase of theatre activity and each work[s] toward an ideal which the Group has not yet been able to develop."

The team of Smith and Kazan ran a unit designed to develop new play-wrights, the Group's most desperate need. Taking their cue from the work-ers theatres, whose scripts were improvised on the basis of a political point to be made, they encouraged aspiring dramatists to create collectively: a playwright presented a scenario and discussed its ideas with the actors, who then improvised characters and scenes; the playwright noted which dialogue or situations seemed to work and went off to write the script; further improvisations could help in revisions. The idea was to get play-wrights out of their studies and expose them to the realities of living theatre, both to give them the benefit of working out their ideas in actual production and to encourage them to write with those realities in mind.

Sandy Meisner worked on a production of *Noah*, a play by the French dramatist André Obey that called for a fantastic, extravagant production style. He used rehearsals to explore the possibilities of Obey's drama and to broaden the Group's acting range. Meisner, strongly seconded by Beany Barker, hoped to create a stylized acting technique that could be used to tackle plays outside the tradition of conventional realism.

Bobby Lewis also wanted Group actors to grow beyond realism, but he believed a heightened formal style could be just as appropriate for contem-porary social drama. He took an uncompleted play about coal miners, *In New Kentucky* by Samuel Ornitz, and used various striking vocal effects to create a vivid theatrical presentation that was more like a choral work than a straight play. In one inspired moment, a train was heard approaching: "I got my actors offstage to repeat the phrase 'somebody said so' over and over, starting low and building to a climax, then fading away. By dividing my voices into sections that overlapped each other and then adding in some clacking sounds, I was able to create an imaginative reproduction of a train passing." When Strasberg saw a run-through after he returned from Russia in late June, he praised it as the equal of anything he had seen at the Vakhtangov Theatre. Lewis also gave individual instruction to some of the apprentices; he was particularly struck by Julie Garfield's creative response to an exercise he assigned based on a Picasso painting.

Morris Carnovsky conducted the fourth workshop. Its purpose, the *Times* reported, was "a fresh interpretation of Shakespeare and a general attempt to restore the values of poetic reading in the theatre." Carnovsky had nurtured a profound love of verse ever since his days at Washington University, where he read Shakespeare and the Latin poets and "dreamed of a life compounded of poetry and theatre." Indeed, his courtly personal style seemed a throwback to a more gracious age, though he saw no contra-diction between gentlemanly behavior and his equally strong interest in the political issues of the day. For him, Shakespeare was the consummate dra-matic artist, a passionate participant in the eternal social and philosophical questions, whose plays had been turned into dreary costume parades by generations of superficial acting. He worked on scenes from *Hamlet*, *Mac-*

beth, and *The Merry Wives of Windsor,* urging the actors to discover "the meaning of every line, the values of the words not only as they applied in their own time, but as they may still have excitement for us today."

Experimentation, exploration, hard work, artistic growth—these had been the bywords of the Group from the beginning. The directors had chosen a company of naturally serious actors; for three years they'd studied together to deepen and broaden their capabilities in professional production and in classroom exercises. The dignity of the actor that Clurman had spoken of in his earliest talks was a reality, their assurance and experience now so great that they could continue their progress on their own. While they investigated new ideas and techniques at home, Strasberg, Clurman, and especially Stella Adler were making discoveries abroad that would shake the Group to the core, permanently alter the internal balance of power, and shape their future in surprising ways.

SEVEN
Conflict

When Strasberg and Stella Adler arrived in Moscow in May 1934, they had reached the mecca of the theatrical world. Since the Moscow Art Theatre first enthralled European and American audiences on its 1923–1924 tour, actors, directors, and designers had looked to the Soviet Union as the home of the most exciting productions and ideas in the modern theatre.

The MAT held a preeminent place in foreigners' estimation, but word had also filtered overseas about the revolt against Stanislavsky-style naturalism led by such directors as Meyerhold and Alexander Tairov of the Kamerny Theatre. Russian theatre in the 1930s was too lively and diverse to be dominated by the vision of a single artist. There was ample room for the mass dramas of Nikolai Okhlopkov's Realistic Theatre, which stressed the interaction of actors and audience in theatre-in-the-round staging; the athletic "bio-mechanics" of Meyerhold's actors; the delicate harmony between inner emotion and external theatricality created by Vakhtangov in productions like *The Princess Turandot*, still being performed twelve years after the director's death. The stifling hand of "socialist realism" as prescribed by Stalin hadn't yet descended in full force, though Meyerhold was already having difficulties with the authorities that would lead to the closing of his theatre in 1938.

What Strasberg and Adler observed during their stay was a theatrical community of amazing vitality, enough to make a Broadway denizen weep with envy. Adler was particularly impressed by the broad variety of classes available to actors: dancing, acrobatics, gymnastics, fencing, diction, and Meyerhold's bio-mechanics, in addition to the improvisations and internal work on a part pioneered by Stanislavsky. She attended classes at the MAT and the Vakhtangov Theatre from nine in the morning until late in the afternoon, then watched rehearsals and saw finished productions at night. She was struck by the respectful response of both audiences and critics to even the most imperfect plays. "The work isn't wasted," she told *New The-atre* on her return. "It's seen. It's criticized seriously. Because serious work has gone into it, it isn't kicked around and annihilated the morning after. . . . It's an actor's paradise."

Strasberg was awed by Meyerhold's genius, even though the Soviet direc-tor's lack of interest in psychological motivation ran counter to the Group's basic technique. The imaginative flair and dazzling stylization of Meyer-hold's productions gave them a theatrical power even Strasberg had to acknowledge. The bold staging of *Camille* and *The Forest*—in the former the figure of Death appeared to Camille, in the latter a love scene was staged on a pair of swings—made him realize that there was more than one way to capture life's richness onstage. "[Meyerhold's style] is not a striving to-wards theatricality," he wrote, "it is a desire to mirror and explore life more fully—though its total effect is one of showing off the art of the theatre. Look at all the life-activity which Meyerhold is able to put into the forest which a seemingly realistic set makes impossible." This approach strongly affected Strasberg's work on *Gold Eagle Guy;* after a talk by a bio-mechanics instructor on "the situation of the body in space [as it] defines the style and national character," he dropped a note to Crawford asking her to research period songs and dances for their forthcoming productions.

But the director closest to the Group's heart was Vakhtangov, who had worked to bring Meyerhold's theatrical bravura to bear on productions rooted in the emotional truthfulness of the original Stanislavsky technique. When Strasberg and Adler visited Vakhtangov's widow, she read aloud two letters from Stanislavsky to his protégé. Strasberg was so moved he had tears in his eyes; the letters confirmed his judgment that Stanislavsky con-sidered Vakhtangov his heir and that the younger man's reformulation of the system, in particular the use of "inner justification" (the technique Strasberg called "adjustment") was a logical extension of the system. This belief allowed Strasberg to reconcile his continued faith in affective mem-ory with his new interest in more stylized work: "Vakhtangov's value," he wrote, "lay in disassociating the Stanislavsky System as a technique for the actor from the Stanislavsky method of production [i.e., strict naturalism]."

The great disappointment of their visit was the Moscow Art Theatre itself. Stanislavsky, then in poor health and spending much of his time abroad, had little to do anymore with the day-to-day activities of the com-pany. Strasberg was appalled by the sloppy direction and lack of acting discipline in MAT productions. When he saw one actor in *Resurrection* looking out into the audience (a total taboo in the system), he was so infuriated he wanted to climb up onstage and kill the offender. The MAT seemed to Strasberg to have abandoned its quest for truthful emotion with-out acquiring a compensating theatricality. "The Moscow Art Theatre has nothing to give," he concluded. "Even if it were inspired simply by its old motto of search for the Truth—it would be more vital and inspiring. Without that—without the straining of the soul of which we've been accused—one would much rather see something more crude—more active—more vigorous—something of today."

Adler may have agreed; certainly she had grave doubts about the Stanislavsky system's effect on her own work. It's a measure of the extent to which Group members could overcome personal feelings and concentrate on more important matters that she and Strasberg spent so much time together in Moscow. Their violent disagreements over *Gentlewoman* weren't forgotten, merely put aside as they explored the Soviet Union's theatrical scene and considered what they could bring back from it to the Group. They might differ bitterly at times over the best way to help the Group grow artistically, but there was never any question about the ultimate goal: the creation of an American theatre that expressed the social and cultural spirit of their country with a creativity and imaginative power equal to that of the Soviet theatre at its best.

Clurman joined them in June. He too was disappointed in the MAT and agreed with Strasberg that the most exciting discovery to be made in the Soviet Union was "that the Group had nothing to 'blush' about *in any respect* as far as its own work of the last three years went . . . what it had created in American terms and under American conditions was something that we had every reason to be proud of." More personally, he learned from the wide range of theatrical styles in Soviet theatre that he could be a good director without working precisely as Strasberg did. Clurman had felt himself in his partner's artistic shadow, and his failure to direct anything except summer workshops had eroded his self-confidence. Now, viewing "the kind of productions that I had always wanted to do myself but never actually seen . . . helped make my ideas more substantial and renewed my confidence, for I realized that certain desires I had expressed which seemed farfetched or 'literary' to some people [probably Strasberg and Crawford] could be worked out quite practically on the stage."

Clurman remained in Moscow for only ten days; he made further discoveries on a longer visit the following spring. For the moment, he took heart from his belief that the Group was on the right track and he himself had something to contribute. Strasberg returned to America in late June. Clurman and Adler stopped on their way home in Paris, where on July 3 they finally met the man whose system of actor training had so deeply influenced the Group.

It was Clurman's old teacher Jacques Copeau who told them Stanislavsky was in Paris. When they called on him, Adler remembered later, she remained in the background, unwilling to reveal the depth of her disenchantment with his methods. Stanislavsky, on the contrary, recalled "a completely panic-stricken woman [who] clutched me and cried, 'You've destroyed me! You must save me!'" That may have come later, for Adler herself noted that when she finally spoke up she said, "Mr. Stanislavsky, I enjoyed acting and the theatre until you came along, and now I hate it."

"If the system does not help you, forget it," the Russian replied. He had given similar advice to other actors confused or troubled by his teaching; he regarded it simply as a tool to help the actor, one to be discarded when it didn't help. But, he suggested to Adler, she might not be using his technique properly. "Since you are in trouble because of the system I must help you. I don't want you to think the system isn't worth anything!" He invited her and Clurman to visit him again, and they returned the next day to explore more specifically the problems Adler had encountered.

After a few days Clurman grew restless. He was fascinated by their discussions, particularly Stanislavsky's remarks about improvisation, which gave him new ideas about how to use it during rehearsals; and he admired Stanislavsky greatly as an artist and a man. But he wanted to go home to America. "There lies my work and my fight," he wrote Paul Strand. "Above all there is where my comrades are." He was never completely happy away from the Group. Over Adler's protests, he departed for New York. She remained for nearly a month, working with Stanislavsky on a single scene in *Gentlewoman* in order to clarify her difficulties with the system.

What troubled Adler was the same thing that bothered Beany Barker, Phoebe Brand, Morris Carnovsky, and many other Group actors: affective memory. She knew the exercises had deepened the Group's acting, bringing to their plays an emotional reality that enriched the text. But she had watched younger, less experienced actors become so obsessed with the quest for real feeling that they were paralyzed, incapable of playing an actual scene. Strasberg had made everyone so afraid of producing clichés —"they were like a profanation of some kind," Carnovsky recalled—that sometimes they couldn't produce anything at all. In *Gentlewoman* Adler had found her own acting tense and joyless because of the system. She felt herself caught between two worlds: dissatisfied with the superficiality of traditional acting, yet unable to achieve the relaxation and concentration that were supposed to go hand in hand with true emotion onstage.

"One must never speak of feeling to the actor," Stanislavsky told her. "We must attack the psychological from the point of view of the physical life so as not to disturb the feeling. Search for the line [of the part] in plans of action, not feeling . . . Find the action and the cliché will disappear. If you act and believe you will begin to feel." He questioned her about her training at the American Laboratory Theatre and with Strasberg and concluded "everything she had learnt was right," but certain aspects of the system had been overemphasized. Stanislavsky's thinking had changed since the period when Boleslavsky and Ouspenskaya had worked with him; their classes at the Lab, from which Strasberg took much of his understanding of the system, stressed emotional memory to an extent that Stanislavsky now considered wrong.

In his work with Adler, the director turned her attention to the through-line of action that should inform her entire performance and the various tasks she had to perform in order to create that line. Truth onstage was still the goal, but Stanislavsky emphasized finding that truth within the given circumstances of the play, not in the actor's personal history. They broke her part into pieces and made a chart of the main stages in the role; he explained each step to her. "When she had learnt this," he recalled, "she acted so brilliantly that we absolutely 'howled' with delight." For Adler, the four weeks had been a revelation and a liberation. "I'll pay you back for this, Mr. Stanislavsky," she said as she left him. "With all my life I'll pay you back." She returned to New York, armed with a chart outlining the various aspects of an actor's work on a part and detailed notes taken at the sessions by a friend, determined to make the Group see the error of Strasberg's ways.

While Adler, Clurman, and Strasberg explored the Soviet theatre, Crawford made plans for the Group's immediate future. She and Helen Thompson finalized arrangements to bring the company to Boston for a six-week season: they would open there October 15 with *Men in White*, then revive *Success Story* for two weeks before presenting the premiere of *Gold Eagle Guy*. Their local sponsor, Marguerite Hopkins, had rounded up an impressive roster of guarantors, including the presidents and faculty members of the city's most prestigious universities and "other persons prominent in the social and civic life of Boston." The press was still reporting that the Group hoped to make its permanent home in Boston, but Clurman recalled later that he and Strasberg were barely aware that this plan existed; it's possible that no one in the Group except Crawford and Thompson took their proposed relocation very seriously.

For their summer retreat, Crawford found an old hotel in Ellenville, New York, about twenty miles west of Poughkeepsie. *Men in White* closed August 4, and the company departed immediately for Ellenville to prepare *Gold Eagle Guy* and the Boston revivals. The rambling wooden hotel, perched 2,000 feet above sea level in the Catskills, was full to the rafters with Group members, spouses, ten apprentices, and no fewer than eight dogs, including Billy Kirkland's hapless pet, Xander, who had lost all his fur. Three Group people weren't there: Virginia Farmer had decided to devote all her time to the Theatre Collective's actor-training program; Grover Burgess had taken a leave of absence to appear in Maxwell Anderson's *Valley Forge* at the Guild; and Alixe Walker, who'd never been entirely happy as Group stage manager, was gone for good.

The Group's stay at Ellenville began with a bang. On August 7 Stella Adler gave the first of two talks on her work with Stanislavsky. The lecture was fairly technical, with Adler going over the chart she had made dividing the actor's work on a part into forty different areas. The main thrust, however, was crystal-clear: the Group had relied much too heavily on affective-memory exercises. The key to a coherent, truthful performance was understanding a character's through-line of action and its relationship to the central purpose of the play. (When the English version of Stanislavsky's *An Actor Prepares* was published in 1936, the translator would call this central purpose the "super-objective.") If the various smaller actions—

"beats," Stanislavsky dubbed them—were properly worked out in each scene, then the appropriate emotion should arise naturally from the given circumstances of the play. There was no need to "take an exercise" for every line in the script; indeed, doing so turned a performance into a series of disjointed moments that interfered with the through-line.

Adler's fellow Group actors were excited and intrigued by her talk. "You could feel the fog lifting as she went from one technical point to another," said Bobby Lewis. "We were all so oppressed by this over-usage of emotional memory." Phoebe Brand agreed: "We had had it up to here with affective memory; we just couldn't stand it anymore. When Stella came back from the horse's mouth, we thought, Oh, thank God! We don't have to do that nonsense anymore!" The actors peppered Adler with questions, interjected their own comments, and began to think about what this meant in terms of the Group's rehearsals and performances. Some of Adler's remarks about the system were corroborated by Eunice Stoddard, who'd met Stanislavsky in 1929 while he was writing *An Actor Prepares* and heard him read portions of it aloud.

One Group member was conspicuous by his absence. Lee Strasberg had refused to attend Adler's lecture, though naturally he heard all about it. This was the first direct challenge to his authority as sole arbiter of the Group's artistic technique, and he wasted no time in responding. The next day he gave a long talk, summarizing the Group's experiences over three years and his observations of the Russian theatre. The gist of it, said Bobby Lewis, was: "We don't use the Stanislavsky system; we use the Strasberg method." Strasberg argued that the Group had gone beyond Stanislavsky, incorporating the innovations of Vakhtangov and Meyerhold to create their own way of working. The dreary MAT productions he had seen in Moscow proved that Stanislavsky was old-fashioned and they had nothing to learn from him.

Strasberg remained firm in his commitment to affective memory, and to justify that he had to make a second argument that very nearly contradicted his first. After claiming that the MAT had failed to keep up with the times, he then turned around and admitted that, yes, Stanislavsky had new ideas, but these ideas were all wrong:

> Action we have always used but the emphasis on action as the main thrust, no. If you are unable to bring in emotion, then what is the point of action? Stanislavsky says clearly, "If your senses are working and if you're in good adjustment with your partner *then all you need is the action.* If everything works perfectly then you don't even need the action! However, if you have only the action and the other things not, then nothing's working."

He utterly disagreed with the main idea Adler had brought back from Stanislavsky: that if the action was performed properly, the appropriate feelings would arise. For Strasberg, true emotion had to be found before the action could be played; his comments indicated that he didn't even necessarily think the action was required at all.

The actors were astonished and dismayed. They had worshipped Strasberg as a teacher and director, and though certainly none of them thought every exercise he gave them came straight from Russia, there was an implicit belief that the Group was working along lines laid down by Stanislavsky. It was shocking to hear Strasberg, confronted by evidence that they'd misunderstood or at least misapplied some aspects of the system, declare that *he* knew how they should work and what Stanislavsky thought was irrelevant. "We thought this was a dictatorial and absurd attitude," said Stoddard.

Strasberg didn't realize how unhappy many Group actors had become with their rehearsal process. "Actors are not guinea pigs, to be manipulated, dissected, 'let alone' in a purely negative way," Sandy Meisner wrote in a memo to the Group after Adler's talk and Strasberg's response. "Our approach was not organic, that is to say, not healthy." They had been thrilled by the discovery of affective memory at Brookfield, and they appreciated the wonders it had done for their acting in plays like *The House of Connelly* and *Men in White*. They knew, and the critics had told them, that Strasberg's direction had molded them into the finest acting ensemble in America. But there was something deeply disturbing about the relentless way he pursued people's private emotions to fuel their public performances. It was distressing to see people so upset by the exercises that they burst into tears. "That was always the test with Lee," said Bobby Lewis. "If you could cry, then you had real feelings and you really cared." A couple of scary incidents where unnerved actors walked around like ghosts for days convinced many Group members that they were unearthing powerful psychological forces which neither the actors nor the directors were equipped to handle. Was all this really necessary to get a truthful theatrical performance?

Strasberg thought so, and the early Group productions and the work of actors who studied with him later proved that his stress on true emotion resulted in an intensity quite unlike anything achieved by more conventional acting techniques. Yet it's telling that Strasberg's method made its greatest impact in the 1950s, a decade when Americans largely turned away from the social concerns of the Depression and war years to immerse themselves in private life and personal preoccupations. The emphasis on action that Adler brought back from Paris suited the mood of the Group and the nation in the mid-thirties. Political events and economic circumstances forcibly reminded people that their lives were governed by larger forces, that they'd better attempt to understand these forces and work to change them if they didn't want to be crushed by them. Action was the cry of the 1930s and of the Group. They had come together to capture the life of their times in the theatre; a unified technique was a means to this end, not an end in itself. They shared Strasberg's desire for true emotion onstage, but true emotion in service to the play, not for its own sake.

The contretemps over Adler's lectures badly damaged Strasberg's prestige and, possibly, his self-confidence; some Group actors felt in retrospect that he never directed again with the same assurance. His work on *Gold Eagle Guy* was definitely different, largely owing to the effect of his exposure to Meyerhold. He continued to explore the individual characters' psychologies, but he had a new interest in the physical aspects of production. He gave a lecture on bio-mechanics, Meyerhold's system of training actors to use stage space three-dimensionally, and incorporated active, athletic staging into his direction; in one scene, Julie Garfield made a spectacular leap down a flight of stairs. Strasberg took time with the actors trying to create a specific tempo in speech and movement that would reflect the rhythms of nineteenth-century American life. Working with Tamiris, who came to Ellenville to teach classes and create the dances required by the script, the actresses explored the ways their clothing would affect their movements. "We spent absolute hours walking with our hands folded on our bustles," Beany Barker remembered.

Strasberg hoped the scenery would have the visual imaginativeness and intellectual substance that excited him at the Meyerhold Theatre. The Group hired Donald Oenslager, a successful and well-respected artist who'd designed more than fifty productions since his professional debut in 1925. Strasberg asked for sets that reflected the transformation of the central character, Guy Button, from a down-and-out sailor to the ruthless and successful owner of a shipping line. "They wanted scenery which would contain ideas," Oenslager explained to the *New York Times*. "So I started off with a scene made up of rough, crude stuff—pieces of wrecked ships, old boards, straw—all of which looked as though it might have been cast up by the sea. In each successive scene, the settings became more and more artificial. Likewise, more and more gold comes into them, so that the last scene —which happens to be a complete abstraction—is practically all gold, with the huge triumphal arch from which the symbolic gold dollar is suspended being nothing the like of which has ever been seen in an office." Strasberg also requested that the set have several different levels to aid his efforts to stage the play more actively than some of the Group's earlier work.

The director viewed *Gold Eagle Guy* as a step in the Group's continuing stylistic evolution. "There are some treatments in the theatre which we feel we are not yet equipped to handle," he told Helen Deutsch, who in her new capacity as the Group's press representative was cranking out stories on their summer activities to be placed in the New York newspapers. "There is no reason why such acting and direction as I saw at the Meyerhold, the Vakhtangov and the Moscow Art Theatres should not be brought into the American theatre, but our actors are not yet prepared to handle them. The Group Theatre is working towards types of production which we hope will be as indigenous to our American theatre as the work I saw abroad was to the continent."

It was clear from the way both Strasberg and Clurman were talking that they hoped *Gold Eagle Guy* would be a vivid, physical, romantic period production extending the Group's technical range in the direction pioneered by Meyerhold. Clurman realized, however, that this style wasn't necessarily best suited to his partner's gifts. Strasberg would never be "a brilliantly 'exterior' (colorful) director," he wrote to a friend, but Meyerhold's influence was nonetheless valuable because it "makes him think more about giving his productions an 'outside' body as well as 'inside' substance." Clurman considered the rehearsals "a sort of test of all Lee's recently acquired knowledge."

The actors weren't sure they and Strasberg were passing the test. They still didn't like the play, and during rehearsals Luther Adler let fly a quip that would be repeated all fall: "Boys, I think we're working on a stiff." Stiff, unfortunately, was also the word for most of the performances. Given a strong script they believed in, the Group actors' careful attention to detail and painstaking work with affective memory gave depth and emotional reality to their characterizations; with a bad script that had no real characters, their conscientiousness could result in highly mannered acting, in which they tried to create personalities out of thin air (and a thin text) by making gestures do the work of inspiration.

Strasberg was right in one sense when he argued that action was no substitute for meaning: all the leaping around à la Meyerhold he had them doing couldn't disguise the fact that *Gold Eagle Guy* was inherently static and undramatic. The only fully drawn character was Guy Button himself, but even Joe Bromberg's skilled and colorful acting couldn't disguise the fact that Button was exactly the same at the end of the script as he had been at the beginning. The "action" Stanislavsky spoke of wasn't merely physical; it was the progression of ideas and feelings that existed in a well-written play. They might be thinking more about the through-line after Adler's talks, but this script had no through-line to follow.

It wasn't exactly the ideal vehicle for Strasberg's desire to prove that his method was superior to Stanislavsky's. Bobby Lewis, Gadget Kazan, Russell Collins, Luther Adler, Tony Kraber, and his wife, Willy Barton, were among those who found Stella Adler's classes more artistically stimulating than anything going on in rehearsal. Over and over again she drove home the point she had made in her first talk: "Feeling for feeling's sake [is] abnormal. . . . *Style must be derived from the content* of a play—not from mood or feeling. . . . If you go to your own memories, you create your own play, not the author's." Improvisation not directly linked to the play was dangerous, she argued, because it encouraged actors to look to their own lives for the through-line instead of concentrating on the play's given circumstances.

Willy Barton's notes from Adler's classes reveal that the actress by no means rejected everything Strasberg had taught the Group. True emotion remained crucial; when listing the different areas of work on a part, she included the "golden box" that contained the actor's personal source for the feelings needed in a scene. But she emphasized the conscious use of emotion, the interconnection between mind, will, and feeling: "One cannot feel without the will and mind being concerned. They are the motor of our psychic life." Adler focused on problem-solving, taking direct steps to make a part *work*. "To know and understand is one thing, to know and do is another," she reminded her students. "A part is a collection of actions." Her practicality, the result of a lifetime spent onstage as much as her studies with Stanislavsky, gave the actors a new sense of command over themselves and their art. "Stella was a good teacher," said Phoebe Brand. "I enjoyed working in her class, because she had a lot of objective actions that were very exciting." When Adler directed her in a part, said Beany Barker, "I felt I'd learned more in a half-hour than I had in all the years with Strasberg."

Adler's classes were the talk of the summer. Sandy Meisner went so far as to suggest that she be given an executive position in the Group to deal specifically with acting problems, but his proposal was swiftly scuttled; most of the company weren't ready to antagonize Strasberg to that extent. Adler wasn't the only actor assuming more responsibility: Meisner, Lewis, and Carnovsky continued the classes they had begun in New York, and Odets taught acting to the apprentices. The Group Theatre was being decentralized, whether Strasberg liked it or not.

The shifts in the Group's power structure made everyone edgy, and the weather didn't help: it was a chilly, damp, miserable summer. "All the dogs died," remembered Barker. "It was a terribly unhappy time. We would wake up under these pine trees in a heavy mist; the floor was so slimy that when Tamiris beat her drum, and we were supposed to run and leap, you took two steps and you were down on the floor, flying around!" The wet climate helped spread ringworm from the dogs to the actors; Billy Kirkland had such a bad case he was sick the entire stay. The failed hotel they'd rented was isolated and gloomy. They were crammed into a decaying Victorian mansion, while all the surrounding buildings were boarded up. Crawford was convinced the place was haunted. The access road climbed 1,200 feet in two miles, discouraging visitors who might have lightened the collective mood. Only the perennially optimistic Bud Bohnen found anything nice to say about the place; he thought the view was lovely.

People's personal lives were as unsettled as the work situation. "Every day or so somebody comes to me with the thought of 'resigning' for one reason or another," Clurman wrote Paul Strand. Luther Adler kept the director up late one night complaining that Strasberg yelled at him during rehearsals and fellow actors like Odets were cold and hostile to him. Carnovsky became briefly infatuated with one of the apprentices, making Phoebe Brand terribly unhappy. Joe Bromberg was having second thoughts about the lucrative movie offer he had turned down to stay with the Group. Kazan missed his wife, too busy with the Theatre Union and her editorial job at *New Theatre* to join him. Strasberg and Stella Adler argued constantly, going over their separate positions on Stanislavsky's new technique again and again, neither one budging an inch. "The fighting went on continuously," Crawford remembered. "Nobody ever solved anything simply in the Group Theatre." She was so fed up with the quarrelsome atmosphere that one day she stomped out to take a week off from the Group. When someone asked if she would be lonely, she snapped, "I hope so!"

Crawford was particularly annoyed by the turn the actors' radicalism took at Ellenville. "There were wearying arguments in which the directors were accused of exploiting the actors, the designers, the kitchen help—in fact, everyone except the animals," she recalled caustically. Art Smith's wife, Betty, was organizing among the kitchen workers, and several actors strongly interested in trade unions invited labor activists up to lecture on the subject. According to Kazan, many of the visitors were prominent members of the Communist party. Sid Benson, a CP organizer for the state of Tennessee, and Andy Overgaard, head of the Trade Union Unity League (a CP-backed rival to the American Federation of Labor), both knew Kazan through the party and later became Odets' close friends. (Benson, who also went by the name Ted Wellman, was thoroughly stagestruck and shared Odets' love of classical music.) The CP presence was accepted enough for Bohnen, whose sister was spending the summer with the Group, to write humorously to his brother that "a couple of fiery young communists have been tying her in knots with dialectical materialism."

"Our neophyte radicals wanted to fix everything," Clurman commented a decade later. "Here, there, everywhere, some social foul play needed our remedying." Their preoccupation with the problems of the nontheatrical world sometimes had a peculiar impact on their own work. Kirkland, who was planning to write a new play, confided to Kazan that "before I do I have to read all of Marx." It was easy in restrospect to make fun of the more bizarre manifestations of the Group's political consciousness.

Yet at the time everyone took them pretty seriously, few more so than Clurman. "The revolution is here—now—today," he wrote to Aaron Copland that summer. Stella Adler accused him of being far more interested in politics than theatre and suggested sarcastically that perhaps he was better suited to a career as a politician than a director. " 'Art' is my field," he told Paul Strand, "but my interest in politics is merely a final expression of my realization of the need of tying up and unifying our conceptions of life and our activities in life so that everything is included."

Clurman seemed to thrive in Ellenville's troubled atmosphere. He patiently grappled with everyone's personal and political dissatisfactions. He worked with individual actors outside rehearsals, trying out some of the new ideas he'd been pondering since his trip to Russia and talks with Stanislavsky. He took over the playwriting workshop Kazan and Smith had run in New York, turning it into a more conventional class on the history of dramatic technique from the Greeks to the present. The Group's aspiring dramatists—Odets, Bohnen, Kirkland, and Alan Baxter as well as Kazan and Smith—used Clurman's analysis to help them deal with the technical issues of constructing a workable play. He was increasingly eager to direct, "but I won't till I feel it the best policy for the Group's sake," he told Strand. "That is, when the play comes along to which my contributions would be a distinct value." As Stella Adler had discovered to her fury on many occasions, the Group always came first with Clurman: before the problems of the woman he loved, even before his own needs.

Clurman's friend Odets was aggressively discontented with the Group and his prospects. He'd been assigned a room all to himself for the first time, which he forlornly hoped meant the directors "had some sense that I had some kind of distinction," but he was frustrated by his lack of progress as an actor and playwright. Once again, he had only tiny parts in the Group's new production. Although Bess Eitingon's partner had promised in May that *I Got the Blues* would begin rehearsals in late August, by the time Odets arrived at Ellenville he had given up hope for that. He was juggling a new affair with Helen Deutsch and his ongoing relationship with the young student he had met the previous winter, but his letters and diary entries expressed as much anger as love toward women.

Only his work on *Paradise Lost* from time to time gave him satisfaction. Though the family drama had many similarities to *I Got the Blues*, Odets was trying to meet Strasberg's objections to his earlier play by moving beyond its explosive naturalism to create a more universal drama, an allegory about the decay of the middle class. The characters, less overtly urban and Jewish, spoke of the dilemmas the Depression imposed in more philosophical terms. If the dialogue lacked some of *I Got the Blues*' bite, it had a poetic lyricism that gave the play a gentler tone, more rueful than angry. Only the character of Kewpie, a gangster whose driving compulsion to "get every single thing he wants" was based largely on Odets' friend Kazan, possessed the fury that seethed in almost every page of the previous script.

Odets worked hard on *Paradise Lost* throughout the summer and early fall, and at times it went amazingly well. One exuberant night an entire scene gushed forth so quickly he didn't dare delay even long enough to find paper; he scrawled the dialogue on the whitewashed walls of his room and typed up a copy later. He was so exhilarated that he went out the next day and spent the rest of his option money on two cases of liquor—Scotch, gin, rye, anything he could lay his hands on—and went on a massive drunk with his closest Group friends. Kazan, Smith, Bohnen, and Odets roared into the nearby town and raised hell; they finally all landed in jail when Kazan started throwing flower pots around.

Odets was drinking a lot that summer. He was desperate for recognition, which he feared the Group would never give him. Sandy Meisner's nervous giggle when Odets stormed into the house one night and declared "I am a genius!" seemed to the drunk and angry playwright to be emblematic of the Group's lack of faith in him; he picked up a gin bottle and hurled it at the actor. Toward the end of their stay in Ellenville, he went to Clurman and said he was going to quit. He'd never had a decent part, he told his friend, the directors had no intention of producing his plays, and he'd had enough. Clurman begged him to stay, vowing to make sure he got a good role during the next season. The director made no promises, however, that the Group would present either of his plays. Nonetheless, Odets allowed himself to be persuaded. His threat, he admitted to an interviewer not long before his death, was basically a bluff. "I wouldn't have known where to go," he said. "All I really wanted was to have the Group Theatre do my plays."

The Group left Ellenville for Boston in early October. Crawford and Helen Thompson spared no effort to make their visit a major event. The papers were full of stories recapping the youthful organization's history and quoting the local sponsors on the great cultural opportunity the Group's proposed move presented to the city. The company attended teas on Beacon Hill, and individual actors spoke at lunches and dinners to muster up interest in their work. They gave a special program of sketches for their well-heeled guarantors; Tony Kraber's cowboy songs and humorous patter made a particular hit. The opening night of *Men in White*, October 15 at the enormous and wholly unsuitable Majestic Theatre, was a highly social affair; the columnists' reports on who attended and what they were wearing occupied almost as much space as the reviews. It wasn't the most comfortable environment for the Group, and the Bostonians' response to their productions confirmed their opinion that this was no place for them to settle permanently. "A few charming and interesting people," commented Dorothy Patten, "but most of them seemed to be shocked by anything more than a Strauss operetta."

Men in White, an established Broadway hit, went over well enough, though attendance was hurt by the fact that the movie version had played in Boston only a few months before. *Success Story*, which followed it on October 29, was another matter. The critics were friendly; the spectators weren't. "You should have seen the opening," Odets wrote to Helen Deutsch. "The frozen silence; the terrorized silence, the stink of boiled cod in the air! . . . even a dull person could feel the antagonism of the aristocratic audience." Clurman felt in retrospect that the rise of the Nazis had made the subject of a ruthless, ambitious Jew uncomfortable for an audience, but it's more likely that Boston's Brahmins simply found the whole play sordid and unpleasant. The directors decided to close it after ten days to allow extra time to rehearse *Gold Eagle Guy*.

The premiere of the Group's new play on November 12 was hardly the triumphant finale to the Boston season their sponsors hoped for. Oenslager's elaborate settings and the colorful costumes designed by Kay Morrison drew more favorable comment than the play, which many critics complained was too similar in theme to *Success Story*. Although the Group's acting was generally praised, a number of reviews criticized the performers' diction; in defense of her adopted company, Marguerite Hopkins noted that the bad acoustics of the cavernous Majestic were responsible for most of the audibility problems. She and the other sponsors were deeply disappointed by their city's lackluster response to the Group; it was clear that their dream of making Boston the company's home base was not to be fulfilled.

Given that the Group had been unwilling to consider moving as far off Broadway as 14th Street, it's unlikely that even the most wildly enthusiastic reception would have tempted them to forsake New York. Heated exchanges in the newspapers' letters' columns after *Gold Eagle Guy*'s less-than-stellar premiere showed how much unease the company aroused. One letter printed in the Boston *Transcript* suggested the Group was simply too strong-minded for Boston. Elinor Hughes, the *Herald*'s theatre columnist, agreed that the Group came across as overly serious, especially in the actors' frequently quoted comments about the opportunities they had all passed up to appear in films. Phoebe Brand, whose good looks and featured role in *Men in White* had garnered her several movie offers, was notably vehement in her scorn for Hollywood. Her devotion to the Group was sincere, but journalists tended to interpret it as pretentious. "Too much high thinking, too much art, have a way of alienating sympathy," wrote Hughes. She urged the company to "give a thought to the public as well as their own aspirations." The Group could get that kind of advice in New York.

The actors' encounters with Boston radical groups and workers theatres were more fruitful than their brush with high society. Joe Bromberg made contact with the local John Reed Club shortly after their arrival; he and several other Group members attended a late October meeting to discuss workers theatre. Stella Adler addressed a Jewish workers group to raise funds to aid those threatened by the spread of Nazism, speaking eloquently about the suffering and fear of Jews she had observed during her trip to Europe. Odets, hard at work on *Paradise Lost*, took breaks by strolling around and visiting the city's union halls. He'd recently joined the Communist party, swept up by a feeling possessing many Group members: the desire to ally themselves with the oppressed and the outcast, the people pushed aside by American society even though their labors had built it. For Odets, like his friend Clurman, art was the most important thing in the world, but he wanted more and more to find a way for art to *change* the world.

He got his chance to make what appeared to be a modest contribution to the class struggle in October, when he met with Smith, Kazan, Kirkland, and Bohnen to discuss writing a one-act workers' play as a collective. (They dubbed this collective SKKOB, the amalgamation of the initials of their last names.) The exact mechanism by which *Waiting for Lefty* was called into being is surrounded by a mist of different, sometimes conflicting, stories. Someone asked Odets to write the play or, alternatively, approached the collective as a whole. It may have been Odets' new friend Joe Kelleher, who was organizing coal-boat workers and needed a play to put on at union meetings. It may have been someone from the League of Workers Theatres, which was sponsoring a contest in *New Theatre* for revolutionary short plays. It may have been a representative of a Boston progressive organization, asking the Group to give a benefit performance.

The point was that *Lefty* grew out of a concrete need in the real world, not the private inspiration of a single artist. SKKOB planned to emulate the methods of groups like the Workers Laboratory Theatre and write the play together. The specific subject, the bitter New York taxi strike of February–April 1934, appears to have been Odets' idea; he'd read about it in the *New Masses*. Odets also came up with the structure: a union meeting called for a strike vote, which the corrupt leaders want to quash, with five individual scenes showing how different workers come to realize a strike is necessary. Each of them would write one scene, he suggested, and he would take care of the framing dialogue as well.

Some of the work may have been done that way; several people recalled that Art Smith wrote a fair amount of material. Some of Odets' students from the Theatre Union thought they recognized snatches of dialogue from improvisations they'd created in his classes. Wherever the bits and pieces came from, the collective method didn't produce a complete play, and in the end, perhaps spurred by an approaching performance date, Odets holed up in the Hotel Bellevue and wrote the final version in a matter of days.

There was no question about who was responsible for the end result. The dialogue crackled with the same furious vitality that informed *I Got the Blues;* the underlying passion for justice and a fair chance in life, though shared by millions of people across America, as expressed in *Lefty* was uniquely Odets' own. It murmured in the sad voice of a taxi driver who tells the girlfriend he can't afford to marry, "You and me—we never even had a room to sit in somewhere." It rang in the words of the wife of another underpaid cabbie, so broke she can't buy orange juice for her children, who says, "My God, Joe—the world is supposed to be for all of us." It shouted out loud in the union rebel's closing speech: "Tear down the slaughter house of our old lives! What are we waiting for. . . . We'll die for what is right! put fruit trees where our ashes are!"

"What's important about *Waiting for Lefty*," Odets said years later, "is how it matched my conversion from a fellow who stood on the side and watched and then finally, with a rush, agreed—in this drastic social crisis in the early 'thirties—that the only way out seemed to be a kind of socialism, or the Communist Party, or something. The play represents that kind of ardor and that kind of conviction."

Odets read the play to the Group actors in the basement of the Majestic Theatre on October 31. Although he mentioned the play to Clurman, the directors weren't invited; he wasn't about to give them another chance to criticize his work. Anyway, this wasn't "art" intended for professional production; this was agitprop, a weapon to be used in the fight for a better life. The actors loved *Lefty*, which vibrated with a fervor and commitment to a new world shared by communist and noncommunist alike. They began working on it in their spare time, with Odets and Sandy Meisner as codirectors. After the tense rehearsals of the ponderous *Gold Eagle Guy*, it was a relief to act in something short, swift, and practical; their work had the casual confidence of their best improvisations. Odets took the same relaxed attitude making changes in the script. "No hugging to the breast here, the writer alone and happy in himself," he wrote to Helen Deutsch. "No, do what you want, boys, change, cut, add. I said to myself—this is *some* thing."

If *Lefty* was originally intended for a Boston meeting of some kind, that plan must have been scrapped—Bobby Lewis recalled that the hall they were to appear in was condemned as unsafe by the fire department. The Group actors continued to rehearse, confident that such a badly needed play would soon be asked for again.

Odets sensed that he stood at the threshold of a new life that would challenge him in dangerous ways. "The temptation is so often on me nowadays to make a quick cheap success," he wrote Helen Deutsch in November. "The bastardly joke is that it would impress even my communist comrades as much as my own parents: Group people too. I burn with a craziness to be out and doing, to smash down the walls of opinion around me, to impress myself on the face of society." Even as he tried to work patiently on *Paradise Lost*, "the boyhood desires intrude, the hunger for success and fame and maybe fifty perfumed women sitting in my lap. I know the bull of it all . . . but still my heart pounds at night with uneasiness and desire, very bad desire. We want really—all our kind—to smash down all opposition to every single part of us. We want to master people's regard for us, want to fix it high and indelibly, no matter if the medals be brass and the clamour tinny."

The similarity of this outburst to the words his cabbies used in *Lefty* showed how inextricably intertwined in Odets' complex personality were his genuine longing for a better world for everyone and his equally burning wish for individual recognition. His Marxism wasn't the carefully thought-out choice of a man like John Howard Lawson, making a lifetime commitment after years of consideration. It was the spontaneous response of someone, bitterly dissatisfied in his own life, who looked around and saw to his astonishment and delight that others suffered too, that he wasn't alone in his anger and frustration. Did working-class people fighting for a decent wage have much in common with a middle-class intellectual yearning for fame and success? Odets thought so, and it was a generous belief. He wanted to be somebody, and so did they: it was the American Dream; it was

their right. The intensely personal motives that led him to communism gave
Lefty its emotional power and freed it (most of the time) from the bonds of
dogmatism. Yet there was a confusion in Odets' mind about what he really
wanted, about whether it was all right to grab for capitalism's glittering
prizes—after all, didn't everybody want them?—or whether he could maintain his integrity as an artist and a communist only by choosing the poverty
the workers in *Lefty* were struggling to escape.

For the moment these were abstract questions, since none of his plays
was even scheduled to be produced and *Gold Eagle Guy* seemed unlikely to
afflict the Group with the problems of success. When they returned to New
York in late November to prepare for their opening at the Morosco Theatre,
morale was low. Even the normally cheerful Kazan was subdued. Strasberg
had raked him over the coals in front of the entire company in Boston for
failing to execute properly the complicated series of cues for the play's
climactic earthquake, and Kazan bitterly resented it; he kept his distance
from the director after that.

Strasberg knew the production didn't display either him or the Group at
their best, and the knowledge made him even more autocratic than usual.
On occasion, he was positively brutal. During one of the final dress rehearsals, an unpleasant incident underscored his capacity for cruelty to actors
and drove one Group stalwart to open revolt.

They were rehearsing a party scene in which Beany Barker, playing Guy
Button's well-born wife, pours tea for a group of visitors. During the scene
one of the women faints, and at this particular rehearsal Barker began to
rise from her chair as though to help her guest. Though this was an entirely
natural response for her character, Strasberg's direction called for Barker
to go on serving tea without interruption; when Barker remembered this,
she checked her half-completed gesture and resumed her scripted action.

Strasberg, sitting out front in the Morosco's auditorium, stopped the
scene. "What were you doing?" he asked Barker in the icy tones that de-
noted an impending storm.

"I'm sorry, Lee, I made a mistake," she replied. "May we go on?"

They might not. Strasberg hammered away at her, demanding to be
given a reason for her movement. As Bobby Lewis saw it, Strasberg wanted
Barker to defend herself by saying that standing up was what a society
hostess would do so he could then blow up and tell her *Gold Eagle Guy*
wasn't a play about etiquette; the director from the impoverished Lower
East Side was expressing an underlying class antagonism toward the actress who'd been a Baltimore debutante. He kept at it until he had reduced
Barker to tears, but she refused to justify her departure from the script,
repeating over and over that it was just a mistake. She hoped Strasberg
would eventually tire of badgering her and they could resume the run-
through without having a major scene.

Strasberg was relentless. He wanted an answer; he may very well have wanted a scene. He didn't precisely enjoy screaming at people during re-hearsals—he was as shaken as anyone by his bursts of uncontrollable rage, though he snapped back from them with surprising ease—but it gave him a chance to assert his authority over the actors, to reassure himself that he could still make them tremble with fear for having displeased him. The reaction he provoked this time around was quite different.

Ruth Nelson was the Group's Good Samaritan: she was always nursing people through bouts of poison ivy, holding their hands through emotional crises, binding up the various wounds inflicted by Group life. Always inclined to put others' problems before her own, she was gentle and seldom assertive. But this time she'd had enough. She looked at her friend Beany's tear-stained face, then out into the orchestra at Strasberg, and said calmly, "Now I'm going to kill him." She started downstage toward the director, so angry that she took no notice of the orchestra pit that lay between them—apparently she planned to walk on air to get her hands on Strasberg's throat. The other actors managed to restrain her before she marched off the edge of the stage, but Strasberg wasn't reassured; he turned tail and ran. He never came back to rehearsals, and Clurman took over the direction for the last few days.

The entire scene was unprecedented. People had fought with Strasberg before; Stella Adler had just mounted a major challenge to his authority. But the look of personal hatred he'd seen in Nelson's eyes was new, a sign that he had finally pushed the actors too far. He was no longer God; they expected him to treat them with common human decency, to recognize that they were adults and artists, not naughty children to be bullied until they behaved. Their rejection was devastating. Strasberg took to his bed, and word of his condition spread widely enough around town to be mentioned in print by one of the Broadway reviewers. The experience was deeply humiliating for someone who had put his trust in art, only to find that art didn't exempt him from the obligation to have some care for his actors' personal feelings.

When *Gold Eagle Guy* opened at the Morosco on November 28, the press was kinder than the Group had any reason to expect. Several of the less astute reviewers were fooled by the lavish visuals and jumpy staging into praising the production as "exciting," "vivid," and "atmospheric." Joe Bromberg was generally commended for his "flesh and blood" performance, though several columnists felt he overacted. Morris Carnovsky, who played another cynical banker, won kudos as usual for his subtlety and intelligence, and Billy Kirkland's ease as a romantic painter was contrasted favorably with the finicky work of his peers. The more discerning critics noticed that underneath all the sound and fury, which climaxed in the spectacular and popular earthquake effect, was a lot of tense, overly detailed acting. Margaret Barker was rewarded for the pains she'd taken with her period gestures by having John Mason Brown complain that she used her arms "as if they were wrapped in invisible slings." In general, remarked Brooks Atkinson, the production was "a little timid and fussy," a comment echoed by many of his colleagues. They blamed the play, which they correctly noted was both schematic and undramatic.

Still, the reviewers felt kindly about the Group and went out of their way to mention how worthy an organization it was even when not living up to its highest goals. Enough favorable comments were mixed in with the criticisms to allow Helen Deutsch to create some impressive ads, and Helen Thompson rounded up a solid four weeks of benefit audiences in hopes that word of mouth would improve business. "It's a pure tour de force of promotion—on paper," Bud Bohnen wrote to his brother. "The Box office is zero . . . The play is like a bottle of ginger ale exposed one night—flat. We lift it up by its bootstraps every night." Business didn't improve; the weekly gross hovered around $7,000, which was nowhere near enough for a large, expensive production.

Still, the Group hung on. A flurry of movie interest in December encouraged them to think they could make some of their money back through a sale to one of the studios. They hoped liberal audiences might be drawn in by *The Nation's* mention of the Group on its 1934 Honor Roll, commending the company "for its consistent and successful effort to take seriously all the arts of the theatre, and, specifically, for its current production, *Gold Eagle Guy."* They cut the top ticket price to $2.00. Deutsch took advantage of her press connections to plant background stories about the scenery, the actors, the Group, in nearly every newspaper in town. Despite all their efforts, the gross dropped so low by late December that they couldn't make the rent at the Morosco and were forced to move to the Belasco, "a crummy old joint, shabby, with uncomfortable seats," said Odets.

They couldn't bring themselves to care very much about *Gold Eagle Guy,* even though they knew if it closed they'd be out of work. The actors were far more absorbed by *Waiting for Lefty,* which was now slated to be performed at a benefit for *New Theatre* magazine on January 6. Strasberg's attitude to this upstart production was almost as hostile as his reaction to *I Got the Blues.* When Odets asked for his advice on handling the ensemble of workers who sit in the background and comment on each scene, he was curt and unhelpful. Odets suspected he didn't like the Group being associated with *Lefty:* "Whenever the Group Theatre name was used or represented, it was as though his honor was at stake." When the actors finally unveiled their independent effort to the directors in the basement of the Belasco, Clurman and Crawford warmly praised the run-through. Strasberg shrugged, saying nothing. "Let 'em fall and break their necks," he told Clurman later; General Lee was still hoping his troops would realize they couldn't get along without him.

The directors, however, had nothing to offer as an alternative to *Lefty.* As *Gold Eagle Guy* limped along in what would clearly be its final weeks, they met to decide what to do next. Strasberg and Crawford agreed the situation was hopeless. They'd killed themselves to make *Gold Eagle Guy* a success, to no avail. They'd scoured New York for scripts and come up empty-handed. It was time to bow to the inevitable and end the Group's season. Clurman vehemently disagreed. He wanted to go ahead with *I Got the Blues*, much improved by Odets' revisions of Act One and retitled *Awake and Sing!* The play was custom-made for the Group, he argued; they could give it a fine production. More important, the Group desperately needed to work: if they shut up shop now they were done for. It was the responsibility of the directors to find a project for the company—to make something up, if they had to.

Clurman's closest friends had noticed his new confidence that fall. "We will have joy in Harold yet," Odets wrote to Helen Deutsch from Boston. "A subtle change is taking place—firmness is coming and underneath he buckles on armor for the coming years! No ordinary man is he, but deeply understanding and perceptive of small and main currents in our stinking desert." Clurman had refreshed himself with work outside the Group; an article on his friend Stieglitz had been published that fall, and the admiring comments of critics had boosted his self-esteem. He had found the inner strength to withstand the disappointment of his partners, who felt he was losing face by his failure to direct, and the more intimate reproaches of Stella Adler, who combined personal and professional criticism in a particularly wounding way. After years of talk, he was finally ready to take action. "I would direct a play if we had one now," he wrote to Paul Strand in mid-December; by the end of the month he believed they did have a play and they should put it on.

His fellow directors were less eager and a lot more tired. Crawford had been worn down by the day-to-day demands of putting on a big, elaborate production in two cities. The summer's arguments over the Group's method and the difficult rehearsals of *Gold Eagle Guy* had left Strasberg in a precarious emotional state. When he responded to Clurman's insistence that the Group must go on by telling him their present path would lead them all straight to the hospital or the psychopathic ward, his words had a distinctly personal application. Crawford felt their force. It was all very well for Harold to say they had to find a way to continue, she and Strasberg might justly have argued. *He* hadn't spent five months wrestling with the production of an imperfect script and coping with a tangle of logistical headaches. They stood firm, and Clurman reluctantly agreed that he would be the one to announce that their season would end with the closing of *Gold Eagle Guy*. No matter what his differences with his partners, he still believed in presenting a united front to the actors.

The actors were outraged. Standing in the gloomy confines of the Belasco's basement, they berated the directors for failing for the second time in two years to live up to their promise of continuous work in a permanent company. Stella Adler led the attack: the Yiddish theatre had shown her it was possible to keep actors employed year-round; she believed passionately it was their most compelling need and their right; she blamed the directors' weakness for denying it to the Group actors. The entire company followed her lead, challenging the directors to keep the Group active no matter what the obstacles. Faced with the objection that the Group had no play to produce, the actors announced that *they* would find a script since the directors had proved themselves incapable.

Odets stepped in to remind them they had at least one play whose author was eager for a Group production. He'd revised the first act of *Awake and Sing!* to meet Clurman's objections, they knew from the performances at Green Mansions that Act Two played beautifully, and he could work on the third act in rehearsals. He even offered to raise the money to put it on. Strasberg, angered and shocked by the actors' rebellion, vented his wrath on the presumptuous playwright. "You don't seem to understand, Cliff," he snapped. "We don't *like* your play."

There was silence, though only for a moment. None of the actors had read or heard *Awake and Sing!* recently enough to be prepared to defend it unconditionally. They were heartily sick, however, of Strasberg's propensity for saying "we" when he meant "I." In the stormy discussion that followed his ill-considered remark, agreement was finally reached that the actors would read every script they could lay their hands on and, come hell or high water, the Group would find a play to rehearse. *Awake and Sing!* was neither selected nor definitively rejected.

At this point, the chronology of events becomes somewhat confused. People's memories don't so much conflict as overlap in contradictory ways. Harold Clurman wrote later that he'd already decided *Awake and Sing!* would be the Group's next production, "but I wanted the actors to affirm my choice, or at any rate appear to force it." Luther Adler recalled that after a week of fruitlessly reading scripts, he was approached by Odets, who begged him to ask the actors to attend a reading of *Awake and Sing!* Kazan claimed in his autobiography that Odets' comrades in the Group's Communist party unit, which met every Tuesday night in Joe Bromberg's dressing room, planned their actions at a subsequent Group meeting to ensure that the company would demand to hear Odets read his play. But such a subterfuge was hardly necessary, since the Group had no other viable scripts and both Clurman and Odets were eagerly promoting his.

The reading of *Awake and Sing!*, to which the directors were not invited, took place sometime between New Year's Day and January 13, 1935, when the New York papers announced it would be the Group's next production. On Sunday night, January 6, an event transpired that made the Group's decision to produce *Awake and Sing!* inevitable: *Waiting for Lefty* had its first performance at the Civic Repertory Theatre.

EIGHT

Theatre Becomes Life

efty was one of several works scheduled as part of an evening organized by the League of Workers Theatres to aid *New Theatre*. The benefit staff assigned it no particular importance: the mimeographed one-sheet program simply said, *"Waiting for Lefty,* presented by the cast of *Gold Eagle Guy,"* with no mention of either author or individual actors. The stage manager, Robert Riley, who booked the entertainment and decided the order of appearance, believed that Anna Sokolow's troupe of dancers was more important than a new play by an unknown actor/writer, and he announced that they would appear last. Odets was furious, arguing vehemently that his play deserved the favored final spot. Riley gave in, only to encounter a new problem. The Group hadn't warned him that the show required lighting cues; he had to work them out hastily with the electrician during the intermissions between the other acts. When the lights went up on the bare stage, with Morris Carnovsky as the corrupt union leader directly addressing the audience as if they were his rebellious membership, no one expected anything except another casual piece of agitprop thrown together for a good cause.

Within moments everyone in the theatre knew better. As the actors began to speak Odets' stingingly authentic dialogue—so radically different from either the affected patter of the Broadway show-shops or the wooden sloganeering of agitprop—audience members found themselves swept up in a drama they seemed to know intimately, from deep inside themselves, even though they'd never heard a word of it before.

They gasped when Ruth Nelson as the angry wife said, "Sure, I see it in the papers, how good orange juice is for kids . . . Betty never saw a grapefruit. I took her to the store last week and she pointed to a stack of grapefruits. 'What's that!' she said." They cheered when Tony Kraber, playing the scientist who refuses to develop poison gas, punches his evil boss (Carnovsky again) in the nose. They murmured sadly when the young lovers Phoebe

Brand and Julie Garfield were forced by poverty to part. They jeered at Russell Collins as a company spy and applauded when Gadget Kazan exposed him as "my own lousy brother!" They laughed sympathetically at Bill Challee as a desperate young actor too ignorant to know what a manifesto is and took Paula Miller to their hearts as the tough producer's secretary who gives him a dollar to buy some food and a copy of *The Communist Manifesto*, telling him, "Come out in the light, Comrade." When Luther Adler, playing a young doctor fired because he is a Jew, closed his scene with the communist salute, more than one person answered him from the auditorium with a clenched fist thrust in the air. It was beyond politics. They used the CP salute as Odets defined it in *Lefty*'s last scene: "the good old uppercut to the chin," a rejection of all the forces that hurt people and kept them down, a commitment to fight for a better life.

To Kazan, seated in the auditorium waiting for his cue, the response was "like a roar from sixteen-inchers broadside, audience to players, a way of shouting, 'More! More! More! Go on! Go on! Go on!' " Swept up by the passion they had aroused, the actors were no longer acting. "They were being carried along as if by an exultancy of communication such as I have never witnessed in the theatre before," wrote Clurman. The twenty-eight-year-old playwright was awed by the emotional conflagration he'd ignited. "You saw theatre in its truest essence," Odets remembered years later. "Suddenly the proscenium arch of the theatre vanished and the audience and actors were at one with each other."

As the play mounted to its climax, the intensity of feeling on- and offstage became almost unbearable. When Bobby Lewis dashed in with the news that Lefty has been murdered, no one needed to take an exercise to find the appropriate anger—the actors exploded with it, the audience seethed with it. They exulted as Joe Bromberg, playing the union rebel Agate Keller, tore himself loose from the hired gunmen and declared their independence: "HELLO AMERICA! HELLO. WE'RE STORMBIRDS OF THE WORKING-CLASS . . . And when we die they'll know what we did to make a new world!"

"Well, what's the answer?" Bromberg demanded. In the audience, as planned, Odets, Herbie Ratner, and Lewis Leverett began shouting "Strike!" "LOUDER!" Bromberg yelled—and, one by one, from all over the auditorium, individual voices called out, "Strike!" Suddenly the entire audience, some 1,400 people, rose and roared, "Strike! Strike!" The actors froze, stunned by the spontaneous demonstration. The militant cries gave way to cheers and applause so thunderous the cast was kept onstage for forty-five minutes to receive the crowd's inflamed tribute. "When they couldn't applaud any more, they stomped their feet," said Ruth Nelson. "All I could think was, 'My God, they're going to bring the balcony down!' It was terrible, it was so beautiful." The actors were all weeping. When Clurman persuaded Odets to take a bow, the audience stormed the stage and embraced the man who had voiced their hopes and fears and deepest aspirations. "That was the dream all of us in the Group Theatre had," said Kazan, "to be embraced that way by a theatreful of people."

"The audience wouldn't leave," said Cheryl Crawford. "I was afraid they were going to tear the seats out and throw them on the stage." When the astounded stage manager finally rang down the curtain, they remained out front, talking and arguing about the events in a play that seemed as real to them as their own lives. Actors and playwright were overwhelmed and a little frightened by the near-religious communion they had just shared. Odets retreated to a backstage bathroom; his excitement was so intense he threw up, then burst into tears. The dressing room was hushed as the actors removed their make-up. They emerged onto 14th Street to find clusters of people still gathered outside, laughing, crying, hugging each other, clapping their hands. "There was almost a sense of pure madness about it," Morris Carnovsky felt.

No one wanted to go home. Sleep was out of the question. Most of the Group went to an all-night restaurant—no one can remember now which one—and tried to eat. Odets sat alone: pale, withdrawn, not talking at all. Everyone was too dazed to have much to say. It was dawn before they could bring themselves to separate, to admit that the miracle was over.

There had never been a night like it in the American theatre. The Group became a vessel into which were poured the rage, frustration, desperation, and finally exultation, not just of an angry young man named Clifford Odets but of every single person at the Civic Rep who longed for an end to personal and political depression, who needed someone to tell them they could stand up and change their lives. The Group had experienced the "unity of background, of feeling, of thought, of need" Clurman had said was the basis for a true theatre: during his inspiring talks at Brookfield, at the thrilling final run-through of *Connelly*, in some of the best performances of *Success Story*. Never before had they shared it with an entire theatre full of people, never before had it seemed as though the lines they spoke hadn't been written but rather emerged from a collective heart and soul. Theatre and life merged, as Clurman had promised they could.

Waiting for Lefty changed people's idea of what theatre was. More than an evening's entertainment, more even than a serious examination of the contemporary scene by a thoughtful writer, theatre at its best could be a living embodiment of communal values and aspirations. Theatre *mattered*, art had meaning, culture wasn't the property of an affluent, educated few but an expression of the joys and sorrows of the human condition as they could be understood and shared by everyone. In a fragmented society of wounded individuals, theatre could bring people together and make them whole. After such a revelation, there was no going back for the Group. They would seek the communion created by *Lefty* in everything they did. Sometimes they found it, sometimes they didn't, but they could no longer be satisfied by anything less.

Only one bourgeois newspaper was fortunate enough to have an eyewitness account of *Lefty*'s historic premiere. The *Morning Telegraph*'s second-string critic, Henry Senber, made a habit of checking out offbeat theatrical events like the New Theatre Nights in search of stories, and on Sunday night, January 6, he was handed the story of a lifetime. The *Telegraph* ran his review on Tuesday, scooping every other paper in New York. After describing the "earthquakes of applause" that greeted the performance, he told his readers, "One left the theatre Sunday evening with two convictions. The first was that one had witnessed an event of historical importance in what is academically referred to as the drama of the contemporary American scene. The other was that a dramatist to be reckoned with had been discovered. . . . It has not been announced just where and when 'Waiting for Lefty' will be presented again, but you can rest assured that it will be . . . soon. A play like this does not die."

Indeed it did not. In the days that followed the offices of the League of Workers Theatres and the Group were deluged with calls from workers theatre groups across the country begging for permission to produce *Lefty*. Moved by the national hunger for the play he had tossed off in three days, Odets allowed amateur groups to use it free of charge and reduced his royalties to semiprofessional organizations in the interests of giving as many people as possible a chance to see it. By June, *Lefty* had been produced in Baltimore, Boston, Chicago, Cleveland, Denver, Detroit, Duluth, Harlem (a black production directed by Rose McClendon), Hollywood, Lansing, Madison, Milwaukee, Morristown, Newark, New Haven, Northampton, Peoria, Philadelphia, Pittsburgh, Providence, Rochester, Syracuse, and Washington. It won prizes all over: *New Theatre*'s fifty-dollar award for best short revolutionary play, the Samuel French Trophy in Pittsburgh, the George Pierce Baker Cup at the Yale Drama Tournament.

It was the most widely performed play in America—and the most widely banned. Authorities were outraged by *Lefty*'s openly communist stance, although that was hardly the primary reason for its wild success. Their usual excuse for forbidding its production was the frank dialogue. ("We have seldom listened to viler language than is here thundered into the face of the public which pays to be amused," spluttered the New York *Enquirer*.) In Boston, four members of the New Theatre Group were arrested while presenting *Lefty* and charged with using profanity; two were eventually fined. Although the John Reed Club's Unity Players won first prize with it at Yale, the production was banned from a New Haven high school auditorium by the School Building Committee of the Board of Education, which found it unfit to be seen in public schools. The New Haven police then turned around and allowed the use of another local school building for a fascist meeting. In Newark, where the city council had voted a grant for a Nazi song festival, the mayor banned *Lefty* on the grounds that it inflamed political passions. When the theatre group went ahead anyway, the police

provoked violence by driving the actors from the stage in front of a large
and angry crowd; it took police from three precincts to subdue the subsequent riot, and nine people were arrested. *Lefty* was an event as much as a
play.

Its stunned author was trying to adjust to the fact that he had suddenly
become public property. "The phone has been ringing off the hook!" he told
a friend who called on Monday to congratulate him. He had become, literally, an overnight celebrity, no longer an unsuccessful actor but an exciting
young playwright with one show the talk of the town and another soon to
open on Broadway. For if the Group hadn't definitely decided to present
Awake and Sing! before *Lefty*'s premiere, there was no question about it
afterward: they announced on January 13 that Odets' play would be their
next production and on January 30 made it official that Clurman would
direct. Odets and the actors had won the day. They'd presented *Lefty* in the
face of Strasberg's indifference and been justified to an extent they could
never have dreamed possible. Now they forced him to accept a play he
disliked, directed by a partner whose abilities he was unsure of.

In the meantime, *Lefty* continued its triumphant course. The Group hastily arranged another performance on January 13, this time pairing it with
Kazan and Smith's *Dmitroff* as a benefit for the taxi drivers' union. The
show sold out without a single advertisement: cabbies packed the balcony,
and the union's secretary addressed them before the curtain rose, reminding them of the bitter forty-day strike they'd endured the previous year and
the struggle they still faced. They were as passionate as *Lefty*'s first audience, and Kraber was so carried away by the mood that at the end of the
scientist scene his punch accidentally connected and broke Carnovsky's
nose. The stage manager rearranged the scenes to give them time to stop
the bleeding, and Carnovsky managed to finish the show. His own doctor,
who happened to be in the audience, set his nose afterward. Carnovsky
probably wasn't entirely sorry that the splint made it impossible for him to
continue as a handsome banker in *Gold Eagle Guy;* Bud Bohnen replaced
him for the last few performances before it closed, to no one's regret, on
January 26.

Lefty was back on the 27th to benefit the Group's sinking fund for future
productions. This time the audience included a good many celebrities—the
play was fashionable now—and some movie scouts, although it's hard to
imagine what possible use a film studio could have made of a revolutionary
drama filled from beginning to end with lines like "The Constitution's for
rich men then and now" and "One dollar buys nine loaves of bread and one
copy of *The Communist Manifesto.*" To fill out the bill the Group added
dances by Tamiris and some of its improvisations, including the ever-
popular "Red Hamlet," Kraber's songs, and the Bromberg/Carnovsky gibberish pieces. The proceeds from a similar program on February 3 were
divided among the company: "28 bucks for yours truly," Bud Bohnen wrote

happily to his brother, "which is bad news for the wolf at the door." The Group had become famous, but they certainly weren't rich.

At a benefit for the *New Masses* on February 9, they added some of their more socially conscious sketches, including the Grosz improvisation and "An Operation on Hitler" performed by Kazan and Lewis. The uptown press was finally invited to see *Lefty* and the improvisations the following night, and for the most part they liked what they saw. They praised *Lefty* warmly —"vigorous, moving and tense," said the *Daily Mirror*; "soundly constructed and fiercely dramatic," Brooks Atkinson wrote in the *Times*—but there was an anticlimactic note to their comments, since nearly everyone in New York had already heard about it.

The improvisations, on the other hand, were a revelation to the critics, who discovered to their astonishment that the Group had a sense of humor. Atkinson, who clearly viewed the Group as worthy but rather dour advo-cates of high art, characterized the sketches with pleased surprise as "win-ningly good-humored." The *Journal*'s John Anderson found them "more interesting than most of the Group's formal Broadway productions." Such remarks were irritating, but there was an underlying grain of truth best expressed by John Mason Brown in the *Post*. "There has been something baffling and labored and slightly put-offish about even the better of their uptown efforts," he commented, noting that some Group actors "seemed to find themselves tied up in bow-knots" by the Stanislavsky system. Stella Adler and many others heartily agreed with the second remark, if not the first. Brown was right when he wrote that this strained quality was gone from the improvisations. The blow-up over affective memory at Ellenville and the relaxed rehearsals of *Lefty* under Odets' and Meisner's hands-off direction had given the Group a new sense of freedom in their acting, and it showed.

With the more easygoing Clurman in charge of *Awake and Sing!* they hoped to retain that sense of freedom in their work on a full-length play. Strasberg's fierce dedication, which had so inspired them at Brookfield, had begun to seem unnecessarily harsh and often counterproductive. There had been artistry in all his productions, but lately there had been very little joy.

There was a great deal of joy in the rehearsals of *Awake and Sing!* and plenty of bickering too. Stella Adler had violently resisted being cast as Bessie Berger, the middle-aged mother of Odets' quarrelsome clan. Adler was proud of her looks and wanted to show them off onstage, not hide them under padding and a gray wig. Clurman finally provoked her by suggesting that she couldn't play such a demanding character role; she took the part, but was touchy and argumentative throughout rehearsals. Her brother, who played the small-time gangster Moe Axelrod, in love with the Bergers' daughter, Hennie, provoked Clurman on occasion with his "gross self-centeredness"—once prompting the director to fling a chair at him.

Momentary storms were subsumed in the general atmosphere of enthusiastic creativity. No one felt oppressed or intimidated by Harold's anger: he threw a fit, then it was over and forgotten—as often as not brushed aside with a burst of laughter over its absurdity. He excited the actors with his enthusiasm for the play; his talks about its significance in their lives and in American society were spellbinding. He made them eager to bring their very best to this funny and moving story, which illuminated the experience of people too often ignored on the American stage.

The essential difference between Odets' original manuscript and the play they were rehearsing could be grasped from the titles: the depressed tone of *I Got the Blues* as opposed to the commanding optimism of a title taken from the Biblical quotation "Awake and sing, ye that dwell in the dust." Both versions vividly portrayed a year in the life of the Bergers, a Jewish family in the Bronx struggling to make ends meet in hard times. The weak father, Myron, doesn't earn enough to support them; domineering Bessie is determined to keep the family together, even if it means sabotaging their son Ralph's love for a young woman because it would take his sixteen-dollar salary out of the house. She forces Hennie, pregnant by a man who has left town, to marry a young immigrant Jew to save the family's reputation. She mocks her impractical father, Jacob, who spouts Marx and advises Ralph to "go out and fight so life shouldn't be printed on dollar bills." If the plot seemed drab, the characters emphatically were not: even minor figures like Bessie's prosperous, self-satisfied brother Morty and the overworked janitor Schlosser were sharply drawn individuals, and their words had a streetwise poetry that was pure Odets.

In revising *I Got the Blues* and turning it into *Awake and Sing!* Odets took Clurman's advice and cut about twenty pages out of the sprawling first act. He made subtle but major changes in the ending, which Clurman had criticized as "almost masochistically pessimistic." In the first version, Jacob commits suicide and leaves his insurance money to Ralph; Bessie tries to keep it for the family but Myron prevents her by revealing that she has $4,100 in the bank; and Moe, who finally convinces Hennie he really loves her, is arrested for making book, so she is forced to remain with her husband. This conclusion expressed Odets' bitterness toward his own family and all the others like them who, as he saw it, stunted their own lives and those of their children with a stubborn adherence to a worn-out and irrelevant code of behavior.

Clurman argued for a more affirmative final statement, and by the winter of 1935 Odets was ready to provide one. Jacob still dies—although whether it is suicide or not is left undecided—but the young people are given a chance. Moe persuades Hennie to go away with him: "Make a break or spend the rest of your life in a coffin," he warns, and she decides to join him in his flight to a place where "the whole world's green grass and when you cry it's because you're happy." Ralph learns from his beloved grandfather's death that there is work for him to do. "Let Mom have the dough," he says of the insurance money. "Did Jake die for us to fight about nickels?" He can start changing the world in his own warehouse: "Get teams together all over. Spit on your hands and get to work . . . Maybe we'll fix it so life won't be printed on dollar bills." As Moe and Hennie leave, the curtain falls on Ralph standing "full and strong" in the doorway, looking toward a better future.

The new ending shared with *Lefty* a romantic faith in the value of struggle as personally fulfilling and politically necessary. What gave *Awake and Sing!* its unique quality, however, were the chaotic, cacaphonous scenes that preceded the lyrical finale. Odets captured the fractious intimacy of the overcrowded Berger household, whose exasperated inmates could be positively brutal in their attempts to carve out some emotional and spiritual space for themselves, in words as fast and funny as they were essentially sad. "No one else alive is writing such dialogue," Waldo Frank remarked at a rehearsal he attended.

The rapid, staccato tempo of the characters' speech was matched by the feverish pace of the rehearsals. Clurman and the actors had only four weeks to prepare the play, and their haste contributed to the warmth and spontaneity of a production that depended a great deal on the training Strasberg had given the Group actors but used it to a rather different end.

In terms of the structure of rehearsals, Clurman worked essentially as Strasberg did. The company began with a lengthy analysis of the play: the director outlined the overall action (Stanislavsky's super-objective), then traced its evolution throughout the script, the major and minor actions that brought the plot forward. They discussed each character's spine, the prime motivation that governed an individual's behavior, and how it related to the overall action. They analyzed relationships among characters and their significance to the play. Only after this lengthy period of talk did they begin to improvise scenes based on situations in the play; learning lines and formal blocking came last.

Strasberg did all this in his productions; indeed, he introduced the Group to this way of working. The difference was a matter of tone and emphasis. Strasberg looked at a text primarily for the emotional qualities it demanded of the actor, then set about to find ways to evoke those emotions in the people playing the parts. Every second was analyzed: what should the actor feel here? what personal experience would help create that feeling onstage? Improvisations, like the burning mine shaft and small-town wedding during *Connelly* rehearsals, were sometimes completely unrelated to the play's content, designed instead to work on the actors' technique. He was less concerned with the author's ideas, or at least he focused on how they were embodied in the characters' emotional development. What he wanted were performances imbued at every moment with true emotion, the sense that life itself was happening onstage.

Clurman wanted that too, but he wanted it in the context of the life of the play and its essential themes. He benefited in *Awake and Sing!* from a number of developments that enabled him to work with greater freedom and vividness toward establishing a through-line of action without sacrificing the depth of feeling that had distinguished past Group productions. He was directing a company whose grasp on their unified technique was firm and assured after four years of hard work under Strasberg's exacting tutelage. Clurman realized, as his partner apparently didn't, that it was no longer necessary to oversee every step of the actor's internal work on a part; often it was enough simply to explain what he was looking for and let the actor figure out the best way to make that quality personally real. He used improvisations more closely related to the play—a typical dinner at the Bergers, or a scene in which Jacob recounts a boyhood memory while sewing a button on his coat—trusting the actors to draw the parallels between what they were discovering about the characters and analogous situations in their own lives.

The actors could do that without using the affective memory exercises they'd grown to hate, because the milieu was so close to their own experiences. They'd observed similar relationships among their friends and families, they'd felt the frustration and anger of young people like Ralph and Hennie, they sensed that the Bergers' quarrelsome bond wasn't so different from the collective intimacy they'd dubbed with the joking name "Groupness." Their knowledge of each other as human beings *and* actors infused the interactions among characters in *Awake and Sing!* with a reality that astonished their audiences. It didn't seem like acting at all, said one admirer: "It simply appeared; it just seemed to be more alive and truer than anything I'd ever seen before." That truthfulness came as much from four years of working and living together as from anything Clurman did.

Clurman's great gift as a Group director was to recognize how much the actors could bring to the production and to invite them to do so as respected collaborators rather than subordinates. "Harold's rehearsals were like parties at which he was the guest of honor," said Kazan, who stage-managed the show. "He didn't hector his actors from an authoritarian position; he was a partner, not an overlord, in the struggle of production." His contribution was his brilliant interpretation of the play and the characters, the creation of an overall vision that unified everyone's work. That was the director's fundamental job, he believed; then, "by asking questions, by stirring the actor's imagination, by indicating the proper channels for the actor's thought, the director can induce a creative response. A good maxim to remember is: the director is responsible for *the what*, the actor for *the how.*"

This was quite different from Strasberg, who was virtually obsessed with the *how* of acting. With a company less skillful than the Group actors, Clurman's attitude could lead to technical problems, for he wasn't much interested in the mechanics of staging; in this area he was less imaginative and accomplished than Strasberg. But as an inspirer he was unequaled. He made theatre seem the noblest art, the greatest adventure and the most fun anyone could be lucky enough to have. Strasberg demanded sacrifice, work, work, and more work; Clurman promised fulfillment. He wrote in 1941:

> [The director] must not sacrifice the individual to the ensemble. *He* must see to it that the ensemble is served by the best efforts of each *individual.* He must show the individual that he—the individual— achieves his truest stature by serving the ensemble.

He backed up his belief that individual and collective fulfillment were complementary, not contradictory, by putting biographies of the actors in the *Awake and Sing!* program—the first time since the ill-fated *Gentlewoman*— stating that "brief accounts of their careers help to clarify the Group Theatre's methods and standards."

The remarkable ensemble in *Awake and Sing!* flourished under this loving approach. Bessie could have seemed vulgar and cruel; as Stella Adler played her, with biting humor and a sense of Jewish tradition, she had the dignity of a woman struggling to hold on to the only values she knew. Art Smith as her husband captured Myron's unassuming shamble with such apparent ease that he seemed actually to be living in the Bergers' shabby apartment. The profoundly moving interplay between the gentle despair of Morris Carnovsky as Jacob and Julie Garfield's fresh, youthful lyricism as Ralph made the crucial relationship between grandfather and grandson the play's emotional center. Jacob's desire to set his grandson on the right path in life drew some of its power from Carnovsky's personal affection for Garfield, one of the many young actors he guided and nurtured within the Group.

As the embittered Moe, Luther Adler was electrifying; his passionate final speech to Hennie, where he reviews his stunted life and begs her to give them both a chance for something more, was one of the single finest pieces of acting the Group ever produced. Phoebe Brand gave Hennie the warmth and sense of deep feeling needed to make the audience sympathize with a woman who abandons her husband and child at the final curtain. Capitalistic Uncle Morty had Joe Bromberg's usual comic zest. In his first good role, Sandy Meisner seized some of Odets' funniest, most characteristic dialogue ("I'm so nervous—look, two times I weighed myself on the subway station") and created an entire life behind it for Hennie's hapless husband. Like Meisner, only with many fewer lines, Bud Bohnen as the janitor gave a small part the weight of the character's life experience. The effect of the actors' superb work was to humanize a play that on paper sometimes seemed harsh without blunting its sharp truthfulness.

The humanism that informed the Group's production came from Clurman, whose love for Odets spilled over into his affection for the characters and their inchoate longings. He didn't try to clean up the script's exuberant messiness; in fact, he made it the production's stylistic motif. To give the audience a stronger sense of the life ebbing and flowing through the Bergers' overcrowded apartment, he decided with the set designer Boris Aronson to eliminate the wall between the dining room and living room so that action could take place simultaneously in both. The props were realistic, but each one was chosen to clarify the play's basic mood: a large wall calendar with a sentimental picture depicting luxurious surroundings made a stark contrast with the Bergers' living conditions and gave rise, Clurman thought, "to a special feeling of almost comic gloominess." Aronson, a Russian immigrant who felt he didn't know enough about American Jewish life, went to visit Julie Garfield's family in the Bronx; his set had the same heavy furniture and clutter of objects he'd observed weighing down the inhabitants there.

Aronson, an innovative designer strongly influenced by the Russian constructivists' ideas about three-dimensional, stylized scenery, viewed his realistic set for *Awake and Sing!* as merely a workmanlike effort. He had created far more interesting scenery for the Yiddish Art Theatre, where he worked regularly in the late 1920s. Like John Howard Lawson, he found the Group's Stanislavsky-based approach rather old-fashioned, and he was appalled by their naïve faith in the Soviet system, which he had fled in 1922. Yet he quickly became close friends with Clurman, Odets, and Kazan, drawn to them and the Group by a shared enthusiasm for American culture. Like Clurman, he saw the raw material for theatre in the city streets. "The American rhythm is expressed in the forms which are the daily visual experience of every American," he wrote in 1930. "These forms have utilitarian motives: to attract, to sell, to please. But as they are the experience of America, they are also the expression of America. Hence they may be called the American art: indigenous and lively rather than borrowed and effete."

As rehearsals of the Group's own indigenous form of American art sped toward conclusion, the company sensed that they were creating something important and new, a play that argued as strongly as *Lefty*, though in less ideological terms, that capitalist society maimed the lives of its less fortunate members. No one else in New York seemed to share their faith in *Awake and Sing!*: although the production cost only $6,000—cheap even in 1935, when the average Broadway show was budgeted at $10,000—neither Clurman nor Odets could raise it. The director finally phoned Hollywood for help; Franchot Tone, who had heard from Crawford about the exciting rehearsals, sent $5,000 without even reading the script. His generosity made it possible for the play to open at the Belasco on February 19.

The critics were cordial, but relatively restrained. Unsurprisingly, they focused a good deal of their attention on the author of the now famous *Waiting for Lefty*. Everyone acknowledged Odets' unique way with words. In the *Post* John Mason Brown praised his "uncommon ability to heighten the idioms of daily speech into dialogue that was as seemingly true to life as it was theatrically effective," although the Brooklyn *Eagle*'s Arthur Pollock complained that "he puts words together rather than ideas." Several were relieved to find *Awake and Sing!* less political than its predecessor. "It is comforting to find that Mr. Odets has not written one of those naive plays in which the right is always on one side," wrote Brown. His more conservative colleagues, however, discerned Odets' point of view in Ralph's closing speech and criticized its radicalism. Whatever the individual reservations, opinion was virtually unanimous that, as John Anderson averred in the *Journal*, "Clifford Odets has the stuff." The press congratulated the Group on finding "a new dramatist of exciting potential . . . the only one the present season has disclosed."

Critics also noted how fortunate Odets was in his cast. "[The Group Theatre] has never presented a more fluent production," said Brown, and Brooks Atkinson commented that the actors "play as if they felt at home inside Mr. Odets' Bronx saga." Luther Adler's performance was generally considered the finest of the season, and Carnovsky got the best notices of his distinguished career. "It is almost an impertinence to praise such a performance, so complete, so perfectly judged and balanced, so authentic in every detail of character, feeling and action," wrote his old friend Virginia Farmer in *New Theatre*. Their personal reviews were only slightly better than those of the other actors, and Sandy Meisner almost stole the show in his small but pitifully moving part.

Despite all their praise, it was clear that the reviewers didn't wholeheartedly like the play, and their strictures about Clurman's direction revealed why. "Brittle," "overwrought," and "shrill" were about the kindest comments his fast-paced staging received. Yet, as Edith J. R. Isaacs admitted in *Theatre Arts Monthly*, it was entirely appropriate to the subject matter. "These people in this wretched Bronx flat are, it is easy to imagine, forever treading on each other's toes, stumbling across each other's sentences, knocking over each other's idols." However, she concluded loftily, "A director with the right restraint would have suggested much of this without actually letting it seem that two of the people on his stage were always trying to occupy the same space at the same time, and continually interrupting or doubling on each other's speech." Ironically, the proletarian *Daily Worker* was as offended by this "messy naturalism" as the bourgeois press.

Isaacs and her peers seemed to be faulting Clurman's direction for qualities in the play itself that made them uneasy. It was so messy, so cluttered, so noisy, so . . . Jewish. "It is as non-Aryan as a Bronx Express and as swift," said Walter Winchell, and if he enjoyed the sensation of being "a neighbor of the Bergers, not a reporter at a play," many of his colleagues did not. The radical critics liked working people to be angry and noble, not confused and quarrelsome. Among their colleagues in the mainstream press the underlying assumption was still that such common folk belonged in the theatre only as the subjects of low comedy or sentimental melodrama. Odets treated them as real people whose lives and aspirations were of general interest, and the Group's acting gave them a dignity not everyone thought they deserved.

In its own more personal way, *Awake and Sing!* was just as revolutionary as *Lefty,* and the audience knew it. There were fifteen curtain calls on opening night; the house shook with bravos, cheers, and applause emanating largely from the balcony, "where I assume authorities [on Bronx life] sit," Burns Mantle noted condescendingly in his unfavorable *Daily News* review. When a young writer named Alfred Kazin saw the show a few months later, he felt the excitement of people discovering that culture was for them, that their lives were worthy of an artist's consideration. "How interesting we all were, how vivid and strong on the beat of that style!" he wrote.

> Listening to Stella Adler as Mrs. Berger in *Awake and Sing!,* I thought that never in their lives would my mother and the other Brooklyn-Bronx mamas know that they were on stage, and that the force of so much truth could be gay . . . Sitting in the Belasco, watching my mother and father and uncles and aunts occupying the stage in *Awake and Sing* by as much right as if they were Hamlet and Lear, I understood at last. It was all one, as I had always known. Art and truth and hope could yet come together . . . I had never seen actors on the stage and an audience in the theatre come together with such a happy shock.

Kazin was wrong about only one thing: a good many Bronx mothers and fathers made the trek down to Broadway to see themselves onstage. Helen Thompson kept the Belasco well filled with benefit parties, and their vocal response to the play often startled the quieter audience members sitting sedately in the orchestra. The balcony especially loved Carnovsky; Jacob's ardent yet passive socialism was a part of a European heritage many of them knew intimately, and his hope that his grandson would fulfill the dreams that had been shattered in his life was personally moving to people struggling to put children through school on working-class incomes. They gave him the warmest reception at the curtain call, and some nights they stopped the show with their applause when he cried out, "Awake and sing, ye that dwell in the dust!" They also adored it when Stella Adler pulled off her gray wig to flaunt her golden hair as she took her bow; it infuriated her fellow actors, but it was the kind of flamboyant gesture Yiddish theatre audiences had always enjoyed. In the early months of its run, *Awake and Sing!* averaged $10,000 a week at the box office, nothing like the money such huge hits as George Abbott's *Three Men on a Horse* pulled in, but more than any other Group production except *Men in White.*

The box-office figures gave no real indication of the stir Odets and the Group created in New York that spring. The one-two punch of *Lefty* followed by *Awake and Sing!* made them the talk of the town. At the center of it all, because the media preferred to spotlight an individual rather than a group, was the delighted and apprehensive playwright. The phone never stopped ringing at the new apartment on University Place he had rented with Clurman. His new agent, Harold Freedman, reported offers from movie studios for his services as a screenwriter; Odets kept turning them down, and they kept upping the ante: $500 a week, $700, $1,250, $2,500. Invitations poured in for lunch, for cocktails, for dinner with people Odets the struggling actor had known only as names on a marquee: Helen Hayes, Charles MacArthur, Moss Hart, Tallulah Bankhead, Billy Rose, Jed Harris, Edna Ferber, Fannie Brice, Beatrice Lillie. He began a romance with a big Broadway star, Ruth Gordon. He attended a lot of parties, often standing in the corner scribbling furiously in his notebook, awed by his inclusion in the revels of celebrities. Everyone wanted to meet him, talk to him, interview him, to find out what he thought about America, about the Soviet Union, about the theatre.

Odets finally had the fame he'd longed for, and it was as disturbing as it was intoxicating. He felt beleaguered and bewildered by all this attention, which seemed to belong to someone else. "A new Odets has come to town," he told a reporter from the Buffalo *Times*. "I see him as a suit of clothes with some utter stranger inside them, who is known as 'Odets, the successful playwright' . . . meanwhile I follow along behind him, exactly the same as I was six months ago, trying to write a good play, appreciating the flavor of good Scotch and suffering like hell from a headache this minute as if the new Odets had never existed."

His friend Clurman warned him of the dangers lurking for an artist who let himself be dazzled by the transitory spotlight of American success, and Odets tried to keep a level head. In interviews, whenever possible, he turned the conversation to his work. He was decidedly ambivalent about being hailed as the fair-haired boy of the revolutionary theatre. On the one hand, he disliked being labeled a propaganda dramatist. "I'm concerned with the realism of the characters and the essential truth of the theme," he explained to the *Herald Tribune*, adding in another interview, "No special pleading is necessary in a play which says that people should have fuller and richer lives." On the other hand, he still cared very much what the left thought of him (both the *Daily Worker* and the *New Masses* found *Awake and Sing!* ideologically muddled) and was eager to reaffirm the commitment that had sparked *Lefty*. "Of course I believe social and economic reform can be accomplished with the aid of the theatre, or I wouldn't be writing for it," he said. You didn't have to be a propagandist, he argued, to make a case for change: "Today the truth followed to its logical conclusion is inevitably revolutionary."

Odets was too intelligent not to realize that part of his appeal for the press and the celebrity hounds lay in his exotic radicalism, something Broadway columnists knew little about. Certainly the Group had drawn the ire of critics in the past for presenting left-wing drama, and Joe Bromberg never made any bones about his opinions. ("My tendencies are extremely radical," he explained to a reporter from the Brooklyn *Eagle* during the run of *Gold Eagle Guy.*) But the political sentiments expressed in *1931—* and *Gentlewoman* had been blamed primarily on their authors. Until now the Group had been viewed essentially as an art theatre; their famous method had drawn more press than their social views. Not until *Lefty* and Odets arrived did articles begin casually referring to the Group's "blood-and-thunder Red melodramas," or to a communist (quoted in the *Post*) "delighted to find the Group Theatre going Red in such a big way" that "its days of being 'The Grope Theatre' [are] safely behind it."

Within a year the directors, at least, were worried enough by the "Red" label to issue a public disclaimer asserting that the Group should not be identified with the views of their playwrights. But that spring the whole Group proudly accepted their alliance with an exciting new force in the American theatre. The left theatre movement had been gathering momentum throughout 1934, and by the time *Lefty* opened a mainstream critic like Brooks Atkinson could note, almost in passing, that "the progress of the revolutionary drama in New York City during the last two years is the most obvious recent development in our theatre." Part of the reason the Group got so much attention was that they were much more accessible to Broadway journalists than those strange people at the Theatre Union and the Workers Laboratory Theatre—at least the Group worked north of 14th Street.

Broadway hadn't been quite ready for radical drama in 1934, when John Wexley's passionate play about the Scottsboro case, *They Shall Not Die,* disconcerted Theatre Guild subscribers and Elmer Rice's ambitious program of socially conscious theatre foundered after two poorly received productions at the Belasco. Rice was so angry that he wrote an article in November declaring he would never work in the commercial theatre again, because the profit motive "stifles the creative impulse and dams the free flow of human vitality." (He talked with the Group briefly about joining them before signing up with the Federal Theatre Project in August.) Nineteen thirty-five was the year Broadway discovered drama with a message: Katharine Cornell appeared in an antiwar play *(Flowers of the Forest),* Leslie Howard starred in a melodrama that was also a parable about the impotence of liberalism *(The Petrified Forest),* and such formerly inconceivable projects as a radical musical revue originally written for the Theatre Union *(Parade* by Paul Peters and George Sklar) and a play dramatizing the plight of Carolina miners *(Let Freedom Ring* by the Group's old friend Albert Bein) could also be seen in Times Square.

And, as of March 26, so could *Lefty*. After months of sold-out benefits, the Group decided to bring the show uptown. Since their share of the *Awake and Sing!* proceeds barely covered the weekly payroll for more than thirty full Group members, they hoped income from an additional production would help them build up some savings for the future. But they needed a second play to round out the evening; the sketches were deemed too informal for a nonbenefit audience, and *Dmitroff* was too much a conventional, speechifying piece of agitprop for the directors to feel comfortable with it on Broadway. They turned to their hot new playwright for a companion piece.

Odets wrote *Till the Day I Die* in five days. It was based on a letter in the *New Masses* about a German communist arrested by the Nazis, who made it appear that he'd betrayed his comrades and eventually drove him to suicide. It wasn't a very good play; the stilted language, so unlike the vibrant dialogue of Odets' two earlier works, revealed his lack of personal experience with the subject matter. Still, it was one of the first anti-Nazi dramas to be produced on Broadway, and it gave some Group members who'd been restlessly inactive their first parts of the year. Billy Kirkland played Ernst Tausig, the violinist turned underground leader; Beany Barker was his lover, Tilly; Eunice Stoddard played another member of the underground; Dorothy Patten was a Nazi wife. Strasberg, who like them had missed out on the excitement of *Lefty* and *Awake and Sing!*, was so eager for some connection with Group life that he took a tiny part as the shattered survivor of a detention camp, his first acting job since the Group was formed. Lewis Leverett and Bud Bohnen played the two principal Nazis, the former a sadistic captain, the latter an anguished major trying to hide his Jewish blood and repress his self-contempt for collaborating with fascism.

Crawford was credited as the director of *Till the Day I Die*, although several people in the production couldn't remember her being at rehearsals. It's likely the play was thrown together in much the same casual fashion as *Lefty*, with the actors basically directing themselves. The minimal set was designed by Paul Morrison, a close friend of Sandy Meisner's and one of the many young theatre folk in New York who hung around eagerly on the fringes of Group life. (He'd been the assistant stage manager of *Gold Eagle Guy.*) Morrison worked for free; he spent $329.64 on construction, painting, and props; and the costumes set the Group back $150. *Lefty* cost essentially nothing, so even after Crawford added in such indirect expenses as publicity and insurance, her total outlay for the double bill was $1,694.95, making it surely one of the cheapest Broadway shows on record. The rock-bottom budget enabled the Group to keep ticket prices unusually low: seats at the Longacre Theatre cost from 40 cents to $1.50, and the ads boasted "two plays for half the price of one!" Even though they'd moved uptown, the Group wanted *Lefty* to remain accessible to their downtown audience.

Group actors not in *Awake and Sing!* replaced the original *Lefty* cast

The Group Theatre's directors—"two Old Testament prophets and a WASP *shiksa*"
—at Brookfield Center in 1931. *Left to right:* Lee Strasberg, Harold Clurman, and
Cheryl Crawford.

"The Group is our life": the entire company at Brookfield Center. *Seated on the steps, clockwise from the front:* J. Edward Bromberg, Lewis Leverett, Sylvia Feningston, Harold Clurman, Phoebe Brand. *Standing on the grass, left to right: (to the left of the steps)* Philip Robinson, Clifford Odets, Paula Miller, Morris Carnovsky, Mary Morris, Stella Adler; *(to right of steps)* Clement Wilenchick, Friendly Ford, Walter Coy, Gerrit Kraber. *On the porch, left to right:* Margaret Barker, Alixe Walker, Dorothy Patten, Sanford Meisner, Franchot Tone, Cheryl Crawford, Robert Lewis, Virginia Farmer, Mab Maynard, Lee Strasberg, Ruth Nelson, William Challee, Eunice Stoddard, Art Smith, Herbert Ratner. (Photo by Paul Strand)

Clurman (seated at far left) at Brookfield Center, giving one of the wide-ranging talks an actor later spoofed as "The Cultural History of the United States and Its Derivations from Europe, the Foundations of the Group Theatre, and the Philosophy of Harold Clurman." (Photo by Ralph Steiner)

The scene from *The House of Connelly* that prompted a startled Guild Theatre doorman to try and toss a bucket of water on Morris Carnovsky. Franchot Tone standing at right center, Carnovsky on the couch upstage with William Challee and Art Smith bending over him, J. Edward Bromberg being restrained in front of the windows.

The class struggle on Broadway: the director of a Bowery flophouse and a group
of well-fed tourists look down on the unemployed in *1931—*.

ABOVE LEFT: "The blood and bones of a living stage must be the blood and bones of the actuality around us." John Howard Lawson. ABOVE: A miscast Dorothy Patten and an uncomfortable Luther Adler in one of *Success Story*'s less successful moments. LEFT: Stella and Luther Adler in *Success Story*, bringing the passion of the Yiddish theatre to a contemporary American play.

The famous operating room scene in *Men in White*, the brilliantly theatrical apo-
theosis of Lee Strasberg's unified production technique.

Theatre becomes life: *Waiting for Lefty* on Broadway. Elia Kazan clenches his fists in defiance at center stage; Russell Collins, second from right, glowers capitalistic menace.

LEFT: Clifford Odets, man of the hour in 1935—"a suit of clothes with some utter stranger inside them, who is known as 'Odets the successful playwright.' " BELOW: Odets' Bronx Jews, "occupying the stage in *Awake and Sing!* by as much right as if they were Hamlet and Lear." Morris Carnovsky comforts Jules Garfield at the window; gathered around the table (left to right) are Art Smith, Luther Adler, Phoebe Brand (back to camera), Stella Adler, Sanford Meisner, and J. Edward Bromberg.

LEFT: Stella Adler in the mid-1930s, displaying the glamorous looks she resented hiding under a gray wig and padding in *Awake and Sing!* BELOW: Stylization in the service of a deeper realism. *Left to right:* Robert Lewis, Morris Carnovsky, and Luther Adler in *Paradise Lost.*

ABOVE: A dubious Morris Carnovsky and a didactic
Lee Strasberg discussing *Case of Clyde Griffiths*,
1936. BELOW: A battered Group tries to look hopefully toward the future at the Pine Brook Club,
Nichols, Connecticut, 1936.

The Group flexing their muscles, Felicia Sorel wielding a drum, and Gluck Sandor (back to camera) exhorting them to greater efforts during a body movement class at Pine Brook. (Photo by Ralph Steiner)

ABOVE: *Left to right:* Art Smith, Russell Collins, and Sanford Meisner, mercifully unencumbered (for the moment) by Donald Oenslager's massive scenery, in *Johnny Johnson.* BELOW: Luther Adler and Frances Farmer in one of the quiet scenes from *Golden Boy* that Adler loved best: "They're closest to me because they contain most of what Clifford Odets is himself."

ABOVE: After the 1937 reorganization: Morris Carnovsky, at left, as the representative of the apprehensive actors to the Group's new powers-that-be (left to right), Elia Kazan, Kermit Bloomgarden, Harold Clurman, Roman Bohnen, and Luther Adler. BELOW: The core of the Group after the shake-out. *Seated, left to right:* Luther Adler, Phoebe Brand, Eleanor Lynn, Frances Farmer, Robert Lewis, Art Smith, Elia Kazan. *Standing:* stage manager Bill Watts, Irwin Shaw, Sanford Meisner, Ruth Nelson, Lee Cobb, Harold Clurman, Leif Erickson, Roman Bohnen, Morris Carnovsky, Michael Gordon, and Kermit Bloomgarden.

ABOVE: Clurman in action, circa spring 1939. Even as they questioned his leadership, the actors could still be enthralled by his spellbinding talks. Here (left to right), Leif Erickson, Luther Adler, Frances Farmer, Ruth Nelson, Sanford Meisner, Phoebe Brand, Eleanor Lynn, Elia Kazan, and Irwin Shaw hang on his every word; only Morris Carnovsky, seated below Clurman, seems impassive. BELOW: William Challee (standing) and Leif Erickson in a scene from *Rocket to the Moon* that was cut shortly after the play opened. Some of Odets' best writing went into scenes that didn't advance the plot; a practical theatre man to his fingertips, he axed this one when he decided it slowed the pace of the third act.

ABOVE: Art nourishing life in *My Heart's in the Highlands*. Art Smith's trumpet calls forth the villagers' offerings, grouped in Robert Lewis' imaginative staging to suggest a tree flowering as it is watered. BELOW: Homeless. Elia Kazan and Jane Wyatt on the streets in *Night Music*, the Odets play whose failure prompted the final breakdown of the Group.

members who were. Russell Collins took over Carnovsky's multiple roles as the various evil incarnations of capitalism. Gadget Kazan got Joe Bromberg's show-stopping turn as Agate Keller. Paula Miller was upgraded to Phoebe Brand's part as Florrie after a bitter quarrel between Strasberg and Odets, who didn't think the director's wife was good enough. (Apparently their common membership in the Communist party didn't inspire Odets with enough revolutionary solidarity to overcome his artistic scruples about Miller.) Dorothy Patten replaced her as the militant secretary, and Bobby Lewis took Collins' role as the labor spy. Odets replaced Luther Adler as Doctor Benjamin; the opening-night audience gave him a standing ovation.

The critics were nice to him too. A surprising number abandoned their usual strictures against propaganda onstage. "Of course [*Lefty*] is propaganda," said a Newark reviewer. "And what's wrong with propaganda intelligently applied and worked out by someone with something to say and the fine, singing words in which to say it?" Richard Watts understood the crucial contribution Odets' beliefs made to his style. "The critics who are telling him that he should outgrow his propagandist purposes are giving him bad advice," Watts wrote in the *Herald Tribune*. "It is to his enthusiasm for the radical viewpoint that almost all his finest qualities, from his fire to his sense of pity and terror, can be attributed, and without his zeal he would not be the flaming dramatist he seems destined to become."

As Hitler's power increased abroad, as industrial strife worsened in the United States and dust storms drove hundreds of thousands of farmers off the land, Odets' political plays seemed too important to be dismissed out of hand, even by those who disagreed with their conclusions. "I don't care what your political religion may be," Whitney Bolton wrote in the *Morning Telegraph*, "nor how thoroughly you may distrust and resent Communists. I think you owe it to yourself and the days of the times you live in to see *Till the Day I Die* and *Waiting for Lefty*. These are plays of today, of now, of this morning, in the warm terms of today. [Odets] is writing about your world and the corners of it you inhabit."

He was also, the press agreed, writing great theatre. "Iron-fisted and exciting stuff," John Anderson said in the *Journal*. "What [Odets] has is an intuitive sense of stagecraft, the sort of easy command of his medium which [Noel] Coward has. . . . His is the theatre of a writing actor." John Mason Brown praised Odets' "extraordinary instinct for theatre" in the *Post*, and even Brooks Atkinson, who disliked *Till the Day I Die*, admitted it was "unmistakably the work of a man indigenous to the theatre." The understanding of craft Odets had gained during his four years with the Group gave even his lesser works a drive and sheer theatrical excitement very few plays, right or left, could boast.

Yet *Lefty* didn't have quite the same electrifying impact on Broadway that it had downtown. Kazan made a huge hit in the rabble-rousing finale —Walter Winchell said he "look[ed] as though he was pulled right off a cab to play the role," and one reviewer later referred to him as a "proletarian thunderbolt"—but the cast overall wasn't so effective. The main difference, though, was the audience. Even with the lower ticket prices, it was still a more conventional crowd, undoubtedly including some people curious about the nation's most notorious play who had been too timid to venture down to 14th Street. The opening-night audience, noted Stanley Burnshaw in the *New Masses*, was "frankly jittery" (one woman fainted) and much less responsive to the play's humor, though they appeared sympathetic to the workers' plight as presented in Odets' warmly human language.

Just as Broadway reviewers were becoming more receptive to revolutionary drama, Burnshaw's article revealed that radicals were now willing to give bourgeois theatregoers the benefit of the doubt. "In every Broadway audience," he wrote, "there are numberless potential friends of the revolutionary theatre movement, a fact which we all too often ignore. While we sneer at these people, the Group does something far more intelligent. It talks directly into their ears, it challenges them with pictures of our world which some among them may come to recognize eventually as their own." In the face of the growing fascist threat abroad *and* at home—it's easy to forget today just how many Nazi sympathizers there were in America in the mid-1930s—the left was slowly beginning to realize it was suicidal to waste time nit-picking with well-meaning liberals when the real enemy was elsewhere. The League of Workers Theatres acknowledged this when it changed its name in February to the New Theatre League and opened admission to anyone who could subscribe to a broad-based credo: "For mass development of the American theatre to its highest artistic level. For a theatre dedicated to the struggle against war, fascism and censorship."

Those were goals everyone in the Group shared, and in the spring of 1935 they participated in a broad spectrum of theatrical activities with the exhilarating sense that everything they did was part of a larger movement fighting to make theatre, and life, more meaningful.

Kazan was the most obsessively busy. His Group work was enough to keep him hopping. He stage-managed *Awake and Sing!* and understudied Sandy Meisner; he played a small part in *Till the Day I Die* before bringing down the house at the end of *Lefty*. When Meisner got sick in May, Kazan spent a week playing Sam at the Belasco, without giving up his crowd-pleasing role as Agate Keller. Every night he exited the Belasco stage early in Act Three and leaped into a cab at 10:38, pulling off his putty nose and changing costumes during the four-block ride to 48th Street, where he rushed into the Longacre to deliver Agate's final speech.

Anyone less consumed with the need for work would have spent his days recuperating, but not Kazan. He taught at the New Theatre League, which had launched an actor-training program; Art Smith, Joe Bromberg, and Cheryl Crawford also gave classes there. He'd always wanted to direct, and the Workers Laboratory Theatre gave him a chance to try. The company had recently given itself a new name, the Theatre of Action, and a new goal, to present full-length plays in a professional manner as the Theatre Union and the Group had done. (It was symptomatic of the temper of the times that the new venture's executive board included not just such workers theatre stalwarts as Albert Maltz and George Sklar, but also Moss Hart, one of Broadway's most commercially successful playwrights.) Kazan joined to help founder Al Saxe direct their first effort, a play about life in the Civilian Conservation Corps called *The Young Go First*. Under the aegis of Nykino, the Theatre of Action's film branch, he codirected a movie called *Pie in the Sky* with his wife, Molly Thacher, and photographer Ralph Steiner. The satire on organized religion featured Russell Collins as an unctuous preacher and Kazan as a destitute wanderer.

Other Group members were almost as active. Collins, Tony Kraber, Bill Challee, and Walter Coy took small roles in a special three-night run of *Panic*, a play about the '29 crash written by poet Archibald MacLeish, produced by John Houseman, and starring nineteen-year-old Orson Welles. "Every actor . . . should definitely make such work part of his experience," said Collins. "It makes him forget stage selfishness, the exaltation of part above play, and makes him realize how co-operative a work of real drama is." No matter where they went, the Group actors took their ideals with them. Sandy Meisner took his to the Neighborhood Playhouse acting program, which had evolved out of the old producing organization; he has taught there, with one five-year break, ever since. Strasberg took his to the Theatre Collective, where he taught directing while Carnovsky, Crawford, and Lewis Leverett offered actor training. Art Smith put his on paper and wrote *The Tide Rises*, a one-act play about the San Francisco general strike the preceding year.

One Group actor was having a hard time making idealism compensate for a dearth of good parts. Alan Baxter played a gunman in the original production of *Lefty*, another in the succession of tiny roles the Group had given him. The problem, in the directors' opinion, was that Baxter was a conventional actor without emotional depth, a drawback exacerbated by his habit of talking through clenched teeth. They were fond of him and needed an actor with his kind of leading-man looks; they sent him to speech teachers to get him to open his mouth, and Crawford worked with him for hours on affective memory. None of it seemed to help—Bobby Lewis gained much amusement from his clandestine observation of Crawford's fruitless attempts to loosen Baxter up—and they kept him in small parts. When the Theatre Union offered him the lead in *Black Pit*, a play about a miner who turns informer after spending three years in jail, he announced he would rather do that than suffer anymore under Group discipline. The actors called a special meeting and begged him to stay, but his mind was made up. He did well enough in *Black Pit* to get a contract in Hollywood, where his impassive delivery worked just fine for his many gangster roles.

The reception of *Black Pit* showed that the radical theatre community's new interest in broader appeal hadn't eliminated their concern that a play's message be politically correct. Many labor activists were appalled that the Union would present a drama that portrayed an informer as someone tragically trapped by circumstance rather than as a plain old stool pigeon. That spring's ideological squabbles proved, if nothing else, that the theatrical left comprehended a spectrum of opinion in which the Communist party's preeminence was obvious but not absolute. When members of the cast of *Sailors of Catarro*, a drama of an Austrian naval mutiny, walked a picket line with striking workers at Ohrbach's department store, a member of the executive board of their own producing group (the Theatre Union again) wrote an article in the socialist *New Leader* criticizing them as naïve and asserting that the office workers union was communist-controlled. Another member of the board answered him angrily in print, but the Union hung on to both men; it was committed to the principle of political diversity within a broadly left-wing consensus.

The Group got a taste of the left's fratricidal tendencies in mid-March, when the *New Leader* ran a bizarre article by Gertrude Weil Klein, who clearly wasn't head of the Clifford Odets Fan Club. Klein titled her piece "Workers Stink," a remark she claimed Odets had made in his Greenwich Village days. After calling *Lefty* "A pretty bad piece of theatrical hokum," she went on to point out (correctly, as it happened) that most of Odets' cabbies weren't workers at all, but declassed professionals. "The regular, ordinary taxi-drivers are a pretty low, ignorant lot," she asserted (incorrectly). "Its bad men are all old-line labor leaders, synonymous with gangsters, racketeers and crooks." Her point was that Odets was a political naïf, led astray by sinister CP agitators, who had slandered that portion of the labor movement that wasn't communist. Since the *New Leader* had been hostile to the original taxi strike and supported a settlement the union membership rejected as a sellout, there was reason to believe Odets was simply a handy target in the ongoing war between the Socialist and Communist parties. (The Communist International's declaration of a united front in August muffled the hostilities, but never quite brought them to a halt.)

Odets sent an angry telegram vehemently denying the quotation. "No one is born class-conscious," he admitted. "But even before I was consciously prepared to express the strong working-class sympathy that is an integral part of my plays, I could not have said such a thing." He affected to disdain sectarian name-calling: "I'll bet there isn't one rank-and-file Socialist out of a thousand who wouldn't recognize in my old-line labor leaders the kind of labor fakers who have sold out one strike after another." However, the pointed references to "rank-and-file" and "labor fakers" (a frequent CP term of abuse for socialist union officials) made it clear which side Odets was on. The Group sent a delegation to the paper to denounce "such an insult to both our organization and to the working class with which the play deals and for whom it was played." The editor, who probably realized that the article made the *New Leader* look both petty and envious, promptly apologized, claiming he hadn't seen the piece before it ran and admitting the justice of the Group's protest, "although we do not agree with its heat."

The whole strange affair was rather exciting for the Group; it gave them a heady sense of being allied with the *real* radicals, while jealous parlor pinks sat on the sidelines and criticized. Plenty of people who weren't communists felt the party was doing important work and could be a valuable source of tactical advice. The revolt within Actors Equity, for example, would never have achieved as much as it did without the shrewd assistance of Andy Overgaard, who'd become friendly with several Group members through the party.

The previous spring, disgusted by Actors Equity's failure to help the cast of *Sailor, Beware!*, an insurgent group had prodded the union to make its procedures more democratic and managed to elect three of their number to the governing Equity Council. In February 1935 the rebels organized themselves formally as the Actors Forum to effect further change. They wanted Equity to create a Cuts Board to review any requests by producers for reduced salaries; they also urged the union to advocate rehearsal pay for actors and the abolition of the junior minimum salary, which allowed managers to pay younger actors twenty-five dollars a week while senior members in equal roles got forty dollars. Six of them agreed to stand for election to the nominating committee that virtually controlled election to the Council.

At a stormy meeting on March 1, Forum members learned that there was no point in having good ideas if they couldn't get them heard. Equity president Frank Gilmore had learned about playing rough during the bitter 1919 strike that gave birth to the union. He packed the meeting with his supporters, he allowed an anti-Forum letter to be read aloud, he refused to let Forum members respond, and when Bob Reed, a Theatre Union actor who headed the Forum, protested, Gilmore had him ejected from the hall. Unsurprisingly, none of the rebels made it onto the nominating committee. Even after the election was over, Gilmore cut off discussion of the Forum's platform. Bud Bohnen was so outraged by Gilmore's high-handed tactics and Red-baiting comments that he began to shake all over; "My God, Bud, calm yourself!" urged the tougher-minded Phoebe Brand.

Shocked and disheartened, Odets and a few others who knew Overgaard went to him for advice. There was no point in trying to get their views across in a hostile environment, he told them. They would have to build support for their platform outside the Equity structure. The Forum held a meeting at Bryant Hall on April 3 and invited all Equity members to attend. Gilmore, of course, didn't, but he sent someone to report on the proceedings. The meeting endorsed an independent slate of candidates for the Council, including Beany Barker, Billy Kirkland, Morris Carnovsky, and Joe Bromberg. Bad feelings and dirty tricks ran rampant during the June election: many actors never received the independent ballot, and none of the rebels got in.

The Forum lost the battle but won the war. The Council, with the exception of the three insurgents elected the previous year, firmly backed Gilmore through the beginning of April. But his support began to erode after the Bryant Hall meeting revealed how many members were fed up with Equity's leaders. Although the Council passed a resolution in June stating that it had complete faith in Gilmore's honesty and handling of the ballots, the three rebels pointedly voted "present" and several others retained nagging doubts about the election's fairness. By July the Council had established a Cuts Board, ruled (over Gilmore's heated objections) that managers must pay actors during rehearsal, and passed a compromise resolution allowing no more than 20 percent of any company to be employed at the junior minimum salary.

The Communist party hadn't handed these gains to American actors, any more than it had told them what to ask for in the first place. But the Council unquestionably felt pressure from the membership, which had been aroused in part by the Forum's skillful organizing as a result of Overgaard's advice. Labor unions across America benefited from CP organizers' tactical expertise as they fought for recognition and decent wages. The great paradox of the 1930s, which many former communists still grapple with uneasily today, is that so much good work was done at home by people who looked overseas for inspiration and direction to a government that was repressing and murdering its citizens on a scale no capitalist country outside of Nazi Germany would have dared attempt.

That uncomfortable realization came later. In 1935 it was still possible to dismiss the stories filtering out of the Soviet Union about the first Stalinist purges as the lies of Trotskyites and the capitalist press. What mattered to Group members caught up in a whirl of artistic and political activism was the feeling that they were accomplishing things, that they were making the world and their own small corner of it better. They had brought their convictions to Broadway with Odets' three plays and shown that audiences, and even some critics, were hungry for meaningful theatre. They gave younger, struggling companies the benefit of their artistic expertise through their teaching and appearances outside the Group. Their benefits raised money for good causes ranging from the Committee for the Defense of Political Prisoners to Jewish charitable organizations. Art and life were one, and they were proving it every day.

No one was happier about it than Harold Clurman, who'd been personally vindicated by the Group's triumph. His closest friend was now recognized as America's most exciting young playwright, and it was Clurman who'd nurtured Odets' talent through four long years of alternating hope and despair. He'd stood firm against the American fever for instant results in every area of Group life: refusing to expel members who were slow to develop or temporarily provoked the collective wrath, reminding the company in moments of both success and failure that their road was long and must be trod deliberately, adamantly insisting that he would direct only when he felt ready. He'd proved that growth took time, that the best results were worth waiting for. The press might criticize his direction of *Awake and Sing!* The actors knew it had been perfect for the play and an important step in the evolution of the Group's creative process. As they rushed around New York on their various missions, they were fulfilling his vision that ideas and actions worked together to make a complete life.

Secure in his achievements, eager for a change of scene, Clurman decided to return to the Soviet Union and explore its theatre in more depth. *Awake and Sing!* continued to do well, and though the double bill was taking in only about $6,000 a week the running costs were so low it hardly mattered. The two productions would sustain the Group financially for a few more months. The newly prosperous Odets gave Clurman the money for the trip, paying him back many times over for the day in 1932 when the impecunious director opened a thin wallet with two dollar bills in it and told his friend, "Take one." Cheryl Crawford decided to come along and see the Soviet stage for herself. They set off on April 13; the Group gave Clurman a new traveling bag and a leather-bound diary to record his impressions.

Lee Strasberg remained at home, prey to bitter thoughts about his diminished prestige. Crawford's status hadn't been changed by the earthquake of *Lefty:* she was still the calm, capable mother who took care of all the practical problems "the boys" (as she frequently referred to her fellow directors) couldn't deal with. She may not have been entirely satisfied with this role, but she'd made her peace with it. Strasberg had fallen from the heights, and he was badly bruised. He wasn't sure he had a future in a company now run more by consensus than by leadership from the top; he wasn't sure he wanted one. He needed time to think things over. He went to the Actors Committee, charged with managing the Group's affairs while Clurman and Crawford were gone, and told them he had to have a leave of absence. If it wasn't granted, he warned, he might have to resign from the Group altogether. The actors were startled and distressed; they might get fed up with Strasberg sometimes, but no one had forgotten how much he'd contributed to Group life. They urged him not to do anything hasty, to wait until his fellow directors returned before making any decisions. He did, and by the time they got back he seemed to have adjusted to the Group's altered power structure.

Virtually inactive since its founding in the wake of *Big Night*'s closing in 1933, the Actors Committee had revived that winter, when the flood of phone calls, letters, requests for interviews, and all the other post-*Lefty* attention made it impossible for Crawford and the Group's tiny business staff to handle everything themselves. The Committee was composed at that time of the same five men who made up the Group's writing collective, SKKOB: Smith, Kirkland, Kazan, Odets, and Bohnen. In addition to such mundane activities as making out the payroll and trying to hustle up radio work for the Group, they read plays, debated policy, and made plans for the future, presumably to be confirmed by the directors.

The Actors Committee members were certain enough of their authority to meet with Michael Chekhov in May to discuss the possibility of his teaching a class at their summer retreat, perhaps even directing a Group production. The distinguished Russian actor, a favorite of Stanislavsky and close collaborator with Vakhtangov, had emigrated from the Soviet Union in 1928 and drifted across Europe for seven years before arriving on Broadway in February to launch a season of productions presented by the impresario Sol Hurok. Group actors were extremely impressed by Chekhov, in particular his famous use of "the psychological gesture," the single movement that revealed a character's basic motivation. Stella Adler, Morris Carnovsky, Bobby Lewis, Phoebe Brand, and many others attended his lectures in New York; it was Adler who suggested the Group might work more closely with him. Molly Thacher edited a translation of his notes on the Stanislavsky technique, which was published in *New Theatre*. None of this sat well with Strasberg, as it marked a further encroachment on his former role as the Group's sole interpreter of Stanislavsky.

In the end, Chekhov's association with the Group remained limited to a few classes. He was uncomfortable with their political orientation. "Morris, don't go in for this wickedness of communism," he told Carnovsky. "It encourages the materialistic impulse in our whole society." Also, he dreamed of creating his own theatre school, and the chronically impoverished Group couldn't offer him the financial security he needed. He found more reliable sponsors in the actress Beatrice Straight and her wealthy parents, who invited him to establish the Michael Chekhov Theatre Studio at their utopian community, Dartington Hall, in England. Yet Chekhov's emphasis on the physical expression of emotional life contributed to the Group's growing awareness that the Stanislavsky system was flexible and could be shaped to meet many different needs.

As the Group's eventful spring surged to a close, their star playwright was feeling the strain of life at the center of the media circus. After Will Geer, an actor who staged *Till the Day I Die* in Hollywood, was abducted and beaten up by "friends of the New Germany," Odets put a heavy lock on his apartment door. He hired his boyhood friend, Herman Kobland, as his secretary to deal with the deluge of mail and phone calls. He left the cast of *Lefty* on April 19 and fled to a Coney Island hotel in search of peace to revise

Paradise Lost. The Group wanted to present the play in the fall, and before Clurman left for Europe he made detailed comments on the changes necessary to get it into final shape. Odets, however, was finding it hard to work. Part of the problem was simply a difficulty in settling down to the quiet life of a writer after the giddy whirl of being a celebrity; a lot of it had to do with his feelings about *Paradise Lost* and his new position in the Group.

Odets doubted the wisdom of following *Awake and Sing!* with a play so similar to it. He would have preferred to work on a new idea, a drama about a factory strike he called *The Silent Partner,* but he knew the Group and Clurman were counting on him. In the first flush of enthusiasm over *Awake and Sing!* they dropped options on three plays they'd been holding for ages without ever really mustering up much desire to produce: the long-neglected John Houseman translation of *Gallery Gods, Fortune Heights* by John Howard Lawson's friend John Dos Passos, and *If This Be Treason,* a drama of the Chicago teacher's strike by Group Associate Philip Barber. They expected one of the many scripts promised to them would materialize by summer, but by April it was clear they'd been overly optimistic. Paul Green's new play, *The Enchanted Maze,* wasn't ready, and no one was sure that a satire on college life was quite in the Group's line anyway. Lawson had temporarily abandoned *Marching Song* to write a book about dramatic technique in an effort to clarify his thoughts about the relationship between society's problems and a playwright's artistic expression of them. They were still waiting to hear from Maxwell Anderson. They scrambled around looking for alternatives, briefly considering a drama on the life of Nijinsky, but nothing definite except *Paradise Lost* was at hand.

Odets both relished and resented the Group's assumption that he would, of course, make sure they had a workable script by fall. After years of feeling marginal to Group life, he was thrilled that now he was important to them, that they wanted and needed his talents. As the reviewers had noted, he was a theatre man to his fingertips, comfortable with the practical requirements of actual production and willing to write to order when necessary, as he had with *Till the Day I Die.* He was the first serious American playwright whose writing grew organically out of life in a working theatre company. O'Neill had benefited enormously from his relationship with the Provincetown Players, but he had a trunkful of plays before he ever met them and they had no impact on his ideas. Odets' philosophy and technique were deeply influenced by the Group: he often wrote with his fellow actors in mind; he noted a "spine" for each character just as any Strasberg-trained actor would; he created plays with six or seven equally important parts, confident that the Group could cast each of them with a good actor who didn't need to be the star; and his plays expressed an idealistic faith in the future, in the need for struggle to create better lives for everyone, that reflected four years of Clurman's lectures and Group discussions as well as Odets' own personal longings.

Yet Odets was discovering what Lawson, George O'Neil, and several others associated with the Group had already learned: collective life wasn't always ideal for a writer, who had to at least begin the creative process in private. Because they placed great importance on a script's ideas, wanting to make them their own, the Group could be especially hard on playwrights. "I had a tendency to attack the problems of a play as if its author was a name in an Encyclopedia rather than a very vulnerable citizen of our town," Clurman admitted, and the actors' willingness to argue about what their parts meant enraged more than one writer. Odets, a veteran of four years of Group-ness, was more used to this approach than most, and his friend- ship with Clurman meant that he was always treated as an individual, not an encyclopedia entry. But the special nature of his relationship with the Group imposed a daunting responsibility. He was *their* playwright, he shared their goals, and they increasingly relied on him to provide the raw material for their dreams.

The burden of their faith weighed on him a great deal that spring, as he put aside a play he wanted to write in favor of one he wasn't even sure he wanted produced, because the Group's needs came first. In later years, he would decide that the Group's chronic hunger for his scripts had forced him to work too quickly, to allow the production of plays with technical and thematic problems he hadn't had time to fix, for which he then took a beating from the critics. There was some truth in this, but Odets was never so productive as in the 1930s, when he had a theatrical home where he felt needed and secure, confident that anything he had to say would be eagerly read and lovingly produced by people who understood his vision.

Through the second half of April he struggled to revise *Paradise Lost*, spurred on by a letter from Clurman (en route to Russia) urging him to be true to his talent and avoid the blandishments of easy Hollywood money. It was slow going, halted completely on May 8 by the shattering news of his mother's unexpected death in Philadelphia at the age of forty-seven. Odets had been closely, ambivalently attached to her, and he was grief-stricken by her death; her unhappy, unfulfilled life, her miserable marriage, seemed emblematic of the human waste he saw all around him and had pledged to fight in his plays. The funeral was made even more painful by Lou Odets' grotesque efforts to justify himself to his children by claiming their mother had had an affair in Atlantic City. His son took some comfort from the presence of Stella Adler, the only Group member to attend. Odets and Adler had quarreled frequently in the past—each resented the other's closeness to Clurman, and the playwright made no secret of his opinion that she was cruel to his friend—but that made no difference to Adler, who revered ritual and tradition; she felt it was her duty to be there. Odets was deeply touched. "No matter how I resented Stella's treatment of Harold," he said later, "I could never hate her after that."

When he returned from the funeral he threw himself into outside activi- ties—anything to keep him away from the troublesome *Paradise Lost*. He spoke at a meeting protesting Germany's military build-up, at another opposing the shipment of iron to Japan; he turned up on lower Broadway to lend his support to picketers from the newly formed Writers Union. He'd attended sessions of the first American Writers Congress, where the union was formed, in late April; the fiery speeches and violent arguments at this CP-organized gathering had revealed how much left-wing American writers respected the party, and how completely unwilling they were to let it dictate their style or subject matter. He signed copies of *Three Plays*, his first published book, and enjoyed the critics' attacks on the Pulitzer Prize committee, which had awarded the 1935 prize to Zoë Atkins' conventional drama *The Old Maid* rather than to the fiercely original *Awake and Sing!* He had a series of expensive lunches with Bennett Cerf, who convinced him to allow Random House to buy out his contract with the small firm of Covici-Friede.

He joined his Group friends in their work for the radical theatre. A Spring Varieties program, held at the Mecca Temple on May 19 to raise money for the seamen's and longshoremen's unions in their "militant fight against war and fascism," included improvisations by Odets, Joe Bromberg, and Walter Coy; the first performance of Art Smith's new play, *The Tide Rises;* and Morris Carnovsky delivering a monologue by Odets called *I Can't Sleep* (a problem the playwright himself had been having all spring). Written in a single night—Odets seemed to work best in short bursts—*I Can't Sleep* was a haunting little piece displaying a characteristic blend of personal and social concerns. The speaker, accosted on the street by a beggar, sees accusation in the poor man's eyes; he reviews his frustrated life, from a bitter marriage ("Even my wife don't talk to me . . . 'Come eat,' she says. Did you ever hear such an insult?!") to the guilt that keeps him awake: "They don't let me sleep. All night I hear the music of the comrades. All night I hear hungry men. All night the broken hearted children. No place to hide, no place to run away." When Clurman read it, he found the playlet "most significant for its indication of the source of [Odets'] inspiration— the troubled conscience of the middle class in the depression period."

The Tide Rises turned up again on May 26 as part of National Theatre week, a seven-day festival of left theatre sponsored by the New Theatre League. Bud Bohnen directed it, and no fewer than twelve Group members were in the cast, including Ruth Nelson as a journalist who joined the San Francisco strikers and cried out at the end, "All the bullets in the world can't stop us! The tide is rising. General strike!" The festival also featured Kazan's directorial debut, *The Young Go First,* and a seminar on acting and directing by Strasberg. There seemed to be no end to the Group's feverish activity: around the same time, Bill Challee directed a production of *Lefty* for the Negro People's Theatre, and Kazan, Steiner, and Thacher completed *Pie in the Sky*. The film had a few public showings, but its creators concluded after discussions with friends that it was no good for revolutionary purposes, as its vitriolic satire of organized religion would offend working-class people. Everything had to serve the revolution that spring, when as mystical and spiritual a writer as Clurman's old friend Waldo Frank could speak at the Writers Congress of "the American capitalist culture that we are sworn to overthrow."

When Clurman and Crawford returned from the Soviet Union in mid-June, they were startled and slightly dismayed to discover just how militant the actors had become. The directors' trip had drawn them closer together. given them new ideas about the Group and their theatre. They attended some thirty-five productions, had long interviews with Stanislavsky and Meyerhold, observed with wonder and envy the firm foundation of public and government support that maintained the Soviet theatre. The Moscow Art Theatre alone employed 240 actors ("What would the Group be like if we had 240 actors?" Crawford wondered wistfully), and the government gave each artist four weeks' paid vacation—most people in the U.S.S.R. got two—to compensate for working more than five days a week. The state could afford this generosity, for each evening 200,000 people attended the theatre in Moscow; most Russians went three or four times a week and rooted for their favorite directors the way Americans rooted for baseball teams. Dazzling productions of *Romeo and Juliet* and *King Lear* made Clurman and Crawford realize that classical productions could be as exciting and important as contemporary dramas. They laughed when a translator told them audiences were sick of revolutionary plays with self-sacrificing heroes and wanted to see comedies and romances with happy endings—it sounded just like Broadway.

They were particularly struck by the courtesy and consideration displayed by theatre people in their dealings with each other. At one theatre Clurman observed a call board plastered with typewritten pages, which turned out to be notes by actors, directors, and technicians offering their comments on each other's work. "That is the most impersonal and at the same time the friendliest way," the company's director explained. "All the actors learn discipline themselves because of this, whereas personal discussions cause bad feelings and do great mischief." Thinking of the Group's highly personal meetings, Clurman and Crawford could only agree. On the long trip home, they discussed everything they had seen and its implications for the Group's future. "The goal of the Group," Crawford wrote, summarizing their conclusions, "should be to move an audience in the ethical, aesthetic sense, not to provide political theatre."

The directors arrived home to find many of the actors immersed in political theatre and inclined to speak of each other and their work as though they too were engaged in a class struggle to the death with unrelenting foes. They weren't disposed to be charitable to those less committed: in a typical incident in late May, Odets got into a violent argument with Maxwell Anderson, who expressed reservations about the Soviet government, and accused him of being a reactionary and a fascist. Helen Deutsch, who'd brought Odets to visit her close friend Anderson, was mortified; she was fed up with both Odets, who'd been openly seeing other women, and the Group, which continued blithely to accept her services as a press agent without ever offering to pay her.

Anderson remained fond enough of the Group to offer them his new play anyway. He completed *Winterset,* a verse drama loosely based on the Sacco and Vanzetti case, on June 1, and there was a copy waiting for Clurman and Crawford when they got back. Crawford agreed with Strasberg, who'd already read it, that although the script was imperfect it was worth doing. The Group should begin their fall season with something other than an Odets play, they felt, and *Winterset* would provide a good contrast to the realistic dramas they were best known for. Clurman wasn't sure. He still disliked Anderson's use of verse, which seemed especially inappropriate to the Lower East Side setting, and found the whole play rather cold. With the success of *Awake and Sing!* and his own improved status, he was less inclined to defer to his partners' judgment than he had been, and they reached a stalemate. They decided to read *Winterset* to the entire Group.

The actors detested it. The more radical members found it sentimental and without contemporary relevance; everyone thought the verse was affected and overblown. The Group was a working theatre, not an organization of critics, Strasberg argued (though he may have wondered about the second statement); they could turn a flawed script into an interesting production. Their recent experience with *Gold Eagle Guy* hardly proved his point, nor had *Night over Taos,* further back in their history, given the actors much confidence in either Anderson's verse or their ability to perform it. Strasberg, deeply conscious of his lessened authority, didn't press the argument, and Crawford was as usual willing to abide by the majority decision. The Group rejected *Winterset.* That fall, under Guthrie McClintic's direction, it was a commercial and critical success, winning the first New York Drama Critics Circle award.

The actors had no regrets. They were very sure of themselves and the Group in 1935, proud of the respect they had won both on Broadway and among the radical organizations many of them believed represented the future of American theatre. Clurman, though he agreed with their verdict on *Winterset,* was troubled by the arrogance he heard underlying their arguments: "Everybody, it seemed, was expanding into a highly vocal authority on art and life, theatre and culture, politics and the state of the world." He also worried over the actors' combative stance toward the outside world and, more dangerously, one another. He could see that less political members of the company were sometimes criticized with a harshness that wounded them deeply; Beany Barker, who'd chosen not to march in the May Day parade, felt she was treated like a pariah by those who had. Clurman, always astute about personal relationships within the collective, sensed that the Group's triumphant progress was leaving behind some of their most devoted members. He feared they were narrowing their horizons, concentrating on social ideals at the expense of the artistic purpose that must be their central reason for being.

Characteristically, he put his thoughts down on paper and read them to the assembled company. He pleaded for better manners and greater kindness, an end to the constant sniping that was undermining Group unity. At the same time, he criticized the Group for being too self-righteous, too certain that their way was the only way, too immersed in the exciting world of radical politics. Their goal, he reminded the actors, was "to become the recognized and honored first theatre of America," known for "the variety of our productions," rather than a particular political point of view. He pointedly defined "popular theatre" (a favorite radical buzzword) as something that "any unspoiled normally sensitive person can come to and enjoy," i.e., not workers theatre, but everyone's theatre.

Although Clurman's address implicitly urged the actors to criticize themselves more and others less, Odets' thunderous seconding of his remarks astonished and embarrassed everyone, including the director. The Group had become complacent and self-satisfied, he shouted; they were making no progress as artists or as human beings. His comments went far beyond anything Clurman intended, and the rage he delivered them with seemed to spring more from Odets' personal worries about *Paradise Lost* and ambivalent feelings about his own success than anything going on within the Group. Clurman tried to calm his friend down, while making it clear that he didn't necessarily agree with him.

The actors were stunned by Odets' diatribe and hurt by Clurman's more measured statement as well. They disagreed with the director's implication that their involvement in political theatre had somehow turned them away from a higher artistic goal. They saw no conflict between the two. "[We] look first for artistic quality," Carnovsky told a reporter earlier in the year.

If another *Hamlet* came along . . . [we] wouldn't reject it because the new Shakespeare was unaware of the defects in our social system. [Yet] we of the Group believe that we can't retain our artistic integrity, even as actors, unless we say something, unless, in short, our work has social significance. We must face conditions, we must face life and the inequalities of life. We can't go on having untruths forced down our throats and glib illusions dealt out to us under the guise of entertainment. We can't afford to disregard what's going on in Washington, or what's going on abroad. Those things are of vital importance. They're reality. They're life.

Hadn't Clurman himself declared the Group's subject matter to be the essential moral and social preoccupations of their time? In the actors' opinion, the Group had moved a long way down the difficult road that led to their goal, and there was no reason not to celebrate. As their miraculous season drew to a close, they could point to any number of events justifying their belief that the Group had achieved a new level of status and security. Even a nontheatrical organization like the New York City Board of Education recognized it: when Helen Thompson got the idea in June to drum up publicity and business for the Group through a symposium on the modern theatre to be given that fall at the New School, the Board approved the symposium as an "alertness course" that teachers could take for credit toward salary advancement. The actors' own union affirmed it: when Equity ruled in July that managers must provide rehearsal pay, it exempted the Group, just as it had relieved them in March of the requirement to post a bond for each production, because their members were paid on a year-round basis. "That's something for which an actor will renounce capitalism any day," joked one Broadway columnist.

Hundreds of actors were eager to renounce the commercial theatre in favor of the Group. In February 200 people applied for twenty unpaid apprentice positions. More yearned for full membership in the permanent company. "The Group Theatre actors are the most envied people on Broadway," Bud Bohnen wrote to his brother in July. "I have been interviewing applicants for membership every Friday afternoon . . . Hundreds of them . . . former stars . . . people whose salaries have been up to $2,000 a week . . . all with their tongues hanging out to be taken into this haven." Bohnen may have been exaggerating a bit—he was always anxious to prove to his skeptical family that he'd made the right decision in joining a noncommercial theatre—but he wasn't inventing the desire of many actors to cast their lot with the Group.

More than the hope of a steady paycheck, which anyone who'd been in New York longer than six months knew the Group hadn't always provided, it was the promise of proper training and attention to each actor that drew aspiring performers. Every review praising the company's unusual depth of acting talent, every outside class taught by a Group member gave their version of the Stanislavsky system additional credibility and prestige. No performer could fail to be impressed by an organization that cared enough about all its actors to switch around parts on occasion simply to give everyone a chance to stretch. In June Ruth Nelson and Bill Challee took the leads in *Till the Day I Die* while Beany Barker uncomplainingly picked up Nelson's smaller but effective role in *Lefty;* Bohnen gave his part as the sympathetic Nazi to Russell Collins, whose villainous roles in *Lefty* went to Tony Kraber; and Eunice Stoddard left her tiny part in *Till the Day I Die* to play Florrie, the young woman reluctantly abandoned by her cabbie lover in *Lefty.*

Hollywood had taken note of the versatility and skill of Group actors before, but the publicity surrounding the Odets plays prompted the studios to dangle even greater rewards in front of them. The playwright himself turned down staggering amounts of money to write screenplays and deliberately sabotaged the possibility of selling *Awake and Sing!* by insisting on a contractual commitment not to change the political dialogue. The actors became experts at saying no to movie agents: Joe Bromberg, Phoebe Brand, and Billy Kirkland declined repeated offers, and Julie Garfield was uninterested in the temptations his featured role as Ralph brought his way. Yet film's potential to reach millions of people intrigued the Group, and they were considering the possibility of trying to make a movie on their own terms as a unit. Crawford found a backer willing to finance an original film and had brief, ultimately fruitless conversations with West Coast studios about distribution. There was no question, however, of filming it anywhere except New York. The Group had no desire to leave the stimulating and nurturing environment they'd created for themselves.

It wasn't just their own work that excited them, though that was fulfilling enough; it was the sense of being at the center of an entire web of relationships among committed theatre people. Their extracurricular activities at the Theatre Union, the Theatre Collective, and the Theatre of Action introduced them to young actors eager to join their ranks. Albert van Dekker, Lee Cobb, Joan Madison, Curt Conway, and Will Lee all worked with Group members downtown before appearing with them on Broadway. Julie Garfield had already made the leap from the Theatre Union to the Group; that summer they added the Yale-educated director of *Sailors of Catarro* and *Black Pit,* Irving Gordon (known to everyone as Mike and soon to change his first name officially to Michael), who was willing to go back to being a stage manager in order to get a chance to work with New York's most important company. The fight to reform Equity linked them up with other friends, old and new: one of the dissident Council members, George Heller, had small parts in the *Lefty/Till* double bill; another was Phil Loeb, who had given many of them their first break at the Theatre Guild; among those who ran for office as reformers were former Group members Mary Morris and Virginia Farmer. They lived and worked in a community of like-minded people who looked to the Group for leadership. Even those who'd left the fold didn't break the Group bond entirely: Franchot Tone still sent them money from Hollywood and spoke wistfully of returning someday; Phil Robinson and Grover Burgess both appeared in *The Young Go First,* and Burgess assured them he would be back for the Group's fall production.

They felt they were the wave of the future. "Dad and I used to talk about the frailties of the Group, the dangers of tying yourself down to a collective," said Bud Bohnen. "But I still feel what I felt then . . . What else is there, barring a movie career? The theatre IS a collective craft, and the only way to achieve satisfaction in it is to control the collective conditions . . . I am proud to be in the vanguard of this movement." Their way of working was so clearly better, how could anyone not want to be part of it? "We are convinced that the Group Theatre is the finest in the country," Billy Kirkland told a union newspaper. "The artists have a common interest, in which we help each other grow. I predict that in five years, the entire New York stage will consist of co-operative Group Theatres."

In 1930 it had been daring and slightly crazy to dream of a single Group Theatre, but five years later Kirkland's hyperbolic statement seemed almost reasonable. Even the government recognized theatre's importance to national life: Roosevelt's new Works Progress Administration, designed to create jobs for the unemployed, included a Federal Theatre Project committed to putting theatre artists to work in their own field. When the determined and resourceful Hallie Flanagan agreed to head the project in August, idealistic theatre people were delighted; under her direction the FTP would be far more than a federal imitation of the Broadway show-shop. As her former students Molly Thacher and Helen Thompson could tell the Group, Flanagan had devoted her ten years teaching and directing at Vassar to advancing the idea of theatre as "a part of, and not apart from, everyday existence." She saw the FTP as an opportunity to create a nation-wide federation of noncommercial theatres; her dreams were even bigger than the Group's.

With the world so clearly going their way, the actors didn't listen very hard to Clurman's words of caution. Odets, slightly abashed by his outburst, turned his bad temper on more deserving targets. He went to Cuba as nominal head of a fifteen-person delegation to investigate conditions under the reactionary Mendieta-Batista regime, but saw nothing except the inside of a prison; the entire group was arrested as soon as they landed on July 2 and deported the next day. Odets was irritated to learn from a communist member of the delegation that the party had expected this all along, in fact had planned the trip to expose the U.S. ambassador's complicity with the regime, but he enjoyed the headlines his arrest provoked. No sooner had he finished telling the press all about his night in a Cuban jail than he joined John Howard Lawson and *New Theatre* editor Herbert Kline in a visit on July 23 to the Italian playwright Luigi Pirandello to urge the Nobel laureate, now safely in New York, to retract his public support for Mussolini's planned invasion of Ethiopia. Odets felt uncomfortable arguing about politics with a man whose plays he admired, but at least it kept him out of his study and away from *Paradise Lost*.

That play, the directors had decided, would definitely be one of the Group's fall offerings, to be joined by the new Green and Lawson scripts, if they were ever finished, or perhaps by *Weep for the Virgins*, a drama of working-class life in California they were considering. Odets tried to work on revisions, but he managed to find distractions: if there were no social wrongs to be righted, he could always devote himself to complicated maneuvers among the five different women he was involved with that summer. He even stepped back into *Lefty* for five final performances before the double bill closed on July 20.

Awake and Sing! ended its run a week later, as the Group prepared to take their first summer off. It had been an extremely hectic season, the directors explained to the press, and they'd decided everyone needed a vacation from the theatre for a month. The Group would reassemble in September to tour *Awake and Sing!* with *Lefty* and begin rehearsing their fall productions.

NINE

The Struggle for Organization

Anything seemed possible in the heady fall of 1935, as Group members returned from their individual vacations with a sense of achievement and anticipation. They'd taken New York by storm the previous season, introducing the most exciting new playwright in a decade and triumphantly justifying their ideals with two productions that were the talk of the town and beloved by their audiences. If they could do all that after their sorry start with *Gold Eagle Guy*, what could they not accomplish this season, when they were beginning with a soaring reputation, a (modest) bankroll, and a new play by Clifford Odets?

But success, the Group discovered, was transitory when not based on solid organization and adequate financing. They'd come a long way on sheer will and determination, but on Broadway, where you were only as good as your last show, the gains they made so slowly and arduously could evaporate with a few bad reviews. In the wake of *Lefty* and *Awake and Sing!* their dreams grew larger and more ambitious; they wanted permanency and continued growth as well as acclaim. Now all they had to do was create an organizational structure capable of making those dreams real.

They gathered in New York in September, refreshed and ready to work. They were happy to be back together, optimistic about the tour of *Awake and Sing!* and *Lefty*, eager to read the scripts of their fall productions. Everyone felt there were great things ahead as they listened to Clurman expound on the Group's future. While they'd been relaxing, he'd used his vacation to think about new projects their recent success would allow them to undertake. He revived his hopes for a Group Center, a place where they could invite friends and supporters in all the arts "to sustain and enrich one another's work," and he excitedly presented his ideas in a paper to his comrades.

Clurman envisioned the Group occupying an entire theatre building, where they would present their plays, conduct an experimental studio, and run a school, which would include courses on acting, directing, body, voice, diction, stage mechanics, playwrighting, theatre history, and theory. The building would also house a Music Center, directed by his friend Aaron Copland; a Dance Section; a division of Art and Cinema, headed by Paul Strand and Ralph Steiner; a magazine; and "a club restaurant . . . where the various collaborators of the Center's activities and their close friends might gather informally," and that might contain a reading room and library as well. "Each door (section) of the Center will be the entrance to a complete 'world,' " he wrote. "None of these activities will exist by or for itself alone and thus a growing, living organism affecting vast bodies of people will be established. . . . The establishment of a Center will release the creative possibilities for our whole cultural life inherent in the Group idea."

It was a lovely vision, characteristic of Clurman's humanistic view of the world of culture as a home for artists who would much rather work together than compete with each other in the marketplace. Though he stoutly insisted the project was "in no way utopian or over-ambitious," it was, of course, both. Yet in the hopeful atmosphere of the early fall, even Harold's wildest fantasies seemed attainable to the Group. If they could run a revolutionary drama on Broadway for four months, and a folk play of the Bronx for nearly six, maybe they could make enough money on tour to rent their own theatre and gather all their friends around them in a Group Center.

The abortive tour brought them face to face with their organizational and managerial deficiencies. They planned to do too much and planned none of it in detail. When they moved the *Lefty/Awake and Sing!* double bill to Philadelphia's Broad Theatre on September 30, after two weeks in New York, the advance sale was so strong the directors decided to extend the run there indefinitely. They would rehearse their fall productions *(Weep for the Virgins* had been added to the roster), revive *Men in White*, then open *Paradise Lost* at the end of October. But they took no account of the fact that Odets had barely begun to make the necessary revisions on his script; moreover, performing two plays, rehearsing two more, and preparing another for revival was a lot of work to be doing all at once. They were also too optimistic about the box office, which after a few fat weeks quickly reverted to the usual Group demographics: sold-out balconies and half-empty orchestras. By the end of October *Variety* reported that the double bill had "stayed too long and skidded to $4500," which would hardly cover their expenses, let alone put money toward a Group Center. They were forced to end the tour and return to New York on November 10.

It was back to Group finances as usual. The New School symposium and a hastily improvised course at the YMHA on the "History of the Experimental Theatre" were their only modest sources of income until the fall productions opened. The actors, well aware of the commercially uncertain nature of both new plays, could already see looming ahead another season of scraping by, living hand to mouth on the proceeds from teaching jobs and radio appearances, all because of their leaders' inability to manage the Group properly. Twelve of them, including Odets, Kazan, and Lewis, got together to discuss the situation; the resulting memo to the directors was the opening round in the season-long debate over the Group's organization.

The two perpetual sore spots of Group life that most concerned the actors were scripts and salaries. "We would like to know what methods are being formulated other than the usual line between agent and producer to contact plays for us," they stated. "If nothing new is being done about it, we would like to discuss and work out possible ways of going about it." They also wanted a "more definite analysis of that rather general phrase 'value to the Group,' " by which the directors set the company pay scale. The actors clearly felt that too often the directors evaluated their worth by the standards of the commercial theatre the Group was supposed to have rejected. They wanted to know: "Are we definitely working toward a basis which will allow Group value to be assessed and rewarded in terms of reality rather than on the partially opportunistic ones now thought to be necessary?"

On the artistic side, the actors expressed their dissatisfaction with the Broadway-oriented production schedule, which limited the Group to a few shows a season and meant that less prominent members were stuck in small parts, with little chance for either recognition or growth. They suggested the establishment of a permanent studio, just as Clurman had in his proposal for a Group Center, but while he had defined the studio's purpose as "the production of plays of special interest; the investigation of new forms of theatre; the creation of new audiences and new talents," they had in mind a more specific goal: "to rehearse plays either old or new which are primarily actors' plays and which are cast for the sake of the development of the actors who are not likely to have the chance to work on long parts in the Broadway productions for some time."

They proposed that Strasberg direct these plays; they were worried that the man who had formed the Group acting style was being neglected and underutilized. They seem to have been the first to realize, however implicitly, that General Lee might be better suited temperamentally to work in a laboratory situation than under commercial pressures. "Lee really only wanted to be a teacher," said Eunice Stoddard. "When he was directing he was always teaching."

Underlying all their comments was their sense that the directors had failed to seize the opportunity presented by their success in the spring, had made no progress toward giving the Group stability and security. Odets was vehement on this subject: though *Awake and Sing!* had run for 209 performances, it had returned no money to its backers and not much to its author. He blamed this on poor business management, which had kept the play running after it stopped making money, although this was less a bad business decision than an expression of the Group's desire to keep working and make sure everyone who wanted to see the play got the chance. Crawford, who was in charge of the overworked and underpaid business staff (the lawyer and press agent both donated their services), resented these criticisms as unrealistic. "All of the requests had merit," she wrote later of the actors' memo, "but there didn't seem to be a lot we could do about them, because we lacked both money and energy to implement them."

The directors promised to think about how the Group could be restructured, but for the moment they had to concentrate on the plays at hand. The only concrete result of the Group's brief flirtation with a film project was that two movie studios came forward to finance their fall productions: appropriately enough, *Weep for the Virgins* was backed by Warner Brothers, which had made many films with a similarly proletarian milieu, while MGM, which took pride in its artistic projects, put up $17,000 for the poetic *Paradise Lost*.

Because Odets was still struggling with the last act of his play, *Weep for the Virgins* was scheduled to open first, a decision by default that was typical of the way the entire production was handled. When the script was submitted by a novelist using the pseudonym Nellise Child, the directors had a hard time making up their minds about it. The story concerned three sisters working in a San Diego fish cannery. Raised by their dreadful mother to hate men and dream of becoming movie stars, all three nearly ruin their lives through an inability to face reality. As written, the play was something of a mess: it was hard to believe the sisters couldn't see how selfish and hypocritical their mother was, and the plot twists were, to put it mildly, melodramatic. Lillian Gerard (the author's real name) knew little about dramatic construction, and it showed in her uncertain handling of the theme: the pernicious effect of Hollywood-influenced dreams on poor people's lives.

Still, the theme itself was worthwhile, and her portrait of working-class life had an authentic grittiness that gave the script a certain savor. Like many writers in the 1930s, a decade when the artistic establishment was unusually receptive to proletarian talent, Gerard had seen more of life than the inside of a university. She'd worked in a cannery herself, also in a soda fountain, a department store, a biscuit factory, and a Western Union office before writing her first novel. She was an ardent trade unionist (and vocal anticommunist) who knew the people and milieu she portrayed in *Weep for the Virgins*. The play throbbed with life—mostly unpleasant, but life all the same—and its humor was bracingly down to earth.

The directors had wavered over the summer about whether or not it was worth doing. Strasberg finally provoked his partners into action by observing, no doubt thinking of *Winterset*, that they read many plays but never seemed to buy any. (The press agreed with him; one columnist in August referred to the Group as "a cautious shopper," and several reporters wondered why the organization seemed to have such a hard time finding scripts.) Stung, Clurman replied, "Well, let's do it." With that rousing vote of confidence, *Weep for the Virgins* became a Group project.

Strasberg didn't think enough of the script to direct it, and once again Crawford was stuck with a job no one else would do. She often annoyed the Group with her air of martyrdom, her frequent complaints that no one appreciated her hard work, but her attitude was more than a little justified. Strasberg and Clurman had the arrogance of self-assured artists. They never did any work they didn't want to or felt they weren't suited for, and if their fellow directors or Group members didn't understand, that was too bad. Crawford spent her life taking care of the details they disdained— raising money, making up budgets, getting the scenery built, renting the costumes (which the Group always seemed to leave to the last minute). Had she been more confident of her own artistic abilities she might have had the courage to insist they find an administrator to deal with the odds and ends, but as it was she used her ceaseless round of caretaking activities as a means of asserting her value to the Group.

She wanted very much to direct, so she tried to suppress her doubts about *Weep for the Virgins* and make the best of the situation. Her confidence wasn't helped by the actors' response when the company read both plays in Philadelphia prior to beginning rehearsals. The actors liked *Weep for the Virgins* well enough—it had some undeniably funny moments—but they loved *Paradise Lost*, which was in many ways Odets' most beautiful and profound work to date. When parts were handed out, it was clear that several actors, Joe Bromberg in particular, were disppointed to be working with Crawford instead of on the Clurman/Odets team.

Still, *Weep for the Virgins* gave Ruth Nelson, Phoebe Brand, and Paula Miller meaty parts as the three sisters, and for once no one objected to the directors bringing in an outsider, the seasoned Broadway veteran Evelyn Varden, to play the girls' monstrous mother. Billy Kirkland and Julie Garfield were Brand's and Nelson's respective love interests, and Bromberg got another comic role as the middle-aged man who lures Miller's chubby character away from her tap shoes with the promise of a decent meal in place of her mother's constant exhortations to diet. If the play's plot was improbable and the motivations of most of the characters absurd, Crawford at least hoped she could bring the atmosphere of the San Diego waterfront vividly to life with the help of a large cast solidly trained in the Group method.

Beany Barker, for one, enjoyed going to the Brooklyn Navy Yard to observe the fleet followers in preparation for her tiny role as a prostitute; she based her performance on a young girl she'd seen there sucking on an enormous lollipop. The Group's new stage manager, Mike Gordon, was impressed by the company's technique. "There was more time taken, there was an improvisatory approach in the course of rehearsals that wasn't characteristic in my experience prior to that time." He could see what a powerful tool that approach could be in Ruth Nelson's sensitive performance as the oldest sister, a classic piece of method work in which her inner conviction and total commitment to the character gave even the silliest lines the ring of truth. He also quickly learned that the Group's artistic philosophy had an effect on his own status: "It was made very clear to me that the stage manager in the Group had a far more subordinate position than the normally prevailing theatre practice: you were regarded as a servant of the actors rather than a foreman."

Gordon believed that Crawford "affirmed the same basic criteria and techniques as Lee and Harold, though the emphases were different in many respects. Cheryl was, I think, less complex or penetrating in her explorations, less imaginative, but nevertheless, very well organized and thorough, very intelligent. I had considerable respect for her, but I don't think in terms of flair or talent, she could rival either of them." Eunice Stoddard, who was fond of Crawford, blamed her fellow directors for not helping her develop. "Cheryl was terribly hardworking, terribly sincere and very idealistic, but she wasn't very self-assured. What she really needed was for either Harold or Lee to come and sit by her and talk with her the way Harold would sit and talk when Lee was directing. But they never came near her. She had a terrible play to direct, and there wasn't much she could do."

When *Weeping for the Virgins* opened on November 30 at the 46th Street Theatre, the critics couldn't imagine why the Group had bothered to do it at all. "It isn't even radical," noted Arthur Pollock in the Brooklyn *Eagle;* virtually every reviewer now identified the Group as a left-wing theatre. They all joined the Brooklyn *Citizen* in wondering "what on earth has happened to the judgment of this otherwise excellent organization." Crawford's careful but hesitant direction received generally negative appraisals, and though a few critics had kind words for the Group's acting, old complaints about too much detail and an overly deliberate approach also resurfaced. There were some nasty cracks to the effect that several of the play's Californians sounded like they came from the Bronx; the press was developing a tendency to speak of the Group as though the entire company were composed of New York Jews who could play nothing else. Yet the glow of last season's triumphs hadn't faded entirely. Critics spoke warmly of the Group's distinguished track record and looked forward to the opening of *Paradise Lost* the following week.

So did the Group. They were disappointed, but not exactly surprised by the reviews of *Weep for the Virgins* and did nothing to prevent it from expiring on December 8 after nine performances. They hoped *Paradise Lost* would save their season and justify their work, as *Lefty* and *Awake and Sing!* had done before.

Odets' new play superficially resembled *Awake and Sing!* in that both were dramas of a family thrown into economic and emotional crisis by the Depression. The essential character of the two families, however, was completely different. The Bergers live at the bottom of the middle class, where unemployment and starvation happen close enough to home to be constant threats. They give no quarter in their ferocious family quarrels because life, so brutal to them, has taught them to be brutal to each other. The Gordons of *Paradise Lost* are better off, one step further removed from the naked struggle for survival. The father, Leo, owns a pocketbook business; one son, Ben, is an Olympic athlete; the other, Julie, works in a bank; the daughter, Pearl, is a pianist. These are gentler people: Leo's wife, Clara, a pragmatist like Bessie Berger, views her impractical, idealistic husband with an amused affection Bessie would find soft-headed.

There are tougher characters: Leo's rapacious partner Sam Katz, and Kewpie, another of Odets' seething gangster figures, who seduces his friend Ben's wife as part of his ruthless drive to snatch everything he can from an indifferent society. But they are drawn to the sensitive, intellectual Gordons even as they victimize them; the relationships and motivations are more complex than the simple, strongly drawn interactions of *Awake and Sing! Paradise Lost* has a dreamy, slightly unreal quality that intensifies as the Gordons are subjected to one disaster after another. Everyone in it except Clara seems slightly nuts, escaping the harsh realities of the world around them through flight into personal fantasies or by attempting to cope with stratagems as bizarre as they are futile. Odets depicted them all with a tenderness and compassion that made the play sing with emotion. It was his most moving work.

When parts were assigned, there were a few storms—most minor, one major. Both Morris Carnovsky and Odets felt that casting Carnovsky as Leo emphasized the similarity between that role and Jacob in *Awake and Sing!* Carnovsky would rather have taken Bud Bohnen's place as Gus Michaels, father of Ben's roving wife, Libby. Luther Adler didn't want to play Sam Katz and suggested that he switch parts with Sandy Meisner, assigned to the role of Julie. Clurman managed to persuade them all to stay where they were, but he had a much harder time with Stella Adler, who was livid at being asked to portray yet another middle-aged mother.

Why Clurman insisted on Adler as Clara is something of a mystery. Granted that he considered her the most accomplished Group actress, it wasn't so difficult a part as Bessie, and was well within the reach of other members of the company. The fact that all the Group's other women were assigned to *Weep for the Virgins* was a joint decision made with Crawford. Some of the outside actresses in *Paradise Lost* could easily have taken parts in the other production to free a Group member to play Clara, if that had been what Clurman wanted. But it wasn't. He argued, rather, that they had to be confident in the Group's ability to create their own world and live wholly inside it. "Theatrically speaking, the Group was to be a law unto itself and should not think of its actors in terms of the market. Our actors, in other words, would never be constrained to go out again and play for commercial managers who would judge them solely on the basis of type; they would stay within the fold, where they would be cast in such a variety of roles that experienced theatre-goers would appreciate their versatility."

In short, he preferred to ignore the actors' unhappiness with their possible typecasting.

As the actors' earlier memo had indicated, some Group members thought they were being relegated to small parts and denied the opportunity to prove themselves. Their pledge to accept Group discipline was voluntary, based on their trust in the directors' concern for their development, but as the Group's history grew longer and the directors' evaluation of people's merits became clearer, they began to feel that a hierarchy was forming and certain people were getting all the best parts. Adler had little to complain of on that score, but she felt in her own way that the directors took no account of her artistic needs and desires. She finally submitted and agreed to play Clara, but she was furious; it was a long time before she forgave Clurman.

The director had other problems. Stirring and poetic as *Paradise Lost* was, its third act was still very rough. The catastrophes that crowded in on the Gordons were so overwhelming that the play closed on a note of despair that Clurman found unworthy of the characters' transcendent humanity and sweetness. He'd been urging Odets since the spring to find a way to make it clear that "with this [sweetness] and a little courage to continue life and learn that their plight was not unique, new hope might be born and a new happiness be achieved." But Odets was having a hard time with a script whose original inspiration was now cold; he diverted himself by alternating between hobnobbing with celebrities and making the world a better place through political action. The same man who dined with Jed Harris and sat on the edge of Tallulah Bankhead's bed, telling her dirty jokes but refusing to climb in with her, also spearheaded a drive to get 100,000 signatures on a petition demanding that the Secretary of State pressure Nazi Germany to free the imprisoned communist leader Ernst Thaelmann.

Perhaps it was his complicated and contradictory desires that gave Odets the ability to portray the confused characters of *Paradise Lost* with such warmth, depth, and understanding. But they didn't help him solve his third-act problem; Odets was always stronger on character and mood than resolution. Only under extreme duress, with rehearsals in their third week and Clurman laying virtual siege to him, did he finally complete the revisions. The play's despair is voiced for the last time by a homeless man, memorably played by Bill Challee, who tells the Gordons, "Why, you're sleeping! All over the country people sleeping . . . You had a sort of little paradise here. Now you lost the paradise. That should teach you something. But no! You ain't awake yet . . . You have been took like a bulldog takes a pussycat. Finished! They left you the dust of the road." Leo's answering speech, as the Gordons are turned out of their house, is rambling, mystical, utterly true to the character, and deeply moving:

No! There is more to life than this! Everything he said is true, but there is more. That was the past, but there is a future. Now we know.

We dare to understand. Truly, truly, the past was a dream. But this is real! To know from this that something must be done. That is real. We searched; we were confused! But we searched, and now the search is ended. For the truth has found us. For the first time in our lives—for the first time our house has a real foundation. . . . Clara, my darling, *listen to me*. Everywhere now men are rising from their sleep. Men, men are understanding the bitter black total of their lives. Their whispers are growing to shouts. *No man fights alone* . . . Yes, I want to see that new world. I want to kiss all those future men and women. What is this talk of bankrupts, failure, hatred . . . they won't know what that means. Oh, yes, I tell you the whole world is for men to possess. Heartbreak and terror are not the heritage of mankind! The world is beautiful. No fruit tree wears a lock and key. Men will sing at their work, men will love. Ohhh, darling, the world is in its morning . . . and *no man fights alone!*

When his wife, touched by his passion, crosses to kiss him, Leo gestures to the windows of the house he no longer owns and cries softly, "Let us have air . . . open the windows," and the curtain falls as a brief fanfare plays offstage.

Paradise Lost remains for many in the Group their favorite production. It was "the play everyone loved," said Stella Adler's daughter, Ellen. "There was never a thought in anyone's mind that *Awake and Sing!* was as deep an experience." In some ways *Awake and Sing!* represented their past, for many of them had come from the same hard-pressed lower-middle-class background as Odets and the Bergers, while *Paradise Lost* examined their present. Whatever their origins, they were now artists and intellectuals, closer in demeanor and world view to the sensitive, bookish Gordons. The spiritual concerns implicit in the author's earlier work—only in Odets plays do revolutionaries talk about planting fruit trees, as Agate did in *Lefty*—were explored at greater length and with more depth in *Paradise Lost*. It was the play closest to the Group's heart.

It had great personal significance for Clurman, who found in the confused, disintegrating world of *Paradise Lost* a dramatic replica of the situation he'd discovered within the Group the summer before:

When I returned from the Soviet Union last June, New York had a strange effect on me . . . my whole environment—my good friends and intimates, the plays I saw, the books I read, the newspapers I scanned, the conversations I heard—all seemed a bit mad! People complained about woes that were mostly imaginary, overlooked conflicts that were immediate, belied their thoughts by their acts, explained their acts by ideas they professed to scorn. Many spoke of saving and spent beyond their means, others talked of sacrifice to ideals and wasted their time, still others clamored for things they had no real interest in, and waxed skeptical over struggles that were essential to their happiness.

This was, it should be pointed out, Clurman's highly selective view of Group life, a reflection of his distress about the actors' immersion in political theatre and activism. He could be a devastating polemicist without seeming like one because he would take views he disagreed with and twist them just enough to make them seem slightly absurd, presenting himself as an amused, objective observer rather than a participant in an argument. But though his analysis of the Group's state of mind might be personal and debatable, there was a good deal of validity to his larger point that "this crazy world that Clifford Odets had wrought . . . was simply the world we live in—or to be more exact the middle-class world of our daily experience."

After the terrifying paralysis of the early Depression years, Americans were moving forward on many different fronts at once by 1935. In the White House, President Roosevelt had taken a pragmatic, improvisatory approach to solving the nation's problems, proposing new programs almost as fast as his staff could think them up to put the economy on a firmer, fairer footing and relieve those whose plight was most desperate. Organized labor, encouraged by the passage of the National Labor Relations Act to guarantee the right of collective bargaining, was more assertive than it had been in years. As the Group was preparing *Paradise Lost*, dissidents from the American Federation of Labor established the Committee for Industrial Organization to unite skilled and unskilled workers within a given industry to fight more effectively for better wages and conditions. While there was hope at home, racism and religious bigotry flourished abroad: the Nuremberg Laws deprived Jews of German citizenship, forbade mixed marriages, and made intercourse between Aryans and Jews punishable by death; riots in divided Ireland killed Protestant and Catholic alike; Italian troops overran Ethiopia, asserting the white man's right to rule Africans. Everywhere there was a sense of movement and change—some of it good, some bad, all of it bewildering.

In Clurman's astute analysis, the American middle class was uniquely confused and adrift at this moment in history. Members of the working and ruling classes knew what they wanted and who their enemies were, whereas people like the Gordons were unclear about where their allegiance and best interests lay. It was a political point, but Clurman was interested in political points only as they illuminated human reality—or, in this case, the lack of reality that made almost every character in *Paradise Lost* seem mildly demented. "This does not make them 'exceptional,'" he told the cast. "On the contrary, it makes them like us." He wanted the audience to see that the characters' foibles were created by a world situation that affected them too, that made their lives as unreal as those onstage.

Clurman's ideas called for a daring and difficult approach that blended naturalism and stylization to make the characters believable and alive, but also to comment on their behavior. He asked Boris Aronson to make the set slightly abstract, "to give some feeling of a 'home' which is the actual milieu of the play without sacrificing the quality of a *stage* as a place where artists have a right to express something more than the 'naked facts.' " He looked for the same duality of intent in the acting.

Aronson, who felt Odets' strength lay in his realistic portrayal of New York Jewish life, had doubts about Clurman's aim of making the play a general portrait of the middle class. The set reflected his ambivalence, and the director later acknowledged he had failed to make his point clearly enough to the designer. In her more jaundiced moments Stella Adler told people that the Group actors too had missed the play's style: "It was semi-realistic, poetic, symbolic—but *we* were all realistic." Adler was overstating her case; the Group had been exploring stylized theatre for years, and that fall some of the actors worked with Strasberg on their ability to comment on a play without violating its structural integrity. They were rehearsing one of Bertolt Brecht's learning pieces, and the author himself, in New York to supervise the Theatre Union's production of *Mother*, came by to observe. In a book written many years later, Strasberg recalled that Brecht had been impressed by the director's explanation of the famous "alienation effect." It wasn't the absence of emotion, Strasberg told the Group actors, but an exact and truthful *description* of emotion without the attempt to re-create it psychologically that actors used in more naturalistic plays.

This wasn't precisely the technique Clurman was looking for in *Paradise Lost*, but Group actors were sophisticated enough about varying degrees of theatrical realism to understand what he was driving at. They used comedy to discourage the audience from wallowing in the play's pathos. Morris Carnovsky took his friend Harold's physical ineptitude as part of his characterization of Leo Gordon to point up Leo's inability to deal with real life or even know what it was. This decision gave Carnovsky a strong line of action to play, as the character developed from a bumbling, rather foolish dreamer into the ardent philosopher of the closing scene. Grover Burgess, as the Gordons' left-wing furnace man, gave Pike's speeches a slightly silly quality to convey Clurman's sense that the character wasn't a real radical at all but "a wraithlike figure as of some wounded but undying spirit of protest in the American soul."

The production's most flamboyantly theatrical performance was Bobby Lewis' tour de force as Mr. May, an arsonist who proposes to solve Leo's financial problems by burning down his factory. Lewis dyed his hair red and combed it up in flamelike plumes, wore a black guard on one finger ("hinting at some unfortunate accident in one of my forays"), and used a weird accent to highlight the character's bizarre quality. Lewis stood at one extreme of the broad spectrum of attitudes toward stylization within the Group—one of the company's more orthodox naturalists asked disgustedly,

"Is he going to start that stuff again?"—but Clurman loved his performance. It revealed, he wrote, "the director's way of making a theatrical comment on the scene, a means of saying, 'What the author has written here is the grotesque and tragic farce of our middle class life.' "

Strasberg and many of the actors thought Clurman was at the peak of his form directing *Paradise Lost*. A striking and unusual production was taking shape, one that blended realism and stylization, poetry and vernacular, irony and deep emotion to create an unforgettable spiritual and political portrait of American life. It was a complex interpretation of a complex script, and much as Odets appreciated the Group's devoted work he worried that audiences were going to be confused by the play's loose, episodic structure. Just before *Paradise Lost* opened on December 9 he decided to send a letter to the press explaining what he was trying to do.

"As the established social order breaks down," he wrote, "the same process is working out in the artist's forms." The hero of *Paradise Lost* was "the entire American middle class of liberal tendency," and they were in a state of disarray similar to that of the Russians Chekhov had portrayed in his tumultuous times:

> It is sinful to violate their lives and aspirations with plot lines. Excuse us if we insist upon life, brought to the stage instead of the stage brought to life! Excuse us if we do not accept the dictum that any deviation from Ibsen and the Pinero form is a deadly sin. . . . Excuse us for our neglect of a thousand tawdry theatre tricks which make primer plays and quick profits. But please allow us to continue to respect the men and women all around us and make the theatre serve an earnest examination of their lives and backgrounds. In interesting new theatrical forms. With poetic conceptions. With character understanding. With fresh dialogue. With love.

Only someone as naïve as Odets could have thought that this warm-hearted, arrogant letter would help his cause with the critics.

Opening night at the Belasco drew wildly varying responses. From the balcony, which was breathlessly attentive and receptive throughout, came shouts, cheers, and applause sufficient for seventeen curtain calls. Several Group members, however, noted with anxiety the stony silence of the orchestra. "The wealthy people in the audience just hated it," said Phoebe Brand. "I was standing in the back and I overheard people saying, 'Oh my dear, why don't you come and buy an apartment in our building, it's only $3,000, you know you would love it, it's just charming,' and this kind of yap yap yap. I listened and thought, 'Good Lord, they won't like this play at all' —and they didn't." When Stella Adler peeped out from behind the curtain before the show and saw rows of affluent New Yorkers, she thought to herself, "They'll die. These business people and bankers have paid loads of money to see a play which said to them, 'Your lives are junk. You will fail.' . . . this audience was at the wrong show."

The critics weren't so hostile as the orchestra, but they certainly didn't share the balcony's enthusiasm. They could feel the company's commitment to *Paradise Lost*, and virtually all of them warmly praised the performances and the direction. But the play itself baffled them, and they seized on Odets' unfortunate letter as an easy way to organize their thoughts. His casual reference to Chekhov became the starting point for six out of the nine reviews that appeared the next morning, and, unsurprisingly, they found the twenty-nine-year-old American not up to the level of the Russian master. It may have been Odets' linking of his characters' milieu with that of Chekhov, who portrayed a world ripe for revolution, that led several critics to insist on seeing Leo's closing speech as communist propaganda. Or they may simply have been unable to conceive that the author of *Waiting for Lefty* could write anything else.

The gentleness and charm of *Paradise Lost* escaped the press, and critics were offended by Odets' claim that his characters were representative. "As a charter member of the American middle class of liberal tendency," wrote Richard Lockridge in the *Sun*, "I assure Mr. Odets that it is not in the least like this; that what he has achieved is a mixture of shrill melodrama and caricature and that his religious faith in the revolution is descending like a curtain between him and the people of the real world, whom it is every dramatist's duty to observe." Reviewers went out of their way to distance themselves from the Gordons and their troubles; they vehemently denied any connection between the life onstage and American life outside the theatre.

Yet even as they jeered at Odets' premise, many critics acknowledged it had prompted his richest, most symphonic writing to date. And no matter how harsh their comments, they took it as a given that they were writing about an important American dramatist. Odets "is still groping," said Arthur Pollock in the Brooklyn *Eagle*. "But his shadow grows bigger and bigger as he gropes, and his skill spreads with the continuous exercise of it." The *Journal*'s John Anderson, after sharply criticizing the plot and voicing the inevitable complaint that the characters were too peculiar to be representative, concluded, "The fact that Odets can write a play to raise such issue is honest measure of the place he has won so quickly in the theatre. We have few enough playwrights who present anything to discuss at all . . . Here is a playwright with a lot on his mind and an instinct for putting it into vivid drama. If he hasn't quite brought it off in *Paradise Lost* he has nevertheless written a miss that may be prouder than many hits."

This wasn't good enough for the Group, and they determined to fight. The day after the reviews appeared, they ran a newspaper ad proclaiming, "We believe Clifford Odets' *Paradise Lost* is a great and important play. We are proud to present it," and quoted the many favorable comments buried in the mixed reviews. Helen Deutsch, expanding their initial advertising plans, bought extra space in the newspapers as the Group fought to reach the play's audience. They invited prominent artists and intellectuals to see *Paradise Lost* and used their guests' praise in later ads.

Odets, in polite but strong letters to every critic, trenchantly defended his view of the Gordons as a representative American family. The press seemed to be unaware of the crisis disrupting contemporary life, he suggested sardonically:

> Some of us are inclined to think that we are surrounded on all sides by normal, well-juiced people. We are apt to forget that day to day millions of intellectuals, professionals and white-collar workers are gently being eased out of comforts they once knew, surely being de-classed and dispossessed. Perhaps many of us living in comfort, well cushioned from reality, know little of what is going on. Little or nothing. Perhaps these comfortable, well-cushioned ones, able to buy drinks at Tony's or 21—surely full of sane, normal people, as John O'Hara has brilliantly shown—are not aware that twenty-eight million Americans are living on relief of varied kinds. Perhaps we have not seen the delicate psychological manifestations of their degradation.

That was only the beginning. The Group objected to more than negative comments about a play they loved; they rejected the entire scale of values implicit in Broadway reviewing, and they did so publicly and militantly. A letter to the press by Clurman, reprinted in many newspapers, laid out the issues:

> It is really astonishing to find plays that reviewers obviously do not think about twice complimented as being a swell evening's entertainment, while they write reviews of a play by an author they unmistakably admire which give the impression that because the play is not quite immortal it is inferior to the run of here-today-gone-tomorrow amusements. We believe it would show far more regard for the theatre and for its best public to hold one's reservations of such a play as *Paradise Lost* for studied critical essays in the future and to say right away that it is one of the truly important contributions to our theatre —one of the plays that place the theatre in the realm of deeply enjoyable art. We believe that when an author of Clifford Odets' caliber writes so rich and varied a play as *Paradise Lost* the least that one might expect is a clear-cut statement to the effect that every sensitive theatre-goer must by all means see it.

Clurman's letter didn't go unchallenged. Joseph Wood Krutch made the lengthiest and most coherent statement of the reviewers' point of view in *The Nation:*

Of course we critics apply different standards to the judgment of different plays. A pretty good tragedy is not better than a very good farce . . . to prefer a pretentious play which doesn't come off to an unpretentious one that does is not to demonstrate refinement of feeling and an exalted mind; it is merely to reveal oneself as a highbrow, a prig, and a "serious thinker." Good intentions in a bad play are not an extenuation but an aggravation. . . . Mr. Odets is a very "promising" playwright, and perhaps more than that. But there is in this very fact every reason for judging him by standards complimentary in their severity.

Krutch had a point, and his debate with Clurman revealed the gulf between their conceptions of what criticism should be.

Clurman had been impressed in the Soviet Union by the fact that theatres often sent reviewers copies of scripts in production and invited them to attend rehearsals so their criticism could be informed by a knowledge of what the director and cast were trying to accomplish. He wanted American critics to be participants in the cultural scene, to evaluate plays not on the basis of their effectiveness but as contributions to the national literature and to vital debates on the issues of the day. Broadway reviewers saw themselves as members of the audience who happened to have a public forum for their views. They believed their mission was to offer a running commentary on the theatre season at hand, to tell theatregoers that Play A, though a mindless comedy, was a lot of fun, while Play B, though palpably serious in intent, didn't quite come off. There was really no way to reconcile those views.

Clurman's letter showed him at his most self-righteous, and it's easy to scoff at his unrealistic expectations. Nonetheless, his criticism of the whole setup of daily reviewing had validity, and Krutch's statement that a pretty good tragedy wasn't better than a very good farce was slightly disingenuous. As Clurman plaintively asked in a letter replying to Krutch's column, "Might we suggest that Chekhov's immature tragedy *Ivanoff* is more important or, if you will, 'better' than a very good farce like *She Loves Me Not*? Is it too much to say that Ibsen's unsuccessful tragedy *When We Dead Awaken* is 'better' than a very good farce like *Seven Keys to Baldpate*?" In fact, the Chekhov and Ibsen plays are still read and performed today, while both farces have vanished into the mists of theatrical history.

The Group's militant defense of their play and the critics' response provoked a storm of controversy. "Just produce 'em—don't explain 'em," said Walter Winchell of the Group's ad. Still, Odets' and Clurman's letters were reprinted in many papers in the belief that such "good, hearty, forthright debate" could only benefit the American theatre. *Paradise Lost* had supporters everywhere. Newspaper columns were filled for weeks with letters urging readers to ignore the reviews and rush to see it. Heywood Broun, who didn't normally discuss theatre in his *World-Telegram* column, took the unprecedented step of devoting an entire day's type to his "not very humble opinon [that there is] no play in New York at present which is as alive and vital and stirring as *Paradise Lost* . . . it is the best thing our stage has to offer." The radical press, which had expressed reservations about *Awake and Sing!*, was surprisingly kind to the more diffuse *Paradise Lost*, possibly because it gave them a chance to excoriate their bourgeois colleagues, whom Robert Forsythe in the *New Masses* characterized as having "the longing of a lost child for security. If any strain of the mind is required, they refuse to follow." Seldom had a play with such mixed reviews garnered so much publicity.

But business wasn't good. Weekly receipts hovered between $4,000 and $5,000, mostly due to Helen Thompson's heroic efforts in the benefit department. "Sandy claims he doesn't need sense memory for his line, 'The house feels kind of empty tonight,' " joked a column in *The Flying Grouse*, the Group magazine Luther Adler and Bud Bohnen inaugurated that winter. The item went on to play on the name of a cut-rate ticket agency: "Morris insists, 'The show's going over with a Leblang!' " The actors took enormous salary cuts, up to 80 percent, to keep the show running.

They knew that most people who saw *Paradise Lost* loved it from the passionate letters they read in the papers and the warm comments of friends like Elmer Rice, who came back over and over again. So, in one more concerted effort to convince the audience to support them and the new play, they organized a "speaking campaign" and sent everyone out on the road. During January Group members addressed more than seventy-five meetings: Billy Kirkland (their best public speaker) went to New Haven to talk to students at the Yale Drama School; Crawford spoke at a Smith Club luncheon; Strasberg addressed the Friends of the Chinese People; Mike Gordon traveled to Yonkers to tell members of the New Workers' Theatre about the Group; Beany Barker turned down Odets' invitation to Artur Schnabel's opening piano recital in favor of a meeting in the Bronx. Behind the scenes, Grover Burgess, Bill Challee, Ruth Nelson, Julie Garfield, and Lewis Leverett sent letters, booked engagements, and wrote speeches. What they were looking for, as Challee pointed out in *The Flying Grouse*, was an *"active* audience" that understood their goals. "If a campaign of this nature could be arranged each year. . . . I feel it will be an important and sane way of cementing our relations with 'our audience.' "

They were killing themselves to keep *Paradise Lost* and the Group alive, and the strain began to show. Russell Collins' drinking, which had been a concern for years, finally incapacitated him altogether. One night onstage in his role as Challee's homeless sidekick he blacked out, forgot his lines, and was too drunk to be prompted. Something had to be done, but the Group were unwilling simply to throw him out, especially since they knew his devotion to the organization was the only thing keeping Collins, a deeply unhappy man with no personal life, from sliding into irreversible alcoholism. At a meeting called by Bud Bohnen the company decided to send him to a sanatorium known for its success in treating drinking problems. Financing this expensive cure out of the anemic Group treasury was impossible; the actors offered to give bimonthly performances for the inmates to pay the bill. The clinic agreed, and for six months the Group shuttled off to the country every few weeks to meet their obligation. Paul Morrison stepped into Collins' role, and around the same time actors from the defunct *Weep for the Virgins* replaced most of the non-Group members in *Paradise Lost*.

Harold Clurman and Stella Adler were in one of their periodic states of crisis as well. She never let their relationship stop her from flirting with other men, but around the time of *Paradise Lost* she became more seriously involved with someone else. It may very well have been a means of taking revenge on Clurman for forcing her to play Clara. Actress and director had first been drawn together through the theatre, and it was the foundation of their life together: they talked about it, argued about it, thought about it constantly. (Other aspects of their relationship appear to have been less satisfactory, at least for Adler.) With their work and personal life so closely intertwined, it was inevitable that problems in one created problems in the other. The Group was their bond and their most bitter bone of contention. Adler believed in a permanent company and shared the Group's reverence for acting, but she had many reservations about Group life—and not just the artistic ones she expressed at Ellenville. Group-ness wasn't her style, and she was tired of being poor. She both loved and resented Clurman for holding her to her ideals: "I feel that I need to sin, and you make me feel I have no right to," she told him. If Clurman wouldn't let her "sin" onstage by playing the glamorous parts she yearned for, she would make him suffer for it offstage.

Adler wasn't the only Group member subject to temptation. Newspaper reports in late December revealed that Joe Bromberg had signed a contract with Fox Films and was due to report to Hollywood in January. Confronted with the news, Bromberg admitted he hadn't told the Group what he was planning because he was afraid they would talk him out of it. He dealt the worst blow to Group morale since Franchot Tone's departure, and they reacted with anger and condemnation. Bromberg was no Alan Baxter, doomed to small parts and not really essential to the ensemble; he was one of their most respected actors and had played leading roles in their best plays. He was leaving for the money, pure and simple, they concluded, and some of them appeared to almost hate him for it. Stormy meetings were held to berate him. Bromberg, shocked and hurt by the savagery of his former comrades' remarks, responded by going on the attack. He had two small children; of course he needed the money. He hadn't been all that crazy about playing Uncle Morty, he hated *Weep for the Virgins*, he wasn't even in *Paradise Lost*. What did the Group have to offer him?

It was an ominous question, revealing that as Group members got older and acquired families and responsibilities, they had to think about what they could get from the Group as well as what they could give. It was also unanswerable, for at the moment, as far as actual productions went, the Group had nothing to offer.

Their play problem was as acute as ever. Sometimes it was due to factors beyond their control. They were considering Paul Green's *The Enchanted Maze*, revised and expanded after a workshop production in North Carolina, but its subject matter didn't seem appropriate and it would make enormous demands on their limited resources, with a cast of one hundred plus eight complicated sets. John Howard Lawson still hadn't completed *Marching Song*. Odets was working on *The Silent Partner*, but that too was unfinished, and no one thought it was a good idea to do a fifth successive Odets play. Sometimes the Group made their difficulties worse. They missed the chance to do *Dead End*, a big Broadway hit that fall, because Sidney Kingsley had neither forgotten nor forgiven their tactless comments about how their production had saved the so-so script of *Men in White*. When Beany Barker submitted an adaptation she'd made with a friend of *The Unpossessed*, a provocative novel by Tess Slesinger about uncommitted intellectuals, she was deeply wounded by the blunt comments made at the meeting held to discuss it. Her fellow members didn't just criticize the play, they attacked its characters as sick, useless people, far inferior to the Group because they hadn't learned to "truly search" for life's meaning.

This kind of ideologically tinged discussion was common in the 1930s, and if they could be brutal they were at least about real issues of content. But the Group hadn't learned that the honesty they inflicted on one another made all but the hardiest playwrights flinch. They'd grown so used to their plain-spoken meetings they didn't realize that for an outsider, who hadn't shared the collective trust and intimacy that informed their candor, these gatherings could be terrifying. Molly Thacher joined them as playreader that winter, and over the years she would try to introduce more supportiveness into the Group's relations with writers.

The directors knew they needed to develop a better way of finding scripts, and now they took a first tentative step toward actually working with artists to develop a play from scratch. Clurman had met the German composer Kurt Weill, Brecht's former partner, who'd fled the Nazis and was now cooling his heels in New York awaiting the long-postponed opening of *The Eternal Road*. This collaboration among Weill, Franz Werfel, and Max Reinhardt, a verse drama depicting the suffering of the Jews in scenes drawn from the Old Testament, turned into a mammoth spectacle whose technical problems delayed the opening several times. It finally premiered at the Manhattan Opera House in January 1937. Meanwhile, Clurman introduced Weill to several Group members, and the idea took shape that they might work together. The Group knew *The Threepenny Opera*, the most famous

Brecht-Weill work, through German-language recordings and the mordant film version made in 1931 by G. W. Pabst. They admired Weill's music and were eager to bring his talents into the Group. Crawford, who loved popular songs, was especially enthusiastic about the Group tackling a musical project. They began to discuss possible subjects, including an American version of *The Good Soldier Schweik*.

But in January 1936 that project was in its very early stages. They were stuck for a script and desperate to find one, as it was clear that despite their best efforts *Paradise Lost* wouldn't run long. When Milton Shubert, nephew of Lee and an active member of the Shubert organization, came to them with an adaptation of Theodore Dreiser's *An American Tragedy* they were disposed to be receptive. The novel had been dramatized once before, in 1926, and presented on Broadway in a version that treated the story of an ambitious young man who murdered his pregnant girlfriend as a sentimental melodrama. The script Shubert bought after seeing it produced in 1935 at Jasper Deeter's Hedgerow Theatre in Rose Valley, Pennsylvania, was quite different. The author, a director named Erwin Piscator, who had headed Berlin's famous Volksbühne, was one of the pioneers of epic theatre, which sought to educate the audience in social and economic realities. His version, based on a scenario by Dreiser's German translator, the producer Lena Goldschmidt, saw the tragedy as ordained by fate—not the mythical fate of Greek drama or the modern psychological fate of flawed protagonists, but the socioeconomic fate that governed the destiny of every individual in a capitalist society. He added the character of a Speaker to drive home this point in a didactic manner appropriate to his view of theatre as a weapon.

Clurman didn't much care for the script, which he found cold, but Strasberg thought it had possibilities. It offered another chance for stylistic experimentation, with its emphasis on telling a story through narration, as opposed to re-creating it through dramatization. He saw the production as an opportunity to explore the epic theatre approach and also to incorporate some ideas he'd developed from his study of Oriental theatre, in which one actor was traditionally delegated to stand at the side and describe the scenes as they unfolded. He was willing to direct, the Shuberts would put up the money, the Group needed to work—it would be crazy to refuse. The directors agreed to present the play, whose title they changed to *Case of Clyde Griffiths* to distinguish it from the 1926 production. They were almost sorry when, only a few days later, a young radio writer named Irwin Shaw offered them his sizzling antiwar drama, *Bury the Dead*. The Group wanted very much to produce it, but they were committed to the Shuberts and Shaw was unwilling to wait. His play caused a sensation when it appeared at a New Theatre Night in March and subsequently ran for several months on Broadway.

As *Paradise Lost* limped along in late January, losing money despite the salary cuts and the Group's intensive audience campaign, everyone was weary and disheartened. The Group felt they'd failed the play; Odets felt he'd failed the Group. They'd dropped back to earth after their skyrocketing rise in the spring, and no one felt the jolt more keenly than the playwright. He was no longer the great Red hope of Broadway; he was just another writer who'd had two hits followed by a flop. It had been hard to be a struggling author, unappreciated even by his beloved Group, but at least then he could devote all his energies to his plays and his furious quest for recognition. Now he was divided: too discouraged by the obtuse reception the critics had given his best play to be very eager to get down to work on the next one, wondering ruefully whether he'd been a fool to turn down all those lucrative movie offers in the first flush of fame. He had more money than ever before, but he'd also assumed responsibility for his extended family and was worrying about finances on a level that would have been inconceivable to the hungry young actor who could be cheered by a dollar from a friend.

Odets needed to get away, from New York, from the theatre, from the Group. Like Stella Adler, he needed to sin. (When she told Clurman she wanted to succumb to temptation and he was preventing her, Odets, who was in the room, shouted, "She's right!") He decided to take a trip to Hollywood—the home of that mortal Group sin, show business as strictly business—and see for himself what it was like. It was all for a good cause, he told himself. He would cut a quick deal, make a couple of fast bucks, send money to the Group, and be home in a few short weeks. The actors were crushed by yet another defection, however temporary, to the Gold Coast. They begged Clurman to persuade Odets to stay, to act as his conscience as the director had done so many times before. In early 1936, however, Clurman was tired of being everyone's conscience, and he refused. He'd retreated from his personal and professional sorrows into a stance of sardonic cynicism that was quite unlike the Harold they knew; it didn't bode well for the Group's future.

Odets departed for California shortly before *Paradise Lost* closed on February 8, leaving the Group to grapple with a series of painful questions about their organization that touched on their very reason for being. On February 16 the *Herald Tribune* reprinted a curious letter Clurman had sent to the New York play agents which revealed some, though not all, of the complex cross currents rippling under the surface of Group life:

Due to the success of *Waiting for Lefty* and the other Odets plays, the impression has arisen that the Group Theatre is primarily interested in the production of so-called "propaganda plays." This is false. The Group is essentially interested in plays that make for exciting and intelligent theatre. To make this clear I might say any of the following types of plays would have been considered by us as possible Group material: *Journey's End, First Lady, Russet Mantle, Winterset, The Petrified Forest, The Road to Rome, Pride and Prejudice, The Children's Hour, The Jest, Dinner at Eight.* In short, we would like to receive a greater variety of plays than have been submitted to us for the past year.

This was a peculiar and, to Group members, depressing list, composed as it was primarily of worthy, thoroughly conventional Broadway dramas. (The inclusion of *Winterset* was, under the circumstances, decidedly disingenuous.) Clurman seemed to be turning his back on the playwright who not only was his best friend but had given the Group three of their most important plays. What was this letter really saying? Was Clurman trying to suggest that no matter what the actors said or what kinds of productions they appeared in downtown, the Group was *not* a political theatre? Was he reminding agents that it was the directors, not the actors, who bought scripts? Probably both, and quite a bit more as well.

The letter aroused a furor among the Group actors, who knew perfectly well what it was all about. The play problem had become a symbol of all the practical and philosophical issues the Group needed to address. Clurman's letter suggested that the Group continue to rely primarily on the conventional source of new plays, agents, and be willing to repudiate their social ideals and finest achievements in a pathetic attempt to get a "greater variety" of scripts. The actors, on the contrary, had been arguing for almost a year that the Group needed systematically to develop new ways to reach playwrights sympathetic to their aims—and they did *not* include among their aims the production of a piece of high-society fluff like *Dinner at Eight*.

They wanted to draw closer to playwrights, to make them understand and share the Group's aims as Odets did. When the Dramatists Guild presented its revised minimum basic agreement to theatrical producers in mid-February, it seemed obvious to the Group actors that they must support the writers. They voted that the Group sign the new agreement, whose most controversial clauses required that the writer get a greater share of the proceeds from film sales and more control over the conditions of sale. They were aware that the movie studios and the League of New York Theatres (the Broadway producers' organization) bitterly opposed the contract, but in a quarrel like this they knew which side the Group should be on.

The directors weren't so sure. The Group's last two productions had been financed with movie money, as had 25 percent of the new plays on Broadway in the 1935–1936 season, and the studios made it quite clear they would never back a show under the terms the dramatists were proposing. The directors delayed signing for months while the League of New York Theatres negotiated a compromise agreement. This was still strong enough to provoke the studios into refusing to invest in Broadway shows for several years, and the Group was one of the first organizations to sign the new agreement, in early April, a month before the League officially settled with the Guild. But the fact remained that the directors had betrayed their principle and ignored the wishes of the members in favor of financial considerations. This was not the Group Theatre Clurman had spoken of so fervently in the winter of 1930.

The directors' reluctance to sign with the Guild prompted a series of tempestuous meetings in February and March at which the Group's power structure was severely criticized. What was the point of voting on Group policy, people shouted from the floor, if their decisions were then ignored? The directors had proved that they couldn't be trusted to act in a manner consistent with the Group's most basic beliefs, and the actors were no longer willing to leave matters exclusively in their hands. The radical suggestion was put forth that all questions concerning Group actions be decided by a vote of the entire membership.

This proposal was in all likelihood first put forward by members of the Group's communist unit, although the sentiments that inspired it were shared by many. In his testimony before HUAC, subsequent interviews, and again in his autobiography, Kazan painted an eloquent and sinister picture of the party's machinations to, as he saw it, take over the Group. His recollection of the chronology shifted over time: in 1952 he said it happened in the winter of 1935–1936 (which is most likely correct); in 1988 he pushed the episode back a year, possibly to minimize the length of time he was a party member. In all versions, the basic course of events remained the same. Higher-ups in the party instructed—not suggested, said Kazan, instructed—the unit to press for greater democracy within the Group, the idea being that once the actors were nominally in charge the party would actually dominate through, in Kazan's words, "the usual tricks of behind-the-scenes caucuses, block voting, and confusion of the issues." With Bromberg and Odets both in Hollywood (Odets in any case having drifted away from the party) the unit now boasted a grand total of seven members, but seven well-organized people in a group of thirty could certainly have a major impact on policy.

In the discussion that followed the unit's receipt of these instructions, Kazan, as he tells it, was the only one to vote against the idea. (The fact that they voted suggests that there was more autonomy, at least in theory, than his use of the word "instructed" implied.) His fellow members were surprised; in the past he'd always been agreeable and eager to go along. They thought they knew the reason for the change. Kazan was no longer the anxious, insecure apprentice who had joined the party in 1933. As stage manager he had gained the confidence and affection of Clurman, who sent him a telegram when *Awake and Sing!* opened calling him "brother." After he rose to the rank of actor he made a great personal hit, first in *Lefty* and then in *Paradise Lost* as Kewpie, a character whose savage pursuit of success brought to the surface feelings Kazan had until then kept carefully hidden. (Odets, who knew his friend Gadget's innermost thoughts better than most, had written the part with him in mind.) He was close to the two men who now wielded the most artistic authority within the Group, and he no longer needed to be so nice to everyone else. "The mask of the ever-compliant-good-kid fell clattering to the floor," he wrote of this transformation in his memoirs. "What was emerging was my true self."

His comrades in the unit distrusted that self. They suspected Kazan of being an opportunist, willing to do anything to get ahead, and his reluctance to challenge the directors confirmed their opinion. At a second meeting, a party activist from the impressive real world of labor organizing was called in to bolster the unit's resolve. He defined Kazan in class terms: the actor, he told them, was a foreman type, trying to curry favor with the bosses. For a long time he tried to convince Kazan of the error of his ways, and they put the matter to a vote again. But as far as Kazan was concerned, it was a farce, "a ritual of submission for me to act out." His was again the only dissenting vote. He walked out and went home, deeply disillusioned. Although he maintained afterward that he wrote a letter that very night resigning from the Communist party, subsequent events suggest that the break wasn't final until later in the year.

It's unfortunate that Kazan's various accounts of these two meetings are the only ones available, for they're strongly colored by his desire to justify not only his resignation but also his subsequent decision to give the names of his fellow party members to HUAC. The reluctance of other surviving Group members who were there to discuss his version suggests that it's roughly accurate and that they have mixed emotions about their actions. "There are certain aspects of my own history that I feel I have, subconsciously or not, deliberately sunk," Morris Carnovsky replied when asked for his comments on Kazan's statements. Phoebe Brand, who found the subject as distressing as her husband, acknowledged that she now felt she had been wrong to believe that more democracy would have solved the Group's problems. "I think there has to be one artistic director. You can have as much discussion as you like, but when it comes to final say, he has to say yes or no."

What Kazan's account lacks, and what those who disagreed with him also find hard to provide, is a sense of context. The Communist party could convince its Group members to press for a democratic, collective power structure, and they could count on the support of many noncommunist actors, only because every aspect of Group life was being reconsidered that spring. The badly managed tour, the half-hearted production of *Weep for the Virgins*, the devastating failure of *Paradise Lost*, had made everyone realize that something had to be done about the haphazard way the Group operated.

The Flying Grouse, whose two issues appeared in February and June, revealed how wide-ranging the debate was, how many options the Group explored in their effort to become more businesslike without abandoning their ideals. "We are all deeply concerned with the problems of securing our future together and at the same time keeping to the line of the principles and objectives we have set for ourselves," Crawford wrote.

They were all scattering their energies too much, she continued, bouncing around town with "a finger in every pie from Broadway to Marx" instead of "hammering away at our fundamental problems until we solve them." As far as plays went, she reiterated the point the actors had made that playwrights "need first to be attached more closely to the Group so that they can share and understand our purpose more clearly."

About money, her specialty within the Group, Crawford had sharper thoughts. She deplored the Group's tendency to hope for "miraculous visitations of public grants and private subsidy. We have ways of getting money —from the radio and from the movies, if not from plays. The problem here is how to still be the Group and engage in either of these activities." She and Clurman were both trying to overcome the actors' resistance to the idea of doing radio programs, or even feature films, as a unit; the actors, on the contrary, believed they made enough sacrifices for the Group in their theatre work and were unwilling to take salary cuts in other media to replenish the company treasury.

Luther Adler, who'd managed a theatre company as a young man and knew something about administration, felt the Group was getting too far away from their basic purpose when they dreamed of radio and movie money as a solution: "They can never give us, as a theatre, the basic security we want and need," he wrote in the *Grouse*. Taking the Group on the road was the better answer. "It not only gives us the opportunity to earn our full salaries, but it might also give us three months work, plus the economic leisure to rehearse new plays. We seem to have developed a 'smash-hit psychology.' What we need is a full season plan; and that the road can do much to provide."

In her article for the *Grouse*, his sister wrote about the potential of a newly created administrative body within the Group: the production committee, on which Stella was serving for *Case of Clyde Griffiths*, along with Kazan and Bobby Lewis. The idea was to take some of the pressure off the director of an individual play by assuming responsibility for areas he didn't have enough time for—work on crowd scenes or the characterizations of actors in small parts—and also to facilitate communication among Group members about the production: to convey complaints by the actors to the director, when the committee judged it appropriate; to report to the directorate on the progress of the production. Adler believed that production committees would also give Group actors who wanted to direct a way to learn the craft in stages, and she hoped their scope would eventually expand to allow experimental productions and workshops in various acting styles. She thought they were good for morale, because "they are able to keep a group together ideologically and artistically."

A lot of ideas were flying around in the magazine and in the Group's meetings. Although Crawford had urged them to focus their energies, the members wanted the Group to consider every possibility. Discussions went on and on, in meetings notable for turbulence and acrimony. A few actors supported the directors wholly, some did in part. Billy Kirkland believed strongly that the Group was best run as a democratic cooperative, but he shared the directors' distaste for the label of political theatre. He described the Group to a reporter as "an organization of dramatic entrepreneurs," claiming, as Clurman had, that "we simply pick the best scripts that are available to us. It doesn't make a particle of difference whether they point a moral or not . . . I'm no more a Communist than a vegetarian." Some actors were confused and couldn't make out what was really going on behind all the yelling. "There was an awful lot of underground politics happening," Beany Barker remembered. "We were terribly aware of some kind of a steamroller."

Grim as the meetings were, the Group could still find humor in them. When the *Grouse* wasn't airing policy issues, it enjoyed poking fun at individual and collective foibles: everything from Julie Garfield's enthusiastic misuse of big words ("I have developed a new atrophicy in my diction. With me this is tantamount"), to Strasberg's erudition ("Lee is reading simultaneously *Die Entwicklung des Basso-Buffo im Weltpolitik des 20 Jahrhunderts* and *The Cadaver of Gwendolyn Gwynne*"), to the Group's varying attitudes toward stylization ("Harold swears all actors can act like Bobby and like it"). Stella Adler would reduce her friends to hysteria with wicked imitations of people's incoherent and rambling speeches. The *Grouse* spoofed Art Smith, who tended to be long-winded—"Well—one, I approve; one-a, I think it's necessary; and two, have I still got the floor?"—and joked about the actors' tendency to consider everything a matter for collective discussion:

> Behind closed doors his Committee meets
> To perform miraculous mental feats
> By settling problems of very great weight
> Like a sudden incline in the Group birth-rate.

(Both the Kazans and the Bohnens were expecting their first babies.) Their ability to laugh at themselves took some of the sting out of the meetings, which continued throughout the spring without coming to any conclusions.

Meanwhile the Group tried to continue their artistic explorations under Strasberg's direction in *Case of Clyde Griffiths*. The director adopted a drastically different approach for this script, which appeared to interest him primarily as a technical problem. "It does not call for psychological progression of acting," he told the actors, "but essentially for full, precise, actors' energy and the strictest kind of relationship to stage space." Tony Kraber's rehearsal notes, reprinted in part in the *Grouse*, indicated that

Strasberg dropped the use of emotional memory and instead worked with the actors to achieve a quality of "narrative emotion," which presented the play's events as if they had already occurred and were being remembered by the performers. This technique was based on Strasberg's understanding of the epic theatre as a didactic rather than emotional experience. He may also have been influenced by the ideas of Max Gorelik, newly reconciled with the Group, who suggested that the entire production be staged as if it were the actual trial of Clyde Griffiths, with the audience acting as jury and the scenes showing Clyde's progression toward the murder being presented as courtroom reenactments.

The Group wanted to hire Gorelik, whose sharp analytical abilities would have aided enormously both in designing and in interpreting a difficult script. But the Shuberts insisted on their house designer, Watson Barrat. His immense, unwieldy set not only did nothing to illuminate the play's themes but also terrified the actors, who were afraid they would fall off one of the numerous badly lit offstage staircases and break their necks. The Shuberts didn't help matters by refusing to pay for more than six weeks of rehearsal, far less than the company were accustomed to and not nearly enough for a production that presented complex technical problems.

Rehearsals were tense. Only Billy Kirkland, playing the unfortunate Clyde, still believed wholeheartedly in Strasberg as a director. Morris Carnovsky didn't entirely succeed in hiding his dislike of the Speaker and his doubts that they could make the audience accept his role as interpreter of the stage action. ("You don't seem to let yourself have faith," Strasberg commented plaintively.) Phoebe Brand, as Roberta Alden, the poor woman Clyde kills, and Beany Barker, as Sondra Finchler, the rich one he loves, worked on their parts primarily with Stella Adler, who saw her place on the production committee as giving her permission to act as an assistant director. Clurman was trying very hard to keep Adler committed to the Group, and him, by giving her more to do. He'd gone so far as to plant stories with friendly columnists that she might play one half of the Speaker or alternate the role with Carnovsky. It's easy to imagine Strasberg's reaction to these published reports, and the idea was dropped—if indeed, it had ever been anything more than Clurman's way of assuring Adler he had her needs in mind.

It's a sign of how listless and apathetic Strasberg felt at the time that he didn't object to Adler's usurpation of his authority with the two leading ladies. He was working with his intellect, not his heart, on the production. For the sake of exploring a new theatrical style, he abandoned his greatest strength as a director: his ability to get the actors to plumb their characters' psychological depths, to make each moment vibrate with emotion. With Gorelik's help he might at least have created a few breathtaking stage pictures, and the production did have some striking visual moments, but his effects were hampered by the unimaginative set and murky lighting.

Though Strasberg and the actors worked conscientiously and hard, *Case of Clyde Griffiths* just wasn't sparking anyone's best efforts. The one exception was Bobby Lewis, who created in a small but important scene a stylized dramatization of Clyde's passage from one class into another. Lewis played a department-store mannequin (in contemporary art, a frequent symbol of alienated modern man) who comes mysteriously to life as a tailor to fit Clyde for his first tuxedo, as three Salvation Army women sing "Silent Night." Lewis fitted Kirkland using ritualistic gestures; the light, which appeared to be coming through a stained-glass window, reinforced the religious imagery, and Kirkland, also using stylized gestures, suggested that he was turning into a mannequin himself. The scene climaxed with Clyde's sudden appearance in a tuxedo—a vaudeville quick-change used to suggest a miracle—and emergence onto the street as a new kind of dummy, a member of the upper class. The religious subtext buttressed the Speaker's references to Clyde as a sacrifice to society, and the mannequin imagery made Piscator's social point far more wittily than the lines.

The Group's low opinion of Broadway critics' acuity wasn't altered by their reaction to *Case of Clyde Griffiths* when it opened at the Ethel Barrymore Theatre on March 13. The reviewers fell all over themselves praising Strasberg's direction, which the Group considered well below his usual level, and Watson Barrat's ugly, unhelpful set. Their warmth for the acting was more appreciated: both Barker and Brand felt they'd done some of their best work with the help of Stella Adler, and Carnovsky took slight comfort from the reviewers' comments that, if anything could have won them over to the Speaker, his mellifluous voice and appealing demeanor would have.

But the press found the Speaker's constant hammering home of the script's political message both tiresome and unnecessary. Even the *Daily Worker*, which heartily agreed with the idea that it was the social system that pushed Clyde to murder, thought the Speaker annoyed the audience by pointing out the obvious: "The play stands nobly on its own legs without the Speaker's commentary." As for the bourgeois reviewers, they vehemently rejected the idea that any factors other than Clyde's personal failings were responsible for his fate. The *Times'* Brooks Atkinson was typical. "This column, which is trying to look as pink as possible this morning," he wrote, "cannot help thinking that Clyde Griffiths murdered Roberta Alden because he was a boy of cheap and sniveling character. . . . *Case of Clyde Griffiths* sounds pretty silly when it is rattling the skeleton of Karl Marx and accusing the audience of conspiracy and high treason."

Despite their own reservations about the play and their work on it, the Group hoped that the critics' lavish praise of the production (if not the concept) would attract audiences. They met with the Shuberts to discuss measures that might be taken to keep the show running while they tried to drum up business, but discovered that the tightfisted organization expected them to make all the sacrifices. "The Shuberts tried to pull a fast one," Bud Bohnen wrote to his brother, "i.e., pay us chicken feed until after Easter, in the hope of a pickup after then. We, however, were to *continue* to get the chicken feed, and he [Shubert] was to get *all* the pickup." Over the weekend of March 27 they negotiated in hopes of taking over the production from the Shuberts, but they couldn't reach an agreement, and on Monday announced that the Saturday evening show had been their last. *Case of Clyde Griffiths* had eked out a scant nineteen performances.

For the third time in the Group's history they were stranded months before the summer with no show on the boards and only the most tenuous prospects for the fall. Clurman departed hastily for North Carolina to talk to Paul Green about *The Enchanted Maze*; problematic though the play was, it was their only possibility at the moment. Also, Crawford had suggested that Green, who used music in his symphonic regional dramas of American history and folklore, might be the right collaborator for Weill. This idea gained added force when Green mentioned in passing that he had fought in the World War. Clurman broached the subject of an Americanized *Schweik*, and Green responded enthusiastically. When the director returned to New York, he told his partners they had a collaborator, and Crawford immediately sent Green a script of *Schweik* to peruse.

In the meanwhile, Luther Adler convinced the company that a well-planned spring tour of *Awake and Sing!* could solve their financial problems, and he and Bud Bohnen took on much of the responsibility for it. Bohnen was also working on rewrites of a radio play the Group was set to present April 23 on "The Rudy Vallee Show." Odets had dashed off a quick sketch allegedly based on an incident in the life of Sarah Bernhardt. In it, the actress refuses to entertain troops during the World War, recalling the guilt she felt when her taunts drove a pacifist lover to his death during the Franco-Prussian conflict. Stella Adler would play Bernhardt in the ten-minute drama; Bohnen, Kirkland, and Carnovsky supported her. None of them was especially thrilled by the script, but it meant work and a paycheck.

Less than a week before the radio piece was broadcast, the actors were thrown into an uproar by a letter printed in several New York newspapers. Although signed by Crawford (stuck with the dirty work as usual), it had in fact been written by Clurman at Strasberg's suggestion. The critical response to *Clyde Griffiths* seemed to the directors to confirm their fear that the press had typecast the Group as a narrowly political theatre, with dire consequences. They felt they must attempt one more time to disassociate themselves from the opinions expressed in the plays they presented, to put themselves on record as a theatre devoted to exploring all aspects of the American experience.

Despite the fact that the letter began, "The directors and actors of the Group Theatre believe that every creative theatre must represent a kind of conviction or collective sentiment . . . a theatre's productions should reveal its basic intentions," its principal statements revealed that in fact the directors *didn't* want to be judged by the plays the Group had done:

> Certain remarks in a few reviews of our recent productions make us wonder whether our general approach to the theatre is not being taken with an almost mechanical literalness, so that the detailed opinions of our playwrights are believed to represent our own opinions point by point. . . . We have produced plays because we felt what they had to say was of interest and value, not because we agreed completely with the playwright's individual philosophy or his individual method of expression. We believe, as you do, in a varied, rich theatre that neglects nothing in the unmeasurable gamut of human experience and imagination, and we believe too in allowing our collaborators— playwrights as well as others—the privileges of their own idiosyncrasies, prejudices and partisanship. As a theatre we cannot be held responsible for all of them.

Clurman accurately described this confused document a decade later as "a prime example of collective bungling in both the tactical and the ideological sphere." It did nothing to convince the press: several critics, after printing excerpts from the letter, ran columns of their own expressing surprise that the Group should object to being considered a left-wing theatre, urging them to stick to their guns and produce what they liked. The actors were as scornful of this example of directorial wishy-washiness as they had been of Clurman's letter in February. Yet the directors' insistence that the Group Theatre could only be hurt by being pigeonholed as a venue for left-wing propaganda appeared to be having some sort of cumulative impact. Surviving memos from this period indicate that ideology was playing less of a role in Group discussions than everyone's strong desire to reorganize the company along more effective lines.

Although many Group members remained sympathetic to the openly political theatres downtown, it didn't escape their notice that these companies were undergoing severe growing pains of their own. The most prominent of them had the worst problems. The Theatre Union had pleased no one with *Mother* (certainly not Brecht, who detested the production), and a well-intentioned antifascist drama, *Bitter Stream*, was little better received in March. The Union had a deficit of $15,000; its executive board was rent by ideological disputes; and, like the Group, it was having trouble finding scripts. Most ominous of all, it was about to lose its home at the Civic Rep because the bank that owned the theatre decided that if it couldn't get more rent it would tear the building down and convert it into a parking lot. The Union limped along for another year, but in the spring of 1936 it was clear the organization's best days were behind it.

Smaller companies were finding it hard to compete with the allure of the Federal Theatre Project, which under Hallie Flanagan's leadership was strongly committed to the goal of presenting socially conscious plays for the masses of people unable to afford Broadway theatre. The Theatre of Action, after an unsuccessful production codirected by Kazan in March, was absorbed into the FTP and then dissolved. Many members of the Theatre Collective and the amateur groups in the New Theatre League also joined the Project. It was not, of course, a Marxist theatre, but Flanagan didn't share her Washington colleagues' paranoia about communism; she kept the FTP open to all unemployed theatre workers and refused to quiz people about their political affiliations. Despite a troubling precedent set when *Ethiopia*, the first Living Newspaper, was banned in January because authorities feared it might offend foreign heads of state, in general the Project was remarkably free from censorship. The Living Newspapers in particular, with their dramatizations of such public events as the agricultural and housing crises, borrowed the techniques used in *Newsboy* and other workers theatre plays to create a nonsectarian form of agitprop whose goal was to provoke informed debate through exciting theatre.

As the Federal Theatre flourished and the left theatre floundered, the Group put their own political commitments temporarily aside to try and solve their organizational problems. Luther Adler wrote a long memo voicing the company's growing realization that "business plans deserve as careful rehearsal as a new play requires" and laid out a list of proposals "aimed at (1) extending the goodwill we possess and (2) consolidating our financial position." As Crawford had in the *Grouse*, he called for "complete concentration on Group activity"—in fact, Kazan's directing stint at the Theatre of Action had been the only significant non-Group work that spring—and urged members to assume responsibility for specific practical tasks, since "we are no longer in a position where we can afford specialists to help us." Among his ideas were special matinees for school groups, reorganization of the long-dormant Group Associates to help drum up backing for Group productions, better solicitation of subscriptions, and sustained efforts to build support for the Group among unions. He held up as long-term goals the founding of the Group school and a European tour.

While the actors were out of town on the Group's American tour, the directors discussed Luther's proposals and all the other suggestions that had been made during their tumultuous spring meetings. Clurman promised to write out a coherent plan for reorganizing the company, and on May 1 Strasberg wrote a letter summarizing his personal feelings about the Group's ongoing evolution:

Much as I agree that the three directors are the most able to lead a theatre—it still seems to me necessary to do something *if the Group is to develop*. When two people marry—one may feel himself competent to run everything—but if the marriage is to be successful some mutual "giving in" is necessary. It cannot remain a "honeymoon" nor remain just as it was before. It is a new step which necessitates a certain amount of rearrangement—and no amount of "pure" logic can change that necessity. When a child grows up it *must* do certain things, possibly with dangerous results. There is no other path in life.

Collective activity despite its mistakes should not be either belittled or condescended to. I do not think that the Group Theatre can be built by the three directors alone—or any other three directors—except by constant replacements. But it can be built by the Group as a whole realizing and solving its own problems, even if thereby certain mistakes are made, mistakes which are inevitable in any case.

This was quite a change from Strasberg's position three years before, when he had argued that government by a directorate was the soundest way to run the Group, whether or not the three current directors retained their titles. His letter suggests that he and Clurman had changed places, with the latter now arguing for greater authority at the top and Strasberg in favor of more participation by the actors. Part of this was because Strasberg, as he said in his letter, wanted to be relieved of all administrative responsibilities:

I am absolutely unwilling to risk my personal sanity in such activity. I think that the three of us have come as near to complete nervous breakdown as I have ever seen people verge on—not because of overwork, or hard work, but because of mental worry and strain. Personally, I do not wish to continue it. . . . if you decide to simply reclarify the group organization and retain the form of directorial responsibility I will have to receive a leave of absence from performance of those functions for at least a year or two.

At the time of Strasberg's letter he was the only Group director in New York. Clurman was in Chicago with the *Awake and Sing!* tour, having followed Stella Adler there. Crawford was in North Carolina, working with Weill and Green on a scenario for their American version of *The Good Soldier Schweik*. They read German novels and plays from the period for general inspiration, and newspaper articles to get the flavor of the period; at night they talked about their ideas. Gradually a rough scenario began to evolve. They decided to call the play *Johnny Johnson* (30,000 American Johnsons had served in the World War, 3,000 of them named John). They envisioned a work that would draw on diverse native American idioms— vaudeville, folklore, homespun satire—and unify them in a form of musical theatre like that Brecht and Weill had pioneered in Germany, with songs and speech flowing naturally together. Crawford was, perhaps for the first time in her years with the Group, truly happy and fulfilled. Green and Weill adored her and gave her all the credit for making the project a reality. "This was the kind of work I really enjoyed," she wrote later, "inspiring new works and being a part of their development."

The Group had released all the actors not in *Awake and Sing!* to take whatever odd jobs they could find until the company reunited for the summer. The tour began in Baltimore on April 27, with Bobby Lewis replacing Joe Bromberg as Uncle Morty and Gadget Kazan subbing temporarily for Bud Bohnen, who was home with his wife, Hildur, awaiting the birth of their first child. (When their daughter, Marina, arrived on April 30, Bohnen's brother, Arthur, cabled jokingly: "DISAPPOINTED IN HILDUR. ANY GOOD COMMUNIST WOULD HAVE AWAITED MAY FIRST.") The week-long engagement went well, owing largely, Luther Adler wrote, to the brilliant publicity effort mounted by Emanuel Eisenberg, a young writer and press agent active in the left theatre who had worked with the Group before on *Gentlewoman*. Helen Deutsch's relationship with the company was increasingly strained, and Eisenberg's work in Baltimore reinforced Luther's belief that the Group needed a reorganized and more effective publicity department. He reiterated in his notes on their week in Baltimore his faith that touring would help them "build for our theatre a 'national' reputation."

A profitable month in Chicago seemed to justify Luther's optimism. Bill Challee, who knew the city, had made an advance trip in April to line up publicity and group sales, and Arthur Bohnen, who lived there, had helped. Business was good, especially in the first two weeks, and the lovely spring weather boosted everyone's spirits. Clurman made contact with a young playwright named Robert Ardrey, a former student and protégé of Thornton Wilder's, and urged him to write something for the Group. The actors had a friendly reunion with Alan Baxter, in town to promote a film. Although they booed Joe Bromberg's first movie effort, *Under Two Flags*, when they saw it in Baltimore, they harbored no grudge against Baxter and threw a party in his honor after the show—graciously allowing him to pick up the tab, since he could afford it on his Hollywood salary. Their reception in Chicago was so enthusiastic that they added special Sunday performances of *Waiting for Lefty* and their experimental skits, which also sold well.

There were a few sour notes in the Windy City. On opening night the actors were alarmed when no one laughed; it turned out the advance publicity had so stressed the Group's seriousness that the rather staid orchestra audience (composed largely of Theatre Guild subscribers) apparently missed the play's humor. The balcony was rowdier but not very friendly: after the first intermission a gang of university students—apparently responding to Luther Adler's closing line, "What the hell kind of house is this, it ain't got an orange!"—began pelting the actors with fruit. As Bobby Lewis remembered it, only Stella Adler's majestic descent to the front of the stage to announce, "It's up to you ladies and gentlemen out there to protect these actors," saved them from being inundated.

By the time the Group arrived in Chicago, Adler, Lewis, and Sandy Meisner had formed an inseparable trio, united by their mutual feelings of discontent. Adler was still angry about her role in *Paradise Lost*. Meisner had been so dissatisfied with his position in the Group he had threatened to resign a few weeks before the tour. Lewis had directed the Sarah Bernhardt radio program, which had been poorly received and prompted a nasty argument within the company over how the fee should be divided; he blamed Clurman for the confusion and for failing to support him properly in his work. The actress and her two pals spent a lot of time offstage together, giggling, gossiping, and directing well-placed satirical barbs at both the Group and Clurman. Though they were careful to couch their remarks in humorous terms, their intent was clear. Clurman called them "the Weird Sisters," a nickname taken up by the rest of the Group as well. The fractious spring meetings and endless debates over policy and organization had strained personal as well as professional relationships—the two were never very clearly distinguished in the Group in any case.

While the Group wound up their stay in Chicago, Clurman went West to see Odets in California. His friend, who'd fallen in love with the Vienna-born actress Luise Rainer, seemed to be drifting. When not working on the screenplay Paramount was paying him $2,500 a week to write, Odets divided his time between hitting the Hollywood hot spots with his new friend John O'Hara and attending meetings to raise money for such good causes as *New Theatre* magazine and the Scottsboro defense. He was as conflicted as ever about where he belonged. Clurman found him oddly eager to impress movie people with the Group's—and his own—importance; he valued their opinion far more than was wise, the director thought.

Clurman was also worried about the progress—or lack of it—of *The Silent Partner*. He seemed intent on molding the labor play to what he perceived to be the Group's needs: at one point he asked Odets plaintively if perhaps a good part could be written into it for Stella Adler, and later he pressed him to give more emphasis to the love story. Odets, who'd been sending part of his salary back to New York for the Group, felt further stirrings of resentment about the company's reliance on him. It was a strained visit, though Clurman enjoyed the ease of Hollywood life and tried to refrain from preaching at his friend. He returned east, hoping against hope that *The Silent Partner* would be finished and in suitable shape for rehearsal by June.

It might be their only hope, for he discovered in New York that the *Johnny Johnson* scenario was very rough; Strasberg considered it not yet promising enough to plan on summer rehearsals, and Clurman agreed. Crawford, who had greater faith in Green and Weill, shielded them from the news of her partners' dissatisfaction as much as she could and told them that Group actors who'd heard bits of the score had loved it. She urged Green to send completed sections as quickly as possible to Weill; while Clurman and Strasberg scrambled around town looking for other scripts, she quietly prepared to bring Green north to continue work on the project at the Group's summer retreat.

The *Awake and Sing!* tour arrived in Cleveland on June 7, just as the Republicans were gathering there to nominate Alf Landon for the futile task of running for president against Roosevelt. Business was terrible; GOP delegates were hardly the most likely audience for Odets' Bronx drama, and no one else wanted to venture into the overcrowded downtown area where the Hanna Theatre was located. Accommodations were almost impossible to find, and when found were prohibitively expensive. The Group lost money, and lost even more in Newark when they moved there on June 15; too many New Jersey residents had seen the play in Manhattan. By the time they shut the tour down on the 22nd, they'd lost every nickel they made in Baltimore and Chicago.

From Newark they went directly to Nichols, Connecticut, where the rest of the Group had assembled on Memorial Day to begin another summer of alternating performances for adult summer campers with rehearsals of their fall projects. Though they had nothing as yet to rehearse, the camp already bustled with Group activity and expectations. Crawford, Weill, and Green had taken a house together and were hard at work on *Johnny Johnson*. Odets was due soon with, he promised, a finished script of *The Silent Partner*. John Howard Lawson swore that *Marching Song* would be completed any day now and he would bring it straight to the Group. Clurman had only been waiting for the arrival of the touring company to present his paper on reorganizing the Group to the entire company. They had problems to solve, but also projects to look forward to—and the whole summer ahead of them.

TEN

Falling Apart

The Pine Brook Club was, according to its advertisements, an adult camp "for the discriminating." Although it was only a few miles from Bridgeport, in 1936 the trip was a long one over dirt roads; residents enjoyed the sense of being way out in the country. There were woods to stroll in, a lake for swimming and boating, horses to ride, huge stretches of lawn with deck chairs for sunbathers. It was a hot, sunny summer; everyone wore a minimum of clothing and spent a lot of time in the water. It was good to be back together in a rural setting, away from the frantic pace of New York, where there was always another letter to write, another meeting to address, another crisis to resolve. The Group hoped that in this unpressured environment they could come to grips with the fundamental problems their difficult season had exposed.

Despite their problems, over the course of five years and fourteen productions they had won a respected place for themselves in the American theatre. Even so fundamentally unsympathetic a critic as the *Herald Tribune*'s Percy Hammond, who was amused rather than inspired by their ideals and mildly annoyed by most of their plays, felt constrained to admit the Group was "the finest acting institution in this if not in any other land." How far they had come could be seen in the terms of their stay at the Pine Brook Club. The management had been only too happy to renovate an entire eighteen-room building, including a large rehearsal space and two classrooms, for their use. They were expected to provide in return a single weekly performance, a far cry from the exhausting four-nights-a-week schedule at Green Mansions in 1934. Conditions seemed to promise a productive summer devoted largely to their own work.

Yet some of the old communal spirit was gone. Stella Adler, who'd had enough of dormitory accommodations, rented a house, and Clurman lived there with her and her daughter, Ellen. They weren't aloof from the company: Adler liked to have people around her, the house was constantly filled with Group members, and she gave wonderful parties where Kurt Weill's wife, Lotte Lenya, would sing with Sandy Meisner accompanying her at the piano. But the Group actors were there as her guests; it wasn't like the old days of gathering in the living room at Brookfield. Odets too had rented a cottage off the campgrounds; he was no longer content to bang away on a borrowed typewriter in any empty room that came to hand, and he wanted some privacy for the visit Luise Rainer had promised to make. The house Crawford shared with Weill, Lenya, and Paul Green was about a mile away, a deliberate decision on Crawford's part: "I had had my fill of living packed like a sardine." They were still a closely knit band, but people were older; they felt the need for more space and more time alone.

The clan assembled at Pine Brook included the usual mix of members, apprentices, spouses, and hangers-on, but a few familiar faces were missing. Everyone felt the absence of Joe Bromberg, whose jolly personality had enlivened previous Group summers. Walter Coy too had defected to the movies and been dropped from the membership roster. Billy Kirkland had taken a leave of absence. Russell Collins, happily, was back, looking more physically fit and at peace with himself than he had in years; the counseling sessions at the sanitorium had apparently freed him from some of the personal demons that had driven him to the bottle.

The twelve apprentices had a closer and more carefully planned affiliation with the company than ever before. The directors hoped to expand the membership, and with that in mind had taken actors with more experience and credentials than ordinary apprentices. In return for their work at no pay, they were promised instruction in the Group method and serious consideration for Group membership at the end of the summer. Some of them were old friends from the left theatre who had worked with the Group before. Curt Conway and Will Lee, long-time members of the Workers Laboratory Theatre, had been directed by Kazan in *The Young Go First*. Lee Cobb appeared in *Mother* and *Bitter Stream* at the Theatre Union and had a small part in *Till the Day I Die*. Albert van Dekker also worked at the Union, but he'd acted with Carnovsky and Meisner long before that in *Marco Millions* and *Volpone* at the Theatre Guild; Actors Forum members knew him as one of the reformers on the Equity Council.

At the moment, classes were about all the Group had to offer anyone, since *Johnny Johnson* was unfinished and neither *The Silent Partner* nor *Marching Song* had yet arrived. The members and apprentices studied fencing and took a dance class taught by Gluck Sandor and Felicia Sorel. Though these two were known primarily for their work in ballet, their course offered a survey of the different styles of dance movement and aimed to "widen the body range of the actor." The Group, used to Tamiris' more laissez-faire approach, thought Sandor's insistence on labeling each movement with a number was rather funny; they giggled as they went from a One to a Three to a Six, though they found the balletic poses refreshingly pretty after the angular attitudes of modern dance.

Strasberg's class emphasized the fundamentals of acting, offering new Group associates in-depth exposure to the exercises that were the cornerstone of the method and giving long-time members a chance to brush up their basic technique. Stella Adler worked on specific problems of interpretation and characterization; she assigned scenes from classic and contemporary plays, then critiqued the performances. Carnovsky continued his exploration of speech and language in poetic drama. Ever-malapropian Julie Garfield broke the class up one day when he climaxed a thunderous rendering of Hamlet's "O, what a rogue and peasant slave am I" monologue with the line "If he do belch, I know my course." The word should have been "blench," but Garfield had more enthusiasm than book learning. "Julie used to walk through the woods at Pine Brook reciting poetry and Shakespeare," said Phoebe Brand. "He loved it—but he always got it a little wrong!"

The one completely new course was Kurt Weill's class in musical theatre. Weill had two tasks to accomplish. First, as it was becoming increasingly clear that *Johnny Johnson* would probably be the Group's first fall production, he had to teach the actors how to sing in a style appropriate to the material. Professional singers weren't necessary—which was fortunate, since few Group members had that kind of training—but the play did require a very definite vocal approach. "It was a way of talking on the note so it was a kind of musical talking," Bobby Lewis remembered. Weill stressed interpretation over vocal beauty. "Don't sing so much," he was always telling them. He didn't want them to smooth out the rough edges in their voices; he wanted the songs to have as personal and immediate a quality as their speech. His wife, who also had no formal musical education, had made her reputation in Germany as the foremost exponent of this special style.

The Sprechstimme technique grew out of Weill's conception of musical theatre, the fundamental subject of his classes. Musical theatre was the purest form of poetic theatre, he told them. It allowed the use of heightened language and emotions without the artificial quality that sometimes crept into verse drama. In his work, songs weren't a musical interlude; they grew naturally from the demands of the script. When characters sang, it was because the play's essential idea at that moment could be better expressed in song than with speech. True musical theatre wasn't a bunch of popular songs strung together by a mindless script; it was an organic mingling of music and speech to express the emotions of the characters and the ideas of the creators. He wanted to restore music to its rightful place in the drama, to go beyond the limits of naturalistic straight plays and artificial musical comedies to create a synthesis that expressed life's deeper reality in vividly theatrical terms.

The actors were excited by his vision, which recalled some of Strasberg's early lectures on the importance of music in primitive religious theatre. They were eager to explore the possibilities of a modern attempt to fuse the two art forms, an impulse that had been mostly lost in the American musical theatre. Jerome Kern's *Show Boat* in 1927 and George Gershwin's *Porgy and Bess* in 1935 were foremost among the very few Broadway shows that integrated songs into a dramatic story. *Johnny Johnson* was in some ways even more ambitious, for the script Green was developing blended comedy, tragedy, and satire to portray the madness of war. It promised to mark a stimulating new stage in the Group's ongoing effort to master a broad range of theatrical styles.

While the Group awaited *Johnny Johnson*'s completion, and the arrivals of Odets and Lawson, they studied and kept the Pine Brook guests entertained with their weekly performances. They revived most of their best-known shows—*Lefty, Awake and Sing!, Men in White, Success Story, Paradise Lost*—and trotted out the popular Dover Furnace improvisations as well. They took the opportunity to work on some plays impossible to present as commercial Broadway productions, dreaming of the day when they would have a repertory theatre and could regularly present such a varied program. Bud Bohnen directed the first American production of Sean O'Casey's *A Pound on Demand*. They did one-acts by Arthur Schnitzler, Ferenc Molnár, and Anton Chekhov. The Chekhov evening included *The Marriage Proposal*, in which Bobby Lewis made everyone howl with his interpretation of the nervous suitor as a little mouse sniffing and nibbling at his intended as though she were a piece of cheese. (Yellow-haired Paula Miller, dressed in a full-length yellow dress, played the cheese.)

The apprentices presented another humorous piece: *Waiting for Odets*, a parody written by the Chicago Repertory Group that depicted a bewildered Mr. Gruhber, who has foolishly bought *Lefty* for Superart Films, trying to figure out how to make it into a movie with the help of Eugene O'Neill and Noel Coward. The scene between the young lovers was written in the manner of O'Neill's *Strange Interlude*, complete with the Freudian asides; it ends with the cabbie realizing he is actually in love with his girlfriend's brother. The hard-pressed married couple are transformed into sophisticated Coward spouses like the ones in *Private Lives;* the actor and the militant secretary become flamboyant Russians; and the prologue is done as an opera. The climactic line spoofed the famous moment when a union rebel announces the discovery of Lefty's death. In this version, it was Odets who was found: "Back of the stage with a bullet through his head!"

The performances were fun, but neither they nor the classes had the Group's full attention. That was devoted to the endless, unpleasant meetings at which they tried to analyze the canker eating away at the Group spirit, to find out why they were all so unhappy with their work and one another. Clurman announced on their first day at Pine Brook that he would read his paper on the proposed reorganization of the company shortly and every member would get a copy. He cleared the ground for this event with some ruthless criticism of Group performances and behavior over the past year, designed to prove how desperately they needed to take drastic measures. Unless they found a way to remedy their basic faults, he warned, life in the Group might well become unbearable.

Clurman used the Group tradition of conducting a post-mortem on the acting and direction of each production to make his larger points. His comments on individual actors were frank and wounding to many. Dorothy Patten heard herself described as a good worker who needed to cultivate greater originality. Beany Barker was criticized for having too idealistic a view of the craft of acting. Bill Challee was too tense, Paula Miller had a grating voice, Luther Adler had no Group technique and didn't know how to improvise. Sandy Meisner and Stella Adler were sometimes too subjective. Phoebe Brand had trouble playing actions; she should try to *do* more. Clurman didn't spare himself in these discussions; he admitted that the direction of the last act of *Awake and Sing!* lacked technical precision, particularly when it came to motivating exits for the actors. Only Morris Carnovsky escaped the general tongue-lashing; his impeccable conduct during rehearsals was held up as an example to his peers.

Clurman's point was that the breakdown in Group discipline was affecting their work. He complained of people coming late to rehearsals, talking to each other when they weren't onstage—behavior that would have been unthinkable in the atmosphere of almost religious dedication Strasberg had created at Brookfield. Group actors were listening too much to outside critics and passing their comments thoughtlessly along to their co-workers, he said. They took the directors' remarks, on the other hand, with an almost brazen skepticism; they lacked respect for their leaders and for each other. They were devoting too much of their time to activities outside the Group, when their theatre ought to come first. If the Group were solidly established and functioning smoothly, then additional work might be all right, but under the present circumstances it dangerously dissipated their energies.

It was a full-scale assault on the actors' presumption in thinking they could dispense with the directors' authority when they displayed no commitment to self-government, and his partners backed him up. Strasberg and Crawford had changed their minds since 1933, when they'd responded to Clurman's proposal that he become the Group's managing director with a flat no. They hadn't believed then he was ready for such responsibility; they may not have believed it now, but they saw no alternative. Harold had directed their most important recent productions, Harold had the actors' trust (as much as any of them did), Harold said he could solve the Group's problems. They were willing to give him a chance.

Strasberg told the company he believed strengthening Group leadership was essential if they were to progress, and because centralization was the best way to accomplish this he was willing to take a place secondary to Harold for the sake of the Group. The actors, who knew perfectly well that Lee would like nothing better than to relinquish all administrative duties forever, were unimpressed by his show of sacrifice. They countered Clurman's criticisms of their behavior with some strong comments of their own on his penchant for taking eight hours on a job that ought to have been done in three, and his distressing tendency to be distracted from work by the complications of his personal life. They wanted to hear his paper's specific proposals before they agreed that more leadership rather than more democracy was the solution to the Group's crisis.

Clurman's paper, entitled "Group Organization," was brief (for Harold) and to the point. Artistic and administrative responsibility were to be vested in a managing director, who would have the ultimate authority to choose plays, select their directors, designate teachers for classes, hire such subsidiary workers as playreaders and publicity representatives, and decide all policy matters. Clurman proposed to take this job, with Strasberg and Crawford becoming associate directors who acted as his immediate advisers. His word would be final: "Nothing shall be considered official Group business of which the managing director is not informed. No decision shall be considered official unless it is stated by or through the managing director [who] shall specify what means are to be taken to deal with every Group contingency, complaint or problem." Group meetings would not be held without his approval of their agenda in advance, and he would act as chairman; in any case, "meetings of the entire Group will be less frequent because this scheme of organization renders them functionally unnecessary."

The managing director was not, however, an absolute dictator. The director of an individual production retained complete control over its casting, design, and artistic direction; the managing director's only recourse in case of a disagreement was to hire a new director. New Group members had to be approved by the associate directors as well as the managing director, and current members could be fired only by the unanimous decision of all three directors and a vote of two-thirds of the Group. If on a specific issue both associates disagreed with the managing director and chose to take their case to the membership, his decision could be reversed by a vote of three-fourths of the Group. A new Actors Committee of four elected members would present the actors' wishes and complaints to the directorate, but it had no formal authority.

Clurman argued that this centralization "should bring more immediate results to anyone with a claim, a complaint, a new plan." He promised that important questions would be taken up with the associate directors and the Actors Committee, but made it clear that the ultimate power to make decisions would be his. He asked them to trust him and approve the reorganization; an assenting vote by three-quarters of the membership was necessary to put it into effect.

Throughout July the Group debated the pros and cons of his paper. The idea of vesting final authority in a single director provoked strong resistance, spearheaded at least in part by members of the Group's communist unit. A fascinating letter scrawled in a notebook that one of the members kept at Pine Brook revealed the conflicts within the unit and the Group. Although unsigned, it appears to have been written by Kazan; the attitude it conveys fits what is known of his opinions during that period. If it is his letter, then his break with the party in the spring was by no means as complete as he later claimed, although the rift was clearly widening.

The letter began by outlining the problems of the Group—casting, salaries, backing, plays—and noted that underlying them was a more serious "sickness" manifested in every area of Group life, including Joe Bromberg's defection and ongoing disciplinary problems with both Adlers. The unit had managed to bring these problems out into the open, it continued, but had as yet offered no solutions (a parenthetical note elaborated, "Rejection of Harold's paper but none of our own"). The letter continued, "I feel that the solution for the Group must come from the unit" and suggested they drop "L" a note asking what to do. ("L" was probably Lewis Leverett, who, judging by his absence from the Pine Brook programs, appears to have pulled one of his periodic disappearing acts.)

The writer was obviously in the middle of sorting out his feelings about the Group and the Communist party, for the letter alternated between praising the party for "fighting for us" and admitting doubts about its course:

> It is no secret to you (as per my attitude at meetings) that I disagree with our "Marxian analysis" and tactics. I believe we are using the old trade union tactics [that] have been banned because they always lead to splits . . . I have a problem—whether to fight in the u[nit] or the Group—I can't do both. At the moment I feel I have to leave one or the other and I can't leave the Group because I believe that the Group Theatre is more important to the *movement* and the world than the unit.

Some noncommunist Group members later came to the conclusion, partly influenced by Kazan's selective retelling of their history, that it was party members in the Group who were responsible for the bitter organizational debates that racked the company during 1936. On the contrary, as the Pine Brook letter shows, the communists were responding with as much confusion as anyone else to the crisis in Group life. Group communists certainly asked for advice from the higher-ups in the party's headquarters downtown; the letter's comments on disruptive tactics suggest that they sometimes followed it. But Group meetings were chaotic and vociferous to begin with, and party members could never have done more than contribute to their fractiousness. Personalities and relationships had at least as much to do with people's behavior in Group meetings as any political affiliation: Luther Adler, who wasn't a communist, was far more openly critical of the directors than Morris Carnovsky, who was.

In the argument between those who wanted greater centralization and those in favor of more democracy, Clurman's opponents, communist and noncommunist alike, failed to come up with any specific proposals of their own. Clurman's plan clearly delineated lines of authority, established subsidiary committees, and defined the areas in which the members would continue to set policy. If those opposing him wanted to be taken seriously, they needed an alternate plan with details of how their ideal democratic organization would function. Lacking that, all they had was an abstract belief in government by the collective. Everyone knew from previous experience how work was duplicated and contradictory decisions made by various committees that had been hastily thrown together in response to one crisis or another. In addition, Clurman had brutally but truthfully driven home the point that collective discipline of late had been less than exemplary.

By late July, when the question was put to a vote, the entire membership assented to the reorganization. The Group's communists, along with everyone else, suppressed their doubts and voted to give Harold a chance to show that he could save the Group. To represent the members' views to the new boss, they elected Stella Adler, Bohnen, Carnovsky, and Kazan to the Actors Committee.

The irony was, as Clurman later acknowledged, that the approval of this document ultimately proved beside the point. The terms of the debate had very little to do with the Group's real problems. Vesting final authority in a managing director might lead to greater efficiency; creating a more democratic structure might make the Group as an entity more responsive to the concerns of the membership. Neither would magically prevent actors from being dissatisfied with their roles, ensure every member of the company a decent salary, or conjure up financial backing and new playwrights out of thin air.

The essential cause of the agonizing personal and professional discontents tearing the Group apart was the inherent difficulty of running a theatre with uncommercial ideals—artistic or political—in a commercial system. They couldn't change Broadway, and they were unwilling to be relegated to the fringe of the American theatre by working elsewhere. They'd set themselves an impossible goal and achieved it for five years in large measure thanks to the extraordinary sacrifices made by every member. But privations endured gladly, even gaily, by people in their early twenties just starting out in the theatre were harder to take five years later, when children and other outside responsibilities made a stable income as important as the Group Idea. (Kazan's daughter, Judy, born that summer, was the second Group baby in three months.) The strain was too much, and it had begun to poison the Group. Political maneuvers, personal rivalries, artistic disagreements were all real enough, but they couldn't have seriously hurt the Group if their theatre had rested on a firmer foundation. It's an indication of how desperate everyone was to find such a foundation that they were willing to believe, or at least pretend, that Clurman's reorganization was more than window dressing.

All they really wanted, all they ever wanted, was a good play to produce, a chance to say something important about American life and grow as artists at the same time. They looked hopefully to *Johnny Johnson*, *The Silent Partner*, and *Marching Song* for this year's shot at salvation. When Odets arrived in late July, just after his thirtieth birthday, they gave him a joyous party and Clurman rushed to read his new script. The director was gravely disappointed. It seemed to him his friend's drama of a factory strike was choppy and incomplete, weak in characterization and story, even though individual scenes were tremendously exciting. Reluctantly, he told Odets that the script was nowhere near ready to put into rehearsal.

Odets was crushed and angry. He was well aware of *The Silent Partner*'s weaknesses; he'd been struggling with the revisions on and off for months. But Clurman's letters to him in California had promised that the Group would rehearse the script that summer if Odets thought it was ready. He was hurt that his best friend and the company his writings had done so much for weren't willing to begin work solely on the basis of their faith in him. He had no desire to repeat the experience of *Paradise Lost*, rewritten under the pressure of an impending New York premiere, but a Group summer was supposed to be a time for experiment and laboratory work. He wanted to shape his new play with the advantage of insights he could gain only by seeing it performed.

John Howard Lawson, who arrived not too long after Odets with a completed script in hand, also needed the Group's support at this difficult moment in his career. *Marching Song* was his first stage piece since the disastrous twin openings of *Gentlewoman* and *The Pure in Heart* in 1934. He'd been making a living in Hollywood, satisfying his political conscience by participating in the bitter battle to establish the Screen Writers Guild and reporting in the radical press on union organizing in the South. But the theatre was his artistic home, the place where he hoped to combine his concerns as a man and a writer. Like *The Silent Partner*, *Marching Song* was an ambitious attempt to write a labor play with spiritual as well as political themes, in language richer and more sophisticated than the strident slogans of agitprop. Only the Group, Lawson felt, could do justice to the complex technical demands of his script, which depicted a group of auto workers planning a sit-down strike in poetic dialogue that stressed the drama's ritualistic aspects.

Unfortunately, Clurman liked *Marching Song* even less than *The Silent Partner*. While he convinced himself that Odets' chaotic and underdeveloped play had potential, Lawson's effort struck him as "cold, artificial, a creature of the author's will—lacking in spontaneity." He couldn't even suggest revisions, as he had with Odets, because he thought the entire play, in theme and subject matter, was a mistake. Lawson wrote best about middle-class life, which was closer to his own experience, Clurman told him; this proletarian drama suffered from being written out of a sense of duty rather than an overriding artistic impulse. Lawson didn't disagree— he was already planning a new play about a middle-class family—but thought *Marching Song* marked an important phase in his development as an artist. "I had to assert the aspect of my experience that arose from my visits to the South in 1934. I could not be myself unless I achieved this enlargement of experience. It was, I believed, necessary for the theatre and specifically necessary for the Group."

Lawson believed that Clurman's reluctance to produce either *The Silent Partner* or *Marching Song* resulted less from their artistic flaws than from his distaste for their subject matter. The letters he had written to the press in February and April revealed how anxious he was to disassociate the Group from the left theatre, and the contretemps over the revised Dramatists Guild agreement proved he and his partners were willing to compromise Group principles in the interests of practical considerations. It's very likely Clurman felt that presenting a labor play, or two, at this point in the Group's history would reinforce a connection he wanted to downplay and that it would be nearly impossible to finance either production. But he also genuinely thought his friends' best talents weren't stimulated by this material, that they wrote most honestly and powerfully about the American middle class, whose moral and political confusion they understood far more deeply than they could ever hope to know the internal struggles of working-class characters.

On a purely artistic level, Clurman was right on both counts. *The Silent Partner*, at least in the incomplete form it exists in today, is a mess, with only some gorgeous dialogue to prevent it from being an utter disaster. *Marching Song*, eventually presented by the Theatre Union in February 1937, was better but problematic; certainly none of the characters had the ferocious intensity and compelling psychological reality of Sol and Sarah in *Success Story*. Yet each was the work of a playwright closely linked to the Group in beliefs and aspirations, writing about matters that greatly concerned America in the mid-1930s. The Theatre Union production of *Marching Song* coincided with the sit-down strikes that swept the automobile industry in early spring; Clurman himself would later remark that the more brutal scenes in *The Silent Partner* were acted out in real life on Memorial Day 1937, when Chicago police attacked a crowd of unarmed people demonstrating in support of striking steelworkers, killing seven and injuring eighty-four. It's hard not to believe that if the Group had been in better shape someone wouldn't have come to Clurman, as Crawford did over *1931*—, and said, "It is our theatre's duty to produce such a play."

But it wasn't 1931. The arguments of the spring and summer had exhausted the Group intellectually and emotionally, though there was enough nervous energy coursing through the camp to light up a small city. They were anxiously marking time, waiting to throw themselves into rehearsals. Clurman decided, rightly or wrongly, that the Group had committed themselves too many times in the past to imperfect scripts on the blithe assumption that problems could be fixed during rehearsal. What they needed right now was to emerge from the summer with a production ready for the fall season. *Johnny Johnson* was the best possibility, he thought, and it was too big a project to allow them to prepare another simultaneously. Loyalty to Group playwrights, dedication to addressing the issues of the day were now secondary matters: the survival of the Group was at stake.

Events in the outside world reinforced the Group's apocalyptic mood. Italian troops had overrun Ethiopia and on May 9, 1936, annexed it to Mussolini's fascist state. When the Ethiopian emperor, Haile Selassie, pleaded with the League of Nations on June 30 to intervene, he warned, "It is us today. It will be you tomorrow." Less than three weeks later, Spain's army officers revolted against the democratically elected Popular Front government; led by Francisco Franco and Emilio Mola, they formed a Junta of National Defense on July 30 and began an armed resistance intended to restore the power of the landowners, the army, and the church. While Britain, France, and the United States stood by, unwilling to help the left-leaning Spanish government, Hitler and Mussolini poured troops and money into Franco's hands. Group members made a grim joke of the situation by dubbing Stella Adler "La Pasionaria" in honor of the communist militant Dolores Ibarruri, whose fiery rhetoric stiffened Madrid's resolve to resist the army. But it wasn't really very funny. Everywhere they looked, nations were marching with frightening speed toward war and fascism. Their own struggles seemed at once insignificant in the face of such catastrophes, and desperately important as their only means of finding some meaning in a world gone mad.

Observers of Group life could see how close to the edge everyone was. Helen Deutsch had had her fill of quarrelsome meetings and criticism of her work; she resigned as the Group's press agent on July 22, to be replaced by Manny Eisenberg. Luise Rainer, who came to see Odets in August, thought the Group actors were pretentious and hostile to outsiders. She was shy, accustomed as a movie star to being handled with kid gloves, and the Group's high-pitched interactions oppressed and wearied her. They in return found her affected and aloof. The assertive Group women were irritated by Rainer's wide-eyed helplessness, which they considered put on. The actress lasted only a few weeks, during which she and Odets bickered about the ugly house he'd rented and his commitment to the Group, before she fled to Los Angeles with a case of tonsillitis and second thoughts about her new romance.

There were plenty of unhappy people roaming around the Pine Brook Club's spacious grounds, but no one, it was obvious to all, was more miserable than Harold Clurman. He could often be observed standing alone and wringing his hands, a habitual gesture of distress; on one occasion he was so unnerved by a cat that had invaded a dormitory room—he disliked animals—that Carnovsky had to remove it before he could enter. As managing director he was now solely responsible for solving the Group's problems, and he knew how serious they were. Even the most immediate task, putting *Johnny Johnson* into rehearsal, raised sticky problems and professional issues.

Paul Green had gone back to North Carolina in early August to whip the script into final shape, and when he returned just before Labor Day Clurman made it official that the musical would be the Group's first fall production. "I feel pretty sure that it will be an important step in our theatrical development," he wrote to a friend, "as it represents an utterly novel problem and form in the American theatre." He was worried, however, that neither he nor Strasberg was well suited to handle the complex technical and artistic challenges *Johnny Johnson* posed. Crawford was closest to the material and had the confidence of both author and composer, but her two disastrous directorial efforts had convinced the Group that her talents lay in other areas; in any case, they would need every ounce of her practical abilities to raise money and deal with the show's logistical demands.

The solution Clurman hit on initially indicated how desperate he was and how his judgment could be clouded by his personal needs. He proposed handing over the Group's most expensive, complicated, and technically demanding project to Stella Adler and Gadget Kazan as codirectors, though Adler had never directed a professional production and the largest budget Kazan had ever handled was the Theatre of Action's minuscule purse. It was an especially absurd suggestion because the two cordially disliked each other, but Clurman was swayed by his desire to find something for Adler to do, as there was no part for her in *Johnny Johnson*. Kazan deeply resented being asked, as he saw it, to act as her subordinate; he wanted to direct a Group play, but not under these circumstances. He was spared the awkward necessity of flatly refusing when Strasberg emphatically vetoed the idea, arguing quite correctly that both candidates were too inexperienced.

Clurman hesitantly decided that he should direct *Johnny Johnson* himself. Both Crawford and Strasberg had doubts that he could master the play's technical problems, but Strasberg thought on the whole he was temperamentally compatible with the material, particularly the script's broad comic moments. Crawford wasn't so confident. When she voiced her reservations to Strasberg, he told her he would support Clurman's decision. Crawford nonetheless called a directors' meeting and expressed her concern to Clurman. He was apparently in one of the cynical, almost nihilistic moods that overcame him with greater and greater frequency, for he shrugged and said, "What difference does it make who directs it?"

Strasberg hit the roof. It was infuriating to hear Clurman passing off the question of who was to direct as if it were of no importance. It was of the very greatest importance, and he wasn't eager to leave the production in the hands of someone who had that attitude. Was Harold too swamped by the duties of managing director to handle *Johnny Johnson* as well? Or was he just indulging in sarcasm at the expense of his colleagues? Strasberg didn't know, but he did know he was angry, and so was Crawford. Relations among the three directors were breaking down.

Strasberg's disenchantment deepened at a subsequent meeting with Donald Oenslager to discuss the scenery. Clurman had already sent the designer a preliminary letter, expressing his general sense about what the basic mood of the settings should be. He believed in inspiring the artist's creativity rather than outlining specifically what he wanted, but this approach worked better with designers like Max Gorelik and Boris Aronson than it did with Oenslager, who was always working on about five productions at once and had little time to come to his own conclusions about a script. He needed firmer guidance, but when the directors met with him at Crawford's house Clurman continued to talk in very general terms. He rambled on about the charming, miniaturelike quality the set should have, leaving Oenslager baffled by his remarks and totally in the dark as to his intentions.

Clurman's associates reacted in characteristic ways. Strasberg barricaded himself behind a newspaper, pretending to read the sports page and refusing to participate in the discussion at all. This was an unprofessional, not to mention extremely rude, manner of expressing displeasure, and it made Clurman stumble all the more. Crawford, sensing a disaster in the making, leaped in to focus the conversation on the production's major technical requirement, a device that would make the script's many scene changes as quickly as possible. Suddenly she and Oenslager were talking about a turntable. The necessary exploration of style and atmosphere had concluded without the designer and the director having made any real artistic contact.

None of the directors appeared at their best in this unfortunate meeting. Clurman was vague, Strasberg was withdrawn, Crawford threw herself into busywork that bypassed the Group's real needs. They were all under terrible strain, filled with doubts about themselves, the Group, their future together. Everything depended on *Johnny Johnson;* it seemed possible that if the show failed, it would be the end of them. The battle over reorganizing the company had been bitter, but the directors had won their point. They got the centralization of authority they wanted; now it was up to them, and especially Clurman, to prove its value. They wondered if they could.

In this tense atmosphere, with the summer already over, rehearsals tentatively began. Clurman cast Russell Collins as Johnny Johnson; Phoebe Brand as Minny Belle, the woman he loves; and Grover Burgess as Anguish Howington, his rival for her affections. They were the only characters who appeared throughout the play, but many Group actors had striking roles in individual scenes. Art Smith did a comic turn as the recruiting sergeant convinced by Johnny's idiosyncratic responses to a ridiculous intelligence test that he is an idiot, Tony Kraber as a soldier at the front sang a cowboy song Weill wrote especially for him, Julie Garfield had a touching moment as a frightened German sniper, and Morris Carnovsky played a psychiatrist who is even crazier than the patients in his asylum. Ruth Nelson had one of the few small female parts as a dreary charity worker who makes an oppressive visit to Johnny in an army hospital. Stella Adler, Beany Barker, and Dorothy Patten had no roles at all.

Clurman sat the actors down for the "table talks" that always inaugurated Group rehearsals. There was a lot to discuss, for *Johnny Johnson* had a special tone, elusive and tricky to capture. "The first act is a comedy, the second a tragedy and the third a satire," Paul Green told a reporter. The hero, an idealistic young tombstone maker who enlists in the war to end all wars, is treated in a gently ironic fashion, though he gains tragic stature at the end. The first act is indeed largely comic: it pokes fun at the mindless jingoism that could turn a peace celebration into a war rally in the twinkling of an eye, the stupidity of military officers, and the hero's naiveté. The mood darkens when Johnny goes to war in Act Two; the bitter reality of life in the trenches doesn't shake his idealism but confirms his determination to make peace. After dosing the Allied High Command with laughing gas and persuading them to sign a cease-fire, he is arrested and sent home to a state mental hospital. The third act makes the point that it is society that is mad, not Johnny, in its portrait of the lunatic psychiatrist and the patients who are saner than the world outside, which in the final scene is again preparing for war. Though Minny Belle marries his rival and their son wants to play with toy soldiers, Johnny's faith in humanity remains; the curtain falls on his wistful song expressing hope for a better future.

Weill's music had many different moods as well. Several songs were affectionate parodies of such American musical genres as pompous military marches and sentimental ballads; others inhabited the modernist territory the composer had explored in his work with Brecht. The entire score was closely integrated with Green's script, sometimes underlining the dialogue, sometimes offering an ironic counterpoint. The music had more punch than the script, which presented its antiwar message in a sweet but extremely general fashion; a few more sharply political points would have given it some much-needed bite. Nonetheless, *Johnny Johnson* had enormous wit and charm; its antiwar theme was all too relevant at a time when the possibility of another global conflict seemed greater every day; the rapid alternation of comic and tragic scenes presented an interesting technical challenge. It was well worth the Group's doing.

But by the time they returned to New York in mid-September, with Al van Dekker and Lee Cobb added to the permanent company, Clurman had succumbed to paralyzing doubts about whether or not he was the man to direct it. He had a nagging sense, which may have reflected his own opinion more than actuality, that Weill and Green thought Strasberg would be a better director for the play. He was overwhelmed by his administrative responsibilities, for which he was neither practically nor temperamentally well suited. Just keeping the Group afloat in New York seemed more than he could handle. "Nobody seems particularly grateful for our efforts," he wrote to a friend in a letter explaining that their season had been delayed "due to the tardiness of our playwrights and to the rotten conditions of our American theatre generally." It was all too much for him; shortly after their arrival, he asked Strasberg to direct *Johnny Johnson*.

Strasberg consented reluctantly; under the circumstances he had no choice. On September 24 the Group announced Strasberg would direct *Johnny Johnson*, and rehearsals began Monday, September 28, at the Belmont Theatre, a little auditorium on 48th Street whose small scale perfectly suited the intimate mood Clurman and Strasberg agreed the play required.

No one had conveyed this idea to Donald Oenslager, however, and when the directors met with him after the change in command Strasberg's sense of foreboding deepened. The sketches Oenslager brought showed scenery that seemed remote from the director's expressionistic concept of the production, and the precisely worked-out ground plan worried him even more; the scale of the settings was much too large. He voiced these objections diffidently, for despite his often autocratic handling of actors Strasberg tended to be deferential to well-known theatre artists outside the Group, and he knew making changes would delay construction of the scenery, which had to begin immediately. Clurman, who shared Strasberg's ideas about the production and should have backed him up, instead assured him that the sets would be very effective; Crawford, who had to worry about getting the set built on time, was also reluctant to alter a design that had the merit at least of being technically feasible. Oenslager agreed to make some stylistic changes, but the basic ground plan was left unchanged. Strasberg had allowed himself to be maneuvered into a position where he felt he was making the best of someone else's bad job, and it didn't improve his mood.

The directors hadn't even begun to solicit backing for the production, so they had no money to make the customary one-third advance payment for the set construction. They benefited from the faith of Bill Kellam, who had been their carpenter for years and agreed to begin without seeing a dime. It wasn't only actors who gave the Group their loyalty and devotion. Many of their technical staff stuck by them through thick and thin, feeling as strong a kinship with the Group's goals as those who received the applause. They had a special relationship with the organization, which made a point of not treating them like employees. There weren't many Broadway companies that arranged interviews for their prop man, as Helen Deutsch had for Moe Jacobs during *Awake and Sing!* (He told a *Herald Tribune* reporter that for him the play was "one long meal.") Jacobs was friendly with several Group members, particularly Kazan, who'd been his drinking buddy during *Men in White*. He made an appearance in *The Flying Grouse*, which quoted his joking comment that the reason *Case of Clyde Griffiths* flopped was its lack of set dressing: "Sure, the chinamen people play without props, but even a chinaman sits down sometimes, no? If you don't figure out a place in it to use beer, you're crazy!"

The actors also remained committed to the Group Idea. It made no difference to them that their financial situation was so bad Clurman had to borrow $1,500 each from the film director Lewis Milestone, who'd worked with Odets at Paramount, and the playwright himself, holed up at Pine Brook to work on *The Silent Partner*, just to give the actors money to eat and pay their rent. When Clurman asked them if they would rather abandon *Johnny Johnson* than risk another failure, they replied that of course the Group must go on.

The going was rough; rehearsals were bumpy and often unhappy. There wasn't anything wrong with Strasberg's basic concept:

> A strange distinction has arisen between the play of ideas and the play of pure entertainment [he wrote after the show opened]. *Johnny Johnson* was an effort to track down this unnatural distinction and perhaps destroy it. . . . We meant to do an American folk legend, full of the humors of old vaudeville and the provincial family album, sharpened with poetic comment on the madness of contemporary life. We felt that fantasy, extravagance, and dramatic music were intrinsic to such an exciting experiment.

The characters lived in "a far freer and easier world than that of routine naturalism"; their heightened, poetic speech flowed easily into song that was an integral part of the drama. The production was supposed to be theatrical but not grand, he told the actors. The style they were looking for was homespun, informal, unpretentious; the scenery (Strasberg must have swallowed hard here, hoping for the best) would be like a series of post-cards by Raoul Dufy, the French Fauvist painter who celebrated the plea-sures of ordinary life.

This all made sense to the actors, but they were gravely disappointed by the implementation of the concept in rehearsals. Ever since the showdown at Ellenville in 1934 over affective memory, Strasberg had seemed to be more interested in exploring various theatrical styles than in working with individual actors on their performances. *Gold Eagle Guy* had been a foray into the physical flamboyance of Meyerhold, *Clyde Griffiths* a stab at epic theatre's use of the stage as an educational device. Neither had been very successful, and what they lacked was what *Johnny Johnson* also badly needed: a strong directorial view of the play's content (as opposed to its style), a statement of the central theme and how each character's emotions and actions contributed to it. Strasberg was always deeply concerned with form, but in the early Group productions—*Connelly, Success Story,* and his masterpiece, *Men in White*—his creation of a unified technique had meant he gave close attention to each actor as well as to the overall style. During *Johnny Johnson* rehearsals, however, many of the actors worried that they hadn't a clue as to their characters' intentions, and their director seemed uninterested in providing any. Strasberg may have been trying to respond to the actors' earlier criticisms of his approach as domineering, to give them the freedom they enjoyed in their work with Clurman. If so, Strasberg forgot that Clurman was generally very clear on what he wanted, though he left it to the actors to figure out how to get there. In their best work the two men directed in very different ways. Clurman began with an idea, excited the actors with his dazzling talks about it, then related their individual efforts to the larger theme. Strasberg built a production from the ground up, creating a mosaic of sharply detailed moments, each one filled with a sense of personal truth and reality through the use of affective memory; the theme emerged from the cumulative impact of these moments. He got to the larger picture through his keen use of detail, and when in *Johnny Johnson* he tried to speak more generally in terms of mood and tone, the actors felt lost.

The effect on morale was disastrous. In scenes with many characters, each actor was left to work out independently his or her character's motivations and actions, and the result was chaos and hard feelings: Actor A, having decided what the scene meant to him, thought Actor B had missed the point and was working in the wrong way. There had always been a certain amount of collective criticism during Group rehearsals, but the level of bitterness rose, a result of their terror over the lack of direction inside and outside the rehearsal hall.

The Group's reorganization, which served to isolate the directors from the company, contributed to the actors' sense of helplessnesss. The long, exhausting, and occasionally destructive group meetings had at least enabled everyone to let off steam; now the Actors Committee received a stream of frightened, angry people demanding to know what Harold was doing to ensure their economic survival, how *Johnny Johnson* was to be financed, whether their rehearsal complaints had been passed on to Lee, what their next production would be, where their next meal was coming from.

The directors were unavailable. Clurman and Crawford had their hands full getting backing for the show; they finally raised $40,000 from Bess Eitingon and another $15,000 or $20,000 from the millionaire John Hay Whitney, but dress rehearsals were so expensive because of overtime costs that Clurman had to go out and scrounge up additional funds at the last minute. Strasberg responded to criticism with fits of rage; he was just as frightened as the actors. *Johnny Johnson* was eating up all their time and energy.

In this ghastly atmosphere, rehearsals progressed better than could have been expected. Strasberg's iron will and fierce demeanor kept the murmurings of discontent below the level of open revolt, and slowly the show began to come together—much too slowly, many of the actors felt; weeks had been wasted in aimless talk and fumbling preliminaries. Nonetheless, enough of the actors had found a center for their performances and enough of Strasberg's gift for imaginative stage groupings came through to create an intriguing, provocative production. The heart of the show was Russell Collins' beautiful performance as Johnny; he moved everyone with his simplicity, warmth, and gentle humor. Visitors to the Belmont Theatre found the final run-throughs touching and charming.

Then came the apocalypse: dress rehearsals at the 44th Street Theatre. This enormous barn of an auditorium (it held more than 1,400 seats as opposed to the Belmont's 500) had been foisted on the Group by the Shuberts, who'd built the theatre and retained an interest in it; they claimed no other was available. At the Belmont the actors' musically untrained voices had carried properly and had just the natural, unstudied quality Weill wanted. "It needed opera singers by the time it got on the 44th Street stage," said Phoebe Brand; the cavernous hall swallowed up sound and made the actors virtually inaudible.

The biggest problem, however, was the scenery, which confirmed Strasberg's worst fears. The set was huge, completely contradicting everything he had told the actors about the style of the production. They felt dwarfed by it, and although one of the play's themes was that of little people ground down by war, having them crushed by the settings wasn't what anyone had in mind. The physical blocking was completely altered when the actors had to climb in and out of enormous trenches, cross distances between objects far vaster than they'd expected, and make costume changes on a whirling turntable.

Only Morris Carnovsky, who'd been floundering around in his role as the psychiatrist, found the steeply raked stage and ludicrously oversized desk for his scene gave him the spark of inspiration he needed; he took his own bewilderment and gave it to the character, which made him all the funnier. The settings shocked and confused everyone else. Tony Kraber mustered up enough courage to buttonhole the harassed director and say, "But Lee, these huge sets are the opposite of what you promised us we would have to work with."

If Strasberg had been a different kind of man, he would have frankly confessed that, yes, the sets were all wrong and not in the least what he'd wanted, but they were stuck with them now and would have to find a way to make them work. But admitting failure was not something that came easily to him, certainly not when he was facing nightmarish dress rehearsals with the aggrieved sense that some of the handicaps they labored under, especially the scenery, weren't his fault. He turned angrily to Kraber and snapped, "Never mind! Donald knows!" before stomping away. Carnovsky, who overheard this interchange, was outraged by what appeared to him to be Strasberg's cavalier attitude.

Dress rehearsals were gruesome. There was no time to think of interpretation, mood, dramatic intent; it was all anyone could do to get in and out of costumes, on and off stage in good order. As well as being inappropriate, the scenery was nearly unworkable. The stage manager, Mike Gordon, struggled valiantly with the crew to make the shifts between the nineteen different scenes as speedy as possible, but it took them days to get the changes even close to performance level. The Group couldn't postpone the previews because they couldn't refund the money, so they appeared, trembling, before their first paying audience on November 13. It was a disaster. Half the spectators left within five minutes of the curtain going up; by the time it rang down, there were some twenty people sitting in a 1,400-seat theatre.

Clurman later remembered the first two previews as "the most distressing experiences I have ever gone through in the theatre." The performances themselves were awful enough, but what really undid the Group were the all-night sessions afterward. Scenery was cut, songs eliminated, light cues redone in an atmosphere of panic in which everyone behaved badly. Strasberg was surrounded by hordes of terrified people, each one hissing in his ear about a detail that had to be fixed right away, and the person at his elbow knew just what to do. When he managed to shake them off with an angry comment, he could be seen standing onstage with Clurman, both screaming at the top of their lungs while an ashen-faced Crawford stood by, watching the script whose creation had given her so much joy sinking into a morass of technical difficulties and personal conflicts.

Relations between Clurman and his associates had been tense for months. Strasberg believed that Clurman hadn't fulfilled his obligation as managing director to protect his colleague from all but artistic worries, while Clurman found Strasberg so hypersensitive as to make it impossible to criticize his work or offer suggestions, even when they were badly needed. Crawford was also impatient with Clurman's inadequacies; she agreed with Strasberg that too often, just when they needed him most, he either disappeared or simply failed to take action. The three had fought before, but they'd always presented a united front to the actors; now everyone was aware that the cohesion of the directorate had broken down.

The primary problem was between Strasberg and Clurman. Crawford's tragedy was, as ever, that her opinions and actions were not given the weight assigned to those of her male colleagues. That the two men had different personalities was one of the Group's strengths; in the old days they'd welcomed and valued each other's point of view. Now they were simply irritable and dismissive, convinced they'd heard it all before. Everything leading up to the previews—the spring's furious debates, the troubled summer at Pine Brook, the difficult rehearsals—had tried their patience and resolve to the limits. *Johnny Johnson* was the breaking point. Things were said at three in the morning, by people who'd had no sleep in days, that might be forgiven but could never be forgotten. "I felt as if everything was giving way underneath me," Clurman wrote, "not only the production, but six years of work." By the time *Johnny Johnson* opened on November 19, the two idealists whose excited conversations about life and art had brought the Group into being were barely speaking to each other.

During the grim week of previews the production regained some semblance of order, as much from simple repetition as from any of the panicky cuts. Opening night went well. The audience was appreciative of the play's special qualities and responded at the curtain's fall with a standing ovation that lasted nearly ten minutes. Paul Green, who'd stayed in town to endure the previews with the Group, came forward to give an emotional speech about Woodrow Wilson's League of Nations and the universal desire for peace, which prompted more warm applause. The exhausted Group seemed to have fended off disaster once again.

But the reviews the next morning gave Group morale its worst blow since *Paradise Lost*—worse, in fact, for they believed wholeheartedly in the Odets play, while the press reaction to *Johnny Johnson* expressed their own reservations about it. The worst thing about the mixed notices was their respectful but disappointed tone, which just about guaranteed bad box office. Every critic noted the script's hybrid nature, what Richard Watts in the *Herald Tribune* called "a disturbing and often hilarious medley of caricature, satire, musical comedy, melodrama, farce, social polemic and parable." Some enjoyed the mix, others thought it confusing, but all found the Group's decision to tackle it praiseworthy.

What hurt, because they so closely paralleled the Group's own feelings, were the reviewers' comments about the execution of the concept. "An in-and-out show if ever you saw one," Watts continued. "It attempts to cover too much ground and rushes off in too many directions at the same time, with the result that the final effect is one of confusion and opportunities missed." Gilbert Gabriel in the *American* found the production "a strange, brave bungle. . . . It could, I suspect, have been kept six months longer in the dill-barrel of the Group's pickling process and been brought out thoroughly great." Most of the critics blamed the show's uneven quality on Green's script, but quite a few faulted the Group ensemble as well; the word "amateurish" was tossed around enough to make the actors seethe—not just at the critics, but at Strasberg.

Although a few cruel comments were made about the Group's lack of singing ability, most critics were fairly kind and noted that Weill's score, which they loved, justified a dramatic, as opposed to a musical, approach. "It is the voice of America singing from coast to coast," wrote one reviewer, "an America which does not expect to appear on anyone's amateur hour, still less professionally, but which sings out of a full heart, sometimes gay, sometimes sad, but always piping up after every catastrophe. . . . Perfect? Heavens no, it's alive!" Phoebe Brand and Morris Carnovsky, who *could* sing, were commended for doing so, and Carnovsky's hilarious turn as the lunatic psychiatrist was universally enjoyed. Russell Collins won the kudos he deserved for his faultless incarnation of Johnny.

Strasberg ground his teeth as he read the warm reviews for Oenslager's disastrous set; had the situation been less dire it would have been funny to read articles like the one that informed readers the designer had "carefully avoided the pitfall of allowing the sets to dominate the play instead of assisting it." The critics generally praised the direction, noting that individual scenes created theatrical effects as striking and powerful as anything Strasberg had ever done. One moment that impressed everyone occurred in Act Two when Johnny and his fellow soldiers lie asleep in the trenches. Suddenly three enormous cannons come into view behind them and swing toward the audience. They lower, aim—but instead of gunshots, one of Weill's most beautiful melodies pours out of the weapons' mouths, as the cannons sing of the deadly work they will do and the better uses their metal might have been put to. This summed up the seductive allure that went hand in hand with war's destructiveness in a single surreal, profoundly disturbing tableau. If every scene had been as imaginatively conceived and flawlessly executed as this one, *Johnny Johnson* might very well have saved the Group.

As it was, enough of the later reviews came vigorously to the production's defense to give the Group some hope they could keep it on the boards. "Since *Johnny Johnson* is the first imaginative and exciting entry in a season of old, dead-tired waxworks, I think it ought to be given a break or two," Robert Benchley wrote in *The New Yorker*. "My God, if we don't grab onto something really big when it comes along, even if it does have its flaws, the theatre may go right on as it has started." Some critics whose initial reaction had been mixed, like the *Telegraph*'s Whitney Bolton, took the trouble to write follow-up columns admitting that *Johnny Johnson* lingered in their memory despite its faults. "Of all the plays of the season thus far produced," Bolton commented, "it is the only one that has clung like a burr and demanded thought hours and days after its production."

The Group believed in the play, if not entirely in their own work on it, and they launched once again into an effort to overcome the reviews and find their audience. The usual round of talks, meetings, and interviews began, and they reached out to their supporters in a questionnaire sent to several thousand people on the Group mailing list and included in the program. "We would like to feel that your attendance at *Johnny Johnson* is not a casual thing," the card began forlornly, "but rather an interest in the development of the American theatre." It went on to ask, "Are there dramatic experiments you would like us to undertake? Would you like us to keep you informed about our production activities, symposia, discussions, entertainments, public dinners, and summers in the country?" It was a measure of how drained the Group felt that they were asking their audience for guidance; they had none to offer themselves.

They made gestures toward a program of continued activity. They promised to present some of the one-acts they had done at Pine Brook in a series of special Sunday-night performances. When Odets returned to New York with a revised script of *The Silent Partner* they held a reading of it on November 24 and announced it would be their next production. Both Strasberg and Crawford argued that it still wasn't ready, and Clurman knew they were right, but he put it into rehearsal anyway. The Group needed to work, and Odets needed to be reassured of their commitment to him.

Despite his financial support, Odets was acting rather distant with his old friends. His relationship with Rainer, who'd come east for the premiere of *Johnny Johnson*, was absorbing most of his energy; his Group comrades were jealous and worried that she would pull him back to Hollywood. Indeed, just as rehearsals began on December 15, Odets departed for California. He needed money and had agreed to do a quick adaptation of a German film for Lewis Milestone. He hoped to convince Rainer to marry him. He was probably eager to put 3,000 miles between himself and the rewrites he knew Clurman would want on *The Silent Partner*. He could feel that the Group looked to his play as their only hope to stay together, and at this point in his life it wasn't a responsibility he wanted. Times had changed: Odets was thinking of himself first and the Group second.

Matters reached a crisis point. Rehearsals of *The Silent Partner*, Clurman himself admitted, were "not properly organized" and "lousy." Morale was at an all-time low, and people's despair spilled over into the performances of *Johnny Johnson*. One night Sandy Meisner whistled rather than sang his song as the recruiting officer; when the conductor, his good friend Lehman Engel, reproached him during intermission Meisner slapped his face.

Just how serious the situation was could be seen when two of the Group's most stalwart members threatened to resign. Actors like Herbie Ratner and Bill Challee were the backbone of the company's ensemble ideal; they uncomplainingly took small parts year after year, living by Clurman's credo that the best kind of actor cared more about the worth of the play than the size of his role. "Herbie the actor," as his comrades teasingly dubbed him after he identified himself that way early in the Group's history, was never much of a performer, but he threw himself into improvisations and collective life with a zest that won everyone's affection. Bill Challee, whose marriage to Ruth Nelson was one of the happiest results of their first enchanted summer, had been a driving force behind the *Paradise Lost* audience campaign and an active participant in all the Group's political and artistic pursuits. Both men had stuck by the Group through every vicissitude of their collective fortunes. Their sudden decision that the company was holding them back as individuals expressed the disillusionment and demoralization of every member.

Clurman was inclined to let them leave and astonished when Strasberg, usually the first to condemn those he perceived as disloyal, begged them to stay. Strasberg, as much as anyone else, needed to believe that the Group would go on. All three directors were trying very hard to overcome their bitterness toward each other for the sake of the goals they still shared and the theatre they still loved. Rehearsals of *The Silent Partner* dragged on, with everyone painfully conscious that there was no way the Group could present it in its current state. The directors met frequently and fruitlessly to try and figure out what to do next.

Any plans they might have made were preempted by the Actors Committee. Stella Adler, Bohnen, Carnovsky, and Kazan had been meeting regularly ever since *Johnny Johnson* opened. Clurman, who even in his most distracted moments always had one ear attentively cocked to the murmurings of Group life, was aware of the sessions (Strasberg and Crawford apparently weren't) and encouraged the committee to write a paper summarizing their findings. "Report of the Actors Committee to the Directors of the Group Theatre" was completed sometime in December and read aloud to the entire company except the directors; the members agreed to send individual copies to Clurman, Strasberg, and Crawford and await their response.

Only the complete and obvious breakdown of the Group's leadership could have provoked this blistering twenty-nine-page document, a collaboration among four very different personalities who weren't especially compatible. Kazan and Carnovsky didn't much like each other: the older actor's well-meaning attempts to act as a mentor to the Group's junior members cut no ice with the ambitious Kazan, quick to take offense when he felt he was being treated as an inferior, and the differences within the Communist party unit had driven them farther apart. Adler viewed Kazan, as she did Odets, as a rival for Clurman's affection and esteem; Kazan found her aggressive and ambitious, and while he might have admired these qualities in a man, he preferred women to be nurturing and supportive, as his own intelligent and well-educated wife was. Adler's and Carnovsky's relationship was complex: each had considerable respect for the other's acting ability, though she sometimes made sardonic fun of his reverence for Shakespeare, and he occasionally found her affected. Good-natured Bud Bohnen was the sole Actors Committee member who got along well with all his peers. It was a mark of just how grave the crisis was that he abandoned his perennial desire to put a good face on things and signed his name to a paper that ruthlessly tore apart not just their most recent production but the artistic and personal failings of the three directors whose vision had brought the Group into being.

"We are writing this paper so that the Group will go on," the Actors Committee began. "We are trying to find the truth regardless of personal feelings. . . . it says what we must say at this time." They prefaced a lengthy analysis of *Johnny Johnson*'s sorry history with the explanation that they were using it as a case study of the Group's chronic faults. "Every director has a right to failures, and every producer also. But we must distinguish between organized failure and UN-organized failure."

Everywhere the committee looked in the production of *Johnny Johnson* they saw people's talents and enthusiasm wasted because there was no organized channel for them. The script, created through Crawford, was "one of the most gratifying incidents in our entire experience," but had flaws that lay undiscovered until the final weeks of rehearsal because no one had been assigned the responsibility of scrutinizing it closely once the working draft was completed. Rehearsals were needlessly hesitant in the beginning because the production director wasn't chosen until the last minute, then changed three weeks later. Performances lacked clarity because Strasberg hadn't told the actors what he wanted from each part. The physical staging wasn't polished because it was left until too late in rehearsals. The scenery was inappropriate because neither Clurman nor Strasberg had communicated his ideas to the designer. The lighting was even more so, not having been worked out in advance at all. Costumes too, left until the last minute, weren't really designed but pulled hastily from the nearest rental company. Dress rehearsals were a shambles because work that should have been done over eleven weeks was crammed into a few chaotic nights.

If Strasberg couldn't deal himself with every aspect of a production in detail, the committee suggested, then he had to learn to delegate authority to people who understood his basic concept and could ensure that it was reflected in the show's individual components. Production committees had been created for that purpose, but "right now the production committee is a kind of a board of proctors, a monitors club and a gang of artistic stool pigeons."

Bitter comments of this sort were scattered throughout the paper. Underlying their criticisms of *Johnny Johnson* was an angry sense that its faults were the result of the directors' basic inability to lead, which threatened the Group's very existence:

It's no secret that Group morale on every front reached its all-time low during the final stages of *Johnny Johnson*. Another period of that sort will beyond question completely destroy the fruits of five years of work and hope and pain. The important fact here is that no longer can morale be engendered by stirring the coals. The fire was laid five years ago. Exhortations, appeals to integrity, etc.—everybody knows 'em by heart. . . . Nobody can invoke a morale in the absence of a *long distance material plan of action.*

Clurman's "so-called 'vast reorganization'" hadn't addressed the fundamental lack of such a plan. At the moment, the approach was what it had always been: "a precarious 'play-to-play' policy—gambling for hits."

Five years of reduced paychecks had taught the actors that this approach simply couldn't sustain the kind of theatre everyone wanted the Group to be. The directors' failure to come up with an alternative had created an "utter lack of confidence in the economics of the Group, and in the administration of their talents." Moreover, the committee argued, the directors continued to treat the actors with a paternalism that was no longer justified:

> We all know that five and a half years ago the Group was wrenched out of the American theatre by the sheer force of the directors' will. . . . Essentially the Group was Cheryl, Lee, Harold, their power, superior vision and above all their greater determination and will to make what they envisioned come true . . . today the Group is no longer the three directors. It is kept together neither by the domineering paternalism of Lee nor the hysterical faith of Harold. . . . The Group Theatre today is the thirty members (including the individual directors). Whatever superior talent and wisdom the directors might have today is no longer *the important factor* in holding the theatre together. . . . If any generalization should be made it is much more true to say that the actors, by their dogged faith and belief in the idea of the theatre (which was planted five and a half years ago by the directors), are keeping each other and the directors together. At certain points it has been absolutely clear that what kept the Group together was *their* determination—seemingly unreasonable—that the Group must go on.

The directors hadn't adjusted to this new reality, the committee said. The detailed individual criticisms that followed distilled in three savagely honest pages the frustrations and the perceptions of their directors' weaknesses that the actors had acquired over nearly six years of collective life. Their portrait of Strasberg seethed with mingled love and hatred.

> There is no doubt that it was Lee who gave the first artistic shape to the Group. For example, the thing that most of the actors still call *the Method* is in reality Lee's own method of work (at least, up until *Gold Eagle*). In this respect, we believe that in actual influence exerted, Lee has been the greatest artistic force in the American theatre during the last five years. Five and a half years ago with the inception of the Group, the revolutionary task was primarily his to do. He had to break down a whole tradition in thirty different individuals and this task really necessitated (as it tended to further harden and bring out) Lee's great courage, his doggedness, his necessity for being right, his cold scorn of artistic compromise, his clannishness, his removal from life,

his hysterical force (used as a threat), his psychotic domineering, and above all, the *brute force of his will.* Lee filled the need of that time— he met the objective circumstances and forged a revolution.

But today, with those objective circumstances changed and the Group, as such, established, the same qualities that once were neces- sary, now, when they manifest themselves, seem unhealthy. The tragic thing about Lee's relation to the Group both for him and for us is that for the many lovable and admirable qualities he does have—and for his real brilliance as a student and teacher of the theatre, he could be the most loved person of the organization. . . . People have left a re- hearsal with Lee pledging themselves eternal allegiance to him, and then left the next rehearsal with the coldest and most corrupting of icy hatreds. Thus Lee, sooner or later, at one time or another, is apt to destroy every breath of *theatre love* that he ever called forth.

We believe that Lee under the new organization should be relieved for some time to come of all but purely artistic tasks, that his produc- tions should be so organized around him that he will be really aided and that all his faults and deficiencies should be actually taken care of and that he really have an opportunity to recreate for himself his true place in the group.

They moved on to Clurman, who got off fairly lightly, considering the administrative failures pitilessly outlined by the actors:

Despite the fact that his regime as managing director is a failure, he is nevertheless the logical man for the position at the head of the theatre, to actually guide our course. It was he, single-handed, who brought the Group alive into the world. He is still the clearest and most whole of the three directors and in him the Group Idea still flourishes the most, in the sense that he still carries the unquenchable appetite for a Group theatre. We feel that it is the only way he can live —that as long as he goes on living, there will be a Group theatre around him.

But Harold has the gravest faults, which he is far from recognizing himself. This is evidenced by the fact that during his term as managing director he DID NOT CREATE THE *THEATRE* ORGANIZATION that was his first and most important task. Now we propose to create it with him and for him. . . . Harold, scorning certain problems, rendered impo- tent by emergencies, lacking craft competence, i.e., *really working* only under the spell of inspiration, crumbling just before rising to the heights and positively lacking certain talents, MUST HAVE AN IRON CLAD ORGANIZATION AND A COMPLETELY WORKED OUT PLAN. We propose that our plan be considered and carried out and an organization be created around Harold to achieve it.

The committee's analysis of Crawford was in some ways the most wounding of all, especially since its acknowledgment of her skills was decidedly perfunctory:

> We know that there probably could have been no Group today without Cheryl's tireless work. She's had six years of dirty jobs. We appreciate this, BUT Cheryl's Group problem is her own personal problem. She strikes us as a disappointed artist, a person who does not get the artistic exercise she craves, but is always forced to do other work in which she is not interested, but which nevertheless provides her substitute satisfaction. Consequently, she always feels she is wasting her life, that she is a "martyr" in the Group, that without her the Group would fold in a minute and worst of all, no one appreciates her. . . .
>
> We say that the Group theatre should drop, once and for all, Cheryl's dummy artistic standing as a *director of productions*. The Group Theatre must find Cheryl's real place in the Group's functioning. Our belief is that the first thing that should be done is that she should be freed from most of her routine jobs, the office work, the details of promotion, advertising bills, etc. etc. We must get a business manager we really trust to take over these tasks. Cheryl, with her adjustments to these tasks, does them not well enough. Secondly, we, the Group Theatre, must give her tasks which will really use her talent and energy and creative side, for example the creation of scripts like *Johnny*, tasks of high finance and promotion which she can do very well.

The Actor's Committee's evaluation of the directors was candid to the point of brutality, far more detailed and devastating than Clurman's onslaught against the actors the previous summer. It was, however, quite accurate and justified, in the actors' minds, by the dreadful conditions of Group life, vividly depicted in their closing pages:

> At least one third of the Group receive what for them is not even a subsistence wage. Another third grub on a debasing wage level. The rest have either outside jobs or outside sources of income. Year after year debts pile up. . . . The Group as it is functioning today is making the *Group* continuing impossible. From the personal point of view, the life of the individual artist in the Group today is simply not worth the tremendous sacrifice. Often, a whole year of one's life adds up to only *one* good part *IF YOU ARE LUCKY*. . . . The actors want and need full artistic lives and they want and need this NOW.

The Group actors' two most basic needs, they concluded, were, "a regular, predictable, sustaining income [and] *sufficient Artistic Exercise*." These needs could not be met, they warned, through "the dream that to the lyric notes in Harold's voice $70,000 will flop in our laps, to be doled out paternalistically to the actors so that they will stop crabbing." What they had to do was "institutionalize ourselves . . . to acquire our own theatre, OUR PLANT, a swift moving yearly schedule of production on a semi-repertory basis, an organized audience, students, a studio, a state charter to permit the solicitation of revolving funds . . . we must set ourselves up for what we are and WHAT WE WANT TO BE—the Moscow Art Theatre of America."

This proposal recalled Clurman's earlier desire to found a Group Center, but the actors believed they had found a way to make his impractical dream a reality. They wanted to found a Group School, an idea that Helen Thompson had been fruitlessly suggesting to the directors for more than a year. "The fact that the school idea is considered old hat around the Group office only indicates to us that our administrators have been blind," they remarked acidly. They attached a report from Thompson outlining the benefits of the project.

In her report Thompson argued that with the money they received from tuition, the Group could rent an entire theatre on a yearly basis and guarantee weekly salaries for the members. Having their own theatre, she pointed out, would save them thousands of dollars because they would have storage space and rehearsal rooms at no extra cost. It would give them a venue for special Sunday-night performances ("for which I always can get an audience") that would raise more money and allow them to try out new playwrights' work and develop new directional talent in an unpressured setting. The school itself, in addition to bringing in an estimated $20,000 a year in tuition, would be an organized way to train young actors in the Group method and add people to the permanent company.

Thompson proposed that she be named executive director of the school, with Bohnen and Kazan acting as codirectors. She pointed out that she was responsible for the Group's benefit program, which regularly boosted their box office through the sale of blocks of tickets, and for the remunerative New School symposium, now in its second year. "I have never undertaken a campaign that has not resulted in success," she stated; she believed the school was as practical and feasible as her earlier efforts.

The Actors Committee, aware that there might be unexpected pitfalls, argued that a school was nonetheless the most immediately practical way to solve the Group's pressing financial problems. "The keynote is OPERATION," they wrote. "We don't urge the school idea AS SUCH. We are really interested in STUDIOS, not schools. But before any of these things can happen we must first of all become a theatre which operates as an institution. If someone has a better means to this end than the school idea," they added rather defensively, "let's have it!"

The entire paper throbbed with indignation, fear, and desperate desire for the Group's survival. Its closing paragraphs revealed how high the stakes were:

Six years are six years! Today thirty people are ready and waiting to FUNCTION. What are we going to do? WE HAVE ONE TATTERED BOND LEFT BETWEEN US ALL—A PASSIONATE CONCERN FOR THE *GROUP IDEA*. AND SO WE PLACE THE CHOICES BLUNTLY BEFORE OUR LEADERSHIP—THEY ARE ONLY TWO.

IMMEDIATE ACTION—thus serving the GROUP IDEA through the present personnel and present organization—and following a plan such as the one we have suggested,

or,

an alternate possibility we have not discussed—DISSOLUTION—to let a new and more fit Group rise from the ashes, to start on a clean slate —reorganize fully, bearing in mind our mistakes.

WHICH WILL SERVE THE GROUP IDEA BEST?

It was fitting that the Actors Committee paper closed with a question. It was at heart an impassioned cry of despair over the Group's current state, not a blueprint for the future, and it made further evasion, prevarication, and self-deception impossible. The Group could no longer limp painfully along, working far below their potential. Reality had to be faced, and the Actors Committee had taken a giant step toward facing it.

The ball was now in the directors' court, and when they met to discuss the paper, there was a sense of relief that matters were finally out in the open. They must have had other feelings as well, but it's very likely that all three were in a state of shock from the "painful juggernaut," as Crawford later described it, that the Actors Committee had run over their characters and abilities. Even the members who voted to send the paper to the directors had been concerned about its savagery: "They wrote this devastating criticism of these people who had killed themselves for the Group," said Beany Barker, "just tore the directors to pieces." How devastating it was can be judged by the fact that neither Clurman, Strasberg, nor Crawford ever discussed in public their personal reactions to this crucial Group document.

Clurman now felt absolved of the responsibility of trying to lead the Group under these impossible conditions. Stella Adler, having contributed her scathing insights to the Actors Committee report, departed for Hollywood on December 22, and he intended to follow her there shortly. In the meanwhile, he suggested that he and his two partners resign as directors and meet with the actors to consider what new organizational structure would best meet their present needs. Rehearsals for *The Silent Partner* should obviously be abandoned, since Odets was not available for the revisions it needed and no one was in a state of mind conducive to work in any case. Strasberg and Crawford agreed, and they announced their decision to the actors. The Group was now officially leaderless.

The actors responded by suggesting that a joint committee of the former directors and three actors selected by the membership—Bohnen, Kazan, and Luther Adler—try to draft a plan for the Group's future. A few meetings took place, but they were crippled by Clurman's indifference (which may have been a mask for anger and pain) and his assertion that no matter what they decided, he intended to stay in Hollywood for six months. He couldn't promise that he would return, and he had no idea what kind of a Group he might be willing to come back to. Strasberg, furious, hinted that the Group might simply decide to go ahead without him, but didn't have the personality to inspire the actors with the will to continue. That had always been Clurman's specialty, and right now he wasn't interested: "The truth is that I did not really know what was troubling me most," he wrote later, "except for the fact that I was tired—very tired."

So was everyone else. Strasberg's notes from one of the abortive reorganization meetings show a demoralized Group unable to do more than deplore the current state of affairs:

> No one is yet quite sure of what they intend for themselves or with each other. Until this condition is cleared somehow it would be unfair to all concerned for people to make sacrifices, including career and financial sacrifices, for something which might *not* come to be in the form they wish for it or demand of it. . . . Following this out it was felt that no commitment for a Group summer should be entered into for the time being.

It was neither a Merry Christmas nor a Happy New Year for the Group. On January 5, 1937, Clurman wrote to Odets, who was to marry Luise Rainer in three days, to break the news that *The Silent Partner* had been "postponed." He acknowledged that some Group actors wanted to continue with the production (Art Smith was the most vocal), but argued that "such insistence (on your part as well as theirs) would lead to a breakdown from which there would be no recovery—for it would mean an effort made under continuously false conditions." A week later the Group announced that *Johnny Johnson* would close January 16 and they would suspend production for the season.

While the mainstream press reacted with surprise, the Group's problems had been an open secret for months to their colleagues on the left. A well-informed article had appeared in *New Theatre* in July—in all likelihood part of the Communist party's efforts to convince the members that the Group "must actually *become* a Marxist theatre" in order to grow, for it covered many of the same points members of the unit had made in the spring. A two-part article in the *Daily Worker* on January 10 and 17, 1937, essentially rehashed the same material; its suggestion that the Group's main task should be to reach middle-class audiences with important social plays was hilariously irrelevant at a time when the company was on the verge of dissolution.

The left might chide the Group, but always had faith in them. Some Broadway columnists, on the contrary, seemed almost pleased by the news of what they took to be the Group's demise. "The Group, which anxiously denied that it had any political philosophy, seems to be going the way proper to all hedgers," sneered the *Sun*. "Clifford Odets—remember the boy wonder?—has married a movie star. There hasn't been a good communist riot in a dog's age. What were the boys and girls of the Left? Merely foul-weather friends, running for cover now that the economic skies have cleared a little?"

The Group's audience didn't share the *Sun*'s ill-natured satisfaction. The office was flooded with phone calls and letters begging them not to shut down, telling them the Group was too important to halt even temporarily. Arthur Pollock, one of the company's warmest supporters in the press, saw in their inability to stay solvent an ominous portent. "With the departure from the Broadway scene of *Johnny Johnson* last night it is possible to reflect with considerable anxiety upon the parlous state of our theatre this year," he wrote in the Brooklyn *Eagle*.

> The Group Theatre is perhaps the most distinguished acting-group in the United States today: a body of young men and women to whom the traditions of the theatre mean more than prestige, glamour and good living (on occasion). . . . But they have not been able to make the sort of success that would guarantee their continuance as an acting-organization. They require support, and this editorial is a piece of special pleading, aimed to direct public attention to what these people can and have given for the money.

It was too late for special pleading. The Group couldn't go on as they were, and at the moment no one could see a way to reestablish themselves on a saner footing. Though an article by Clurman in the *Times* was head-lined "The Group Halts, But Only to Think It Over," its content was primarily a depressed and depressing list of the insuperable obstacles the organization faced. It could have been written five years earlier; indeed, Clurman's very first article about the Group, in December 1931, had warned of the same difficulties. Since then they had triumphantly justified their acting technique with *Success Story* and *Men in White*, proved that radical theatre could be great theatre with *Waiting for Lefty*, affirmed their commitment to the most exciting playwright of the day with *Awake and Sing!* and *Paradise Lost*, won the grudging respect of a largely hostile press, discovered a devoted audience—and solved precisely none of their underlying problems. Unable to change their situation, they had torn one another apart with criticisms that, while largely justified, had destroyed whatever shreds of resolve the Group still possessed.

Those who were left standing scrambled for jobs in the outside world.

Julie Garfield got the lead in Arthur Kober's *Having Wonderful Time;* Tony Kraber and Herbie Ratner had smaller roles. Bobby Lewis landed a part in a play called *His Excellency*, while Morris Carnovsky considered an offer of the starring role. Grover Burgess and Curt Conway went to the Theatre Union to do Lawson's *Marching Song*, the play Clurman had turned down. Russell Collins went back to the Cleveland Playhouse to headline in a stock production of *Johnny Johnson* on his old home turf. Art Smith went home too, to direct a WPA production in Chicago. Bud Bohnen also got employment through the Federal Theatre Project, working as assistant to the Group's old friend Philip Barber, who was director of the New York City project. Odets wangled jobs for Clurman and Kazan on the film he was writing, and there were hints that the producer, Walter Wanger, might be willing to hire several Group actors for the project. Strasberg, Crawford, and Molly Thacher would stay behind in New York, to cheerlessly hold down the fort at the Group offices and pretend they might have a future.

On January 17, most of the Group went down to Grand Central Station to say good-bye to Clurman and Kazan as they boarded the Twentieth Century for California. It was the bleakest moment in their collective history. None of them knew if they would ever work together again. Among those present at this forlorn farewell gathering was Lee Strasberg. Never one who voiced his feelings easily, he'd dipped into his cherished book collection to find something that expressed his desperate hope that somehow they would find a way to renew the commitment to the theatre that had sustained them for six enthralling, impossible years. As the train was about to depart, he pressed into Clurman's hands a rare copy of Henrik Ibsen's *Letters.*

ELEVEN
Regrouping

Clurman and Kazan had hardly stepped off the train in California when they were joined by Crawford and the Group's attorney, John Wildberg, who'd flown out to negotiate a deal for the Group with Walter Wanger, formerly chief of production at Paramount and now an independent producer. Crawford and Wildberg worked out an agreement they hoped would give the actors and the Group modest financial security while they were sorting out their future. Wanger agreed to pay the performers $150 a week each as an advance against their salaries when they got parts in specific films. They would receive $750 a week when they worked in his movies, and if he loaned them out to other studios (a common practice with independents) at a higher price, actor and producer would split the additional money. To keep the Group offices in New York solvent, Crawford proposed that the actors send 10 percent of their salaries back east.

Luther Adler, Bud Bohnen, Phoebe Brand, Morris Carnovsky, Lee Cobb, Ruth Nelson, and Dorothy Patten arrived in Hollywood in early February to make screen tests for Wanger. They were joined in these tryouts by Kazan, who also wanted to see if there was a place for him as an actor in Hollywood, and by the apostate Group member Walter Coy, whose film career to date hadn't been exactly thrilling and who hoped he might do better with the Group. They were pleased to have the tests supervised by Lewis Milestone; most of them knew him through his friendship with Odets, and he was slated to direct *Castles in the Air*, the screenplay Odets was currently writing about Spaniards in Paris who wanted to go home and fight for the Loyalist government.

When Wanger, satisfied with the test results, ratified the Group deal and cast Adler, Bohnen, Brand, Carnovsky, and Nelson in *Castles in the Air*, they were delighted. It seemed an opportunity to work on a project more meaningful than the run-of-the-mill studio offering, with two of the most cultivated men in Hollywood. The sensitive, intellectual Milestone had directed the antiwar classic *All Quiet on the Western Front*; Dartmouth- and Oxford-educated Wanger had made his reputation at a studio known for its well-written scripts and a commitment to allowing its directors to fulfill their artistic visions.

Some of the Group's screen tests have survived, and they offer an intriguing glimpse of the acting style the company had forged through six years of hard work. In their silent tests, both Adler and Carnovsky are remarkably relaxed and focused; the "circle of attention" exercises they had done with Strasberg made it easy for them to create the mood of "solitude in public" Stanislavsky called for as a prerequisite to behaving naturally onstage. Their scene together from *Success Story* shows Group acting at its pre-Odets peak: Carnovsky's brilliant vocal characterization, a slightly nasal American upper-class accent, gives his performance a tone of jovial cynicism that contrasts perfectly with Adler's nervous, aggressive rhythms as the driven Sol.

Adler is more flamboyant in his intense *Awake and Sing!* monologue, which demonstrates that his personal style owed at least as much to the Yiddish theatre as to Stanislavsky. Odets' dialogue, which could look flowery on the page and had sounded artificial when delivered by movie actors in his first film to reach the screen *(The General Died at Dawn)*, seems natural, true, and touching when spoken by someone who understood the life experiences that lay behind it. Ruth Nelson's scene from *Weep for the Virgins* shows how much the method could bring even to a bad script; her character's every move is charged with inner meaning, despite the dreary dialogue and an unhelpful, affected supporting performance by Walter Coy, who seems to have forgotten everything he'd ever learned about Group technique. Kazan is too nervous and eager to please in his test, apparently based on an improvisation, to show how good he could be in the right part; in any case, one exposure to the way he photographed and the sound of his New York accent on film was enough to convince him he had no future as a movie actor.

One Group member was noticeably absent from the screen tests: Dorothy Patten had had a severe nervous breakdown and been confined to a sanitorium. Her crisis was prompted by a complex tangle of personal and professional worries. The immediate cause had been an ugly fight with Crawford shortly before her return to New York; Patten wanted to break off their lengthy relationship. But there was more to it than a lovers' quarrel. Patten was one of the Group's most idealistic and devoted members: she'd worked hard on the audience campaigns, taken pride in her succession of small but challenging roles, and in lean times generously doled out portions of the allowance from her wealthy family to less affluent comrades. Despite this commitment, over the years she'd been quietly relegated to the fringes of the acting company; a certain amount of class consciousness existed within the Group, and people like Patten, Beany Barker, and Eunice

Stoddard, who had some family money and outside personal lives, felt they weren't considered true Group members by those more single-mindedly focused on collective life and work. The Actors Committee paper had shaken Patten badly, exposing divisions within the company she'd hardly been aware of.

The trip to California reinforced her feelings of insecurity. Her proposed test scene, from *Success Story*, brought back unhappy memories of her failure in a part she'd been unsuited for. She felt she was included in Wanger's deal only as an afterthought and that unless her test were brilliant she would simply languish in California, drawing her salary until the contract ran out. She looked in vain to her Group comrades for reassurance of her femininity and appeal for the camera—"the Group is no place to get that 'thing' back from other people in *the form you need it in,*" said Bud Bohnen, analyzing Patten's breakdown in retrospect. The quarrel with Crawford brought everything to a head, and after a few weeks in which Bohnen and Nelson dashed back and forth to the sanitorium, hoping she would recover quickly, it became clear she needed a long rest. She was dispatched with a nurse to Baltimore, where Barker, her closest friend in the Group aside from Crawford, arranged for a consultation at Johns Hopkins with her father. After a course of treatment there, Patten went to a ranch in Wyoming to recuperate.

"I've had a ten percent dose of the same disturbance," Bud Bohnen admitted, attributing both his and Patten's nervous state to the tensions created by the screen tests. "All the people have felt this to a degree, but all the circumstances are more acute in Dorothy's case. For all the rest of us have some outside concern or responsibility to focus on, to shake ourselves with . . . except Ruth, perhaps, who creates it for herself by rushing around taking care of everybody and his dog, filling her own need in a self-consuming frenzy, which I suppose she'll have to pay the piper for later on." The slightly acid quality of these remarks, so untypical of the normally sweet-tempered Bohnen, showed how edgy everyone was. Nelson needed to find ways to feel useful; her marriage to Bill Challee had come apart under the strains of the Group's disintegration. They weren't the only Group couple in trouble; scarcely a month after his wedding, Odets was having stormy scenes with Luise Rainer.

Patten's collapse and other Group members' personal problems revealed the terrible pressure they were all operating under. They hated Hollywood. "It's truly capitalism gone mad out here," Bohnen wrote his brother. "Everybody talks salary, pictures, graft, drag, the whole spirit of the place is fake, the acting is fake, the art is synthetic." They noted with alarm that former Group members like Franchot Tone and Joe Bromberg hadn't saved a nickel during their lucrative California sojourns—so much for dreams of financing the theatre on their movie earnings. Aware that some of the Group remaining in New York had resented the departure of a large faction for the golden West, Bohnen wrote to Crawford, "If there is anyone under-foot who envies us out here tell them they're crazy—that we all curse the circumstances that make it necessary."

It was bad enough sitting around waiting for *Castles in the Air* to begin shooting. What was really intolerable was the uncertainty about the Group. Most of the actors viewed their visit to California as merely an interlude, a pause while they regathered their forces for a new and better-organized theatre. The abrupt postponement of the Odets picture just as they were about to go into production in early March—there were rumors that Wanger, who was trying to make a film in Italy, feared it would offend Mussolini—added to their sense of Hollywood as a place profoundly hostile to the Group Idea, an environment in which it was impossible for them to do any meaningful work.

To the Group members on the West Coast, *Castles in the Air* had been a partial justification of their flight to California; to Wanger, it was just an-other project, to be canceled or reworked as he saw fit. Under the terms of the Group contract, they had no legal redress against this change in plans. They began to feel Crawford had cut a lousy deal: the salaries, so enormous in comparison to their meager wages in New York, were pitiful by Holly-wood standards; Wanger seemed to have no immediate plans to use any of them; and their contract with him made it difficult to find work elsewhere. Kazan, who had a nose for sniffing out shady maneuvers, believed their lawyer, Wildberg, was actually working for Wanger; that, he claimed, was why the deal was so bad.

Bohnen could see what happened to those who succumbed to the lure of California's easy lifestyle: "[You] drink yourself to death in the glorious sunlight with oranges dropping into your mouth." They had to find a way to bring the Group back into active existence. Luther Adler mounted yet another fund-raising campaign, offering "life memberships" at $100 each; he managed to get pledges from some of the Group's movie-star friends, and Crawford drummed up a few more in New York, but the total came laughably short of their announced goal of a $100,000 endowment.

Money wasn't what they needed—or at least, they needed it no more badly than at any other time in the Group's history. What they had to have was the belief that there was still a reason and a chance to go on. The Group Council, composed of Luther, Bohnen, and Kazan, was charged with man-aging the organization's practical affairs, but for inspiration they looked to Clurman. He was completely uncooperative, too exhausted by the bitter debates of the previous year to be willing to do anything but wait for con-ditions to somehow improve. He was wrapped up in his relationship with Stella Adler, who'd signed a contract with Major Pictures and was still bitterly angry with the Group. He virtually shunned his former comrades, resisting all attempts to make him discuss their future as a theatre.

Even more troubling was his apparent determination to sabotage Craw-ford's and Strasberg's attempts to keep the Group afloat. Shortly after the actors' arrival in California, Crawford tried to hold meetings about the Group's reorganization; Clurman refused to attend. He stirred up trouble about the 10 percent the actors and he had agreed to send back to New York, telling them he thought it was ridiculous for them to sacrifice any part of their paychecks after the privations they had endured for years. When stating his opinions for the record, he was more evasive. Bohnen, charged with collecting the tithe to support the Group offices, reported to Crawford on her former partner's position:

1. he doesn't feel the 10% thing should be mathematically imposed, 2. that the sum can be more or less than 10% depending on the capacity of the individual as determined *by* the individual, 3. that he himself needs a breathing spell before he starts remitting—of at least a week or two due to the morass of immediate obligations, 4. that he will hold up his end at the earliest opportunity.

Most of the actors sent what money they could, but the checks were sporadic and insufficient to cover office expenses. Crawford and Strasberg sat anxiously in New York, stewing in their enforced inactivity. With Clurman, the entire Council, and most of the Group's important actors on the West Coast, any steps to restore and reorganize the company had to be taken out there. Judging by the letters Crawford and Strasberg were receiving, not a thing was being done. Paula Miller, who joined the other actors under contract to Wanger in early March, wrote to her husband that everyone seemed to be eager to find work in the movies and no one knew what shape the new Group should take. Clurman and Stella Adler were waiting before coming to a decision about their participation, she added. Kazan, in a letter to Strasberg written ten days later, was blunter:

I told [Harold] frankly that I thought he was in a comatose state, that he seemed to have lost his own appetite, desire and personal dynamics . . . that he seemed to be further embedded in his concern for Stella than he had ever been before. To this he simply answered that I was right. . . . Everyone longs for the Group; all await leadership.

It was increasingly clear to Crawford and Strasberg that this desperately needed leadership was not forthcoming in California and that circumstances prevented their providing it in New York. On March 17, Crawford sent the Council a letter of resignation from the Group:

The shock and surprise of my determination is perhaps greater to me than it will be to you, but I have tried to deal with my problems logically and sanely and unsentimentally. . . . I hope very much that you will not feel I am failing in responsibility to the Group in making this step, for if my interpretation of the reports I have received from the Coast is correct, I have not done so. I would like to say that I still believe with all my heart in a Group Theatre and that the objective or outside situations which have caused us so much strain and difficulty *can* be slowly solved, but the inner situation seems to me incapable of solution at least at this time. Believe me that I more deeply regret this than anything I have ever had to do, but it truly seems to be necessary and inevitable.

The following day Strasberg unofficially notified Group members in New York that he would also be leaving, and on March 23 he formally resigned in a letter to the Council. A personal note to his wife revealed his bitterness over the step that he, like Crawford, felt he'd been forced to take:

My own point is simple. If time is needed to carry out any plan that we have I wouldn't mind waiting 10 years and 10 summers. But to wait because fundamentally the people aren't up to action (that's what I feel) and so they can rest up etc. seems to me valueless. . . . I do feel very strongly however that for the people of the Group to have gone ahead and wrecked the Group organization without any immediate and definite plan and assumption of responsibility was a criminal act. It leaves me speechless and breathless to realize that that's what all their talking and complaining came to. It is an interesting comment on the situation that two of the three Group elected representatives (Bud and Luther) are people who were approached to join the Group and didn't join it except at their convenience.

Strasberg and Crawford continued for years to believe, and state publicly, that the actors had destroyed the Group with their inability to submit to leadership from above. This wasn't quite fair, for in the Group's early history they had unquestioningly accepted the directors' right to make all important decisions. Every incident of revolt by the membership—the creation of the Actors Committee following the closing of *Big Night* in 1933, the drive for a more democratic structure in the spring of 1936, and the devastating Actors Committee paper the following December—had been sparked by the actors' feeling that the directors had put the Group in mortal jeopardy. Because of his temperament, Clurman found it easier to accept the members' criticisms, which were indeed often unfair, as a natural consequence of their passion for the Group Idea. At this painful juncture in Group life, he may have been more prescient than his former partners in realizing that there were times when retreat was both inevitable and necessary.

Crawford's and Strasberg's desire for action was commendable, and their irritation at Clurman's passivity understandable. But their desire to bustle around and hold meetings, to get the Group back in action *right now*, ignored the fact that the wounds of the previous year were too deep to be healed by another reorganization on paper. "In this intermediary period, many people are being motivated by a certain kind of fear," Kazan wrote to Strasberg just before his resignation.

> This impulse says, "Let us cling to what we have, it is better than nothing . . . we can slowly iron out our faults as we work along . . . we had the best people and we had the best relation and adjustment between these people . . . for chrissake let's not lose what we have." I believe this attitude to be a panicky one and also extremely dangerous. I believe that if we got together this summer, the same people in the same relations etc.—the same clashes and diseases would grow up and then there would come a really terrible explosion!

Clurman's letter to Strasberg accepting his resignation made it clear that he was still unready to make plans for the Group's future. The Council had asked him to write, he explained: "It is taking over the job of running the Group and will do everything in its power to keep it going and to build it up." He himself, at this sad moment, preferred to celebrate their past. "The years since I have known you personally and professionally have really been the years that have *made* me," he wrote to the only man whose dreams in 1925 had matched his own. "I look back at them gratefully and proudly. They were years of a wonderful creative collaboration that, we need not doubt, have stamped themselves permanently on the American Theatre." When he looked ahead, it was only in the most general terms. "Despite the fact that we now 'part' I feel sure that, because we reflect the maturest thinking and experience in the American theatre, we may still be of invaluable assistance and service to one another in whatever work in the theatre we may undertake from this point on. Best of luck in everything. Always, Harold."

The resignations were announced in the *New York Times* on April 12. "Miss Crawford plans to become an independent producer with a small group of associates," the article stated. "Mr. Strasberg will direct plays for her and for other managers, and may return to the Group occasionally to stage a production. According to Mr. Strasberg, the nucleus of Miss Crawford's acting company will include some players now with the Group."

Strasberg's comment that he might direct plays for the Group expressed his lingering hope that the break would not be final rather than any real possibility, but the idea that some Group actors might join Crawford wasn't totally unfounded. The contingent of the Group remaining in New York— which included such founding members as Beany Barker, Tony Kraber, Herbie Ratner, and Eunice Stoddard—was even more in the dark than Strasberg and Crawford as to what was going on out west. Only Julie Garfield, starring in *Having Wonderful Time* and being pursued by Wanger for a film contract, was in close touch with the Hollywood contingent. The rest worried that the future of the organization was being decided without them, and they were hurt and angry.

A well-informed article by Henry Senber, the *Telegraph* reporter who'd scooped New York on the premiere of *Waiting for Lefty*, presented the opinion of New York Group members about recent events:

> Three factions have figured in recent manipulations. [The revolt of actors against directors was only] one fight. The actors themselves are divided between the "stars," including members of the Group who went to Hollywood recently to make a picture for Walter Wanger, and the other players. The non-stars resented this "desertion," feeling that if the Group aristocrats had stayed on it might have been possible to continue with another production. . . . Another cause for complaint on the part of the rank-and-file members of the company was the alleged practice of the Group's hierarchy in passing out choicer parts to a group-within-the-Group. As one member of the company said yesterday, "It was just a case of the Group Theatre presenting the Adler family."

Since Stella hadn't appeared in the last two Group productions and Luther had only small roles in *Johnny Johnson,* this last comment wasn't accurate, but it expressed the New York actors' perception that they were less valued members of the company, and their fear that the new Group would not include them. When Kazan returned to New York shortly before the resignations were made public, he was besieged by actors asking if they were still in the Group. He reassured no one by saying he didn't know.

He was telling the truth, more or less. He, Luther Adler, and Bud Bohnen were determined that the Group should have a fall season, and they persuaded the reluctant Clurman to agree that the four of them could lead the new Group Theatre. "We take over the name, the properties, and small debts, and any of the old Group members that we think deserve to be in the new set up," Bohnen wrote to his brother in mid-April. "The 'Group Idea' will have continuity, but the personnel will be altered." Kazan agreed that "we need fresh blood; we need to take chances again with new people." He believed, as he'd written to Strasberg a month earlier, "Loyalty is no longer enough. The struggle is too fierce." Inasmuch as he was certain some members would be dropped, it wasn't entirely honest not to tell people in New York of that decision.

Yet Kazan wasn't lying when he told people he didn't know whether they were in or out. The Council had the will to go on, but no specific plans and no scripts. Most important of all, they had only the vaguest commitment from Clurman, who still seemed content to collect his salary as Wanger's assistant and live in the eternal present. Kazan saw no future for himself in Hollywood: he would never make it as an actor there, and though he was intrigued by the possibility of directing films, he concluded that there was no way to do sustained good work under the studio system. Its idiocies were summed up for him by the production chief who suggested he change his name to Cézanne; when Kazan remarked that there was a rather famous painter by that name, the executive assured him, "After you make two pictures, they'll never know he existed." He detested southern California and missed his baby daughter and wife, who spent most of her time in the Group offices reading plays and writing severe letters reproaching him and Clurman for abandoning the theatre. In early April he threw up his hands and came home, leaving it to Luther and Bud to find a way to spur the indolent Clurman into action.

Every Group member in California was essentially waiting for Harold to find his way, and they discovered that in the meanwhile Hollywood's fat paychecks and easy lifestyle weren't so hard to take and in fact provided a much-needed respite from the rigors of Group life. Morris Carnovsky got the role of Anatole France in the Warner Brothers film *The Life of Emile Zola;* he and Phoebe Brand rented a pretty little house on Graciosa Drive. Bohnen and Ruth Nelson had small parts in Wanger's *Vogues of 1938*, a picture Clurman also worked on, "teaching John Powers models how to walk," as one theatrical magazine rather nastily noted. Bohnen and his wife took the opportunity to concentrate on improving their health: getting their teeth fixed, arranging their schedule so they slept and ate regularly, something there hadn't always been time for in the Group, and cutting down on their drinking. "We have both been pretty physically demoralized for about two years," he wrote his brother, "like floundering swimmers in a choppy lake. California is a crucially welcome sandbar." Even Luther Adler, who was frustrated to find his friend Odets placidly working on another film after the cancellation of *Castles in the Air,* was willing enough to compromise with the film world to have his nose fixed and take a part in a film called *Lancer Spy.*

His sister, who'd always had a taste for luxury, thoroughly enjoyed Hollywood and her lavish digs at the Beverly Wilshire Hotel. She and Clurman could be seen eating in expensive restaurants where the headwaiters greeted them by name. Group moral indignation against the actors who had deserted to the movies earlier lapsed, and they had friendly dinners with Joe Bromberg and Alan Baxter. Sundays with Franchot Tone and his wife, Joan Crawford, became a weekly Group get-together. Bobby Lewis, who'd come west to direct a WPA production, remembered that Crawford always retired for bed promptly at nine-thirty to get a good night's sleep before her early call in the morning; guests were admonished not to say anything unsettling that might disturb her slumbers. The Sunday routine was a pleasant one of badminton, dips in the pool, drinks, and dinner followed by private screenings of new films. One afternoon, floating lazily in the water, Clurman looked up, squinting in the warm sunshine, to find Tone observing him with amusement. "The life of a prostitute is pretty comfortable, isn't it?" his friend remarked sardonically.

Everyone was in a state of suspended animation. When they looked east to New York, there seemed hardly any reason to go home. The warm, supportive environment of socially minded theatres they had helped to create was all but gone. The Theatre Union, closest of the left-wing companies to the Group in the scope of ambition and desire to reach a broad audience, gave its last gasp with *Marching Song* in February 1937, though its demise wasn't officially announced until August. *New Theatre* magazine, the lively champion of the alternate stage Luther Adler had poured so much time and energy into, had suspended publication in November 1936, racked by debts and a victim of the movement's declining energy. It reemerged briefly the following March, with a more sober format, as *New Theatre and Film*, but folded for good in April. Even the Federal Theatre Project, which for more than a year had been triumphantly fulfilling the left theatre's goal of bringing socially conscious plays to the masses, was under attack. Hostile congressmen used the business recession of 1937 as a pretext to make a 25 percent cut in the budget of the WPA, the New Deal program most hated of all by conservatives for its presumption in asserting that artists were people in need of jobs just like anyone else. Only in the fund-raising efforts of the Theatre Committee to Aid Spanish Democracy, founded by members of the *Marching Song* company, did the old fighting spirit seem alive.

Spain was on everyone's mind that spring, as it became increasingly obvious that the civil war was a testing ground for fascist armies and weapons that would later be used against other nations. The defenseless Basque town of Guernica, destroyed by German bombers on April 26, was a symbol of ordinary people everywhere threatened by the Nazi military machine. It was incredible to many Americans that their government, and those of other Western democracies, refused to aid the Spanish Loyalists while Hitler sent 10,000 German soldiers and Mussolini more than 50,000 Italians to fight with Franco. Only the Soviet Union contributed advisers and equipment to the Loyalist cause, a fact most leftists were far more comfortable discussing than the disquieting questions raised by the Moscow show trials, which had begun in January to purge the old Bolshevik leadership. Spain was a battleground where right and wrong seemed clear, and *New Theatre* editor Herbert Kline was one of the many Group friends who joined the thousands of Americans in the Abraham Lincoln Brigade, one of the volunteer International Brigades fighting in support of Spanish democracy.

Much of the Group's social life in California centered around efforts to raise money for the Loyalist cause. In retrospect, Clurman saw the zeal to aid Spain that swept Hollywood's artistic and intellectual community as deriving from "an emotional hunger whose cause was first of all deeply American . . . [a] desire to bring ourselves in some way into the main stream of the true life of our time." As he often did, he somewhat slighted people's political beliefs with his emphasis on their psychological needs, but it was true that for many in the Group their work on behalf of the

Loyalists satisfied a longing their well-paid, trivial film jobs and agreeable afternoons by the pool could never fulfill. As the spring progressed, their demands that concrete steps be taken to revive the Group increased in urgency. Luther Adler's and Bud Bohnen's efforts in California, and Kazan's in New York, were a beginning, but they needed Clurman and were convinced that he needed the Group. Even Stella Adler, who had no intention for the moment of returning to embattled collective life and a theatre she believed offered her nothing as an actress, turned to him one night with tears in her eyes and said, "You shouldn't be here. You should be back in New York where your real work is."

Clurman continued to stall for time. He couldn't proceed without a suitable script, he told his comrades, and despite his work with Odets *The Silent Partner* remained unready. He candidly admitted that he was reluctant to leave Stella alone in California; their newly tranquil life together had been the happiest part of his stay in Hollywood, and he feared she would start seeing other men if she felt bored or neglected. He was still tired, unready to assume again the monumental task of leading the Group.

Kazan broke the impasse in early May with a long, impassioned letter masterfully conceived to jolt his friend and mentor into action. It was a shrewd mix of flattery, subtle criticism of Clurman's subservience to Adler, and a barely veiled threat that the Group would go on without him if necessary. "There's nothing that could make me happier than if you, Bud and Luther would all get on the train on July 28th, choo-choo back here, and we'd all unleash and build the theatre anew," Kazan wrote. "But, I SAY STAY THERE TILL YOU REALLY WANT TO COME BACK, TILL YOU REALLY FEEL *YOUTHFUL* AGAIN, TILL YOU WANT TO *REBUILD FOR CHRISSAKE A THEATRE* AND NOT PRODUCE A PLAY OR TWO." There was no one he'd rather work with, Kazan wrote. "I think you and I have the motor, the energy, the brains, the experience, the ruthlessness, the richness, the emotion, the appetite to build the greatest theatre ever built, and I think we can do it in America, today. But we can't do it with you split up, un-resolved, hesitating, *un-youthful.*"

On the thorny subject of Adler, he commented:

> I told you when I was there that I believe that Stella's personal problem can never be solved in any Group Theatre in the USA. There's no Group Theatre possible in this country today that can meet the requirements of an actress who says, "I never want to be poor again." . . . I don't see how any Group Theatre, now, can give Stella her rightful place as an actress. It's impossible. Also, to make this one of the primary problems of the theatre, I'd say, would very much distort the case.

He went on to make his point clearer, that undue concern with Adler's needs "would reinforce your adjusting to the theatre scene like an individual producer, rather than like the leader and builder of a Group Theatre." He pricked Clurman's conscience by reminding him of the Group's ideals, saying that he was convinced there was "NO theatre which dealt with the real world. Except ours tried to . . . you were one of those who taught me to see this more clearly [that] the Theatre Union and such theatres deal with just as putrid, unlifelike conventions as do the [commercial] theatres." The Group had vital work to do in New York, and sooner or later Clurman would be back to do it:

> What I say to Bud and Luther is this: You seem determined as I am to go on. Don't delay too long. There's tremendous work to be done here, plans to be laid, plays to be prepared, talent to be found, leadership to be adjusted and welded. . . . For the sake of a few hundred bucks earned out there, don't handicap or endanger the enterprise from which you expect to live all next fall, winter, spring. We four are now the leaders. Nothing will happen except through us.

Having made it clear that he was committed to the Group whether the directors came back or not, Kazan closed with an urgent plea to Clurman to fulfill the best in himself through rededication to the Group:

> Harold, I've looked up to you for five years. You've epitomized for me —as I told you—the artist. The completely resolved person, with direction fixed everlastingly and therefore with terrific personal momentum. You were always surrounded with a miasma of incompetences, like a cow is with the swarm of gnats, but they never mattered fundamentally to me. The cow was always there in the middle. You *were* the Group Idea; that was and is your significance. That, as religious folks used to say, is your *call*. Well you've won me and converted me. I say *All or nothing*, and I say (after Lee) I'd rather have half an apple if I want an apple and I do. To me the Group is not so much a career. IT'S A WAY TO LIVE A LIFE! THAT'S WHY I'VE GOT TO HAVE IT. LOVE. GADGET.

It was a brilliant piece of work, displaying Kazan's enormous charm and his formidable ability to manipulate people. He used everything he knew about Clurman: his boredom in Hollywood, his belief that the Group had a special role to play independent of both the commercial and the left theatre, his love for New York, his desire to work surrounded by friends, even the opinion he tried to keep to himself that he, and not Strasberg, had always represented the true spirit of the Group. The letter had its desired effect. "I answered as if there had never been any question of what I would do," Clurman wrote later. "There were no two choices. There was only one course: to begin work again next season with the Group." If Stella wouldn't go east, he would have to go without her, and it's easy to imagine her bitterness at discovering, not for the first time, that when it came down to a choice between her and the Group, Clurman would always—hesitantly, reluctantly, but always—choose the Group. On May 10 the New York papers announced that Clurman would leave California for New York in August to begin rehearsals immediately for the Group's seventh season.

He brought the Group back to life with nothing but the will to go on. Despite all his previous intentions, Clurman made the announcement without having either a script or financial backing for the company. But the promise of a future was all Group members asked for. Within two weeks of the announcement, Odets showed the director a sheet of paper with a play outline he had scribbled down in a cab coming home from Paramount the day before. It concerned a young Italian-American whose father wants him to be a musician, but who decides to make his fortune as a boxer. Clurman thought the idea was intriguing, and that same night Odets roughed out half of the first ten scenes. A note the playwright wrote to Bobby Lewis gave an indication of the new Group's priorities: "If we have a good popular play (and this one has more audience appeal than even *Awake and Sing!*) we don't need to work out new Group problems and plans—the success of the first production will take care of so much!"

In the meetings held to discuss the reorganized Group, Clurman made it clear that many of the old ways would be abandoned. As the May 10 press release had announced, all decisions would now be made by a board consisting of him, Luther Adler, Bohnen, and Kazan. Furthermore, only actors in an actual production would receive a salary. He would no longer burden the Group with the responsibility of maintaining a permanent company year-round, nor would he promise to cast only Group actors. He was looking for new talent, and members who had failed to prove their usefulness wouldn't be kept on for old times' sake.

Some of the actors, Clurman later admitted, were deeply disturbed by this last statement. Dropping people who'd given six years of their lives to the Group, they told him, was not just wrong, but bad for the organization. "This was something more than sentimentality, I was assured; it was a feeling that our strength lay in the fact that down to the last bit player in the cast all our people were animated by a single faith and spirit." How much Clurman had been changed by the stresses of previous years could be seen in his response to this simple restatement of the Group Idea: "I remained firm in the conviction that I had to proceed without any further 'religiosity.' "

Clurman didn't identify the actors who made these objections, but of the Group members in California the most likely would have been Brand, Carnovsky, or Nelson. Kazan's and Bohnen's letters made it clear that they were in favor of some drastic personnel housecleaning, and Adler worked so closely with them that they would surely have noted in their correspondence if he disagreed on such a basic issue. Nelson, on the other hand, famous in the Group for her selfless care for others and considered by Paula Miller a fanatic on the subject of the Group Idea, would probably have found this new policy distasteful. Brand and Carnovsky, whose political life

was animated by their strong sense of responsibility toward those less fortunate, were also unlikely to have approved, although Carnovsky later said
he'd felt the Group was getting a little ingrown.

Their protests went unheeded, and the board went ahead to discuss with
a number of film actors the possibility of their appearing in future productions to give the organization some star power. It was disheartening for
members of the finest acting ensemble in America to see that their leaders
felt the Group needed movie stars to attract an audience, but in fact the
people they approached were, in general, appropriate additions to the company. Franchot Tone, of course, wasn't an addition at all; everyone was
delighted by his promise to return to the Group. Sylvia Sidney, who was
romantically involved with Luther Adler, had been a stage actress before
she came to Hollywood; she was an ardent admirer of the Group's ensemble
acting and eager for firsthand experience with the famous method. Bill
Anderson, a handsome young singer who had appeared in Max Reinhardt's
A Midsummer Night's Dream, was also drawn to the Group by his desire to
study the craft of acting seriously, a chance seldom presented by his routine
work as a contract player for Paramount, whose main contribution to his
career was giving him an improbable new name: Leif Erickson.

Clurman was most immediately interested in Erickson's wife, a fiery
young actress named Frances Farmer who seemed perfect for the female
lead in the new Odets play. As intelligent as she was beautiful, Farmer
promised to make a lively addition to the new Group. Born in Seattle, the
daughter of a lawyer, she kicked up her first public stir when she was
seventeen, in 1930, by winning a national high-school creative-writing contest with an essay entitled "God Dies." Her parents were mortified by the
hostile headlines in the local papers, but Farmer was undaunted. She entered the University of Washington the following year as a drama major,
studying the Stanislavsky system and dreaming of working with an acting
company like New York's famous Group Theatre. Her senior year she won
a trip to Moscow by selling the largest number of subscriptions to a radical
Seattle weekly called *The Voice of Action*. Her mother was hysterical and
threatened to commit suicide; Farmer was unimpressed and went anyway.
She got back in the summer of 1935, eager to work in the New York theatre,
but found Broadway unreceptive to a neophyte with no professional credentials. Her breathtaking good looks attracted the attention of movie
agents, however, and she signed a seven-year contract with Paramount in
September.

Her first two films marked her as a promising starlet with considerable
audience appeal, and her third, *Come and Get It*, was a hit. But Farmer
found movie acting superficial and unsatisfying; she loathed the mandatory
social life and enforced publicity appearances required of a rising young
actress. She quickly acquired a reputation as an eccentric who wore slacks,
disdained make-up, drove a six-year-old car, and gave brusque interviews.

Her marriage to Erickson was largely a matter of convenience, though she was fond of him; it absolved her from the necessity of making public appearances with a succession of boring male escorts, fellow contract players, for the sake of their careers. By the time she met Clurman, who'd admired her in *Come and Get It*, she was dying to get out of Hollywood. She hated working on films where hours were spent fussing with her clothes and hair while she had to fight every inch of the way for time to develop a performance. She was awed by the Group and eager to be part of their theatre.

As Group members got to know Farmer at dinner parties and the various rallies for Spain—she was active in support of the Loyalist cause—they grew very fond of her. "She was a wonderful girl," said Phoebe Brand, "very idealistic, like the rest of us." Her enthusiasm for the Group was especially appealing; it rekindled their own excitement, damped by the terrible stresses of 1936, and reminded them that despite all their difficulties they'd created a body of work that meant a great deal to ardent young people like Farmer. Perhaps Clurman and the Council were right; new blood would give them the determination they needed to resume the struggle in New York.

Luther Adler and Clifford Odets departed for the front line in early July, Adler to help Kazan set up the new Group offices, Odets to complete his play in an environment more conducive to creation than the troubled atmosphere of the house he shared with Luise Rainer. The marriage was disintegrating, torn apart by the conflicting demands of two careers and the clash of two strong personalities who each wanted the other to drop everything and act as helpmate to a needy spouse.

As he'd done before, Odets was fleeing his real family to take refuge with his adopted kin. But the situation was very different than it had been in 1931. Odets was no longer the idealistic young man who wanted nothing more than to have the Group Theatre produce his plays. His season as the toast of New York and his sojourn in Hollywood had made commercial success more important than ever to someone whose desire for mainstream recognition had always been strong. He didn't want to be a curiosity, a left-wing adornment at Broadway cocktail parties; he wanted the people who had lionized him after his early success to accept him as one of them, an important New York playwright in conventional terms.

His ideals remained, and the Group Theatre was a symbol of them, but his relationship to the company that had given birth to *Lefty* and *Awake and Sing!* was now more complicated. He felt a mixture of love and resentment, a desire that they should hold fast to the faith that had brought them together in 1931 and exasperation that they were (in his view) incapable of giving his work the polished performances required to win him the respect he deserved on Broadway. He wholeheartedly agreed with Clurman's and the Council's plans for a more professional Group, but he had an uneasy sense that something was being lost in the process, as it had been lost in his own life. He poured these feelings into his new play, which he called *Golden Gloves*, while Adler and Kazan protectively shielded him from outside upsets; he *had* to finish it in time for the Group's fall season.

Back in California, Clurman threw himself into the task of finding more scripts. He'd maintained a close friendship with Irwin Shaw, despite the Group's failure to produce *Bury the Dead*. The two men had very different temperaments—Shaw was hearty and athletic, with an unabashed desire for commercial success—but shared a gusto for life's pleasures that drew them together. Shaw gave Clurman *Siege*, a script set against the backdrop of the Spanish Civil War, but the director didn't care for it; he warned Shaw, as he had Odets and Lawson, about the dangers of subject matter unrelated to his own experiences. He was excited, however, by Shaw's work in progress, a fantasy called *Quiet City* that explored the troubled conscience of a New York department store executive. This seemed like a promising possibility for the Group, and he urged Shaw to complete it.

Hollywood was filled with playwrights making an easy, if artistically barren, living as screenwriters. Clurman held a meeting and urged them to return to the theatre, as he was. He wasn't contemptuous of the movie industry, nor did he think it was killing the theatre. On the contrary, "Since the stage today is hardly a business at all compared to pictures, it had better become an art—in practice as well as in theory. . . . Hollywood will force the theatre to be itself or die." They could make a contribution to that art, he told them:

> If you feel you are really represented by what you write for pictures, forget the theatre. But if you feel that there is something more, something beyond, something essentially different that you want to say . . . you must write for the theatre [which] demands a richer, stronger, fuller expression than ever before. We [in the Group] have chosen this because it is the most insistent urge we feel. There is no other or better reason for such a choice.

Clurman's belief that only in the theatre could playwrights most deeply fulfill and most freely express themselves was unquestionably sincere. Despite his lofty comments on the theatre as an art, however, the administrative reorganization of the Group in New York was proceeding, with his approval and cooperation, along lines designed to make it more of a business. Adler, Bohnen, and Kazan had rented new offices on 44th Street in the Sardi Building, home of the restaurant of the same name, a highly publicized watering hole for Broadway stars. They fired John Wildberg and hired Arthur Krim, a partner in the successful law firm Phillips, Nizer and "the finest theatre and film attorney in the business," Bud Bohnen told his brother. Phil Adler resigned as business manager to cast his lot with Crawford; they replaced him with the savvy and shrewd Kermit Bloomgarden, whose association with the Group didn't prompt him to relinquish his well-paid job as general manager for producer-director Herman Shumlin. They fired Claire Leonard, Group secretary since their second season, intending to replace her with Carolyn Slasky, an experienced administrator from the musicians' union.

In the end Slasky didn't join them, and the executive secretary's job devolved by default on Ruth Young, a Brooklynite barely out of her teens who'd been doing odd jobs around the Group offices. Young was, by her own admission, "a lousy typist and stenographer"; the new Group wasn't always more efficient than the old. But the intent of all these changes was clear: "to put this theatre on a healthy, attractive, exciting, popular level," in Bud Bohnen's words. Though he stoutly insisted this would be "without sacrifice of [our] fundamental intentions," his subsequent remarks made it clear how much the Group's basic values had changed. He spoke of suing the various amateur companies who had named themselves Group theatres back in the heady days of 1935 to indicate general sympathy with the organization that produced *Waiting for Lefty*. "It is well to remind oneself that this is big business," he wrote to his brother. "Our next *Men in White* for instance will be handled entirely differently, for we will send out a flock of road companies, and in general exploit it as a piece of theatrical property . . . we will be more cagey and more box office than we have been in the past."

This was not the institutional theatre the Actors Committee, including Bohnen himself, had called for in their report. This was a commercial enterprise whose leaders happened to believe in doing serious American drama. Clurman, Adler, Bohnen, and Kazan felt the only way to put the Group Theatre back on its feet was to recognize that, like it or not, they were part of the Broadway system and had to organize themselves to work as effectively and profitably as possible within its confines. "We were now veterans with hard experiences behind us," Kazan wrote, "and we'd decided to accept certain realities."

But the Group had been founded on the idea of opposing those realities; some of their best work had been done in defiance of them. The old setup, with the Group committed to sustaining a permanent acting company without a permanent endowment, had been impractical, idealistic, and, in the end, unworkable. Everyone knew they couldn't continue on that basis. Perhaps the idea of supporting thirty people from the proceeds of a Group school was utopian; the Group Theatre Studio the board planned to establish after *Golden Gloves* opened, with Bobby Lewis as director, was considerably more modest in scope and seemed designed primarily to bring new talent into the Group rather than to provide an income for members they already had. Clurman's and the Council's main energies were focused on the reorganization of the Group offices and administration; they proceeded on the assumption that a more pragmatic, businesslike approach, rather than an institutional one, was needed.

There had been a fundamental harmony between form and content in the old Group, a reflection of the dynamic interaction between Clurman's and Strasberg's complementary personalities and interests. Under Strasberg's exacting tutelage, they'd worked and studied together to create a unified technique, with Clurman always reminding them that the technique was necessary because it enabled them to give the fullest expression to plays whose ideas were personally meaningful to them—in the case of Odets, plays that literally grew out of the entire company's thoughts and feelings. With Strasberg gone, technique became less important to Clurman, who'd always felt the Group's fundamental purpose was to present important American plays, that the means to this end were less important than the goal itself. He thought he could discard the less skillful practitioners of the method, keep the Group's best actors, instill their technique in new people, and still call the Group a permanent company. He should have known that means and ends are always inextricably intertwined, that a drastic change in one inevitably affects the other.

Indeed, he may have known it, for it appears from the confused and contradictory newspaper reports published throughout August that he was leaving the details of the Group's reorganization deliberately vague. Reporters scrambling for information relied on sources who obviously weren't sure themselves what was going on. "When thoroughly revamped, organization will be 100% co-op," *Variety* told its readers, whatever that meant. Stella Adler would remain on the West Coast, it continued, and "several other members of the acting company will be out, some in pictures, some on their own, details of this not being clear yet." The *Times* identified Odets as a member of the executive board, a mistake that probably arose from the fact that he was an officer in the new nonprofit corporation whose other members were Clurman and the Council. The *Daily News* reported that the new Group had financial backing and six plays to produce (both statements were untrue) and went on to tag Clurman as the Group's managing director and the Council as an advisory body. This was the arrangement Clurman preferred to remember when he wrote the Group's history in 1945, and in fact was pretty much how it operated in practice.

But with Clurman still on the West Coast, there was no way to judge what relation all these different stories had to reality. For the actors who had been waiting anxiously in New York since January to find out what was going to happen to the Group, this confusion was intolerable. They could see for themselves major changes were being made, and they feared their attachment to the Group would go the way of John Wildberg's, Phil Adler's, and Claire Leonard's. When Clurman arrived in New York on August 23 and shortly thereafter announced his preliminary decisions on the casting of *Golden Gloves*, their concern deepened. The Hollywood contingent were virtually all in: Luther Adler, Bohnen, Brand, Cobb, Carnovsky, and Kazan all had parts, Frances Farmer got the female lead, Nelson understudied her and Brand. Garfield and Lewis, who'd been periodic visitors out west, were also cast. A few Group members who hadn't made the trek were retained:

Art Smith came back from Chicago to take a featured role, and stage manager Mike Gordon got his first acting assignment. Sandy Meisner, though not in the cast, would act as Clurman's assistant. The rest of the small roles went to people new to the Group.

Some Group members were clearly out. Russell Collins had publicly announced he would join Crawford's new efforts. Paula Miller naturally wanted no part of the company her husband had resigned from. Billy Kirkland too remained loyal to Strasberg. The position of people like Beany Barker, Grover Burgess, Bill Challee, Tony Kraber, Herbie Ratner, and Eunice Stoddard remained unclear, and when asked for a clarification of their status Clurman made no promises. He still believed in a permanent company, he said, but the Group could no longer afford to make a permanent commitment to thirty people. There might be roles for them in future productions; there might not.

It was a bitter moment, made more so by the fact that it was extremely ambiguous. Clurman hadn't done anything so simple as drop people as Group members; he'd redefined the entire idea of membership, which now appeared to be contingent on being cast in a Group play. The "permanent company" consisted of a core of actors he believed in; he would add to it as he saw fit. Long-time members he felt hadn't grown sufficiently or improved long-standing faults could no longer count on the Group. "They had to prove their value elsewhere," he told them, which meant he was tossing them back into the commercial theatre he'd promised them as recently as the fall of 1935 they would never have to work in again. Many of them never forgave him for this betrayal of the original Group Idea.

Group members who did have parts in *Golden Gloves* struggled with a painful mixture of emotions. After eight months of uncertainty, they were happy to be back in the theatre, relieved that the Group would go on with a new play by their favorite writer. But they were extremely upset by Clurman's abandonment, whether temporary or permanent, of people who had worked and suffered with them for six years, who were their friends as well as co-workers. Some of them had protested this move; they'd been ignored. They had no choice but to trust that Harold knew what was best for the Group—not all of them felt the same about the Actors Council—for there was no future without him and *Golden Gloves.*

"We didn't know what was going to happen exactly," said Phoebe Brand, her face twisted with distress more than fifty years after the fact at the memory of this difficult time. "What we came back with was a play that Harold had cast." If *Golden Gloves* was a hit, it would partly justify the hard decisions Clurman had made, perhaps even allow him to bring the rest of the old band back into the fold. If it flopped, they were back where they'd been in January, with the additional burden of having discarded their ideals to no purpose.

Rehearsals began on September 13. Once again, it was up to Clifford Odets to save the Group Theatre.

TWELVE
A New Agenda

To the end of his life, Odets would have mixed feelings about *Golden Boy*, as his new play was retitled in October 1937. With most of his theatre pieces, he told an interviewer shortly before his death, "I simply sat down to express a 'state of being.' " On occasion, however, he would write a play where "I would like to get it across in a very commercial way. So I will kind of put blinders on and not express the entire spread of what I feel about this material, but just try to make it theatrically entertaining, and try to get across something that people will like, that will excite them." *Golden Boy* was that kind of work, written deliberately to make money so the Group could stay together, and as such its author held it slightly in contempt, as a work of craftsmanship rather than inspiration. Yet he was proud of his skill: "Before [*Golden Boy*] I was a kind of nutty artist who had some kind of wild gift, and now, only now, was I a man with a ten-million-dollar arm who could really direct the ball just where I wanted it to go."

The play justifies his ambivalence. It is straightforward and appealing, his most carefully constructed work to date. It has a quintessentially American subject: Joe Bonaparte, the young violinist turned boxer, tempted away from his true nature not so much by the desire for money and possessions, though that plays a part, as by the desperate yearning to "be someone," to escape from the ranks of the poor and despised, to achieve recognition and respect in a society where financial success is the only measure of worth. The dialogue is marvelous, with a characteristic Odets mix of humor and shrewd observation: Joe speaking to his manager's mistress, Lorna Moon, one of those rootless, restless women Odets viewed with special tenderness, "The city is full of girls like you who look as if they never had parents"; his brother-in-law describing Eddie Fuseli, a notorious gangster: "He shoots you for a nickel—then for fifty bucks he sends you flowers!" Lorna is neither a floozy nor a good girl gone wrong but a flesh-and-blood woman, trying to do her best for others because she no longer cares much for herself. Eddie is no ordinary thug but a terrifying predator, a homosexual in love with Joe who thinks he can buy him with "good times and silk shirts."

Few of the other characters have that depth. Siggie, the none-too-bright brother-in-law, and Joe's sister, Anna, who spend their time alternately fighting and making love, come perilously close to conventional comic relief. Papa Bonaparte, with his awkward Italian dialect and the burden of carrying the play's moral message, is basically an idea waiting to be fleshed out by a performance. The denizens of the fight world are almost stock figures: the harassed manager, Tom Moody; the wise, kindly trainer, Tokio; the venal club owner, Roxy Gottlieb; the dumb boxer, Pepper White. Because Odets knew little about boxing and not a whole lot more about Italian-Americans, the milieu lacks the sharp authenticity of *Awake and Sing!* and even, in its more diffuse way, *Paradise Lost.* The plot development is simple, almost crude—if not quite melodrama, then certainly, as Odets had subtitled an earlier draft, "a modern allegory."

It is, though, an allegory with considerable emotional power, stemming from Odets' intense identification with Joe and his struggle. *Golden Boy,* as Clurman immediately noted, wasn't really a play about boxing at all; its subject was the ambivalent position of an artist in America. Some of Joe's speeches were nakedly autobiographical: "People have hurt my feelings for years. I never forget. You can't get even with people by playing the fiddle. If music shot bullets I'd like it better"—Odets had been widely quoted as saying works of art should shoot bullets—"artists and people like that are freaks today. The world moves fast and they sit around like forgotten dopes . . . I'm out for fame and fortune, not to be different or artistic! I don't intend to be ashamed of my life!"

As he had so many times before, Odets was expressing the Group's feelings as well as his own. The Actors Committee paper had revealed how tired they were of being regarded as peculiar idealists whose brand of acting, though impressive, was outside the mainstream. As they had written:

> The actors of the Group resent being called "Amateurs" so widely in the press. What the newspaper critics perceive and label amateurism is not the deeper problems or elements of acting that we know of— but rather the lack of simple cleanness and dexterity that a George Abbott show has on first night . . . our productions can achieve entirely EXTERIOR PROFESSIONALISM without sacrificing of "Group content," within the method . . . for our own protection let's adopt the motto, "At Least as Slick as the Best of Broadway."

Hollywood was tempting not just because it offered financial security, though everyone in the Group desperately needed that, but because it bestowed recognition of their skill, it proved that their rejection of the commercial theatre stemmed from a desire for something deeper, not an

inability to meet Broadway standards. The trap of Hollywood under the
studio system was that status and a fat paycheck were all it could provide;
the kind of work they wanted to do wasn't possible there except in very rare
instances.

The parallels between Joe's situation and theirs were obvious, and some
of the joy that infused rehearsals of *Golden Boy* came from their sense of
having met temptation and conquered it—for the time being. The play's
commercially acceptable form and the new business orientation of the
Group management, neither of which stemmed from cynical motives, were
pointing them down a path even more fraught with potential pitfalls than
the difficult, impoverished one they had followed for six years. The Group
had always been by instinct and belief a populist as well as an art theatre,
and Odets argued implicitly that they could be both.

In " 'Democratic Vistas' in Drama," an article published shortly after
Golden Boy opened, the playwright took as his theme the plea in Whitman's
famous essay, a favorite of both Odets and Clurman, for a theatre that spoke
to the masses of ordinary people:

> Let us, for once, give the movies some credit. They have spoken to this
> people. The movies have explored the common man in all of his man-
> ifestations . . . [they] are now the folk theatre of America. But they are
> still not what Whitman asked for in 1871. Hollywood has a great
> genius for business and technical organization. More important, it has
> a great talent for picking important American types and interesting
> and vital themes—in order to exploit them for business purposes . . .
> it is about time that the talented American playwright began to take
> the gallery of American types, the assortment of fine vital themes away
> from the movies. Great audiences are waiting now to have their own
> experiences explained and interpreted.

Odets had a point. The huge audiences who flocked to the Federal Theatre, where ticket prices ranged from a dime to a dollar and many performances were free, had proved how hungry people were for live theatre,
when they could afford it. But the Group was pursuing popular success on
Broadway; to be a hit *Golden Boy* had to appeal to people who could pay
anywhere from one to three dollars for a seat. There is never more than a
fine line between accessibility and compromise, and the forum the Group
worked in remained a problematic one for their ideals, especially given
their newly urgent need for box-office success. Odets believed he could "tell
the truth" and still appeal to this audience: *Golden Boy* ends not with Joe's
realization of where he's gone wrong, but with his death in a car crash;
boxing has ruined his hands and rendered him unfit for the world he abandoned—only death is left for him. Whether comfortable Broadway theatre-

goers would get the point, or see the play as merely a sad story of a poor kid from the slums, remained to be seen.

In casting the play, Clurman grappled with the delicate task of ensuring box-office appeal and also choosing actors capable of the emotional complexity the play required. The touchiest question was the title role. Odets had promised it to Julie Garfield, who on the surface seemed perfect: at twenty-four he was closest to the character's age (twenty-one), he had Joe's tough streak and animal magnetism, and by virtue of his starring role in a hit play he would be a box-office draw as well. But Clurman felt Garfield lacked the pathos and variety the part demanded, and after seeing him in *Having Wonderful Time* Odets agreed. Nonetheless, he was startled by the director's choice: Luther Adler, thirty-four years old, a bit jowly and none too thin. Joe was a sensitive kid searching for meaning, not a fighter, Clurman argued, and Adler could best reveal that quality. Kazan, who wanted the role himself, thought the director cast Luther to please Stella, never far from his thoughts even though 3,000 miles away. Odets may have wondered about this himself, but Luther was his friend and unquestionably one of the Group's finest actors; he went along with Clurman. Garfield swallowed his anger and pride—it had been widely reported in the papers that he would play the lead—and left a $300-a-week star's salary to take the supporting role of Siggie and a $100 paycheck. His belief in the Group Idea was still strong.

Odets also consented to Frances Farmer as Lorna, after some initial hesitation prompted in part by his wife's vehement opinion that Farmer was all wrong. (Rainer, in town to try and patch up her marriage, may have been worried about her husband being placed in close proximity to a gorgeous blonde.) He wasn't happy, however, with Clurman's selection of Morris Carnovsky for Papa Bonaparte and Phoebe Brand as Anna. The director was convinced that what Odets really wanted was "a good Broadway cast," while he, on the contrary, was committed to using as many members of the Group company as he could. He managed to persuade Odets to see things his way, and the final cast included Kazan as Eddie Fuseli, Bud Bohnen as Tom Moody, Art Smith as Tokio, Bobby Lewis as Roxy Gottlieb, Lee Cobb and Mike Gordon in small roles.

Clurman's belief in a permanent company didn't extend to using old Group members in bit parts, which he handed out to a group of newcomers. The only one with much previous experience was Howard Da Silva, who had played the proletarian hero, Larry Foreman, in *The Cradle Will Rock*, the controversial labor musical that got John Houseman and Orson Welles fired from the Federal Theatre Project. But Clurman's eye for talent was keen; among the youngsters were Harry Bratsburg, who later changed his last name to Morgan; Mladen Sekulovich, who reworked his entire name into Karl Malden by the time the *Golden Boy* program was printed; and Martin Ritt, who hung on to his own name.

These new arrivals were awed by the select company they'd been admitted to. "It was easily one of the most exciting experiences of my life," said Ritt. "It's still the best acted play I've ever been around. And Harold was a wonderful, passionate, artistic man; I was impressed by how perceptive he was, humanly, and the things he saw in the play that I hadn't quite seen when I first read it." Malden remembered a superb, utterly self-confident director who knew exactly what to say to help an actor find the right emotion for even the briefest line of dialogue. Malden played a manager whose fighter has been killed by Joe; in his single scene, he pushes his way into the dressing room and cries out, "You murdered my boy!" Just as he was about to deliver the line for the first time, Clurman drew the young actor aside for a chat.

"You told me you came from Chicago by bus," he said; Malden agreed. "And you told me it took two days and a night to get here." Malden agreed again. "Now listen carefully," the director said. "On that bus you were riding, you rode all day and into the night, and suddenly the bus is in an accident—it goes over on its back, rolls over, and it's dark and it's black and you crawl out of the bus, you can't find your suitcase, you're helping other people out, and in about an hour the fire engines come, the ambulances come, and there are rumors around that one person died in the bus, but you don't know who. You're just helping people; there's an excitement, kind of a hysteria going. And another bus comes to take you on your way, and you all get on the bus and you all sit in the seats that you had before, and suddenly in about fifteen minutes you turn and you look over, and you realize the man that was sitting next to you is the man that died. *That's* the moment I want. That realization is what I want—not a completely hysterical kind of thing that would normally be done. No, I want that moment when you just look over . . . and then you come on and you say, 'He's dead. You killed him.' "

"I've never forgotten it," said Malden. "It was the greatest piece of direction I think I've ever had." That was Clurman at his best: the endless, rolling stream of talk dedicated to helping each actor in a uniquely personal way.

Experienced Group actors also credited Clurman with the looseness and creativity of rehearsals. "We felt a kind of freedom and a joy in working that Harold brought to it," said Phoebe Brand. "We'd been up to our ears in classes and experiments with Lee, and I think everybody said, 'Let's do a *show*, let's get a *show* on.' " There was some improvisation, but not much; the emphasis was on the play and its meaning for all of them as a delineation of "a great fight—a fight in which we are all engaged, whatever our profession or craft, [to find] a place in the world as an individual." Max Gorelik, happily back with the Group after a year in Europe on a Guggenheim fellowship, took Clurman's explication of the basic theme and made the play's central visual metaphor the boxing ring, although not a single scene took place there. Joe's dressing room had a diamond-shaped floor plan, like the ring itself, and each separate setting moved onstage on a platform that stood out sharply on the stage, "giving a hint of a prize ring in every scene."

The core of the acting company had been working together so long that they spoke in a kind of shorthand about "spine," "action," and "objective." Farmer, who'd studied the Stanislavsky system in college, knew the terminology but lacked the depth of technique her elders had gained from years of experience. It didn't matter too much in *Golden Boy* because she was so well suited for the part of Lorna, although her inability to alter her basic speech patterns gave the "tramp from Newark" an oddly well bred way of talking. She had an instinctive gift for using her personal feelings in her character's interactions, and her scenes with Luther Adler sizzled with a mutual attraction obvious enough that several Broadway columnists commented on it in print. Sylvia Sidney, who'd come east to be with Adler and was getting indifferent personal notices in a Ben Hecht play called *To Quito and Back*, can't have been pleased, although it's impossible to know now whether Adler and Farmer had anything more than the kind of emotionally intense but essentially professional relationship common among actors in rehearsal.

Adler's performance was, once again, dazzling. Any doubts that he could look the part were quickly dispelled. Ritt, who'd been hired partly because he knew something about boxing, took the star around to the local fight gyms, where he soaked up atmosphere and worked out to give himself a boxer's physique. By the time the show opened he could make the audience believe he was twenty-one. More important, Adler brought to Joe an intimate understanding of the conflicts and yearnings that drove him—and his creator. The actor liked best the scenes in the park, where Joe talks to Lorna about his love for music and his counterposing desire to be rich and famous. He explained his preference to an interviewer after the play opened: "They're closest to me because they contain most of what Clifford Odets is himself. . . . I know what the author means there more richly than I do in any other part of the play—and when you thoroughly understand an author's intention, it's far easier and more of a joy playing those scenes."

The swift pace and confident mood of rehearsals were marred only by the fact that there was no money to finance the show. The Council, which had promised Clurman he would no longer have to shoulder the onerous burden of fund-raising, had been unable to get backing prior to his arrival in New York; he had no better luck. In the end, Odets and Rainer put up most of the money themselves, Walter Wanger settled his contractual obligations to the Group for $2,000, Sidney Kingsley threw in a small sum, and a number of Clurman's friends in Hollywood contributed the additional amount necessary to make up *Golden Boy*'s modest $19,000 budget.

The play opened November 4 at the Belsaco Theatre to a fashionable audience who arrived in limousines, couldn't be bothered to return to the auditorium until well after the intermissions had ended, and when they did finally reclaim their seats, continued talking as though they were still at the bar. This was a real Broadway crowd, attracted by the opportunity to see a movie star in person and to find out whether the Hollywood fleshpots had made any change in the philosophy of America's most famous left-wing playwright. When they could be induced to listen, however, they appeared to like what they heard; the company drew a healthy number of curtain calls, and Odets was cheered when he nervously appeared to take a bow.

Also in the audience were Cheryl Crawford and Lee Strasberg, both prey to extremely mixed emotions. One look at the program told them how much things had changed: on the page that formerly listed first the directors and then every member of the Group, in alphabetical order, they now saw, under the heading "The Group Theatre, Inc.," the names of Harold Clurman as director, the three members of the Council, Molly Thacher as playreader, Bobby Lewis as director of the Group Theatre School and the entire Group business staff. The actors weren't mentioned at all (although they got conventional bios further back in the program). This wasn't the same Group they had worked with and believed in.

The real question was, what did they think of the production? The actors' slangy, gunfire-rapid delivery was certainly nothing like a Strasberg-directed production, and the hearty laughter the early scenes provoked wasn't something they'd heard much of in *The House of Connelly* or *Success Story*. *Golden Boy* definitely had the exterior professionalism the Actors Committee had called for. Had they done it without sacrificing the inner life that was the cornerstone of the Group method?

I went to the opening night of *Golden Boy* in a very odd mood [Strasberg remembered later]. I didn't know whether to root for it or to hope that it was bad. If it was bad, it would show that I was needed. I really didn't know in what way I'd react. I really went with the kind of implied question to myself, Was it worth it? If I had it now to do over again, knowing that I would go through the same thing and then ultimately resign, would it be worth it? And at the end of the performance I came out with something that was a very warming kind of thing, because it seemed to me that it *was* worth it! That if I had it to do over again, knowing that this would be the end result, that it would be worth doing and I would do it. Because what I saw on that stage was something that we had worked for, something that I could appreciate objectively because I had not directed it . . . the work I had done, that I had been part of, had not been wasted.

The critics, by and large, weren't thrilled by *Golden Boy*, though they continued to praise Odets' brilliant way with words. "Few men in our theatre—certainly none of the younger playwrights—can touch him in writing the salty common talk," the *Journal's* John Anderson said in a typical review. "It has limber, it has the steel tension of girder-work, it has the same faultless joining, and it moves the story with smooth precision. . . . It just seems a pity to waste such dialogue and the extraordinarily sharp and persuasive production the Group has given the play." Anderson, like most of his colleagues, found the story trite, and several remarked that it could easily have been a movie. (Playwrights returning to the stage after lucrative absences in California often heard this criticism.) Odets' delineation of the boxing world was strongly criticized for being phony and unconvincing.

The production was almost universally admired, more for the acting than for Clurman's direction, mildly praised in passing. Luther Adler's powerful portrayal of Joe was the focus of every review. "You will go far before seeing a more sincere or a more compelling performance," wrote Sidney R. Whipple in the *Telegram*. "He seems to be Joe Bonaparte, not to play him." Burns Mantle in the *Daily News* went out of his way to note, "none of the younger actors could have done better." Farmer won restrained praise for her sincerity and simplicity—a considerable achievement, since the press always lay in wait for movie stars who presumed they could act. Carnovsky added another stack of raves to his scrapbook for his heartbreaking characterization of the gentle father, though several reviewers noted that an Italian accent wasn't his strong suit. ("I'm not very good at most dialects," the actor admitted years later. "That kind of naturalistic detail doesn't interest me.") The press also liked Kazan's spooky incarnation of Fuseli, Garfield's sharp comic turn as Siggie, and Brand's funny, sexy stint as Anna. The actors in smaller parts received an unusual amount of attention; the ensemble playing, critics commented, was in the best Group tradition.

If they didn't much like the play itself, their criticisms weren't the sort that would keep audiences away; everyone noted *Golden Boy*'s energy and the excitement it generated. It was an immediate box-office smash, pulling in $13,000 in its second week and shooting quickly up to an average of $16,000 to $17,000 by the time it settled into its run. The receipts weren't in the league of a megahit like *I'd Rather Be Right*, the satirical musical spoofing the New Deal to the tune of $35,000 a week, but well within the range of such other current successes as the George S. Kaufman–Moss Hart comedy *You Can't Take It With You* and the dramatic version of John Steinbeck's *Of Mice and Men*. Clurman heaved a sigh of relief that the Group was for the moment on sound financial footing and fled to California a week after the opening, ostensibly to see writers but primarily to try and restore himself to Stella Adler's good graces.

His parting shot, presumably in response to the continued inquiries of old Group members desperately trying to find out what their current status was, was a sign posted on his office door: "Nobody is in the Group Theatre but the cast of *Golden Boy*." It was the first thing Beany Barker saw when she returned from an extended trip to the Soviet Union and strolled into the offices, thinking she was still a member of the Group. She was devastated; she'd had no warning, no letter, it hadn't even occurred to her that there wouldn't be a place for her in the new Group. She tore out of New York, too upset to demand an explanation, and went home to Baltimore, where she worked briefly in radio before winding up in an alcoholic sanitorium for eighteen months.

Barker, a teetotaler today, freely admits she'd been drinking heavily in the tense months before and after the Actors Committee paper. But this was hardly the reason for her fall from grace; Art Smith's and Bud Bohnen's fondness for the bottle hadn't kept them out of *Golden Boy*. Nor was the sign directed at her personally, for it also excluded such Group stalwarts as Grover Burgess, Bill Challee, Tony Kraber, and Eunice Stoddard. In fact, all of them except Barker would work with the Group again, though none would ever have a major part. Stoddard, who had an active life outside the Group and didn't come into the offices when she wasn't working, still considered herself a member; she drifted slowly away from the company rather than making a definite break. Kraber was still taking small roles with the Group more than two years later. The sign meant very little, and yet it meant a lot. It was Clurman's way of making explicit what he had already said rather vaguely on his return from Hollywood: the Group Theatre was now a producer, not a home; actors had to bring more to it than devotion to the Group Idea, and those who in Clurman's judgment did not were more or less out.

The rejected actors sought for years to come up with a reason for their relegation to the sidelines. Some thought it was political, but that seems unlikely: Tony Kraber and Bill Challee were among the most socially active members of the company, while Luther Adler was about as apolitical as it was possible to be in the 1930s. Some had a sneaking suspicion it was sexual—one actress remarked, only half in jest, that she wasn't an easy lay —and indeed Barker, Stoddard, and Patten were among the few Group actresses who'd never been involved with any of the men in the company. But the hard fact was that Clurman's decision was part and parcel of his determination to remake the Group on a new, artistically and commercially healthier basis, retaining only those elements of the past he considered useful.

The actors who'd been retained weren't entirely happy with the new Group either. They thought the Council and business manager Kermit Bloomgarden had too much power and made too many of the important decisions that should have been considered by the whole company. The actors had agreed to allow Clurman to reconstitute the Group as he saw fit, but they were by no means prepared to grant the same privilege to Adler, Bohnen, Kazan, and a newcomer like Bloomgarden. They protested to Clurman that these four had become a clique within the Group, a confederation of would-be managers assuming authority they had no right to.

Clurman dismissed these complaints as prompted by jealousy, and it's true that personal factors entered into it. Bohnen was well liked, but he wasn't perceived as having the same clout as the others. Adler's relationship with the Group had always been stormy: there had been complaints for years about his laziness, his unprofessional behavior in rehearsals and general lack of dedication. To have him turn up as a member of Clurman's inner council was galling. He was a great actor, but was it his administrative know-how or Clurman's desire to please his sister that prompted the director to place him so high in the Group ranks? Bloomgarden's refusal to give up his job with Herman Shumlin fed the suspicion that he wasn't entirely committed to the Group Idea. Some actors feared he would make commercial considerations too much of a factor in choosing scripts; they wondered if the six-week rehearsal period for *Golden Boy*, much shorter than the Group norm, had been his idea and might become standard.

Kazan was a particularly troubling personality for many of the old Group members, who'd never quite adjusted to his transformation from the affable, eager-to-please apprentice they'd patronized (perhaps unconsciously) to the driving, ambitious man who'd won Clurman's affection, respect, and a place at the director's right hand. "He's always true to himself—good or bad," Kazan's friend Odets said of him later. "He just can't be bothered living by any of the made-up rules." For someone like Carnovsky, a believer in the rules of good behavior and human beings' better instincts, this kind of character was both unappealing and disturbing. Kazan's open affair with a young dancer working at the Belasco as an usher sparked resentment on behalf of his wife, Molly, warmly liked by Group members for her sweet personality as well as her tireless devotion to the job of Group playreader.

But Clurman tended to overestimate the importance of these personal aspects. The original Group members had never quite reconciled themselves to the organization's new structure, and now that *Golden Boy* had given them some financial security they hoped for a return to the old, democratic ways. Had Clurman told them unambiguously that he was now absolutely in charge and they could like it or lump it, they might have learned to live with the new order, but that wasn't his style. "A man who used the methods of even a benevolent 'boss' with the Group company would have been unable to hold it," he believed. So he pleaded for their trust, told them he couldn't lead the Group without it, and never really forced them to face the fact that the organization had changed.

The left was worried about the new Group too, particularly as their values were manifested in *Golden Boy*. The *Daily Worker* criticized the Odets drama as "just another Broadway play," plaintively noting that the workers theatres *Lefty* had inspired were waiting for Odets' return to commitment. V. F. Calverton, an independent noncommunist radical, felt *Golden Boy* was "interesting and arresting . . . but certainly not one of his best social plays by any means." Yet there was support for Odets' new ecumenicalism as well. The *New Masses* applauded Odets for taking a great step forward in radical theatre by writing "a play rich in social implications but cast in a new mold: not a strike play, not a soap-box exhortation, not a 'conversion' drama, but a story that grips for its own sake and yet plants its meaning squarely in any eye that can see." This was the mood of the Popular Front in the late 1930s, when ideological debates were muffled in order to draw as many people as possible into the fight to save democracy in Spain and prevent the spread of fascism in Europe.

Group members were very much a part of this effort, submerging any doubts they had about their own organization in a whirl of activities in support of the beleaguered Loyalists. Frances Farmer appeared in "Stars for Spain," a benefit performance in mid-December. She and Erickson, who came east to join her in September and replaced Howard Da Silva in *Golden Boy* in January, sent ten dollars a month to Spain to feed a needy orphan. Odets donated a portion of the *Golden Boy* manuscript to the League of American Writers auction to raise funds for the Medical Bureau to Aid Spanish Democracy; he also peddled tickets to a New Year's Eve benefit at the Waldorf for the same organization. Sylvia Sidney appeared there, as did Luther Adler, Carnovsky, Brand, and the Group's old friend Curt Conway, who'd replaced Garfield in *Having Wonderful Time*. The *Golden Boy* company banded together with a number of other socially conscious theatres to send cigarettes, chocolates, and coffee to the Abraham Lincoln Brigade.

Spain wasn't the only good cause the Group supported. They gave performances to raise money for the Newspaper Guild, the Actors Fund, the Stage Relief Fund, and the Little Red School House. Carnovsky did a Chekhov monologue at an Artef memorial honoring Yiddish author Sholem Aleichem. To protest the Japanese invasion of China, Farmer and Brand gave up silk stockings and wore lisle. (A note to that effect appeared in the *Golden Boy* program.) They stuck to their principles closer to home as well: when the Board of Theatrical Managers, Agents and Treasurers picketed the Belasco as part of its efforts to organize box-office employees, the Group issued a statement of sympathy and pressured Belasco manager Sam Grisman to recognize the union; the pickets were later called off by special arrangement, though other Grisman theatres continued to be barricaded. The benefits arranged by Helen Thompson were good for the Group because they guaranteed an audience, but they also enabled the organizations that participated to make a profit on their resale of the tickets; she booked everything from the Emmanuel Sisterhood to the fraternity Alpha Sigma Tau. The New School symposium Thompson had organized entered its third year, bringing small sums to Group members and friends who lectured there and keeping the Group name constantly before the theatregoing public. "I simply do not know where the time goes," wrote Bud Bohnen, who had a finger in virtually all these pies.

It was wonderful to feel again the sense of living and working in a community inspired by shared ideals. Even the alternative theatre, which had so recently seemed moribund, showed new signs of life. *New Theatre* was dead, but the New Theatre League still operated on a reduced scale, sending scripts and advice to workers groups across the country. New Theatre Nights to benefit the League continued to give Group members a chance to work on experimental plays; Art Smith directed a cast including several members of the *Golden Boy* company in *Plant in the Sun*, a drama about a sit-down strike in New York that played Sunday-night performances through the winter and spring. The Federal Theatre Project proved that reports of its impending demise were greatly exaggerated with a bold, innovative production of *One-Third of a Nation*, a Living Newspaper dramatization of slum conditions that won kudos from *Variety* for the professionalism of its presentation as well as the power of its theme.

Just how eclectic and nondogmatic the alternative theatre had become could be seen in two new productions that opened in the same month as *Golden Boy*. *Pins and Needles* was a satirical revue produced by the International Ladies Garment Workers Union, one of the militant CIO unions that, encouraged by the example of the workers theatres, had set up companies of their own. Harold Rome's lively music and pungent lyrics were performed by an all-union cast (directed in the dances by former Group instructor Gluck Sandor) at the ILGWU's own theatre, the Labor Stage on 39th Street. Audiences adored the humor and snap of numbers like "Sing Me a Song of Social Significance" and "One Big Union for Two," which showed that you could have fun with the movement without abandoning your principles, and they seemed equally receptive to the stronger political satire provided by contributors like the Group's press agent, Manny Eisenberg. You didn't have to be a Marxist to be prolabor anymore, nor did warnings against the dangers of accommodation with Hitler automatically mark you as a dangerous radical.

The most talked-about production of the season was *Julius Caesar*, the inaugural effort of the Mercury Theatre, the classical repertory company formed by John Houseman and Orson Welles after their unceremonious departure from the WPA. Performed on a bare stage in modern dress, this *Caesar* depicted the Roman general as a prototypical fascist and Brutus as a liberal intellectual who comes reluctantly to realize that only violence can stop a dictator. Enthusiastically reviewed and well attended (at a top ticket price of $2.00), it offered dazzling proof that the classics could be as relevant as a director chose to make them. It was both an inspiration and something of a goad to the Group, who talked a lot about wanting to perform the classics but never actually did anything about it. There was a more or less amicable rivalry between the two theatres; Houseman regarded his friend Clurman's company as stylistically stodgy, while the Group director preferred to view the Mercury's success as more a result of the extensive media coverage of Welles's flamboyant personality than any real public interest in the classics or a repertory theatre.

Yet Clurman still believed in institutional theatre. He told himself that in the changes made to revive the Group the organization "had not deviated in its purpose or basic methods, but had made a sane synthesis of its years of experience." With *Golden Boy*'s revenues steadily fattening the Group treasury, he hoped once again to give the Group actors both continuity and opportunities for growth. Upon his return from California in early December, he gave a number of interviews stating that the Group intended to expand its permanent company to thirty or forty, "made up of a nucleus of regulars surrounded by auxiliaries, all on a salary basis of 30 weeks a year." (The *Golden Boy* company had standard run-of-the-play contracts.) "The financial advantage provided by *Golden Boy*," the *Herald Tribune* reported, "makes it possible to invite players the Group has wanted for a long time, provide employment for all the regular members and recall a number of others to the old stand." He also talked of experimental Sunday-night performances to present plays too special for regular Broadway runs; he hoped to begin with an Odets one-act about Cuba, *The Law of Flight*.

These were all just dreams at the moment, but one project affirming the Group's desire to become an institutional theatre was actually in operation: the Group Theatre School, or Studio, as it was more often called. Bobby Lewis had selected fifty students out of the thousand who applied, and classes began on November 15. The Studio was a scaled-down version of the school Helen Thompson had been proposing for two years—tuition was $100 for a twenty-week semester, as opposed to the $400 for a full-year course she'd suggested—but the aims were essentially the same. Lewis and Kazan taught most of the classes, with assistance from dance and speech instructors, and the students included younger members of the *Golden Boy* cast like Will Lee and Martin Ritt as well as other New York actors eager to learn more about the Group method. The Studio added some modest amounts of money to the Group treasury, but it wasn't intended to be the full-scale financial support Thompson had envisioned. The organization's first commitment was to produce Broadway shows with the Group acting company, and the Studio lasted only one semester.

Clurman had commercial prospects on his mind as well as permanence and continuity. At the same time he was talking about experimental programs and an organization of forty actors, he and Sandy Meisner were looking for movie stars to cast in a road tour of *Golden Boy*, which would contribute nothing to the Group's technique or permanent company but potentially a great deal to their coffers. The actors could hardly be blamed for being confused about the Group's intrinsic nature when their director himself was trying so strenuously to ride two horses at once.

The Group's second production of the season revealed the complex mix of old and new forces working within the organization. *Casey Jones* was written by Robert Ardrey, a young playwright Clurman had been cultivating since they'd first met in Chicago nearly two years earlier. Its theme—the tendency of skilled workers to identify themselves with the company they work for rather than their fellow employees—was extremely topical in light of the bitter ongoing division between the craft-oriented AFL and the CIO's militant believers in industrial unionism. The money for it was raised with relative ease; a divorcee named Dorothy Willard, from Chicago's wealthy McCormick family, put up $20,000 because she admired the Group. It gave

Kazan his first opportunity to direct a Group production—Meisner stepped into his role in *Golden Boy*—and he hired his old friend Tony Kraber as assistant stage manager and Eunice Stoddard and former apprentices Curt Conway and Frances Williams as actors. But the leads were given to outsiders: a novice actress Kazan thought had potential, Katharine Bard, and two movie stars, a rising young actor named Van Heflin and, in the title role of an aging engineer losing his eyesight, a hard-bitten veteran, Charles Bickford. "We were beginning, all of us, to feel this wasn't fair," said Stoddard of the decision to use non-Group actors in major roles for the second time. "It wasn't following the whole precedent of the Group."

Rehearsals began on January 17. Kazan was extremely nervous. Directing professionals in a commercial production was very different from working with the amateurs who worshipped him down at the Theatre of Action; he felt pressured by the amount of money involved and his need to prove himself to Clurman and the rest of the Group as a Broadway-caliber director. He saw rehearsals as a power struggle between himself and the strong-willed Bickford, and he believed the actor was winning. None of this was apparent to Stoddard, who found Kazan confident and sure of what he wanted, nor to an Associated Press reporter who visited a rehearsal and saw a relaxed atmosphere; the director's problems with Bickford may have been largely in his own head. His nerves weren't helped when early run-throughs revealed Katharine Bard's performance wasn't taking shape as quickly as those of the other actors and Clurman brought in Stella Adler to coach her.

Adler had returned from Hollywood in late December with Clurman's promise that, if the Group still had no decent parts for her, she would at least get the chance to develop as an assistant director on forthcoming productions. Group actors who'd done scene work with her during the summers found her a superb coach, so Clurman's action, though undoubtedly prompted by his desire to find something for her to do, wasn't unreasonable. But Kazan, though he pretended to go along with the idea, was furious. Always touchy on the subject of his status within the Group, he felt Adler's arrival undermined his authority. He also believed she would merely frighten the sensitive, inexperienced Bard with her forceful personality, and in this he may have been correct, for the actress finally had to be replaced. Shortly before *Casey Jones* opened, a Broadway pro named Peggy Conklin stepped into the part. Kazan was very bitter in retrospect about the production, feeling he'd been betrayed by his friend Clurman and forced to make his Broadway directorial debut with less than his best work.

The critics who attended opening night at the Fulton Theatre on February 19, however, liked Kazan's vigorous direction. He divided the little praise *Casey Jones* garnered with Max Gorelik, whose imaginative locomotive set was everyone's favorite element of the production. Using completely nonrealistic components—the engine was constructed of black velour flats mounted on a platform—the designer created the illusion of movement with forced perspective and a hefty assist from Mike Gordon's production staff, who shook the platform to and fro, blew steam in the actors' faces with an offstage fan, and ran the sound-effects tape (recorded at a New York Central switching station) at a volume so loud that by opening night Bickford was hoarse from shouting above it. Gorelik gave his locomotive "so much dynamic power," wrote Brooks Atkinson in the *Times*, "that nearly every member of the audience longed to drive it."

Like most of his colleagues, Atkinson was less impressed by the play, which he found "long on character and short on sustained drama." The press had been to another Ardrey opening only eleven days earlier, when *How to Get Tough About It*, a drama of a cement factory strike, opened at the Martin Beck. Richard Watts noted in his *Herald Tribune* review of *Casey* that it had the same virtues and defects as its predecessor. "Again [Ardrey] demonstrates his talent for individual scenes, freshly observed characters and vigorous, racy prose. But, unfortunately, with this indisputable skill, there still goes that strange inability to turn so many excellent parts into a satisfying and properly integrated whole." Kazan's direction, "more professional than most Group offerings of the past," helped a lot, observed Wilella Waldorf in the *Post;* she went on to note that *Casey* hardly seemed like a Group production at all, with a cast composed primarily of movie stars and newcomers to the company.

In the face of reviews like those, *Casey* managed to eke out a three-week run only because Helen Thompson had arranged enough theatre parties to carry it that long. But this quick failure had been worth doing, Clurman felt, if for no other reason than that it gave Kazan a chance to direct and cemented the Group's relationship with a talented new playwright.

Ardrey had been inspired in his writing by the example of Clifford Odets. He remembered his excitement at reading the reviews of *Waiting for Lefty* with his mentor, Thornton Wilder: "A theatre engaged with its times had arrived in New York, and the fresh wind blew all the way to Chicago." Yet Ardrey's work, though it often dealt with labor subjects and shared Odets' buoyant faith in the common man and woman, had a tentative, anti-ideological tone that was as typical of the late 1930s as *Lefty* had been of the the decade's stormy, militant early years. The point of *Casey Jones* wasn't "the heartlessness of corporations," he told a reporter just after it opened. It was the personal story of a man who used his job to escape from a world he didn't understand. "Mr. Ardrey . . . has no crack-pot ideas about reforming the world through the theatre," his interviewer wrote approvingly.

Ardrey had a genuine affection for ordinary human beings, whose language he loved and captured beautifully in his dialogue. He wanted to write about them because they were the essence of America, and he had his own ideas about the proper way to do it.

It has never been an American tradition to speak truly of the people [he commented in the *Times*]. Always we have thought of them wishfully, according to our own ends. A social evangelist, in a far-away temple, shouts loudly of the people and class solidarity. Are these Americans class conscious? I can only show them to you and say, judge for yourselves. A fascist leader condemns them as stupid. Are they stupid? It would seem to me that an unschooled man who is aware and puzzled is frequently more intelligent than a man with an educated mind, convinced and closed. But that's merely my judgment, so don't accept it. Accept only my people and judge for yourself.

This was a far cry from *Lefty*, which for all its humanism had asked audiences to accept its conclusions, not judge for themselves. As the threat of a second World War increasingly overshadowed every other political problem, Ardrey was not the only creative writer to feel the need for more compassion and tenderness in public discourse, to recoil from the harsh rhetoric of the worst Depression years.

His style suited the mood of the new Group, and they hoped for more plays from him. Clurman was aware of the danger posed by depending too much on Odets for material, especially now that the playwright was bouncing back and forth between New York and California, trying to salvage his shaky marriage, make a living in films, and write for the theatre all at the same time. The Group was still promising to produce *The Silent Partner*, and Odets had a new idea for a play about a dentist, but there was no guarantee that either would be ready any time soon.

The other playwright most closely attached to the Group seemed lost forever to the movie industry. Clurman had arranged for John Howard Lawson to be hired to rewrite Odets' *Castles in the Air* screenplay, which emerged from Lawson's pen as a surprisingly political (for Hollywood) Spanish Civil War film called *Blockade*. The director may well have rued the day he did so when he visited Lawson in California that fall, for the playwright now felt the constraints on screenwriters were no worse than those imposed by Broadway investors; he intended to stay where he was and write movies.

Molly Thacher had been working hard all season to develop new writers for the Group. Just after *Golden Boy* opened she and Clurman met with some New York playwrights to discuss their potential association with the company. Several turned over works in progress to be performed at the Studio, and some continued to talk with Thacher about their ideas.

Clurman was still eager to do *Quiet City*, which had been announced throughout the winter as the Group's next production, but Irwin Shaw was having trouble with it. He'd been distracted by rehearsals for *Siege*, the Spanish Civil War play Clurman disliked, which had been picked up by a commercial manager and given an unsuccessful production. Disappointed by its failure, Shaw was now ready to get back to *Quiet City* and the Group; on March 15 he departed with Thacher and Clurman for a two-week visit to Cuba to iron out a final script. Shortly after their return, Thacher announced a contest for playwrights under age twenty-five: the prize would be $500 and the possibility of a Group production. Manuscripts weren't due until January 1, 1939, so this would do nothing to solve the Group's immediate lack of plays, but it was a step toward building a core of Group playwrights.

Meanwhile, *Golden Boy* continued to pack audiences in at the Belasco. "Our present plan is to continue through the summer," Bud Bohnen wrote his brother. "Not that we aren't pretty sick of it, but we have a certain objective to build a subsidy of $50,000 by fair means or foul, so we are going to plough on." The projected non-Group road tour had fallen through, but Clurman made a deal with a West Coast manager for a limited engagement directed by Stella Adler, who began rehearsals in California on March 11. Cast with solid film and theatre actors but no big stars, the production did only so-so business during its three weeks in San Francisco and only somewhat better in Los Angeles, where it closed May 14 without having noticeably enriched the Group.

The New York company had settled into the comfortable routine of appearing in a hit. Luther Adler spent most of his free time with Sylvia Sidney, trying vainly to duck photographers when they went out. Their affair was now public knowledge, though they denied rumors that they were about to get married. A *Daily News* columnist tried to stir up the old story about Adler and Farmer by reporting that the costars were no longer speaking to each other offstage. Sidney and Farmer were used to this kind of scrutiny —Farmer had always detested it—but it was quite a novelty for Group actors to see their personal lives covered in the gossip columns.

Farmer and Erickson were living quietly on the unfashionable Upper West Side, less interested in having their picture taken in smart restaurants than in their work for the Theatre Arts Committee, as the Theatre Committee to Aid Spanish Democracy had just been renamed. They weren't the only Group members active in TAC; Clurman and Garfield were both on the executive board, and Brand, Carnovsky, and Gorelik did a lot of work there as well. Some of the liveliest theatre that spring happened, not in a Broadway house, but in an old nightclub on East 55th Street called Chez Firehouse, where "Cabaret TAC" was offering a decidedly different kind of after-hours entertainment to raise money for the cause. The lively political revue changed from week to week, borrowing material from shows like *Pins and Needles* as well as offering new sketches that spoofed movies and the Broadway theatre in addition to pointing up the vicious absurdities of fascism. With the help of stars like Farmer and Erickson, who often acted as M.C., "Cabaret TAC" attracted chic and well-heeled viewers who could afford to assist the Loyalists generously. TAC's concerns weren't confined to foreign affairs; it urged support for the Federal Arts Bill, designed to make the Federal Theatre Project permanent, and issued a magazine that covered the arts from a leftist but broadly nonsectarian point of view.

Erickson was now firmly enough attached to the Group to turn down a featured role in a Shubert production to keep his forty-dollar-a-week part in *Golden Boy*. He did leave in late March, along with Meisner, to act in *All the Living*, a drama set in an insane asylum produced by Cheryl Crawford and directed by Lee Strasberg. Clurman's relations with his former colleagues, though strained, weren't hostile; he released both actors and urged Erickson to profit from Strasberg's instruction. Kazan stepped back into his old role as Fuseli; the enthusiastic audience response that his chilling performance always inspired boosted his self-confidence after the battering it had taken from *Casey*.

Collective Group morale got a bad blow in April, when Julie Garfield announced he'd signed a two-picture deal with Warner Brothers. Garfield had never really forgiven Clurman for casting Luther Adler instead of him as Joe Bonaparte, and he'd been pursued avidly by movie studios ever since he'd first made a splash in *Awake and Sing!* Three years of turning down lucrative offers was enough. The Group's promise of artistic fulfillment rang slightly hollow to someone who'd lost out on the part of a lifetime; Warner Brothers was a studio where the street-smart, socially conscious actor could feel comfortable; he decided to take his chance. But his fellow Group members were stunned and angry. They held a meeting to tell him he still had a lot to learn as an actor—he hadn't been all that great in *Having Wonderful Time*—and in any case it was wrong to tear a hole in the seamless fabric of the *Golden Boy* ensemble by leaving in the middle of the run.

Most upset of all were Morris Carnovsky and Bud Bohnen. Carnovsky had poured his own passionate idealism into his performance as Papa Bonaparte, and he saw Garfield's departure as just the kind of tragic mistake Joe had made. "Many of our most genuinely talented young people prefer to make their marks as successes in the conventional and material sense of the word to retaining their integrity," he'd told an interviewer that winter, describing *Golden Boy* as an indictment of ambition. "They prefer the meretricious, immediate rewards, the popular recognition of success to the best uses of their own peculiar genius." It was painful for him to see his words verified by an actor he'd loved and regarded as a protégé; he barely spoke to Garfield after the meeting. Bohnen was so worked up that on the day Garfield was to leave he rushed down to Grand Central, still in make-up after a matinee, fell on the actor's neck, pleaded with him not to stay in Hollywood, then burst into tears. He shook Garfield badly, but couldn't change his mind. Will Lee took over the defecting actor's role in *Golden Boy*.

Clurman refused to badger Garfield to stay and viewed the meeting held to dissuade him with alarm. "What made me impatient . . . was not the unfairness to the individual involved (who I was sure could take it) but a certain deaconish smugness that crept into the proceeding," he wrote later. "I not only disliked this quality, I feared it. It did not represent clarity of mind or strength of character, but rather self-protective turning from reality. It was as if the people who indulged themselves in these virtuous homilies were not so averse to the sin in the person they belabored as to the temptation his sin aroused in themselves." Clurman had given plenty of virtuous homilies in the past, but he was no longer prepared to bind actors to the Group with moral imperatives.

Clurman was mulling over an offer from RKO to direct films; he thought he might try working six months of the year in Hollywood and spending the other six in New York with the Group. In late April he went west to find out if Selznick was willing to consider such a deal and to see Stella Adler's *Golden Boy* production. It didn't take him long to decide that he couldn't run the Group and make movies at the same time; the fact that he'd even considered it, he realized uneasily, was a sign of how much the 1937 sojourn in California had affected the Group. Before then, Hollywood was largely an abstract concept, a mythical place that offered ludicrous sums of money but didn't seem quite real. It had tempted away a few comrades, and the departures of Franchot Tone and Joe Bromberg had been protested and regretted, but no one who remained with the Group had immediate personal experience of just how pleasant life in California could be.

Hollywood offered an alternative to the Group that Broadway even in its best days never had. When the company was formed in 1931 the directors promised the actors the security of permanent employment (however ill paid) as well as artistic fulfillment, contrasting this with the on-again-off-again rhythm of work in the New York theatre. The decision Group actors like Beany Barker made to abandon their dreams of Broadway stardom in favor of a higher goal was difficult, but they were helped at least in part by the knowledge that a career on the New York stage was a chancy thing for all but the biggest stars. The movie studios, by contrast, offered long-term contracts and large salaries even to lower-ranked actors; it was the only way they could assure the steady supply of talent they needed for the hundreds of films they cranked out each year. "The theatre—why, it's just an art," Clurman had remarked to Walter Wanger during his first visit to Hollywood. "But this—this is an industry!"

There was never any possibility that movie careers could fulfill them as actors the way the Group did: the industry required employees, not artists. Good acting happened in Hollywood, but it was mostly at a professional, craftsmanlike level which was antithetical to the Group's way of working. Frances Farmer had told them how unreceptive film directors were to any leisurely exploration of a part in depth, and Carnovsky had experienced the same haste even in a "prestige" production like *The Life of Emile Zola*. The pace of filmmaking made a four-week Broadway rehearsal period look positively slow. It took a very special kind of talent to work quickly and still give a good performance and it wasn't necessarily a talent Group actors wished to develop. When they returned to New York to do *Golden Boy*, they'd made a choice; as Clurman put it, they preferred "a hazardous path of personal expression [over] generally lucrative employment in a craft." They had no regrets, but this new sacrifice put an additional burden on their relationship to the Group. They had given up a lot for their theatre, and they expected a lot in return.

Their belief that they'd made the right choice was reinforced May 13 by the happy news that Franchot Tone would be rejoining the Group for the 1938–1939 season. In his nearly six years in Hollywood, Tone had made more than thirty pictures, most of them thoroughly undistinguished; he looked east to the achievements of his old friends with nostalgia and an increasing desire to be part of their work. His marriage to Joan Crawford was on the rocks, his contract with MGM would be up soon, there seemed no reason to stay. He was ready to make a commitment to the Group even though they had as yet no plays definitely set for fall. Clurman still hoped to do *Quiet City*, with Stella Adler as codirector and Tone in the lead, but the script remained problematic. Odets was in the middle of his worst crisis ever with Rainer; the dentist play he'd spoken of as his next project was only an outline. Nonetheless, Clurman returned to New York with renewed faith that the Group was back on course with a program of continuous activity.

He arrived in the midst of a serious business crisis. The *Golden Boy* box-office receipts had taken an unexpected nose dive. The Group had counted on the play carrying them through till the fall, when they planned to re-hearse their new productions while on the road with a previously arranged seven-city, three-month tour of *Golden Boy* with the original cast. The Group's share of the *Golden Boy* movie rights, which had just been sold to Columbia for $70,000, wouldn't keep the actors solvent for three months. Suddenly they were faced with the equally unattractive alternatives of be-ginning the tour in the summer, never a good time to tempt people away from their vacations and into hot theatres, or disbanding until fall to allow the actors to pick up what movie work they could. No one wanted to scatter the Group again, but they turned down an offer to take *Golden Boy* to London when the manager insisted on an unlimited engagement that would have delayed or even precluded a fall season in New York. In the nick of time, a second English manager offered to finance a two-month visit, com-plete with a 30 percent salary raise for the actors to cover British taxes. The Council even managed to convince *Golden Boy*'s American backers to allow the actors to divide the Group's share of the London profits.

There was one small hitch. The money for the trip was being put up by Lillian Emerson, an American actress living in London on the proceeds of her family's investment in Bromo Seltzer. Emerson wanted to play Lorna Moon, and after some hesitation Clurman agreed. Frances Farmer's release from her Paramount contract was only for the New York run of *Golden Boy* and the fall tour with the original company; technically, she was obligated to go back to Hollywood for the summer if the play closed. This was true, but Farmer had been negotiating with the studio all spring to get out of her contract altogether; she wanted to stay with the Group, and she was hurt when they made a deal without her. In fairness to Clurman, it should be noted that Farmer was also in the middle of a lawsuit with her former agent, and there was no way of knowing if the case would be settled before the Group was scheduled to leave for England. (In fact, she won the suit on July 1, only ten days after *Golden Boy*'s London opening.) Under the circumstances, he "did not think it too mean a compromise" to agree to star an actress known more for her good looks than her ability in a production based on ensemble acting for which she would only have three or four rehearsals before opening night. The Council agreed, but not every other Group member did: "one or two people informed me in no uncertain terms that this decision betrayed a thoroughgoing opportunism on my part," the director later admitted.

Golden Boy closed in New York on June 4. Farmer and Erickson went back to California to make a dreary film called *Ride a Crooked Mile*. On the 8th the rest of the Group sailed for England. Phoebe Brand and all the men in the company save Luther Adler boarded the *President Harding* for a leisurely cruise cross the Atlantic, while Clurman, Odets, and both Adlers took the swifter *Queen Mary* in order to have a few additional days for rehearsal with Emerson.

Sylvia Sidney, who went to see them off, returned home to discover the afternoon papers proclaiming "Luise Rainer Sues Odets for Divorce." The couple's seventeen-month marriage had been troubled from the start, and their savage quarrels throughout the spring climaxed in a ghastly exchange of telegrams on May 28, the first from Rainer announcing she was pregnant, the second from Odets stating coldly, "Dear Luise Will wire you Monday because now I don't know what to say Love Clifford." Shattered, the actress had an abortion and informed Odets three days before his departure that she was going to see a lawyer. He'd told his Group friends none of this, though they noted his brooding silence and obvious emotional distress; apparently he wasn't expecting Rainer to take public steps so promptly.

Sidney put a radio-phone call through to the *Queen Mary* to warn Clurman and Stella Adler of the press reception undoubtedly waiting for Odets in London. (Rainer, who in March had won the Academy Award for best actress for an unprecedented second year in a row, was a big star, especially in Europe.) Adler broke the news to Odets, and when Clurman went on deck to see how his friend was taking it, the playwright had just removed his wedding ring and was throwing it into the ocean. It was fitting that Odets got the word in the company of his closest Group companions; one of the issues that had most bitterly divided him from his wife was his commitment to the Group and her despairing sense that she would never truly be welcomed into the intimate circle of friendship created by years of shared struggle and achievement. The Tone-Crawford marriage had also broken up in part because she tired of hearing him complain about how much he hated Hollywood and how badly he wanted to go back to the Group.

Greeted on his arrival by the anticipated hordes of reporters, Odets, who was often intemperate and indiscreet when he gave interviews, managed to keep his cool. "It's a pity," he told the press. "I did know something like this was planned, but all the same it is very sad. . . . I hope we shall remain friends."

Though sorry for Odets, the Group actors were rather relieved that his stormy marriage was at an end; they hoped he could now devote his full attention to his work. There wasn't much time to spend commiserating with him, for the *Golden Boy* premiere was only a few days away. They were excited and nervous about their invasion of the London stage. Then as now, it was considered the fountainhead of the English-speaking theatre; London productions were frequently imported to Broadway with great success, and half the bad actors in America affected phony British accents and stagy gestures in their efforts to imitate the polished, stylized sweep of English classical acting. Yet there was another side to the British theatre, a loose confederation of working-class amateur companies that looked to America, and especially Odets, for their inspiration. *Lefty* had been performed more than 2,000 times up and down the country by groups like the Merseyside Left Theatre Club in Liverpool and London's Unity Theatre club, the most famous and well established of the insurgent companies. Group members were eager to exchange ideas with their overseas allies in the progressive theatre.

They wondered, however, if the audience at the St. James Theatre in the West End, London's equivalent of Broadway, would be as sympathetic to the Group. *Golden Boy* was scheduled to open there on June 21, and the alterations made by the Lord Chamberlain, the British stage censor, who insisted on the removal of such incendiary lines as "Did you sleep with her?" and "I don't believe the bull about the meek will inherit the earth," made them worry lest the play was too strong for the apparently delicate-minded West End crowd.

Their fears increased during the opening-night performance—but were happily dispelled at the end. The audience "didn't make a sound during the entire play, didn't say a word," remembered Phoebe Brand. "We said, 'They don't like it,' but at the end they just stood up and yelled. They were just quiet, listening; I've never heard anything quite like it." Part of the breath-less attention was due to Odets' highly colloquial American dialogue, which was hard for some of the audience to understand; the *Morning Post* noted that not until the plot began to emerge unmistakably in the third scene did the spectators really begin to follow the play. But they were thrilled by the passion of Group acting. "The speakers may sometimes leave one guessing as to the precise significance of what they have said, but never in doubt as to what they feel," commented the *Observer*.

The British press was overwhelmed by the intense realism of the Group's performance. "Even those who appear on the stage only to vanish are not simply decorations to the plot but people who think and feel, and whose thoughts and feelings are sensitively conveyed to the audience," wrote the critic for the *Spectator*. "If the acting of the members of this cast is typical of acting in America, dramatic writing is not the only form of theatrical accomplishment in which England, compared to America, loiters several leagues to the rear." The *Times* spoke of "a furious energy of acting as though that art had just been invented, totally unlike the English duplication of esteemed successes."

The box office took a few weeks to build, but by early July *Golden Boy* was breaking house records at the St. James. The production was such a smash that the producers persuaded the Group to arrange for a second American company to come over and continue the engagement when the original cast departed in August; they expected the play to run for a year.

The Group Theatre was the toast of the town. When a number of the actors walked into the Ivy Restaurant, London's equivalent of Sardi's, Dame May Whitty loudly informed fellow British thespians gathered at the bar, "You may as well stop trying, boys and girls, the Yankees are here." Bud Bohnen wrote to his brother:

It's hard to describe how this play has hit London between the eyes! The *ensemble acting* has been lauded up and down and the Group is regarded as the fountain-head of all true health of the English speaking theatre. . . . We [are] truly the *rage* here—international artistes— ambassadors of virile culture from America, etc. It's all very good for us at this time.

Bohnen's oblique final comment may have baffled his brother, for the rest of his letter made no mention of the tensions that plagued the company despite their London triumph. Odets, deeply unhappy over his failed marriage, channeled his bitterness into a brooding consideration of everything he felt was wrong with the Group Theatre. He and Luther Adler, who were sharing a flat in Mayfair, spent a lot of time discussing the personal and professional weaknesses of their friend Harold, the terrible effect they were having on the Group, and how they might be remedied. They called a meeting with Clurman, Bohnen, Kazan, and Bloomgarden, the four men who with them constituted the Group's self-appointed leadership, to present their thoughts on the organization's future.

Adler began by declaring that now the Group was in such good financial shape thanks to *Golden Boy*, they should make plans to establish themselves as a repertory theatre. He and Odets had drawn up a list of great American plays that should be included in their repertory, along with notes on possible Group casting; they wanted to start work immediately. Clurman agreed that repertory was the Group's ultimate goal, but argued that at this moment they still couldn't afford it. They hadn't had an easy time simply raising money for individual shows, he reminded them, and repertory was far more expensive. Did they have any kind of a budget, outlining in specific dollars-and-cents terms how they could pay for it?

Adler and Odets responded with a flurry of personal recriminations that appear to have been the real message they intended to deliver all along. Clurman was lazy, they shouted, he had no respect for his talent, he was jeopardizing the Group with his subordination to Stella Adler. Odets began to rant about Group actors; he had long since lost his sense of solidarity with the company and acquired the aggrieved feeling, common in playwrights, that the performers he was stuck with weren't bringing out all the values of his plays. Group actors weren't working to develop as artists, he stormed. He was sick of all of them; a movie star like Jimmy Cagney could do more for his plays than anyone in the company. Considering that he was in a room with three members of the *Golden Boy* cast, it wasn't the most tactful thing to say, and Kazan jumped into the battle to support Clurman. He accused Odets and Adler of being blind to hard economic realities and inventing problems to satisfy their own need for emotional excitement. Tempers rose, fists and furniture flew, and the meeting degenerated into a shouting match where people said a lot of things they hadn't thought through and didn't really mean. Clurman was left with the unpleasant sense that his closest associates in the Group didn't trust him or his judgment.

He was terribly torn between the Group and Stella Adler, and his effort to draw her back into the organization by making her director of the second-string company was only partly successful. Adler was willing to coach a new set of actors, most of them from her West Coast production, and spend another few months in Europe. She had no intention, however, of returning to the Group and an impoverished life-style in New York. Her taste in accommodations ran to London's Dorchester Hotel, where she and Clurman were living cheek by jowl with groups of visiting Nazi officials and reactionary supporters of Franco. Adler, who was active in the clandestine movement to get endangered Jews out of Germany, apparently wasn't troubled by the contradiction between her political beliefs and her neighbors at the Dorchester, but it bothered Clurman. Europe was a grim place to be in the summer of 1938, only a few months after the Anschluss made Austria part of the Third Reich. He had no desire to stay longer than necessary, and when Adler moved on to Paris, he joined her only briefly—with Odets, Kazan, and Bloomgarden in tow—before embarking with them on the *Champlain* July 20 for New York. Adler remained behind, her feelings about Clurman and the Group just as complicated and painful as they had been in 1931.

Back in England, the *Golden Boy* company had been keeping busy. Bobby Lewis went to Dartington Hall the last weekend in June to attend classes and observe Michael Chekhov's work with young English actors. The Group heard his report with great interest: Lewis continued to admire Chekhov's emphasis on movement and visual stylization, but he thought the students often merely reproduced the master's physical gestures without capturing the inner emotional force that inspired them. "A great actor might also be a great teacher," he told them, "but it ain't necessarily so." Lewis probably didn't tell them what a relief he found the serene, spiritual mood at Dartington in contrast to the Group's embattled atmosphere. Despite his generally light-hearted attitude and the stream of witticisms with which he enlivened Group gatherings, Lewis was sensitive and easily upset by the stresses of Group life. He was so unnerved by the arguments flying back and forth before Clurman's departure that he collapsed and had to be sent home at the end of July.

The more politically minded Group members tried to take their minds off their leaders' quarrels by immersing themselves in the British alternative theatre and making a contribution to the class struggle in this horrifyingly class-bound nation. Will Lee visited Glasgow to address a workers theatre company; back in London, he founded a Playwrights' Forum and Conference to discuss the problems of the labor stage and tell English groups about such American experiences as the Federal Theatre's Living Newspapers and the New Theatre League. Moe Jacobs, who'd come along to do the Group's props, spent his spare time in the London pubs—organizing a bartenders union. The whole Group went to Lancashire to study industrial conditions, and they attended a meeting of the Left Book Club Theatre Group, an offshoot of the famous club founded in 1936 by the publisher Victor Gollancz. Even Luther Adler, less active than some though by no means without a social conscience, made a special trip to the House of Commons to praise the Unity Theatre at a meeting of M.P.'s.

Sylvia Sidney arrived on July 25 to visit him, and although the couple refused to comment on the frenzied press speculation about their possible nuptials, that in fact was why she was there. They were married quietly at the Caxton Hall Register Office on August 13. The brief ceremony took place at 8:00 a.m. to avoid reporters. The only guest was E. J. O'Bryen, one of *Golden Boy*'s London producers; when they realized they needed a second witness, a painter working on the hall was pressed into service.

On this cheerful note, the Group's stimulating, turbulent London visit ended. *Golden Boy* closed on August 20. The company crossed the channel to Paris for a quick vacation before boarding the *Champlain* for America on August 25. They arrived in New York September 1, less than two weeks before the road tour was set to open in Chicago. They were delighted to hear that Odets' dentist play, now titled *Rocket to the Moon*, was definitely slated as their first fall production. Clurman had also acquired a new script from Irwin Shaw, *The Gentle People*, and a play by a young short-story writer named William Saroyan, *My Heart's in the Highlands*. With Shaw's *Quiet City* also scheduled, that gave the Group four productions to prepare and a busy season to look forward to. It was good to be home.

THIRTEEN

Fame and Its Discontents

Golden Boy opened at the Harris Theatre in Chicago on September 12, with Frances Farmer resuming the role of Lorna. The local press loved the show, and business was brisk; receipts topped $16,000 for the second week of the Group's month-long stay.

The actors would have been happier, however, if they'd had a completed script of *Rocket to the Moon* in hand. Toward the end of the Chicago run a letter from Odets arrived telling them that the play wouldn't be ready for a reading there, but promising to bring it to Detroit, their next stop on the tour.

Odets had been in an odd mood ever since his return from London. He'd rented a house in the country with Clurman and the Kazans (now expecting their second child), but he worked there only intermittently. He spent most of August commuting erratically between New York and New City in his brand-new Cadillac, which he could barely drive. One night he stormed into the living room of their country retreat, pointed an accusing finger at Clurman, and launched into a lengthy monologue designed to refute the director's criticisms of *Golden Boy*. The problem with the play wasn't his unfamiliarity with boxing, he shouted angrily, but rather the difficulties inherent in trying to explore the characters' psychologies in depth while also creating a strong narrative line. The outburst, which came out of the blue, was probably prompted by anxiety over similar issues in *Rocket to the Moon*.

It was Odets' first play without violent incident—no strikes, no suicides, no evictions, in particular none of the plot-driven twists and turns that in his mind had marred *Golden Boy*. Like *Awake and Sing!* it takes place in a single setting, but, unlike the Bergers' crowded home buzzing with life, the dentist's office is a stifling, confining spot, its air heavy with the abandoned dreams of the characters, who drift listlessly in and out. The original outline, written in the stormy days shortly after Odets' wedding, focused on the dentist, Ben Stark, awakened from a sterile marriage and a dull career by an affair with his receptionist. By the time Odets got to work on the story in earnest, he found his interest had shifted to Cleo, the foolish, affected, but essentially sound young woman, and the general theme of the search for love in the modern world.

The subsidiary characters gained depth from this change in emphasis. Ben's wife, Belle, formerly a conventional shrew, became (mostly owing to Clurman's suggestions) a more sympathetic figure trying in her own way to keep her husband's love. Her father, Mr. Prince, shouldered his way onto center stage: a worldly yet not entirely cynical man who urges his son-in-law to "take a rocket to the moon! Explode! You'll die soon enough—" and who is also eager to snatch Cleo away from Ben to assuage his own loneliness. The play had a rueful, rather sad tone, closer to *Paradise Lost* than any other Odets play, but with a smaller cast of characters and greater attention paid to individual psychological development. The relationships were carefully drawn and satisfyingly complex, but Odets worried that the play's slow pace wouldn't hold an audience's attention, that they would find the characters drab. He was also having a terrible time deciding how to end it: Should Cleo accept Mr. Prince, as Luise Rainer had argued? Does Ben return to his wife because he is too weak to do otherwise, or does he really love her? In fact, who is the protagonist—Cleo or Ben?

Progress on the script was slow, impeded not only by these unresolved questions but also by Odets' personal despair over the collapse of his marriage and the worsening situation in Europe. The same day the *Golden Boy* tour began, a violent speech by Hitler insisting on self-determination for the German-speaking minority in Czechoslovakia's Sudetenland launched the worst diplomatic crisis since the end of the Great War. Odets followed the developments as he drove south to attend Thomas Wolfe's funeral in North Carolina. His grief over the death of a novelist he'd admired and known personally, combined with his anger over the appeasement of Hitler, completely undid his rudimentary driving skills; outside of Asheville he lost control of the car and crashed, demolishing the vehicle and cutting himself up badly. The controversial settlement of the international crisis on September 29 in Munich, where the leaders of Great Britain and France forced Czechoslovakia to hand over the Sudetenland to Hitler, prompted his letter to Chicago postponing the arrival of *Rocket to the Moon* because he was "too dispirited to work well."

After further wanderings through Canada—in a new Cadillac—he finally got to Detroit, where *Golden Boy* was playing for a week, in early October. The company was delighted to see him, though slightly discouraged to learn that he'd brought only the first two acts of *Rocket to the Moon*. (Third acts were a chronic problem for Odets, who once said, "Show me a playwright with third-act trouble and I'll show you a man who cannot make a commitment.") Nonetheless, everyone agreed the characters were among his most complicated and interesting, the writing his most mature.

They gave the play its first full-scale reading when they moved on to Boston on October 16; Clurman and Kazan made some preliminary cuts in the overly long script. One week later Luther Adler, Carnovsky, Meisner, and Smith left the *Golden Boy* cast to begin rehearsals for the new play in New York. The tour continued: Kazan finally got his chance to play Joe, Lee Cobb took over the role of Papa Bonaparte, Meisner and Smith were replaced by Curt Conway and Grover Burgess—the Group management was still trying to provide for former members when possible. The new company played to a healthy box office in Philadelphia, Baltimore, Washington, D.C., and Pittsburgh before closing in mid-December.

Clurman had warned the actors on their return from London that a big hit like *Golden Boy* was bound to be a rare occurrence in their theatre and that the Group couldn't count on its revenues to sustain them indefinitely. (He was proved right when the London production closed in October and a second tour, with a new company directed by Bobby Lewis, was forced to fold after only a few weeks on the road around Christmas time; the play didn't draw without a Group cast.) Clurman set about trying to capitalize on *Golden Boy*'s success by drawing up a plan to raise a subsidy of $100,000, that magic number he'd been trying to hit since his first article about the Group's finances in 1931. He wanted backing for the Group as an institution so they could proceed with their season free from the arduous necessity of raising money on a show-by-show basis. Created with the help of Kermit Bloomgarden and the Group's lawyer, Arthur Krim, the proposal guaranteed the production of at least four plays and promised investors half of the Group's profits, not just on those plays but on all Group productions for several years. The terms were generous—Odets protested when he saw the plan that he could make a better deal for a single work of his own, let alone an entire season—and Clurman hoped the Group's seven-year track record, capped by an international hit, would give backers confidence in the proposal's feasibility.

He was disappointed. Broadway angels weren't in the habit of investing in a theatre, as opposed to an individual show, and they wanted to see scripts before they put down their money. This was an unwelcome request: *The Gentle People*, though Clurman believed it was worth doing, posed tricky stylistic questions and was unlikely to encourage backers; *Quiet City* and *My Heart's in the Highlands* were both experimental works calculated to make the average investor recoil; and *Rocket to the Moon* wasn't finished. Clurman tried to whip up enthusiasm for the idea of supporting the Group as a whole, but he had little success. Ironically, the one Wall Street figure who did express interest was lost to the Group because of the international situation; he'd been juggling his currency holdings, counting on a war in Europe, and the Munich settlement ruined him.

Rehearsals for *Rocket to the Moon* began without financing, without a third act, and without a female lead—the last problem being the most pressing and potentially divisive. Odets had written the script with an actress named Ruth Gilbert in mind for the part of Cleo. She wasn't a Group member, though she'd married Bill Challee after his divorce from Ruth Nelson, but Odets no longer cared about that. His diatribe in London showed how much he'd changed since the days when all he wanted was to have the Group Theatre produce his plays. Now he resented the Group's need for his work: not only did he feel that because they rushed him his scripts weren't as polished as they should be—that was an old complaint— but he also believed Group actors weren't always the best choice for his roles. He insisted on the freedom to go outside the Group when it served the best interests of his plays.

Group actresses bitterly noted that it was always the women's parts that were cast with outsiders. Somehow, Clurman could always convince Odets that thirty-four-year-old Luther Adler could play a twenty-one-year-old fighter or that Morris Carnovsky, best known for his work as older characters, was the right choice for Ben Stark. But he didn't seem to make the same effort to find leading roles for Nelson, one of the Group's finest actors of either sex but not a physically glamorous woman, or for Brand, who wasn't yet thirty and felt she deserved a chance to prove she could play nineteen-year-old Cleo. The Group's new commercial imperatives weighed more heavily on the female members—on Broadway, an actress in her late twenties was either a star or over the hill—and they resented it. They liked Frances Farmer personally and agreed she'd been good as Lorna, but it was demoralizing to learn that Clurman and Odets were again seeking new female faces, both for *Rocket* and *The Gentle People*, for which he was considering Sylvia Sidney.

Their resentment deepened when Clurman decided Gilbert wouldn't do for Cleo and, instead of considering Group actresses, flew to Hollywood to interview candidates. They had to admit, however, when he returned with a young actress who'd just been released from her MGM contract, that Eleanor Lynn was perfect for the part. Born Echika Lin in the Williamsburg section of Brooklyn, she'd changed her name while appearing in a bit part in the Theatre Guild production of *The Good Earth* in 1932, when she was only sixteen. She'd always wanted to be an actress, but after a few years of summer stock and forgettable Broadway productions she married a cellist and took six months off to tour Europe with him before signing a short-term contract with MGM. She made nine films in a single year, but when she arrived in New York for *Rocket to the Moon* rehearsals she was bursting with the same energy and enthusiasm that made Cleo such an appealing character. She'd studied the Stanislavsky system, and her political sympathies were in line with the Group's; Clurman heard about her from Julie Garfield, who'd appeared with her in a satirical review sponsored by TAC's West Coast branch to raise money for Spain. Even the most embittered Group actresses couldn't help but like this tiny dynamo—she was five feet two and weighed barely one hundred pounds—when they looked into her merry brown eyes and heard her gay, easy laugh.

"I never felt like an outsider," Lynn said later. "I was embraced, and I embraced them." She was thrilled by rehearsals: "I was an actress who worked instinctually, but I found that I had clear ideas of what I wanted to do. We did lots of improvising"—Clurman apparently revived this old Group practice for a play that depended heavily on psychological interactions—"and it was wonderful, because we took the spine of the characters and really knew what we were doing. I knew exactly the way Cleo lived and what she had done and how she dressed—everything about her."

Being new to the company, Lynn wasn't aware that not every member of the cast was as happy as she about rehearsals. Sandy Meisner, who disliked his small part as a womanizing dance director, was appalled by the short amount of time they had to prepare *Rocket to the Moon;* when Lynn arrived in early November, the scheduled opening was less than three weeks away. Meisner loved the play, but he believed it was being rehearsed too quickly, not in the Group spirit, and they weren't bringing out its full value.

Morris Carnovsky felt miscast as Ben; he struggled throughout rehearsals to find a way to make the character personally meaningful to him. "The spine of the play has to do with the search for love," Clurman told him. Ben's individual spine was "to make things different (that is, closer to the condition of love) . . . he is boyish." This didn't help Carnovsky much; not until the day they opened, when they were having the Group's customary sitdown "talk-through" of the play to relax and refresh them before the premiere, did a line about Ben being raised in an orphanage suddenly strike him as the key to the character. Finally he could *feel* Ben as a yearning boy, stuck behind the bars of an orphanage; that image made real for the actor both Ben's longing for life and his feeling of being separated from it. But opening day was rather late in the game to be discovering such a crucial element of his characterization. Carnovsky too wondered why Clurman allowed the Group to be rushed into performance.

It was especially baffling because Clurman was clearly worried about the play. He feared the audience would see it as merely a drab story about a trivial affair between a dentist and his secretary. On the contrary, he told the actors, "The loneliness in Cliff's play is social. . . . The theme of the play: love in the middle-class world. . . . The thesis: Free love—romance—the free exercise of the passion of love is impossible in middle-class life today." This was a long stretch to give Odets' most personal work a social significance; Clurman may have been trying to counter the criticisms of Group actors who thought the entire season as planned was much too mild and lacked the commitment to exploring important contemporary issues that had always been a Group trademark. Odets, who would have liked to direct the play himself (though he never told Clurman this), for the first time found himself critizing his friend's staging; he went so far as to redirect a scene in the second act after the play opened because he felt Clurman had missed its point.

Personal feelings simmering under the surface of rehearsals made them the most emotionally fraught the Group had ever had. Ruth Nelson, cast as Belle Stark, had to work with her former husband, Bill Challee, now married to the actress Eleanor Lynn had beaten out for the role of Cleo. Leif Erickson, who played a featured role, was anxious about leaving Frances Farmer to her own devices on the *Golden Boy* tour; their marriage, never much more than a companionship on her part, was increasingly shaky, and there were rumors that she was playing around with other men in the Group.

Most disturbing of all was the fact, obvious to everyone, that Morris Carnovsky was falling in love with his costar. His relationship with Phoebe Brand was the most stable and devoted in the Group; it was hard to believe he was jeopardizing it for a woman nearly twenty years his junior. Odets took a certain pleasure in seeing the dignified Dean prove himself as fallible as other men. Carnovsky might think he was miscast in *Rocket to the Moon*; the playwright thought he was just like Ben: "For years [Morris] had been trying to keep his life orderly and clean (simplified), in form no matter if the form fitted or not," Odets wrote in his diary. "Now he found he was unable to control his impulses, could not deny 'queer' and contradictory manifestations of himself which were beginning to assert themselves despite his conscious plans." Odets viewed this as Carnovsky's much-needed liberation from the stifling grip of a woman—a strange attitude, considering that he himself had just been reconciled with Luise Rainer, at his initiative, but Odets' attitude toward women was composed just about equally of tenderness and hostility.

Distressing though these personal concerns were for those involved, they gave the performances an emotional intensity that served the play well; no one could ever think the characters drab as they were incarnated by Group actors. Lynn, flattered and excited by the attentions of someone she revered as an artist as well as a man, shone with an inner glow as Cleo. When she said the lines, "Talent!—I'm talented. I don't know for what, but it makes me want to dance in my bones!" she made Mr. Prince's final assertion that this often silly young woman was in fact "an artist" understandable. Carnovsky's own painfully mixed emotions, invested in the passive Ben, made the character's indecisiveness touching when it might very well have been irritating. Nelson was so moving as Belle that during one rehearsal she made Mike Gordon, the stage manager, cry: "I looked down and I saw a tear drop from my eye onto the script! She was so very, very good."

Clurman had a hard time raising money for *Rocket to the Moon*, partly because the last act wasn't completed until ten days before they opened. A few small investors from *Golden Boy* helped back it, Odets put up some of the money himself, and Sylvia Sidney provided the rest. When she finally heard Act Three, she was horrified; Cleo's emergence as the central figure at the end seemed to her to have no connection with the preceding two acts, and she was sure the play would lose money. She overreacted: Cleo's decision to walk away from Ben and to reject Mr. Prince's offer of marriage because "none of you can give me what I'm looking for: a whole, full world, with all the trimmings!" was in fact foreshadowed, though perhaps not so clearly as it should have been. Odets himself, though he defended the ending, agreed with Sidney that the play would flop; he didn't think audiences were ready for such a quiet character study.

Perhaps not, but they were certainly eager for a new play by Clifford Odets. Helen Thompson sold $22,000 worth of theatre-party tickets before the show opened on November 24, and the Belasco was packed for the premiere, despite a severe snowstorm complete with lightning and thunder so violent it occasionally drowned out the actors. The reviews were better than the Group had expected; many critics agreed with the *Post*'s John Mason Brown that the first act, "warmly human and extraordinarily revealing," was Odets' finest work to date. "By the sheer magic of his dialogue, by the almost dental precision with which he can lay bare the nerves of his characters, and by the skill of his planning no less than his portraiture, Mr. Odets fills his stage with people who are quiveringly alive," Brown wrote. "When the curtain lowers on this act you feel the exhilaration which can come only from the theatre. . . . You are fascinated and to a certain extent stunned by the impact of the man's skill."

This paean, however, was followed by a major qualification made by almost every reviewer. Brown not only shared Sylvia Sidney's dislike of the third act, but didn't think Act Two was very good either. There were flashes of brilliance throughout, the press agreed: Bill Challee's single scene as a happily married salesman was greatly admired, as was the wrenching moment when Art Smith as a patientless dentist revealed he'd become a blood donor so he could pay his rent. If the play as a whole didn't quite work, critics were content to judge it gently as a noble failure. "Odets is approaching profounder subjects which he himself has not completely digested," Walter Winchell wrote in the *Mirror*. "But he is on the right track."

The Group's production fared better than the play, and many reviews emphasized the fruitful symbiosis that had developed between playwright and company over the past four years. "If Mr. Odets is its greatest asset the Group Theatre is just as valuable to him," Brooks Atkinson commented in the *Times*. "It knows what he is writing and believes in it." Richard Lockridge in the *Sun* applauded the "amazing sensitiveness and intelligence" of the acting, as did most of his colleagues. Eleanor Lynn's Cleo caused a sensation—the critics appeared to be almost as much in love with her as Ben Stark was—and everyone else was warmly commended as well. The press also liked the physical production: the "easy naturalness" of Clurman's direction; a typically thoughtful set by Max Gorelik, who used seemingly realistic details to "build toward an abstract pattern which aims at interpreting the inner meaning of the drama"; and the moody, evocative lighting. Mike Gordon was now lighting as well as stage-managing Group productions, and in him the company had finally discovered a designer who was more than a technician and who understood the Group Idea as Gorelik did.

The mixed nature of the notices, however, made *Rocket to the Moon*'s commercial fate uncertain. It survived due to the loyalty of the Group's audience, developed over seven years by first Cheryl Crawford's and then Helen Thompson's tireless organizing. Labor unions, community groups, social clubs, and charitable institutions came back year after year to buy blocks of tickets at slightly reduced prices; they felt a kinship with the Group's aims and a warm, almost proprietary affection for the actors and the plays. They knew the Group as intimately as anyone outside the company, and reviews meant little to them. They were touched by the characters in *Rocket*, each one so fully imagined and burningly alive, and they followed the progression of the plot without the critics' restless dissatisfaction over its lack of thematic clarity. There weren't enough of them to make the show a hit, but week after week it grossed from $8,000 to $9,000, enough to make a small-cast, one-set play reasonably profitable. More important, their quiet attentiveness and fervent applause at the curtain calls reminded the Group that there was more to theatre than reviews and box-office receipts; they had created a body of work that had personal meaning and importance for a great many people.

Just how strong an attachment the Group could prompt was evident in the words of Franchot Tone shortly after he arrived in New York on December 11 to begin rehearsals of *The Gentle People*. "I'd better not get started on the Group Theatre," he told an audience at a Town Hall Club lunch, "because I know I'll get too emotional about it and then I won't be able to talk at all." He spoke fondly of his early days with the company, the satisfaction he'd felt as part of an effort "to produce plays in a really collective and jointly creative way and to develop an attitude towards life . . . which was affirmative and constructive." He'd sorely missed that spirit in Hollywood, and he was glad to be back among his old comrades.

But the Group Theatre Tone rejoined was very different from the one he'd left in 1933. Instead of comradeship, he found anger and hostility, not so much toward him personally, for many Group members were genuinely glad to have him back, but toward a production that seemed to cave in completely to the desire for commercial success. The cast featured no fewer than three movie stars: Tone, Sylvia Sidney, and Sam Jaffe, who'd recently appeared as the High Lama in Frank Capra's *Lost Horizon*. (Clurman had wanted to cast another one as well, but the newly rechristened John Garfield had made such a hit with his first film, *Four Daughters*, that he decided to stay in Hollywood; Gadget Kazan got the part.) "That was a whole new batch of people that you could hardly call the Group anymore," said Phoebe Brand. "It was casting like it used to be on Broadway. I think a certain opportunism crept in at that point with Harold." When Group members read newspaper articles claiming that "they prefer not to be compared to organizations which depend more on subscribers for financial returns than on commercial plays. ... Yes, the Group Theatre is on par with Gilbert Miller, Guthrie McClintic or Sam H. Harris and just as commercial," they shuddered. The Group seemed to be turning into everything they most despised.

The Gentle People as a play was cause for concern as well. It told the story of two humble men, a Jewish lens grinder (Jaffe) and a Greek cook (Bohnen), whose only pleasure in life is fishing off a pier in Coney Island and dreaming of the day when they might afford to indulge their hobby down in the Gulf Stream. Tone played the gangster who shakes them down for protection money, then seduces the lens grinder's daughter (Sidney) and demands their life's savings, which he intends to use to take the daughter to Havana. Pushed to the limit, the two men eventually kill the gangster in a clumsy scene that mixes farce and melodrama as they grapple with him on a small boat. Shaw intended the story as a parable of the struggle against fascism, pointing the moral that ordinary people could protect themselves against dictators only by meeting violence with violence. But the play's tone was uneven, ranging from whimsy to fairly pedestrian realism; topical references to the Anschluss and Czechoslovakia weren't effectively integrated into the script. Only in a hilarious, though basically extraneous, scene in a steam bath did the dialogue have any real life. "It was full of plot, yet somehow more narrative than dramatic," Clurman admitted, "heavier than it was meant to be, yet lighter than the author's and the Group's reputation promised."

By the time Tone arrived in New York, Clurman again had barely three weeks to shape this problematic script into a coherent production. As he had in *Paradise Lost*, he tried to blend naturalism and stylization to point up the story's broader relevance. He wanted the mood to be tender, intimate, never harsh, firmly rooted in the physical details of ordinary life, yet not prosaic. Boris Aronson designed a marvelous set, essentially realistic yet stylized enough to suggest the play's fairy-tale nature. The Coney Island pier, built in perspective with the water effect produced by gauze, created just the atmosphere of dreamy yearning Clurman was looking for.

There simply wasn't time, however, for the in-depth work needed to develop the same qualities in the actors. Rehearsals were superficially pleasant enough, but no one was excited by them. Sidney had expected to do the kind of detailed, introspective study of character the Group was famous for; when she went to Clurman privately and complained she wasn't getting that opportunity, he told her to relax: all he wanted was the personality she projected in the movies. Sidney, a Hollywood rebel who had spent years fighting with studio executives to escape typecasting, was shocked and deeply hurt. She angrily concluded that the Group cared about her and Tone only as box-office draws, whereas she had come to them sincerely as an artist wanting to grow. Tone himself was disappointed in Clurman's direction, although he didn't say so until after the production opened; he wanted very much to believe in the Group.

Irwin Shaw worried about the director's rather cavalier attitude toward physical staging. He used to amuse his friends with a slightly malicious tale of how, when Tone stopped a rehearsal to ask a technical question about the tricky blocking of the murder scene, Clurman responded with an hour-long lecture on fascism. Kazan, who acted as Clurman's assistant as well as playing Sidney's boyfriend, often got stuck with cleaning up the staging; he was both pleased by his friend's reliance on him and resentful of Clurman's implicit assumption that these were mere details, unworthy of the director's attention but suitable work for the ever-faithful Gadget.

If the regular Group actors were less than thrilled by the casting of *The Gentle People* and Clurman's uncharacteristically superficial direction, they were horrified by the circuslike atmosphere surrounding the play's premiere on January 5. The sidewalks in front of the Belasco (*Rocket to the Moon* had moved to the Windsor Theatre) were jammed with movie fans. Inside, they shrieked and sighed when Tone entered, commented loudly on Sidney's clothes and acting ability, giggled and chattered whenever the pair were offstage. They cheered lustily at the end, but probably not for the triumph of gentle people over gangsterism. Tone and Sidney had to exit via the Belasco's fire escape to avoid the mob of screaming autograph hunters.

Reviewers weren't quite so impressed as the fans. They liked the acting well enough: many thought Sidney gave her best stage performance ever; Tone's return to the theatre was hailed; Jaffe and Bohnen were praised for their charm and humor; and everyone loved Lee Cobb's sidesplitting bit in the steam-bath scene as a failed businessman turned thundering anarchist. They were surprisingly cordial to Clurman's direction, although several noted the awkward staging of the murder scene. What they heartily disliked was the play itself, "a synthetic and rather shopworn job," as Robert Anderson called it in the *Journal-American*. They noted the parallel with the situation in Europe, but found it unconvincing as embodied in stock characters and clichéd dialogue. Shaw had the dubious distinction of being compared to Odets in nearly every review, always to his disadvantage. Unfortunately, the critics were right: *The Gentle People* had neither the depth of insight into character nor the dazzling dialogue of *Rocket to the Moon*, or indeed even the weakest Odets drama.

It was, however, a modest hit, thanks to the presence of Tone and Sidney. It grossed $15,000 its first week, and although business tapered off slowly it continued to take in anywhere from $10,000 to $12,000 well into the spring. For the first time since the exhilarating days of *Awake and Sing!* and the *Lefty/Till the Day I Die* double bill in 1935, the Group had two plays running simultaneously on Broadway.

The Group Theatre was now an institution. The program covers of both

Rocket to the Moon and *The Gentle People* displayed small photographs of the eighteen productions they'd presented on Broadway over eight seasons, and the press was not unmindful of the extraordinary achievement this represented. Even the most critical reviews of their current offerings noted the "vivid characterizations executed in the Group's best tradition of ensemble playing," and Brooks Atkinson spoke for all when he declared, "In its eighth season the Group Theatre has become our leading art theatre by sheer persistence and hard-won ability." Their house playwright was widely considered the most promising young writer for the stage in America, and that winter Odets received more attention than he had since the heady spring of 1935: he was the subject of a *Time* cover story in December, and in January *The Nation* placed him on its 1938 Honor Roll, "for a series of increasingly powerful plays, of which the current *Rocket to the Moon* is perhaps the best."

On the surface, the permanence and continuity the Group had always aimed for were firmly in their grasp. Clurman was confident enough of their finances by the time *The Gentle People* opened to put thirteen members on an annual salary. Luther Adler, Bohnen, Carnovsky, Cobb, Erickson, Gordon, Kazan, Meisner, Nelson, Smith, and Tone were all in the Group shows already running, but Brand and Farmer weren't. There would soon be work for everyone, however; Clurman planned to add one more full-scale production—John Howard Lawson's new play, *Parlor Magic*, with Farmer and Erickson in the leads—and to present *Quiet City* and *My Heart's in the Highlands* as experimental Sunday-night performances before the end of the season. In addition, an article in January announced, "The Group Theatre is getting that collective urge again and for the first time in more than a year is holding those intensive jam sessions in which everybody from Leif Erickson to Bobby Lewis has a say about the past, present and future of the organization."

If such meetings were held—no one in the Group now remembers them —they must have been stormy. The reality behind the press releases about annual salaries and ambitious future plans was a demoralized, divided company, harshly critical of Clurman's artistic leadership and bitterly unhappy about the direction in which he was taking the Group. Virtually no one liked *The Gentle People*. The actors were cold to Irwin Shaw as the author of a play they considered a grossly commercial venture unworthy of the Group and his talent. They made no effort to conceal from Clurman their opinion that he'd done a so-so job of directing it. They attributed many of the production's failings to the too-brief rehearsal period, and they blamed Kermit Bloomgarden for that. Their attitude infuriated Clurman, and he was even more annoyed by their criticisms of *Rocket to the Moon*, most of which were voiced only after the production opened and, Clurman believed, were influenced by the left-wing papers' reservations about it.

In fact, a review of the play that appeared in the *New Masses* did reinforce the uneasiness many felt over the play's lack of a social message, and several actors repeated its main premise to Clurman. Ruth McKenney wrote:

> The people of our country have learned how to be bold and brave in the last three years—and Clifford Odets has not. The little dentist in the Bronx, and his wife, and his friends have been jolted out of their narrow vision of life by history, but Mr. Odets sees them today as they were long ago, before the workers of Spain went out to fight fascism, before the workers of America organized to fight reaction in our nation. The great playwrights must be teachers, leaders. Mr. Odets has still to learn from his own characters before he can instruct as well as excite. The people of America are writing Clifford Odets' third acts.

The personal nature and sad, indecisive tone of *Rocket to the Moon* were more representative of the national mood in the late 1930s than either McKenney or the more radical members of the Group cared to recognize. The militant faith in a better future that had animated plays like *Lefty* was hard to maintain in 1939. Madrid fell to Franco's troops on March 28, marking the triumph of reaction in Spain. It was obviously only a matter of time until the next European war started, with fascist Germany and Italy lined up against capitalist Britain and France, possibly making a reluctant alliance with the Soviet Union. No one could be confident that the right side would win this war; many Americans, for wildly varying political reasons, weren't sure there *was* a right side. At home, the pace of social reform had slowed, due in part to a determined counterattack mounted by conservative congressmen like Martin Dies, who established the Committee to Investigate Un-American Activities in 1938 largely to prove that New Deal programs were riddled with communists.

The Communist party itself no longer had the influence on Group life it once did, though that influence had always been part of the members' more general desire for the Group to be meaningfully engaged in issues of the day. The unit in the Group still met to discuss contemporary events, and presumably Group life as well, but the links that had bound together their political and artistic lives in the mid-1930s had been shattered by the breakup of 1937 and the subsequent reorganization of the company. The Group's communists no longer expected their political views to affect Group policy; the past two seasons had made it clear that Clurman decided the Group's course, with assistance from Luther Adler, Bohnen, Kazan, and Bloomgarden.

Virtually all Group actors were distressed by their exclusion from the decision-making process and by the substance of those decisions. The Group, once a secure home base from which they could fight for artistic and political change, now seemed to many of them to be infected with commercialism and complacency. When they insisted that Clurman had to find stronger plays, when they sniped at the movie stars in their midst, they were expressing their underlying unhappiness over the changed nature of the Group. They desperately needed their theatre to make the world right for them, to give them the satisfaction they could find nowhere else. When it couldn't, they tore themselves and each other apart trying to find out why.

It was a dreadful spring for everyone. Odets and Rainer quarreled again, and he fled south to Florida with the manuscript of *The Silent Partner;* his secretary was instructed to tell no one where he was. Devastated by Carnovsky's affair with Eleanor Lynn, Phoebe Brand went home to her parents, then took a long boat trip to the Virgin Islands to think things over. The Bohnen marriage had been rocked by a crisis as well; it's unclear what exactly happened, but a letter from Hildur to a friend spoke of being a fool and nearly throwing her life away. By spring they were trying to patch things up, and Bud was on the wagon. Sylvia Sidney was miserable in *The Gentle People,* which was literally making her ill; she missed three performances in mid-March, reportedly owing to a bad cold, and was out for a whole week later in the month as well. It may have been morning sickness —she and Adler were expecting their first child—but her physical condition was certainly affected by the stress of Group life.

Franchot Tone was finding his reunion with the Group far less ecstatic than he'd expected. He kept aloof from the company outside the theatre, drinking and dancing after performances until the small hours of the morning in New York's most fashionable watering holes. He resisted Clurman's efforts to persuade him to take part in either *Quiet City* or *My Heart's in the Highlands.* It was increasingly obvious that he was disillusioned with the Group and shared Sidney's suspicion that they were using him for his drawing power as a star. Irwin Shaw warned Clurman that the Group had treated Tone tactlessly; although he'd invested $22,000 in *The Gentle People,* he hadn't been invited to Council meetings during rehearsals to discuss its progress. They should try to draw him into Group life more, argued Shaw, a warm, gregarious man with more common sense about personal relations and commercial imperatives than most Group members had. If they didn't make Tone feel an integral part of the organization, they were going to lose him.

An awkward meeting at Carnovsky's apartment, with Clurman, Bohnen, Kazan, and Tone in attendance, didn't help the situation. Tone was evasive when Clurman asked him to share their collective life more fully, to work to make himself truly a Group member again. Clurman was equally evasive when the actor asked him if he respected the reputation Tone had made in films. "That is not why we want you," he replied. But they were willing to use his name to make *The Gentle People* a commercial success, Tone rejoined. Clurman admitted this was so. It wasn't a response calculated to fill Tone with good feelings about the Group.

Relations were further strained when it was discovered that Sam Grisman, who managed both the Belasco and the Windsor and hence was responsible for paying the Group their portion of the box-office receipts, had been dipping into the advance sale monies to meet his other financial obligations and had no means of repaying them. The Group was out $17,000, and Tone, as the principal backer of *The Gentle People*, lost money too. He blamed the Group's poor business management, with some justification. Grisman had been slowly going under for nearly a year, and sometime during the run of *Golden Boy* he began calling up Ruth Young, the Group's executive secretary, after he'd sent the weekly check and telling her, "Listen, don't deposit the check today, wait until tomorrow." Young was just a kid, too inexperienced to realize what this meant, and Kermit Bloomgarden, who would have known better, was too often out of the Group offices performing his duties for Herman Shumlin to keep a close eye on the Group's daily affairs.

Tone might not have been so annoyed by the Group's ineptitude in business matters had he been more satisfied artistically, but he'd convinced himself that he was miscast as a gangster, that Clurman hadn't given him enough guidance, that he'd really wanted to act in the Odets play with his old Group friends Carnovsky, Adler, and Smith—in short, that he'd been mistreated and exploited. By late March the gossip columnists reported he'd told the Group that when *The Gentle People* closed he was through.

It was a painful moment for Clurman, who'd had a bad spring in general. Stella Adler returned from Europe in January to renew her ceaseless recriminations about how bad the Group was for her and how much his commitment to the company hurt their relationship. She was by no means entirely wrong, nor was she completely self-centered; she'd been distressed by the way the Group had used actresses like Beany Barker, Eunice Stoddard, and Dorothy Patten, then, in her view, cast them aside. She wasn't imagining the Group's hostility toward her; her own brother told Frances Farmer, "Harold must be perfect. He can't afford a girl like Stella." Clurman could neither answer her criticisms nor do anything about them. "He couldn't give her up for the Group, and he couldn't give the Group up for her," said Adler's daughter, Ellen. He needed them both, and he drove everyone crazy with his efforts to bring them together, whether they liked it or not.

He hoped to draw Adler back into the Group with a part in *Parlor Magic*, but when Lawson arrived with the completed script in January, Clurman was deeply disappointed. It seemed to him that Lawson's involvement in the Communist party had ruined him as an artist. The script was mechanical, its characters strait-jacketed by the author's desire to point a political moral. Clurman was in sympathy with the moral—the need to fight fascism at home as well as abroad—but that was beside the point. He couldn't commit the Group to a script devoid of the passion and human perceptiveness that had made *Success Story,* and even the incoherent *Gentlewoman,* so stirring.

Lawson was hurt by this reaction, but it did nothing to shake his faith in the new life he'd made for himself as a well-paid screenwriter who justified his salary with the political work it enabled him to do. He'd faced a dilemma felt by many artists in the 1930s, when writing plays or painting pictures seemed to the most sensitive and caring people an inadequate response to the dire problems of the times, and he'd made the hard decision that activism was more important than art. Clurman thought he was wrong, but understood the forces that drove him to it. Many members of the Group, which had been founded on the idea that the greatest art must inevitably reflect and comment on its times, believed their theatre had gone too far in the opposite direction from Lawson, producing commercial plays with only the most facile things to say about the struggles taking place in the world.

They did what they could to support a socially committed theatre and to act as citizens to pressure their government to take a stand against Nazism. In the wake of Germany's horrifying Kristallnacht riots in November, when Jewish shops, homes, and synagogues were burned and looted and tens of thousands of Jews deported to concentration camps, TAC sponsored an anti-Nazi rally and a petition, signed by many Group members, asking Roosevelt to protest Hitler's new anti-Semitic laws. In January 1939, Sylvia Sidney and Franchot Tone hosted a cocktail party to raise money for the Committee of 56, an organization of actors lobbying for a total boycott of German trade. Sidney and Tone were also active in the battle to defend the WPA, and especially the Federal Theatre Project, against budget cuts imposed by hostile congressmen. They flew to Washington in mid-January, accompanied by Phoebe Brand, Frances Farmer, and Helen Tamiris, to present Roosevelt with a petition signed by 200,000 people protesting the cuts. Farmer and her husband, appearing on a radio show to plug the Group, infuriated their host by spending the entire time criticizing the WPA cuts instead. All this work was important, but it was defensive, an attempt to protect people and programs against the onslaughts of conservatives at home and fascists abroad. There was an air of grim necessity about it, none of the exhilarating sense of moving forward and changing the world that had inspired them in the early 1930s.

It amused very few in the Group that, as far as the press was concerned, these were their greatest days. When *Awake and Sing!* was revived in early March, to run in repertory with *Rocket to the Moon,* the reviews were glowing, far more enthusiastic than they'd been in 1935. "The more I see of the Group Theatre which, in truth, seems to have undergone a spiritual awakening, the greater becomes my admiration for its collective talent," wrote Sidney Whipple in a typical review in the *World-Telegram.* Most critics found Julia Adler, who took the role of Bessie when her sister refused to play it again, and Alfred Ryder, a young actor stepping into Julie Garfield's part as Ralph, inferior to their predecessors, but in general they felt the performances had deepened since the first production. The Group knew better. They judged the revival, with Clurman, as "relaxed to the point of glibness . . . distinctly inferior to the original." Nonetheless, they were pleased to have Joe Bromberg among them again; he'd returned from Hollywood in January, eager to rejoin the Group, and threw himself into rehearsals for *Quiet City* as well as *Awake and Sing!*

The press could hardly be blamed for seeing the Group at the peak of their achievements, for the company was bustling with activity and laying the groundwork for future productions, most notably in Molly Thacher's efforts to cultivate new playwrights for the Group. On March 15, she announced the winners of the Group's playwriting contest. Ramon Naya, a twenty-five-year-old Mexican, won $500 for his play *Mexican Mural*, which the judges (Thacher, Clurman, and Shaw) praised as "outstanding in the scope of its achievement, the richness of its color and the mature projection of character in a social setting." The Group had planned originally to present only one prize, but Thacher and her colleagues were so enthusiastic about a series of three sketches called *American Blues* that they voted a second award of $100 to the author, a twenty-seven-year-old named Tennessee Williams.

In addition, Thacher kept up an active correspondence with some twenty other young playwrights, hoping to bring new writing talent into the Group. The problem was, she told a *World-Telegram* reporter, their agents all wanted to ship them off to Hollywood to make money; they'd hardly begun in the theatre before they were pushed into an entirely new craft. "I weep for the theatre," she said, "if we don't hold onto these babies." They needed to be nurtured, to learn about the particular requirements of writing for the stage: "Mr. Shakespeare and Mr. Molière were actors first. Mr. Shakespeare knew his company and he knew his box office. These guys sit at home and they don't know anything." What she didn't say to the reporter was that she was also frustrated by Clurman's lack of interest in most of these young people. With the exception of *My Heart's in the Highlands*, which she'd sent him when he was in London, she'd never been able to convince him to produce plays by any of the writers she developed. She did manage to get a commitment that if the Group went away for the summer she could bring along six of the most promising playwrights to attend classes and get the experience they needed.

While Thacher was doing this work, her husband was grappling with *Quiet City*. Clurman had decided to use Group money to produce both that play and *My Heart's in the Highlands* for limited Sunday-night runs. *Highlands* was too unusual, he thought, to attract a large audience, while *Quiet City* had technical problems that needed to be explored in a workshop before it was given a full-scale production. He and Shaw agreed that Kazan should direct it, Max Gorelik was hired to design the scenery, and Aaron Copland wrote an evocative musical score. Rehearsals began in late February.

Quiet City was a much more ambitious and interesting play than *The Gentle People*. It explores the troubled conscience of Gabriel Mellon, president of a New York City department store, who has just been appointed ambassador to Finland. The threat of a truckers' strike prompts him to reexamine the choices he has made in his life. In 1928, he'd been an idealistic young poet named Gabriel Mellinkoff. He'd changed his name, abandoned his Jewish girlfriend, and married a wealthy woman in order to get his start in business. As he prepares for his departure for Finland, old memories come flooding back; the play mingles scenes from his past and present to show how the thought of what he gave up torments him. "The city cries out to me, it howls, it calls with five million voices," he shouts in an odd but moving scene where he phones the mayor to beg him to make those insistent voices keep quiet. He feels he's betrayed his race and his class, and the example of his bohemian, trumpet-playing younger brother (who joins the Communist party in the last act) rebukes his own opportunism and cowardice.

Politically, *Quiet City* was tougher than anything Shaw had written since *Bury the Dead;* it made a militant analysis of the labor situation not unlike that of *Waiting for Lefty,* and it brought the agony of Europe home in the painful personal story of Gabriel's father, who rejects his German-American wife because the Nazis' actions lead him to believe Jews can no longer trust Gentiles. The play had a dark, brooding tone shot through with fierce poetry quite different from the forced fantasy of *The Gentle People* or the lyrical lilt of Shaw's popular *New Yorker* stories. It was a project the Group could be proud of, a worthy successor to *Success Story* and *Paradise Lost,* as honest an expression of its historical moment as they had been of theirs. Virtually every prominent Group actor was cast in it, and Clurman hoped that when they ironed out the stylistic difficulties posed by the script's shifting time frame and nonrealistic elements they could present it as a regular production in the fall.

But Kazan felt from the first day of rehearsals that the actors weren't giving him their trust, that they expected a lengthy, passionate analysis of the script such as Clurman always provided when he directed a play. This wasn't Kazan's style, and although he seemed very confident to Eleanor Lynn, who was in the cast, he was inwardly uncertain and worried about getting his vision across to the company. He needed Clurman's support, and he was furious when his friend disappeared with Stella Adler for two weeks, first to Florida to see how Odets was progressing on *The Silent Partner,* then to Bermuda and Cuba for a vacation.

To make matters more difficult, Kazan had a discipline problem with Morris Carnovsky, who was chronically late for rehearsals. Carnovsky always apologized, but Kazan didn't believe he meant it; he interpreted the tardiness as a challenge to his authority. It may have been—there was certainly little love lost between Carnovsky and Kazan—but it may just as well have been an expression of the actor's troubled state of mind. His affair with Lynn had ended, he and Phoebe Brand were reconciled, but the scars remained; it must have been uncomfortable for all three to be rehearsing *Quiet City* together. Unlike Kazan and Odets, who both had numerous affairs almost as a matter of course, Carnovsky didn't take such things lightly; he'd hurt someone he loved very deeply and lost a young woman who meant a great deal to him. He was one of the actors most disturbed by the Group's new direction, and although he'd been added to the Council along with Odets that season, it's unlikely he felt as much a part of Clurman's inner circle as Odets, Luther Adler, Bohnen—or, for that matter, Kazan himself. When someone as professional and reliable as Carnovsky began behaving erratically, it was a sign of how badly disjointed Group life had become.

The company worked hard on the play and gave two performances, squeezed onto the Belasco stage in front of *The Gentle People* sets, on April 16 and 23. The extent of their apprehensions can be judged by the fact that the press wasn't invited. The audience response was unenthusiastic, and Clurman decided there was no point in making further efforts on the production. Everyone was saddened by this decision, for with all its problems it had been a major Group effort on an important script.

My Heart's in the Highlands, by contrast, was regarded by most of the Group as a virtual stepchild. Clurman was enchanted by this whimsical tale of a poet's struggle to survive in a hostile world—written in the gentle, slightly surreal style familiar to readers of William Saroyan's short stories —and saw it as the perfect project for Bobby Lewis, whose perpetual frustration over the Group's lack of interest in stylized theater had finally erupted in early 1939 in a lengthy memo that argued, "Group productions lack music, color, rhythm, movement—all those *other* things in the theatre besides psychology." The very qualities that appealed to Clurman and Lewis were what put off the rest of the Group; Mike Gordon thought it was "a piece of fluff," Kazan found it weak and defeatist, and Max Gorelik said it had "a not very robust grasp of a serious problem." Art Smith was the only long-time Group actor who would consent to appear in it; Harry Bratsburg, one of the company's younger, post-1937 regulars, also took a small part. Lewis hired Phil Loeb, the Group's old friend from the Theatre Guild, to play the poet and a fourteen-year-old named Sidney Lumet for the role of the son; he assembled most of the rest of the cast from his former students at the Group Studio.

Unlike the tense, difficult preparation of *Quiet City*, rehearsals for *My Heart's in the Highlands* were swift, sure, and light-hearted. Lewis knew exactly what he wanted, and he worked closely with the actors, designers, and Paul Bowles, who wrote the musical score, to synthesize speech, movement, scenery, costumes, light, and sound for a unified, highly theatrical effect. The opening scene set the mood for the entire evening. As the poet kneels on an upper platform of the stylized house set, searching for the right word to make a rhyme, his son below tries to turn handstands. Each attempt and fall of the son's is synchronized with the discovery and discarding of a new rhyme by the father, while music plays underneath. Just as the poet finds the perfect rhyme, his son manages to stand on his hands. In another scene, to make the point that people are nourished by art, Lewis arranged the villagers bringing food to an old man playing the trumpet to create the image of a plant blossoming as it is watered. "Bobby was a wonderful director, very imaginative," said Sidney Lumet, a successful child actor who'd never appeared in a production quite like this one. "I must say it struck me as very odd! It excited my imagination enormously, but it was very surprising."

Lewis knew exactly how surprising the more psychologically oriented members of the Group would find it, and when the Council (in Clurman's absence) asked to attend a rehearsal, he refused. Not only was he sure they wouldn't approve, but he'd prepared the play so quickly that by the third week of rehearsal the company was doing full run-throughs, which took only ninety minutes or so, and filling up the rest of the day with egg hunts for the children and similar antics—not anything he wished to be caught doing by the Council. The Council, annoyed, instructed Kermit Bloomgarden to wire Clurman, stating that due to the Group's losses in the Grisman affair the organization must retrench and *My Heart's in the Highlands* should be canceled. "The Group is not a bank," Clurman telegraphed in response. "Proceed with the Saroyan play."

When Clurman saw it upon his return, he was so pleased that he felt it deserved more than a Sunday-night run. He tried to convince the Guild to pick it up as a subscription offering, but the board feared its subscribers might feel cheated by such a short play. The Group opened it on April 13 at the Guild Theatre, intending to give only five performances; they did, however, invite the press to take a look at it.

The reviews were wildly mixed, the "most sharply divided opinions of the season," *Variety* noted. Critics either loved or hated Saroyan's wistful, rather insubstantial tale. Sidney Whipple called it a "crackpot fantasy" in the *World-Telegram,* asserting that "you will search in vain for any trace of truth, beauty or moral in it," while the *Post's* John Mason Brown was "interested and moved . . . and I surmise from those around me who had tears in their eyes that they were no less touched than I was by what is poignant, charming, and yet indefinable in *My Heart's in the Highlands.*" No one seemed very sure what the play was actually about; they either responded to the enchanted mood Lewis had created, or they didn't.

Everyone agreed the direction was brilliant, "every bit as creative as the play," wrote Brooks Atkinson. "What [Mr. Lewis] has accomplished in the responsive and inventive direction of *My Heart's in the Highlands* will long be remembered as one of the gems of the unhackneyed theatre." Given that the production had been disdained by so many of his fellow Group members, it gave Lewis a good deal of sardonic pleasure to read reviews that saw *Highlands* as "just the sort of work that such an organization as the Group Theatre, after a successful theatrical year, should be doing" and praise of the acting (by a largely non-Group cast) as "of typical Group excellence." Many critics cited the decision to present the play as evidence that the Group's "growing reputation for good judgment is well deserved."

The Group extended the run for an additional six nights, and the Guild was finally shamed by all the good reviews, several of which noted it had turned the play down, into adding *My Heart's in the Highlands* to its subscription series. The board's apprehensions were justified; the Guild's subscribers didn't much care for the play, and it closed on May 20 after forty-three performances. The play's director, however, was as happy as if it had run for years. Lewis had achieved precisely the artistic and stylistic effects he'd aimed for, he'd had the satisfaction of proving the validity of his vision to a skeptical, at times actively hostile Group, and after years of playing small parts he'd finally stepped into the spotlight, hailed by virtually every major critic as the most innovative director of the year.

The closing of *Highlands* brought the Group's season to an end. *Rocket to the Moon* had shut down on April 4, *Awake and Sing!* continued for only three more weeks before folding as well, and *The Gentle People* closed suddenly on May 6, despite the fact that it was still grossing $8,000 a week. Possibly the Group's decision was prompted by problems with their leading man: Franchot Tone had been in and out of the show in late April with bronchitis, one of the many Group actors requiring hospitalization during that strained season, and wasn't eager to continue.

Although *Rocket to the Moon* and *The Gentle People* had both been modest moneymakers, the Group's profits were swallowed up by the experimental productions and *Awake and Sing!*, which failed to draw despite the enthusiastic notices. Around the time *Rocket* closed, Clurman had begun seriously to consider the possibility of signing a contract for the entire acting company to make films as a unit. Eastern Service Studios, a Wall Street–backed corporation aspiring to break into the movie business, had leased Paramount's enormous Astoria studio and was trying to convince New York stage producers to work there. ESS offered to put up 80 percent of the financing and give the Group complete artistic control of the product, and Clurman was tempted. In early April the New York papers reported that contracts were being drawn up for the Group to make three movies, the first to be an original script by Odets or Shaw.

This announcement prompted a furious letter from Odets, who'd halted his restless wanderings in Mexico to work on *The Silent Partner* and was enraged by the idea that the Group might devote their summer to a movie instead of to his script. (He hadn't read the press very carefully, for the articles clearly stated that filming would begin in September.) The letter revealed how unhappy Odets was about his relationship with the Group:

> For years now I have had the very difficult lonely task of sitting in an empty room and writing plays for months of nights. When the plays were finished they were promptly seized and put in other hands, myself cast away and out like you throw old furniture out. . . . Next, when vital decisions were to be made, concerning my plays or others, or any other Group affairs, I was consulted concerning them to an even less extent than was the office secretary, the girl, Ruthie. Again, in short, I am in the anomalous position of being the Group's main dynamo and at the same time as far out of the texture of the Group as I was eight years ago in Brookfield Center. . . . Don't answer back with the old saw—none of you want to bother me—for, I'm bothered very promptly when someone wants something.

It was unfair of Odets to complain about not being consulted about Group matters when he'd been out of town since January; this was his first letter to Clurman since he'd left. It showed the playwright at his least attractive: self-centered, querulous, and threatening:

> What are you going to do about this problem, Harold? I want, psychologically and materially, to be in the Group Theatre. You will have to assume more responsibility towards my personal welfare than you've been doing. You will have to see to it that I get some personal pleasure out of the Group. You will have to include me more in all organizational plans. Believe me, Harold darling, this letter contains one of the most serious problems of the Group Theatre, although you or no one else may be aware of it. My growing discontent is going to shortly become an unpleasant explosion.

He went on to criticize savagely the Group's recent work ("last production with any depth was *Paradise Lost"*) and to express the fear so many felt that the organization was preoccupied with success and not with its members' spiritual and artistic welfare—although in Odets' case he clearly meant *his* welfare. Odets was "sick with 'togetherness,' " he told Clurman. "You and I are the indispensable members of the Group Theatre, no others."

Odets was expressing, with his characteristic candor, some of the most unappealing emotions the Group's breakdown was prompting, and not in him alone. The selfless dedication that had animated their early years, the painful struggle to subdue their egos and work for the collective good, no longer seemed justified. If the Group Theatre was to be a commercial producer, hiring bankable movie stars and doing superficial work (that was how many of them viewed the season's efforts), then why should they make sacrifices for it? Personal problems and desires loomed disproportionately large in this troubled atmosphere. There had been disruptive love affairs, individual ambition, and intra-Group rivalries before *Golden Boy*, but they never seemed to threaten the collective life as they did now. There was no question that everyone desperately wanted the Group to go on, but people were thinking more about what they needed to get from their theatre, less about what they could give. This wasn't because anyone in the Group had suddenly become calculating and selfish: times had changed, and people changed with them.

Clurman shot back a loving but tough letter, promising Odets that there would be a Group summer and declining to argue with him about whose fault it was that they weren't as close as they all wished. "I will consider that we have *Silent Partner* when a script is in my hands," he stated, noting that the Group was, as usual, bereft of viable plays and that he was for the first time seriously considering a revival of a classic, something Group actors had been agitating for over a period of years. He and Odets corresponded about the possibility of staging an Elizabethan drama; both *The White Devil* and *The Duchess of Malfi*, Odets commented, had good parts for Stella Adler, and their apocalyptic setting in "a world on its way to doom, breaking down with corruption and greed," had obvious relevance in their troubled times.

Clurman would have preferred to find a contemporary drama, however, and he was beating the bushes for scripts. He rued the hasty moment when he'd turned down William Saroyan's new play, which the playwright brought to him after *Highlands* opened. Clurman found it self-indulgent, mawkishly emotional where *Highlands* had been delicately lyrical, and even more structurally undisciplined than Saroyan's earlier work. He urged the author to revise it, but Saroyan replied that he couldn't write any other way. Clurman realized a few days later that the play's strengths outweighed its weaknesses and called Saroyan to say he'd like to buy it after all. Too late, the playwright replied; he'd just sold *The Time of Your Life* to a commercial producer.

Irwin Shaw was reworking *Quiet City*, and Lawson was doing the same with *Parlor Magic*, but Clurman didn't expect either project to turn into a workable script. The Group had an option on *Mexican Mural*, winner of the playwrights' contest, but he didn't think that was suitable either. He read every script he could lay his hands on in New York: a satire about dictators set in Biblical times, another one about war profiteering, an Irish play, a social drama about New York delinquents. None of them seemed right. He went down to North Carolina to see if the Group's old friend Paul Green would write something; Green was receptive, but wouldn't make a definite commitment. If Odets didn't come through with a finished version of *The Silent Partner*, Clurman realized, it would be a classic or nothing for the summer.

In an effort to keep as much of the Group together as possible, they took *Rocket to the Moon* on a short tour in early May. Unseasonably warm weather kept audiences away from the theatre in Baltimore despite good reviews, and business was bad in Philadelphia as well. Luther Adler told a reporter there that he'd taken a role in the film of *The Hunchback of Notre Dame* and planned to take a leave of absence from the theatre. "I've been an actor for 32 years, since I was four," he said. "I want to get away from the stage for a year." His wife, who'd had such an unpleasant experience in *The Gentle People,* may very well have been urging him to think of their future and the child they were expecting, but if so she couldn't shake his commitment to the Group just yet. He intended to join them for the summer, he said: "We're going to collect our thoughts, get a perspective. . . . We want to get away and think and decide just where we're going."

The Group waited anxiously for Odets to arrive with *The Silent Partner,* having very little else to do. Kermit Bloomgarden was negotiating with the popular "Kate Smith Show" for a regular radio spot in the fall featuring excerpts from Group productions, but this was mere moneymaking; they needed the promise of a future. While they took odd jobs and wondered disconsolately what lay ahead, the press showered praise on the season that had been so unsatisfactory to them, so impressive to the outside world. George Jean Nathan, not one of their admirers in the past, listed the Group in his *Newsweek* column as "the most progressive theatrical organization," citing *My Heart's in the Highlands* as the most interesting new American play, *Awake and Sing!* as the best revival and among the best pieces of ensemble acting, Clurman as one of Broadway's best directors. The New York Drama Critics Circle, unable to agree on the season's best play, included on its short list both *Rocket to the Moon* and *Highlands.* Several critics contrasted the idealism and collective faith of the Group with the egotism of Orson Welles, whose Mercury Theatre had folded in November after a disastrous production of *Danton's Death.* The Group, said one syndicated columnist, "came this season as close to developing an American art theatre, along the lines of the Moscow Art Theatre, as anybody ever has this side of the Atlantic."

The contradictions of their situation were encapsulated in a blurb in *Fortune* magazine, which thought enough of the Group's business savvy to place Clurman in its "Faces of the Month" column, where his picture adorned a page that also featured a wealthy Spanish supporter of Franco. "Analysts say 37-year-old Clurman has shrewdly combined Art (Stanislavsky technique), Hollywood names (Tone, Farmer, Sidney), quick-moving plays (Odets, Kingsley), and a vaguer but more important 'what makes money on Broadway,'" the anonymous caption writer declared. This was hardly the kind of praise the Group wanted.

June was a terrible month. Phoebe Brand and Hildur Bohnen were both in the hospital, Brand recovering from a siege of pneumonia, Bohnen with a dangerous kidney infection. On his way to the hospital in a cab to give blood for his wife's transfusion, Bud was in an accident and badly shaken, though unhurt. Odets smashed up yet another car (a Pontiac this time) in Mexico before returning to New York, with a beard hiding his scars, to confess that *The Silent Partner* was still unfinished. He loaned money to several actors, wrote a check to cover *Rocket* losses on the road, argued with John Howard Lawson at the Third Congress of American Writers about artists' social responsibilities, and departed for Maine, promising a complete script by July 1.

While their organization drifted, uncertain of its values and without a coherent program, other theatres they admired were being destroyed. The Federal Theatre Project was shut down on June 30, specifically singled out to be eliminated from WPA funding as the result of the hostility of Republican congressmen like J. Parnell Thomas and Clifton Woodrum (the latter told reporters he was going to get the government out of show business if it was the last thing he did). The Soviet government proved it was prepared to go even further to punish those who defied its notions of what acceptable art was. Meyerhold, whose dazzling stylistic innovations had inspired so much of the Group's early experimental work, was arrested on June 24. The dreams of a decade seemed to be coming to an end, art increasingly irrelevant in a world poised on the brink of war.

What could they do but go on, clinging desperately to the hope that they could remake their theatre and themselves to face a new age? Eight years of work couldn't be for nothing, they told themselves; all they needed, as Luther had said, was time to collect their thoughts. Odets missed his July 1 deadline but swore the script would be ready for rehearsal in just a few weeks. Clurman decided to go ahead and make plans: if *Silent Partner* didn't appear, perhaps Irwin Shaw would return from San Francisco with the new script he'd promised the Group; if not, they would rehearse a classic instead. They had to work. They rented a Christian Science children's school near Smithtown, Long Island, about ninety minutes from New York. On July 15 they packed up and headed east.

FOURTEEN

A Season in Hell

The stakes were high in the summer of 1939, and everyone in the Group knew it. To uninformed observers, the organization seemed poised for its greatest achievements, with the largest company of actors they'd ever assembled, Odets and six new playwrights in attendance, lavish accommodations to work in. The Winwood School, their Christian Science–owned retreat, boasted two dormitories (renamed the Belasco and the Windsor), a central rehearsal hall, an administration building, a gym, and one hundred acres of grounds, including tennis and basketball courts and a nearby lake. They had two acts of *The Silent Partner* (as usual, Odets was still working on the third) and hopes for additional scripts from Irwin Shaw and Paul Green.

But the Group knew their most important task was to straighten out the underlying organizational and artistic problems that had made their previous season so unhappy. Clurman got right down to essentials. Their first night at Smithtown he made it clear he intended this six-week retreat to include a fundamental reexamination of the structure, goals, achievements, their very reason for being. The old Group Theatre was dead, he told the actors. This was, he believed, an opportunity for them to create the Group anew, to organize themselves on the basis of the experience gained from the struggles and achievements of the past eight years. They had to think of themselves as students, still unfinished as artists and human beings; he hoped in a few years they would look back on their early accomplishments as mere child's play, a formative stage in their development, just as he hoped Clifford Odets would look back on *Awake and Sing!*, *Paradise Lost*, and *Rocket to the Moon* as "minor works of his young years." He invited the actors to "talk to me and advise me on the various problems of the Group, the things that disturb you, the things you want to know, the things you want to remedy."

He got the ball rolling with a vengeance the next afternoon, when he asked them a single question: "Is the Group willing to give me, for the period of eight months, the absolute right to act as arbitrator of their artistic, professional and personal destiny?" The word Clurman probably intended to use was "arbiter," and it's possible that Mike Gordon's wife, Elizabeth, who was taking notes at the meetings, simply misheard him, but the mistake was significant. He wanted to be an arbiter, someone with total authority to decide all matters pertaining to the Group without the advice or reproaches of the membership. What he felt he'd become was an arbitrator, mediating between warring Group factions, forced to listen to people's endless complaints about how others had compromised the Group Idea. He was sick to death of these wrenching demands on his time, his patience, and his emotional energies; they were killing him. The only solution he saw was to become the absolute dictator of Group policy. Would the actors agree?

The answer was no. "I believe that the fact that so many of us are here tonight after nine years and the fact that you are sitting in the director's chair is one of the greatest American miracles," said Bobby Lewis. But: "If you say to me that you would like to know whether I would place my artistic life and my personal life in your hands I would say, unqualifiedly and unreservedly no. Not you[rs] or anyone else's." Phoebe Brand felt that "what's needed now is more democracy not less. One person hasn't the time, one person can't possibly do everything that you want to do. . . . If I would trust anybody in the world it would be you, but it's against all my ideals and principles to agree to such a set up." Luther Adler and Bud Bohnen both wondered what Clurman wanted that he didn't have already. "As far as I'm concerned," said Adler, "the last two years have been something which falls in line with what you ask."

"I want more," Clurman replied. Pressed to be specific, he backed off, saying, "I'll talk about that later." This was the director's constant refrain at meetings; he was in such a state of personal and professional turmoil that his thoughts were even more disorganized than usual, exacerbating his tendency "to believe that to answer one question fully, one has to answer all questions." However, in the process of covering "The Cultural History of the United States and Its Derivations from Europe, the Foundations of the Group Theatre, and the Philosophy of Harold Clurman" (as one actor dubbed his talks), he usually returned, circuitously and elliptically, to the issues the actors were raising. Two days later, he made a startling statement followed by a rambling explanation that indicated indirectly what he wanted from the Group.

"Lee Strasberg has been getting a rough deal the last day or two around here," he said, referring to a comment Odets had made describing Strasberg's problems with the Group as symptomatic of the way personal relations were affected by the social system they operated in:

And I was thinking a few days ago of how I could bring Lee back to work with us. I haven't made any decision. I'm not going to do anything about it. The idea is fraught with dangers. All I want to tell you now is that this bad boy, Clurman, [who is] so vindictive that behind everybody's back he talks about everybody, with the full knowledge that the same compliment is paid to him by all concerned. This same person is always trying to figure how all the people he believes in creatively, who have something to give, can really come to give it in this organization. I say Stella has never ceased to be a Group member and you fight me because I didn't attach her to the Group. But it isn't Stella alone about whom I feel this way. It's about Lee Strasberg too. . . . Morris used to say, "Harold, once you said that if a Group member wants to leave the Group, you said you would struggle with them like Jacob with the angel. Now you don't struggle so much." True, I don't struggle quite as much. Because now I have come to the point after eight years of work, *you can't make the new world of the Group Theatre with people who are resistant.* You can't make it with people who spit in my face, with people who get sore at me. [Italics added.]

This sad, angry speech touched on almost every aspect of Group life that was troubling Clurman: the gossiping and backbiting he felt was damaging the company spirit, Stella Adler's equivocal relationship with the organization, the larger question of how to keep people attached to the Group. His mention of Strasberg and his final comments were extremely revealing. In the Group's early days, especially at Brookfield Center, the actors' belief in the directors had been absolute and unshakable. Strasberg's work in rehearsals and Clurman's afternoon talks had created an atmosphere of dedication and devotion that made the actors willing to be molded, artistically and personally, because the Group Idea meant more to them than their individual egos. Clurman believed the Group needed to recapture that mood. He didn't want more power; he wanted more faith, the total trust the actors had placed in all three directors at Brookfield. Strasberg had always been, by temperament and circumstance, the kind of authority figure Clurman was asking the actors to make him; perhaps he thought only a dictator could inspire the selfless commitment the Group required.

Clurman had never been that sort of leader. In the days of the triumvirate he was the director the actors counted on to grapple with their doubts, their problems, their fears. His formidable intellect was coupled with an enormous gift for friendship, an ability to make people believe their personal fulfillment was important to him (which it was) and that the ideas he spoke of so eloquently had an immediate, individual impact on their lives. His increased authority after the breakup of 1937 was accepted, with varying degrees of apprehension, but it didn't mean anyone viewed him as remote, infallible, or above the fray. If Bobby Lewis kiddingly referred to him as Der Führer, the joke being that no one was as patently un-Führerlike as Harold. The actors still came to him with their dissatisfactions; the problem for Clurman was that with the difficult, demanding Strasberg gone and the responsibility for the Group squarely on his shoulders, their complaints were now directed at him, or at policies and personnel problems they expected him to fix.

There was no going back to Brookfield. The young people fired with a passion to change the theatre and change the world were eight years older now; they'd had eight years of hard lessons in just how difficult the task they had set for themselves was, how many obstacles stood between them and their goal of creating an institutional theatre that would give them both artistic satisfaction and economic security. They couldn't possibly have the same faith that they'd had in 1931; their collective history bound them together with love and mutual respect, but it had also given them an intimate knowledge of each other's weaknesses. Real differences of opinion—artistic, organizational, and political—had arisen, and they couldn't be glossed over or wished away. They all came to a head on Long Island: if Brookfield had been the Group's summer in heaven, Smithtown was their season in hell. "It was awfully messy," said Phoebe Brand. "It just all fell apart in every direction: money problems, personality clashes, all kinds of terrible things. It was very sad."

Clurman might complain, as Crawford and Strasberg had before him, that the members were destroying the Group with their criticisms of the leaders, but the fact was they were just as critical of themselves. One major concern, raised over and over again, was the actors' sense that they were stagnating. "I have been troubled for a long time and have felt that I as an individual had died artistically," Morris Carnovsky said. "When I say we are the best actors in America, I say O.K., but that's not enough. . . . Our acting is not as good as it should be, and I know how good it is." Other members agreed. "I feel I haven't developed, and I'm interested in finding out why," remarked Ruth Nelson.

They missed the spirit of exploration and inquiry that had animated their early years. "It's sort of à la mode to pooh-pooh any discussion of these things among us," Mike Gordon said at one meeting. "To turn any question of technique into a laugh." Bud Bohnen felt they'd been wrong to give up classroom exercises and outside work. "Think of the period [of] *Dmitroff* and [the Grosz improvisations] and midnight trips to present things," he said. "When our lives were full of practical activity there was much more relish. Whenever we've had extra curricular life is where [our development] reaches its highest form." The basic problem, Phoebe Brand concluded later, was, "We were not working on our craft enough, we were riding on our past reputation, not experimenting enough, not investigating new forms."

What the actors were implictly calling for was a return to the regimen of classes, exercises, and more exercises that Strasberg had initiated. They'd resented his autocratic attitude that they were children in need of firm guidance; many of them had serious philosophical objections to his emphasis on emotional memory, sharpened in 1934 by Stella Adler's report on her work with Stanislavsky. But those creative clashes had strengthened them as artists, forcing them to examine and defend their beliefs and their acting choices. The freedom Clurman gave them in the Odets plays, especially *Golden Boy*, stood on the foundation of that discipline; it had been a necessary step in their evolution, but now they were feeling what they'd lost. Phoebe Brand's description of her personal progress was a paradigm of the journey every long-time Group actor had taken. "It has to do with the training I had with Lee in which he worked inside me all the time and a rebellion I had against that," she said. "I passed through a period of wanting to be left alone and trying to work out my own development, which I did to a great extent, but now I feel I have to get out of that. I want to go on from there. . . . I don't want to be coddled anymore. Yet I resist not being coddled."

Brand put her finger on the basic problem. She wanted to be challenged, yet she wasn't prepared to return to the days when she sat worshipfully at the feet of General Lee. The Group actors had learned and achieved too much to be treated as students—or at least, not as beginning students. Strasberg had tried to maintain the old paternalistic relationship and been rejected. Clurman had treated them as adults, but he'd also limited their creative work to specific productions, where the time constraints imposed by the Group's shortened rehearsal periods made it difficult to make the detailed, leisurely explorations of character and theme they'd come to expect. They needed to find a new basis for collective growth, one that acknowledged their independence and individual ideas yet yoked people together in a freely accepted discipline.

Everyone felt the absence of such discipline. Meetings were sprinkled with references to "irresponsibility in behavior," "failure of integrity," "a peculiar kind of lack of democracy in our dealings with each other." The younger actors thought their elders didn't respect them because they didn't have the same level of technical knowledge. Morris Carnovsky complained of cliquishness: "little Grouplets within the Group, preferences which exclude other actors too much. . . . sidelong glances, looks, smiles, which immediately consign that person to a lower level." This was not a healthy basis for collective life.

In retrospect, it seems obvious that the actors' destructive behavior was a response to the confusing combination of Clurman's approachable, non-directive personal style and his decision in 1937 to narrow the circle of authority to include only himself and a few close associates. He was still telling them at Smithtown that his desire for absolute authority didn't mean they wouldn't be consulted: "I want to make the entire Group, without exception, to always be my counsellors and never have to make a decision, or very rarely, without trying before hand to tell them what the problem was and without listening to their advice and without giving everybody the right to fully express their advice to me. The two things are not contradictory." Well, the two things *were* contradictory, and by sending such mixed signals, he created an atmosphere of bewilderment and frustrated hopes in which the sniping he deplored was virtually inevitable.

Yet the Group's problems went deeper than Clurman's failings as a leader. He was the same man whose passion had brought them together in 1930, whose friendship and support had sparked Odets' emergence as a writer, whose benevolent tempering of Strasberg's domineering tantrums had given them the confidence they needed to assert their individual worth as artists. Strasberg's departure, and the passing of the Group's business administration from a woman they loved and knew shared the Group Idea (Crawford) to a man they suspected of injecting commercial considerations into the organization (Bloomgarden), had changed their relationship to their management, but the issue was more basic than that.

The Group Theatre wasn't Harold Clurman any more than it had been Harold Clurman, Lee Strasberg, and Cheryl Crawford. It was a collective, founded, as Clurman wrote in describing their early days, on "a unity of background, of feeling, of thought, of need." Every issue raised at Smithtown, every specific discussion of Group problems, in the end came down to the members' agonized feeling that this unity was gone, that they were no longer a collective. They had been one, they wanted to be one, they had no idea how to make it happen. "There's no mechanical way of creating this communal life we're talking about," Art Smith said.

When they discussed the perpetually thorny subject of casting, Lee Cobb insisted it wasn't just the natural desire for better parts that made actors in small roles discontented:

> For instance, and this might seem silly, if I personally thirst for the friendship and understanding of Clifford Odets and haven't got it, I will be unhappy when you're casting me. There's a connection. If Clifford says he likes to write plays for us because he wants to understand us and does, and I can't share in that, then I am not part of that collective. So that when you cast me in the small part, I am unhappy not because of the small part but because it's part of something of which I'm not a part.

Ruth Nelson believed actors could be reconciled to subordinate roles if they were made to feel important to the Group: "I think that things can be done in the way of asking people who understudy actually get to play the parts. There's also direct personal contact in making an actor realize that he is valuable and has his use." Gadget Kazan suggested every actor have a personal interview twice a year with Clurman "so that we can know what you think of us and our problems in relation to the various parts we play."

The question of working outside the Group was particularly volatile because it touched on the essential nature of people's commitment to the collective. "I want a Group Theatre that is extremely tight," said Mike Gordon.

I want a Group in which because there are no outside commitments that Sandy is dying to play a Willy Wax [the role Meisner had disliked in *Rocket to the Moon*]. . . . I want a kind of theatre where a small part is played by a prominent actor. You don't have to know his name, you know he is a developed actor. I want the kind of theatre where there is no longer conventional casting, in which there is crazy casting, in which Frances Farmer is playing character parts and I am playing an ingénue, in which Morris is playing a much younger man than Stark, because I know they can do it. It will be a much better production. That is the kind of psychology that will produce the kind of work that the actors will get great satisfaction and growth out of. If there is an organization where the orientation is outside, that will never happen.

It wasn't so simple, replied Luther Adler. He used himself as an example:

I feel I am stale. I want to rest . . . the reason I am here is what I really want, with a capital R, is this kind of theatre, even though I myself now don't feel up to working in it. As I said to Harold, let me go. Let me have a period where I don't act in the theatre. Maybe I will do something else. Maybe I will come back. You don't want it all the time. That is why it is difficult to say whether we are going to have a tight or loose theatre. I've never been worried about the people who go. I think it is anti-life to have people who never leave. [On the other hand] if we have a kind of "you go and do as you please," we won't have a permanent company and we won't have a theatre. We don't want either of these things and yet we want both. When people want to go, let them go. One of the faults I have always found with our theatre is that we watch the other fellow too much.

The debate went on all summer. The issue was raised in a specific, particularly difficult form when Bud Bohnen asked for a leave of absence of five weeks to take a featured role in the film version of Steinbeck's *Of Mice and Men*. Bohnen had already refused, with great reluctance, Lewis Milestone's offer to test him for the part; the salary was $1,500, which he desperately needed, but he believed that "the summer was sufficient to make it unGroupy to even entertain the idea." When Milestone convinced the studio to hire Bohnen without a test, the actor was sorely tempted; he decided, with Clurman's approval, that it should be a matter for general Group discussion.

The discussion was tense, combining a considerable degree of sympathy for the well-liked Bohnen with resentment that he was playing on that sympathy. Morris Carnovsky and Bobby Lewis, who'd both turned down other offers so they could join the Group for the summer, were understandably annoyed that Bohnen's case should be presented as more urgent. "I feel that I am as staunch as Bud is and he might just as well have been talking about me," said Lewis. "I was just trying to sit here and think of why I am not up there. . . . I haven't thought it out except that I have a certain emotional feeling." Sandy Meisner argued, "The principle seems to be primarily the fact that we have got to keep our theatre and our actors. When Julie [Garfield] goes and you release the principle it is very clear in everybody's mind that you have lost an actor. If Bud goes it is very clear in my mind we haven't lost an actor. . . . I have no fear that he will violate the principle." Lewis and Carnovsky might well have concluded from this line of reasoning that they were being judged as somehow more susceptible to the temptations of Hollywood than Bohnen, yet in the end they too agreed that he should be allowed to make up his own mind, which in essence meant they felt it was all right for him to go.

The decision left a bad taste in everyone's mouth. Even Frances Farmer, who felt "the Group as a whole is never wrong," worried that the decision set a bad precedent. "We are all in agreement that Bud should go," she said. "The only thing that is before us is, if Bud can go, why can't everybody go?" Gadget Kazan summed it up, speaking directly to Clurman: "I have an uneasy feeling about any loosening of the fabric of this organization. If I were in your shoes as director I would be extremely worried because Bud is a very important person in the Group not only as an actor but in charge of radio work, on the Council, and so forth. I just can express a terrific concern about this general tendency to loosen things." Clurman admitted that he'd thrown the question open to the whole Group because "I'm getting more and more to the point where I can no longer make decisions of a certain kind because I don't know completely whether that is what I am supposed to do."

The discussion of Bohnen's release was confused because the members were confused about the most difficult question of Group life. How could they precisely define the reciprocal obligations of the individual and the collective? When did personal sacrifice stop being a necessary contribution to the whole and become destructive self-abnegation? How much personal fulfillment did the collective have to provide the individual for the relationship to be worthwhile? Clurman's frequent attempts to clarify his own position—he often seemed to be thinking out loud rather than stating a definite attitude—were symptomatic of the whole Group's uncertainty.

Clurman knew that communal life could flourish only when it satisfied individual needs, and he was well aware that in the past two years the Group Theatre had been a source of pain rather than pleasure to many members. "We have to find an individualism which is collective and a collectivism which respects the individual," he said at one meeting. "The people in the Group have a sense of not wanting the collective of the Group Theatre to so dominate me that I am lost." Yet, he argued, "Nothing is incompatible with the Group idea and the idea of individual development. . . . Who is the Group Theatre, they? It is not they. It is us. It will live through each individual realizing himself through it. . . . The Group must satisfy all of us, each of us. Unless it does, the Group won't exist."

At the same time, Clurman resented the actors' criticism of him and Group policy, seeing it as a rationalization for succumbing to the temptations of the outside world. He warned the actors against

> saying I will work for this as long as it is ideal or as long as it satisfies my artistic sense of what should be. Everybody who has ever gotten out of an idealistic movement has gotten out of it on the basis of idealism. . . . Everybody will agree that *Quiet City* was not thorough, and therefore people say that the way it is done makes a theatre artistically unthorough. If people want to go into movies and work for George Kaufman on the grounds that *Quiet City* was unthorough, there is a basic fallacy.

It was impossible to resolve this fundamental question through debate. In a way, it was a matter of fact, not opinions. When people believed that they shared a set of values, that they were making progress toward a common goal, then collective life was healthy and individual sacrifices, no matter how difficult, were made with a sense that they were justified. When the consensus broke down or the goal was too far off, individual problems and dissatisfactions became paramount and the collective dissolved. There was no clear dividing line between these two states, only a vast gray area of confusion and distress. The Group lived in that gray area at Smithtown, and no one could tell if they would emerge with renewed purpose or scatter to the four winds as alienated, lonely individuals. All they knew that summer was, they were miserable. "This is a very difficult theatre," said Sandy Meisner, speaking for them all. "It's the most painful thing I ever hope to contend with in all my life and I would like very much not to leave this theatre but there are certain things which tend to force me in other directions."

Clurman tried to convince them their suffering was worthwhile, indeed inevitable:

> We are the only theatre really going in America which recognized the possibility of pain and failure in our work. This is not a theory. We have lived through very difficult periods. We are the only theatre which said it is impossible for us to go on without difficulty in the theatre, to see ourselves in the theatre as producers of a series of successes. We must be prepared for these difficulties and ride through these periods. Because we have been able to weather the storm we are today in a better position than we have ever been before.

After all, sorrow wasn't the sum total of their experience over the past eight years. Clurman gave a series of talks on the foundations of the Group Theatre, hoping to inspire them with the desire to renew the Group just as his words at Steinway Hall in 1930 had inspired them to create it. "This theatre is a theatre of meaning," he reminded them at the first of these talks, on July 19:

> The Group Theatre is one of the few who said at the beginning of its work, Plays have a meaning, theatres have a meaning. We fight for the meaning of these plays because they are good for our life, they are good for the life of those who love us and those whom we love and the theatre is one clear, strong definite form of the expression for us of the meaning of our life which is also the life of our families, of our city, of our state, of our United States, of our world.

Unfortunately, more typical than this moving summation was the incoherent way Clurman opened the next night's session. Even allowing for the fact that Elizabeth Gordon's verbatim notes tend to make people's comments seem more disjointed on the page than when spoken, Clurman sounded out of control:

> Yesterday I said it's your life we are dealing with. I found it was very difficult, I had a headache, so I stopped because I couldn't go on in that particular state. I also thought of beginning classes, but I've decided only to begin when I was sure of the process so that the process would be very sure and not tentative because that would start it off in the right way. Then I thought we would continue a discussion of organizational problems we had begun but left off. Then I felt that in a sense I wasn't up to it. Then I thought I might give you an evening off and we could all go to the movies or do anything else we wanted. Then I thought no, I don't want to do that tonight because I told Gadget that in a few days I will have to leave camp for a day just to be alone for a while so I could come back and be clearer about a number of things because while I'm throwing questions in the air all the time, these are questions that form into a zero and I'm throwing questions at myself too. I decided that I wasn't going to call off the evening meeting even though I'm still woozy—it's not sleepiness, just wooziness—and we would have a conversation piece. By which I mean that a lot of things have been going on for a few days, talks, discussions, thoughts, suggestions, and it might be good for us just to meet and have a little talk together, less official than something that was prepared in advance.

The Group actors looked at each other, embarrassed and frightened. Clurman had always been a rambler, but in the past it was because his mouth simply couldn't keep up with the exuberant gush of his thoughts. This was like watching someone have a nervous breakdown in public. "He was very disturbed emotionally the final summer, very disturbed," said Phoebe Brand. "We never understood completely why."

There were many reasons. He and Stella Adler were fighting nonstop: about the Group, about their relationship, about whether they should do a classic if *The Silent Partner* didn't work out (she was pushing for Chekhov's *The Three Sisters*), about anything and everything. Almost more unbearable was the constant stream of well-meaning advice from the rest of the Group. "It is simply not the Group's business if I've had a fight with Stella," he shrieked at one meeting. "And it's not your business, either, if I want to make up with her."

But Clurman had lived through crises with Adler before—they defined the relationship—and he'd been warding off Group complaints about his obsession with her ever since their first season. There was more on his mind than that. The Group's expectations of him filled him with dread. "I sometimes want the whole Group to flop," he confessed. "I want everything to go wrong because that would relieve me of [a] certain responsibility. Then I will cry and pretend to be heartbroken, but I will really be happy because I won't have this thing hanging on my mind. I push on because that is what is expected of me, but I want it to fail. I have just as much need of its failing as for it to succeed."

Harold Clurman had given birth to the Group Theatre, had kept it alive against virtually insurmountable odds with his warmth, his humor, his passionate faith that such a theatre was artistically and spiritually vital, not just for the people who worked in it but for American society as a whole. To hear him admit that part of him wanted it to fail was a terrifying confirmation of just how bad things were. He'd been exhausted by this monstrous task before, but there had always been someone else to help him shoulder the burden: Crawford to raise money and run the office, Strasberg to direct a production and (not at all incidentally) act as a lightning rod for the actors' criticisms. For two years Clurman had been on his own. Bloomgarden might keep an eye on business matters, Kazan or Lewis might direct an individual play, but they weren't the leaders of the Group. He was, and the institutional and personal responsibilities he'd borne for nearly a decade had worn him down:

> Everybody has to solve his own problem. A problem that has been solved for you has not been solved. The only thing I can do is to aid, abet and make less or more painful the solution to the problem. I'm a social factor in relation to you in the sense that I try to preserve the Group Theatre which I still believe will be a creative thing for the people engaged in its work and also the fact that certain guidance I think I can give. Because that's my function and I hope my talent.

Don't forget I have never meant to give the feeling to any of you that I'm going to solve your problem. If I do I'm misrepresenting myself, and if you believe and hope for that thing you are doing yourself an injustice.

Clurman was overwhelmed by the complex, bitter tangle of personal and professional discontents that were giving collective life an ugly aspect that summer. "We are fighting for our lives in building this theatre," said Art Smith, and like most life-or-death struggles, it got pretty vicious. Their fear that the Group might not survive prompted outbursts of the kind of personal nastiness most likely to kill it. Bud Bohnen made sneering reference to Lee Cobb's new Packard, bought with Hollywood money. Morris Carnovsky was elegantly sarcastic, his usual mode of expressing anger, and infuriated his fellow actors by making veiled comments about people's inadequacies, then refusing to specify exactly what he meant. A few men vented their hostilities in the Winwood School's well-appointed sports facilities. "Some of the guys would play basketball and just barely escape murdering each other," Ruth Young remembered. "Mike Gordon and Gadget Kazan were the kind of competitive athletes where losing was the most tragic thing in the world; you had to kill each other." Kermit Bloomgarden didn't bother to sublimate: given an ultimatum to choose between the Group and his work with Herman Shumlin, he told Clurman, in public, to "kiss my ass and beg me to stay." Sylvia Sidney was so horrified by the way Group members went at each other that she left in disgust after a few weeks and went home to her farm in New Jersey; the Group informed Luther Adler that his wife was selfish.

These ghastly proceedings were leavened by a certain desperate gaiety. Phil Loeb, the Group's old friend from the Guild who'd given a wonderful performance in *My Heart's in the Highlands*, kept them in stitches with his antics. During baseball games, if he didn't like the umpire's call he would take off his pants and wave them in the air. The Group gave him a birthday party, complete with a lavish cake, and while he delivered a lengthy thank-you speech he reduced everyone to hysterics by absent-mindedly picking up pieces of the cake and smearing them all over his body. The actors would assemble at night in the Belasco lounge to recite bawdy limericks or get up a game of charades. Sandy Meisner interpreted the phrase "public solitude" by coming downstairs stark naked with a chamber pot tied around his hips. "It was a crazy, wild summer," said Ruth Young. "You could cut the temperament with a knife, but in addition to all the tragedies, the *Sturm und Drang* and the divisiveness, there was a spirit of fun." Sidney Lumet, who'd been invited to visit by Bobby Lewis, agreed: "They were some of the funniest people in the world."

Lumet didn't attend the evening meetings and wasn't aware of the conflicts racking the Group. What he saw was a dedicated company of artists who took their work, but never themselves, utterly seriously. Incredibly, despite the dreadful pain felt by almost every member of the Group as they watched their collective bond disintegrate, they were still holding classes and preparing scenes, hoping that if they continued their work as though nothing were wrong they could keep the Group alive by the sheer force of their will and the strength of their need.

They took a speech class, faithfully intoning tongue twisters like "Charge, Chester, Charge" and "99 Nuns in an Indian Nunnery" as if they were still beginners rather than seasoned veterans acclaimed as the finest acting company in America. They began studying movement with Maria Ley Piscator, wife of the famous German director who was now living in exile, but her minimal English made it difficult to understand what she was getting at, and the actors didn't much like the exercises. Will Lee's wife, Rebecca Rowen, was asked to offer a more accessible class based on her work as an Anna Sokolow dancer. Bobby Lewis gave a course on acting fundamentals for the younger Group members; Stella Adler and Sandy Meisner assisted him from time to time. Bud Bohnen gave a talk to the new actors on the Group's history. There was even an attempt to revive the old Group spirit of social inquiry; Odets had spent a good portion of the spring with Sid Benson, a labor organizer many in the Group had first encountered back in 1934 at Ellenville, and the playwright brought his friend along to Smithtown to give lectures on contemporary issues.

Molly Thacher kept her six playwrights sequestered on the second floor of one of the dorms, instructing them never to answer the phone or let anyone distract them from their work. She had great hopes for her protégés, who included Arnold Sundgaard, author of *Spirochete*, one of the Federal Theatre Project's most controversial Living Newspapers; Jerome Weidman, whose satirical novel of the garment industry, *I Can Get It for You Wholesale*, had been a best-seller in 1937; and Charles O'Neill, a young playwright whose adaptation of a Danish play called *The Melody That Got Lost* she'd been pleading with Clurman to produce for more than a year. Thacher knew how unwise it was for the Group to depend so heavily on Odets; she was trying to prepare for the company's future.

Odets himself was feeling as ambivalent about the Group as ever. "When I think of home, I think of the Group Theatre," he told the company at one of their early meetings that summer. "It's my contention, by the fact of the Group Theatre's being together and being what it is, that men must not be alone, they must not be unconnected . . . they must work and live together." He relied on the Group, he said. "I can't write plays in a void. I must write because you need my plays." At the same time he was harshly critical. "It becomes increasingly difficult for me to write plays for the Group Theatre actors. When I thought of how a certain actor would play a certain part, in each case I checked off a name and said, well, from this person I don't get such a feeling because to my mind this person is no better actor than he was six years ago. This man is holding me back."

Odets unhesitatingly supported Clurman against the actors, several of whom had come to his room after the first talk to express their fear that Harold was turning into a tyrant like Lee Strasberg:

> Harold Clurman has seen—and has seen with very good eyes—certain twentieth-century idiosyncracies in all of our people or most of them which slowly and surely engulf and devour the Group Theatre. [He] has for years been watching the individual growth or retrogression of all of the members of the Group and he has seen that even in the case of the most deeply socially minded members of the Group there still are elements, I am saying this advisedly, of what goes to make a fascist and by that I mean what goes to make an irresponsible uncreative person because essentially that is what fascism is.

Several actors commented at meetings that the only truly creative partnership in the Group was the one between Odets and Clurman; underpinning these remarks was an uneasy sense that the two considered themselves to be the Group Theatre and were prepared to do without anyone else if they had to. Yet Clurman and Odets weren't getting along all that well at Smithtown either. There may have been personal tensions: Odets had embarked on an intense, stormy affair with Frances Farmer, whose marriage to Erickson had finally broken down, and if he hadn't already heard the rumors running through the company that the actress had been involved with Clurman during Stella Adler's absence, he certainly would have heard them now. He continued to resent the director's easy willingness to take money from him for the Group; he was paying for the summer, as he had subsidized rehearsals of *Johnny Johnson*, the closing costs of *Rocket to the Moon*, and countless other Group expenses in the past.

The principal bone of contention, however, was *The Silent Partner*. Odets had been grappling with the script for four years, but it seemed to Clurman that the version the playwright handed him on July 15 was only slightly different from the one the Group had rehearsed unsuccessfully in late 1936. He still found the characterizations, especially those of the working-class protagonists the audience was supposed to admire, dangerously weak and the love triangle involving the two brothers who lead the strike insufficiently compelling. Added to this old complaint was a new concern: the sweeping New Deal labor legislation enacted since Odets had written the first draft, he believed, dated the play. He told Odets of his doubts, yet continued to assure the actors the play would be put into rehearsal that summer. Odets read the first two acts to the company on July 17.

The discussion the following day (Odets' thirty-third birthday) revealed that the rest of the Group too had mixed feelings about *The Silent Partner*. Some were enthusiastic. "I feel this to be a very deeply and basically antifascist play," Carnovsky said. "To me this play is like a celebration of the good in life, a belief in the final emergence of the good forces in the world against the evil. . . . To me this is a very poetic play." Max Gorelik was delighted by the script because "it seemed to show a definite movement on the part of Clifford and the Group Theatre"—i.e., it dealt with "real" issues instead of the kind of messy psychological themes the tough-minded and highly political Gorelik disdained.

Sandy Meisner was moved by Odets' passion: "The feeling I got from the play was that this comes from Clifford. It was a heroic thing, his feeling for the workers, his feeling for justice for the working people." Yet, Meisner added, after the devastating scene in which armed thugs pour containers of milk onto the ground rather than let the strikers' wives have it for their children, "I got very tired and bored. I said, now the suffering is on a different level. Now it's just suffering . . . [it] doesn't move you anymore." Several actors were troubled by the later scenes; they worried that the defeat of the strike would encourage the audience to see the workers as misguided and foolish, that Odets' intended point—the characters had learned from their mistakes and would do better next time—was unclear. Mike Gordon noted, as Clurman had, that the central love story didn't quite work. Nonetheless, the actors were clearly excited by the play and profoundly in sympathy with its theme, which captured the basic spirit that had animated so many of them throughout the 1930s. It would be many years before a group of actors preparing a play would again so matter-of-factly assume their kinship with working-class people fighting for a better life.

Clurman's comments at the July 18 meeting made it clear that his worry about the play had as much to do with tactical as artistic considerations. The play had forty-three characters and five sets, he noted; it would be costly to produce:

I ask myself still, do people pay $1.50 in New York to learn the strategy of a strike? If you ask me today if I think the play will be a success I would say I don't think so. I think we're going to lose money. . . . Then I say to myself there is the problem of the public ideologically. You must have heard once in a while that we are . . . a Red theatre. It is not good—we [w]ould be non-essential as that. . . . this play will not diminish or wipe out that impression that we are a certain type of theatre.

Clurman's private comments to Odets were even stronger:

This play at the present time would do the very opposite of what it's intended to do. [It] would put the Group Theatre in its attempt to meet the American situation today three years back in its effort to move forward and be the honored first theatre in America and with the most creative audience possible to have.

Clurman had never wanted the Group to be a narrowly political theatre; he'd made the same comments about their goal being recognition as America's first theatre upon his return from the Soviet Union in 1936. The difference three years had made, however, could be seen in the fact that he had gone on in 1936 to direct a deeply political, though nondogmatic, interpretation of *Paradise Lost*, whereas it was now clear that he preferred not to produce *The Silent Partner* at all. It would be easy to see his reluctance, as several actors did, as a commercially motivated desire to keep the Group noncontroversial and successful along the lines of *Golden Boy* and *The Gentle People*. That would be unfair. In his view, the mood in America had changed, and the Group must change with it:

> Plays are not of protest now. They are plays of affirmation. I think that because of the type of anger that is represented in *Silent Partner* a noisy, raucous impression is made which is bad for the present day, bad for our theatre because our theatre's problem is the problem of asserting itself [as part of] the most healthy elements of the creative American life and the creative American tradition. . . . It's impossible for a theatre to fight its audience, contradict its audience in a violent fashion. A theatre is successful in a social and artistic way when it brings the audience what it wants, what it deeply needs, what it is thirsty for at that particular time.

Waiting for Lefty had met a certain need in 1935, Clurman acknowledged, but now America's needs were different. Underlying everything he said about art and propaganda was the sense that a broad audience was no longer receptive to angry, openly class-conscious plays like *Lefty:*

> No political theatre can exist at all in the American theatre today as a professional theatre. We are an American theatre because our Americanism is an attempt to permeate into the problems of America today and understand those problems. If you do that in the form of bad art and art that is too eager, you are too eager to get didactic results, very often you are fooling yourself, it is satisfying to your ego but it isn't telling the people the things that are important so that they hear and are willing to go where we want them to go. We must constantly respect that outside situation.

Clurman was trying to reassure the actors that he still believed in the same things they did—he identified himself over and over again as an antifascist and a liberal—but not everyone was convinced. Smith, Gorelik, and Bohnen strongly disagreed with some of his statements about the impossibility of political theatre: Gorelik challenged his assertion that Piscator's famous *Volksbühne* had produced nothing but flops; Smith, in a series of sharp questions, forced him to admit that it was possible to take a promising play with flaws (like *The Silent Partner)* and learn something by working on it with actors; and Bohnen pointed out that it was sometimes valuable to be in the vanguard of public opinion. "In the heat of certain strife you may be the first one to go to the trenches and you know you have to go," he said. "That is not didactic art. It falls into a complete category which I would like to see developed sometime."

Odets could see that there was considerable support within the Group for producing *The Silent Partner.* The opinion that mattered to him, however, was Clurman's. The director finally told him that the Group would produce the play if he insisted, but mentioned again the prohibitive expense, the likelihood of commercial failure, and its potential to bankrupt the organization. Hurt, angry, yet still loyal, Odets consented to a postponement. "He doesn't intend to rewrite this play at the moment," Clurman told the actors on August 8:

> He is too close to the old script to be able to do that. He intends to write a new play which takes place in New York, unlike anything he has done before, which he hopes to have finished in December. He doesn't wish to be rushed. He doesn't wish to bring me incomplete scripts which I then spoil, but he wishes to have plays which are as complete as he can make them. This intention seems also extremely wise, and I for one shall be happy to spoil plays only by directing them.

Odets had bowed under pressure, but he wasn't happy, nor was he particularly gracious about it, as Clurman's rather bitter asides revealed. More than twenty years later, the memory of *The Silent Partner* still rankled. "I should have insisted that the play be produced," Odets told an interviewer in the early 1960s. "It's the kind of writing that I have not done since, and I don't think I'm capable of it now . . . if I had continued writing from there on, after its production, in the same way, something extraordinary might have come out. The production was absolutely necessary for me. But I was not mature enough to insist upon it." It's doubtful that the production of *The Silent Partner* would have altered Odets' destiny, but there's no question that its abandonment for the second time drove a wedge between the two men whose creative relationship had fueled the Group's artistic life for four years.

Clurman tried to put a good face on things. Odets was preparing a new acting version of *The Three Sisters* for them, he told the actors, and they would begin rehearsing it within ten days. The Group would divide their efforts between that and a new play by Irwin Shaw, who'd promised to deliver the script by August 15. Clurman knew Shaw's general theme already, he said; it was "extremely interesting and exciting," and he expected the script would be "satisfactory for production almost immediately on receipt." *The Golden Years*, like Lawson's *Parlor Magic*, dealt with the rise of a native form of fascism among the American middle class—a theme of only too obvious relevance, as the Group could see from their encounters at a local bar with the unpleasant and arrogant members of a nearby camp of Nazi sympathizers. Unfortunately, Clurman's optimism about the play's producibility proved unfounded. When he read the script, he concluded that it too was not yet ready for rehearsal and rejected it.

That left them with *The Three Sisters*. Clurman's divided feelings about the advisability of proceeding with it can be judged by the fact that he didn't begin rehearsals until August 22, a week after he'd rejected the Shaw play and a scant ten days before they were slated to return to New York. He'd made it clear in earlier discussions about staging a classic that he didn't believe such a production could be financed in the commercial theatre, and he was uncertain that his gifts as a director were well suited to Chekhov. He decided to have Stella Adler act as his codirector since her years in the Yiddish theatre had given her a greater familiarity with the production of European plays.

Rehearsals got off to a wobbly start, with Clurman admitting that he hadn't definitely decided on the cast. He was still hoping that a contemporary script would materialize, and he was reluctant to make final decisions about *The Three Sisters* when he might need some of the actors for this hypothetical production. "I decided for the time being to disregard the other play," he said—a wise decision since there *was* no other play—

and to proceed on the basis of the casting of this play only, with the knowledge that I may have to take certain people out of this play [and] put them in another one. . . . That much is set. It's particularly the women's parts which are not set. However, I don't want to delay another day or two to get to work. So bear in mind, I know this is not the best way to proceed, but under the circumstances I can see no other course. It doesn't mean that anybody is being tried out. It means I'm actually not certain.

The three sisters were Stella Adler as Masha, Frances Farmer as Olga, and Phoebe Brand as Irina. Luther Adler was cast as their brother Andrey, Ruth Nelson as his grasping wife, Natasha. Morris Carnovsky played Vershinin, Masha's lover; Phil Loeb was Kuligin, her husband. Sandy Meisner played Baron Tusenbach, in love with Irina; Gadget Kazan was Solyony, the angry, destructive captain who kills Tusenbach in a duel. Sidney Lumet noticed, as parts were handed out, how disappointed younger actors like Alfred Ryder and Marty Ritt were to be passed over, but it was hardly surprising that Clurman had chosen the Group's most experienced members for this complex play.

Working under less than ideal circumstances, with organizational and personal disagreements still dividing the Group and his relationship with Stella Adler a constant source of anguish, Clurman nonetheless began work with aplomb. He invited a Russian émigré to spend time with them explaining the background of the play: what kind of school Kuligin would have taught in, the architectural style of the houses the characters inhabited, the cultural atmosphere of a small Russian town at the turn of the century. It had been a long time since the Group had done this kind of extensive research; it was exciting for the actors, who felt they were getting the chance to challenge themselves they'd been longing for.

Clurman stressed the links between this provincial Russian town and a world the Group actors knew better:

> To me, *Three Sisters* is the most American play, because it deals with young people. It's about people in the old life talking constantly about the future, about getting away from this old life and not accepting it at all, or at least completely. That is the basic environment in which this play takes place. When I saw the Civic Repertory production, I said, this reminds me of an American town, with its high school, its teachers, its Rural Board and a good deal of the atmosphere we got in a small town in 1925.

Many American actors, taking their cue from the Theatre Guild's rather stodgy classical productions, tended to play all foreigners as languid, world-weary sophisticates, and Clurman thought in the first reading that the Group cast was being more "sensitive" than the play required:

> [The characters] are just guys, they want what they want and they are very normal, the most normal people you could meet. These people are fundamentally full-bodied, energetic, full of the juice of life, full of humor, passion, appreciation. As you observe, the tragedy of these people is certainly not that they are a bunch of depressed people but rather that they are a bunch of wonderful, healthy people whose health and fullness is not given an opportunity to expand in the world in which they live. . . . The spine of the play might be to find a full life in a world that has no opportunity.

That was the key, the theme that had drawn Clurman to the play, the source of the actors' feeling of kinship with it. There were many technical reasons why Chekhov was an especially suitable playwright for the Group: the Stanislavsky system, after all, had been developed working on his plays; the fully imagined characters, each with a personal history and philosophy resonating under and around the text, offered scope for the detailed exploration that was the cornerstone of the Group's method; the fact that every part was rewarding solved their perpetual problem of casting good actors in thankless roles. But the love they all felt for *The Three Sisters* went deeper than that: it stated, in the most warmly human, well-rounded way, with all the complexities and contradictions of life itself, the single idea that informed the Group's greatest work.

It had been implicit in *The House of Connelly* until the Group persuaded Paul Green to change the ending so that Will Connelly, who has the opportunities, joins forces with Patsy, who has the will, to defy the dying society crushing them both. It took its most agonized form in *Success Story*, in which Sol destroys himself and the woman who loves him because America gives him no productive outlet for his burning energies. It came to fruition in the Odets plays, which affirmed with passionate optimism that men and women could *create* the life they wanted, even in the face of an indifferent or hostile world—through militant political action in *Lefty*, through the characters' deeper understanding of themselves and their society in more mature works like *Paradise Lost* and *Rocket to the Moon*. It was the great struggle of the Depression years, it was the American dream in any decade, it was the Group's very reason for being: to make a better life.

The fundamental source of the Group's fratricidal conflicts at Smithtown was their knowledge that this better life was hardly any more within their grasp in 1939 than it had been in 1931. The specific causes of their quarrels —personality clashes, disagreements over the best way to run their theatre, Clurman's weaknesses as a leader, the painful problem of reconciling collective commitment and individual ambition—were important, and their role in shattering the Group shouldn't be underestimated. They couldn't have killed a theatre firmly rooted in a welcoming and supportive environment.

The disheartening truth was that their eighth season had brought them showers of praise and not one step closer to institutional security. They'd emptied their treasury financing two experimental productions because not a single Broadway investor would even consider backing such risky ventures, even as the critics applauded the Group's decision to mount them. They'd killed themselves to link playwrights more closely to the Group and assure a steady supply of worthwhile scripts, then confronted the hard fact that only the most conventional, commercial writers could make a living on Broadway; everyone else had to bounce back and forth to Hollywood, a commute which made impossible the kind of intimate, profound understanding Odets had once shared with the Group. Their theatre had been founded on the premise of a permanent company engaged in continuous full-time work; in eight years they'd had exactly two such seasons, during *Men in White* and *Golden Boy*. Their only reward for all the work they had done was a flood of Hollywood offers that would reduce them to the level of well-paid employees and, if enough of them left, put an end to the Group Theatre.

Clurman saw this problem as clearly as anyone. More than his problems with Stella Adler, more than his worries about the actors' insubordination, that was what was tearing him apart. "There was no ground for a Group Theatre in New York; there never had been," he wrote a few years later, describing his troubled state of mind. "There was the material, the need, the value, the chance; all this had been amply proved. We had done the impossible. Yet, at the zenith of our efforts, we were as far from being a truly established, rooted organization as we had been as unknown beginners in 1928." He didn't say this directly to the actors, but they could see how worried he was. "Almost the last view I had of Harold that summer," said Morris Carnovsky, "was when I was out walking around, and I came to an opening in the grass, and there he was, standing in the middle of a field wringing his hands. I knew that we were doomed."

"The three sisters are the light that shines in darkness," Clurman told the actors, offering a central image to illuminate the play. Their theatre, he believed, was like the sisters:

> [An] organization which is trying to carry out some aspiration, through some particular medium, any such job which is aspiration of that kind in this country which is not yet in full light, be it said without too much pessimism is a light that shines in darkness. . . . We are in the Group Theatre as symbolic not just of a group, but of a certain healthy sector of the American middle class, and though we go forward now—and we should and must and will—with loud cries of revolt, that has about it the quality of exasperated youth, and marching songs and battle hymns. It's valuable to us to hear the quiet faith, expressed in the perfect lyric of an artist who perhaps lived in even greater darkness than ourselves.

The darkness of the outside world was closing in on the Group. The day *Three Sisters* rehearsals began, radio reports announced that Hitler's foreign minister, Joachim von Ribbentrop, was headed to Moscow. On August 23, Germany and Russia signed a nonaggression pact, each nation promising to remain neutral toward the other in the event of a war. The shock to American radicals can hardly be overstated. For ten years, with a few notable exceptions, they'd looked to the Soviet Union and the Communist party as the leader of the world's progressive forces. American communists had been prominent leaders in the battle for trade unions and civil rights; their European comrades were in the vanguard of the struggle against fascism. Russia had supplied aid and arms to democratic Spain while the capitalist West stood aloof. Suddenly, the nation they'd viewed with naïve veneration as the home of a brave new experiment in better, fairer social relations had made an alliance with a government they regarded, with every justification, as the incarnation of reaction and evil.

When the news reached Smithtown, a pall settled over the company. Sidney Lumet saw Odets standing on the dining-room porch, tears rolling down his face. Eleanor Lynn remembered lying in the grass with Gadget Kazan, who tried to explain to the shocked and angry young actress that the Soviets must have had their reasons. Frances Farmer, too, asserted defiantly and disconsolately, "Stalin must know what he's doing." All over the Winwood School, small clusters gathered to talk in hushed, pained tones of what the pact meant. War in Europe was obviously inevitable; Hitler had only been waiting to secure Germany's eastern flank before he invaded Poland, and Britain and France had made it clear they would not back down a second time as they had at Munich.

The need of the Group's more committed radicals to believe in the Soviet Union was great, especially at a time when their ideals at home seemed beleaguered and incapable of realization. By the next afternoon Odets had come up with a justification for this incomprehensible step. "Clifford said the Russians knew that England, France and America wanted Germany to attack the Soviet Union and do away with it," Phoebe Brand remembered. "The only hope they had of staying alive was to make a pact and push them the other way, which they did. It made sense to me at the time." There was a certain amount of truth to Odets' statement; the Russians had decided after the Munich settlement (which they'd been excluded from) that the West couldn't be counted on to stand up to Hitler and that Tory-ruled Britain, in particular, was at least as hostile to communism as to fascism. Nonetheless, no amount of rationalization could hide the fact that a government they'd believed was different had been revealed as a power monger like all the rest, willing to sacrifice principles for the sake of political and territorial gain.

In the bleak week that followed the Hitler-Stalin pact, the Group gathered after rehearsals around the radio, waiting to hear when—no one any longer said if—war would be declared. Their organizational meetings had ground to an exhausted halt, coming to no conclusions. Clurman closed with a grimly determined assertion: "This thing has to go on one way or another. I say the solution . . . is the ultimately complete relaxation that comes from an understanding of the fundamental collectivity here, a fundamental belief in the honesty of the people. Then there won't be any dissension about going or staying. But that kind of relaxation which says, something is wrong here, let's fix it, but by joining together with a 'yes' to the Group work." But their work on *The Three Sisters* had begun to falter, with Clurman more uncertain and rising tension evident between Stella Adler and Morris Carnovsky. On Friday, September 1, their last day of rehearsal in Smithtown, Hitler's armies marched into Poland. On Sunday, as they returned to New York, England and France declared war on Germany.

FIFTEEN

Homeless

A demoralized and apprehensive Group straggled back into New York in early September. The bruising summer at Smithtown had solved nothing. No decisions had been made about the form their organization would take; it seemed for the moment they would simply stumble along with Clurman trying to hold them—and himself—together. A couple of their most stalwart members were gone: Bud Bohnen was still in Hollywood, and Bobby Lewis had taken a leave of absence to direct *The Time of Your Life*, the Saroyan play Clurman had turned down. After his separation from Frances Farmer, Leif Erickson resigned from the company. Manny Eisenberg, the press agent, was out as well: though he had worked with the Group off and on for five years, Eisenberg was, in Clurman's view, too rooted in the now moribund left theatre; the director hired the more Broadway-oriented James Proctor. Ruth Young, who was close to Eisenberg, felt bad about the change, especially when Clurman handled the firing by sending Eisenberg a letter—his preferred way of avoiding confrontations.

Clurman couldn't be blamed too harshly for his shabby treatment of Eisenberg; he needed every scrap of his limited emotional resources to deal with the messy disintegration of *The Three Sisters*. To begin with, he discovered with dismay that it would be nearly impossible to finance the production. Even the Group's most loyal backers had no interest in subsidizing a classic, which they assured him would lose money. Clurman had expected this difficulty; far more disturbing, because unanticipated, was the bitter feud that had broken out between Stella Adler and Morris Carnovsky.

In Carnovsky's view, Adler was giving an extremely affected performance as Masha. Under Clurman's direction, with an acting script prepared by Odets, the Group was trying to present Chekhov in a modern, fairly idiomatic way that stressed the play's links to America in 1939. This may not have been a comfortable approach for Adler, raised on the European classics in the Yiddish theatre, where the grand manner and big gestures weren't considered incompatible with emotional reality. Her personal style tended to the flamboyant, and though Strasberg had managed to rein her in for *Success Story,* it had been a struggle. She might take criticism from a director; she didn't appreciate it from a fellow actor, especially since she was the codirector. Her niece, Pearl Adler, remembered her being "in a state of turmoil and anguish" during the preparation of *The Three Sisters.* Tempers rose, and heated exchanges disrupted rehearsals. Clurman couldn't control the battling pair. The rest of the company held worried meetings, took sides, and quarreled themselves. The gruesome climax came at a rehearsal when Carnovsky lost his temper and shouted, "You are not a truthful actress. I just don't believe you!"

This wasn't something you said to Stella Adler. Her entire life as an artist had been dedicated to the search for truth in acting. It was what had led her to study first with Boleslavsky and then with Stanislavsky himself. It had pushed her away from Broadway, even though she loved the glamour and luxury of the Great White Way. It had drawn her to the Group and, for the most part, kept her there, despite her discomfort with collective life and the perpetual financial hardships involved. She was deeply wounded by Carnovsky's remark, and of course she was furious. There was no hope they could work together after that.

Adler resigned from the cast. Clurman, worn out by the conflict, his authority compromised by his inability to prevent this confrontation, quit too, and persuaded Kazan to take over the production. The women's parts were shuffled: Frances Farmer replaced Adler as Masha; Ruth Nelson took Farmer's place as Olga; Pearl Adler, who'd been well reviewed in small parts with the Group under her stage name, Katherine Allen, came in to play Natasha. Rehearsals proceeded without further incident for a few more days, but the company's spirit was broken. On September 25, *The Three Sisters* was abandoned.

It was a bitter moment for the Group. For years they'd wanted to challenge themselves with a classic, and until the Adler/Carnovsky struggle erupted they'd been excited by Clurman's direction and pleased with their own progress. Phoebe Brand, who believed she was doing her best work to date as Irina, saw her chance to become a recognized leading actress slip away. Carnovsky was appalled by the holocaust his hasty words had wrought. The outburst was utterly out of character for him, prompted as much by the inner dynamics of the disintegrating collective as his dissatisfaction with Adler. The incident was so traumatic that fifty years later he and Brand were both convinced there had been no other Group productions after *The Three Sisters.*

In fact, the Group plunged immediately into a new play: *Tower of Light* by Robert Ardrey. Kazan had remained friendly with the playwright despite the failure of *Casey Jones,* and while paying a visit to Ardrey late in the summer of 1939 he read the script and liked it. The idea came to Ardrey during the grim days of the Munich crisis, when he was living on Nantucket. Looking out into the vast Atlantic Ocean, worried about the war that seemed inevitable but disgusted by the self-interested maneuvers of the politicians at Munich, he wondered what people of good will could do in a world gone mad. He got the idea to write of a man tormented by the same question, and over the course of 1939 the play gradually took shape.

The protagonist is Charleston, a former combatant in Spain who's retreated to a job as keeper of a lighthouse, where he can live in isolation from political problems he's concluded can't be solved. Ardrey introduced a fantasy element by confronting his hero with ghosts from a vessel shipwrecked off the coast in 1849, disillusioned idealists who have also fled their dreams. Their unhappy stories teach Charleston that men and women must stand up and fight for what they believe in, and *Tower of Light* closes with him leaving his ivory tower, an obvious symbol for the traditional refuge of intellectuals.

When the play was produced by the Group on Broadway, Charleston's final big speech was an impassioned plea for peace:

America's not going to war. She's got a bigger job than war. Peace. Peace in the face of war, that's the job, and she can do it. . . . Don't force the world to go our way, force won't work. Show them, show them that our way's best. Do the things we've always done, every man to his peacetime job. But go to work with a new responsibility. We've got to show others what freedom means, freedom of speech, freedom of conscience. A nation at peace can put men to work at better jobs than destruction. A people at peace can have butter to eat and the luxury of justice. America's got one high obligation: to preserve the last peace on earth.

That was not, however, the original closing. In an essay written nearly thirty years after the fact, Ardrey laconically noted that the Hitler-Stalin pact "left only a line or so to be written into my third act to complete the play." This was disingenuous: the Group's final prompt script shows three new pages on different paper, inserted into the third act to replace nine deleted pages. A Baltimore newspaper, after the play opened, reported that "as originally written—or, so we have been told—much of the last act was a hymn to Russian ideology and had to be hurriedly rewritten when Russia, by its treaty with Germany, let the Leftist author down." This seems overstated; Ardrey had never been a communist, and his earlier work displayed suspicion of pat ideology of any kind. Nonetheless, it seems clear that he, like most of the American left, was stunned and bewildered by the pact, and the changes he made in *Tower of Light* were expressive of the disarray among American radicals.

The official Communist party line was that America should stay out of a capitalist war, and this was insisted on so slavishly that thousands of people quit the party in disgust. The Theatre Arts Committee, which followed the same line, was so discredited by its abrupt about-face—one month it was criticizing isolationists as capitalist stooges, the next it was preaching the same philosophy itself—that Equity ordered its members to leave the organization in April 1940. Yet in the winter of 1939–1940 many radicals who were by no means dogmatic communists allowed their suspicions of Tory England and anti-Semitic France, nations only too willing to parley with Nazi Germany in the past, to persuade them that the United States was better off on the sidelines. It was the period of the "phony war," with Hitler apparently content to hold his army in Poland and rumors circulating that the European powers had made a deal: a few face-saving months of stalemate, followed by peace on the basis of Germany's recent gains.

It was in this context that Ardrey wrote his call for vigilant neutrality. It embarrassed the author later; the published version of the play concludes with Charleston urging an armed struggle against Nazism, presumably the speech used when the play was a hit in besieged London during the Battle of Britain the following year. But in the fall of 1939, Ardrey's argument that Americans could best combat fascism by strengthening democracy at home was an honest expression of the uncomfortable position many left-wing intellectuals took, one that soon became untenable.

Clurman shared Ardrey's views, but he had other concerns about *Tower of Light*. Though he liked the theme and thought the use of ghosts offered interesting theatrical possibilities, he found it lacking in "lyric inspiration," which may have been his way of acknowledging the somewhat hollow ring of the closing oration. After the debacle of *The Three Sisters*, however, he knew the Group needed to work—now. He accepted the play and was annoyed by the actors' cool response to it; he'd put aside his doubts and expected them to do the same.

Ardrey and Kazan had agreed that Clurman should direct *Tower of Light*, but during the preparation period Kazan took it over. According to Ardrey, this was because Clurman had a nervous breakdown; though neither Clurman nor Kazan mentions this in his memoirs, it seems very likely. Clurman had been under intolerable strain for at least eight months, since Stella Adler's return had reconnected his personal and professional difficulties, and the buffeting of the summer months followed by his painful failure to keep *The Three Sisters* alive might very well have been more than his nerves could stand.

Kazan directed the play at arm's length, he recalled in his autobiography, uncertain that either he or the cast were suited to Ardrey's cool Midwestern style. And indeed, Ardrey was yet another playwright taken aback by a full-scale exposure to the Group's rehearsal methods. (*Casey Jones* had been cast primarily with non-Group actors, while *Tower of Light* featured Luther Adler, Bud Bohnen, Morris Carnovsky, Art Smith, Lee Cobb, Ruth Nelson, Frances Farmer, and Harry Bratsburg.) In a funny article with a bitter undercurrent that appeared in the *New York Times* just before the play opened with its new title, *Thunder Rock,* he described his experience. What happens to the author of a Group play? he asked:

> They give you what amounts to temporary membership in the Group Theatre. You have all the innocence of a bystander on the Maginot Line. If somebody in the company gets a divorce, you discover yourself on the witness stand. If the switchboard girl has a baby, you find yourself in labor pains.
>
> The light man has a brainstorm. He floods the stage with evil red light. You run shrieking to the director. Go talk to the light man, says he. So you wring the light man's neck, personally. An actor discovers a bad line in his part. Do you find out about it, in nicely tempered tones, from the director? No, in the midst of rehearsal the actor speaks the line, comes to a halt, looks about. "Where's the author? Ardrey, this line stinks." You find yourself with the business manager, worrying about the budget. You find yourself with the publicity man, worrying about the press release. You share [Max] Gorelik's headaches, while he works over the model of the set, trying to find room in the base of a lighthouse for half a dozen vital Group actors to express their vitality. And while you're biting your fingernails . . . you're confronted by Morris Carnovsky. For ten minutes, says Morris, I sit over there on the left without anything to say. What am I supposed to be thinking about? So you go to bed at night—if you go to bed at all—worrying not about Carnovsky's lines, but about his thoughts. . . . A regular Broadway production finds the author on the outside, looking in. A Group Theatre production finds the author on the inside, looking cross-eyed.

Playwrights in the past had been startled by the actors' commitment to exploring the total reality of a play, which meant confronting the script in a less well-mannered, more turbulent way than many writers were accustomed to. The cast was particularly high-strung for *Thunder Rock* owing to the Group's unsettled state and the personal problems of individual members. Luther, who was playing Charleston, had to contend with his wife's antipathy toward the Group and their shared concern over their new baby. Their son, Jacob, was born on October 22 and shortly thereafter developed an alarming fever that didn't subside for several days. Adler was worried enough that the Group nearly had to cancel *Thunder Rock*'s scheduled out-of-town premiere; the infant recovered in the nick of time, and the show went on.

Frances Farmer, who played one of the ghosts, was clearly in bad shape. She drank heavily throughout rehearsals in a misguided attempt to cope with the breakup of her marriage and her tumultuous affair with Odets, and the cast watched in dismay as her clothing got sloppier, her personal hygiene more negligent, her approach to the part more and more uncertain. The final blow came at the end of October, when Luise Rainer turned up in New York and Odets callously sent Farmer a telegram that read, "My wife returns from Europe today, and I feel it best for us never to see each other again." She was devastated, and rehearsals did little to help her regain her equilibrium; she knew she wasn't very good in the part.

Nothing in Farmer's training had prepared her for a tricky period role, and her admiration for the Group actors and their technique only made her more critical of her own performance. "Frances was an extremely intelligent woman, who understood all of the things that the Group was striving for," said Mike Gordon. "But she wasn't ever really equipped through the practice to implement it for herself. I think that one of her greatest assets, her self-confidence as a luminous, beautiful young woman, was impaired by the fact that she knew what the goals were but did not have the technical resources to accomplish them in her own work."

The Group never solved the problem of how to integrate into the ensemble new and younger actors who hadn't shared the intensive classes of the early years. Clurman wasn't by inclination a teacher as Strasberg had been, and although several Group members were—Bobby Lewis, Sandy Meisner, Stella Adler, Morris Carnovsky—the company simply didn't devote the time to study that it once had. The established Group actors felt the lack too, but it weighed most heavily on new members like Farmer. A permanent Group Studio would have enabled these actors to develop, but the fruitful dual focus of the company's early years, as a training ground and a place to present individual plays, had narrowed; the Group Theatre was now primarily a producing organization.

Farmer had other problems, many of them a product of her stormy personal history, but some reflecting stresses within the Group as a whole. During *Thunder Rock* she hung a star on her dressing room identifying herself as Lucy Stone, a feminist gesture about thirty years ahead of its time. She resented the way women were treated in the Group and she wasn't shy about saying so. One evening with Clurman, Irwin Shaw, and Phoebe Brand she mercilessly badgered the director about his indifference to the actresses' problems as compared with his constant concern for the men's artistic development. She expressed herself violently and almost incoherently, but Brand knew what she was talking about; Group women had been feeling like second-class citizens for years.

Despite her troubled state of mind, Farmer somehow managed to struggle through the final rehearsals, and the company arrived in Baltimore on October 31 to give three performances before *Thunder Rock*'s New York premiere. Bobby Lewis, who'd quit *The Time of Your Life* because of artistic differences with the management, rejoined them to play a small part. Luther Adler spent the train ride to Baltimore complaining to Clurman about Kermit Bloomgarden's supposed incompetence and bad manners. Adler rather fancied himself as an actor-manager along the lines of his famous father, and he viewed his actions as giving his friend Harold the benefit of his experience. Clurman, heartily sick of well-meaning advice from the Group actors, aware that Adler disliked *Thunder Rock* and was worried about his interpretation of Charleston, attributed the whole episode to pre-opening nerves and paid little attention. Group members didn't seem to be listening to each other much anymore.

The Baltimore reviewers found the play well acted but static. "Perhaps too much good talk and too little sustained action," noted the *Sun*, "but it will command the respectful attention and provide a stimulating evening for thoughtful theatregoers." When it opened at the Mansfield Theatre on November 14, the New York critics were less impressed by the talk, and a few were positively contemptuous of the action. (One asserted that the special visual and sound effects associated with the ghosts "belong in tank-town drama.") The closing speech prompted the most sharply divided opinions; many agreed with Joseph Wood Krutch of *The Nation* that it was merely a "grandiloquent pep-talk," while a minority found it, with Richard Watts in the *Herald Tribune*, "a cry of hope for humanity that cannot be repeated too often." Only Max Gorelik's imaginative set sparked general enthusiasm. The reviewers' customary words of praise for the Group's acting were more restrained than usual, and Robert Rice in the *Telegraph* agreed with Kazan that the Group's approach was wrong for Ardrey: "All in all the production is a trifle too Russian Arty for a play that requires a straightforward American treatment." Luther Adler's apprehensions were justified; he got the first generally bad notices of his Group career, although kinder critics attributed his melodramatic acting to an understandable lack of faith in the implausible script.

Discouraged by the reviews, lacking a profound commitment to the play themselves, the Group decided to close *Thunder Rock*. To their surprise, this announcement prompted a small flurry of the kind of ardent protest that had kept *Success Story* and *Paradise Lost* running despite bad reviews. Some Group friends who had scorned *Golden Boy* as too commercial, *Rocket to the Moon* as too personal, and *My Heart's in the Highlands* as too strange assured Clurman that *Thunder Rock* was in the best Group tradition of serious contemporary drama. The playwrights Philip Barry and Elmer Rice, neither of whom knew Ardrey personally, wrote letters to the *Times* defending the play; Barry noted that the second-night audience gave it seven curtain calls. Attendance picked up over the weekend, and Helen Thompson's phone started to ring with inquiries from theatre parties eager to book evenings. As they had so many times in the past, the cast took cuts, and the run was extended.

But *Thunder Rock* was no *Paradise Lost*, and it was 1939, not 1935. Clurman's description of the efforts to keep it open—"fervent zealots in the audience cried out: 'Don't close the play! Don't close it!' "—had a weary tone. He was as tired of others' "breathless professions of faith" as Strasberg had been tired of his in 1934. When Luther Adler balked at taking a second pay cut to keep the show running, sparking the resentment of his fellow actors and the author, Clurman refused to insist: "I no longer considered it wise to make actors play at half or less than their regular salaries in plays that hardly deserved such sacrifice." *Night over Taos* had been no more worthy, yet the actors had willingly worked at minimum to keep the Group together, and Clurman had applauded their commitment. This time around, he just didn't care enough. *Thunder Rock* closed on December 2 after twenty-three performances.

Even the news that Odets had finished his new play, *Night Music*—third act and all—didn't cheer the Group much. An unsigned paper entitled "An Analysis of the Problems," preserved in Odets' files from the period, reveals the company's disconsolate state of mind. This document may be "Harold's desperate paper in December," referred to six months later by the actors, though the language doesn't sound like Clurman; on the other hand, he wasn't sounding much like himself that fall. More probably, however, it was written by someone else, perhaps Bud Bohnen. The authorship hardly matters, for the paper's importance lies simply in its voicing of the feeling that had spread through the Group since Smithtown that "things simply cannot continue in the same old way any longer. To relegate the Group Theatre to just sort of a producing organization would be to relegate the actor from a participant in a vital and living organism for which he would make any sacrifice into an employee, playing in plays as they are produced and nothing more." The basic task was one of "radically overhauling the whole method of work and inner life of the theatre."

The paper acknowledged that the Group's program required "a high degree of planning and organization [and] these in turn demand a high degree of authority in the leadership," but, it warned, "the leadership must also recognize the voluntary nature of the association of the Group, and that leadership cannot be won or maintained by force." It urged annual or semi-annual meetings at which the members would discuss major policy issues and assist in the formulation of plans for the future.

Some in the Group wanted more say in the decision-making process than this, but the one point everyone agreed on was that individual productions by themselves could never satisfy the Group or create the institutional theatre they all wanted. The sticking point, of course, was money, and the paper looked to Odets once more as the Group's potential savior. "The present burning problem is the production of *Night Music* in the most efficient and most effective way. . . . The successful production of *Night Music* opens the opportunity of reorganizing the Group to ensure its future existence as a Group."

Clurman had high hopes for *Night Music*, a play he retained special affection for throughout his life. He thought the rambling, picaresque drama of Steve Takis, a young movie studio employee adrift in New York, perfectly captured the nervous, aimless mood of this unsettled moment in history, then dug deeper to explore the emotional and spiritual homelessness at the core of the American experience. Indeed, there were wonderful things in the play. Each of the minor characters thronging its many scenes is a complete, marvelously quirky individual, observed by Odets with surprisingly gentle humor. Detective Rosenberger, the kindly policeman who befriends Steve, was an honorable addition to Odets' gallery of nurturing father figures (so unlike the playwright's own crass progenitor). Fay Tucker, the young actress Steve falls in love with, is basically a conventional ingenue part, but she has a sweetness rare in Odets' female characters.

Night Music has two major technical shortcomings. The plot premise is absurd: Steve, sent to collect two trained monkeys and bring them back to Hollywood, lands in jail and then on the streets when one of the animals throws away the wallet containing his tickets, credentials, and money, while the other steals Fay's locket. It's necessary to swallow this nonsensical device whole in the first scene before enjoying the atmospheric comedy that follows. Unfortunately, the first act isn't as enjoyable as it might be, because the leading character is so irritating. Odets deliberately paints Steve as a hostile, unpleasant young man; by the time the second act reveals the uncertainty behind his arrogance, the damage has been done and it's hard not to wish the charming Fay would give her abrasive suitor the brush-off.

Clurman was aware of this, but hoped to tone Steve down in rehearsals. He believed *Night Music*'s commercial prospects were good. It was Odets' first real comedy, though its undercurrents were deeply sad, and the narrative moved at a lively clip. *Night Music* was as mainstream in its aspirations as *Golden Boy*, but the earlier play challenged basic American assumptions about success in a way that the new one never did.

Odets was no longer the fiery young man who'd written *Waiting for Lefty*. In his journal during rehearsals of *Night Music*, he wrote:

Communism needs to be Americanized before it will have any effect in America. My personal feeling about social change is this. I have one opinion as a private citizen. But in the world of theatre, in relation to my plays and audiences for them, leftism as understood by the Communists is impossible. Any excessive partisanship in a play defeats the very purpose of the play itself. . . . To be socially useful in the theatre, one cannot be any more left than, for instance, LaGuardia. Unless one is writing pamphlets or agitational cartoons, only clear but broad generalizations are possible. But one must make sure to write from a firm core even though, in my opinion, an attempt to reach as broad an audience as possible should always be taken into consideration. I thought once that it would be enough to play in a small cellar, but I soon saw that those who would come to the cellar were not the ones in need of what I could say.

How much the Group too had changed could be seen in the casting of *Night Music*. Clurman used the core of the Group company, including many of the younger actors: Kazan as Steve, Carnovsky as Rosenberger, and Bohnen, Meisner, Nelson, Smith, Loeb, Bratsburg, Lee, and Pearl Adler in smaller parts. He cast Tony Kraber and Walter Coy, who'd both been absent from Group productions and Group life for a while. But he also hired a lot of people who'd never worked with the Group before and released Luther Adler to take a leading role in a new Elmer Rice play, *Two on an Island*, rather than requiring him to stay and play a small part as had been Group practice in the past. "Now that Group methods and discipline had been established," Clurman wrote of this decision a few years later, "I had no desire to continue to apply them in a doctrinaire fashion by making first line actors play bits that might just as well be played by young aspirants seeking their first chance."

Yet even Adler, who would make more money in his non-Group role, had reservations about this policy. The Group wasn't strong enough to lightly permit its members to make outside commitments. Why, for example, was Clurman encouraging Kermit Bloomgarden to produce *Heavenly Express* as a non-Group production, with Bobby Lewis as director, when both men's talents could well have been used within their own organization? The loosening of Group bonds aroused as much unease that winter as the discussion of the issue had at Smithtown.

The casting of the female lead once again created hurt feelings and bitterness. Frances Farmer was out of the question; after *Thunder Rock* closed she barricaded herself in her apartment, refused to see anyone, then took a starring role in Ernest Hemingway's *The Fifth Column*, a Theatre Guild production directed by Lee Strasberg. (Strasberg couldn't cope with the troubled actress either; she was drinking more than ever and finally simply stopped showing up at rehearsals. She quit the play in January and fled the following month to Hollywood.) Clurman wanted a movie star for the part, possibly because he hoped it would help him raise money for the show, which was proving difficult. In December he, Stella Adler, and Bobby Lewis took turns flying to California, where almost every second-level actress in films read for the part. Phoebe Brand was so angry about the way they were proceeding that she refused to take a small role in *Night Music*, declaring for the first time in nine years that she would look for work outside the Group.

The Hollywood visits proved fruitless, and on January 7 the *Daily News* announced that "at the moment, Eleanor Lynn has been assigned to the role"—a phrasing that could hardly have reassured Lynn. Her worry was justified. A scant nine days later, Odets had decided she was "way off type." (Typecasting, a dirty word in the Group's early days, was apparently now acceptable.) He and Clurman called Lynn into the Group office and fired her. She wasn't womanly enough, they told her. After a few more days of auditioning and waiting for word from Margaret Sullavan, who was trying to get out of her MGM contract to play the part, they finally settled on Jane Wyatt, an ingénue with considerable stage experience better known for her work in such films as *Lost Horizon*.

Clurman loved *Night Music* and enjoyed directing it. The play meant a great deal to him personally, and he thought it was significant for the Group as well. "The Group Theatre believes with Fay Tucker 'We're more than them and we can sing through any night!' " he said, quoting one of *Night Music*'s loveliest speeches. "We are living in the night of civilization [but] small voices like Fay's (a real American voice) give us hope." The play's spine as defined by Clurman—"the search for a home"—was a resonant one for the Group actors, who feared they were losing their own home in the theatre and would soon be cast adrift to roam New York as aimlessly and unhappily as Steve Takis did.

The basic conflicts of Group life hadn't been resolved, simply put aside for the more pressing task of preparing *Night Music*. Everyone knew that the play's commercial success was their only hope for a breathing spell to reconsider and reshape the Group. "If they did not have my script, there would be no Group Theatre," Odets wrote in his journal. He was more and more resentful of the Group's need, weary of a company that seemed incapable of supporting his plays financially. He'd had to arrange *Night Music*'s backing himself by agreeing to write a screen version for the independent film producers Al Lewin and David Loew in exchange for a $20,000 investment in the stage production; Odets put up the rest of the money, some $21,000, himself.

He was no longer sure the Group's artistic contributions to his work justified such sacrifices, and he wasn't happy about rehearsals. He still admired Clurman's work as an analyst of the play's values and the characters' psychology, but he became impatient with the director's less-than-assured physical staging and inability to impose discipline during rehearsals. "Harold is very overindulgent as a director," he wrote in his journal. "The actors are on a holiday, feeling, as they do, in a friendly relaxing atmosphere."

Until the Group arrived in Boston on February 5 for *Night Music*'s out-of-town tryout, Odets' pleasure in the production outweighed his misgivings; he liked Wyatt's and Kazan's work, admired many of the actors in smaller parts, and thought Carnovsky was "shaping out one of the best performances he will ever have given." Yet he was more and more worried about *Night Music*'s prospects in New York, despite the Boston audiences' enthusiasm and generally favorable reviews. He began to think that Kazan lacked variety and was slightly mechanical as Steve and that Clurman was doing nothing to correct the problem. On February 17 he wrote:

We haven't profited from the tryout period. Twice [Harold] sat in afternoon rehearsals and permitted the company to rattle through their lines. Later, when I asked him why he hadn't used each rehearsal for some particular purpose (work on characterizations, etc.), he stammered out some feeble apology, flushed into silence, and that was the end of that. . . . As you watch, week after week, you discover that the actor needs a firm hand to guide and tie up his ideas into proper forms and finished performances. This last half Harold is unable to control or direct up to practically eighty percent.

Like the Actors Committee in 1936, Odets wanted the psychological depth of a Group to be combined with the slick Broadway finish he thought would ensure critical respect.

Clurman had a lot on his mind besides *Night Music*. He'd been brooding about the Group's organizational problems ever since Smithtown, and the day the play opened in Boston he decided the time had come to take action. He'd already informed the actors who'd been given a thirty-week contract the year before that this arrangement would not be continued, and on February 8 he followed up that disheartening news with a bombshell. From now on he would run the Group alone, he told the company; the Council was abolished, and performers would be hired solely on the basis of their suitability for specific productions. This was the authority he'd asked them to grant him at Smithtown, but now he wasn't asking; he was telling. A well-informed *New York Times* article reported the actors' reaction:

> The dissidents hold that Mr. Clurman has established himself as a "dictator" with the support of Clifford Odets and Elia Kazan, whereas the Group was originally formed as a collective unit whose policies were to be determined democratically. The others hold that the transition was necessary to the smooth functioning of the Group and that the new set-up is not at variance with the Group's original tenets.

The Kazans' home life must have been decidedly uncomfortable in this period, for while he was identified as Clurman's supporter, Molly Thacher was one of those most outraged by the director's actions. Many of the actors were angry, but inclined to think that once *Night Music* had opened in New York Clurman would calm down and they could convince him of the error of his ways. Thacher was skeptical; at a meeting held to discuss the situation she declared the Group had been transformed by fiat into a one-man theatre she wanted no part of. She resigned, and her name was conspicuously absent from the *Night Music* program when the show premiered at the Broadhurst Theatre on February 22.

Clurman had argued for the Lyceum, a smaller house he believed was better suited to *Night Music*'s intimate tone, but Odets kidded him about his love for old theatres and insisted on the more fashionably located Broadhurst. Despite his criticisms of the direction and Kazan's performance, Odets still hoped for a commercial success. He said little to Clurman and nothing to Kazan of his misgivings about their work. The three were virtually inseparable in the weeks before the opening, dining in chic restaurants like Barbetta (a far cry from Stewart's Cafeteria), drinking bottles of fine wine selected by the budding oenophilist Odets, and puffing on the cigars they all loved. They shared a belief that only strong leadership would save the Group and an impatience with the members who wanted more democracy; it drew them, temporarily, closer together.

The reviews quickly drove them apart. In the all-important *Times* notice, Brooks Atkinson sneered, "Now that Odets writes like Saroyan, Doomsday is near. Mr. Odets, who has always clung to the erratic, is now writing entirely without discipline and listening fondly to the sound of his voice. . . . [he] has been around long enough to improve instead of subside into mannerism; there is no reason why we would take comfort at this late date from a new playwright who has not yet learned how to use the theatre expertly." There was a note of almost personal hostility in Atkinson's review; he seemed to be criticizing an entire trend in the theatre as much as Odets' play. His fellow critics, though generally more restrained, took the same approach. Perhaps the most wounding aspect was that Odets, once acclaimed as sui generis, a theatrical law unto himself, now saw his work lumped by virtually every critic in an "interesting but undisciplined" category that included, in the current season, Rice's *Two on an Island* and Saroyan's *The Time of Your Life* as well.

"It is not merely that Messrs. Saroyan, Rice and Odets have all abandoned realism for romantic extravaganza," wrote Joseph Wood Krutch in *The Nation*, "but also that they have adopted the same theme—namely the triumph of youthful spirits over the confusions and cruelties of contemporary life." Reviewers found that theme banal, and they objected to the impressionistic, nonlinear way the playwrights expressed it. Only Stark Young in *The New Republic* sensed that the press was blaming the artists for truthfully expressing their times. "Can we demand from a dramatist, in an age like ours, scattered, distracted, surging, wide, chopped-up and skimmy, that he provide his play with a background of social conceptions that are basic, sound, organized, prophetic, deep-rooted?" he wondered. "We should remind ourselves that there is no reason to ask any theatre to surpass its epoch in solidity, depth or philosophic summation."

With the exception of Atkinson, the critics were fair to *Night Music* within their limited frame of reference. If their comments were geared to the conventional Broadway audience rather than more adventurous theatregoers, who enjoyed the play's offbeat tone and picaresque structure, that should hardly have come as a surprise. Yet Clurman and Odets were devastated. They resented having their production pigeonholed as part of a social trend; Clurman loathed the critics' habit of comparing authors and believed it had led them to miss *Night Music*'s basic theme of homelessness —"so simple, clear and direct . . . that we ought to assume that everyone save perhaps the professional reviewers can easily appreciate it," he wrote in an angry article responding to the notices. Odets' reaction was even more emotional. "I felt as if a lovely delicate child, tender and humorous, had been knocked down by a truck and lay dying," he wrote in his journal the day the reviews appeared.

The play meant so much to them, its success was so crucial to the Group's future, that anything less than a rave struck them as a vicious attack. They were confronting, as they had throughout the Group's history, the paradoxical nature of the critics' dual role as reporters to the general public and opinion makers with enormous power to create or kill a healthy theatrical scene. The villain in the *Night Music* affair, as Robert Rice pointed out in an intelligent article in the *Telegraph*, was not the press, which was right to judge the play as not Odets' best. It was

a theatrical set-up that in the first place makes commercial success the measure of merit and in the second place makes perfection a precondition of commercial success. There is no room for in-betweens on Broadway these days. The play must be tops in its own category to get anywhere, and it doesn't matter whether the category is the most driveling and infantile variety of slapstick—vide, *Hellzapoppin*—or the most exalted variety of art—vide, the Maurice Evans *Hamlet*. It's got to be perfection in its own sphere before success is assured.

Such a state of affairs leads to the discouragement and failure of important young authors. . . . It becomes, if carried to its ultimate point, the death of the living theatre, because it puts a quick and unkind quietus on everything that has potential promise. . . . As long as [playwrights'] first and initial gleams of talent are met with a stony and ungrateful nonchalance, nine out of every ten will perish by the wayside. As long as the theatre is in the hands of real estate operators, and is supported by $3.30 customers, there will be barriers to creativity that will prove too difficult for all but a few to overcome.

The Group knew all this; for nine years they'd worked within a system fundamentally hostile—or, worse, indifferent—to their ideals. They'd created a great theatre, but they couldn't create a welcoming theatrical environment that would nourish it. A company could run for only so long on sheer will; the struggle had exhausted them all.

In the climate of confusion and anger created by the reception of *Night Music*, they took out their frustrations on each other. Odets was typical. He rushed down to the Group office with $15,000 he wanted to spend on advertising to counteract the reviews, only to be infuriated by the business staff's "ugly passivity." He found them "quite inured there to the humdrum commercial aspect of doing a play this way—close if the notices are bad," but reluctantly agreed in the end that his money would be better spent covering the actors' salaries so the show might run a few weeks. Yet he resented Clurman's refusal to mount a splashy ad campaign, or even the kind of determined fight they'd made for *Paradise Lost*. Clurman's explanation that "the audience that would enjoy *Night Music* enough to turn it into a popular success was not a large one at Broadway prices" was maddening —what, then, were they doing on Broadway?

Clurman didn't know. He was hurt by the reviews of a production he'd felt was one of his best and even more wounded by Odets' after-the-fact criticisms. All the misgivings the playwright had kept to himself were now poured on his friend's head: Kazan was miscast and misdirected; the minor characters were "torturing to death a few delicate deft lines"; Max Gorelik's settings were too elaborate; and so on and so on. Clurman, who'd heard little of this during rehearsals, could only conclude that Odets was rationalizing the play's failure by blaming him. "After being repeatedly treated to this refined analysis," he wrote of his friend's heated remarks, "I lost all perspective. I had very little idea of what I had done or failed to do. I simply felt a dull ache."

Clurman had no more fight in him. "We are closing *Night Music* on Saturday night," read the ad that announced the end of the run after twenty performances. "In spite of the fact that it is being acted by the best acting company in America: the Group Theatre. In spite of the fact that it includes some of the best performances of the season. . . . You playgoers who are interested in the best the American theatre has to offer have this week to see *Night Music*." On March 9, after the last audience member had left the auditorium, Clurman sat down on the stage and sobbed. It seemed the end of everything he had hoped and worked for in the American theatre.

Nonetheless, he stoutly denied the widespread rumors that the organization was disbanding. The Group would be "associated" with the production of *Heavenly Express*, he said, which meant that Kermit Bloomgarden was producing it independently and Bobby Lewis was directing a cast including Art Smith, Phil Loeb, Harry Bratsburg, and such former Group members as Russell Collins and Julie Garfield, lured back from Hollywood for the starring role. Clurman admitted, however, that "unless a suitable script was forthcoming most of the actors would be free to take other assignments until the fall."

No one in the Group was satisfied with this. In the turbulent weeks just before and after *Night Music*'s closing, they held a series of meetings, desperately struggling to come to some conclusions about how to continue. The first one, on March 6, was held without Clurman; many of the actors blamed him for their current rout, and the sense of the meeting was that it was up to them to create a stronger, more democratic Group. Although Odets doubted this would solve their problems—"If you are not strong enough to stand alone, you are not strong enough to stand together," he told them—they elected him, along with Bud Bohnen, Morris Carnovsky, and Jim Proctor, the company's press agent, to a committee charged with drawing up a plan for a new Group Theatre.

When Clurman spoke the next night, he "impressed no one, not even myself." He tried to stir the old embers of devotion and dedication into a flaming belief that the Group could, would, must go on, but the response was a weary shrug. "People do not believe in his ability to perform any of the ideas or work he outlines," Odets commented in his journal. In addition, Clurman's talk of the Group Idea as something shared by people outside the organization, who might profitably be brought in to help them, aroused suspicion; the actors had seen little evidence that others in the New York theatre shared their goals, or cared whether the Group lived or died. They wanted Clurman to acknowledge his failings, to admit that he needed their help. He did neither; he thought they were destroying what remained of Group life with unfair criticisms that masked their own lack of discipline and need for strong leadership.

Everyone was thrashing around, casting blame, and seeking confusedly for new plans. Odets, Bohnen, Carnovsky, and Proctor met on March 8 to discuss the Group's problems, but came to no definite conclusions. By March 14, the planning committee had dropped Proctor and added Phoebe Brand, but had no better luck in deciding on specific actions. Odets concluded the situation was hopeless, at least for the present, and after a bitter dinner with Clurman at which he aired his dissatisfaction with *Night Music*'s production one last time, he left town on March 20 to lick his wounds in private. Clurman too was fed up with meetings and reproaches. He bought a play, *Trouble in July*, an adaptation of a novel by Erskine Caldwell about a lynching in a small Southern town. Having ensured at least the raw material for a Group fall season, he departed for Hollywood, where a big agent assured him there was a job lined up for him.

The Group had no intention of waiting for the word from Harold or a script from Clifford to revive their theatre. They elected a new committee —Carnovsky, Brand, Bohnen, Meisner, and Gorelik—to create a constitution and a formal program of reorganization. Clurman always deflected their criticisms by saying they complained about his decisions but offered no alternative plans—well, they would present one to him and force him to respond.

Odets blew back into town on April 6, refreshed after a visit to his family in Philadelphia and a jaunt through North Carolina with his friend Bill Kozlenko. One evening at Paul Green's house, Odets and Hallie Flanagan, herself without a theatrical home after the destruction of the Federal Theatre Project, had a long talk about the need to decentralize the American theatre, to start small companies all over the country along the lines of the Group and the FTP, abandoning the sterile New York stage forever. It was a visionary idea, but Odets wasn't ready to give up on New York just yet. He met with Strasberg for dinner several times in April and May to discuss the Group and the possibility of Strasberg's return. Cheryl Crawford joined them for one meeting but although she was curious about what her old comrades were up to, she had plans of her own for a stock company in New Jersey and no interest in rejoining the Group.

Strasberg was more ambivalent. If the Group had been battered in the three years since his departure, he'd been at loose ends, an equally unhappy state. He'd directed a number of Broadway productions, none especially successful, and paid the rent with a scattered variety of teaching jobs. The fragmented life of a free-lance director wasn't for him; he missed the Group and the sustained activity that had nourished him there. In his talks with Odets, he was eager and wary. The Group was the only place in America where a theatre artist could truly function, he told the playwright, but he could never go back to the organization unless substantive changes were made. Odets was noncommittal; he had no authority to invite Strasberg back in any case. But he hoped something might come from their contact. "[Lee] is still the most talented theatre director in the English-speaking theatre," he wrote in his journal, "and it is my opinion that the only place in the country for him is within the walls of the Group Theatre. By all means the contradictions of his and Harold Clurman's natures should be resolved into what must necessarily be a higher level of synthesis for the Group."

The constitutional committee was thinking about Strasberg too; the plan they drew up mentioned him as a potential director for future Group productions. When they met with Odets on May 6, however, he expressed grave reservations about the results of their labors. They'd created an elaborate mechanism "calculated to effect a broadly democratic centralism": a board of five directors elected annually by the members; monthly membership meetings; rules for the conduct of those meetings; provisions for adding new members and expelling old ones; a process by which directors could be removed; the designation of officers—a president, treasurer, and secretary—to handle the Group's administrative affairs, and a series of appointees to perform specific tasks, including a Group Studio director, business manager, promotion manager, playreader, and directors of specific Group productions.

This structure, the committee acknowledged, was "A FORM, not a content." In that area, they offered a "Plan for 1940" that reiterated solutions to the Group's economic and artistic difficulties that had been proposed since 1936: rental of a theatre on a yearly basis; a season of five productions, planned as a coherent package; a permanent Group Studio; experimental productions and classics; a program for new playwrights; a full-time business manager (resentment of Kermit Bloomgarden's refusal to commit himself wholly to the Group ran deep); etc., etc. ("An Analysis of the Problems" in December had suggested exactly the same steps.) Odets pointed out loudly and angrily that this was all mere talk: "All of the practical workings of the theatre they had neglected to chart." Who would actually choose the plays, a committee of five directors? What if the actors disliked the selection, as they had so often before? Was the director of a specific production constrained to hire only Group actors? If not, what was to prevent the same resentments that had disrupted the Group in the past? Most important of all, where was the *money* going to come from? Odets, who knew from bitter experience how hard it was to get backing for a single show, doubted the feasibility of planning to have a collective group of investors finance a whole season as a single project.

The irritated committee replied that it was at least worth a try. Nothing could be worse than the scramble from play to play that had characterized the Group's entire history. If Odets reminded them that Clurman had tried as recently as 1938 to get backing for a four-play season and failed utterly, they may have believed that it failed because Bloomgarden and Arthur Krim, who had helped draw up the proposal, lacked a real commitment to it. Max Gorelik, for one, thought he could do better. He got into a shouting match with Odets when the latter caustically expressed his doubts as to his business abilities. Phoebe Brand was distressed by Odets' open contempt for their "sick and timorous fixation on a 'constitution of democracy.' " One of the Group's most politically committed members, she couldn't understand why the playwright had backed away from convictions he'd expressed so forcefully only a few years earlier. Odets, for his part, regarded Brand with a good deal of hostility as someone desperately clinging to rigid, outmoded left-wing ideas.

Noticeably absent from the meeting were two members of the now defunct Council: Gadget Kazan and Luther Adler. Kazan went straight from *Night Music* into a supporting role in a successful revival of *Liliom;* he spent his free time trying to raise money for a fund to encourage new playwrights, but had little success. When *Liliom* closed, he took an acting job in Hollywood. He wasn't sure he wanted to work with the Group anymore. His friendship with Odets had cooled. Kazan had received excellent reviews for his performance as Steve Takis, and he resented hearing of Odets' complaints about it through the grapevine instead of directly from a man he'd considered one of his closest friends. Kazan was fed up with the Group for the moment and glad to get away.

Adler, like Kazan, had a wife who bitterly disapproved of the Group, though Thacher's reasons were ideological while Sylvia Sidney had more personal resentments: she felt they'd treated her badly during *The Gentle People* and thought her husband's devotion to the organization hindered his career. Adler had just finished a comfortable stint in a modest success— *Two on an Island,* unlike *Night Music,* had survived mixed reviews and run for three months—and was uncertain how he felt about the Group. He saw a lot of Odets, but kept his distance from the ongoing debate.

The May 6 meeting ended inconclusively. Odets shared the committee's suspicion that Clurman, still in Hollywood, was too wrapped up in his personal problems to come up with a suitable reorganization plan, but he was skeptical theirs would work either. When the majority of the Group assembled on May 10 to hear the committee's proposal, however, they voted to accept it. At least the new constitution provided a way to move forward. The solutions offered were nothing new, granted, but it could be argued that they'd never been seriously attempted and it was up to the Group actors to insist this attempt be made. Referring to the stormy days of the Actors Committee paper, the constitutional committee's report noted:

> We demanded violently that a certain kind of theatre be made— whether it included us or not—but make it. Somebody make it. Or else God help us. So we reassembled, expecting it to be made. We sat quiet. Patiently. It hasn't been made. Why? Because that kind of patience is not a virtue! Because if it's going to be made, somebody has to MAKE it. We must cease asking for it, and set about making it. It is OUR PROBLEM, each of us in this room, and the others to come.

Despite these brave words, the Group was still waiting for Clurman. Although the constitutional committee declared in its report that "we, at this meeting, along with others not present, regard ourselves and each other as qualified for this functional type of Group membership, with its franchise and voice in the administration of the Group," they could think of no clearer way to define who was a member than to demand that "a specific Group membership be immediately declared by our present artistic leadership"—i.e., Clurman.

They couldn't conceive of a Group Theatre without the man whose fiery talks had brought it into being, who with all his faults had kept them together when it seemed impossible. Clurman had nurtured their best playwright and directed the productions that gave most eloquent voice to their shared vision of what life as an artist in American could be: a transcendent union of public and private concerns, of form and content, of good citizenship and individual fulfillment. If many of them felt he'd compromised that vision, they couldn't bring themselves to imagine that his actions reflected a fundamental change in his thinking. The Group Idea was Harold's idea; Group life was his life. To reject him, to say that the Group Idea no longer sustained him would be to admit that perhaps it couldn't sustain any of them. No one needed and wanted the Group Theatre more than Harold Clurman, and the actors knew it. "I don't think we would have wanted to go on without Harold," said Phoebe Brand. "We were trying to hold him in."

The only concrete step taken in his absence was a letter from Helen Thompson to David Stevens at the Rockefeller Foundation inquiring about the possibility of a Foundation grant to support the Group's activities. Clurman had tried for nine years, off and on, to raise a subsidy from individual sources; Thompson hoped an institution would be more receptive to their need. Stevens's reply, dated June 17, regretted that the Rockefeller Foundation wasn't set up to finance professional companies. Once again, the Group found themselves caught in the contradiction between their aims and the necessity of pursuing them in the commercial theatre.

Clurman returned in mid-June, no wealthier or happier from his Hollywood sojourn. He'd blown his seemingly certain job prospect by treating an MGM executive to a violent harangue about the Group Theatre's importance and his own stature as a director. He concluded in retrospect that he'd succumbed to the actors' "desire for this-and-that": a need for financial security and worldly fame, combined with a bitter feeling that the show-business industry ought to respect the Group's achievements more than it did. If he had learned of the Rockefeller Foundation's rejection, it would only have reinforced his unhappy sense that there was no institutional way to solve the Group's problems, that in fact they'd come to the end of the line.

It was hard to look toward the future in the bleak summer of 1940. On May 10, the day the Group forlornly ratified their constitution, Hitler's armies invaded the Low Countries; Holland surrendered on May 13, Belgium followed suit on the 28th. France was next, and British and French troops were helpless to prevent the Nazis' lightning sweep through the countryside. Mussolini, eager to share the spoils, brought Italy into the war on June 10. As Clurman crept disconsolately into New York on June 14, the Germans marched into Paris; Marshal Pétain, the new French head of state, signed an armistice with Germany on June 22. Great Britain now stood alone against the Axis powers, and in the terrifying six-week air assault that began July 9, no one could be sure the English would repel the invaders. "I experienced a curious sensation of nervous exhilaration," Clurman wrote of those days. "The outside world in its crack-up appeared to justify the sense of breakdown within me."

Clurman saw no other course for the Group but to hold on grimly as Britain was doing. He planned to proceed with a new season on the basis of whatever individual scripts he could acquire. He avoided the Group, not even getting in touch with Odets until nine days after he'd arrived. Their subsequent meetings were tense; Odets was incredulous that Clurman thought he could simply forge ahead without addressing any of the Group's underlying problems. The director had no intention of getting bogged down in debate again: he refused to discuss the constitution, quarreled angrily with Carnovsky about the war—Clurman now favored U.S. involvement, Carnovsky still opposed it—then disappeared to Cape Cod for a visit with Irwin Shaw.

Shaw had written a new play, *Retreat to Pleasure*. Disenchanted with the Group after *The Gentle People* and *Quiet City*, he'd angered Clurman by selling it to George S. Kaufman, but by the time Clurman arrived at Cape

Cod, Kaufman had dropped his option. Shaw was now prepared to consider a Group production, provided Clurman agreed to cast the parts as he saw fit, without regard to Group membership. The director was willing. He'd decided, as Odets told him accusingly before he left for Cape Cod, that the Group would have to adjust to existing conditions in the theatre rather than challenge them. He would meet Shaw's terms because it was the only way he could acquire *Retreat to Pleasure*, which he liked, discerning beneath its flimsy plot and highly artificial dialogue a genuine document of their troubled times.

It's difficult to understand in retrospect what Clurman saw in *Retreat to Pleasure*, Shaw's least successful script to date. It has a veneer of social concern: the heroine, Norah Galligan, is a young New Dealer disenchanted with her job as head of Home Relief in Ohio and tempted to marry a wealthy businessman so she can give up the struggle to make a better world. But it is essentially a comedy of manners without the assured touch required for such material. The principal male character, a young rebel who persuades Norah to reject her suitor, then abandons her at the final curtain, seems light-minded as well as light-footed, with no coherent values to oppose to the businessman's conventional stance. The plush settings in New York and Miami undercut whatever message the play may have had. Perhaps, as Clurman believed, Shaw captured the cynicism and escapism of a brief historical moment, but he did so with little artistry. The play's mood was deeply antithetical to the Group spirit. They'd come together in 1930 to reject the nihilism of the 1920s; cynicism wasn't an emotion the Group expressed comfortably or well. Clurman had never before evinced any interest in expressing it at all.

But *Retreat to Pleasure* suited his mood in 1940. He understood only too well Norah's weariness with a thankless, impossible task. He had a cynical streak of his own, developed over the years as a self-protective device to ease the pain inspired by the yawning gap between the Group's aspirations and the conditions they struggled under. Looking around him on his return to New York on July 31, he saw no reason for optimism. The Group Theatre, the most acclaimed company of the day, had not a nickel in its coffers to support its actors or writers. Odets, the most important playwright of the decade, could make a living only by heading for Hollywood, which he did on August 22. Clurman drifted, unable to muster the resolve to take up his backbreaking burden again.

When he roused himself on September 1 to write an article denying persistent reports that the Group was breaking up, he found himself listing for the hundredth time obstacles that blocked their course: the difficulty of financing a theatre with long-term goals on a show-by-show basis, the perils inherent in taking artistic risks in a world where commercial success was the only measure of worth, the lack of continuity in American theatre and life. When he asserted that the Group "can function and thrive even as a business in this art which dare not speak its name," it was more a reflex gesture than a genuine statement of belief. The problems were the same as they had always been, the solutions no closer at hand. How much longer could he go on kidding himself?

Not much longer. On Thursday, September 5, Clurman called a meeting to discuss the Group's fall season. The actors were furious when he dismissed the proposed constitution out of hand. What he proposed as an alternative seemed to many a complete betrayal of everything the Group Theatre stood for.

They lived in a world of capitalist relationships, Clurman told the actors. Continuity of work and paycheck was not in the nature of things. Therefore, it was unrealistic, corrupting, and fundamentally sick to try and maintain the Group on their old, mutually supportive basis. It was time for them all to grow up, to become independent and self-supporting, to run their lives on the basis of what was best for them as individuals. In terms of the Group Theatre, that meant that he would proceed as if he were a conventional producer: he would direct *Retreat to Pleasure,* casting the four or five Group members he felt were suitable for it, then *Trouble in July,* which he warned them also contained few parts for Group actors. The rest of them would have to find work elsewhere. The Group Theatre could survive only if they all became practical and resigned themselves to living and working within the limitations imposed by the commercial theatre.

His remarks caused an uproar. This wasn't the Group Theatre the actors had worked for and suffered with for an entire decade; the organization he was describing sounded like any other Broadway show-shop. By abandoning the idea of a permanent acting company, Clurman was rejecting one of the two central tenets on which the Group Theatre had been founded. If he thought he could maintain the other—the production of plays expressing the vital social and moral issues of their times—without it, he was contradicting what he himself had said in 1930. Then he'd scornfully dismissed the efforts of organizations like the Theatre Guild to present serious drama as fatally flawed by their lack of an acting ensemble committed to the ideas in those dramas. They might offer better wares, he'd declared, but without a unified technique and shared philosophy of life they would never create a truly successful alternative to the commercial theatre. Now he seemed to be saying that he could instill the Group Idea in any actor he chose to work with—that the Group Theatre, in fact, was any production directed by Harold Clurman.

The actors were dumbfounded. How could there be a Group Theatre production, Sandy Meisner asked, without Group actors in it? Mike Gordon pointed out that everything Clurman said about the capitalist theatre had been equally true in 1930, but then the same conditions had led him to a completely different conclusion: namely, that they would have to build a new theatre where those conditions would not prevail.

Gordon was right, and in his heart of hearts Clurman knew it. "For ten years I had been an idealist," he wrote. "Despite my knowledge of the facts, I had been impelled by the feeling that if one's will is strong enough, if one's desire is sufficiently hot, these alone can mold events." What ten years had taught him, what the actors weren't willing to admit, was that molding events, which the Group had certainly done, wasn't the same as altering the fundamental nature of the American theatre. He'd decided it couldn't be done, and he desperately wanted the actors to come to the same conclusion and leave him alone: "I had had enough of hearing this agonized echo of my own words hurled at me in accents of accusation." The Group hadn't changed; Clurman had. It's easy to imagine his feelings as he tried to dismiss the beliefs of a younger, more confident self.

As he often did when confronted by arguments he knew were basically sound, Clurman turned his opponents' strengths against them by taking their line of reasoning to absurd lengths, then rejecting it. When someone passionately stated that the Group's theatrical aims couldn't be realized without the permanent company of fifteen actors with an annual contract they'd finally achieved in the 1938–1939 season, he replied that he couldn't agree more. In fact, he went on, what they really needed was a company of twenty-five, forty, no, fifty actors. But obviously they couldn't afford to keep fifty actors on year-round salary; therefore, the idea of a permanent company was unworkable.

The actors were infuriated by this kind of argument, which seemed both frivolous and contemptuous of their distress. They felt Harold was mocking them, playing with the ideas that were life and death to them and their theatre. If they sensed the pain and fatigue behind his wild comments, that only frightened and angered them all the more. The meeting degenerated into a melee of shouted accusations and reproaches. Did Harold really think he would get the same quality of performances from non-Group actors? some asked. Were Sam Jaffe in *The Gentle People* or Jane Wyatt in *Night Music* as profound, as centered, as emotionally true as Luther Adler in *Awake and Sing!* or Morris Carnovsky in *Golden Boy* or the entire company in *Paradise Lost*? Was he such a great director that he didn't need them? Clurman begged them not to look to him for magical solutions to the Group's dilemma. He'd told them what he felt had to be done. If they thought they could do better, if they wanted to create a theatre based on their constitution, then they should go ahead; he might even apply for a job there. If they'd reached the point in their development where they could tell him to go fuck himself, that was all right with him. Clurman was famous for his uninhibited recourse to four-letter words, but he uttered this one with real venom.

The Group Theatre received a mortal wound that September afternoon, though the death throes would last another eight months. The actors could neither accept Clurman's despairing vision of what the Group had to be nor imagine a Group Theatre without him. No matter what he said in the heat of the moment, he couldn't imagine a theatre without them either; he would go through the motions one more time, but it was as if his heart had been cut out.

Retreat to Pleasure, which opened December 17, wasn't a Group production at all, despite being billed as one. Of the four Group actors in it, only Art Smith and Ruth Nelson were current members (if that term had any meaning anymore); Leif Erickson and Dorothy Patten were hired as freelance talent, like the rest of the cast. More to the point, the production was in spirit, intention, and execution nothing like a Group Theatre effort. It had no vital central theme for Clurman to analyze for the actors, no cohesive ensemble to apply a shared technique to their roles, no characters, in fact, of sufficient depth or reality to warrant an intensive exploration of their internal life. Clurman directed the script in the competent, uninspired fashion it deserved. The critics were indifferent; many didn't even bother to mention the Group's supposed connection with the production. Stella Adler had the last word: "Sad, isn't it?" she remarked on opening night.

It *was* sad, and it was the end. This time the Group would not pick up the pieces as they had in 1933 and 1937. For a while Odets thought he could revive the organization with a new play, *Clash by Night*, and an old director, Strasberg. Although Luther Adler, who'd been promised the lead opposite Sylvia Sidney, urged Odets not to give it to the Group—Adler was very bitter about Clurman after the final meeting—the playwright decided to go ahead. When he told Clurman in December that he wanted to use the Group Theatre's name as producer, though he in fact would own most of the show himself, his friend gave apathetic assent. Clurman planned to take a six-month contract at Fox; he told the Group's office staff that they would remain on salary for *Clash by Night* and could now consider Odets and Strasberg their employers. He couldn't bring himself to see any of the Group actors personally, but he dropped each of them a note saying that he was leaving for Hollywood and they were "free to do what they would or could" about the Group Theatre, which at the moment consisted of *Clash by Night*, Odets, and Strasberg.

But a single play was no substitute for an organization, and Odets found himself constrained by commercial imperatives to keep chipping away at the Group Theatre's connection to the production. First, theatrical impresario Billy Rose insisted on such a large share of the profits in return for his financing that there would be none left for the Group; Clurman, consulted by wire, shrugged and said that was fine. Then Rose declared he wanted sole billing as producer, with no mention of the Group at all; that was fine with Clurman too. By the time *Clash by Night* finally opened in December 1941, the Group's only association with it was the presence of Art Smith and Lee Cobb in the cast.

By then, everyone had reluctantly acknowledged the fact of the Group's demise. Carnovsky, representing the actors, met with Odets and Strasberg in late 1940 and early 1941 to try and establish a new Group Theatre, but nothing came of it. Clurman returned to New York in May to close the Group offices for good. Bobby Lewis and Gadget Kazan went with him to the Sardi Building so he wouldn't be alone when he shut the door on ten years of hopes and dreams.

Clurman's obituary for the Group appeared in the *New York Times* on May 18, 1941. For the last time he pointed out that "our means and our ends were in fundamental contradiction . . . while we tried to maintain a true theatre policy artistically we proceeded economically on a show-business basis." To continue on that basis, he believed, "would be artistically misleading, financially disastrous, personally heart-breaking." He was no longer willing to struggle along without the sustained financial support that symphony orchestras, ballet companies, and European theatres received as a matter of course. He still believed in the theatre with all his heart, but he'd had enough of show business. "Until a method of raising a subsidy for our kind of theatre can be evolved, until a real working basis can be created, I would rather our offices remained closed. There can be no institutional product without an institutional foundation."

For ten years the Group fought against insurmountable odds to create the kind of theatre they believed in. If in the end they were defeated, they could still look back with pride on a remarkable record of achievement. It wasn't just that their twenty-three productions included *The House of Connelly, Success Story, Men in White, Waiting for Lefty, Awake and Sing!, Paradise Lost,* and *Golden Boy,* plays that captured the spiritual essence of their times. Nor was it solely that they revolutionized the craft of acting with their insistence on emotional truth, forging through hard work and constant experimentation an ensemble regarded with reverence as the finest in America. The Group defined what serious theatre must be: a permanent company dedicated to presenting plays that revealed in the deepest, most complex way the unshakable connection between theatre and real life. The Group reminded people that art was not just entertainment, but an expression of living ideas that could be carried out of the theatre, the library, or the museum to affect the world. Art and life were one, just as the actors and the play were one, the means and the end were one. Achieving that unity was difficult; maintaining it in the commercial arena where the Group had been forced to operate proved impossible. That didn't mean there was anything wrong with the idea.

In the winter of 1940–41, as *Retreat to Pleasure* limped toward its inevitable closing, Morris Carnovsky ran into a friend who congratulated him on his featured role in the hit comedy *My Sister Eileen.* How did it feel to be in a success? the man tactlessly inquired. Carnovsky looked at him with surprise. "I've been in a success for ten years," he replied.

The Group Theatre was dead; the Group Idea remained.

EPILOGUE
After the Fall

When members spoke in later years of the Group's breakup, they all used the same metaphor: they'd lost their home, they said; their family was gone, and they felt terribly alone. Without the Group, the theatre seemed a cold, forbidding place, a commercial arena where they had to compete as individuals, cut loose from the collective that had sheltered and nourished them for ten years. Many of them would spend large portions of their lives trying to create another Group, a place where they could feel at home.

What was the alternative, really? The position of the serious artist forced to struggle as an individual in the American theatre was—and remains—frustrating, unproductive, and, as Clurman wrote, heartbreaking. No matter how hard life was in the Group, life outside, as pungently described in a letter written by Eugene O'Neill in November 1940, was worse.

The letter was addressed to Kenneth Macgowan, an old friend from the Provincetown Players:

> The memory of the old P.P. days moved me to sad nostalgia. There was a theatre then in which I knew I belonged, one of guts and idealism. Now I feel out of the theatre. I dread the idea of production because I know it will be done by people who have really only one standard left, that of Broadway success. I know beforehand that I will be constantly asked, as I have been asked before, to make stupid compromises for that end. The fact that I will again refuse to make them is no consolation. The fact that I will have the final say on everything is also no consolation. The fact that I like these people personally and the relationship is always friendly and considerate, is no consolation. The big fact is that any production must be made on a plane, and in an atmosphere to which neither I nor my work belongs in spirit, nor want to belong; that it is a job, a business within the Showshop, a

long, irritating, wearing, nervous, health-destroying ordeal, with no creative enthusiasm behind it, just another Broadway opening—the Old Game, the game we used to defy in the P.P. but which it is impossible for me to defy now, except in my writing, because there is no longer a theatre of true integrity and courage and high purpose and enthusiasm.

This was the judgment of America's most eminent playwright, who for twenty-eight years had dedicated himself single-mindedly to his art and achieved enough commercial success to be able to virtually dictate his terms to the producers of his plays. If O'Neill, by nature a lonely and isolated man, still longed for a theatre inspired by shared ideals, how much greater was the need of the former Group members, who had made such a theatre and brought their plays to life with a unified technique far more theatrically exciting than the often amateurish work of the Provincetown Players. Those who had lived for ten years in a warm, supportive atmosphere of collective work and belief could never be satisfied by the fragmented life of a free-lance theatre worker.

They wasted no time in trying to create alternatives. Clurman's pained obituary for the Group appeared on the front page of the *New York Times*'s entertainment section. Right next to it was an announcement of the Dollar Top Theatre, a new venture launched by Lewis and Kazan, with Molly Thacher acting as playreader. Since the Group's cheapest tickets had always sold best, the team planned to rent a theatre large enough to offer every seat for a dollar. They hoped to combine the Group's seriousness of purpose with the populist appeal of the Federal Theatre, scheduling children's plays and holiday entertainments as well as contemporary drama. They got scripts from Irwin Shaw, Ramon Naya, and Victor Wolfson and promises from Odets and Paul Green. Unfortunately, neither Lewis in New York nor Kazan in Hollywood (where he was acting in a movie) could raise the money they needed to begin production. Just as they were about to sign a long-term lease on a theatre in the fall of 1941, the Dollar Top Theatre was reluctantly abandoned.

Barely two weeks after the first announcement of the Dollar Top, on May 30, 1941, the Actors Laboratory in California issued its Statement of Policy. The Lab had its roots in both the Group and the Federal Theatre Project. It grew out of the Hollywood Theatre Alliance, formed by members of the Los Angeles section of the FTP after it closed. At the time the Statement of Policy appeared the Lab's executive board included three former Group members: Virginia Farmer, Joe Bromberg, and Bud Bohnen. They intended it to be a more realistic version of the Group; members were professional actors employed in films (the Lab didn't assume the Group's responsibility to provide a living for its members) who wanted to challenge themselves by exploring advanced acting problems in classes and public performances.

By 1945 the Lab was virtually a West Coast Group, in personnel at least, with Bohnen, Bromberg, Carnovsky, Brand, Nelson, and Smith all on the executive board. (Will Lee and Mike Gordon joined the board in 1947.) Old friends dropped by as well: Bobby Lewis directed a production of André Obey's *Noah* and rehearsed *The Lower Depths* with Charles Laughton; Clurman and John Howard Lawson gave lectures.

The Lab flourished for nearly ten years, with its fingers in many different pies. It was active in war work, producing shows that were performed at army camps, hospitals, and overseas bases under the auspices of the USO. After the war, it drew much of its income from a separate school called the Workshop, which offered classes for studio contract players and veterans taking advantage of the GI Bill's tuition appropriations. The professional members continued their studios and appeared in the Lab Theatre Wing's full-scale commercial productions: among the more notable were *Volpone*, directed by Carnovsky; a revival of *Awake and Sing!*, directed by Bromberg; and a series of evenings dedicated to one-act plays, including several by Tennessee Williams. Young Lab associates who went on to make their mark in the theatre included Joseph Papirofsky, better known as the New York Shakespeare Festival's Joe Papp, and Bernard Gersten, now executive producer of the Lincoln Center Theater.

The Lab was finally done in by the ugly postwar political climate. Numbering among its members some of the Group's most socially conscious actors, it had always stressed "a real understanding of and participation in the life of our times . . . as people who consider the preservation of democracy and a democratic culture a matter of life or death." This stance, which seemed commendably patriotic during the war years, was viewed as suspiciously subversive by 1945, when the *Hollywood Reporter* called the Lab's leaders "as red as a burlesque queen's garters." That kind of nonsense could be laughed off for a few more years, but in February 1948 the California Senate Fact-Finding Committee on Un-American Activities, chaired by state senator Jack B. Tenney, subpoenaed Bromberg, Bohnen, and Lee. All three refused to answer questions about whether or not they had ever been members of the Communist party. The Lab was now firmly labeled Red, and the results were disastrous. The movie studios had already yanked their contract players from the Workshop at the first whiff of controversy in 1947; in October 1948 the IRS revoked the Lab's tax-exempt status, and in 1949 it was forced to withdraw from the veteran training program. Its other sources of revenue dried up as well: attendance at performances dropped precipitously, and the subpoenaed members lost their film jobs.

Beleaguered from without, beset by internal difficulties, the Lab foundered. It had never been very well organized. Phoebe Brand, one of the most persistent advocates of democratic structure within the Group, found to her dismay at the Lab that democracy entailed a lot of meetings that wasted everyone's time and a proliferation of committees that sabotaged the lines of authority. It was held together largely by the passion and commitment of Bohnen, the driving force behind all its activities, beloved by members and students alike. The combination of political ostracism, the Lab's organizational difficulties, and his own personal problems as sole support of his father and daughter finally killed him. He died of a heart attack, onstage during a Lab performance, on February 24, 1949. The Lab struggled along for another year before closing its doors forever in 1950.

The Lab actors weren't the only former Group associates uprooted by the political whirlwind that swept through Hollywood and New York in the postwar decade. John Howard Lawson was one of the Hollywood Ten cited for contempt of Congress in late 1947, when they refused to answer questions by the House Committee on Un-American Activities about their affiliation with the Communist party on the grounds that such questions violated the First Amendment's protection of the right to free speech. After a legal battle that went all the way to the Supreme Court, which refused to review their convictions in the spring of 1950, the Ten went to jail.

By the time HUAC got to work in earnest in 1951, when it subpoenaed several former Group members, the basic issues confronting those forced to testify before the committee were starkly clear. Although membership in the Communist party had been perfectly legal in the 1930s and '40s, the 1951 Smith Act convictions of the party's American leadership established the principle that the United States government now viewed such membership as by definition a commitment to armed revolution. Two Supreme Court decisions in 1950 laid out the equally unappealing alternatives for those subpoenaed. In *Rogers v. U.S.*, the Court declared that any witness who discussed his or her personal involvement in the Communist party could not then refuse to name others involved without risking a contempt citation and jail sentence. In *Blau v. U.S.*, the Court affirmed that those unwilling to admit membership in the party could safely invoke the Fifth Amendment's protection against self-incrimination in refusing to answer questions.

Julie Garfield, Morris Carnovsky, Joe Bromberg, Mike Gordon, and Virginia Farmer, who all appeared before the committee in 1951, faced an intolerable situation. Many had been communists in the 1930s; some still were, some had drifted away. They all considered themselves patriotic Americans who'd taken actions that seemed logical at the time to support a political party they believed was dedicated to the best, most progressive aspects of the American way of life: justice for working people, equal rights for black Americans, a militant struggle against European fascism. They could do what the committee wanted—beat their breasts, repent of their communist associations (implicitly admitting that membership in the party was the hideous offense HUAC claimed it was), and inform on friends and co-workers who'd made the same commitment—or they could take the Fifth (which also implied that being a communist was a crime) and rest

assured that they would not work in film, television, or the New York theatre for a very long time.

Carnovsky, Bromberg, Gordon, and Farmer all took the Fifth and suffered the consequences. Bromberg, forced to appear despite an affidavit
from his doctor that he had a severe heart condition and should be excused,
died of heart failure in December 1951. Farmer never worked in films again;
Carnovsky wouldn't make another one until 1962. He and Phoebe Brand
moved back east, where they lived for two years on the proceeds of the sale
of their Hollywood home. He acted in the burgeoning off-Broadway theatre
before the blacklist eased enough so that mainstream producers would take
a chance on him again. Gordon didn't work in Hollywood for seven years;
after two heart attacks he reluctantly made a deal in 1958, when he appeared in a private session and confirmed names read to him by a court
reporter, a ritualistic act of self-abasement that freed him to direct *Pillow
Talk* with Doris Day. Garfield, who'd never been a communist, said so and
avoided giving names by the simple expedient of claiming no one had ever
discussed the party with him at any time. The committee—which seemed
particularly anxious to nail Garfield, a big star in 1951—wasn't satisfied,
and refused to give him the political OK required by the movie studios
before anyone could go back to work. He died of a heart attack in 1952, not
long after his thirty-ninth birthday.

It was clear to all the anxious Group alumni who waited to see if they
would be subpoenaed that their decisions about what to say to HUAC could
literally be a matter of life and death. (Phil Loeb, one of the many Group
associates smeared by HUAC who was never even called, killed himself in
1955 after losing a series of jobs because of his alleged Red connections.)
Former communists were in particular jeopardy, but plenty of noncommunists whose worst sin consisted of signing petitions against segregation
or in support of Loyalist Spain also found themselves hauled in for private
grillings by HUAC investigators who promised not to subpoena them if they
would name names then and there. It was a terrible dilemma: they could
violate everything they'd ever believed about personal loyalty and collective
solidarity, or they could stand firm and quite probably never work in their
chosen profession again. There was no Group to support them now; they
faced the committee alone.

The stakes were particularly high for Clifford Odets and Elia Kazan, who
were both subpoenaed in the spring of 1952. Odets had written only one
play *(The Big Knife)* since *Clash by Night;* he was a well-paid, successful
Hollywood screenwriter who would lose his principal means of support if
he refused to testify. Kazan was the hottest director in Hollywood and New
York in 1952. He'd directed *A Streetcar Named Desire* and *Death of a Salesman,* two of the most successful and important Broadway productions of
the late 1940s. He'd also made seven films, with his adaptation of *Streetcar*
cementing his reputation in that medium, and just completed an eighth,

Viva Zapata! His boss at Twentieth Century-Fox was putting enormous pressure on him to cooperate with the committee and save his unreleased movie from extinction.

Kazan horrified his former comrades by not only naming the eight Group actors who'd been in his CP cell, but also loudly condemning communist thought-control and heartily seconding HUAC's assertion that the party remained a menace to the American way of life. He went so far as to take out an ad in the *New York Times* defending his decision as a necessary step in the battle to "protect ourselves from a dangerous and alien conspiracy" and urging others subpoenaed to do likewise. "Secrecy," he argued, "serves the Communists. At the other pole, it serves those who are interested in silencing liberal voices." Odets was considerably less friendly toward the committee—he had to be persistently prompted before he would admit, in even the most qualified manner, that party members had tried to influence what he wrote—but he too gave names and a detailed account of CP meetings and procedures. When Lee Cobb appeared the following year, he followed their example and gave the names of Carnovsky and Brand, as well as several other non-Group communists.

Former Group members were distressed by Odets' and Cobb's testimony and contemptuous of their cowardice, but the man they really hated was Kazan. His actions were bad enough, but his sanctimoniousness about them was unbearable. Many of them never spoke to him again. Tony Kraber, finally dragged in front of HUAC in 1955—four years after he'd lost his job at CBS because the network management thought he'd be called—replied when asked if he knew Kazan, "Is this the Kazan that signed the contract for $500,000 the day after he gave names to this committee? Would you sell your brothers for $500,000?" (Kazan vehemently denies that he signed any such contract, although he did go to work for Fox on an anticommunist film shortly after he testified.) Kazan got hate mail and anonymous phone calls. His secretary quit. People crossed the street to avoid him. The sometimes uneasy solidarity between radicals and liberals that had existed from the 1930s through World War II was definitively shattered by HUAC's witch hunts, and for many Kazan incarnated anticommunist liberalism at its most self-righteous and self-serving. To Group alumni who'd disliked his driving ambition nearly twenty years earlier, his actions confirmed their worst suspicions about his character.

There would be no further efforts to create a theatre that combined artistic and political activism, at least not by alumni of the Group Theatre. The Group's most renowned and long-lived offshoot, the Actors Studio, became identified through the successful young movie actors who studied there with a certain social attitude, but it was one of personal rebellion rather than systematic criticism. (It was best exemplified by the famous line in *The Wild One*, a 1954 film starring Marlon Brando as the leader of a motorcycle gang. Asked what he was rebelling against, he wisecracked,

"What've you got?") The Studio was most famous not for any political point of view, but for the Method, a version of the Group's actor-training system that acquired a capital M and worldwide recognition in the 1950s.

Kazan, Bobby Lewis, and Cheryl Crawford founded the Studio in 1947. Although each of them was doing quite well in the commercial theatre, Lewis and Kazan as directors, Crawford as a producer, all three missed the opportunity the Group had provided to work on the actor's development at leisure and in depth, as they never could during rehearsals for an individual production. They agreed to set up a studio for professional actors, with Kazan and Lewis teaching the classes and Crawford handling the administrative details. There would be no tuition fees for the members and no payment for the staff; admission would be based on talent alone, and the directors' reward would be a growing cadre of trained actors they could draw on for their productions in the commercial theatre. The Actors Studio opened its doors in the fall of 1947, with a roster of students that included Marlon Brando, Montgomery Clift, Julie Harris, Anne Jackson, Sidney Lumet, Karl Malden, E. G. Marshall, Patricia Neal, Jerome Robbins, Maureen Stapleton, and Eli Wallach.

Lewis resigned after the first year following a dispute with Kazan, who'd advised Lewis to decline Crawford's offer to direct a Broadway musical called *Love Life*, then turned around and agreed to direct the play himself. The Studio was left without its principal acting teacher, as Kazan was too busy with his film and stage work to be able to devote full time to the organization. For a few years, various teachers, including Sandy Meisner and Marty Ritt, taught classes, but what the Studio needed was someone to bring coherence and continuity to the training program. Crawford lobbied hard for Lee Strasberg—she'd been his warmest admirer and strongest supporter in the Group—and she managed to convince a dubious Kazan that he was the man for the job. It took them a while to persuade Strasberg, who'd been insulted by not being included at first, but he finally became artistic director of the Actors Studio in 1951.

It was a classic case of the right man in the right place at the right time. Although Lewis, one of the Group's severest critics of affective memory, was horrified that his erstwhile partners had handed the Studio over to the man who was obsessed with it, in fact the acting style Strasberg forged in his classes perfectly suited the temper of the 1950s. What came to be regarded as the typical Method performance was moody, introspective, neurotic, withdrawn, yet seething with internal emotions that burst to the surface in moments of cathartic power. Although Studio members like Maureen Stapleton, Eli Wallach, Kim Stanley, Julie Harris, Paul Newman, and Geraldine Page had an enormous impact on Broadway in *The Rose Tattoo*, *Bus Stop*, *Sweet Bird of Youth*, *I Am a Camera*, *Camino Real*, and other landmark productions of the 1950s, the Studio's real fame came from members who moved on to film, particularly Marlon Brando and James

Dean in the Kazan-directed movies *On the Waterfront* and *East of Eden* (which both featured dozens of other Studio- and Group-trained actors). Just as Group acting in 1931 had seemed a rebuke to the stodgy, phony posturing of conventional Broadway performances, so the Method intensity evoked a warm response from audiences bored with the schematic good guy/bad guy characterizations of standard Hollywood movies.

More important to the actors themselves, the Studio became a home, a place where they could intensively study their craft and grow as artists. They worshipped Strasberg as the man who could unlock the doors to real feeling; his Tuesday and Friday scene classes were both the mecca and the nightmare of every Studio member, for criticism could be savage. No one questioned Strasberg's right to be cruel: Group actors had been his peers; Studio actors were his followers. This relationship suited a man who'd always been more comfortable lecturing than engaging in a dialogue; the Studio was like Brookfield Center year after year.

Former Group members didn't see it quite that way. Though the Studio was repeatedly described as the Group's successor, many of Strasberg's past comrades expressed deep ambivalence about it. Sandy Meisner, Bobby Lewis, and Stella Adler, themselves among America's most prominent acting teachers (Brando credited Adler, not Strasberg, as the greatest influence on his work), continued to believe Strasberg's emphasis on internal emotion was dangerous and destructive. Adler in particular, who founded her own school in 1949 and runs it to this day, became the most vocal opponent of Strasberg's Method, referring to it publicly as sick, damaging to actors' psyches as well as their craft. Nonetheless, the Studio was a dominant influence on American acting for more than two decades; a second generation of Studio-trained actors, including Robert De Niro and Al Pacino, became stars in the 1970s. Strasberg and the other Group alumni who turned to teaching ensured among them that the Stanislavsky system, in one version or another, became and remains the basic technique of most American actors.

But the Studio wasn't the Group, nor was it ever intended to be. Lewis, Kazan, and Crawford agreed when they founded it that it would be a workshop, not a producing organization. The Group had been on the Broadway battlefield, struggling to achieve commercial success with the unified technique they knew was the only way to create true theatre. The Studio was a refuge, a place where you did your real work and then tried to bootleg as much of it into commercial productions as you possibly could. Group Theatre members had believed they could change the world; Studio members, by and large, had to accommodate themselves to the realities of commercial theatre and film. A two-year attempt to present professional productions, though it featured some interesting efforts, came to an end with a Strasberg-directed production of *The Three Sisters*, which received mixed reviews in New York and was an unqualified disaster when imported to London in

1965. In any case, the Actors Studio Theatre had never developed the permanent ensemble that was its professed aim; it relied on the participation of stars who had too many other obligations to make a full-time commitment to the company.

The Actors Studio Theatre was in part an angry response to the Studio's exclusion from the Lincoln Center Repertory Theatre, the last attempt involving a number of Group alumni to create a permanent repertory company. The Studio's three directors had several talks with the Lincoln Center board about the organization's possible participation in the new cultural complex. Strasberg, with the arrogance and commercial naiveté that often characterized his thinking, assumed that the Studio would be incorporated intact into Lincoln Center, particularly after Kazan was named codirector of the theatre company, joining producer Robert Whitehead, in 1959.

But although Kazan initially pushed for Strasberg to be named head of the actor-training program, he ran into determined opposition from Whitehead, who felt the Studio's emphasis on internal psychology was unsuitable for a company that intended to present classics as well as contemporary plays. Kazan, who harbored the same reservations he always had about Strasberg's teaching and knew the Lincoln Center board distrusted his old colleague as dogmatic and incapable of compromise, elected not to fight. He and Whitehead offered Bobby Lewis the job of training the company's actors in 1962 and the following year asked Harold Clurman to serve as executive consultant and adviser on the theatre's program. Arthur Miller promised a new play for their first production, and for a while it seemed, as Miller wrote in his memoirs, that Lincoln Center would be "the old Group Theatre resurgent two decades after its demise, but this time with public financing and a permanent home."

The Lincoln Center Repertory Theatre, however, lacked both a unifying vision and the wholehearted support of the businessmen who wielded the financial power. Kazan, as he freely admitted, had no feeling for the classics, yet the organization was committed to presenting them. Only half of Lewis' students were taken into the permanent company, largely in supporting roles, and a new group of better-known actors were hired for the theatre's first season, largely on the basis of their suitability for Miller's *After the Fall*. Kazan tried to recruit some Studio actors, but found most uncooperative; they regarded his failure to get the Studio included in Lincoln Center as a betrayal. When the Actors Studio Theatre was announced in 1964, Kazan resigned as a Studio director.

The first Lincoln Center Repertory Theatre season, which opened in early 1964 in Greenwich Village while its fancy new home uptown was being completed, was a bumpy one. *After the Fall*, directed by Kazan, was unfavorably reviewed as a thinly disguised account of Miller's marriage to Marilyn Monroe, though it was a commercial success for that very reason. A revival of O'Neill's *Marco Millions* was poorly received, and the third play,

But for Whom Charlie by S. N. Behrman, was scornfully regarded as a production that could easily have been done in the commercial theatre. The fall season was equally uneven. Kazan's direction of the Elizabethan tragedy *The Changeling* proved his point that he was ill-suited to the classics, although Miller's *Incident at Vichy*, directed by Clurman, had better notices, and the season's final effort, Molière's *Tartuffe*, with an outside director, proved the company could successfully extend its reach.

But the Lincoln Center board, which appeared not to have heard Whitehead's candid advance warning that a repertory theatre would always lose money, panicked at the first sight of red ink and bad press. Unwilling to give Whitehead and Kazan the time needed to find their way, the board squeezed them out. By the time the Vivian Beaumont Theatre opened in 1965, the Lincoln Center Repertory Theatre had new artistic management and the same old problems that had dogged every effort to create a national theatre in America: inability to maintain a permanent acting ensemble, lack of a coherent philosophy about what this theatre was actually trying to do, and a touchy relationship with its financial backers.

If so many Group actors turned to teaching—Sandy Meisner at the Neighborhood Playhouse; Stella Adler at her own conservatory; Bobby Lewis at Yale and other universities; Carnovsky, Brand, Nelson, and Smith at the Lab and elsewhere—it was partly due to their sense that the kind of acting they cared about was simply impossible in the commercial theatre. Of course, not every Group actor gave up performing. Younger people like Lee Cobb and Karl Malden had their greatest success after the Group, particularly in Kazan-directed productions: Cobb in *Death of a Salesman*, Malden in the stage and screen versions of *Streetcar*, both men in *On the Waterfront*. Carnovsky continued to act with distinction for many years, notably in a series of Shakespearean roles at John Houseman's American Shakespeare Festival. Luther Adler, Bill Challee, and Will Lee were active into the 1970s; Margaret Barker and Ruth Nelson are still working today. But many others chose to teach, lacking the heart for the grind of auditions, too-brief rehearsals, and incompletely realized productions that too often characterized the working actor's life. For ten years, they'd had a *real* theatre, and nothing else ever quite lived up to it.

For the man who cared the most about the Group Theatre, who'd been its heart and soul for ten years, one Group was enough for a lifetime. In 1941 Harold Clurman took a job as an associate producer in Hollywood, where he spent a few quiet years socializing with other intellectuals ill at ease in the Golden West and writing *The Fervent Years*, his moving and extremely subjective history of the Group. He and Stella finally legalized their tempestuous union in the early 1940s (they were divorced in 1960). Back in New York, he formed a producing company with Kazan. In 1946 they presented Maxwell Anderson's *Truckline Café*, directed by Clurman with Marlon Brando in a small part, and in 1947 mounted Arthur Miller's

All My Sons, directed by Kazan. Then Kazan took a job in Hollywood and ended the partnership. Clurman directed several Broadway productions in the 1950s, including Carson McCullers' *The Member of the Wedding,* Lillian Hellman's *The Autumn Garden,* William Inge's *Bus Stop,* Jean Anouilh's *The Waltz of the Toreadors,* Tennessee Williams' *Orpheus Descending,* and O'Neill's *A Touch of the Poet.* It was obvious after *The Fervent Years* that he wrote as well as he talked; he joined *The Nation* as drama critic in 1953 and became, in his friend John Houseman's words, "the best theatre critic writing today in the English-speaking world," distinguished by "his sensibility, his cultural experience and the depth of his theatrical knowledge." His columns, as sensitive and provocative today as when they were written, were collected in *Lies Like Truth, The Naked Image,* and *The Divine Pastime;* he also wrote *On Directing* and *All People Are Famous (instead of an autobiography).*

Clurman continued to relish a life surrounded by friends and family, but he remained amicably aloof from post-Group collective endeavors. He was too traumatized by the breakup to have any energy for the Dollar Top Theatre; the Lab was too political for his taste; the Studio was Strasberg's domain. He was more closely involved in Lincoln Center, but his connection ended with Kazan's and Whitehead's. The Group remained the central experience in his life, the intoxicating ten-year moment when all the varied aspects of his personality—his formidable intellect, his love for theatre, his need for a warm collective environment—found outlet within a single organization. Like Odets (though Clurman's later years were far more joyous and professionally fulfilled than those of his tormented friend, who died in 1963), he would never again fly quite so high as he had in the 1930s.

As Group members looked back on their careers in a flock of autobiographies and acting manuals that appeared in the 1970s and '80s, they too saw the Group as a formative influence. Cheryl Crawford, Bobby Lewis, and Elia Kazan all devoted portions of their memoirs to the Group. Lewis' book was dedicated to Clurman; Kazan wrote about the Group as though he were still a resentful twenty-two-year-old apprentice instead of one of the most famous directors of the century and a best-selling novelist *(The Arrangement)* to boot. Strasberg's *A Dream of Passion* chronicled the evolution of the Method and described his work with the Group in detail, devoting a good deal of space to justifying his emphasis on affective memory and refuting the charge that the Method worked only in strictly naturalistic productions. Sandy Meisner's *On Acting* paid tribute to Clurman, Strasberg, and Stella Adler as the people who introduced him to the Stanislavsky system, adding that "without the Group I would have been in the fur business." Morris Carnovsky's thoughtful treatise on his craft, *The Actor's Eye,* was filled with warm references to the Group and his comrades there; he closed by describing their work together as "an act of love." All these books showed how deep and strong their authors' feelings for the Group still ran;

they restated arguments about the Stanislavsky system and political commitment as though those battles had taken place only yesterday.

They all had their own ideas about what the Group meant, and few were satisfied by Clurman's evocative rendering of their history in *The Fervent Years*. The book's publication in 1945 caused a lot of bad feeling. Many Group actors regarded it scornfully as Harold's mystical account of his own philosophical preoccupations. Even worse, it seemed to be essentially the story of how Harold Clurman created the Group Theatre all by himself. He mentioned few Group members at any length other than Strasberg, Odets, the Adlers, and Carnovsky, and those left out resented being relegated to bit parts in their own story. They thought Clurman's critical, often pessimistic tone misrepresented what had, in their minds, been a fundamentally positive experience. "The Group Theatre," Irwin Shaw complained to his friend, "was a glorious crusade, not a funeral." Cheryl Crawford was so enraged by the factual errors she believed the book contained that she flung her copy in the fireplace, though she admitted she later fished it out and finished it. A lengthy, unpublished essay by Bud Bohnen revealed how wounded he was by the way Clurman subtly downplayed everyone's contributions to the Group but his own. Ruth Nelson spoke for all when she told an interviewer, "Harold has written a lovely book in *The Fervent Years*. But it's his book; it's not the book of the Group Theatre whatsoever."

The question, then, is: what *was* the Group Theatre's significance?

Some of the answers are fairly obvious. In their best plays—*The House of Connelly*, *Success Story*, *Awake and Sing!*, *Paradise Lost*—the Group brought the tumult of life in the 1930s onstage, reconnecting the theatre to the world of ideas and action in the society around them. *Waiting for Lefty* was more than a play; it was a historic event: actors and audience literally tore down the walls between theatre and real life, performer and observer, artists and ordinary people, asserting for one thrilling moment a unity of emotion and belief that is the greatest joy the theatre can offer. Their two biggest commercial hits, *Men in White* and *Golden Boy*, weren't quite at that level, but they were superb productions of scripts that made defensible compromises for the sake of getting their message across to a larger audience. Some of the Group's failures, despite their artistic imperfections, were as interesting and important in their own way as the successes. *1931—* captured the terror of the early Depression years; *Gentlewoman* expressed the agonizing ideological uncertainties of one of America's most politically charged decades; *Johnny Johnson* was a warm-hearted piece of Americana and an important stylistic experiment that suffered more from the Group's internal problems than any basic flaws in its conception. The post-1937 plays marked a retreat from the Group's earlier intensity, but *Casey Jones* and *Thunder Rock* were both worthy attempts to grapple with important issues of the day, *Rocket to the Moon* was Odets' most psychologically profound drama, and *My Heart's in the Highlands* was a triumphant exercise in

sheer theatricality. The Group's record of productions remains an example
of how much good work a theatre with a well-defined credo and a commitment to continuous activity can create.

It must be admitted that many of the Group's most famous efforts
haven't aged well. It's possible to read *Lefty* and still be moved by its passion, but it's doubtful that it could be performed today with any credibility.
The other Odets plays *can* be done, as witness a lovely public television
version of *Paradise Lost* in the early 1970s and a recent English production
of *Rocket to the Moon* with John Malkovich, but too often they're turgid and
stagy, with the actors and directors unable to find any living significance in
scripts written fifty years ago. Most of the Group's plays have vanished from
the repertory, but that's the usual fate of contemporary drama, especially
in America. For every Eugene O'Neill, Arthur Miller, Tennessee Williams,
or even Clifford Odets, there have been dozens of playwrights who did good
work that meant something to audiences of their day but for a variety of
reasons haven't been admitted into the canon of writers whose plays continue to be read and performed. (The politics of who gets into the canon
and who doesn't is the subject for another book.) The Group's guiding
principle was the desire to present plays reflecting the life of their times,
which they did in the most exciting way. If most of their plays were ephem-
eral, that's more because theatre is primarily an art of the moment than
because of any Group failing. Though many in the company argued passionately that the Group should assay the classics, it's unlikely such an
effort would have prolonged the organization's life.

The Group's impact on American acting was more lasting. The sincerity,
realism, and emotional depth of their performances were a revelation to
audiences and fellow actors alike. True, their strange exercises prompted
considerable mockery from more cynical theatre folk—not to mention the
press, which loved to poke fun at the Group's intense seriousness—but
there was no arguing with the results. In play after play, Group actors
proved that characters onstage need not be a series of conventional attitudes, but could speak, move and even feel with the quirky individuality of
real people. Because they looked as well as acted like ordinary men and
women, not stars, and because the plays they produced assumed that the
problems of these people were worthy of serious attention, the Group asserted the dignity and importance of a class that had been previously excluded from Broadway and drew in new audiences, thrilled to discover that
culture was for them too.

These audiences didn't necessarily know how the Group created such a
compelling sense of reality; they simply sensed the presence of ideas and
emotions that gave each character an inner life of absolute authenticity
resonating under the text and enriching it. By the late thirties, even critics
who formerly disdained the Group's arty ways routinely paid tribute to their
brilliant acting. The Group had the last laugh over the skeptics. The com-

bination of the Actors Studio, which made the Method a household word, and the work of other Group alumni who became teachers exposed a huge number of American actors to the Stanislavsky system. Different teachers emphasized different aspects of it—affective memory in particular remains as controversial today as it was within the Group—but the *idea* of a systematic approach to the craft of acting was firmly implanted in the vast majority of American actors.

Emotional truth was the foundation, but it was only part of what the Group expected from an actor. Strasberg and Clurman urged the actors, and they in turn told their students in later years, to go out and read books, look at paintings, listen to music, study history, philosophy, and geography. Reading Nietzsche would give them insight into the tormented soul of O'Neill and his characters. Knowing that it was dark most of the time in Norway during the winter, that the towns were surrounded by mountains, would help them feel the claustrophobia of an Ibsen play. A German Expressionist painting gave vivid physical particularity to the edgy, explosive nature of early-twentieth-century German society as it shaped the world view of Brecht. The Group brought these techniques to bear largely on contemporary plays, but they had broader application. They gave new dignity to the acting profession with their insistence on the actor's stature as a creative artist who must bring more to a script than the ability to say lines pleasingly.

A distinguished list of productions offered over ten years; an acting technique that remains enormously influential; a new emphasis on ordinary experience—these were the Group's specific contributions to the American theatre, and they weren't trivial ones. To this day, no other American theatre has managed to sustain the Group's fruitful decade-long balancing act as a place where actors could study their craft, then apply the results of their classroom work in professional productions of important contemporary plays for paying audiences. The Group's ideal of a permanent company working year-round in the theatre is, if anything, further from reality today than it was in 1931. Given the economic conditions that now govern both New York and regional theatres, it's hard to believe a modern equivalent of the Group could ever be created—at least, not until another Harold Clurman comes along to convince another group of actors to do the impossible.

More than their actual achievements, impressive though these were, it's the Group's vision of the theatre that continues to inspire. They believed that true theatre was the greatest of all the arts because it was the most human: a collective endeavor in which writers, directors, actors, and scenic artists animated by a common idea worked together to create productions that spoke passionately and personally to an audience of the hopes, fears, dreams, doubts, and passions we all share. Theatre was a communion for the Group, one of the most direct, exciting, and *alive* means of communication possible among human beings. When it was reduced to the level of

an expensive entertainment, accessible only to those who could afford
Broadway ticket prices, it betrayed its real purpose: to bring people together, to examine the forces within the human spirit and in society at large
that shape our lives.

This vision had implications that extended beyond the stage door. Art
had meaning, the Group believed; ideas were real and they mattered. They
argued with their playwrights, their directors, the press, and each other
because they felt what their plays said was important. They understood that
culture is political, that all art implicitly or explicitly expresses an understanding of human nature and the world order that has political implications. Their theatre was part of a society in the throes of wrenching social
dislocation and change; they had a responsibility to comment on that society and offer their ideas on how it could be made fairer, more humane,
more fulfilling for all its citizens. The idea of art as a social force, so prominent in the intellectual life of the 1930s, remains a vital element of any
healthy cultural scene.

The Group's position well to the left on the political spectrum and the
involvement of several actors in the Communist party (in the days when the
party could still be viewed with some justification as an advocate for working people) was no accident. Nor was it, as Clurman preferred to believe, a
romantic gesture made by people who were essentially apolitical. It grew
out of the same concerns and beliefs that led them to the Group in the first
place. The Group rejected the idea of the theatre artists as employees who
bounced from job to job with no opportunity for coherent development;
they asserted that by working together as a permanent company they could
control their professional lives and create the continuous activity that
would give them economic security and the potential for artistic growth on
a long-term basis. Naturally they believed men and women in every line of
work deserved the same dignity and opportunity to make a better life.

What all this adds up to is a quest for unity, an insistence that people's
work should be a fulfillment and an expression of their personal needs and
beliefs. It's here that the Group's significance goes beyond the theatre and
justifies Harold Clurman's assertion that "the Group Theatre was a symptom and an expression of a profound impulse in American life, an impulse
that certainly did not begin with the Group Theatre, and did not end with
it." Other Group members often teased Clurman about his metaphysical
turn of mind, as evidenced in grandiose statements like that one, but as
usual he'd unerringly grasped the essential. The Group Theatre's appeal for
people who weren't part of it lies deeper than the plays it produced or the
actors it nurtured. It's the Group as a way of life that continues to fascinate
and compel. The Group's story is so interesting, so exciting, and ultimately
so sad because it incarnates ongoing issues in American life.

We are, so the cliché goes, a nation of rugged individualists. What Americans treasure above all is freedom: to go anywhere, do anything, be any-

one; to liberate outselves from the confines of tradition, family, and social class, to invent ourselves along any lines we choose. The Group responded to this intoxicating ideal with two observations. First, they noted that this freedom was largely illusory. Individual achievement in their own line of work, as in so many fields, was both contingent on and hindered by factors the individual had no control over, including typecasting and an economic setup that made financial security, let alone artistic growth, almost impossible to attain. Second, in some ways more crucially, they saw that individual success was often lonely and empty. The determined men and women who overcame all the obstacles and seized the prize of stardom assumed to be every actor's ultimate goal simply continued the same scattered journey from play to play, director to director, role to role, at a higher salary level. They were alone in their success as they had been alone in their struggle; a few bad plays or poorly chosen parts, and they dropped right back down into the lower echelons of a system they'd never really escaped.

How much more satisfying it was, said the Group, to join together with like-minded people and work collectively toward a mutual goal. Not only did a group have a better chance of altering fundamental conditions than an individual did, but the struggle itself was fulfilling when shared with others. The means were as valuable as the end. The Group never got the stable, institutional theatre they wanted, but they got something else instead: Group-ness, the warmth and intimacy of a collective life that united their personal and professional concerns, a web of classes, meetings, and performances that enabled them to show the world what a true theatre could be, even as they struggled to make that theatre viable on a lasting basis.

The Group's difficulties offer an instructive case study, both of the internal problems inherent in communal life and of the external pressures imposed by a society set up to offer individual rather than collective rewards. The Group's enormous critical success and modest box-office prosperity in the mid-1930s made it no easier to raise money for specific plays, nor did it convince investors to back the organization on an institutional basis. It did, however, prompt offers to particular Group actors from Broadway producers and Hollywood studios, eager to pay them a great deal more money than the Group ever could to be stars instead of members of an ensemble. The Group actors' stubborn loyalty to the Group Idea was legendary, but they got little support for it in the outside world. The fact that some of them eventually succumbed to temptation is hardly surprising: you can't eat an ideal, and it's even more indigestible when large numbers of your acquaintances are saying you were a fool to swallow it in the first place.

Group members made very real sacrifices to stay with the company, and there's no question that collective life was difficult in ways that went far beyond money. The Group asked people to subjugate their egos to the collective will, to take small parts, undergo personal criticism, and accept decisions they might not agree with, all as part of the larger effort. There were actors—actresses, for the most part—whose careers never really recovered from the Group; a decade of playing in an ensemble, however rewarding it was, didn't give them the credentials Broadway managers expected when hiring for featured roles. Month after month, year after year, Group actors grappled with the question: was the work worth it? For most of them, the answer was yes. "Everybody had their frustrations," said Eunice Stoddard. "I stayed because it was more interesting theatre than anywhere else. Rehearsals were always so exciting: the whole analysis of the play, of the parts, of what the play was saying in terms of our era, was just so much more stimulating than anything you'd ever get on Broadway. You didn't want to leave that for what you knew you'd be getting outside, which might satisfy your ego as an actress but not necessarily create very interesting theatre. It was a very difficult choice."

Because the Group demanded such choices as the price of service to a collective goal, reciprocal obligation was implied to give everyone a say in decisions affecting its operation. Their dream was a theatre that spoke with one voice, and to achieve it they had to listen to every voice. The directors had never pledged themselves to run the Group as a democracy, but they were impelled by the logic of their situation to move in that direction: to take a vote on whether or not an actor should be permitted a leave of absence, to ask for the company's opinion on the plays they were considering, to give actors administrative and publicity responsibilities because there was no one else to assume them. The Group functioned best as a peculiar combination of dictatorship and democracy, with the actors content to leave most matters in the hands of the directors because they felt confident of their leaders' adherence to basic Group values and certain they would be consulted on any crucial or difficult issues. The bitter organizational struggles that racked the Group in later years resulted first from the actors' realization that the directors couldn't deliver everything they'd promised—no one could have—then, after the 1937 reorganization, from an uneasy sense that the Group Idea had in some essential way been violated, that it was up to them to force their leaders to bring it back.

In a collective where people worked closely and often lived together, policy discussions could take on a very personal tone, informed by people's intimate knowledge of each other's character and beliefs. Outsiders tended to view the Group as a bunch of eccentrics and neurotics who fought all the time because they were crazy, not because there were real issues to fight about. Even Group members themselves sometimes in retrospect credited individual failings as contributing factors to the organization's demise, and they weren't entirely wrong. It could certainly be argued that the Group needed the productive tension that existed among the three original directors to create an effective leadership: that Strasberg's authoritarianism and emotional bullying were mitigated by Clurman's warmth and willingness to listen; that Clurman's fits of lassitude and inability to impose discipline were counterbalanced by Strasberg's high seriousness, which encouraged the Group's active program of classes and continued artistic growth; that both men relied on Crawford's tireless handling of details and shrewd understanding of the way you had to talk with commercial producers in order to get backing.

Of course the directors argued among themselves; naturally there were Group members who disliked each other, disruptive love affairs, unpleasant ideological clashes, personal and artistic sniping inside and outside the rehearsal hall, nervous breakdowns, and bitter feuds. Collective life was difficult; they were dealing with real issues and real people. No one had ever said it would be easy.

Yet for ten years this diverse and often ill-assorted group of people found their differences less important than the vision they shared: of a theatre that spoke powerfully and truthfully to a broad audience about the moral and social concerns of their times, of collective action that would make the theatre and the world a better place, of art and life inextricably intertwined. They changed the American theatre, they changed their own lives, and they did it together. Morris Carnovsky was right: the Group Theatre was an act of love.

The House of Connelly by Paul Green.
Opened September 29, 1931, at the Martin Beck Theatre.
Directed by Lee Strasberg and Cheryl Crawford. Scenery by Cleon Throckmorton. Costumes by Fania Mindell.
Cast included Franchot Tone (Will Connelly), Margaret Barker (Patsy Tate), Stella Adler (Geraldine Connelly), Eunice Stoddard (Evelyn Connelly), Morris Carnovsky (Robert Connelly), Mary Morris (Mrs. Connelly), Rose McClendon (Big Sue), Fannie de Knight (Big Sis).

1931—by Paul and Claire Sifton.
Opened December 10, 1931, at the Mansfield Theatre.
Directed by Lee Strasberg. Scenery by Mordecai Gorelik.
Cast included J. Edward Bromberg (Foreman), Franchot Tone (Adam), Phoebe Brand (The Girl).

Night over Taos by Maxwell Anderson.
Opened March 9, 1932, at the 48th Street Theatre.
Directed by Lee Strasberg. Scenery and costumes by Robert Edmond Jones.
Cast included J. Edward Bromberg (Pablo Montoya), Franchot Tone (Federico), Walter Coy (Felipe), Ruth Nelson (Diana), Stella Adler (Dona Josefa), Morris Carnovsky (Father Martinez), Luther Adler (Don Fernando), Art Smith (Captain Mumford).

Success Story by John Howard Lawson.
Opened September 26, 1932, at the Maxine Elliott Theatre.

Directed by Lee Strasberg. Scenery by Mordecai Gorelik.
Cast included Stella Adler (Sarah Glassman), Franchot Tone (Raymond Merritt), Morris Carnovsky (Rufus Sonnenberg), Luther Adler (Sol Ginsberg), Dorothy Patten (Agnes Carter).

Big Night by Dawn Powell.
Opened January 17, 1933, at the Maxine Elliott Theatre.
Directed by Cheryl Crawford. Scenery by Mordecai Gorelik.
Cast included Stella Adler (Myra Bonney), Lewis Leverett (Ed Bonney), J. Edward Bromberg (Bert Schwartz).

Men in White by Sidney Kingsley.
Opened September 26, 1933, at the Broadhurst Theatre.
Directed by Lee Strasberg. Scenery by Mordecai Gorelik.
Cast included J. Edward Bromberg (Dr. Hochberg), Alexander Kirkland (Dr. Ferguson), Margaret Barker (Laura Hudson), Phoebe Brand (Barbara Dennin), Dorothy Patten (Nurse Mary Ryan).

Gentlewoman by John Howard Lawson.
Opened March 22, 1934, at the Cort Theatre.
Directed by Lee Strasberg. Scenery by Mordecai Gorelik.
Cast included Stella Adler (Gwyn Ballantine), Lloyd Nolan (Rudy Flannigan).

Gold Eagle Guy by Melvin Levy.
Premiered November 12, 1934, at the Majestic Theatre in Boston.

Opened November 28, 1934, at the Morosco Theatre in New York.
Directed by Lee Strasberg. Scenery by Donald Oenslager. Costumes by Kay Morrison.
Cast included J. Edward Bromberg (Guy Button), Margaret Barker (Jessie Sargent), Morris Carnovsky (Will Parrott), Stella Adler (Adah Menken), Alexander Kirkland (Lon Firth), Russell Collins (Ed Walker).

Waiting for Lefty by Clifford Odets.
First performance January 6, 1935, at the Civic Repertory Theatre.
Directed by Clifford Odets and Sanford Meisner.
Cast included Morris Carnovsky (Fatt), Art Smith (Joe), Ruth Nelson (Edna), Gerrit Kraber (Miller), Walter Coy (Irv), Phoebe Brand (Florrie), Jules Garfield (Sid), Russell Collins (Clayton), Elia Kazan (Clancy), Paula Miller (Secretary), William Challee (Actor), Roman Bohnen (Dr. Barnes), Luther Adler (Dr. Benjamin), J. Edward Bromberg (Agate Keller).
Opened March 26, 1935, at the Longacre Theatre.
Cast changes included Russell Collins (Fatt), Lewis Leverett (Joe), Paula Miller (Florrie), Herbert Ratner (Sid), Robert Lewis (Clayton), Dorothy Patten (Secretary), Clifford Odets (Dr. Benjamin), Elia Kazan (Agate Keller).

Till the Day I Die by Clifford Odets.
Opened March 26, 1935, at the Longacre Theatre, with *Waiting for Lefty*.
Directed by Cheryl Crawford. Scenery by Paul Morrison.
Cast included Alexander Kirkland (Ernst Taussig), Margaret Barker (Tillie), Walter Coy (Karl Taussig), Lewis Leverett (Captain Schlegel), Roman Bohnen (Major Duhrer), Eunice Stoddard (Zelda), Lee Strasberg, under the name Lee Martin (Stieglitz).

Awake and Sing! by Clifford Odets.
Opened February 19, 1935, at the Belasco Theatre.

Directed by Harold Clurman. Scenery by Boris Aronson.
Cast included Art Smith (Myron Berger), Stella Adler (Bessie Berger), Morris Carnovsky (Jacob), Phoebe Brand (Hennie Berger), Jules Garfield (Ralph Berger), Luther Adler (Moe Axelrod), J. Edward Bromberg (Uncle Morty), Sanford Meisner (Sam Feinschreiber), Roman Bohnen (Schlosser).

Weep for the Virgins by Nellisse Child.
Opened November 30, 1935, at the 46th Street Theatre.
Directed by Cheryl Crawford. Scenery by Boris Aronson.
Cast included Art Smith (Homer Jobes), J. Edward Bromberg (Oscar Sigsmund), Ruth Nelson (Ruby Jones), Alexander Kirkland (Danny Stowe), Paula Miller (Clarice Jobes), Evelyn Varden (Cecelia Jobes), Phoebe Brand (Violet Jobes), Jules Garfield (Hap Nichols).

Paradise Lost by Clifford Odets.
Opened December 9, 1935, at the Belasco Theatre.
Directed by Harold Clurman. Scenery by Boris Aronson.
Cast included Morris Carnovsky (Leo Gordon), Stella Adler (Clara Gordon), Walter Coy (Ben), Sanford Meisner (Julie), Joan Madison (Pearl), Roman Bohnen (Gus Michaels), Blanche Gladstone (Libby Michaels), Luther Adler (Marcus Katz), Frieda Altman (Bertha Katz), Elia Kazan (Kewpie), Grover Burgess (Mr. Pike), Robert Lewis (Mr. May), Russell Collins and William Challee (Homeless Men).

Case of Clyde Griffiths by Erwin Piscator and Lena Goldschmidt.
Opened March 13, 1936, at the Ethel Barrymore Theatre.
Directed by Lee Strasberg. Scenery by Watson Barrat.
Cast included Morris Carnovsky (Speaker), Alexander Kirkland (Clyde Griffiths), Phoebe Brand (Roberta

Alden), Margaret Barker (Sondra Finchler).

Johnny Johnson by Paul Green. Music by Kurt Weill.
Opened November 19, 1936, at the 44th Street Theatre.
Directed by Lee Strasberg. Scenery by Donald Oenslager. Costumes by Paul Du Pont.
Cast included Phoebe Brand (Minny Belle Tompkins), Russell Collins (Johnny Johnson), Grover Burgess (Anguish Howington), Sanford Meisner (Captain Valentine), Lee Cobb (Dr. McBray), Jules Garfield (Johann Lang), Morris Carnovsky (Dr. Mahodan), Kate Allen (Mahodan's Secretary).

Golden Boy by Clifford Odets.
Opened November 4, 1937, at the Belasco Theatre.
Directed by Harold Clurman. Scenery by Mordecai Gorelik.
Cast included Roman Bohnen (Tom Moody), Frances Farmer (Lorna Moon), Luther Adler (Joe Bonaparte), Art Smith (Tokio), Jules Garfield (Siggie), Morris Carnovsky (Mr. Bonaparte), Phoebe Brand (Anna), John O'Malley (Frank Bonaparte), Elia Kazan (Eddie Fuseli).

Casey Jones by Robert Ardrey.
Opened February 19, 1938, at the Fulton Theatre.
Directed by Elia Kazan. Scenery by Mordecai Gorelik.
Cast included Van Heflin (Jed Sherman), Charles Bickford (Casey Jones), Peggy Conklin (Portsmouth Jones).

Rocket to the Moon by Clifford Odets.
Opened November 24, 1938, at the Belasco Theatre.
Directed by Harold Clurman. Scenery by Mordecai Gorelik.
Cast included Morris Carnovsky (Ben Stark), Ruth Nelson (Belle Stark), Eleanor Lynn (Cleo Singer), Luther Adler (Mr. Prince), Leif Erickson (Fren-

chy), Sanford Meisner (Willy Wax), William Challee (A Salesman).

The Gentle People by Irwin Shaw.
Opened January 5, 1939, at the Belasco Theatre.
Directed by Harold Clurman. Scenery by Boris Aronson.
Cast included Sam Jaffe (Jonah Goodman), Roman Bohnen (Philip Anagnos), Franchot Tone (Harold Goff), Sylvia Sidney (Stella Goodman), Elia Kazan (Eli Lieber), Lee Cobb (Lammanawitz).

Awake and Sing! by Clifford Odets.
Revival opened March 7, 1939, at the Windsor Theatre.
Cast changes included Alfred Ryder (Ralph Berger), Julia Adler (Bessie Berger), William Challee (Schlosser).

My Heart's in the Highlands by William Saroyan.
Opened April 13, 1939, at the Guild Theatre.
Directed by Robert Lewis. Scenery and costumes by Herbert Andrews.
Cast included Philip Loeb (Ben Alexander), Sidney Lumet (Johnny), Art Smith (Jasper MacGregor).

Thunder Rock by Robert Ardrey.
Premiered November 2, 1939, as *Tower of Light* at Ford's Theatre in Baltimore.
Opened November 14, 1939, at the Mansfield Theatre.
Directed by Elia Kazan. Scenery by Mordecai Gorelik. Costumes by Paul Morrison.
Cast included Luther Adler (Charleston), Morris Carnovsky (Captain Joshua), Frances Farmer (Melanie).

Night Music by Clifford Odets.
Premiered February 8, 1940, at the Shubert Theatre in Boston.
Opened February 22, 1940, at the Broadhurst Theatre.
Directed by Harold Clurman. Scenery by Mordecai Gorelik.

Cast included Elia Kazan (Steve Takis), Morris Carnovsky (A. L. Rosenberger), Jane Wyatt (Fay Tucker).

Retreat to Pleasure by Irwin Shaw. Opened December 17, 1940, at the Belasco Theatre.

Directed by Harold Clurman. Scenery by Donald Oenslager.

Cast included Leif Erickson (Peter Flower), John Emery (Chester Stack), Hume Cronyn (Lee Tatnall), Edith Atwater (Norah Galligan), Dorothy Patten (Gretchen Tatnall).

ACKNOWLEDGMENTS AND
NOTES ON SOURCES

First and foremost, my thanks must go to the people who shared their memories of the Group with me, in personal interviews, by letter or phone: Ellen Adler, Stella Adler, Margaret Barker, Phoebe Brand, Morris Carnovsky, Helen Deutsch, Ruth Young Eliot, Jean Garlen Fox, Michael Gordon, Eleanor Lynn Helprin, the late John Houseman, Elia Kazan, Sidney Kingsley, Wilhelmina Barton Kraber, Robert Lewis, Sidney Lumet, Arthur Miller, Charles O'Neill, Pearl Adler Pearson, Wendell Phillips, Martin Ritt, the late Philip Robinson, Sylvia Sidney, Eunice Stoddard.

Several institutions have significant collections of material pertaining to the Group Theatre. Principal among them is the Billy Rose Theatre Collection of the Performing Arts Research Center at the Lincoln Center branch of the New York Public Library. Not only does the collection house the Group Theatre scrapbooks, containing virtually all press coverage of the organization from 1931 through 1940, it also contains a substantial number of documents and papers from the collections of Luther Adler, Roman Bohnen, Harold Clurman, Cheryl Crawford, and Dorothy Patten. The Theatre Collection staff were without exception helpful above and beyond the call of duty in tracking down obscure and uncatalogued material; I thank them one and all. A complete list of the materials there would be lengthy and tedious; the footnotes list specific items as they are quoted in the text. Among the more crucial documents are Roman Bohnen's letters to his family from 1932 to 1940; Luther Adler's copy of the 1937 Actors Committee report to the Group directors; a manuscript of *The Fervent Years* containing material cut from the published version; the notebook Harold Clurman kept while preparing to write the book; three long and important papers written by Clurman in 1931, 1935, and 1936; the directors' paper replying to the actors' complaints in 1933; Elia Kazan's letter urging Clurman to return to New York in 1937; the two issues of *The Flying Grouse;* Cheryl Crawford's budgets for the early Group productions; speeches given by Dorothy Patten and Alexander Kirkland in 1936; and a number of memos, minutes, and letters that give a wonderfully intimate sense of the texture of Group life. The library also has selected issues of *Workers Theatre* (1931–1933) and complete collections of *New Theatre* (1933–1937) and *Theatre Workshop* (1936–1938) on microfilm.

The Rare Book and Manuscript division of Butler Library at Columbia University also has a copy of the deleted material from *The Fervent Years*, as well as an additional notebook kept by Clurman that contains an account of Stella Adler's meeting with Stanislavsky. The Columbia University Oral History Project, also located in Butler Library, includes interviews with Harold Clurman, Robert Lewis, Sidney Lumet, and Lee Strasberg. The Robert F. Wagner Labor Archives, in the Tamiment Library at New York University, contain letters from Clurman to Jay Leyda, as well as the minutes of the Actors Equity Council meetings; my thanks to Marty Lomonaco for making me aware of this material. The Kurt Weill Foundation in New York

City has a long and very useful videotaped interview with Phoebe Brand and Morris Carnovsky about the rehearsals and production of *Johnny Johnson;* John C. Mucci, who filmed the interview, kindly loaned me his copy, which contained some informative outtakes not in the Weill Foundation version. The Paul Strand Archives in the Center for Creative Photography at the University of Arizona, Tucson, contain letters written by Clurman to Paul Strand from 1928 to 1934. I thank Anthony J. Montoya for arranging to have copies of the correspondence made available to me at the Strand Archives in Millerton, New York, and for allowing me to reproduce a Strand photograph. I found the scripts of plays produced by the Group that were never published in book form at the Copyright Division of the Library of Congress; they are listed in the bibliography.

A number of individuals generously assisted me in my search for Group documents. Margaret Brenman-Gibson loaned me her copy of the Brookfield Diary. Anna Strasberg allowed me to examine her late husband's notes on Group meetings, letters to his first wife about the Group's painful 1937 breakup, and a fascinating notebook kept at the Pine Brook Club. Susan Amanda Lawson let me borrow and copy pertinent portions of her late father's unpublished autobiography. Phoebe Brand and Morris Carnovsky did the same with their copy of the notes taken at Smithtown in 1939. So did Helen Deutsch with letters written to her by Clifford Odets in late 1934. Mel Gordon, now chairman of the drama department at the University of California, Berkeley, but at the time a professor at New York University, loaned me copies of interviews conducted by him and his students with Stella Adler, Phoebe Brand, Tony Kraber, Wilhelmina Barton Kraber, and Will Lee; he also gave me copies of Ms. Kraber's notebook on Stella Adler's classes at Ellenville, a speech given by Harold Clurman in 1932, and outtakes from interviews conducted by Alan Kaplan and Thomas Klein for their documentary "Harold Clurman: A Life of Theatre." Mr. Kaplan and Mr. Klein permitted me to quote from both the outtakes and the documentary itself. I thank them all, in particular Mel Gordon, whose support and encouragement were invaluable; his sharp ideas about the Group fueled many enjoyable afternoons of conversation. Robert Lewis met with me several times and cheerfully answered minor factual queries over the phone. Margaret Barker was also generous with her time and frank in her discussion of the sometimes stormy personal relationships within the Group. Phoebe Brand and Morris Carnovsky, who like Ms. Barker and Mr. Lewis consented to be interviewed more than once, were as gracious and welcoming to a total stranger as I knew they would be from hearing their friends in the Group talk about them; they never once inquired about the direction my book might take, even though it clearly covered issues that were both important and painful to them. I hope I've done justice to their candor.

I'm grateful to the executors and surviving relatives of deceased Group members who allowed me to quote from or reproduce material: Stella Adler, Harold Clurman's first wife, and his widow, Justine Compton-Wentworth, who jointly hold the Clurman copyrights; Paul B. Berkowsky, co-executor of Cheryl Crawford's estate; the Brandt & Brandt Agency, acting for Walt and Nora Odets; Marcia Bromberg, daughter of J. Edward Bromberg; Arthur Green, lawyer for the Irwin Shaw estate; Alex Guerry, a cousin of Dorothy Patten; Susan Lawson, daughter of John Howard Lawson; Pearl Pearson and Lulla Rosenfeld, nieces of Luther Adler; Marina Bohnen Pratt, daughter of Roman Bohnen; Jacqueline Rice, executor of Dawn Powell's estate; Caroline Steiner, widow of Ralph Steiner; and Anna Strasberg, widow of Lee Strasberg.

I'm extremely grateful to my agent, Steve Axelrod, and my editor, Elisabeth Sifton, for believing in the value of a project that virtually everyone else in the New York publishing world thought was worthy but commercially unfeasible. My personal thanks go to my husband and dearest friend, Joe Mobilia, who was endlessly patient about sharing an apartment with someone spending most of her time in the 1930s; he pulled me through the customary bouts of authorial hysteria with his good humor and good sense. He was also the first reader of every chapter, and his perceptive comments and questions immeasurably improved the manuscript. This book is dedicated to him and to Alberta Magzanian, whose classes in European history and political thought taught me that history is about living ideas real men and women argued over and fought for, that we study the past for what it can tell us about how to live our lives today.

NOTES

ONE: GENESIS

Page

3 "I changed": Outtake from "Harold Clurman: A Life of Theatre," documentary by Thomas Klein and Alan Kaplan.

4 "You are lost here": From documentary footage accompanying an early 1970s PBS broadcast of *Paradise Lost*, replayed at "A Tribute to the Group Theatre," held at Williamstown, Massachusetts, August 9, 1987.

Looking at the American theatre: The text of Harold Clurman's Friday-night talks has not survived. Rather than quote from his eloquent, polished summation, written fifteen years after the fact, in *The Fervent Years*, I've used the text of an article and an unpublished proposal written at the time of the talks for a closer approximation of his youthful style.

"If we were providentially": "Critique of the American Theatre," article by Harold Clurman in *The Drama* magazine, April 1931.

5 "The creation, as carefully and lovingly as lies within one's power": Quoted in *The Theatre Guild: The First Ten Years* by Walter Prichard Eaton, New York: Brentano's, 1929, p. 5.

"The only fundamental difference": Clurman, "Critique of the American Theatre."

"Americans don't really talk to each other": From a taped conversation between Cheryl Crawford and Harold Clurman, early 1970s. Uncatalogued portion of the Cheryl Crawford Collection at the Lincoln Center Performing Arts Research Center, Billy Rose Theatre Collection. (Unless otherwise noted, all citations of Lincoln Center refer to material in the Billy Rose Collection.)

6 "We feel the individualism of self-assertion": "Plans for a First Studio," unpublished proposal by Harold Clurman, written in 1931 in response to the Theatre Guild's questions about his Friday-night talks. Roman Bohnen Collection, Lincoln Center.

"How dare you say these things": Margaret Barker, interview with author.

7 "A theatre is created": Clurman, "Plans for a First Studio."

"Words are so inadequate": Ibid.

8 "The essential moral and social preoccupations of our time": "The Group Theatre Speaks for Itself" by Harold Clurman, *New York Times*, December 13, 1931. (Unless otherwise noted, all newspaper articles cited dating from 1931 to 1941 are from the Group Theatre scrapbooks at Lincoln Center.)

"The criterion for excellence": Clurman, "Plans for a First Studio."

"Citizens of a community": *The Fervent Years* by Harold Clurman, New York: Harcourt Brace Jovanovich, 1975 reprint of 1945 Knopf edition, p. 33.

"Isolated purveyor[s] of literary goods": Clurman, "Plans for a First Studio."

Page
9 "A superb ensemble": "Renaissance?" by Lee Strasberg, *New York Times*, July 20, 1958.
11 "To me, theatre is like a light": Quoted in Clurman, *The Fervent Years*, p. 8.
   "Acting which really dug at me": *Sanford Meisner on Acting* by Sanford Meisner and Dennis Longwell, New York: Vintage Books, 1987, p. 6.
12 "Picturesque" . . . "disagreeable though effective": Clurman, *The Fervent Years*, p. 10.
13 "That it was a person": *A Dream of Passion: The Development of the Method* by Lee Strasberg, Boston: Little, Brown, 1987, p. 16.
14 "Obviously, this truth and reality": Ibid., p. 38.
   "There are no laboratories": Quoted in "The American Laboratory Theatre, 1923–1930," Ph.D. dissertation by Ronald A. Willis, University of Iowa, 1968, p. 42.
   "This is it": Strasberg, *A Dream of Passion*, p. 64.
15 "A living social force": Quoted in *A Method to Their Madness: A History of the Actors Studio* by Foster Hirsch, New York: W. W. Norton, 1984, p. 55.
16 "In those days": Quoted in *Lee Strasberg: The Imperfect Genius of the Actors Studio* by Cindy Adams, Garden City, N.Y.: Doubleday, 1980, p. 92.
   "We were drawn together": Clurman, *The Fervent Years*, p. 11.
19 "She was roundly laughed at": *Bright Star of Exile: Jacob Adler and the Yiddish Theatre* by Lulla Rosenfeld, New York: Thomas Y. Crowell, 1977, p. 351.
   "Thorough and complete": Quoted in Hirsch, *A Method to Their Madness*, p. 56.
20 "[Stieglitz] was committed": *All People Are Famous* by Harold Clurman, New York: Harcourt Brace Jovanovich, 1974, p. 54.
22 "Made a damn nuisance of myself": *The Actor's Eye* by Morris Carnovsky with Peter Sander, New York: Performing Arts Journal Publications, 1984, p. 32.
   "I had good instincts": Ibid., p. 101.
   "Man had to face living realities": Clurman, *The Fervent Years*, p. 21.
   "Insufficiently secure, technically speaking": Unpublished material deleted from the original manuscript of *The Fervent Years* (hereafter referred to as unpublished *Fervent*), p. 54.
   "What is this hocus pocus?" Morris Carnovsky, interview with author.
23 "The work of my group": Harold Clurman to Paul Strand, July 20, 1928, in the collection of the Paul Strand Archives, Center for Creative Photography, University of Arizona, Tucson. (All letters from Clurman to Strand are from the Strand Archives.)
   "Here was the personification": Clurman, *The Fervent Years*, p. 28.
   "I can't compete with a dead man": Stella Adler, interview with Mel Gordon.
   "Hazardous interdependence": *One Naked Individual: My Fifty Years in the Theatre* by Cheryl Crawford, Indianapolis, Ind.: The Bobbs-Merrill Company, 1977, p. 93.
   "Strasberg and I": Clurman, *The Fervent Years*, p. 24.
24 "Ethical Culture people": Interview with Harold Clurman by Louis Sheaffer for the Columbia Oral History Project, Butler Library.
   "They had a fixation on pessimism": Harold Clurman, taped conversation. Cheryl Crawford Collection, Lincoln Center.
   "America demands": *Democratic Vistas* by Walt Whitman, London: George Routledge & Sons, 1888, p. 62.
25 "Slightly depressed air": Unpublished *Fervent*, p. 64.
26 "Just blustered through": Eunice Stoddard, interview with author.
   "A theatre closer and more literally faithful": *The Nation*, February 5, 1930.
   "The American drama of today": *Vogue*, February 15, 1930.

"The death watch": *Vintage Years of the Theatre Guild, 1928–1939* by Roy S. Waldau, Cleveland, Oh.: The Press of Case Western Reserve University, 1972, p. 65.

27 "With tragic intensity": Quoted in Clurman, *The Fervent Years*, p. 20.

28 "The conclusions we drew": From an unpublished autobiographical sketch by Dorothy Patten, Lincoln Center.

"This may be all right": Quoted in *Slings and Arrows* by Robert Lewis, New York: Stein and Day, 1984, p. 38.

"Clearly about the best part": Margaret Barker, interview with author.

29 "If you want to be a star": Ibid.

"We needed thinking actors": From a talk by Cheryl Crawford at the Lee Strasberg Theatre Institute, March 9, 1983, tape at Lincoln Center.

"The real basis of choice": Unpublished *Fervent*, p. 86.

"I feel you definitely have a place": Quoted in Lewis, *Slings and Arrows*, p. 33.

30 "I'm laughing": Quoted in *Clifford Odets: American Playwright, the Years from 1906 to 1940* by Margaret Brenman-Gibson, New York: Atheneum, 1981, p. 166.

"Let's take Odets": Clurman, taped conversation with Cheryl Crawford, Lincoln Center.

31 "A unity of background": Clurman, *The Fervent Years*, p. 33.

32 "Collaborating . . . accomplished": Clurman, "Plans for a First Studio."

"It had taken four years": Crawford, *One Naked Individual*, p. 51.

"Vacation resort": *The Danbury Times*, May 15, 1931.

"Beany, if I were twenty years younger": Margaret Barker, interview with author.

"A chance to invest": Lewis, *Slings and Arrows*, p. 39.

33 "Let us step out": *Our America* by Waldo Frank, New York: Boni & Liveright, 1920, pp. 220–21.

TWO: FIRST LOVE

34 "Now closes another . . . day": The nine subsequent quotations are all taken from the Brookfield Diary. They are by, respectively, Phoebe Brand (June 26); Friendly Ford (July 5), Herbert Ratner (July 1), Stella Adler (June 16), Bobby Lewis (June 21), Cheryl Crawford (June 22), Eunice Stoddard (July 26), Clifford Odets (July 12), and Dorothy Patten (June 18).

35 "*What* kind of people": Dorothy Patten, autobiographical sketch.

"Be as personal as you like": Brookfield Diary, Helen Deutsch, on a typewritten page accompanying the notebook.

"They spoke of the meaning": Brookfield Diary, Lewis Leverett, June 8, 1931.

36 "Plays representing . . . native theatre": *New York Herald Tribune*, September 23, 1931.

"Cut it": Cheryl Crawford, talk at Lee Strasberg Theatre Institute.

37 "Lee took it upon himself": Phoebe Brand, interview with author.

"First thing you know": Quoted in "Acting Experiments in the Group" by Mel Gordon and Laurie Lassiter, from *The Drama Review*, Cambridge: MIT Press, Winter 1984, p. 9.

38 "The play in which I think": Lee Strasberg, interview with Peter Jessup, from the Columbia Oral History Project Collection, Butler Library.

"One quavers before the 'method' ": Brookfield Diary, Friendly Ford, July 5, 1931.

39 "General Lee": Brookfield Diary, Eunice Stoddard, June 25, 1931.

"Dr. Strasberg . . . masks": Brookfield Diary, Art Smith, June 17, 1931.

Page
39 "A curious, priest-like quality": Morris Carnovsky, quoted in *A Player's Place: The Story of the Actors Studio* by David Garfield, New York: Macmillan, 1980, p. 31.

"He was God": Bobby Lewis, interview with author.

"He hardly seems a person": Harold Clurman to Paul Strand, August 24, 1931.

40 "All my acting training": Phoebe Brand, interview with author.

"It was that sense": Margaret Barker, interview with author.

"Now we throw out . . . to tell": Brookfield Diary, Art Smith, June 17, 1931.

"Rich with all the possibilities": Brookfield Diary, Mary Morris, July 15, 1931.

"Battering": Crawford, *One Naked Individual*, p. 54.

41 "Making her contribution": Unpublished *Fervent*, p. 122.

42 "It wasn't easy": Brookfield Diary, Cheryl Crawford, June 22, 1931.

"Human relationships": Harold Clurman to Paul Strand, August 24, 1931.

"For the first time": Brookfield Diary, Stella Adler, June 16, 1931.

43 "The thing to do": Ibid., Sanford Meisner, June 23, 1931.

"After we've reformed": Quoted in Lewis, *Slings and Arrows*, pp. 41–42. My reconstruction of this talk is largely based on Bobby Lewis' recollections, assisted by his notes and Herbert Ratner's entry in the Brookfield Diary.

44 "To watch life": Ibid., Lee Strasberg, June 27, 1931.

45 "Never have I so desired": Ibid., Harold Clurman, June 19, 1931.

46 "No, you can't expect pathos": Ibid., Eunice Stoddard, June 20, 1931.

"Pay more attention": Ibid., Joe Bromberg, June 9, 1931.

"Shall we interfere": Clurman, *The Fervent Years*, p. 46.

47 "We have not yet" and "Art is not a plaything": Brookfield Diary, Herbert Ratner, July 1, 1931.

"Osculation Prohibited": Ibid., Fannie Belle De Knight, July 8, 1931.

48 "Slops together": Phoebe Brand, interview with author.

"You don't know how": Morris Carnovsky, interview with author.

"Gain valuable clarity": Brookfield Diary, Gerald Sykes, August 9, 1931.

"I think I expected": Eunice Stoddard, interview with author.

49 "I can't stand *your* noise": Clurman, *The Fervent Years*, p. 47.

"*Required* to be personal": Brookfield Diary, Bill Challee, June 14, 1931.

"He was very good": Phoebe Brand, interviewed by Barbara Wolkoff and Nina Levine, May 19, 1981, collection of Mel Gordon.

"The individual actor's total personality": "The Actor in the Group Theatre" by Stella Adler, in *Actors on Acting*, edited by Toby Cole and Helen Krich Chinoy, New York: Crown Publishers, 1949, p. 603.

50 "There were no failures": Stella Adler, interview with Mel Gordon.

"We loved each other": Phoebe Brand, interview with author.

"This book fairly sings" and "good humbleness": Brookfield Diary, Helen Deutsch, July 19, 1931.

"Naturally we feel more impelled": Ibid., Art Smith, July 20, 1931.

"More than a touch of smugness": Ibid., Helen Deutsch, July 20, 1931.

51 "We will act": Ibid., Margaret Barker, July 15, 1931.

"We were all sort of teary-eyed": Margaret Barker, interview with author.

52 "In the 'method' ": Brookfield Diary, Bill Challee, July 16, 1931.

"I came in this group": Ibid., Walter Coy, July 13, 1931.

"How long do you think": Clurman, *The Fervent Years*, p. 54.

"Ah, well—we have twenty years": Brookfield Diary, Sanford Meisner, June 23, 1931.

Page

"It's nice": Ibid., Herbert Ratner, July 1, 1931.

53 "I was not in a working mood": Harold Clurman to Paul Strand, August 24, 1931.

"You are all my constant concern": Brookfield Diary, Harold Clurman, July 26, 1931.

54 "My small pride": Margaret Barker, interview with author.

"Purity and sweetness": Brookfield Diary, Harold Clurman, July 26, 1931.

"None of us": Ibid., Dorothy Patten, June 18, 1931.

"Hard, exciting": Harold Clurman to Paul Strand, August 24, 1931.

"To grow and live": From *The House of Connelly*, act II, scene iii.

"Too slow": Clurman, *The Fervent Years*, p. 54.

55 "No director—not even Stanislavsky": Brookfield Diary, Harold Clurman, June 19, 1931.

"A new thing": Harold Clurman to Paul Strand, August 24, 1931.

"Your life is going to be *hard!*": Conversation between Cheryl Crawford and Harold Clurman, Cheryl Crawford Collection, Lincoln Center.

"There is no need": Brookfield Diary, Gerald Sykes, August 9, 1931.

THREE: THE REAL WORLD

57 "Some of them": Clurman, *The Fervent Years*, p. 55.

"You have murdered the play": Conversation between Cheryl Crawford and Harold Clurman, Cheryl Crawford Collection, Lincoln Center.

58 "The passing of the experimental group theatre": Quoted in *O'Neill: Son and Artist* by Louis Sheaffer, Boston: Little, Brown, 1973, p. 386.

60 "If you're not satisfied": Quoted in Harold Clurman's notebook for *The Fervent Years*, Lincoln Center.

61 "What beauties Mr. Green has imparted": All reviews are from September 30, 1931, except "It has a group feeling," which is from October 8, 1931.

62 "Happy as a lark": Cheryl Crawford, talk at Lee Strasberg Theatre Institute.

"The incontrovertible fact" and all other quotations from the Group-Guild meeting are taken from Clurman, *The Fervent Years*, pp. 68–69.

63–4 "The contrapuntal design": From the preface to *1931—* by Paul and Claire Sifton, New York: Farrar & Rinehart, 1931.

64 "To give the most expert": "The Group Theatre Speaks for Itself" by Harold Clurman, *New York Times*, December 13, 1931.

"A caricature of all I had said": All quotes in this paragraph are from Clurman, *The Fervent Years*, p. 65.

"It is our theatre's duty": Ibid., p. 69.

66 "It gave evidence": Ibid., pp. 67–68.

67 "Why can't you work": Phoebe Brand, interview with author.

68 "Please don't interfere": This anecdote is told by almost everyone who ever worked with the Group. My amalgamation is drawn from Clurman, *The Fervent Years*; Lewis, *Slings and Arrows*; Adams, *Lee Strasberg*; and an interview with Michael Gordon.

69 "If propaganda drama is your dish": All reviews are dated December 11, 1931, except *Commonweal*, December 23, and *The New Republic*, December 30.

"The Group, though fully aware": *New York Post*, January 26, 1932.

70 "Smoldering conviction": Clurman, *The Fervent Years*, p. 71.

"When an audience": In an article entitled "What the Group Theatre Wants" in the program for *1931—*, Lincoln Center.

Page

71 "In order to put": Quoted in *Producing the Play*, edited by John Gassner, New York: The Dryden Press, 1941, p. 319.

"A machine": From an article by Gorelik in *New Theatre* magazine, September–October, 1933.

"All iron and spit": Margaret Barker, interview with author.

73 "The self-appointed spokesman": From "The Group Theatre and How It Grew" by Morton Eustis, an undated and unidentified newspaper clipping in the Group scrapbooks. The text makes it clear it appeared shortly after *The House of Connelly* opened on September 29.

"Preparing plays" and subsequent quotes: From Clurman, "The Group Theatre Speaks for Itself."

74 "Contracting minor diseases": Harold Clurman to Paul Strand, February 12, 1932.

75 "I succeeded": Ibid.

"The feeling didn't last": Quoted in Clurman's *The Fervent Years*, p. 89.

"Struggled with her doubts" and subsequent quote: Ibid., pp. 85–86.

76 'This is what Death is for": From *Night over Taos*, last scene.

"I think it is a shame": Quoted in Waldon, *Vintage Years of the Theatre Guild*, p. 132.

"Group Theatre Now Independent": *New York Times*, February 19, 1932.

78 "Stories about the Group": "The Group Theatre Laughs Off Some Rumors," *New York Post*, March 5, 1932.

"The Group Theatre insists": Article by Clurman in *The New Leader*, March 12, 1932.

79 "At the end of the fiscal year": From "The Group Theatre Seeks Its Audience," a brochure issued in spring 1932. In the collection of the Paul Strand Archives.

"New plays": Ibid.

"The audience is just as much a part": Interview with Crawford in the *Brooklyn Eagle*, September 11, 1932.

80 "It is our intention": Clurman, "The Group Theatre Speaks for Itself."

"We prefer": Quoted in the *Springfield Sunday Union*, December 20, 1931.

"American plays rather than foreign": Clurman, "The Group Theatre Speaks for Itself."

"Through a form of subsidy": Ibid.

82 "Lee sat there": Quoted in Brenman-Gibson, *Clifford Odets*.

83 "The word 'America' ": Unpublished *Fervent*, p. 187.

"The Awakening of America": All quotes in this paragraph are taken from a typescript draft of Clurman's speech in the author's collection.

FOUR: NEW HORIZONS

86 "That the most precious": *Elia Kazan: A Life* by Elia Kazan, New York: Alfred A. Knopf, 1988, p. 29.

87 "Why? Because he's a Jew": Lewis, *Slings and Arrows*, p. 43.

"Roaring defiance": Kazan, *Elia Kazan*, p. 62.

88 "It is an intrinsic part": From "The Group Center: A Project," unpublished manuscript by Harold Clurman dated August 28, 1935, Lincoln Center.

89 "Really a terribly ghastly exposé": Roman Bohnen to his father, undated, from Dover Furnace. In the Roman Bohnen Collection, Lincoln Center.

"In this way": Ibid.

90 "It is not my object": Interview with Tamiris in the *New York World-Telegram*, December 26, 1936.

Page

"The floor is your friend": Kazan, *Elia Kazan*, p. 65.

93 "Was not to copy": Phoebe Brand, interview with Barbara Wolkoff and Nina Levine, courtesy of Mel Gordon.

"Very daring": Wilhelmina Barton Kraber, interview with Vincent Metzo, courtesy of Mel Gordon.

94 "The social system": Quoted in *Since Yesterday: The Nineteen-Thirties in America* by Frederick Lewis Allen, New York: Bantam Books, 1961, p. 57.

95 "Hasten the day": Brenman-Gibson, *Clifford Odets*, p. 233.

"The class nature": From John Howard Lawson's unpublished autobiography, p. 517, courtesy of Susan Amanda Lawson.

"Doomed to inevitable failure" and "would have just about the same effect": *The Modern Quarterly*, Summer 1932, p. 11.

"The marked movement": *New Masses*, September 1932.

96 "Like a fever": Clurman, *The Fervent Years*, p. 91.

"Every action": Quoted in *Stage Magazine*, September 1932.

"The hope of our theatre": Clurman, *The Fervent Years*, p. 93.

"The grotesque of the American environment": From the introduction to *Processional* by John Howard Lawson, New York: T. Seltzer, 1925.

97 "The blood and bones": Ibid.

"An indictment": Lawson autobiography, p. 239.

"Sarah must *tell* Sol": Ibid., p. 242.

98 "Heart's ease" and "When Clurman wrote": Ibid., p. 243.

"I'm so high-strung": Ibid., p. 242.

"Guided by the idea of moral integrity": Ibid., p. 245.

99 "A more revolutionary point of view": Ibid., p. 243.

"I had no answer at all": Ibid., p. 246.

"The camp had become": Unpublished *Fervent*, p. 211.

"The Group was a free-love farm": Clurman, *The Fervent Years*, p. 97.

101 "No actor's emotion": Kazan, *Elia Kazan*, p. 64.

102 "The most commercial figure": Lawson autobiography, p. 532.

"We believed in those days": Clurman, *The Fervent Years*, p. 100.

103 "Blood sister to a streetwalker": Cited in Lawson autobiography, p. 520.

105 "She was serious" and "began a drunk": Quoted in Brenman-Gibson, *Clifford Odets*, p. 237.

"It's the first time": Ibid., p. 238.

106 "It wasn't until": Quoted in the *New York Times*, August 14, 1932. The playwright is not identified.

FIVE: HARD TIMES

108 "The Group's poorhouse": Clurman, *The Fervent Years*, p. 104.

"For the first time": *The Nation*, October 12, 1932.

"Moral fervor": *New York Times*, September 27, 1932.

"But because they were confused": Harold Clurman to Paul Strand, October 9, 1932.

"Represent[ed] nothing definite": Clurman, *The Fervent Years*, p. 99.

109 "Unlike other people": Ibid., p. 100.

"Mr. Lawson has chosen": *Commonweal*, October 12, 1932.

"A sad, sick genius": *New York Telegram*, September 27, 1932.

"Murky manifestoes" and "good theatre": *New York Post*, September 27, 1932.

"A large part of the audience": *New York Sun*, September 28, 1932.

Page
109 "It was hard to tell": *New York Post,* September 30, 1932.
110 "The message": *The New Leader,* March 12, 1932.
"They regard": *New York Herald Tribune,* January 18, 1933.
"A smooth and effective performance": *Commonweal,* October 12, 1932.
"Precision, definition and rich fury": *The New Yorker,* October 8, 1932.
"Even better": *New York Post,* September 27, 1932.
"[The Group Theatre] has done better": Ibid.
"Everyone seems to be trying": Quoted in the *New York Telegraph,* undated clip from October 1932.
111 "The 24 hour a day system": Roman Bohnen to his brother, September 29, 1932.
"Some improvement": *Variety,* October 11, 1932.
112 "I'm the only actor": Quoted in Adams, *Lee Strasberg,* p. 153.
"The Group has been tense and tired": Harold Clurman to Paul Strand, November 21, 1932.
113 "I was sore": *Brooklyn Times,* March 8, 1935.
114 "Keep your line": Quoted in Lewis, *Slings and Arrows,* p. 77.
115 "Ed, did you ever feel": "The Party" ("Big Night") by Dawn Powell, in the manuscript collection of the Copyright Division, Library of Congress, Act I, p. 9.
"Isn't that remarkable?" Quoted in *Advice to the Players* by Robert Lewis, New York: Harper & Row, 1980, p. 129.
"Felt better": Quoted in *The Political Stage: American Drama and Theatre of the Great Depression* by Malcolm Goldstein, New York: Oxford University Press, 1974, p. 86.
116 "Miss Powell": All quotes from the *Big Night* reviews are dated January 8, 1933, except "Are we only to have high-class cads" from *The New Yorker,* January 29, 1933. The two reviews unidentified in the text are from the *New York Herald Tribune* ("as sordid a play") and the *New York Evening Journal* ("realistically tiresome").
"They ran from it": Clurman, *The Fervent Years,* p. 107.
117 "Hemmed and hawed": Harold Clurman to Paul Strand, February 28, 1933.
"The establishment": All quotes from Clurman's letter are from the *New York Times,* January 29, 1933.
118 "As going up there": From the minutes of a Group meeting, January 27, 1933, in the Cheryl Crawford Collection, Lincoln Center.
"Never before" and quotes in subsequent paragraph: In letter from Roman Bohnen to Arthur Bohnen, February 4, 1933.
119 "All of [these schemes]": Harold Clurman to Paul Strand, February 28, 1933.
120 "I'm not certain": Roman Bohnen to Arthur Bohnen, February 4, 1933.
"We were very poor": Phoebe Brand, interview with author.
121 "If that's the kind of theatre": Quoted in *Stage Left* by Jay Williams, New York: Charles Scribner's Sons, 1974, p. 66.
"I honestly couldn't think": Quoted in Brenman-Gibson, *Clifford Odets,* p. 245.
123 "Poor little Arthur Gordon Smith": Roman Bohnen to Arthur Bohnen, February 4, 1933.
"The world around you": Quoted in *Educational Theatre Journal* (an entire issue devoted to the Group Theatre), December 1976, p. 519.
124 "You couldn't help but say": Ibid.
126 "In the first act": Quoted in Williams, *Stage Left,* p. 124.
128 "My own bleak state": Clurman, *The Fervent Years,* p. 114.

Page

"We began to see each other": Ibid., pp. 114–15.

129 "A middle-class shrinking": Ibid., p. 117.

"No Adler": Ibid., pp. 118–19.

"Reacted to everything": Ibid., p. 119.

132 "Complete freedom from the domination": All quotes from Strasberg's paper are taken from a draft copy in the author's collection.

134 "I don't care what you say": The exchange between Strasberg and Odets is described in unpublished *Fervent*, p. 269.

138 "The Group's life too" and "The Group is still together": Harold Clurman to Paul Strand, June 16, 1933.

SIX: BROADWAY SUCCESS

140 "While each of [us]": Lee Strasberg, interview with Peter Jessup, from the Columbia Oral History Project Collection.

141 "Five weeks": Quoted by Harold Clurman in conversation with Cheryl Crawford, Lincoln Center.

"For six weeks": Patten: autobiographical sketch.

142 "You couldn't blame the poor folk": From an interview with Bromberg by Lucius Beebe in the *New York Herald Tribune*, undated but published during the run of *Gold Eagle Guy* in late 1934.

"A very studious young man": Quoted in "Sidney Kingsley's *Men in White*" by Evangeline Morphos, *The Drama Review*, Winter 1984, p. 13.

"The FBI adjustment" and "He could not": Strasberg, *A Dream of Passion*, p. 89.

"The circumstances of the scene": Ibid., p. 85.

143 "You know": Quoted in Morphos, "Sidney Kingsley's *Men in White*," pp. 20–21.

"You too?" and "Up to here": From *Men in White*, act I, last scene.

"But I don't always": Quoted in Morphos, "Sidney Kingsley's *Men in White*," p. 18.

"I'd be sitting": Margaret Barker, interview with author.

144 "Those damned exercises": Phoebe Brand, interview with author.

146 "The Group has only one director": Clurman, *The Fervent Years*, p. 128.

"Which all were highly emotional": *Run-Through* by John Houseman. New York: Simon and Schuster/A Touchstone Book, 1972, p. 92.

"My goal that summer": Kazan, *Elia Kazan*, p. 102.

147 "The actors are all suffering": Cheryl Crawford, taped conversation with Harold Clurman, Lincoln Center.

"The professional adjustment": Adams, *Lee Strasberg*, p. 161.

148 "The mere reproduction": *New York Herald Tribune*, January 14, 1934.

"As painful": Crawford, *One Naked Individual*, p. 65.

149 "To say that [*Men in White*]": *The Nation*, October 11, 1933.

150 "A joint effect": *Theatre Arts*, December 1933.

"Not much of a play": *New York Post*, September 27, 1933.

"Professional in every meaning": *New York World-Telegram*, September 27, 1933.

151 "Dad was very superior": Roman Bohnen to Arthur Bohnen, October 16, 1933.

"All the methods and theories": *New York Sun*, December 14, 1933.

"I have never": *New York Telegraph*, December 13, 1933.

152 "A new direction": *Long Island City Star*, November 3, 1933.

"It's a swell organization": *Gotham Life*, undated, from fall 1933.

"When planning productions": *New York Herald Tribune*, December 17, 1933.

153 "Wished to avoid" and all other quotes in this paragraph: From "The Group Theatre and Its Audience," an article in the *Men in White* program, Lincoln Center.

"A pastime": Quoted in Kazan, *Elia Kazan*, p. 65.

154 "Maybe someday": Quoted in the *New York Evening Post*, November 3, 1933.

"Plays which could never" and "We feel": *New York Herald Tribune*, December 17, 1933.

156 "Expert trivia": *New Masses*, March 20, 1934.

"Merely good Broadway theatre": *New Theatre*, January 1934.

157 "A central and common purpose": Odets' speech "Toward a New Theatre" is quoted at length in Brenman-Gibson, *Clifford Odets*, pp. 651–54. This citation is from p. 652.

"Smartness, cynicism, negativism": From Clurman, "Plans for a First Studio."

"Our theatre's work" and all other quotes: From "Toward a New Theatre" in Brenman-Gibson, *Clifford Odets*, pp. 653–54.

"I was instrumental": Elia Kazan, testimony to the House Committee on Un-American Activities, April 10, 1952.

158 "Reacting all over the place": Philip Robinson, interview with author.

"In all the meetings": Phoebe Brand, interview with author.

159 "There was a certain kind": Clifford Odets, testimony to the House Committee on Un-American Activities, May 19, 1952.

"Not distinguished" and "We hope that the Group Theatre": *Daily Worker*, October 3, 1933.

"Only by such compromise": Harold Clurman to Paul Strand, October 25, 1933.

160 "All I fret about" and "to freshen": Ibid.

"Written from a Group standpoint" and "I know I could run": Ibid., January 2, 1934.

"What indifference of feeling": *Daily Worker*, November 14, 1933.

"The whole set-up": Ibid., October 16, 1933.

"There is no creative way": Ibid., November 14, 1933.

"Sense of joy": Ibid., November 10, 1933.

161 "Marxist objectivity": Ibid., October 16, 1933.

"Our cause": Ibid., November 10, 1933.

"Workers' splendor": Ibid., February 2, 1934.

"Today the choice is clear": Ibid., October 10, 1933.

"Their whole idea": Ibid., February 28, 1934.

"Applause and cheers": Ibid., March 16, 1934.

162 "De-Jewished": Quoted in Brenman-Gibson, *Clifford Odets*, p. 280.

163 "[It] gets worn out": Morris Carnovsky, interview with author.

"A more vital theatre": From a proposed constitution for the Group, drawn up in May 1940 and reproduced in "The Group Theatre of New York City, 1931–1941," master's dissertation by W. David Sievers, Stanford University, 1944. The constitution makes brief reference to these meetings, but provides no details.

164 "Their dependence": Lawson autobiography, p. 302.

"People who work": From the last act of *Gentlewoman*, in *With a Reckless Preface: Two Plays by John Howard Lawson*, New York: Farrar & Rinehart, 1934.

"It was the end of my life": Lawson autobiography, p. 302.

"Cities burning": From *Gentlewoman*, last act.

"Brain workers" and "muscle workers": These phrases were used in the September 1932 pamphlet signed by fifty-three American artists urging people to vote for William Z. Foster for president (see Chapter Four). It is quoted at length in

Page

   Writers on the Left: Episodes in American Literary Communism by Daniel Aaron, New York: Harcourt, Brace and World, 1961, pp. 196–97.

   "Books are all right": From *Gentlewoman*, last act.

   "You went in there": Eunice Stoddard, interview with author.

165 "Of great potential value": Harold Clurman to Paul Strand, March 30, 1934.

   "The whole idea of the Group": Eunice Stoddard, interview with author.

166 "Practically collaborated": Harold Clurman to Paul Strand, December 30, 1934.

   "To a point": Lawson autobiography, p. 302.

   "Beautiful thoughts" and "It seems to me": *Brooklyn Eagle*, December 18, 1934.

   "Jewish emotionalism": Quoted in Garfield, *A Player's Place*, p. 34.

   "In trying to immerse herself": Lawson autobiography, p. 308.

167 "Comes straight out": *The Nation*, April 11, 1934.

   "You may disagree": From a letter reprinted in the *New York Daily Mirror*, March 28, 1934.

   "A Bourgeois Hamlet of Our Times": All quotes in this paragraph are from Gold's article in the *New Masses*, April 10, 1934.

168 "Unhesitatingly admit[ted]" and "I have not demonstrated": *New Masses*, April 17, 1934.

   "I could not bear": Clurman, *The Fervent Years*, p. 134.

   "Every year around this time": Harold Clurman to Paul Strand, April 6, 1934.

170 "Go over and punch Harold": Clurman, *The Fervent Years*, p. 135.

171 "I pointed out": Clurman, *The Fervent Years*, p. 136.

   "Strict discipline" and "The paper did its work": Harold Clurman to Paul Strand, April 6, 1934.

172 "There was a good deal" and all other quotes in this and the following paragraph: In Harold Clurman's letter to Cheryl Crawford, May 24, 1934, Lincoln Center.

   "Smell the lilies": Dorothy Patten, autobiographical sketch, Lincoln Center.

173 "First concerted and sustained effort": *New Theatre*, July–August, 1934.

   "Represent[s] a different phase": *New York Times*, May 20, 1934.

174 "I got my actors": Lewis, *Slings and Arrows*, pp. 69–70.

   "A fresh interpretation": *New York Times*, May 20, 1934.

   "Dreamed of a life": Quoted in the Chicago *News*, June 3, 1936.

175 "The meaning of every line": *New York Times*, May 20, 1934.

SEVEN: CONFLICT

177 "The work isn't wasted": *New Theatre*, October 1934.

   "[Meyerhold's style]": From Strasberg's Moscow diary, reprinted in *The Drama Review*, March 1973.

   "The situation": Ibid.

   "Inner justification" and "Vakhtangov's value": Ibid.

   "The Moscow Art Theatre": Ibid.

178 "That the Group had nothing": Harold Clurman to Paul Strand, July 4, 1934.

   "The kind of productions": Ibid.

   "A completely panic-stricken woman": Quoted in *Actors Without Make-up* by Boris Filippov, Moscow: Progress Publishers, 1977, p. 59.

   "Mr. Stanislavsky": Stella Adler, interview with Mel Gordon.

179 "If the system does not help you": Clurman, *The Fervent Years*, p. 138.

   "Since you are in trouble": Harold Clurman to Paul Strand, July 4, 1934.

Page
179 "There lies my work": Ibid.

"They were like a profanation": Morris Carnovsky, interview with author.

"One must never": Quoted in Harold Clurman's notes on Stella Adler's talks with Stanislavsky, in a notebook at the Rare Book and Manuscript Division of Butler Library, Columbia University.

"Everything she had learnt": Filippov, *Actors Without Make-up*, p. 59.

180 "When she had learnt": Ibid.

"I'll pay you back": Stella Adler, interview with Mel Gordon.

"Other persons prominent": *New York Times*, September 2, 1934.

181 "You could feel the fog": Robert Lewis, interview with author.

"We had had it": Phoebe Brand, interview with author.

"We don't use": Robert Lewis, interview with author.

"Action we have always used": Quoted in Adams, *Lee Strasberg*, p. 179.

182 "We thought": Eunice Stoddard, interview with author.

"Actors are not guinea pigs": In a typewritten memo signed by Sanford Meisner, part of the Luther Adler Collection, Lincoln Center.

"That was always the test": Robert Lewis, interview with author.

183 "We spent absolute hours": Margaret Barker, interview with author.

"They wanted scenery": *New York Times*, January 13, 1935.

"There are some treatments": *New York Herald Tribune*, September 2, 1934.

184 "A brilliantly 'exterior' (colorful) director": Harold Clurman to Jay Leyda, in the Robert F. Wagner Labor Archives, Tamiment Library, New York University.

"Boys, I think we're working on a stiff": This oft-repeated wisecrack can be found in many accounts, including Lewis, *Slings and Arrows*, p. 82; Clurman, *The Fervent Years*, p. 142; and Kazan, *Elia Kazan*, p. 111.

"Feeling for feeling's sake": All quotes from Stella Adler's classes are taken from Wilhelmina Barton Kraber's notebook. I consulted a typed copy in the collection of Mel Gordon.

185 "Stella was a good teacher": Phoebe Brand, interview with author.

"I felt": Margaret Barker, interview with author.

"All the dogs died": Ibid.

"Every day": Harold Clurman to Paul Strand, August 20, 1934.

186 "The fighting": Cheryl Crawford, talk at Lee Strasberg Theatre Institute.

"I hope so": Crawford, *One Naked Individual*, p. 68.

"There were wearying arguments": Ibid.

"A couple of fiery young communists": Roman Bohnen to Arthur Bohnen, October 9, 1934.

"Our neophyte radicals": Clurman, *The Fervent Years*, p. 140.

"Before I do": Kazan, *Elia Kazan*, p. 111.

"The revolution is here": In Harold Clurman's notebook for *The Fervent Years*, Lincoln Center.

" 'Art' is my field": Harold Clurman to Paul Strand, July 4, 1934.

187 "Had some sense": Interview with Clifford Odets by Arthur Wagner, published in *Harper's*, September 1966.

"Get every single thing": Quoted in Brenman-Gibson, *Clifford Odets*, p. 294.

188 "I am a genius!" Ibid., p. 299.

"I wouldn't have known": Ibid., p. 297.

"A few charming": Dorothy Patten, autobiographical sketch, Lincoln Center.

Page

"You should have seen": Clifford Odets to Helen Deutsch, October 30, 1934, courtesy of Helen Deutsch.

189 "Too much high thinking": *Boston Herald,* November 25, 1934.

190 "You and me": *Waiting for Lefty,* scene III.

"My God, Joe": *Waiting for Lefty,* scene I.

"Tear down the slaughter house": *Waiting for Lefty,* final scene.

"What's important": Odets interview in *Harper's,* September 1966.

191 "No hugging to the breast": Clifford Odets to Helen Deutsch, October 27, 1934, courtesy of Helen Deutsch.

"The temptation": Clifford Odets to Helen Deutsch, November 21, 1934, courtesy of Helen Deutsch.

192 "What were you doing": All direct quotes in this account of the *Gold Eagle Guy* rehearsal are taken from Bobby Lewis' version of this oft-repeated story in *Slings and Arrows,* p. 82.

193 "Exciting": *New York Sun,* November 30, 1934.

"Vivid": *New York Evening Journal,* November 30, 1934.

"Atmospheric": *New York Daily Mirror,* November 29, 1934.

"Flesh and blood": *New York Times,* November 29, 1934.

193–4 "As if they were wrapped": *New York Post,* November 30, 1934.

194 "A little timid": *New York Times,* November 29, 1934.

"It's a pure tour de force": Roman Bohnen to Arthur Bohnen, December 9, 1934.

"For its consistent": *The Nation,* January 1935.

"Whenever the Group Theatre name": Odets interview in *Harper's,* September 1966.

"Let 'em fall": Ibid.

195 "We will have joy": Odets to Helen Deutsch, November 21, 1934.

"I would direct": Harold Clurman to Paul Strand, December 12, 1934.

196 "You don't seem to understand": This remark is quoted in Clurman, *The Fervent Years,* p. 144; Brenman-Gibson, *Clifford Odets,* p. 311; and Kazan, *Elia Kazan,* p. 120.

"But I wanted": Clurman, *The Fervent Years,* p. 145.

EIGHT: THEATRE BECOMES LIFE

197 "Sure, I see" and all other quotes in this paragraph: *Waiting for Lefty.*

198 "Like a roar from sixteen-inchers": Kazan, *Elia Kazan,* p. 114.

"They were being carried": Clurman, *The Fervent Years,* p. 148.

"You saw theatre": From an interview with Clifford Odets in *Theatre Arts* May–June, 1963.

"HELLO AMERICA!" "Well, what's the answer?" and "Strike": *Waiting for Lefty.*

"When they couldn't applaud": *The Drama Review,* Winter 1984, p. 40.

"That was the dream": Kazan, *Elia Kazan,* p. 114.

199 "The audience wouldn't leave": Cheryl Crawford, talk at Lee Strasberg Theatre Institute.

"There was almost a sense": *The Drama Review,* Winter 1984, p. 40.

"Unity of background": Clurman, *The Fervent Years,* p. 33.

200 "Earthquakes of applause": *New York Morning Telegraph,* February 8, 1935.

"We have seldom": *New York Enquirer,* April 7, 1935.

201 "The phone has been ringing": Jean Garlen Fox, interview with author.

"The Constitution's" and "One dollar": *Waiting for Lefty.*

Page
201 "28 bucks": Roman Bohnen to Arthur Bohnen, February 4, 1935.
202 "Vigorous, moving and tense": *New York Daily Mirror*, February 11, 1935.
     "Soundly constructed": *New York Times*, February 11, 1935.
     "Winningly good-humored": Ibid.
     "More interesting": *New York Evening Journal*, undated.
     "There has been something": *New York Post*, February 18, 1935.
     "Gross self-centeredness": Unpublished *Fervent*, p. 319.
203 "Awake and sing": *Awake and Sing!*, act II.
     "Go out and fight": *Awake and Sing!*, act I.
     "Almost masochistically pessimistic": Clurman, *The Fervent Years*, p. 128.
     "Make a break" and all other quotes in this paragraph: From *Awake and Sing!*, act
        III.
204 "No one else alive": Quoted in Brenman-Gibson, *Clifford Odets*, p. 321.
205 "It simply appeared": Sidney Lumet, interview with author.
     "Harold's rehearsals": Kazan, *Elia Kazan*, p. 121.
     "By asking questions": Article by Harold Clurman on interpretation in *Producing the
        Play*, edited by John Gassner, New York: The Dryden Press, 1941, p. 296.
     "A good maxim": Ibid., p. 300.
206 "[The director] must not": Ibid., p. 302.
     "Brief accounts": In the program for *Awake and Sing!*, Lincoln Center.
     "I'm so nervous": *Awake and Sing!*, act II.
207 "To a special feeling": Gassner, *Producing the Play*, p. 284.
     "The American rhythm": Quoted in *The Theatre Art of Boris Aronson* by Frank Rich
        and Lisa Aronson, New York: Alfred A. Knopf, 1987, p. 13.
     "Uncommon ability": All reviews identified in the text appeared on February 20,
        1935.
208 "A new dramatist": *New York Times*, March 10, 1935.
     "It is almost an impertinence": *New Theatre*, March 1935.
     "Brittle": *New Masses*, March 5, 1935.
     "Overwrought" and "shrill": *New York Times*, February 20, 1935.
     "These people": *Theatre Arts Monthly*, April 1935.
     "Messy naturalism": *Daily Worker*, in an undated review.
     "It is as non-Aryan": *New York Daily Mirror*, February 20, 1935.
209 "Where I assume": *New York Daily News*, February 20, 1935.
     "How interesting we all were": *Starting Out in the Thirties* by Alfred Kazin, Boston:
        Atlantic Monthly Press, 1962, pp. 81–82.
210 "A new Odets": *Buffalo Times*, April 13, 1935.
     "I'm concerned with the realism": *New York Herald Tribune*, March 31, 1935.
     "No special pleading": *New York Daily Mirror*, February 25, 1935.
     "Of course I believe": *New York Herald Tribune*, March 31, 1935.
     "Today the truth": *New York Daily Mirror*, February 25, 1935.
211 "My tendencies": *Brooklyn Eagle*, December 9, 1934.
     "Blood-and-thunder": *Time*, February 11, 1935.
     "Delighted to find": *New York Post*, February 18, 1935.
     "The progress": *New York Times*, February 11, 1935.
     "Stifles the creative impulse": *New York Times*, November 11, 1934.
213 "Of course [*Lefty*] is propaganda": *Newark Times*, March 27, 1935.
     "The critics": *New York Herald Tribune*, March 2, 1935.
     "I don't care": *New York Morning Telegraph*, March 28, 1935.

Page
"Iron-fisted": All quotes in this paragraph are dated March 27, 1935.

"Look[ed] as though he was pulled": *New York Daily Mirror,* March 31, 1935.

214 "Proletarian thunderbolt": *New Masses,* undated clip from fall 1935.

"Frankly jittery" and all other uncited quotes in the following paragraph: From *New Masses,* April 9, 1935.

"For mass development": *New Theatre,* February 1935.

215 "Every actor": *New York Post,* March 9, 1935.

216 "Workers Stink" and all quotes in this paragraph: From the *New Leader,* March 16, 1935.

"No one is born class-conscious" and all quotes in this paragraph: From an account of the controversy in the *Daily Worker,* March 27, 1935.

217 "My God, Bud": Phoebe Brand, interview with author.

219 "Take one": Harold Clurman, in a letter printed in the *Saturday Review,* September 14, 1963.

220 "Morris, don't go in": Morris Carnovsky, interview with author.

222 "I had a tendency": Unpublished *Fervent,* p. 347.

"No matter how I resented": Quoted in Brenman-Gibson, *Clifford Odets,* p. 352.

223 "Militant fight against war and fascism": From an ad pasted in the Group scrapbook, Lincoln Center.

"Even my wife" and "They don't let me sleep": From *I Can't Sleep,* published in *New Theatre,* February 1936.

"Most significant": Clurman, *The Fervent Years,* p. 155.

"All the bullets in the world": Quoted in the *New York Daily News,* May 5, 1935.

224 "The American capitalist culture": Quoted in Aaron, *Writers on the Left,* p. 286.

"What would the Group be like": Crawford, *One Naked Individual,* p. 77.

"That is the most impersonal": From an article by Harold Clurman on the Soviet theatre, *New Theatre,* August 1935.

"The goal of the Group": Crawford, *One Naked Individual,* p. 89.

225 "Everybody, it seemed": Clurman, *The Fervent Years,* p. 162.

226 "To become the recognized and honored": Ibid., p. 163.

"[We] look first": *Brooklyn Eagle,* February 17, 1935.

227 "That's something for which": "New York Inside Out," a United Feature Syndicate column. Undated clip in Group scrapbook, from mid-1935.

"The Group Theatre actors": Roman Bohnen to Arthur Bohnen, July 7, 1935.

228 "Dad and I": Ibid.

"We are convinced": *The New Voices,* July 1935.

229 "A part of, and not apart from": *Arena: The History of the Federal Theatre* by Hallie Flanagan, New York: Arno Press, 1980 (facsimile of the 1940 edition), p. 7.

NINE: THE STRUGGLE FOR ORGANIZATION

231 "To sustain and enrich" and all other quotes in this and the subsequent two paragraphs: From "The Group Theatre Center: A Project" by Harold Clurman, Cheryl Crawford Collection, Lincoln Center.

232 "Stayed too long": *Variety,* October 31, 1935.

233 "We would like to know" and other quotes in this paragraph: From a document reprinted in Crawford, *One Naked Individual,* p. 92.

"The production of plays": From Clurman, "The Group Theatre Center: A Project."

"To rehearse": Crawford, *One Naked Individual,* p. 92.

Page
233 "Lee really only wanted": Eunice Stoddard, interview with the author.
234 "All of the requests": Crawford, *One Naked Individual*, p. 92.
"A cautious shopper": *New York Times*, August 28, 1935.
"Well, let's do it": Clurman, *The Fervent Years*, p. 164.
235–6 "There was more time taken" through "affirmed the same:" Michael Gordon, interview with author.
236 "Cheryl was terribly hardworking": Eunice Stoddard, interview with author.
"It isn't even radical": *Brooklyn Eagle*, December 2, 1935.
"What on earth": *Brooklyn Citizen*, December 2, 1935.
237 "Theatrically speaking": Clurman, *The Fervent Years*, pp. 165–66.
238 "With this [sweetness]": Ibid., p. 166.
"Why, you're sleeping" and "No! There is more": *Paradise Lost*, act III.
239 "The play everyone loved": Ellen Adler, interview with author.
"When I returned from the Soviet Union": From "Interpretation and Characterization" by Harold Clurman, in *New Theatre*, January 1936.
240–1 "This crazy world," "this does not make them," and "to give some feeling": Ibid.
241 "It was semi-realistic": Quoted in Rich and Aronson, *The Theatre Art of Boris Aronson*, p. 56.
"A wraithlike figure": Quoted in the *New York Herald Tribune*, December 22, 1935.
"Hinting at": Lewis, *Slings and Arrows*, p. 86.
242 "Is he going to start that stuff": Ibid., p. 88.
"The director's way": *New Theatre*, January 1936.
"As the established social order" and all other quotes in this paragraph: From Odets' letter, reprinted in the *New York Times*, December 15, 1935.
"The wealthy people": Phoebe Brand, interview with author.
"They'll die": Quoted in Brenman-Gibson, *Clifford Odets*, p. 385.
243 "As a charter member": All reviews identified in the text appeared on December 10, 1935.
"We believe": A copy of the ad is pasted into the Group scrapbook, Lincoln Center.
244 "Some of us": Odets' letter was reprinted in the *New York World-Telegram*, December 14, 1935.
245 "Of course we critics": *The Nation*, January 1, 1936.
"Might we suggest": *The Nation*, January 15, 1936.
"Just produce 'em": *New York Mirror*, January 2, 1936.
"Good, hearty, forthright debate": *New York Herald Tribune*, December 22, 1935.
246 "Not very humble opinion": *New York World-Telegram*, December 19, 1935.
"The longing of a lost child": *New Masses*, undated review of *Paradise Lost*.
"Sandy claims": *The Flying Grouse*, February 1936, p. 14. In the Group Theatre collection, Lincoln Center.
"Speaking campaign": Dorothy Patten, autobiographical sketch, Lincoln Center.
"*Active* audience": *The Flying Grouse*, June 1936, p. 15. In the Group Theatre collection, Lincoln Center.
247 "I feel that I need to sin": Clurman, *The Fervent Years*, p. 170.
248 "Truly search": *The Flying Grouse*, February 1936, p. 5.
250 "She's right": Clurman, *The Fervent Years*, p. 170.
"Due to the success": *New York Herald Tribune*, February 16, 1936.
252 "The usual tricks": Elia Kazan, testimony to the House Committee on Un-American Activities, April 10, 1952.
253 "The mask of the ever-compliant": Kazan, *Elia Kazan*, p. 149.

"A ritual of submission": Ibid., p. 131.

"There are certain aspects": Morris Carnovsky, interview with author.

"I think there has to be": Phoebe Brand, interview with author.

254 "We are all deeply concerned": *The Flying Grouse,* February 1936, p. 8. All subsequent quotes attributed to Crawford are from the same article.

"They can never give us": Ibid., p. 11.

"They are able": *The Flying Grouse,* June 1936, p. 15.

255 "An organization of dramatic entrepreneurs": *New York Herald Tribune,* March 8, 1936.

"There was an awful lot": Margaret Barker, interview with author.

"I have developed": *The Flying Grouse,* February 1936, p. 5.

"Lee is reading": Ibid.

"Harold swears": Ibid., June 1936, p. 14.

"Well—one, I approve": Ibid., February 1936, p. 13.

"Behind closed doors": Ibid., June 1936, p. 10.

"It does not call for": Ibid., p. 5.

256 "Narrative emotion": Ibid.

"You don't seem": Ibid., p. 20.

257 "The play stands nobly": *Daily Worker,* March 17, 1936.

"This column": *New York Times,* March 14, 1936.

258 "The Shuberts tried": Roman Bohnen to Arthur Bohnen, April 2, 1936.

258–9 "The directors and actors" and "a theatre's productions": Different portions of the letter were reprinted in various newspapers. These two quotes are from the *New York World-Telegram,* April 17, 1936. "Certain remarks" is from the *New York Post,* April 17, 1936.

259 "A prime example": Clurman, *The Fervent Years,* p. 175.

260 "Business plans deserve": From an untitled memo by Luther Adler, in the Luther Adler Collection, Lincoln Center.

"Much as I agree" and all quotes in these three paragraphs: From Strasberg's letter, reprinted in Crawford, *One Naked Individual,* pp. 93–93.

262 "This was the kind of work": Crawford, *One Naked Individual,* p. 94.

"DISAPPOINTED IN HILDUR": Arthur Bohnen to Roman Bohnen, undated.

"Build for our theatre": From a memo, "Notes on the Group Theatre Tour of Spring '36" by Arthur Adler, Luther Adler Collection, Lincoln Center.

"What the hell kind of house": *Awake and Sing!,* act II.

"It's up to you": Lewis, *Slings and Arrows,* p. 84.

TEN: FALLING APART

265 "For the discriminating": *Midweek Pictorial,* October 17, 1936.

"The finest acting institution": Quoted in the *New York Times,* August 2, 1936.

266 "I had had my fill": Crawford, *One Naked Individual,* p. 94.

"Widen the body range": *New York Times,* August 2, 1936.

267 "If he do belch": Morris Carnovsky, interview with author.

"Julie used to walk": Phoebe Brand, interview with author.

"It was a way": Robert Lewis, interview with author.

"Don't sing so much": Margaret Barker, interview with author.

268 "Back of the stage": *Waiting for Odets* was reprinted in a pamphlet, *New Theatre League's Skits and Sketches,* published April 1939, Lincoln Center.

Page
270 "Nothing shall be considered": From "Group Organization" by Harold Clurman, typescript in the Luther Adler Collection, Lincoln Center, p. 2.

"Meetings of the entire Group": Ibid., p. 7.

"Should bring more immediate results": Ibid., pp. 6–7.

271 "Sickness" and all quotes in this and the subsequent paragraphs: From an unsigned letter in a private notebook kept at Pine Brook that somehow came into Lee Strasberg's hands. It remains in the possession of his widow, Anna Strasberg.

273 "Cold, artificial": Clurman, *The Fervent Years*, p. 186.

274 "I had to assert": Lawson autobiography, p. 791.

275 "It is us today": Quoted in *The People's Chronology: A Year-by-Year Account of Human Events from Prehistory to the Present* edited by James Trager, New York: Holt, Rinehart and Winston, 1979, p. 921.

276 "I feel pretty sure": Harold Clurman to Jay Leyda, August 31, 1936, Tamiment Library, New York University.

"What difference does it make": Lee Strasberg, quoted in Kaplan and Klein, "Harold Clurman: A Life of Theatre."

278 "The first act": *Newsweek*, November 28, 1936.

279 "Nobody seems": Harold Clurman to Jay Leyda, August 31, 1936.

280 "One long meal": *New York Herald Tribune*, June 23, 1935.

"Sure, the chinamen": *The Flying Grouse*, June 1936, p. 21.

"A strange distinction" and "a far freer": *Daily Worker*, January 5, 1937.

282 "It needed opera singers": Phoebe Brand, in an interview conducted on September 14, 1987, at Pine Wood Lake Lodge Theatre, on deposit at the Kurt Weill Foundation, New York City.

"But, Lee": Quoted by Morris Carnovsky, ibid.

283 "The most distressing experiences": Clurman, *The Fervent Years*, p. 188.

284 "I felt as if": Ibid., p. 189.

"A disturbing and often hilarious medley": All reviews of *Johnny Johnson* identified in these two paragraphs appeared on November 20, 1936.

285 "It is the voice of America": *The Sign Post*, November 26, 1936.

"Carefully avoided": *Manhattan Quadrangle*. The clipping in the Group scrapbook is hand-dated November 10, 1936, which must be incorrect as it would have preceded *Johnny Johnson*'s opening; the piece probably appeared on December 10.

"Since *Johnny Johnson* is": *The New Yorker*, December 1, 1936.

"Of all the plays": *New York Telegraph*, November 24, 1936.

"We would like to feel": From a program card in the Group Theatre clipping file, Lincoln Center.

286 "Not properly organized" and "lousy": From notes on the rehearsals kept by Odets' secretary, included in a file accompanying a copy of the script at Lincoln Center.

"Herbie the actor": Phoebe Brand, interview with author.

288 *"We are writing this paper"*: All quotes from the Actors Committee report are taken from a copy in the Luther Adler Collection, Lincoln Center.

293 "Painful juggernaut": Crawford, *One Naked Individual*, p. 97.

"They wrote this devastating criticism": Margaret Barker, interview with author.

294 "The truth is": Clurman, *The Fervent Years*, p. 197.

"No one is yet": From notes taken by Lee Strasberg, in the collection of Anna Strasberg.

"Postponed" and "such insistence": Quoted in Brenman-Gibson, *Clifford Odets: American Playwright*, pp. 442–43.

Page

"Must actually *become*": *New Theatre*, July 1936, in an article entitled "Case of the Group Theatre."

295 "The Group, which anxiously denied": *New York Sun*, January 16, 1937.
"With the departure": *Brooklyn Eagle*, January 17, 1937.
"The Group Halts": *New York Times*, January 17, 1937.

ELEVEN: REGROUPING

298 "Circle of attention" and "solitude in public" are phrases that can be found in *An Actor Prepares* by Constantin Stanislavski, translated by Elizabeth Reynolds Hapgood, New York: Theatre Arts Books, 1936, pp. 77, 79.

299 "The Group is no place": Roman Bohnen to Cheryl Crawford, undated, from late February to early March 1937, Lincoln Center.
"I've had a ten percent dose": Ibid.
"It's truly capitalism gone mad": Roman Bohnen to Arthur Bohnen, February 16, 1937.

300 "If there is anyone": Bohnen to Cheryl Crawford, February–March 1937.
"[You] drink yourself to death": Roman Bohnen to Arthur Bohnen, February 16, 1937.

301 "1. he doesn't feel": Ibid.
"I told [Harold]": Elia Kazan to Lee Strasberg, March 15, 1937, reprinted in Brenman-Gibson, *Clifford Odets*, pp. 456–57.
"The shock and surprise": Crawford's resignation letter is reprinted in Crawford, *One Naked Individual*, p. 100.

302 "My own point is simple": Lee Strasberg to Paula Miller, March 21, 1937, collection of Anna Strasberg.

303 "In this intermediary period": Kazan to Strasberg, March 15, 1937.
"It is taking over": Harold Clurman to Strasberg, April 2, 1937, collection of Anna Strasberg.
"Miss Crawford plans": *New York Times*, April 12, 1937.

304 "Three factions": *New York Telegraph*, April 13, 1937.
"We take over": Roman Bohnen to Arthur Bohnen, April 12, 1937.
"We need fresh blood": Kazan to Strasberg, March 15, 1937.

305 "After you make two pictures": *New York Post*, November 9, 1937.
"Teaching John Powers models": In "The Fabulous Fanatics" by John Paxton, an article in *Stage* magazine, December 1938.
"We have both been": Roman Bohnen to Arthur Bohnen, June 8, 1937.
"The life of a prostitute": Clurman, *The Fervent Years*, p. 201.

306 "An emotional hunger": Ibid., pp. 202–03.

307 "You shouldn't be here": Unpublished *Fervent*, p. 421.
"There's nothing that could make me happier" and all quotes in the subsequent four paragraphs: From a letter from Elia Kazan to Harold Clurman, undated but identified by Clurman as being from early May, in the Cheryl Crawford Collection, Lincoln Center.

308 "I answered as if": Clurman, *The Fervent Years*, p. 206.

309 "If we have a good popular play": Quoted in Brenman-Gibson, *Clifford Odets*, p. 459.
"This was something more" and "I remained firm": Unpublished *Fervent*, p. 438.

311 "She was a wonderful girl": Phoebe Brand, interview with author.

312 "Since the stage today": *New York Times*, September 26, 1937.

Page

312   "The finest theatre and film attorney": Roman Bohnen to Arthur Bohnen, August 22, 1937.

313   "A lousy typist": Ruth Young Eliot, interview with author.

"To put this theatre" and all subsequent quotes in this paragraph: From Roman Bohnen's letter to Arthur Bohnen, August 22, 1937.

"We were now veterans": Kazan, *Elia Kazan*, pp. 162–63.

314   "When thoroughly revamped": *Variety*, August 18, 1937.

315   "They had to prove their value": Unpublished *Fervent*, p. 448.

"We didn't know": Phoebe Brand, interview with author.

TWELVE: A NEW AGENDA

316   "I simply sat down": *Theatre Arts*, May–June 1963.

"Before [*Golden Boy*]": *Harper's*, September 1966.

"The city is full of girls": *Golden Boy*, act I, scene iv.

"He shoots you for a nickel": *Golden Boy*, act II, scene iv.

317   "Good times and silk shirts": *Golden Boy*, act III, scene i.

"A modern allegory": From an introduction by Harold Clurman to *Golden Boy*, included in *Six Plays by Clifford Odets*, New York: Random House, 1939, p. 429.

"People have hurt my feelings": *Golden Boy*, act I, scene iv.

"Artists and people like that": *Golden Boy*, act II, scene iv.

"The actors of the Group resent": Actors Committee report, Luther Adler Collection, Lincoln Center.

318   "Let us, for once": *New York Times*, November 21, 1937.

319   "A good Broadway cast": Clurman, *The Fervent Years*, p. 209.

320   "It was easily": Martin Ritt, interview with author.

"You murdered my boy": *Golden Boy*, act III, scene ii.

"You told me": Karl Malden tells this story in Kaplan and Klein, "Harold Clurman: A Life of Theatre."

"We felt a kind of freedom": Phoebe Brand, interview with author.

"A great fight": From Harold Clurman's program notes for *Golden Boy*, included in *Six Plays by Clifford Odets*, p. 430.

321   "Giving a hint": From a chapter by Gorelik in Gassner, *Producing the Play*.

"Tramp from Newark": *Golden Boy*, act I, scene i.

"They're closest to me": From printed transcript of an interview on WINS, November 23, 1937, in the Group Theatre scrapbooks.

322   "The Group Theatre, Inc.": *Golden Boy* program, Lincoln Center.

"I went": Lee Strasberg, interview with Peter Jessup, from the Columbia Oral History Project Collection, Butler Library.

"Few men in our theatre": All reviews identified in the text appeared on November 5, 1937.

323   "I'm not very good": Quoted in "Morris Carnovsky: Actor and Teacher" by Michael Allan Berkson, Ph.D. dissertation, University of Illinois at Urbana-Champaign, 1975, p. 32.

"Nobody is in the Group Theatre": Margaret Barker, interview with author.

325   "He's always true to himself": *New York Times*, January 24, 1964.

"A man who used the methods": Unpublished *Fervent*, p. 449.

"Just another Broadway play": *Daily Worker*, November 12, 1937.

"Interesting and arresting": *Current History*, April 1938.

"A play rich in social implications": *New Masses*, November 16, 1937.

Page

326 "I simply do not know": Roman Bohnen to Arthur Bohnen, April 16, 1938.

327 "Had not deviated": Clurman, *The Fervent Years*, p. 214.

328 "Made up of a nucleus": *New York Times*, December 12, 1937.

"The financial advantage": *New York Herald Tribune*, January 16, 1938.

329 "We were beginning": Eunice Stoddard, interview with author.

330 "Long on character": All reviews identified in the text appeared on February 27, 1938.

"A theatre engaged with its times": From the introduction to *Plays of Three Decades* by Robert Ardrey, New York: Atheneum, 1968, p. 14.

"The heartlessness of corporations": *New York World-Telegram*, February 27, 1938.

"It has never been": *New York Times*, February 27, 1938.

332 "Our present plan": Roman Bohnen to Arthur Bohnen, April 16, 1938.

333 "Many of our most": *New York Herald Tribune*, November 21, 1937.

"What made me impatient": Unpublished *Fervent*, pp. 463–64.

334 "The theatre—why, it's just an art": *New York Post*, November 15, 1937.

"A hazardous path": Clurman, *The Fervent Years*, p. 222.

336 "Did not think it too mean" and "one or two people": Ibid., p. 223.

"Dear Luise": Quoted in Brenman-Gibson, *Clifford Odets*, p. 504.

337 "It's a pity": *London Evening News*, June 13, 1938.

"Did you sleep with her?": *New York Telegraph*, June 22, 1938.

"Didn't make a sound": Phoebe Brand, interview with author.

"The speakers may sometimes": *London Observer*, June 22, 1938.

"Even those who appear": *London Spectator*, July 1, 1938.

338 "A furious energy": *London Times*, June 26, 1938.

"You may as well stop trying": This anecdote appears in an interview with Luther Adler by the *Philadelphia Record*, June 22, 1939.

"It's hard to describe": Roman Bohnen to Arthur Bohnen, August 1, 1938.

340 "A great actor might": Lewis, *Slings and Arrows*, p. 97.

THIRTEEN: FAME AND ITS DISCONTENTS

342 "Take a rocket to the moon": *Rocket to the Moon*, act I.

"Too dispirited": Brenman-Gibson, *Clifford Odets*, p. 512.

"Show me a playwright": Ibid., p. 371.

345 "I never felt": Eleanor Lynn, interview with author.

"The spine of the play": Notebook kept by Harold Clurman during *Rocket to the Moon*, Lincoln Center.

"The loneliness in Cliff's play": Ibid.

346 "For years [Morris] had been trying": *The Time Is Ripe: The 1940 Journal of Clifford Odets*, introduction by William Gibson, New York: Grove Press, 1988, p. 233.

"Talent": *Rocket to the Moon*, act II, scene 1.

"An artist": *Rocket to the Moon*, act III.

"I looked down": Michael Gordon, interview with author.

347 "None of you": *Rocket to the Moon*, act III.

"Warmly human": *New York Post*, November 25, 1938.

"Odets is approaching": *New York Mirror*, November 25, 1938.

"If Mr. Odets": *New York Times*, December 4, 1938.

"Amazing sensitiveness": *New York Sun*, November 25, 1938.

"Easy naturalness": *New York Daily News*, November 25, 1938.

"Build toward an abstract pattern": *Theatre Arts Monthly*, January 1939.

348 "I'd better not get started": *New York Herald Tribune*, January 1, 1939.

Page
348 "That was a whole new batch": Phoebe Brand, interview with author.
349 "They prefer": *Journal of Commerce*, December 19, 1938.
   "It was full of plot": Clurman, *The Fervent Years*, p. 229.
350 "A synthetic and rather shopworn job": *New York Journal-American*, January 6, 1939.
351 "Vivid characterizations": *New York Post*, November 25, 1938.
   "In its eighth season": *New York Times*, December 6, 1938.
   "For a series": *The Nation*, January 1939.
   "The Group Theatre is getting": *New York Herald Tribune*, January 22, 1939.
352 "The people of our country": *New Masses*, December 6, 1938.
353 "That is not why we want you": Clurman, *The Fervent Years*, p. 243.
354 "Listen, don't deposit the check today": Ruth Young Eliot, interview with author.
   "Harold must be perfect": In Harold Clurman's notebook for *The Fervent Years*, Lincoln Center.
   "He couldn't give her up": Ellen Adler, interview with author.
355 "The more I see": *New York World-Telegram*, March 8, 1939.
356 "Relaxed to the point of glibness": Clurman, *The Fervent Years*, p. 245.
   "Outstanding in the scope": *New York Telegraph*, March 21, 1939.
   "I weep for the theatre": *New York World-Telegram*, May 6, 1939.
357 "The city cries out to me": *Quiet City*, act I, p. 82, on deposit in the Library of Congress Copyright Division.
358 "Group productions lack": Lewis, *Slings and Arrows*, p. 100.
   "A piece of fluff": Michael Gordon, interview with author.
   "A not very robust grasp": *New Theatres for Old* by Mordecai Gorelik, New York: Samuel French, 1940, p. 261.
359 "Bobby was a wonderful director": Sidney Lumet, interview with author.
   "The Group is not a bank": Clurman, *The Fervent Years*, p. 249.
   "Most sharply divided": *Variety*, May 17, 1939.
   "Crackpot fantasy": *New York World-Telegram*, April 14, 1939.
   "Interested and moved": *New York Post*, April 14, 1939.
   "Every bit as creative": *New York Times*, May 7, 1939.
360 "Just the sort of work" and "of typical Group excellence": Ibid., April 14, 1939.
   "Growing reputation": From a review on WOR Radio, April 13, 1939, copy in Group Theatre scrapbooks, Lincoln Center.
361 "For years now": All quotes from Odets' letter, dated April 8, 1939, are taken from Brenman-Gibson, *Clifford Odets*, pp. 553–55.
362 "I will consider": Ibid., p. 556.
   "A world on its way to doom": Ibid., p. 559.
363 "I've been an actor": *Philadelphia Bulletin*, May 22, 1939.
   "The most progressive": *Newsweek*, May 15, 1939.
   "Came this season as close": From a syndicated column by Ira Wolfert, May 27, 1939. The clipping in the Group scrapbook at Lincoln Center is from the *Dayton News*.
   "Analysts say": *Fortune*, June 1939.

FOURTEEN: A SEASON IN HELL

365 "Minor works": The primary document for the Group's last summer is a typed transcript of the notes taken by Elizabeth Gordon at the company meetings. The

Page

author's copy was obtained from Phoebe Brand and Morris Carnovsky. Unless otherwise identified, all direct quotes in this chapter are taken from that transcript.

366 "The Cultural History of the United States": Quoted in the *Chicago Midwest Daily Record*, October 12, 1939.

368 "It was awfully messy": Phoebe Brand, interview with author.
"We were not working": Ibid.

370 "A unity of background": Clurman, *The Fervent Years*, p. 33.

375 "He was very disturbed emotionally": Phoebe Brand, interview with author.
"It is simply not the Group's business": Quoted in Brenman-Gibson, *Clifford Odets*, p. 566.

376 "Some of the guys": Ruth Young Eliot, interview with author.
"Kiss my ass": Quoted in Brenman-Gibson, *Clifford Odets*, p. 566.
"It was a crazy, wild summer": Ruth Young Eliot, interview with author.
"They were some of the funniest people": Sidney Lumet, interview with author.

377 "Charge, Chester, Charge": *Chicago Midwest Daily Record*, October 12, 1939.

381 "I should have insisted": From an interview with Odets in *Harper's*, September 1966.

385 "There was no ground": Clurman, *The Fervent Years*, pp. 256–57.
"Almost the last view": Morris Carnovsky, interview with author.

386 "Stalin must know": Quoted in Brenman-Gibson, *Clifford Odets*, p. 572.
"Clifford said": Phoebe Brand, interview with author.

FIFTEEN: HOMELESS

388 "In a state of turmoil and anguish": Pearl Adler Pearson, interview with author.
"You are not a truthful actress": This story was told to me by several people who preferred not to be identified. This direct quote comes from Brenman-Gibson, *Clifford Odets;* the author doesn't identify her source.

389 "America's not going to war": From the final prompt script of *Thunder Rock*, on deposit in Lincoln Center.
"Left only a line or so": In the preface to Ardrey, *Plays of Three Decades*.
"As originally written": *Baltimore Sun*, November 16, 1939.

390 "Lyric inspiration": Clurman, *The Fervent Years*, p. 258.

391 "They give you": *New York Times*, November 9, 1939.

392 "My wife returns": *Will There Really Be a Morning?* by Frances Farmer, New York: Dell Publishing, 1982, p. 226. (Originally published by G. P. Putnam's Sons, 1972.)
"Frances was an extremely intelligent woman": Michael Gordon, interview with author.

393 "Perhaps too much good talk": *Baltimore Sun*, November 3, 1939.
"Belong in tank-town drama": *New York World-Telegram*, November 18, 1939.
"Grandiloquent pep-talk": *The Nation*, November 25, 1939.
"A cry of hope": *New York Herald Tribune*, November 26, 1939.
"All in all": *New York Telegraph*, November 16, 1939.
"Fervent zealots": Clurman, *The Fervent Years*, p. 260.
"Breathless professions of faith": Clurman, *The Fervent Years*, p. 143.

394 "I no longer considered": Unpublished *Fervent*, p. 543.
"An Analysis of the Problems": This document is reprinted in Brenman-Gibson,

Page

Clifford Odets, pp. 672–76. All quotes in the subsequent three paragraphs are taken from that reprint.

394 "Harold's desperate paper": From a proposed constitution for the Group, drawn up in May 1940 and reproduced in "The Group Theatre of New York City, 1931–1941," master's dissertation by W. David Sievers, Stanford University, 1944. The document is referred to in subsequent footnotes as 1940 Constitution.

395 "Communism needs to be Americanized": Odets, *The Time Is Ripe*, p. 15.

396 "Now that Group methods and discipline": Unpublished *Fervent*, p. 543.
"At the moment": New York *Daily News*, January 7, 1940.
"Way off type": Odets, *The Time Is Ripe*, p. 6.

397 "The Group Theatre believes" and "the search for a home": From Harold Clurman's notebook on *Night Music*, Lincoln Center.
"If they did not have my script": *The Time Is Ripe*, p. 24.
"Harold is very overindulgent": Ibid.
"Shaping out": Ibid., p. 27.
"We haven't profited": Ibid., pp. 41–42.

398 "The dissidents hold": *New York Times*, February 2, 1940.

399 "Now that Odets": *New York Times*, February 23, 1940.
"It is not merely": *The Nation*, March 2, 1940.
"Can we demand": *The New Republic*, March 8, 1940.
"So simple, clear and direct": *New York Times*, March 3, 1940.

400 "I felt as if": Odets, *The Time Is Ripe*, p. 48.
"A theatrical set-up": *New York Telegraph*, March 11, 1940.
"Ugly passivity": *The Time Is Ripe*, p. 48.

401 "The audience that would enjoy": Clurman, *The Fervent Years*, p. 265.
"Torturing to death": Odets, *The Time Is Ripe*, p. 50.
"After being repeatedly treated": Clurman, *The Fervent Years*, p. 266.
"We are closing *Night Music*": This ad is pasted in the Group Theatre scrapbook for *Night Music*, Lincoln Center.
"Associated" and "unless a suitable script": *New York Times*, March 1, 1940.
"If you are not strong enough": Odets, *The Time Is Ripe*, p. 57.

402 "Impressed no one": From Clurman's notebook for *The Fervent Years*, Lincoln Center.
"People do not believe": Odets, *The Time Is Ripe*, p. 59.

403 "[Lee] is still the most talented": Odets, *The Time Is Ripe*, p. 111.
"Calculated to effect": 1940 Constitution.
"A FORM, not a content": Ibid.

403–4 "All of the practical workings": Odets, *The Time Is Ripe*, p. 144.

404 "Sick and timorous fixation": Ibid., p. 143.

405 "We demanded violently": 1940 Constitution.
"We, at this meeting": Ibid.
"I don't think": Phoebe Brand, interview with author.

406 "Desire for this-and-that": Clurman, *The Fervent Years*, p. 266.
"I experienced": Ibid., p. 270.

407 "Can function and thrive": *New York Times*, September 1, 1940.

409 "For ten years": Clurman, *The Fervent Years*, p. 274.
"I had had enough": Ibid., p. 273.

410 "Sad, isn't it?": Ibid., p. 277.
"Free to do what they would": Clurman, *The Fervent Years*, p. 278.

Page
411 "Our means and our ends" and all other quotes in this paragraph are from the *New York Times*, May 18, 1941.

"I've been in a success": Quoted in Williams, *Stage Left*, p. 253.

EPILOGUE: AFTER THE FALL

412 "The memory": *Selected Letters of Eugene O'Neill*, edited by Travis Bogard and Jackson R. Bryer, New Haven: Yale University Press, 1988, pp. 513–14.

414 "A real understanding": Quoted in *"The History of the Actors' Laboratory, Inc. 1941–1950,"* Ph.D. dissertation, by Salvi Delia Nora. University of California, Los Angeles, 1969, p. 241.

"As red as a burlesque queen's garters": Ibid., p. 70.

417 "Protect ourselves" and "Secrecy . . . serves the Communists": *New York Times*, April 12, 1952.

"Is this the Kazan": From Tony Kraber's testimony to the House Committee on Un-American Activities, August 18, 1955.

420 "The old Group Theatre resurgent": *Timebends: A Life* by Arthur Miller, New York: Grove Press, 1987, p. 529.

422 "The best theatre critic": *Washington Post*, May 5, 1974.

"Without the Group": *On Acting*, p. 8.

"An act of love": *The Actor's Eye*, p. 202.

423 "The Group Theatre was a glorious crusade": Clurman, *The Fervent Years*, p. vi.

"Harold has written": *Educational Theatre Journal*, December 1976, p. 526.

426 "The Group Theatre was a symptom": Clurman, *The Fervent Years*, p. viii.

428 "Everybody had their frustrations": Eunice Stoddard, interview with author.

Aaron, Daniel. *Writers on the Left: Episodes in American Literary Communism.* New York: Harcourt, Brace and World, 1961.

Adams, Cindy. *Lee Strasberg: The Imperfect Genius of the Actors Studio.* Garden City, N.Y.: Doubleday, 1980.

Adler, Stella. "The Actor in the Group Theatre," in *Actors on Acting,* edited by Toby Cole and Helen Krich Chinoy. New York: Crown Publishers, 1949.

Allen, Frederick Lewis. *Since Yesterday: The Nineteen-Thirties in America.* New York: Bantam Books, 1961.

Anderson, Maxwell. *Night over Taos.* New York: Samuel French, 1932.

Ardrey, Robert. "Casey Jones." Playscript in the Library of Congress Copyright Division, Washington, D.C.

———. *Plays of Three Decades.* New York: Atheneum, 1968.

———. "Thunder Rock." Final production script in the Billy Rose Theatre Collection, Lincoln Center Performing Arts Research Center, New York City. (The published version is in *Plays of Three Decades.)*

Bentley, Joanne. *Hallie Flanagan: A Life in the American Theatre.* New York: Alfred A. Knopf, 1988.

Berkson, Michael A. "Morris Carnovsky: Actor and Teacher." Ph.D. dissertation, University of Illinois at Urbana-Champaign, 1975.

Boleslavsky, Richard. *Acting: The First Six Lessons.* New York: Theatre Arts Books, 1933.

Booth, John E., and Funke, Lewis. *Actors Talk About Acting: Fourteen Interviews with Stars of the Theatre.* New York: Random House, 1961.

Brenman-Gibson, Margaret. *Clifford Odets: American Playwright, the Years from 1906 to 1940.* New York: Atheneum, 1981.

Brown, John Mason. "Minor Parsifals." *The Saturday Review of Literature,* June 30, 1945.

Carnovsky, Morris. "Yours for a Better Life." *Theatre Arts,* June–July 1948.

Carnovsky, Morris, with Sander, Peter. *The Actor's Eye.* New York: Performing Arts Journal Publications, 1984.

Child, Nellisse (pseudonym of Lillian Gerard). "Weep for the Virgins." Playscript in the Library of Congress Copyright Division, Washington, D.C.

Chinoy, Helen Krich, ed. "The Way We Were, 1931–1941." *Educational Theatre Journal,* December 1974. (Entire issue devoted to the Group Theatre.)

Ciment, Michael. *Kazan on Kazan.* New York: The Viking Press, 1974.

Clurman, Harold. *All People Are Famous (instead of an autobiography).* New York: Harcourt Brace Jovanovich, 1974.

———. "Critique of the American Theatre." *The Drama,* April 1931.

———. *The Fervent Years: The Story of the Group Theatre and the Thirties.* 1945. New York: Harcourt Brace Jovanovich, 1975.

———. "The Idea Behind Production." *Theatre Guild Magazine,* December 1930.

———. *On Directing.* New York: Macmillan, 1972.

Colum, Padraic. *Balloon: A Comedy in Four Acts.* New York: Macmillan, 1929.

Crawford, Cheryl. *One Naked Individual: My Fifty Years in the Theatre.* Indianapolis, Ind.: The Bobbs-Merrill Company, 1977.

Crowley, Alice Lewisohn. *The Neighborhood Playhouse: Leaves from a Theatre Scrapbook.* New York: Theatre Arts Books, 1959.

Deutsch, Helen, and Hanau, Stella. *The Provincetown: A Story of a Theatre.* New York: Russell & Russell, 1931.

Eaton, Walter P. *The Theatre Guild: The First Ten Years.* New York: Brentano's, 1929.

Engel, Lehman. *This Bright Day: An Autobiography.* New York: Macmillan, 1974.

Eustis, Morton. *B'way Inc! The Theatre As a Business.* New York: Dodd, Mead, 1934.

Farmer, Frances. *Will There Really Be a Morning?* 1972. New York: Dell Publishing, 1982.

Federal Writers' Project. *The WPA Guide to New York City.* 1939. New York: Pantheon Books, 1982.

Filippov, Boris. *Actors without Make-up.* Moscow: Progress Publishers, 1977.

Flanagan, Hallie. *Arena: The History of the Federal Theatre.* 1940. New York: Arno Press, 1980.

Frank, Waldo. *New Year's Eve.* New York: Charles Scribner's Sons, 1929.

———. *Our America.* New York: Boni & Liverright, 1920.

Garfield, David. *A Player's Place: The Story of the Actors Studio.* New York: Macmillan, 1980.

Gasper, Raymond D. "A Study of the Group Theatre and Its Contributions to Theatrical Production in America." Ph.D. dissertation, Ohio State University, 1955.

Gassner, John, ed. *Producing the Play.* New York: The Dryden Press, 1941. (Includes essays by Harold Clurman, Mordecai Gorelik, and Robert Lewis.)

Goldstein, Malcolm. *The Political Stage: American Drama and Theatre of the Great Depression.* New York: Oxford University Press, 1974.

Gordon, Mel. *The Stanislavsky Technique: Russia.* New York: Applause Theatre Book Publishers, 1987.

Gorelik, Mordecai. *New Theatres for Old.* New York: Samuel French, 1940.

Gornik, Vivian. *The Romance of American Communism.* New York: Basic Books, 1977.

Green, Paul. *Out of the South: The Life of a People in Dramatic Form.* New York: Harper & Brothers, 1939. (Includes *The House of Connelly* and *Johnny Johnson.*)

Hethmon, Robert. *Strasberg at the Actors Studio.* New York: The Viking Press, 1965.

Himelstein, Morgan Y. *Drama Was a Weapon: The Left-Wing Theatre in New York, 1929–1941.* New Brunswick, N.J.: Rutgers University Press, 1963.

Hirsch, Foster. *A Method to Their Madness: A History of the Actors Studio.* New York: W. W. Norton, 1984.

Houseman, John. *Run-Through.* New York: Simon and Schuster/A Touchstone Book, 1972.

Kaplan, Alan, and Klein, Thomas. "Harold Clurman: A Life of Theatre." Documentary broadcast on public television July 3, 1989. Available from Famous Productions, 19 Wavecrest Ave., Venice, CA 90291.

Kazan, Elia. *Elia Kazan: A Life.* New York: Alfred A. Knopf, 1988.

Kazin, Alfred. *Starting Out in the Thirties.* Boston: Atlantic Monthly Press, 1962.

Kempton, Murray. *Part of Our Time: Some Ruins and Monuments of the Thirties.* New York: Simon and Schuster, 1955.

Kingsley, Sidney. *Men in White,* in *Best American Plays 1918–1958, Supplementary Volume,* edited by John Gassner. New York: Crown Publishers, 1961.

Kirchon, V., and Ouspensky, A. "Red Rust." Playscript in the Billy Rose Theatre Collection, Lincoln Center Performing Arts Research Center, New York City.

Lawson, John Howard. *Success Story.* New York: Farrar & Rinehart, 1931.

———. *With a Reckless Preface: Two Plays by John Howard Lawson.* Foreword by Harold Clurman. New York: Farrar & Rinehart, 1934. (Includes *Gentlewoman.*)

Le Gallienne, Eva. *With a Quiet Heart.* New York: The Viking Press, 1953.

Levy, Melvin. "Gold Eagle Guy." Playscript in the Billy Rose Theatre Collection, Lincoln Center Performing Arts Research Center, New York City.

Lewis, Robert. *Advice to the Players.* New York: Harper & Row, 1980.

———. *Method—Or Madness?* New York: Samuel French, 1958.

———. *Slings and Arrows.* New York: Stein and Day, 1984.

Lifton, David S. *The Yiddish Theatre in America.* London: Thames and Hudson, 1965.

Meisner, Sanford, and Longwell, Dennis. *Sanford Meisner on Acting.* New York: Vintage Books, 1987.

Miller, Arthur. *Timebends: A Life.* New York: Grove Press, 1987.

MIT Press. *The Drama Review,* Winter 1984. (Entire issue devoted to the Group Theatre.)

Navasky, Victor. *Naming Names.* New York: The Viking Press, 1980.

Nora, Salvi Delia. "The History of the Actors Laboratory, Inc. 1941–1950." Ph.D. dissertation, University of California, Los Angeles, 1969.

Odets, Clifford. *Night Music.* New York: Random House, 1940.

———. "The Silent Partner." Playscript in the Billy Rose Theatre Collection, Lincoln Center Performing Arts Research Center, New York City.

———. *Six Plays by Clifford Odets.* New York: Random House, 1939. (Includes *Waiting for Lefty, Awake and Sing!, Till the Day I Die, Paradise Lost, Golden Boy,* and *Rocket to the Moon.*)

———. *The Time Is Ripe: The 1940 Journal of Clifford Odets.* Introduction by William Gibson. New York: Grove Press, 1988.

O'Neill, Eugene. *Selected Letters of Eugene O'Neill.* Edited by Travis Bogard and Jackson R. Bryer. New Haven: Yale University Press, 1988.

Piscator, Erwin, and Goldschmidt, Lena. "Case of Clyde Griffiths." Playscript in the Billy Rose Theatre Collection, Lincoln Center Performing Arts Research Center, New York City.

Powell, Dawn. "The Party" (original title of "Big Night"). Playscript in the Library of Congress Copyright Division, Washington, D.C.

Rabkin, Gerald. *Drama and Commitment: Politics in the American Theatre of the Thirties.* Bloomington, Ind.: Indiana University Press, 1964.

Reynolds, Steven, C. "The Theatre Art of Robert Lewis: An Analysis and Evaluation." Ph.D. dissertation, University of Michigan, 1981.

Rich, Frank, and Aronson, Lisa. *The Theatre Art of Boris Aronson.* New York: Alfred A. Knopf, 1987.

Rosenfeld, Lulla. *Bright Star of Exile: Jacob Adler and the Yiddish Theatre.* New York: Thomas Y. Crowell, 1977.

Sanders, Ronald A. *The Days Grow Short: The Life and Music of Kurt Weill.* New York: Limelight Editions, 1980.

Saroyan, William. *My Heart's in the Highlands.* New York: Samuel French, 1941.

Shaw, Irwin. *The Gentle People: A Brooklyn Fable.* New York: Random House, 1939.

———. "Quiet City." Playscript in the Library of Congress Copyright Division, Washington, D.C.

————. "Retreat to Pleasure." Playscript in the Library of Congress Copyright Division, Washington, D.C.

Sheaffer, Louis. *O'Neill: Son and Artist*. Boston: Little, Brown, 1973.

Shivers, Alfred S. *The Life of Maxwell Anderson*. New York: Stein and Day, 1983.

Shnayerson, Michael. *Irwin Shaw: A Biography*. New York: G. P. Putnam's Sons, 1989.

Sievers, W. David. "The Group Theatre of New York City, 1931–1941." Ph.D. dissertation, Stanford University, 1944.

Sifton, Paul and Claire. *1931—*. New York: Farrar & Rinehart, 1931.

Stanislavsky, Constantin. *An Actor Prepares*. Translated by Elizabeth Reynolds Hapgood. New York: Theatre Arts Books, 1936.

————. *My Life in Art*. Translated by Elizabeth R. Hapgood. 1934. New York: Theatre Arts Books, 1948.

Strand, Paul. *Sixty Years of Photographs*. Introduction by Calvin Tomkins. Millerton, N.Y.: Aperture, 1976.

Strasberg, Lee. *A Dream of Passion: The Development of the Method*. Boston: Little, Brown, 1987.

————. "Moscow Notebook." *The Drama Review*, March 1973.

Telchin, Stanley S. "The Group Theatre: Its Significance and Influence." Ph.D. dissertation, Catholic University, 1950.

Waldau, Roy S. *Vintage Years of the Theatre Guild, 1928–1939*. Cleveland, O.: The Press of Case Western Reserve University, 1972.

Weales, Gerald. *Clifford Odets: Playwright*. New York: Pegasus (a division of Bobbs-Merrill), 1971.

Whitman, Walt. *Democratic Vistas*. London: George Routledge & Sons, 1888.

Williams, Jay. *Stage Left*. New York: Charles Scribner's Sons, 1974.

Willis, Ronald A. "The American Laboratory Theatre, 1923–1930." Ph.D. dissertation, University of Iowa, 1968.

Wilson, John. *The Dorothy Patten Story*. Chattanooga, Tenn.: The Chattanooga News–Free Press, 1986.

INDEX

Grateful acknowledgment is made to the following for permission to reprint previously published and unpublished material:

Paul B. Berkowsky, Co-Executor of the Estate of Cheryl Crawford: *Excerpt from* One Naked Individual *by Cheryl Crawford, Bobbs-Merrill, 1977; Excerpt from tape of lecture given by Cheryl Crawford at Lee Strasberg Institute on deposit at Performing Arts Research Center, Lincoln Center Library; taped conversation between Cheryl Crawford and Harold Clurman on deposit at Lincoln Center Library; entry by Cheryl Crawford from Group Theatre Brookfield Diary, 1931; and excerpt from an article by Cheryl Crawford from* The Flying Grouse, *February, 1936.*
Brandt and Brandt Literary Agents, Inc.: *Excerpts of letters from Clifford Odets to Helen Deutsch, October 10, 30, and November 21, 1934; entry by Clifford Odets in Group Theatre Brookfield Diary, 1931. Permission of Walt Odets and Nora Odets.*
Justine Compton-Wentworth: *Excerpted material by Harold Clurman. Permission of J. Compton-Wentworth, widow of Harold Clurman.*
Alan Kaplan and Thomas Klein: *Excerpts of filmed interview "Harold Clurman: A Life of Theatre" by Alan Kaplan and Thomas Klein, produced by Famous Productions 1988, 19 Wavecrest Ave., #10, Venice, CA 90291.*
Elia Kazan: *Excerpt of letter from Elia Kazan to Lee Strasberg, March 15, 1937, and excerpt of letter from Elia Kazan to Harold Clurman, May 1937.*
Alfred A. Knopf, Inc.: *Excerpts from* A Life *by Elia Kazan. Copyright © 1988 by Elia Kazan.*
Wilhelmina Kraber: *Excerpted material by Tony and Wilhelmina Kraber.*
Anthony J. Montoya, *Strand Archives: One photograph by Paul Strand.*
John Mucci: *Interview with Morris Carnovsky and Phoebe Brand, September 14, 1987.*
Caroline Steiner: *Three photographs by Ralph Steiner.*
Yale University Library: *Letter from Eugene O'Neill to Kenneth Macgowan, November, 1940. Courtesy of the Yale Collection of American Literature, Beinecke Rare Book and Manuscripts Library, Yale University.*

Grateful acknowledgment is made to Anna Strasberg, Executrix of the Estate of Lee Strasberg for permission to quote from the following letters, diaries, and unpublished writings of Lee Strasberg, as well as from Peter Jessup's interview with Mr. Strasberg, and all rights therein are reserved by the Estate of Lee Strasberg:

A Dream of Passion *by Lee Strasberg, New York: Little, Brown, 1987.*
Letter by Lee Strasberg dated May 1, 1936 (reproduced in One Naked Individual *by Cheryl Crawford, Indianapolis: Bobbs-Merrill, 1977).*
An interview with Lee Strasberg conducted by Peter Jessup, in the collection of the Columbia University Oral History Project.
Lee Strasberg's entry in the Group Theatre Brookfield Diary, 1931, in the collection of Anna Strasberg.
Lee Strasberg's unpublished notes on a Group Theatre meeting in December 1936, in the collection of Anna Strasberg.
Lee Strasberg's paper on the organization of the Group Theatre, from the spring of 1933, on deposit at Lincoln Center.
Lee Strasberg's letter to Paula Miller Strasberg, dated March 21, 1937, in the collection of Anna Strasberg.

A Note About the Author
Wendy Smith has written about literature and the arts for The New York
Times, *the* Village Voice, *the Chicago* Sun-Times, *and many other
publications. She is a frequent reviewer for* Publishers Weekly *and a
contributing editor of* Art and Auction.*-She lives in Brooklyn with her
husband.*

A Note on the Type
*The text of this book was set in a digitized version of Aster, a type face designed
by Francesco Simoncini (born 1912 in Bologna, Italy) for Ludwig and Mayer,
the German type foundry. Starting out with the basic old-face letter forms that
can be traced back to Francesco Griffo in 1495, Simoncini emphasized the
diagonal stress by the simple device of extending diagonals to the full height of
the letter forms and squaring off. By modifying the weights of the individual
letters to combat this stress, he has produced a type of rare balance and vigor.
Introduced in 1958, Aster has steadily grown in popularity.*
Composed by Dix Type, Syracuse, New York
Printed and bound by Halliday Lithographers, West Hanover, Massachusetts
Designed by Iris Weinstein